Microsoft
Exchange Server 2010
Administration

Microsoft®
Exchange Server 2010 Administration
Real World Skills for MCITP Certification and Beyond

Joel Stidley

Erik Gustafson

WILEY

Wiley Publishing, Inc.

Acquisitions Editor: Jeff Kellum
Technical Editor: Bob Reinsch
Production Editor: Christine O'Connor
Copy Editor: Judy Flynn
Editorial Manager: Pete Gaughan
Production Manager: Tim Tate
Vice President and Executive Group Publisher: Richard Swadley
Vice President and Publisher: Neil Edde
Media Project Manager 1: Laura Moss-Hollister
Media Associate Producer: Josh Frank
Media Quality Assurance: Shawn Patrick
Book Designers: Judy Fung and Bill Gibson
Compositor: Craig Woods, Happenstance Type-O-Rama
Proofreader: Scott Klemp and Louise Watson, Word One New York
Indexer: Robert Swanson
Project Coordinator, Cover: Lynsey Stanford
Cover Designer: Ryan Sneed

Library of Congress Cataloging-in-Publication Data

Stidley, Joel, 1976-
  Exchange server 2010 administration : real world skills for MCITP certification and beyond / Joel Stidley, Erik Gustafson.
    p. cm.
  ISBN-13: 978-0-470-62443-2 (pbk.)
  ISBN-10: 0-470-62443-4 (pbk.)
  ISBN: 978-0-470-94733-3 (ebk.)
  ISBN: 978-0-470-94735-7 (ebk.)
  ISBN: 978-0-470-94734-0 (ebk.)
  1. Microsoft Exchange server. 2. Client/server computing. 3. Electronic mail systems. 4. Electronic data processing personnel—Certification. I. Gustafson, Erik, 1971- II. Title.
  QA76.9.C55S797 2011
  005.7'1376—dc22
                                        2010036021

Dear Reader,

Thank you for choosing *Microsoft Exchange Server 2010 Administration: Real World Skills for MCITP Certification and Beyond*. This book is part of a family of premium-quality Sybex books, all of which are written by outstanding authors who combine practical experience with a gift for teaching.

Sybex was founded in 1976. More than 30 years later, we're still committed to producing consistently exceptional books. With each of our titles, we're working hard to set a new standard for the industry. From the paper we print on, to the authors we work with, our goal is to bring you the best books available.

I hope you see all that reflected in these pages. I'd be very interested to hear your comments and get your feedback on how we're doing. Feel free to let me know what you think about this or any other Sybex book by sending me an email at nedde@wiley.com. If you think you've found a technical error in this book, please visit http://sybex.custhelp.com. Customer feedback is critical to our efforts at Sybex.

Best regards,

Neil Edde
Vice President and Publisher
Sybex, an Imprint of Wiley

This book is dedicated to our friendship, our loving families, and our friends; all of which make us who we are today.

Acknowledgments

This book, like all publications, took a lot of hard work and patience on many levels. We would like to thank Jeff Kellum, Christine O'Connor, and the others at Sybex for their commitment to this book and their vision for this new series of books. Also, a sincere thank you goes out to the entire Microsoft Exchange development team for making a truly awesome product and doing so much to meet the needs of their customers.

One of the most critical pieces of a successful technical book is the accuracy. Thankfully, we had the best editors, Judy Flynn and Bob Reinsch who worked hard to make this book accurate both technically and grammatically.

We are also indebted to a number of other people who were crucial for providing honest and direct guidance and assistance along the way: Joseph Nguyen, Brian Tirch, Joézer Cookey-Gam, Jules Yacho, Kory Sebby, and Jon Webster.

About the Authors

Joel Stidley has been working in the IT field for 15 years, and he has been a computer fanatic for much longer. He obtained his first Microsoft certification in 1999 and is currently an MCSE, MCTS, and Exchange MVP. At the beginning of his IT career, he was supporting MS-DOS and Windows for Workgroups clients on a Novell NetWare network at a small manufacturing company. Shortly thereafter, he discovered the joys of Windows NT Server. Joel worked with Microsoft Exchange on the Exchange Server 5.0 beta releases. Since that time, he has done migrations from legacy messaging systems such as Lotus cc:Mail to Exchange as well as numerous migrations from Exchange 5.5 to 2000 and 2003 versions. He also led an engineering team to create a shared Exchange 2000 hosting platform before Microsoft released guidance on how to do so. Since then, he has been working extensively with Exchange in a variety of environments.

In 2004, Joel founded ExchangeExchange.com, a Microsoft Exchange-focused community website, where he blogs and provides forums for discussing Exchange, PowerShell, certification, and general Windows topics. In the last few years, he has also been writing extensively. He contributed content to *MCITP: Microsoft Exchange Server 2007 Messaging Design and Deployment Study Guide: Exams 70-237 and 70-238* (Sybex, 2007) and served as lead author on *Professional PowerShell for Exchange Server 2007 SP1* (Wrox, 2008), *MCTS: Windows Server 2008 Applications Infrastructure Configuration Study Guide: Exam 70-643* (Sybex, 2008), and *Microsoft Exchange Server 2010 Best Practices* (Microsoft Press, 2010). Currently, he is the principal systems architect at Terremark Worldwide Inc., where he works with a variety of cloud computing and messaging technologies.

Joel lives near the Dallas, Texas area with his wife and two children. You can contact him at joel@mailtask.com or read his blog at http://exchangeexchange.com/blogs/joel.stidley/.

Erik R. Gustafson is a nine-year veteran of IT consulting and IT support. He started working professionally with Microsoft products while running a successful signage business in 1995, and after selling the business a few years later, he refocused his career on providing IT services. He obtained his first Microsoft certification in 2002 and is currently an MCSE and an MCSA. For the last few years he has helped grow an IT consulting business and set up an IT managed service provider from the ground up. Recently, he has relocated to the Dallas area with his wife, Kelly, and now works as a solutions architect for Terremark Worldwide Inc.

Erik also was a contributing author of *MCTS: Windows Server 2008 Applications Infrastructure Configuration Study Guide: Exam 70-643* (Sybex, 2008) and writes Microsoft exam simulation questions for Ucertify.com.

You can contact Erik at erikrgustafson@gmail.com or read his blog at www.blueskwer.com.

About the Contributing Authors

Joseph Tuan Nguyen, MCITP, is a systems architect with 13 years' experience working with Exchange Server. He has worked as a system administrator, consultant, author, and trainer covering various Microsoft server technologies for messaging, communications, and collaboration. He has worked in small, medium, and enterprise organizations and is currently employed at the University of Oklahoma, where he puts his professional and technical experience to work serving the needs of the campus community. He resides in Oklahoma City with his wife, Jessica, and two daughters, Natalie and Claire.

Jules Yacho has over 13 years of IT experience. He is currently employed as a regional sales engineer at Terremark Worldwide Inc. and is responsible for designing and architecting solutions for complex challenges using his knowledge of networks, security, systems, storage, co-location, and cloud computing.

Jules has worked extensively with all versions of Exchange, from Exchange Server 5.0 all the way to Exchange Server 2010. Prior to Joining Terremark, he was an infrastructure consultant with Dell Inc. specializing in Active Directory and Exchange deployments, and prior to that, Jules was a senior messaging engineer with Turner Construction.

When he is not busy working with technology, Jules enjoys watching his sons play competitive soccer. Jules is married and currently lives in Irving, Texas, with his wife, Erin, and their four children.

Kory Sebby grew up in a small town in Illinois with two loving and supportive parents and three obnoxious younger siblings. While Kory was growing up, he was always taking things apart and rebuilding them or building new items from the parts. After being introduced to computers, things just took off. Kory learned from gaming on PCs new ways to do things and ways to reprogram the games to make them a little easier or play smoother. Kory started his computer training in high school and continued his education at a technical school in Phoenix, Arizona. Using this technical training, Kory started his computer career working at a computer retail store and then worked hard to qualify for his current position as a technical analyst at Verity Three in the suburbs of Chicago. He has since obtained a number of certifications (MCSA, MCDST, VSTP, CCA) and has become a proud father. Kory continues to work hard and learn new technology; he is often the one analyst chosen to learn a new technology. As such, he was chosen to deploy the first Exchange Server 2007 servers for his company's customers a few years ago.

Brian Tirch has been working in the IT field for over 11 years and currently works as a technology architect for Microsoft, where he provides guidance on a number of Microsoft technologies like Exchange Server. Brian currently holds a bachelor of science degree in computer networking and has multiple Microsoft certifications; he obtained his first in 1999.

Brian has been the technical editor of a number of Exchange books over the years: *Mastering Microsoft Exchange Server 2007* (Sybex, 2007), *Mastering Microsoft Exchange Server (2007 SP1 Sybex, 2009)*, and *Microsoft Exchange Server 2007:*

Implementation and Administration (Sybex, 2008). He was awarded the honor of being a Microsoft MVP in Exchange Server before joining Microsoft. Brian also hosts a blog dedicated to Microsoft Exchange Server, located at http://exchange-genie.com.

Brian's most recent achievement is fatherhood. He has become the proud father to his son, Tyler Nicholas Tirch (TNT). He is always appreciative of his family and friends for their support. He is especially appreciative for his wife, Jodie Tirch, who makes it possible for him to spend long hours on the computer.

Joézer Cookey-Gam holds a bachelor of technology degree in electrical engineering from the Rivers State University of Science and Technology in Nigeria. He is a Microsoft Certified Systems Engineer and an IT professional with focus on messaging. He began his IT career as a network engineer and Exchange administrator, supporting medium to large enterprise networks. In this role, he provided solutions for LinkServe Limited, a leading Internet service provider in Nigeria. He joined Microsoft in 2001 and is currently a technical support lead, supporting both Microsoft vendors and partners.

Contents at a Glance

Contents

Table of Exercises

Introduction

Over the years, Exchange Server has become a complicated messaging solution that many organizations rely on. Many companies have not upgraded to Exchange Server 2007 and are still using Exchange Server 2003. With the release of Exchange Server 2010, they are now contemplating upgrading to take advantage of this new version's larger mailbox support, advanced high availability options, and simple archiving and retention features.

Administrators who have been in the trenches supporting Exchange Server 2007 and previous versions of Exchange for the last few years must now upgrade their skills in preparation for the upgrade to Exchange 2010. For example, many administrators will be unfamiliar with the concept of server roles, PowerShell administration, and continuous replication. For Exchange Server 2007 administrators, Client Access servers, Exchange Control Panel, and the new high availability options will be new.

In addition, new Exchange administrators will need to understand the basic components of Exchange and how to perform common administrative tasks. This book aims to cover the information that both new and experienced Exchange administrators need to be successful working with Exchange Server 2010. Since this book was not rushed to market to coincide with the release of Exchange Server 2010, additional time was taken to validate the content. In fact, many chapters include features and updates included with Exchange Server 2010 Service Pack 1.

This book was written from two perspectives. First, it covers the most important design, deployment, and administrative tasks that any messaging administrator will need to perform. Second, both the book and the contents of the CD (videos and practice exams) cover the objectives for the MCITP: Enterprise Messaging Administrator 2010 exams, 70-662 and 70-663. Whether you're preparing for these exams or preparing for your career as a messaging administrator, you'll find this book a useful reference.

Who Should Read This Book

As you can probably tell by the title, *Exchange Server 2010 Administration: Real World Skills for MCITP Certification and Beyond*, this book is primarily aimed at two groups: those seeking real-world Exchange Server administration and design knowledge and those preparing for the Exchange MSITP exams.

- Exchange administrators and professionals: If you are an Exchange administrator, you will find information on the day-to-day management of Exchange. The book will take you through all the steps required to prepare your environment for Exchange 2010 and deploy it. It will also cover the changes and new features included in Exchange Server 2010. If you are a professional, you will find detailed information on how to plan for deployment, securing and providing high availability of Exchange 2010 servers within your organization. You will find information for controlling change in the environment and how to evaluate new features and then deploy them.

- Exam candidates preparing to take the MCITP: Enterprise Messaging Administrator 2010 exams (70-663 IT Pro: Designing and Deploying Messaging Solutions with

Microsoft Exchange Server 2010; 70-662 TS: Microsoft Exchange Server 2010, Configuring). You'll find that all of the objectives are covered when you use the complete training kit this book provides. It's important to note that what you hold in your hands is more than just a book. The CD that accompanies this book includes video training and memory-jogging flashcards as well as practice exams and more to help you master the objectives of both MCITP exams.

As you can see, this book has been developed for a wide range of people. Both the authors as well as the contributing authors have real-world experience as administrators, so the book is written from the reader's standpoint rather than from the perspective of how it is supposed to work or how it works in a lab environment. All of the people involved with the book also have Microsoft certifications, so we understand the testing process and how to prepare for those types of exams. We believe that this book provides a solid basis for passing the Exchange exams while preparing the reader for something far more important, the real world and being successful in your career.

What You Will Learn

This book starts out with an introduction to Exchange server and a short tour of what has changed for readers who have experience with older versions of Exchange. We encourage all readers to review this information before continuing to other chapters in the book.

The second section of the book focuses on the administrative tasks that a messaging administrator needs to know how to perform. This includes preparing Active Directory, deploying the Exchange roles, managing Exchange objects, and configuring Exchange features. Each of the chapters in this part of the book covers the "how to" of Exchange server.

The third section of this book covers situations in which messaging professionals are involved. The chapters in this section focus on what needs to be done and why it needs to be done rather than on the details on how it is done because the latter is covered in the second part of this book.

Throughout the book, you'll find real-world exercises that walk you through the processes required to implement and support commonly used features of Exchange Server 2010. For many people, having this hands-on experience helps to solidify the material learned. We have provided videos on the CD for some of these exercises as well. You'll also find notes to help you understand more detailed concepts and find more information. Additionally, the real-world scenarios provide you with insights on how to apply the information in the chapter in the real world.

This book was written to address the needs of messaging administrators and messaging professionals as they design, deploy, and manage Exchange Server 2010. The book will help you understand what you need to know to get by in the real world as well as to pass the MCITP exams.

Each chapter has the following features:

Hands-on exercises   In each chapter, you'll find exercises designed to give you important hands-on experience. The exercises support the topics of the chapter, and each exercise walks you through the steps necessary to perform a particular function.

Real-world scenarios   Because reading a book isn't enough for you to learn how to apply these topics in your everyday duties, we have provided real-world scenarios in special sidebars. They explain when and why a particular solution would make sense in a working environment you'd actually encounter.

Interactive CD   This book comes with a CD complete with video training, bonus exams for both exams (70-662 and 70-663), electronic flashcards, and the book in electronic format. Details are in the following section.

Chapter essentials   To highlight what you learn, you'll find a list of chapter essentials at the end of each chapter. These sections briefly highlight the topics that need your particular attention.

Glossary   Throughout each chapter, you will be introduced to important terms and concepts that you will need to know for the exams. These terms appear in italic text within the chapters. At the end of the book, a detailed glossary defines these terms as well as other general terms you should know.

What You Need

You should verify that your computer meets the minimum requirements for installing Exchange Server 2010 as listed in Table 2.1 in Chapter 2. We suggest that your computer meet or exceed the requirements for a more enjoyable experience.

The exercises in this book assume that you have performed a clean installation of Exchange Server 2010 into an empty forest. To complete all of the exercises, you will need to have multiple machines available. Rather than deploying multiple physical machines, we recommend using virtual machines with Microsoft Hyper-V R2, VMware ESXi, or another hypervisor capable of running a 64-bit operating system. If you do not have resources available, consider using an online service that allows you to run virtual machines in the cloud. Services like Terremark's vCloud Express, Amazon's EC2, and others may be cost-effective solutions for you to deploy virtual machines to use to complete the exercises.

If you do not already have software available for the exercises, you can obtain the software from the following resources:

- You can download Microsoft's free Hyper-V Server 2008 R2 from www.microsoft.com/hyper-v-server.

- You can also download a trial version of Windows Server 2008 R2 to run as virtual machines or to run the Hyper-V role from www.microsoft.com/windowsserver2008/en/us/trial-software.aspx and create a virtual machine. We recommend using a Hyper-V machine with at least 4 GB of RAM.

- You will need the Exchange Server 2010 media for installation. If you do not have a licensed copy of SQL Server 2008, you can download a trial version from Microsoft's website at www.microsoft.com/exchange/2010/en/us/try-it.aspx.

- You will also need a copy of Outlook 2010 so that you can test client connectivity. If you do not have a license for Outlook 2010 or Office 2010, you can download a trial version from Microsoft's website at http://office.microsoft.com/en/us/try.

We recommend signing up for a Microsoft TechNet subscription, which gives you access to evaluate most of the software Microsoft releases. You can find more information on subscribing to TechNet at http://technet.microsoft.com/en-us/subscriptions/default.aspx

Once you have the installation media available and the hypervisor or physical hardware configured, to be ready for the exercises you should create the servers listed in the following table:

Server Name	IP Address	Windows Version
EX01	192.168.1.10	Windows Server 2008 R2 Enterprise
EX02	192.168.1.11	Windows Server 2008 R2 Enterprise
EX03	192.168.1.12	Windows Server 2008 R2 Enterprise
EX04	192.168.1.13	Windows Server 2008 R2 Standard
ET01	192.168.1.25	Windows Server 2008 R2 Standard

Before beginning the first exercise, you will need to install the Active Directory Domain Services role on EX01 and then promote it to a domain controller for the Mailtask.com domain. Also be sure to install Outlook 2010 on the EX01 so you can test Outlook connectivity. After the domain is functional, join EX02, EX03, and EX04 to Mailtask.com.

What Is Covered in This Book

Exchange Server 2010 Administration: Real World Skills for MCITP Certification and Beyond is organized to provide you with the information you need to effectively administer your Exchange 2010 Server instances. The following list provides an overview of the topics covered in each chapter.

Part I—Introduction to Exchange Server 2010

Chapter 1—Introduction to Exchange Server 2010: This chapter starts out with a brief history of Exchange. You will then learn what is new, what has changed, and what features of Exchange have been discontinued.

Part II—Messaging Administrator's Guide to Exchange Server 2010 (70-662)

Chapter 2—Installing and Configuring Exchange Server 2010: You will master the Exchange Server installation process by actually doing it in this chapter. You will also install the Exchange prerequisites and prepare the environment for Exchange.

Chapter 3—Configuring Connectors, Routing and Transport, and Connectivity: This chapter shows you how to configure connectors, message routing, transport and how to configure Client Access for Exchange 2010.

Chapter 4—Managing Exchange Server 2010 Mail-Enabled Objects: This chapter teaches you how to create new mailboxes and understand the differences between mailbox types. You'll learn about the new Exchange Control Panel and how to work with move requests.

Chapter 5—Configuring and Managing Public Folders: To give you a better understanding of public folders, this chapter will help you to create, manage, and replicate your public folder environment.

Chapter 6—Configuring Security, Compliance, and Policies: In this chapter, you'll learn how to configure Role Based Access Control (RBAC), message compliance and records management, transport rules, and address lists.

Chapter 7—Configuring High-Availability Solutions for Exchange Server: Making sure your Exchange environment is available to end users is one of the most important jobs a messaging professional has. This chapter will help you to understand high-availability solutions for Exchange.

Chapter 8—Disaster Recovery Operations for Exchange Server: You will learn to ensure that you can recover your Exchange server if a failure occurs. Configuring backups and recovering messaging data are just a few of the things covered in this chapter.

Chapter 9—Monitoring and Reporting with Exchange Server 2010: To ensure that your Exchange servers are performing at high levels, monitoring and reporting are necessary. This chapter walks you through the steps of monitoring databases and client connectivity and how to create a server report.

Part III—Messaging Professional's Guide to Exchange Server 2010 (70-663)

Chapter 10—Planning the Exchange Server 2010 Migration and Infrastructure: Much work goes into preparing and planning for a migration or deployment. This chapter will help take some of the guesswork out of the planning stage and give you practical advice and direction for migrating or planning your Exchange environment.

Chapter 11—Designing and Deploying Mailbox Services: This chapter will help ensure that the mailbox services and public folder configuration meet and will continue to handle the needs of the users.

Chapter 12—Designing Routing and Client Connectivity: Exchange Server 2010 provides some advanced functionality right out of the box, and this chapter gives direction on how to design message routing, transport, client access and connectivity.

Chapter 13—Designing Security and Compliance: In this chapter, you will learn the importance of email security and compliance. You can use this chapter to help design your security standards.

Chapter 14—Designing High Availability and Recovery: This chapter introduces you to the process called risk management and helps you understand how designing a high-availability solution will ensure that your environment continues during and after a failure.

Appendix A—This includes a mapping of all the 70-662 and 70-663 exam objectives to the chapter where the objective is covered.

Appendix B—This appendix identifies the contents of the companion disk and how to use it.

Glossary—The final element of the book is the glossary. You'll find definitions of important terms related to Exchange Server 2010. If you're preparing for the exams, be sure to read the glossary on the morning of the exam. This action will ensure your understanding of the most important topics covered.

What's on the CD

With this book, we are including quite an array of training resources. The CD offers sample videos, a PDF of the book, and bonus exams and flashcards to help you study if you're a certification candidate. The CD's resources are described here:

Sample videos   Throughout the book, we have included numerous hands-on exercises showing you how to perform a variety of tasks. For some of these tasks, we have also included a video walk-through. Look for the CD icon for exercises that include a video walk-through.

The Sybex e-book   Many people like the convenience of being able to carry their whole book on a CD. They also like being able to search the text via computer to find specific information quickly and easily. For these reasons, the entire contents of this book are supplied on the CD, in PDF form. We've also included Adobe Acrobat Reader, which provides the interface for the PDF contents as well as the search capabilities.

The Sybex test engine   Since this book is also a supplement for MCITP: Enterprise Messaging Administrator 2010 exam candidates, we have included two bonus exams, one practice exam for the TS: Microsoft Exchange Server 2010, Configuring exam (70-662) and one for IT Pro: Designing and Deploying Messaging Solutions with Microsoft Exchange Server 2010 exam (70-663).

Sybex Flashcards   The "flashcard" style questions offer an effective way to quickly and efficiently test your understanding of the fundamental concepts.

How to Contact the Authors

If you have any questions about your certification or administration voyage, please contact us. If you have questions or comments, you can visit http://exchangeexchange.com or feel free to send us email at erikrgustafson@gmail.com or joel@mailtask.com. We love hearing from our readers.

Introduction to Exchange Server 2010

Chapter

1

Introduction to Exchange Server 2010

THE FOLLOWING TOPICS ARE DISCUSSED IN THIS CHAPTER:

- ✓ Brief history
- ✓ New features
- ✓ Improvements
- ✓ Discontinued features
- ✓ Comparison between 2007 and 2010
- ✓ Client benefits

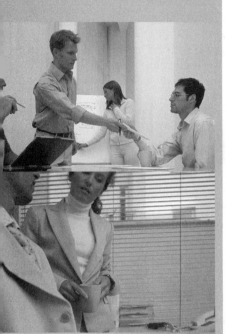

Ninety trillion. That is the estimated number of emails that were sent in 2009. Staggering isn't it? While many of those emails were used to send jokes or argue sports, a large portion of them were used in business and deemed vital for the success of an organization.

It is no wonder, then, that Exchange Server administrators and messaging professionals are in high demand, and it is our goal, in this book, to get you comfortable with Exchange 2010. This chapter's aim is to bring you up to speed on the latest versions of the Exchange administrator tools as well as help you understand the important changes since—and even the smallest improvements over—Exchange Server 2007.

Brief History of Exchange Servers

Exchange Server 2010 is a calendaring and email solution that runs on Windows Server, and like Exchange Server 2007, it can also integrate with your phone system. This is the seventh major release of the product, and the Exchange teams continue to make improvements and add features with every version.

Exchange started out as an upgrade to Microsoft Mail in 1996. Over the next several years, releases 5.0 and 5.5 introduced Lightweight Directory Access Protocol (LDAP), which was a precursor to what would become Active Directory (AD) in Windows 2000. To take advantage of AD in Windows 2000, Microsoft also included Exchange Server 2000, which was a robust platform that included chat and instant messaging (IM) services. In 2003, another version of Exchange was released, aptly named Exchange Server 2003. Features such as chat and IM were removed and they were marketed as separate services in Live Communications Server. The release of Exchange Server 2007 continued the tradition of adding more features and expanded the storage of this email server even more than its predecessors. Let's look briefly at some of the historical milestones:

- 1996 Exchange 4.0
  - Client/server architecture
  - X.400 based
- 1997 Exchange 5.0 and 5.5
  - Clustering introduced
  - LDAP introduced

- Standard and expression versions introduced
- Connectors to allow Exchange to talk to any email server provided
- Administrative console added
- Support for stand-alone SMTP
- Outlook introduced as the preferred client
- Outlook Web Access introduced
- 2000 Exchange 2000
  - Designed to work with AD
  - Scheme management services for sending and receiving secure email
  - Enhanced storage and administrative tools
  - Chat and IM services introduced
- 2003 Exchange 2003
  - Exchange ActiveSync introduced support for blacklisting addresses
  - Enhanced Outlook Web Access module added
  - Enhanced spam control introduced
  - Management console enhanced
- 2006 Exchange 2007
  - 64-bit performance
  - Exchange Management Shell (EMS) added
  - Maximum database size increased to 16 TB
  - Maximum number of storage groups increased to 50 per server

Why use Exchange Server? Exchange is certainly not the only email server on the market. In fact, there are dozens of email servers available, and each one would have a group of individuals who would argue strongly in their favor. There are many of small and medium-sized businesses that want an in-house email system. These businesses want to be up and running in only a few steps and with only a little maintenance.

Simplicity and ease of use are the major contributors to the success of Exchange. Exchange installs and configures simply, and anyone can be trained in a relatively short period of time to use it effectively. Because it also sets up Web access automatically for all mailboxes, it makes it easy for users to check email from home or even while on vacation. Features like these have made Exchange the choice of many organizations. This rich feature set and the ability to scale has led to its dominance in the enterprise market.

While the first version of Exchange, code-named Mercury, was just a Microsoft internal release and could not scale past 25 users, Exchange 2010 has become the mode of transport for a major chunk of the 9 billion emails sent each day.

New Features in Exchange Server 2010

Exchange Server 2010 is available in three editions, Trial, Standard, and Enterprise. The same installation media is used to install each edition. If no license key is supplied, the Trial edition features are enabled. To enable Standard or Enterprise features, an appropriate license key must be provided. Exchange Server 2010 is 64-bit only, therefore you will need 64-bit capable hardware for your production, test, and management systems.

In addition to server licenses, client address licenses (CALs) are also required. The two different types of CALs are as follows:

- Standard CAL will provide access to ActiveSync, email, Outlook Web App, and calendaring.

- Enterprise CAL provides unified messaging and compliance functions, functionality for Exchange hosted filtering for antispam and antivirus, and Forefront Security for Exchange Server.

Whenever new versions of software such as Exchange are released, we want to know what's new! Exchange 2010 includes some very nice changes and additions that will make an Exchange administrator's job a little bit easier, as the following list shows:

Storage improvements   In an effort to provide greater flexibility and higher performance, Microsoft has made some big adjustments in storage architecture. Estimates indicate that you will see an additional 50 to 70 percent reduction in *database storage I/O* over Exchange 2007. The benefit of this to you is that it will reduce the need for additional or more costly storage to retain performance levels. Also, the new high availability (HA) options may reduce the need for RAID in some deployments.

In Exchange 2007, high availability (HA) solutions used continuous replication to copy the transaction logs to another disk or server. You might be familiar with them; these features were called local continuous replication, cluster continuous replication, and standby continuous replication (LCR, CCR, and SCR). These required you to put a single database within a single storage group because multiple databases within a storage group.

LCR, CCR, SCR, and single copy cluster (SCC) have been removed in Exchange 2010 in favor of database availability groups (DAGs). DAGs is an evolution of the Exchange 2007 continuous replication features.

With DAGs, as seen in Figure 1.1, you can create up to 16 different replicas of the database across multiple servers or even sites. This will give you the additional option of not having a RAID solution in place. You will learn more about DAGs in Chapter 7, Configuring High Availability Solutions for Exchange Server.

Unified messaging   Unified messaging (UM) has also matured in Exchange 2010. For example, you now can create up to nine calls or answer rules. This provides a personal auto attendant for the user's mailbox, which will then transfer the call to another user, another number, or voicemail. Figure 1.2 shows the UM interface.

FIGURE 1.1   Exchange 2010 Database Availability Groups

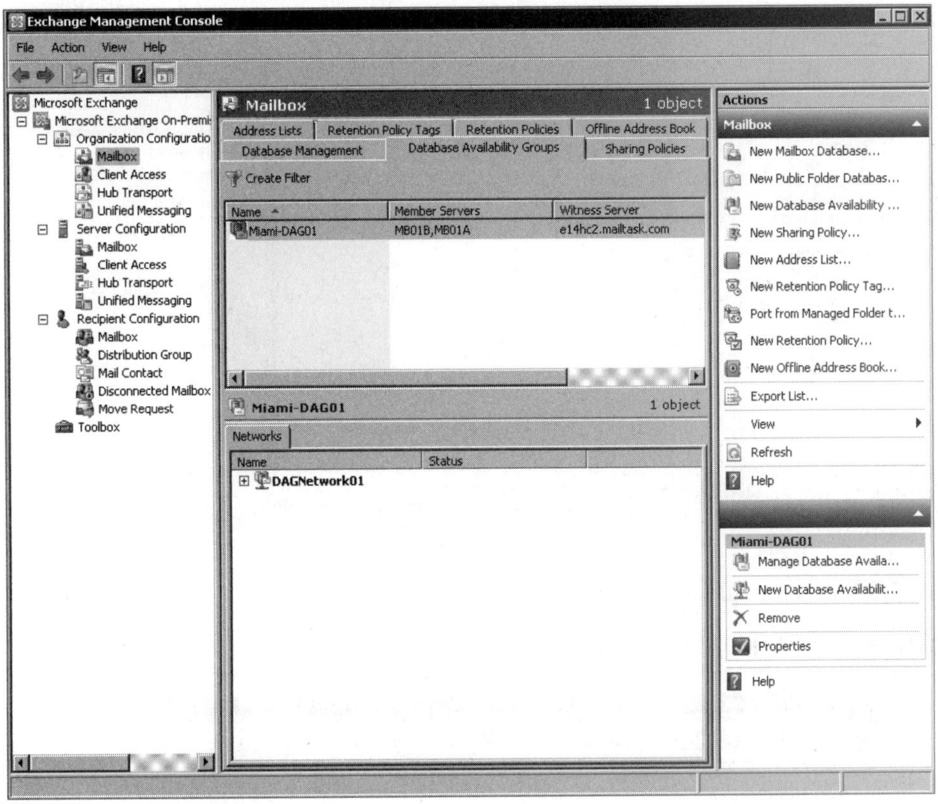

UM also has more language-support features, and the name lookup from a caller ID has been enhanced. Third-party solutions were needed to provide a message waiting indicator in Exchange 2007, but in Exchange 2010 the feature has been added.

Another new UM feature is a voicemail preview. Using Automatic Speech Recognition technology, voicemail messages are transcribed and the text is attached to the voicemail in your inbox. This allows you to be able to respond to voicemail messages, often without having to listening to them on your phone or your computer's speakers.

Role-based permissions   Large organizations will see an immediate value in the new permissions structure with a variety of administrators that handle different administrative roles. This new model gives you granular control over who does what, which gives you better control over a person or group.

FIGURE 1.2 Unified messaging interface

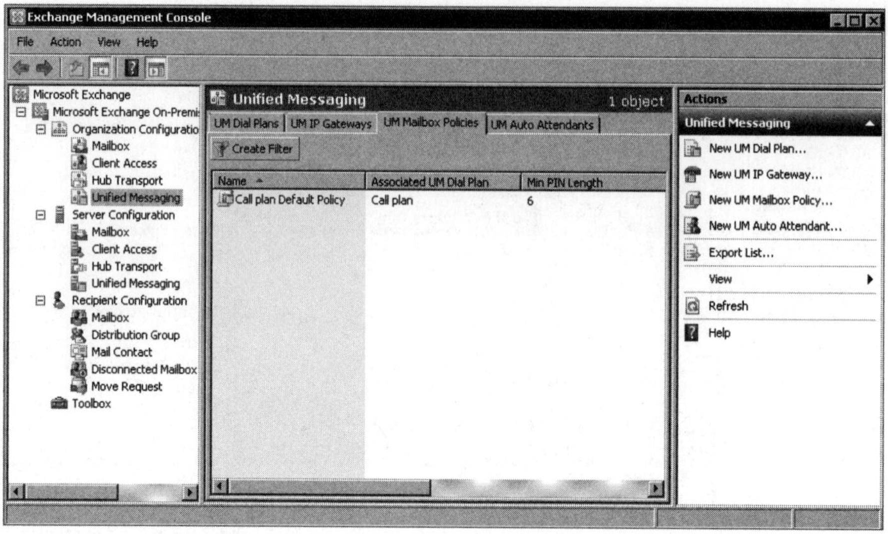

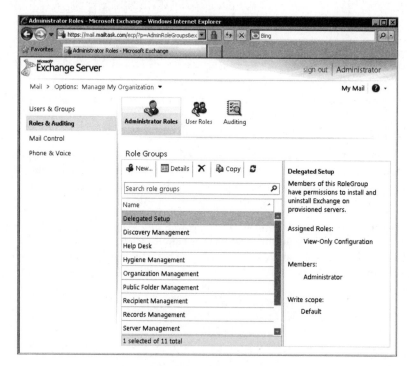

Figure 1.3 shows the Administrator Roles control panel.

FIGURE 1.3 Roles and auditing interface

There are also new management-role assignment policies that will define what users can configure within their own mailboxes, and every mailbox has one of these polices. This is a welcome addition because it allows the administrator to control how much a user can change personal information, contact information, and distribution group membership. The goal of these changes is to give detailed control while also reducing the number of small changes that users need to make.

Improvements in Exchange Server 2010

With any new release of an established product like Exchange Server, Microsoft includes new (and improved) features that benefit both the administrative side of the product and the end-user experience. We briefly highlight some of the key features that are new or improved in Exchange Server 2010 (this list is certainly not all-inclusive):

Outlook Web App   A major change or upgrade for end users is Outlook Web App (OWA, previously known as Outlook Web Access). It now has a seamless flow across browsers, so an OWA user running Safari should have the same experience as one running Internet Explorer. See Figure 1.4 to see what the new interface looks like.

FIGURE 1.4   Outlook Web App

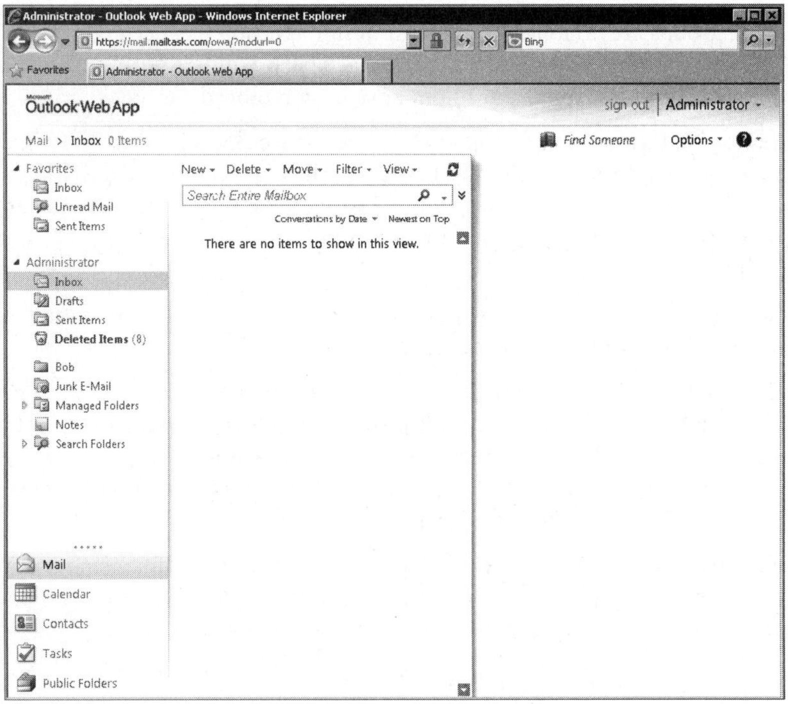

One of the complaints against OWA, especially in the earlier versions, was about the differences between the Outlook client and OWA. Users would complain that OWA was missing features that they needed. In an effort to provide a rich client experience and reduce the gap between the client and OWA, new features have been introduced, including favorites, attaching messages to a message, search folders, integration with Office Communicator and Lync, a new conversation view, and integration with Short Message Service (SMS) messages.

Microsoft Online Services   Many providers of services are moving "into the cloud," and Microsoft is no exception. With Exchange 2010, it is now possible to host mailboxes in a datacenter or host them with your own ISP or even host them with Microsoft Online Services.

Exchange 2010 provides the flexibility to be mixed between hosted and on premises, it can also be 100 percent hosted or 100 percent on site. The users may not notice any difference, however you will be able to manage mailboxes across both the on premises deployment and the hosted environment. In this way you will be able to take advantage of the cloud for a portion of your mailboxes, while maintaining control of other mailboxes by hosting them on premises.

Administration   The Exchange Management Console (EMC) has changed to keep up with the changes to the major features, like HA. Due to the new replication functions, the mailbox database object is now tied to the Exchange Server 2010 organization and is no longer tied to the Exchange Server object.

Because storage groups are no longer used, their administration has been removed from both the EMC and the EMS. Cmdlets you might have been familiar with, such as New-StorageGroup, Get-StorageGroup, and so on, have been removed.

Exchange Server 2010 now runs on top of Windows PowerShell version 2. This version not only has a command-line interface (CLI), it also has an interactive development environment (IDE). This change allows you to easily create scripts and use variables. An output window has been added where you can quickly view the results of your cmdlet or script.

Another new feature is Send Mail, shown in Figure 1.5, which allows you to send mail directly from the EMC, which is great for testing.

Exchange Control Panel   A new options page in OWA now makes it possible to perform some basic Exchange management tasks, not just with the user's own properties, but also at an organizational level. Using this new control panel makes it possible to create users, mailboxes, distribution groups, mail-enabled contacts, management email addresses, and so forth. Figure 1.6 shows the OWA Control Panel.

Active Directory Rights Management   Active Directory Rights Management Services (AD RMS) lets you have greater control with what users can do with emails messages. For example, you can disable the "Forward" options to prevent your messages from being sent to other recipients.

FIGURE 1.5   Send Mail

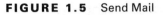

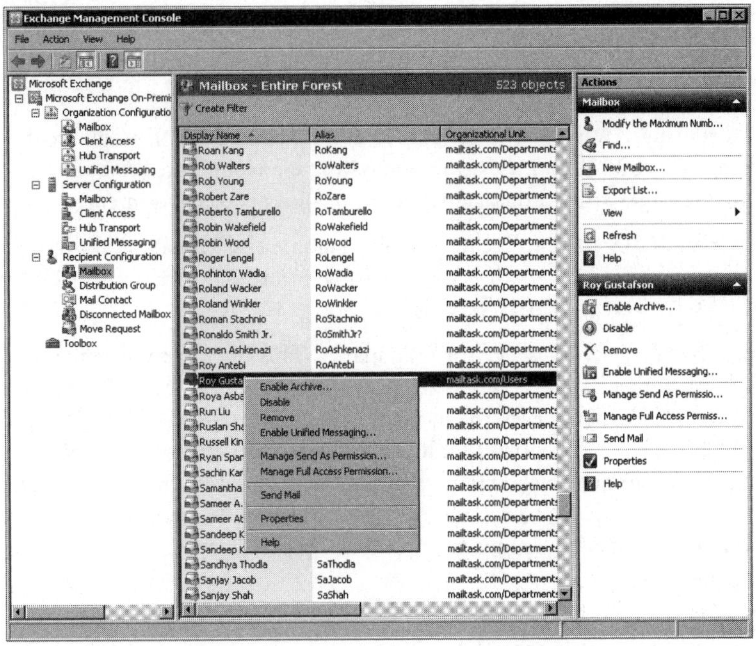

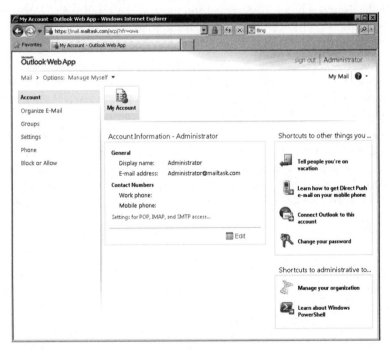

FIGURE 1.6   OWA Exchange Control Panel

With Exchange Server 2010, new features have been added to the AD RMS:

- Integration with transport rules, which is a template for using AD RMS to protect messages over the Internet
- AD RMS protection for voicemail messages coming from the UM server role

Transport and routing   With Exchange Server 2010 it is possible to implement cross-premises message routing. If you use a mixed hosting environment, Exchange Server 2010 can route messages from a datacenter to an on-premise environment.

In Exchange Server 2010, you can create enhanced email disclaimers, making it possible to add HTML content to disclaimers. It is even possible to use AD attributes (from the user's private property set) to create a personal disclaimer.

A new feature in Exchange 2010 is shadow redundancy. This feature protects messages in transit from being lost due to a server or network failure. Instead of deleting a message immediately after sending it to the next hop server, the message is maintained in a shadow redundancy queue until the next hop server reports that it was successful in delivering the message. If the next hop server does not report a successful delivery, the first server will resubmit the message in the shadow redundancy queue to another transport server in the organization for delivery. More information about shadow redundancy can be found in Chapter 3, Configuring Client Access for Exchange 2010.

When you have HA messaging support, the messages stay in the transport dumpster on a Hub Transport server and will be deleted only if they are successfully replicated to all database copies.

Messaging policy and compliance   As email continues to grow and evolve as the number one means of business-critical communication, the need to manage and enforce certain policies on email content and usage also grows.

As part of a general compliance regulation, Microsoft introduced the concept of managed folders in Exchange Server 2007. This has been enhanced in Exchange Server 2010, with new features such as the option of tagging messages, cross-mailbox searches, new transport rules and actions, and the new retention policies.

Mailbox archive   Exchange Server 2010 also introduces personal archive; this is a secondary mailbox associated to a user's mailbox. Because Exchange Server 2010 now supports lower cost storage configurations, the personal archive is a great replacement for locally stored, easily stolen, and damaged PST files. This allows administrators to keep control of messaging data on the corporate servers.

Discontinued Features

In any new release of a software product, discontinued or de-emphasized features are inevitable. The items that follow in no way represent every change that has occurred in Exchange Server 2010, but it does represent some of the most prominent changes.

Features That Have Been Removed

The following key features and functionality have been removed from Exchange Server 2010:

- Storage groups are no longer a feature in Exchange Server 2010. The concepts of a database, log files, and a checkpoint file are still valid, but they are now just referred to as a database. You can think of an Exchange 2010 mailbox database as being a single database in a single storage group.

- Exchange Server 2007 had LCR, CCR, and SCR—three different forms of replication. All three of these features are no longer available in Exchange Server 2010.

- Mailbox databases no longer save storage space by storing the same item in multiple mailboxes using single instance storage. This means that when you send a 1 MB message to 100 recipients, the database could potentially grow by 100 MB. This may have an impact on storage space, however the performance improvements made to the database schema that caused this feature to no longer be feasible are an excellent trade off.

Table 1.1 shows the discontinued Exchange Server protocols.

TABLE 1.1   Discontinued Exchange Server 2003 protocols

Feature	Replacement
X.400 and Network News Transfer Protocol (NNTP)	No migration plan. If this functionality is required, you will need to keep Exchange Server 2003 in your environment.
SMTP virtual server instances	Has been replaced with Exchange Server 2010 SMTP connectors.

In addition, some of the Exchange 2003 connector features have been discontinued. Table 1.2 lists them.

TABLE 1.2   Discontinued Exchange Server 2003 connectors

Feature	Replacement
Microsoft Exchange Connector for Lotus Notes	No migration plan. If this functionality is required, you will need to keep Exchange Server 2003 in your environment.
Microsoft Exchange Connector for GroupWise	No migration plan. If this functionality is required, you will need to keep Exchange Server 2003 in your environment.

Management features and tools that have been discontinued are listed in Table 1.3.

TABLE 1.3   Discontinued Exchange Server 2003 management tools and features

Feature	Replacement
Migration Wizard	Move Request Wizard
Clean Mailbox tool	Export-Mailbox and New-MailboxExportRequest cmdlets (SP1)
Message Tracking Center node	Tracking Log Explorer and Message Tracking tools
AD Users and Computers snap-in	Recipient management included in the EMC
ExMerge	Export-Mailbox and New-MailboxExportRequest cmdlets (SP1)
Recipient Update Service (RUS)	Update-EmailAddressPolicy cmdlets that perform some of the RUS functions
Mailbox Recovery Center	Restore-Mailbox cmdlet
Mailbox Management Service	Messaging records management (MRM)
Exchange Profile Redirector tool (ExProfRe)	AutoDiscover service

Discontinued Exchange OWA features are listed in Table 1.4.

TABLE 1.4 Discontinued OWA features

Feature	Replacement
Web Parts	SP1 of Exchange Server 2010 adds Web Parts back. They were removed with Exchange Server 2010 RTM.
Reading pane at the bottom	No replacement. This is no longer possible.
SharePoint document libraries and Windows file share	No replacement. This is no longer possible.

A De-emphasized Feature

Public folders, a key feature, continues to be de-emphasized in Exchange Server 2010. Starting with Exchange 2003, Microsoft has started to steer away from public folders.

If your organization requires features such as non-MAPI top-level hierarchies in public folder stores, public folder access with NNTP, or IMAP4, you will need to retain Exchange Server 2003 in your organization.

Comparison between Exchange Server 2007 and Exchange Server 2010

Table 1.5 compares Exchange 2007 and Exchange 2010.

TABLE 1.5 Exchange 2007 and 2010 comparison

	Exchange 2007	Exchange 2010
Release date	December 2006	November 2009
Supported operating system	Windows Server 2003 SP2 64-bit and newer	Windows Server 2008 64-bit SP1 and newer
Management tools in client operating system	Windows XP Professional and newer	Windows Vista 64-bit and newer
Supported domain controllers	Windows 2003 and higher	Windows 2003 SP2 and higher

TABLE 1.5 Exchange 2007 and 2010 comparison *(continued)*

	Exchange 2007	**Exchange 2010**
Domain and forest functional level	Windows 2000 Native or higher	Windows 2003 Native or higher
Enterprise Edition	50 storage groups or databases	No storage groups
		100 databases per server
Standard Edition		No storage groups
	5 storage groups or databases	5 databases
	No clustering support	
Hardware requirements	Processor: 64-bit processor Intel EM64T and AMD64	Processor: 64-bit processor, Intel EM64T and AMD64
	RAM: 2 GB + 5 MB per mailbox	RAM: 4 GB + 5 MB per mailbox
	Disk space: At least 1.2 GB on the drive to install Exchange and 200 MB for system drive; 450 MB if Hub Transport server	Disk space: At least 1.2 GB on the drive on which you install Exchange and 200 MB of available disk space on the system drive; 500 MB if Hub Transport server
Software prerequisites	ASP .NET Framework 2.0	.NET Framework 3.5
	IIS	IIS
	WWW	Windows Remote Management
	MMC 3.0	Windows PowerShell v2
	Windows PowerShell	
Options that are de-emphasized	CDOEx	
	WebDAV	

TABLE 1.5   Exchange 2007 and 2010 comparison *(continued)*

	Exchange 2007	Exchange 2010
	ExOLEDB	
	Store events	
	IMF	
Removed options	Outlook Mobile Access	
	Administrative groups	
	Coexistence with Exchange Server 5.5	Storage groups
	Routing groups	Clustered mailbox server
	Outlook Web Access to public folders	
	Mailbox Recovery Center	CDOEx
		WebDAV
		ExOLEDB
		Store events
		Streaming backups
Coexistence and upgrade paths	No Exchange Server 5.5. No in-place upgrade	No Exchange Server 2000 Must upgrade to Exchange Server 2003 or 2007 before transition to Exchange 2010
	Coexistence with Exchange Server 2000 and Exchange Server 2003	Coexistence with Exchange Server 2003 and Exchange Server 2007
	No in-place upgrade	Upgrade Exchange Server 2003 to 2007 and to Exchange Server 2010
	Migration options for Lotus Notes and GroupWise	

TABLE 1.5   Exchange 2007 and 2010 comparison *(continued)*

	Exchange 2007	Exchange 2010
Management and monitoring tools	EMC	Exchange Control Panel
	EMS	Role Based Access Control (RBAC)
	ExBPA	Remote PowerShell
	Database Recovery Management	
	Database Troubleshooter	
	Mail Flow Troubleshooter	
	Message tracking	
	Queue Viewer	
	Performance Monitor	
Administrative roles	Exchange Organization Administrators	Exchange Organization Administrators
	Exchange Recipient	Exchange Recipient
	Administrators	Administrators
	Exchange Server Administrators	Exchange Server Administrators
	Exchange View-Only Administrators	Exchange View-Only Administrators
		RBAC

TABLE 1.5   Exchange 2007 and 2010 comparison *(continued)*

	Exchange 2007	Exchange 2010
Clustering with high availability	Cluster continuous replication	
	Single copy cluster	
	Standby continuous replication	Database availability group
		Mailbox database copy
		Database mobility
Recovery options	Deleted item retention	Deleted item retention
	Mailbox retention	Mailbox retention
	Dial tone recovery	Single Item Recovery
	Recover CMS (CAS)	Dial tone recovery
	Recovery storage group	Recovery database
Compliance	Journaling	Journaling
	Disclaimer	Disclaimer
		MailTips
		Legal Hold
	SSL certificate automatically installed	SSL certificate automatically installed
	Secure RPC for Outlook	Secure RPC for Outlook
	HTTPS access for Outlook Anywhere	HTTPS access for Outlook Anywhere

You can look at the entire list of new and discontinued features in Exchange Server 2010 by visiting the Microsoft Exchange product site at http://www.microsoft.com/exchange/2010/en/us/whats-new.aspx.

Client Benefits to Exchange Server 2010

Microsoft spent much time listening to its customers, consultants, and messaging professionals to find out what features were missing or needed to be enhanced from earlier version of Exchange. The benefits of this feedback are shown in the many new features and enhancements. While we will not cover every modification, we will review some of the major changes.

Large Mailbox Support

Previous versions of Exchange required a significant investment in memory and a robust storage infrastructure to make large mailbox support a reality. Even if organizations had enough memory and storage to support large mailboxes, performance degradation typically started when mailboxes grew beyond 2 GB in size or when the individual folders contained more than 5,000 items. Outlook 2007 SP2 included some changes in how the software handled large mailboxes, making it more efficient to support mailboxes that grew larger than 10 GB. These improvements were helpful but still didn't solve all the issues or specific errors that might be encountered as mailboxes approached 20 GB in size.

Exchange 2010 reduces the I/O requirements of the underlying storage by some 70 percent over Exchange 2007. This results in optimization for mailboxes over 10 GB in size and folders with 100,000 items. Microsoft now supports, and even recommends, deploying Exchange on a properly sized, low-cost SATA-based storage. This can represent a significant cost savings and allow organizations to size Exchange for capacity instead of performance.

Native Archiving Features

With Exchange 2010, Microsoft introduced basic archiving features natively. Figure 1.7 shows the archiving feature enabled.

The native *archiving* feature of Exchange 2010 allows an administrator to create an archive mailbox for each user; content can be moved automatically via policies or manually by end users. Here are a few caveats about Microsoft's native archiving features:

- Access to the archive is online only, there is no support for synchronizing the archive data for offline use.

- No automated PST ingestion tools are currently available.

- The initial release of Exchange 2010 had no ability to store archive data in a different database or on different storage than the primary mailbox. Exchange 2010 Service Pack 1 introduced the ability to store the archive on a seperate database or even host the archive in the cloud.

- Archiving policies may not be as granular as some third-party solutions.

- Removing attachments and storing them elsewhere ("stubbing") is not available.

FIGURE 1.7   Archiving feature enabled

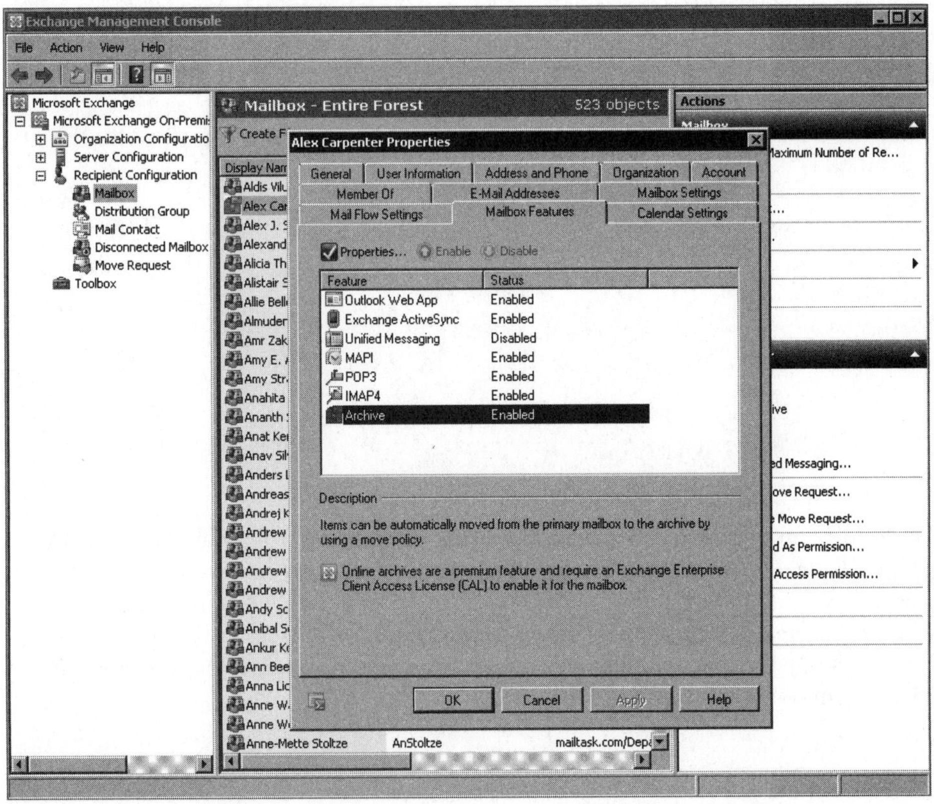

Microsoft's native archiving feature provides basic archiving functionality along with a unified search that will query both the primary, live mailbox and the archive mailbox simultaneously.

eDiscovery Features

In previous versions of Exchange, external tools are required for basic multi-mailbox searching. With Exchange 2010, this is provided by default, as seen in Figure 1.8.

FIGURE 1.8   Multi-Mailbox Search

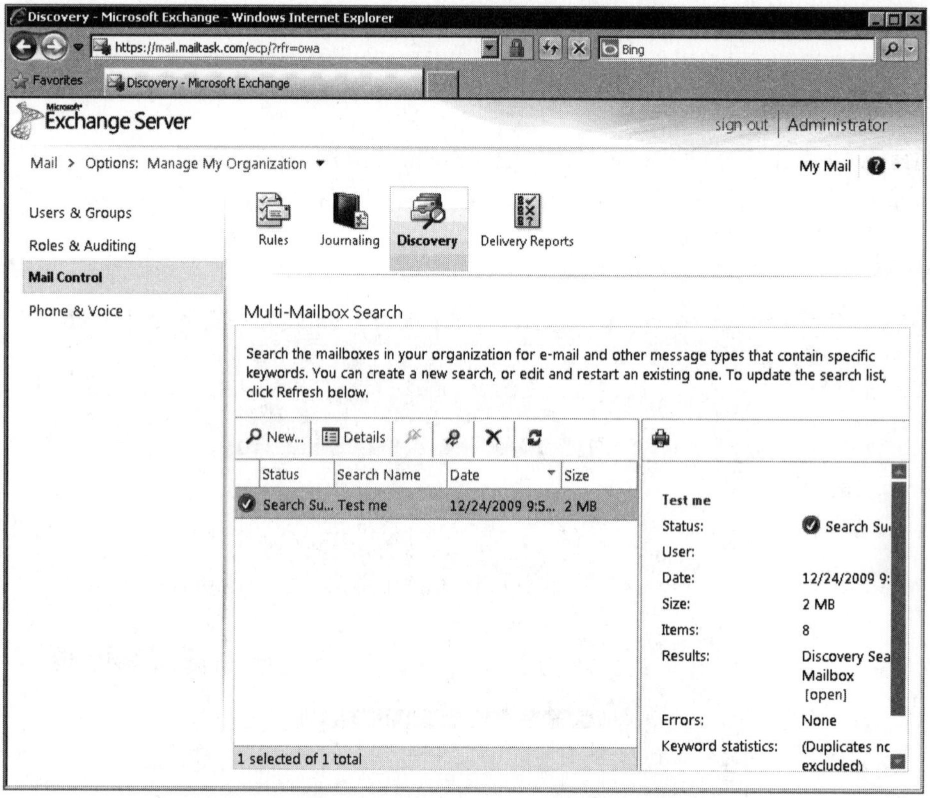

This allows for users—like a user in the Legal department, for example—to search across specific mailboxes or even across all mailboxes based on criteria such as sender, recipient, expiration policy, message size, send and receive date, and information rights management protected items. These searches can be applied across both the primary and archive mailboxes and can also be applied to email, contacts, calendars, and instant messaging conversations.

The results of the specific query, once obtained, may be sent to either a mailbox or a specific SMTP address. Because these functions are also exposed with the API, third parties are able to create tools that integrate with the native features.

Retention Policies and Legal Holds

While basic retention functionality has existed for years in the form of mailbox management policies (Exchange 2003) and managed folder policies (Exchange 2007), granularity of application was restricted to just folders. With Exchange 2010, retention policies exist that can be applied per folder or per individual message. These policies can be applied and managed centrally, or users can be allowed to select an appropriate retention policy using a convenient drop-down menu. If a retention policy applies to a specific item, a notification will be sent to the user when the item is set to expire.

An administrator can configure these policies so that upon expiration, the items are either deleted or moved to the user's personal archive. You can use this functionality to provide a true life cycle of an item by moving it to the archive after a certain period of time and then deleting the item from the archive after a longer period of time. Figure 1.9 shows some of the options that are now available within retention policies.

FIGURE 1.9   Retention policies

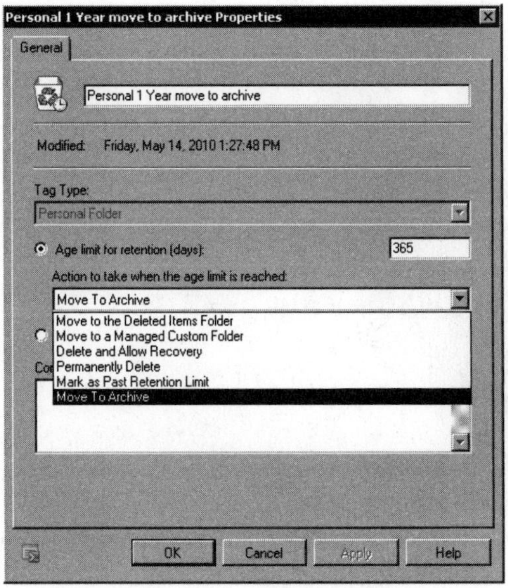

User-Specific HTML Disclaimers

Exchange 2007 provided simple email disclaimer functionality with trasport rules. Exchange 2007 disclaimers are limited to static text and could be difficult to manage. Besides email disclaimers, many companies also want to have standardized email signatures. To accomplish this, many companies would turn to third-party software or email gateways to provide this functionality. Smaller organizations would just manually create Outlook signatures. This content had to be managed outside of Exchange and proved to be difficult to update.

Exchange 2010 can define dynamic signature text that leverages AD-defined attributes such as name, title, and phone number in addition to HTML formatting. As a result, organizations can define a standard format that includes dynamic information specific to each user. Figure 1.10 shows the Specify disclaimer text dialog box.

FIGURE 1.10   Specify disclaimer text dialog box

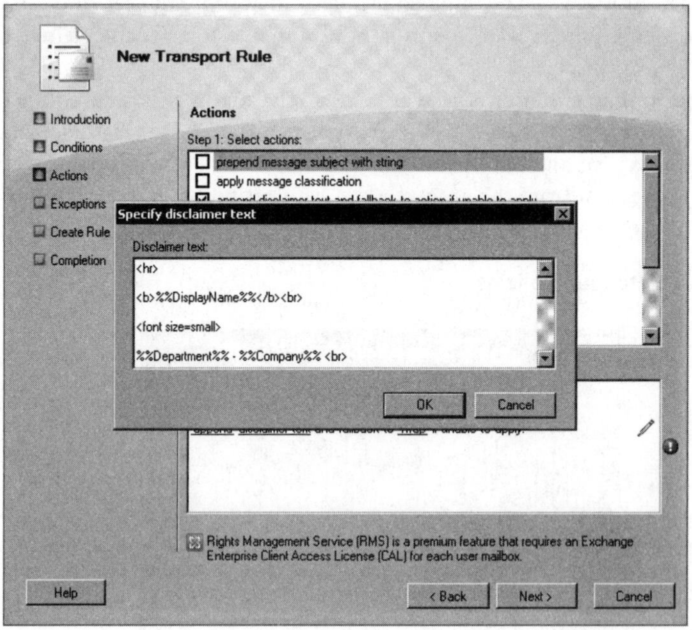

MailTips

MailTips are a new feature in Exchange 2010 that can help a user become more productive with email and can prevent Outlook and OWA policy infractions. MailTips provide suggestions to users about any potentially unanticipated results that will occur if a message was to be sent. In addition, it can prevent specific messages or even content from being sent entirely. There are a number of situations in which MailTips can prove to be useful:

- If a user is about to send a message to a distribution list that contains more than 1,000 recipients or to a distribution list that contains an external email address

- If a user is about to send a message to another user that has enabled their out-of-office auto-reply
- If a message exceeds the maximum configured sending/receiving size limits configured within Exchange
- If a recipient's mailbox is full due to a storage quota
- If a custom MailTip has been configured for a recipient or distribution group
- If a user replies to all but was Bcc'd on the original message
- If a user is attempting to send a message to a user or distribution list to which they are not allowed to send (ethical wall or defined client conflict)

Summary

Exchange 2010 has many improvements focused made to provide better support for large-scale deployments. The much reduced storage I/O requirements and flexible storage options have increased the administrators' or messaging professionals' design options and have allowed them to plan based on both capacity and performance. There is also a much richer set of permissions, allowing work to be pushed down to user-level administrators or to the users themselves.

Many features have created a seamless coexistence between OWA and Outlook 2010. In addition, features such as the ability to define tags and control what items get archived, eDiscovery support, policy enforcement through user intervention and provide solutions for many companied looking to get a handle on email content..

Chapter Essentials

Know what administrative changes have been made in Exchange 2010.   Understanding the changes within Exchange 2010 will help administrators who are coming from an Exchange 2007 environment. Understanding how the management interface has been redesigned will make finding features and components a lot easier.

Know the requirements for Exchange 2010.   A thorough knowledge of the requirements, both in server hardware and network configuration, will help in the planning stages of your Exchange 2010 rollout. These requirements are important because they will shape not only what hardware you will be able to utilize but also the amount of effort required to ensure that your organization's environment is ready for Exchange 2010.

Understand the benefits of the new features in Exchange 2010.   The new features, and even the enhancements to features, provide many benefits to the end users and Exchange administrators. A deep understanding of these features and how to properly configure them will ensure that the deployment will be successful and that your users will be fully prepared to take advantage of them.

Messaging Administrator's Guide to Exchange Server 2010

PART

II

Chapter

2

Installing and Configuring Exchange Server 2010

THE FOLLOWING TOPICS ARE DISCUSSED IN THIS CHAPTER:

- ✓ Understanding the job role of the administrator

- ✓ Installing Exchange prerequisites

- ✓ Preparing the infrastructure for Exchange Server 2010

- ✓ Preparing the infrastructure for Exchange Server 2010 deployment

- ✓ Introducing the server roles

- ✓ Installing Exchange Server 2010

- ✓ Understanding Role Based Access Control

As an administrator, you can spend countless hours just keeping up with the day-to-day tasks of your job. Very little time is left to devote to keeping up with the latest versions of products that are released to market, but this does not stop the push from your organization to stay current when it comes to software and technology. In a perfect world, an administrator, especially a Microsoft Exchange administrator, would have ample time to research the latest version of Microsoft Exchange and then be able to spend the time it takes to really get to know the product. In reality, though, the administrator often gets little or no warning that the messaging environment is going to be upgraded to the latest version of Microsoft Exchange.

It is our hope that this chapter and the rest of the book will make the process of installing and configuring Microsoft Exchange Server 2010 a simple task. Normally, the Exchange administrator would have to scramble to understand all the prerequisites and the preparation involved, not to mention finding all the resources needed to make the deployment a success. This chapter aims to ease that process.

Understanding the Administrator's Job Role

Depending on the size of an organization, the Exchange Server *administrator's* job role can vary. In small to medium-sized companies, the administrator may be directly responsible for both the implementation and management of the Exchange server. In larger, enterprise-sized companies, the Exchange administrator functions are typically split up into several parts. One group of administrators might implement the Exchange servers and another group of administrators might provide the day-to-day management.

Typically, an entry-level Exchange administrator focuses on day-to-day management of the server. This includes performing tasks such as new mailbox creation, troubleshooting mailbox problems, and assisting users with Outlook-related issues. As the administrator's skills grow, they branch out into planning for new Microsoft Exchange Server deployments and *Active Directory* configuration and maintenance. Exchange administrators also integrate disaster recovery and security, vital elements for a properly configured messaging environment, into their company's support and planning processes. After years of experience, the administrator's skills develop to a professional level, and then they begin to take part in the overall planning and designing of the messaging environment. An administrator also spends a considerable amount of time on the configuration of the Exchange server as well as the network.

The following list gives a basic breakdown of the tasks that an Exchange administrator might perform based on skill level:

Entry Level

- Active Directory management

- Exchange Server maintenance

- Exchange Server monitoring

- Exchange Server management

Intermediate

- Exchange services design

- Exchange security design

- Exchange Server installation

- Exchange Server infrastructure configuration

Professional

- Active Directory configuration

- Exchange Server planning

- Messaging security planning

- Disaster recovery planning

The end goal of an Exchange administrator, regardless of their skill level or career path, is to ensure that the messaging environment provides a secure, highly available messaging infrastructure. Part II of this book focuses on preparing you to succeed as a messaging administrator, whereas Part III of this book focuses on the messaging professional role.

Installing Exchange Prerequisites

If you are planning to deploy Exchange Server 2010, you need to make sure all of the following requirements are met. These requirements and limitations encompass much of what you need to know to be successful in preparing to install Exchange Server 2010:

- The schema master must be running Windows Server 2003 Service Pack 1 or later. Since Windows Server 2003 Service Pack 1 is no longer supported by Microsoft, it is recommended that all Windows Server 2003 computers be running at least Service Pack 2.

- A *global catalog* running Windows Server 2003 Service Pack 1 or later must be available in each Active Directory site into which Exchange will be deployed. This cannot be a Windows Server 2008 read-only *domain controller*.

- The Active Directory forest must be set to at least the Windows Server 2003 functional level.

- The Active Directory domain that Exchange will be installed into, or that contains Exchange recipients, should use at least the Windows Server 2003 native domain functional level.

- All Exchange Server 5.5 and Exchange Server 2000 computers must be removed from the domain and the Exchange organization must be set to Exchange 2003 native mode.

- Exchange Server 2007 and Exchange Server 2010 do not support renaming the Active Directory domain. If you are considering performing a domain rename, you must do so before deploying Exchange Server 2010.

- Any Exchange Server 2003 computers and machines with the Exchange 2003 management tools installed must have Service Pack 2 applied.

- Be sure that you have verified that your backup, file-level antivirus, third-party mobile messaging, and alert monitoring systems will support Exchange Server 2010.

Table 2.1 looks at the hardware requirements for Exchange 2010.

TABLE 2.1   Hardware requirements for Exchange 2010

Component	Requirement
Processor	X64 architecture-based computers, which must have an Intel processor that will support Intel 64.
Memory	This changes based on the roles or features that you plan to use.
Paging file size	Minimum and maximum must be set to physical RAM plus 10 MB.
Disk space	At least 1.2 GB on the drive that has the Exchange installation bits. 200 MB free on the system drive. You will need a minimum 500 MB of free space for the message queue database, which will reside on the Edge Transport server or Hub Transport server.
Drive	DVD-ROM drive or network access to the installation bits.
File format	NTFS.

Now that you have a basic understanding of the requirements for installing Exchange Server 2010, let's look at the software requirements:

- Windows Server 2008 with Service Pack 2 or higher
- Microsoft .NET Framework 3.5 with Service Pack 1
- Windows PowerShell 2.0
- Windows Remote Management

These prerequisites are to be installed on the servers on which you plan to install Exchange Server 2010.

Installing the Exchange prerequisites is a fairly straightforward four-step process. Each of these four steps is covered in an exercise. In Exercise 2.1, you'll perform the first step, installing .NET Framework 3.5.1.

EXERCISE 2.1

Installing Microsoft .NET Framework 3.5.1

The following steps walk you through the installation of .NET Framework 3.5.1 on Windows Server 2008 R2. To install the .NET Framework on Windows Server 2008 SP2, you must download and install an update for the .NET Framework 3.5 Service Pack 1 from http://www.microsoft.com/downloads/details.aspx?familyid=AB99342F-5D1A-413D-8319-81DA479AB0D7&displaylang=en. You will also need to download and install the update found at http://www.microsoft.com/downloads/details.aspx?FamilyID=98E83614-C30A-4B75-9E05-0A9C3FBDD20D&displaylang=en.

To install Microsoft .NET Framework 3.5.1 on Windows Server 2008 R2 follow these steps:

1. Open the Server Manager by clicking Start ➢ Administrative Tools ➢ Server Manager.

2. In the Features pane, choose Add Features.

3. In the Add Features Wizard, put a check mark in the .NET Framework 3.5.1 features box.

4. Choose Add Required Role Services.

5. In the Add Features Wizard, choose Next.

6. Click Next on the Web Server IIS page.

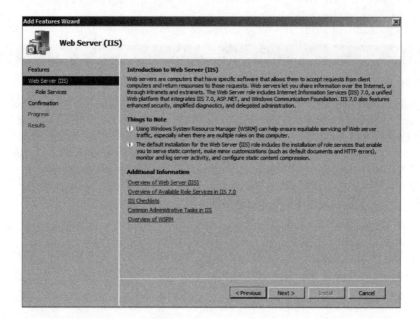

7. Click Next on the Select Role Services page.

8. On the Confirm Installation Selections page, click Install.

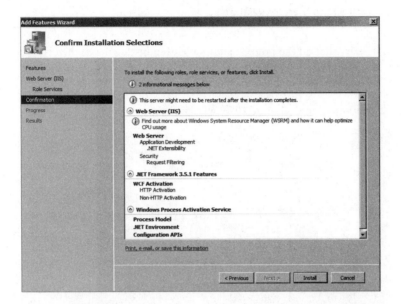

9. After the installation completes, review the installation results to ensure that the installation was successful. Then click Close to close the Add Features Wizard.

The next step is to install the Windows PowerShell 2.0. If you are installing Exchange 2010 on a Windows 2008 R2 server, Windows PowerShell 2.0 is already installed and you can skip the following exercise. If you are installing Exchange 2010 on a Windows Server 2008 SP2 computer, follow the steps in Exercise 2.2 to complete the installation of PowerShell.

Windows PowerShell 2.0 is now part of the Windows Management Framework Core and you can download it from the knowledge base article 968929 at the following URL:

`blogs.msdn.com/powershell/pages/download-windows-powershell.aspx.`

Installing Windows PowerShell 2.0

Perform the following steps to install Windows PowerShell 2.0. Installing PowerShell2.0 on Windows Server 2008 SP2 requires that you download and install the update from `support .microsoft.com/kb/968929`. Windows PowerShell 2.0 must also be installed on Windows Server 2008 R2, this is done by installing the PowerShell 2.0 feature. To install the Windows Management Framework that includes Windows PowerShell 2.0 follow these steps.

1. Click Next on the Windows PowerShell Setup Wizard Welcome screen.

2. On the License Agreement screen, choose I Accept and then click Next.

3. Choose Install on the Start Installation screen.

Now you'll verify that all the prerequisites have been installed and then run the Exchange 2010 setup. It will show you what requirements still need to be installed, as indicated in Figure 2.1.

FIGURE 2.1 Verifying Exchange 2010 prerequisites

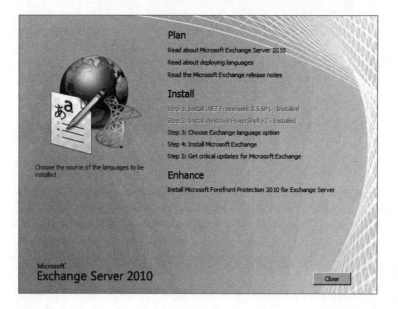

As you can see, steps 1 and 2 are grayed out, which indicates that these prerequisites have already been installed. In Exercise 2.3, you'll complete step 3 of installing the prerequisites, choosing a language option.

EXERCISE 2.3

Choosing Exchange Language Option

Perform the following steps to install the language options for Exchange 2010 installation:

1. Click Step 3: Choose Exchange language option in the Exchange 2010 setup dialog box.

EXERCISE 2.3 *(continued)*

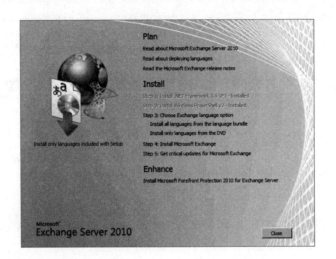

2. For this exercise choose, Install only languages from the DVD.

The steps to verify Windows services, perform network diagnostics, and run /PrepareSchema and /PrepareDomain are all part of the regular installation sequence for a new Exchange Server 2010 organization.

Finally, in Exercise 2.4, we'll show you how to install required services and components on Windows Server 2008 R2.

EXERCISE 2.4

Installing Required Services and Components on Windows Server 2008 R2

Perform the following steps to prepare a Windows Server 2008 R2 computer with the required services and components:

1. From the Start menu, navigate to All Programs ➢ Accessories ➢ Windows PowerShell. Right click and click Run as administrator to open an elevated Windows PowerShell console and run the following command:

    Import-Module ServerManager

2. Now use the Add-Windows Feature cmdlet to install the necessary Windows components. Run the following command to install the components needed for a typical Exchange 2010 installation:

Add-WindowsFeature NET-Framework,RSAT-ADDS,Web-Server,Web-Basic-Auth,Web-Windows-Auth,Web-Metabase,Web-Net-Ext,Web-Lgcy-Mgmt-Console,WAS-Process-Model,RSAT-Web-Server,Web-ISAPI-Ext,Web-Digest-Auth,Web-Dyn-Compression,NET-HTTP-Activation,RPC-Over-HTTP-Proxy -Restart

3. After the system reboot, run the following cmdlet to configure the Net.TCP Port Sharing Service for automatic startup:

Set-Service NetTcpPortSharing -StartupType Automatic

4. Download and install the following updates:

If installing the initial release of Exchange 2010 the Microsoft Filter Pack 2007 from the following URL:

www.microsoft.com/downloads/details.aspx? FamilyID=60c92a37-719c-4077-b5c6-cac34f4227cc&displaylang=en.

Or if installing Exchange 2010 SP1 install the Microsoft Filter Pack 2010 from: http://www.microsoft.com/downloads/details.aspx?familyid=5CD4DCD7-D3E6-4970-875E-ABA93459FBEE&displaylang=en

Also the following updates must also be downloaded and installed:

Win7 rollup package (PR for WFE 81029) from the following URL:

http://code.msdn.microsoft.com/KB98344

FIX: An application that is based on the Microsoft .NET Framework 2.0 Service Pack 2 and that invokes a Web service call asynchronously throws an exception on a computer that is running Windows 7 from the following URL:

http://support.microsoft.com/kb/977020

WCF: Enable WebHeader settings on the RST/SCT

§ http://code.msdn.microsoft.com/KB982867

Optionally you can download and install the following update:

FIX: A System.NotSupportedException exception is thrown when you run an IIS hosted WCF service that uses a client certificate for SSL authentication.

You can learn more about the cmdlets available for installing Windows components and a list of cmdlets based on Exchange Server roles by visiting the Microsoft TechNet article at technet.microsoft.com/en-us/library/bb691354.aspx.

Preparing the Infrastructure for Exchange Server 2010

The importance of preparing the *infrastructure* for Exchange Server 2010 cannot be understated. When you install Exchange Server, good preparation is not only the key to a successful installation, it is also vital. Simply stated, an improperly prepared infrastructure can cause installation failures and result in countless hours of troubleshooting to solve a problem that could be easily avoidable with proper preparation. As with previous versions of Microsoft Exchange, preparing Active Directory and the domain is one of the first steps.

In versions prior to Exchange Server 2000, Exchange maintained a directory of its own through a service known as *Directory Service*. Directory Service maintained a copy of the directory in a database file on each Exchange server and took care of replicating changes in the directory to other Exchange servers.

Since Exchange Server 2000, Exchange has been completely reliant on Active Directory Domain Services (AD DS) to provide directory services. This reliance caused a shift in the way the Exchange directory was maintained. The first item below examines how an *Active Directory forest* contains an Exchange organization. Then, the section "Domain Name Service" looks at the interaction of DNS in an Exchange organization.

Active Directory Forests

An Active Directory forest is a logical boundary for Active Directory. There can be multiple *domains* in a forest; however, outside the forest there are no implicit trusts and there is no built-in ability to replicate with other forests. There is a global catalog that is shared by all global catalog servers in a forest. Therefore, an Exchange organization is also contained within the boundaries of a forest. This is different from earlier versions of Windows NT and Exchange Server 5.5. In previous versions, an Exchange organization could span domains that did not even trust one another because Exchange 5.5 did not rely on the underlying security structure of a Windows NT domain. With Active Directory and Exchange Server 2010, the security structure is integrated, which means a single Exchange organization cannot span multiple forests but can span multiple domains within a single forest.

Because Exchange Server relies so heavily on AD DS, it is essential that it be configured and operating properly in your organization. Outlook Web Access, *SMTP* connectivity, and Internet connectivity all rely on DNS.

Active Directory in Exchange Server 2010 is often called a *namespace*, which is similar to the directory service in earlier versions of Exchange and means any bounded area in which a given name can be resolved. The DNS name creates a namespace for a tree or forest, such as wiley.com, to function properly.

A valid Active Directory namespace such as exchangeexchange.local is not a valid Internet namespace, since the .local top level domain cannot be registered with a domain registrar. Although a user's logon name might be user@exchangeexchange.local, you can use address generation policies to assign email addresses for valid Internet namespaces like exchangeexchange.com. Although, many administrators find it easier to use an Active Directory namespace that does work on the Internet and employ the use of split DNS to segregate internal and external resources.

Active Directory Partitions

Within AD DS, there are three main partitions: *Schema*, Configuration, and Domain. Recall that there can be only one Exchange Server organization within an entire forest. Here are some specific examples of how Exchange Server 2010 uses Active Directory:

- The configuration partition stores all configuration information about the Exchange organization. This information includes items such as recipient policies, address lists, and Exchange settings. The configuration partition is replicated to every domain controller in the forest; therefore, this critical Exchange configuration information is available to every domain user irrespective of which domain holds their user account.

- The domain partition stores information about the basic blocks of Exchange Server 2010: its recipient objects. Recipient objects include the users, contacts, and groups that have configured email addresses.

- The schema partition is modified by the Exchange Server 2010 setup routine to add attributes to existing objects, such as users and groups. Additionally, the schema is extended to include Exchange Server-specific objects that are required for Exchange Server to function properly.

- The global catalog receives many new items of information as a result of the installation of Exchange Server 2010 in a forest. Exchange uses the global catalog to generate address lists for usage by Exchange recipients, and Exchange also uses the global catalog to locate a recipient to aid in the delivery of mail items to that recipient. Exchange Server automatically generates the *global address list (GAL)* from all recipients listed in the global catalog.

Message Flow

Prior to the release of Exchange Server 2007, a complex link-state routing algorithm was used to route messages between geographically separated Exchange servers. Exchange used routing groups that were connected with routing-group connectors to perform this routing. With the elimination of routing groups and link-state routing starting in Exchange Server 2007, all Exchange message routing is performed by Hub Transport servers using the Active Directory sites and site links that service Active Directory itself. As such, message routing (both within the same site and across site links) is significantly less complex in Exchange Server 2010. This also means that proper configuration of sites and subnets is very important to the function of Exchange Server.

Active Directory

Active Directory contains information and data about a network or domain. Active Directory can contain objects that represent users, computers, printers, and other resources.

Because of Exchange Server 2010's involvement with Active Directory, its installation involves a number of Active Directory user and group security accounts. To be able to install and manage Exchange Server, it is important to understand these groups and when you will need to have the permissions assigned to them. Some of the more pertinent groups are as follows:

Schema Admins   Members of this group have the rights and permissions necessary to modify the schema of Active Directory. To run the setup with the `/PrepareSchema` or `/PrepareAD` option, both of which modify the schema for Exchange Server 2010 and are described later in this chapter, you must belong to the Schema Admins group, the Enterprise Admins group, and the local Administrators group on the computer on which you actually run the command.

Enterprise Admins   Members of this group have the rights and permissions necessary to administer any domain in a forest. To run setup with the `/PrepareSchema`, `/PrepareLegacyExchangePermissions`, `/PrepareDomain`, or `/PrepareAD` option, you must be a member of the Enterprise Admins group and the local Administrators group on the computer running the tool.

Domain Admins   Members of this group have the rights and permissions necessary to administer any computer or resource in a domain. You must be a member of this group to run setup with the `/PrepareDomain` option, which prepares each domain for Exchange Server 2010 installation.

Administrators   Members of this local group are given the rights necessary to administer a local computer and install software on it.

The installation of Exchange Server 2010 will also create several new security groups. The following list includes the security groups that you will want to become familiar with:

Organization Management   Members of this group have full access to all Exchange Server properties throughout the Exchange organization. By default, the administrative account that is used to install Exchange Server 2010 is placed into this group.

Recipient Management   Members of this group have the required permissions to modify any Exchange-related property on all Exchange recipients. By default, the Exchange Organization Administrators group is placed into this group.

Exchange Servers   Members of this group are the computer accounts for all Exchange servers. This security group provides Exchange servers with the permissions necessary to access one another and perform necessary Exchange functions.

View-Only Organization Management   Members of this group have view-only access permissions to all Exchange Server properties and recipient objects in the Exchange organization.

UM Management   Members will be granted access to manage the Unified Messaging (UM) features. Features such as mailbox properties as it relates to UM, auto attendant and UM server configuration.

Discovery Managment   When users or administrators are added to this group they will be given access to perform searches on Exchanged mailboxes. Members of this group can search by specific criteria.

Records Management   Members of records management have the required permissions to configure features such as transport rules and retention policy tags.

Server Management   Members of this group are given the access needed to administer the Exchange 2010 server configuration. This group will grant access to the physical servers so as to allow configuration of mailbox features such as database copies, transport queues and Send connectors. This group is similar to the Exchange Server Administrators role in Exchange Server 2007. This group will not give them rights to administer the Exchange 2010 recipient configuration.

Help Desk   Limited access will be granted to members of this group to manage Exchange 2010 recipients.

Hygiene Management   Permissions to configure antivirus and antispam features are granted to members of this group.

Public Folder Management   Members of this group have the required permissions to manage public folders and databases. By default this role group is assigned management roles, which can be added or removed to meet the needs of your organization.

Delegated Setup   Members of this group can deploy Exchange 2010 servers that have been previously provisioned. This group does not have rights to manage the server after it has been deployed.

Active Directory does not, by default, have definitions for what mailboxes, distribution groups, public folders, or other Exchange-related objects are. As mentioned earlier in this chapter, the Exchange installations must create a number of groups and permissions in order to function. To create the definitions for Exchange Server objects and to create the needed groups and permissions, Active Directory Domain Services needs to be properly prepared. So before you install the first Exchange server in an organization, you need to prepare the forest and each domain into which Exchange will be installed. For these tasks, use the following commands available within the Exchange Server 2010 `setup.exe` commands:

/PrepareSchema   /PrepareSchema must be run once in a forest. It should be run on the domain controller that is configured with the schema master role, but this is not a requirement. It extends the Active Directory schema with the objects necessary to run Exchange Server 2010.

/PrepareAD   The /PrepareAD command must also be run within the domain root of the forest and is used to create the global Exchange objects and configuration. If the schema has not yet been extended, the /PrepareAD command will accomplish that. Additionally, the /PrepareAD command accomplishes the tasks performed by the /PrepareDomain command in the domain root.

/PrepareDomain   The /PrepareDomain command must be run in each domain where Exchange Server 2010 will be installed to identify the domain's address list server and to create special domain accounts that Exchange needs in order to run properly.

/PrepareAllDomains   Alternatively, the /PrepareAllDomains command will perform the /PrepareDomain command against each of the domains in the forest provided the account with which you are running the command is a member of the Enterprise Admins group.

In previous versions of Exchange Server, you had to run the ForestPrep and DomainPrep commands. Starting with Exchange Server 2007, these commands were removed and replaced with other options, allowing greater flexibility in how Exchange Server is deployed.

Though this seems like a complicated installation routine, it does provide a significant advantage. Many businesses separate the administrative responsibilities of domain management, schema management, and Exchange management. For example, one group might be in charge of administering the schema and the primary domains of the forest, another might be in charge of managing the child domains, and still another group might be in charge of managing Exchange.

If a single administrator or group runs the network and has all the appropriate permissions (or if there is only one domain in your forest), this simplifies the installation of Exchange. If the account with which you install the first Exchange server belongs to the Schema Admins, Enterprise Admins, and Administrators groups for the local computer, you do not need to run /PrepareAD, /PrepareSchema, or /PrepareDomain manually because you will run them during the regular Exchange setup process.

These additional setup tools provide the ability for separate administrators to perform their necessary part of the Exchange installation and simplify the Exchange deployment. For example, the group in charge of managing the schema will have the permissions required to run the /PrepareSchema command to extend the schema. Domain administrators will have the permissions required to use the /PrepareDomain command that modifies domains. To run the /PrepareAD command, the administrator will need both Schema Admins and Enterprise Admins permissions because this command is all-encompassing. After you complete these tasks, Exchange administrators can install and manage Exchange without receiving permissions for the other preparation tasks.

> ### 🌐 Real World Scenario
>
> **Planning an Active Directory Deployment**
>
> If you are planning a completely new Active Directory deployment for your organization, then you should be certain to place domain controllers and global catalog servers in locations that make sense for how your company is organized and how it operates. When planning how and where to locate these key servers in your Active Directory environment, there is no absolute answer that works for all scenarios. The saying "the more, the better" is not necessarily true, especially if replication over slow WAN links becomes too much for those links to handle. Conversely, saying "less is more" is untrue when it comes to implementing a solid Active Directory infrastructure. Remember, this will be the foundation of your entire network, so you should take however long you need to get it right the first time.
>
> Keep in mind the following guidelines as you work in different scenarios:
>
> - Every domain in the Active Directory forest should have at least two domain controllers. This is for both client load balancing and disaster recovery in case one domain controller should fail.
>
> - You should place additional domain controllers in domains as organizational structures (such as physical location or client groupings) dictate.
>
> - You should be aware that additional domain controllers will cause additional replication traffic, which can be problematic for intersite replication across slow *WAN* links.
>
> - Every Active Directory site must have at least one domain controller, and that one domain controller must be configured as a global catalog if Exchange servers or users are in that site.
>
> - If a site has multiple domain controllers, consider using a Bridgehead server for Active Directory replication to other sites.
>
> - Install the right number of global catalog servers in each site to support the applications. When using 64-bit domain controllers, the ratio of global catalog processor cores to Exchange Mailbox server processor cores is 1 to 4.

Domain Name Service

For Active Directory and Exchange Server 2010 to function, DNS must be properly functioning in your organization.

The DNS name creates a namespace for a tree or forest, such as mailtask.com. All child domains of mailtask.com, such as sales.mailtask.com, share the root namespace. In Exchange Server 2010, Active Directory forms a namespace in which the name of an object in the directory can be resolved to the object. All domains that have a common root domain form a *contiguous namespace*. This means the domain name of a child domain is the child domain name appended to the name of the parent domain.

Before proceeding with any installation of Exchange server, all clients and servers must be able to reliably resolve DNS queries. This is the reason for the underlying requirement for DNS to be properly installed and configured. DNS is used to find email domains. In simple terms, when a user sends an email, a server does either an internal or external request for information on the email domain. This request will return the information about what IP address to send the email to. It works the same way that our snail mail system works today; you cannot send a letter to your friend without knowing their address. So if you don't know it, you will either call your friend or look it up in an address book. The big difference is that the Exchange server can be configured to use any Internet DNS name for email addresses, but your friend's home address is fixed to the location of his house. But the principle is the same, so if DNS is not set up right, the email message has no place to go and you will have unhappy end users.

Some steps can be taken, in the planning stages, that will help make Exchange deployment easier for you. For example, Exchange deployment is a lot easier if you have a domain name that matches your email domain. This simplifies the Exchange deployment for your end users also because their login name matches their email address. So, even though it's hard not to, don't skip over the steps that will verify you have a properly configured DNS setup. If you find any issues or errors, take the time to ensure that they are resolved before you proceed with installing Exchange. This will save you a lot of headaches later on in the installation steps.

Verifying Name Resolution

It should go without saying that functional name resolution within an Active Directory forest is absolutely critical. Because Exchange Server 2010 extends the existing foundation provided by Active Directory, functional name resolution is thus absolutely required for the proper operation of the Exchange organization. In short, you're not likely going to be at the stage of deploying Exchange Server 2010 if your name resolution isn't functioning at that time.

All Exchange Server 2010 servers must be able to resolve names and IP addresses for all other Exchange Server 2010 servers, all domain controllers, and all global catalog servers. For organizations using the Edge Transport role in a perimeter network or the *demilitarized zone (DMZ)*, this also means that all Edge Transport servers must be able to contact all Hub Transport servers inside the protected internal network and vice versa. To that end, functional name resolution becomes more than just an issue of making sure you've done your job within Active Directory; it is also a task in which the network administrator in charge of configuring and maintaining your organizational firewalls and external DNS must be involved.

You can perform quick network resolution testing using the nslookup command from an Exchange Server 2010 server. Figure 2.2 shows how the nslookup command is used to resolve both internal and external names.

FIGURE 2.2   Using nslookup to verify functional name resolution within the network

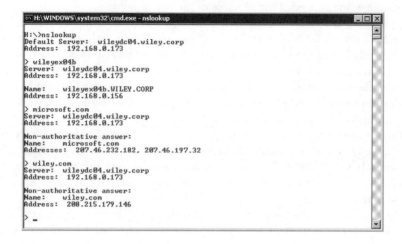

Running Network and Domain Controller Diagnostics Tests

Previous versions of Windows server did not include the support tools, such as dcdiag. Windows Server 2008 now includes these support tools as part of the base installation, thus eliminating the need to download and install them before being able to take advantage of them. In Exchange Server 2003, these tools were linked in the setup preparation tasks and running them was recommended. You should run these commands manually before even getting to the setup process of the first Exchange Server 2010 server.

The dcdiag command performs the following types of checks (among others):

- Connectivity, to verify proper DNS records and LDAP/RPC connectivity

- Replications, to check for replication errors

- NetLogons, to verify that the proper permissions exist to allow for replication

- RIDManager, to verify that the RID master is accessible and functional

- KCCEvent, to verify that the Knowledge Consistency Checker (KCC) is functional and error free

- Topology, to verify that an accurate and functional replication topology has been generated by the KCC

- DNS, to verify proper operation and health of DNS

Figure 2.3 presents some sample output from the dcdiag command.

FIGURE 2.3 Using the dcdiag command to verify domain functionality

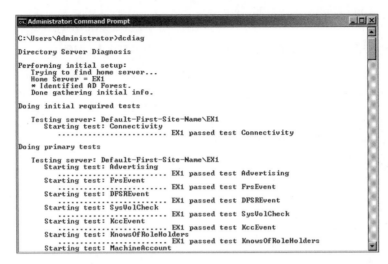

You should resolve any issues noted with any of the tests before you install and configure Exchange Server 2010.

You can get more information about the tests performed, usage of the dcdiag tool, and corrective actions to perform as a result of using the dcdiag tools by searching the Microsoft website for "Windows support tools."

Preparing the Infrastructure for Exchange Server 2010 Deployment

Before you proceed with the deployment of Microsoft Exchange Server, you must take some time to review your current infrastructure and make any changes that are necessary. You will want to review the following sections and examine your current infrastructure, which will help ensure that your organization is ready for Exchange 2010.

This preparation is a must if you want a successful deployment. At times this is something you might want to skip over and get right to the fun of installing your first Exchange server, but if you skip over it, you run the risk of having to deal with a lot of troubleshooting later or of the installation of Exchange failing.

Verifying Domain and Forest Functional Levels

The version of Windows Server that your Active Directory domain controllers are running will directly affect what forest and domain functional levels you can set. The forest and domain functional levels limit the functionality of the domain to the features available in the version of Windows Server that correlates to the level.

The forest functional levels are as follows:

- Windows 2000

- Windows Server 2003

- Windows Server 2008

- Windows Server 2008 R2

The domain functional levels are as follows.

- Windows 2000

- Windows Server 2003

- Windows Server 2008

- Windows Server 2008 R2

To deploy Exchange Server 2010, you need to have a forest functional level of Windows Server 2003, which requires that the domains have a functional level of Windows Server 2003. In Exercise 2.5, we show you how to verify the domain and forest functional levels. You must ensure that they are at the Windows 2003 native functional level or higher.

> Before you adjust the domain or forest functionality, be sure that your domain and forest are able to support it.

EXERCISE 2.5

Verifying the Domain and Forest Functional Levels

Perform the following steps to verify the domain and forest functional levels:

1. Log into EX01 with Domain Admins credentials.

2. Open the Active Directory Users and Computers console.

3. Right-click the domain name in the console and select Raise domain functional level. The dialog box shown here opens.

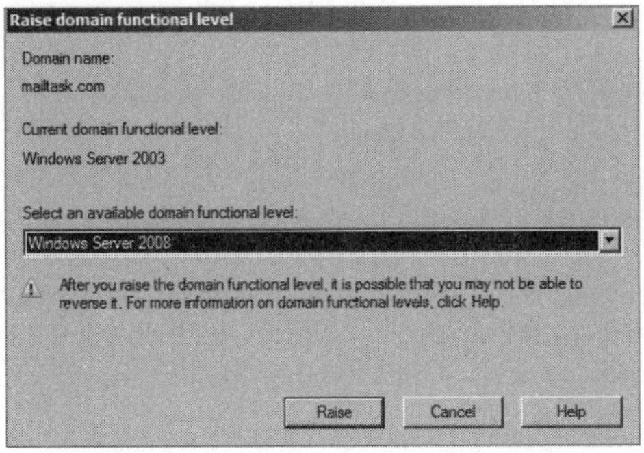

4. If the domain functional level is less than Windows 2003 native, select Windows 2003 native (ideally if there are no Windows 2003 domain controllers), Windows Server 2003, or Windows Server 2008, and click the Raise button.

5. When prompted to make the change, click OK. This is a one-way change that cannot be undone.

6. Repeat steps 1 through 5 for every other domain in the forest.

7. To change or verify the forest functional level, open the Active Directory Domains and Trusts console while logged into a root domain controller with Enterprise Admins credentials.

8. In the console, right-click the root of the Active Directory Domains and Trusts node and select Raise Forest Functional Level. The dialog box shown here opens.

9. Raise the forest functional level to at least the Windows Server 2003 option, and click the Raise button. You are prompted to accept the change here as well.

Preparing the Windows Active Directory Forest

Before you install the first server Exchange 2010 in your organization, you must prepare Active Directory. This allows Active Directory to know that an Exchange server is now part of the organization and how to work with Exchange objects.

Active Directory uses the schema to define a set of rules that define Active Directory and any objects it contains. A schema can control things like naming structures, data types, object types, and so forth. So one of the first things you'll want to do is to prepare Active Directory so that it knows that an Exchange server is coming. To do this update to Active Directory, run the /PrepareSchema command.

To run the /PrepareSchema command, you must belong to the Schema Admins and Enterprise Admins security groups. In addition, you must belong to the local Administrators group on the server on which Exchange will be installed. If you are not a member of these groups, the appropriate administrator will have to run the /PrepareSchema command before you can install Exchange Server 2010.

When you run the /PrepareSchema command, it performs only one task: It extends the Active Directory schema with Exchange-related information and this schema is shared by all domains in the Active Directory forest.

> **WARNING**   Do not run the /PrepareSchema command as your first preinstallation step if you have an existing legacy Exchange Server 2007 or Exchange 2003 Server organization. You must run the /PrepareLegacyExchangePermissions command first. See the section "Modifying Existing Exchange Organizations to Support Migration" later in this chapter for additional discussion on this scenario.

In Exercise 2.6, we walk through the steps to run the /PrepareSchema command.

We'll discuss the process to prepare a forest and domain for Exchange Server 2010 to coexist with Exchange Server 2007 or Exchange 2003 Server later in this chapter.

EXERCISE 2.6

Running the /PrepareSchema Command

Perform the following steps to run the /PrepareSchema command:

1. Log into a server in the same site as the schema master operations role with an account that is a member of both the Schema Admins and Enterprise Admins groups.

2. Insert the Microsoft Exchange Server 2010 DVD into the server's DVD-ROM drive. If the server does not have a DVD-ROM drive, you can copy the files to a network location and then proceed using that location.

3. Open a command interpreter window by selecting Start ➤ Run, enter **CMD**, and press Enter.

4. In the command interpreter window, enter the command

   X:\setup /prepareschema

   where *X* represents the location of the Exchange Server 2010 setup files, local or remote. Press Enter to start the schema preparation process; the command is shown here. When you use the /PrepareSchema command, you can shorten it to /ps, which saves a small amount of typing but performs the same command.

EXERCISE 2.6 *(continued)*

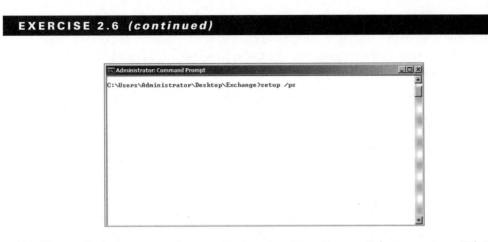

5. If setup finds any errors, they are displayed and the /PrepareSchema process will fail. You will need to rerun the command after you correct the noted errors.

You can run the /PrepareSchema portion of setup while you install the first Exchange Server 2010 computer. This situation is typically encountered only in smaller organizations where only one domain exists within the Active Directory forest. Once the forest has been prepared by extending the schema with the /PrepareSchema command, you need to ready the forest for an installation of Exchange Server 2010. This step involves preparing the root-level domain in the forest and creating the Exchange global objects in Active Directory so that Active Directory understands that there is an Exchange server in the domain and what to do with it. You accomplish this process by issuing the /PrepareAD command, which will also prepare the root domain with the /PrepareDomain command, which means if you have a single domain forest, you do not have to run both commands.

When you run the /PrepareAD command, it performs the following tasks:

- If the forest contains no existing versions of Exchange Server, it prompts you for an Exchange organization name and then creates the organization object in the Active Directory. The organization is at the top of the Exchange hierarchy. This case-sensitive field can be up to 64 characters in length. The organization name is associated with every object in the Exchange directory, such as mailboxes, public folders, and distribution lists. It is important to note that the organization name cannot be modified after installation.

- Creates the universal security groups that were discussed previously in this chapter.

- Creates the Microsoft Exchange container and organization, if they do not already exist.

- Verifies that the schema and the organization are up-to-date.

- Creates the default Accepted Domains entry if it does not already exist.

- Assigns permissions throughout the configuration partition.

- Imports the `Rights.ldf` file to add the extended rights that are required for Exchange to install into Active Directory.

- Creates the Microsoft Exchange *Security Groups* organizational unit (OU) in the root domain of the forest and assigns permissions on this OU.

- Creates the following universal security groups (USGs) in the Microsoft Exchange Security Groups OU:

    - Organization Management

    - Recipient Management

    - Server Management

    - View-Only Organization Management

    - Public Folder Management

    - UM Management

    - Help Desk

    - Records Management

    - Discovery Management

    - Delegated Setup

You can run the `/PrepareAD` portion of setup while installing the first Exchange Server 2010 computer. This situation is typically encountered only in smaller organizations where only one domain exists within the Active Directory forest. We show you how to run this command in Exercise 2.7.

EXERCISE 2.7

Running the `/PrepareAD` Command

Perform the following steps to run the /PrepareAD command:

1. Log into a domain controller of the root domain with an account that is a member of the Enterprise Admins group.

2. Insert the Microsoft Exchange Server 2010 DVD into the server's DVD-ROM drive. If the server does not have a DVD-ROM drive, you can copy the files to a network location and then proceed using that location. Alternatively, the files may have been downloaded and extracted from Microsoft's Volume Licensing portal.

3. Open a command interpreter window by selecting Start ➢ Run, enter **CMD**, and press Enter.

4. In the command interpreter window, enter the command

    `X:\setup /preparead /organizationname:NAME`

EXERCISE 2.7 *(continued)*

where *X* represents the location of the Exchange Server 2010 setup files, local or remote, and *NAME* represents the name you want for the Exchange organization. In this example, we will call the new organization mailtask. Press Enter to start the root domain preparation process; the command is shown here.

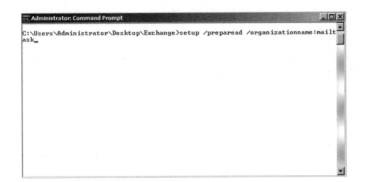

5. If setup finds any errors, they are displayed and the /PrepareAD process will fail. You need to rerun the command after you correct the noted errors.

After the /PrepareAD command has been completed and replication has occurred between domain controllers, you can check two places to quickly identify changes that have been made within Active Directory. The Active Directory Users and Computers console will contain a new organizational unit named Microsoft Exchange Security Groups, as shown in Figure 2.4; it holds the universal security groups discussed previously.

As shown in Figure 2.5, the Active Directory Sites and Services console (Services node) displays the Exchange organization that was created and several configuration items for it. To enable the Services node, click the Active Directory Sites and Services root node and then select View ➢ Show Service Node.

FIGURE 2.4 Viewing changes in Active Directory Users and Computers after running the /PrepareAD command

FIGURE 2.5   Viewing changes in Active Directory Sites and Services after running the /PrepareAD command

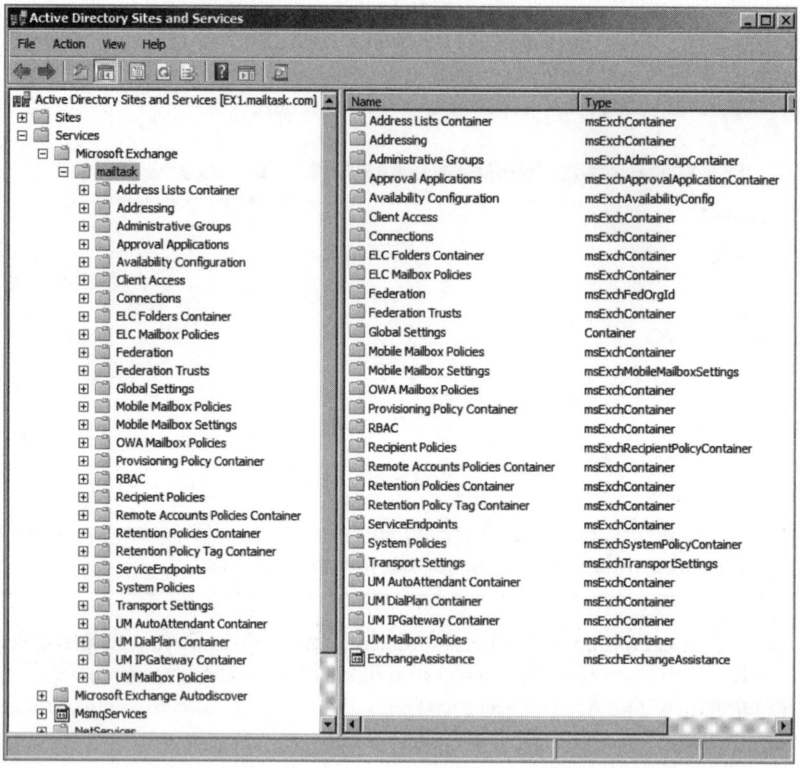

Preparing Other Windows Active Directory Domains

In an Active Directory forest with multiple domains, after running setup using the /PrepareSchema and /PrepareAD commands, you may also need to use the /PrepareDomain command to prepare each additional domain in the forest that will run Exchange Server 2010 or include Exchange recipients. This is only required if the account used to run PrepareAD does not have the necessary permissions to modify the other domains in the forest. PrepareAD is run to set the permissions Exchange Server can run properly. You must run the /PrepareDomain command in each domain that will contain Exchange Server 2010 servers or recipient objects or that has users or groups that will manage Exchange Server 2010 computers. You do not need to run this command on the same domain you used the /PrepareAD command because it automatically prepares the local domain.

You can run the /PrepareDomain portion of setup while you install the first Exchange Server 2010 computer. This situation is typically encountered only in smaller organizations where only one domain exists within the Active Directory forest.

To run the /PrepareDomain command, you must be a member of the Domain Admins group for the domain and the Administrators group on the local computer where you will be running the command, also known as DomainPrep.

DomainPrep performs the following tasks:

- Configures the required permissions on the domain container for the Exchange Servers group, Exchange Organization Administrators group, Authenticated Users group, and Exchange Recipient Administrators group.

- Creates a new container named Microsoft Exchange System Objects and sets permissions on the container for the Exchange Servers group, Exchange Organization Administrators group, and the Authenticated Users group.

- Creates a domain global group in the domain called Exchange Install Domain Servers. This group is then added to the Exchange Servers universal security group in the root domain.

We show you how to run the /PrepareDomain command in Exercise 2.8.

EXERCISE 2.8

Running the /PrepareDomain Command

Perform the following steps to run the /PrepareDomain command:

1. Log into a domain controller with an account that is a member of the Domain Admins group.

2. Insert the Microsoft Exchange Server 2010 DVD into the server's DVD-ROM drive. If the server does not have a DVD-ROM drive, you can copy the files to a network location and then proceed using that location.

3. Open a command interpreter window by selecting Start ➢ Run, enter **CMD**, and press Enter.

4. In the command interpreter window, enter the command

   X:\setup /PrepareDomain

   where *X* represents the location of the Exchange Server 2010 setup files, local or remote. Press Enter to start the root domain preparation process; the command is shown here.

EXERCISE 2.8 *(continued)*

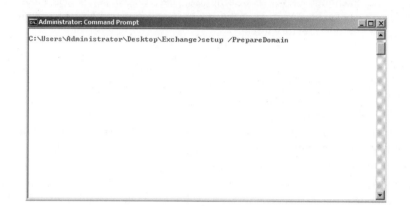

5. If setup finds any errors, they are displayed and the /PrepareDomain process fails. You need to rerun the command after you correct the noted errors.

As shown in Figure 2.6, the Microsoft Exchange System Objects container now exists, although it cannot be clicked and opened like other containers or organizational units. You need to select View ➢ Advanced Features to enable viewing of advanced objects such as the Microsoft Exchange System Objects container within Active Directory Users and Computers.

FIGURE 2.6 Viewing changes in Active Directory Users and Computers after running the /PrepareDomain command

Active Directory Users and Computers [EX1.mailta:	Name ▲	Type	Description
Saved Queries	Builtin	builtinDomain	
mailtask.com	Computers	Container	Default cont
Builtin	Domain Controllers	Organizational Unit	Default cont
Computers	ForeignSecurityPrincipals	Container	Default cont
Domain Controllers	Infrastructure	infrastructureUpdate	
ForeignSecurityPrincipals	LostAndFound	lostAndFound	Default cont
LostAndFound	Managed Service Accounts	Container	Default cont
Managed Service Accounts	Microsoft Exchange Security Groups	Organizational Unit	
Microsoft Exchange Security Groups	Microsoft Exchange System Objects	msExchSystemObjectsContainer	
Program Data	NTDS Quotas	msDS-QuotaContainer	Quota speci
System	Program Data	Container	Default loca
Users	System	Container	Builtin syste
Microsoft Exchange System Objects	Users	Container	Default cont
NTDS Quotas			

Modifying Existing Exchange Organizations to Support Migration

If you will be installing Exchange Server 2010 into an existing Exchange Server 2003 organization, additional configuration changes are made to Active Directory and the legacy Exchange organization. By default PrepareAD will perform the changes done by the /PrepareLegacyPermissions command if it detects that Exchange 2003 has been installed. You may run the /PrepareLegacyExchangePermissions command manually in every domain in which Exchange Server 2003 DomainPrep has been run previously to ensure that the legacy *Recipient Update Service (RUS)* continues to operate correctly on the older Exchange 2003 servers prior to running PrepareAD. The RUS is required in legacy Exchange Server 2003 environments to update some attributes on a recipient, such as the proxy address and the email address. If you have previously created a new mailbox-enabled user in an Exchange Server 2003 organization and had to wait a few minutes for an email address to be stamped on it, then you were waiting on RUS to run.

In these legacy Exchange environments, RUS runs in the context of the local server account for the Exchange server on which it is running. Each Exchange server's computer account is a member of the Exchange Enterprise Servers security group that is created during the DomainPrep process. The attributes that RUS needs to be able to modify and update are grouped together into a property set, and DomainPrep grants the Exchange Enterprise Servers security group the required permissions to modify the attributes in question. Since Exchange Server 2010 no longer uses this legacy Exchange Enterprise Servers security group, a solution is needed to allow RUS to continue to operate properly.

As outlined earlier, Exchange Server 2010 now uses a universal security group named Recipient Management. The members of this group have the required permissions to manage the email-related attributes of all recipients. The legacy Enterprise Servers security group does not provide access, by default, to the property set that is created to allow the Recipient Administrators group access to these email-related attributes. To that end, when the schema modification is performed as part of the preinstallation of Exchange Server 2010, RUS will no longer have permission to manage recipients' email attributes and stops functioning entirely. The workaround to this problem is to run the setup /PrepareLegacyExchangePermissions command before starting any other setup steps when integrating Exchange Server 2010 with legacy Exchange organizations. If setup detects an earlier version of Exchange has been installed, it will automatically perform the /PrepareLegacyExchangePermissions process.

🌐 Real World Scenario

Deploying Exchange Server 2010 in a Large Organization

You are the lead network administrator for a large manufacturing corporation that has 45 geographical locations within North America. In the past, your company has never had a real company-wide network that spanned all locations and linked all users and resources together. You have just completed installing a new Windows Server 2008 Active Directory network that provides one unified network to all users and all locations within your organization.

Your network consists of a single Active Directory forest and, under the root domain, five child domains named canada.manufacturing.com, mexico.manufacturing.com, west. manufacturing.com, central.manufacturing.com, and east.manufacturing.com.

The root domain of manufacturing.com contains no user accounts or member servers. For each of the five child domains, you have two assistant administrators that have the Domain Admins permissions for their applicable child domain. Only your user account has the Enterprise Admins and Schema Admins permissions configured. Also, only your user account has the Domain Admins permissions for the root domain. You have local administrative access on the servers in the root domain, and your assistant administrators have local administrative access on all computers and servers in their child domains. Your office is located within the east.manufacturing.com child domain.

To facilitate the process of installing Exchange Server 2010 on six Windows Server 2008 SP2 computers in each child domain, you have provided network shares in each child domain that contain the installation source files. Also, you have run /PrepareSchema to extend the Active Directory schema to support the installation of Exchange Server 2010. After you run the /PrepareSchema command, you will need to run the /PrepareAD command and specify the Exchange organization name.

After you complete these tasks, you should run the /PrepareDomain command for the east. manufacturing.com child domain. You can then start to install Exchange Server 2010 servers in the east.manufacturing.com child domain if desired. Also, your assistant administrators might begin to install the remaining Exchange Server 2010 servers using the installation source files located on their local network shares. As you can see, the Exchange installation process can be quite lengthy and complicated in a large network environment; however, careful planning and execution can lead to first-time success. In reality, this process can actually be simpler than the ForestPrep and DomainPrep process of Exchange Server 2003, which required you to delegate permissions from within the Exchange System Manager before the assistant administrators could start installing Exchange servers.

You need to be a member of the Domain Admins group and the Exchange Organization Administrators group in each domain in which this command is run. To run the /PrepareLegacyExchangePermissions command as shown in Exercise 2.9, in which it runs against all domains in the forest, you need to be a member of the Enterprise Admins group as well.

EXERCISE 2.9

Running the /PrepareLegacyExchangePermissions Command

Perform the following steps to run the /PrepareLegacyExchangePermissions command:

1. Log into a domain controller in the root domain with an account that is a member of the appropriate groups, as specified earlier.

2. Insert the Microsoft Exchange Server 2010 DVD into the server's DVD-ROM drive. If the server does not have a DVD-ROM drive, you can copy the files to a network location and then proceed using that location.

3. Open a command interpreter window by selecting Start ➢ Run, enter **CMD**, and press Enter.

4. In the command interpreter window, enter the command

   `X:\Setup /PrepareLegacyExchangePermissions`

   where *X* represents the location of the Exchange Server 2010 setup files, local or remote. Press Enter to start the root domain preparation process.

5. If setup finds any errors, they are displayed and the `/PrepareLegacyExchangePermissions` process fails. You need to rerun the command after you correct the noted errors.

You will notice that the word role is used a lot in discussions of Exchange Server 2010. In the following sections, we'll provide an introduction to each of the Exchange server roles.

Introducing the Server Roles

Starting with Exchange Server 2007, Microsoft Exchange no longer uses the front-end and back-end nomenclature to designate a server's primary function. Microsoft has moved to a roles-based installation model (and thus increased functionality and security). This architecture offers five distinctly different server roles for deployment. Some, such as the Mailbox, Hub Transport server, and Client Access server and roles, are mandatory. Others, such as the Edge Transport and Unified Messaging roles, will vary in usage from organization to organization.

Mailbox Server

The *Mailbox server* role is the first of three required Exchange Server 2010 roles. As its name implies, the primary function of the Mailbox server role is to provide users with mailboxes. In all previous versions of Exchange, clients would connect directly to the Mailbox servers. In Exchange Server 2010, direct *MAPI* connectivity has been removed and all client connectivity is now done through the Client Access servers. The Mailbox server also contains the databases that hold public folders if you are still using them in your organization. As a point of comparison, the Mailbox server is most like the back-end server from previous versions of Exchange.

The Mailbox server can host up to 100 databases per server when using the Enterprise version of Exchange. Each database has its own set of transaction logs.

In Exchange Server 2010, messages are not actually routed between mailboxes by Mailbox servers. All message routing, even between mailboxes on the same Mailbox server, is now the responsibility of the Hub Transport server, which is covered next. Because of the nature of the data contained on Mailbox servers, they do not need to be directly accessible from the Internet. Additionally, Mailbox servers must be members of Active Directory domains that have been prepared for the installation of Exchange Server 2010 and they must have fast, reliable connectivity to global catalog servers and domain controllers in the same Active Directory site.

Hub Transport Server

The *Hub Transport server* is the second mandatory Exchange Server 2010 role that must be deployed. The primary function of the Hub Transport server is to route messages for delivery within the Exchange organization. Because message routing is performed outside the Mailbox server role, many new and needed features and functions become available. For example, while messages are being routed through the Hub Transport server, you can apply transport rules and filtering policies that determine where they will wind up, such as in a compliance mailbox in addition to the recipient's mailbox, or what they will look like, such as every outbound message having a disclaimer stamped on it.

Along with message routing, all message categorization is now performed on the Hub Transport server. Hub Transport servers are thus a critical part of your healthy and functioning Exchange Server 2010 organization. Although Hub Transport servers cannot be clustered for *high availability*, multiple Hub Transport servers can (and should) be placed in each Active Directory site where Exchange Mailbox servers exist. In this arrangement, all Hub Transport servers will distribute work load and provide failure redundancy.

Another key role that Hub Transport servers fill is providing *antivirus* and *antispam* controls inside your internal network. Although the Edge Transport server (or some other hardware or software third-party device) is intended as the primary defense against virus-infected and spam messages, the Hub Transport server allows you to put internal controls in place to prevent virus-infected messages from being sent from within your Exchange organization. Also, as part of an in-depth defense strategy, it places extra layers of protection around your most critical data.

Hub Transport servers must be members of Active Directory domains and must have fast, reliable connectivity to Mailbox servers. There must also be at least one Hub Transport server in every Active Directory site that contains a Mailbox or Unified Messaging server. If not, messages will never be sent to or from the servers in that site.

Client Access Server

The *Client Access server (CAS)* is the role that has changed the most in Exchange 2010. Now all client connectivity is done through the Client Access server role. Outlook clients as well as non-MAPI clients, such as POP3, IMAP4, mobile, and web-based clients, must connect to the Mailbox servers via a Client Access server. In this way, the Client Access server is most like the front-end servers utilized in previous versions of Exchange Server. One major difference with the Client Access server role is that, rather than proxying most requests from the client to the back end, the CAS server will process the requests directly.

In addition to providing client access to the Exchange databases, the Client Access server provides other features, such as *Autodiscover*, which allows an Office Outlook 2007 and higher client to configure a user's profile automatically without the need to enter the server and mailbox information as with previous versions of Outlook.

Client Access servers also need to be members of Active Directory domains and should typically be located on the internal portion of your organization's network. If the Client Access server must be accessible from the Internet, it should be presented to the Internet via some sort of application-layer firewall to secure connections to and from the Client Access server and the Internet.

Edge Transport Server

The *Edge Transport server* is an optional role in Exchange Server 2010. Designed to be deployed in the DMZ, or the *perimeter network,* portion of your network, the Edge Transport server is used to provide a secure SMTP gateway for all messages entering or leaving your Exchange organization. As such, the Edge Transport server is primarily responsible for antivirus and antispam controls as well as for protecting the recipient data held within Active Directory.

When an inbound message is received by the Edge Transport server, it scans the messages and then takes the appropriate actions if it determines that the message is a virus or if it appears to be a spam message. Normal, clean messages are delivered to a Hub Transport server for policy and compliance enforcement as well as for delivery to the final recipients.

Unlike all other Exchange Server 2010 roles, the Edge Transport role cannot be deployed on a server with any other roles—it must be deployed by itself on a completely separate server. This is done to increase Exchange security and the overall security of the internal network. The Edge Transport server, because of its specialized role, is not intended to be a member of the corporate Active Directory. Since the Edge Transport servers are supposed to be placed in the DMZ portion of the network, you would not want to open all of the TCP ports into your Active Directory domain controllers, nor would you want any security compromise of an Edge Transport server to expose your corporate Active Directory. To simplify password management in larger organizations, some have chosen to create a separate Active Directory forest for the servers in the DMZ.

Because recipient information is needed for proper message acceptance and routing, the Edge Transport server uses an instance of Active Directory Lightweight Directory Services (AD LDS) in Windows Server 2008 to store its configuration and recipient information. The Hub Transport server then initiates one-way replication from Active Directory to the Edge Transport server to stay up-to-date.

Because of its specialized role, the Edge Transport server requires two-way SMTP access only through the external firewall. Only two-way SMTP and one-way (from the inside) Active Directory synchronization traffic is required through the internal firewall.

Unified Messaging Server

The last of the Exchange Server 2010 server roles is the *Unified Messaging server.* Seeing the increased integration with Exchange Server by third-party voice and fax messaging companies, Microsoft raised the bar and built these functionalities, and much more, into Exchange Server 2010.

The Unified Messaging server role provides the following functionalities to an Exchange Server 2010 organization:

- Voice call answering, voicemail recording, and delivery of voicemail to Exchange mailboxes
- Voicemail access via a phone connection
- Voicemail preview
- Message read-back via a phone connection, including replying to the message or forwarding it to another recipient
- Calendar access via a phone connection, including meeting request acceptance
- Out-of-office messages in voicemail via a phone connection

Unified Messaging servers are intended to be deployed only in the internal network and must be deployed in sites that contain at least one Hub Transport server. Additionally, the Unified Messaging server must have reliable, high-speed connectivity to the Mailbox servers, domain controllers, and global catalog servers in the organization. An IP PBX or VoIP gateway device is required to tie the Unified Messaging server to the phone system.

Installing Microsoft Exchange Server 2010

Microsoft has made the Exchange Server 2010 setup process easier and more error-proof than ever before. As part of the setup process, you are prompted to verify and install, as necessary, the key services that are required to support the installation of Exchange Server 2010. Before you can install Exchange Server 2010 on a server, however, you must install the required services and components that we discussed previously.

As discussed in the previous pages, there are five different Exchange Server roles:

- Mailbox
- Hub Transport
- Client Access
- Edge Transport
- Unified Messaging

We start with the Typical Exchange Server Installation option, where the Hub Transport, Client Access, and Mailbox server roles, plus the Management tools, are automatically installed. If you chose the custom installation, you have the option of selecting just the server roles you want to install.

In Exercise 2.10, we review the process of a typical Exchange Server 2010 installation. This exercise assumes that you already have a working domain named mailtask.com and a Microsoft Windows 2008 R2 domain controller named EX1. As this is the first Exchange Server 2010 installation in the domain, we must use an account that is a member of the Enterprise Admins group.

EXERCISE 2.10

Installing the First Exchange Server 2010

Use the following steps to perform an Exchange Server 2010 installation using the media CD or setup files located on a network share:

1. Insert the Microsoft Exchange Server 2010 DVD into the server's DVD-ROM drive. If the server does not have a DVD-ROM drive, you can copy the files to a network location and then proceed using that location.

2. Run Setup.exe from the DVD or network location.

3. An installation dialog box opens and the first three steps are grayed out. Click the Step 4: Install Microsoft Exchange option.

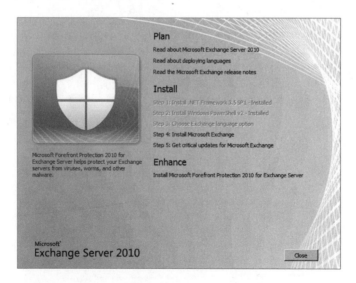

4. On the Introduction screen, click Next.

5. On the License Agreement screen, click "I accept the terms in the license agreement" and the click Next.

6. On the Error Report screen, choose whether or not you will allow Exchange to send error reports to Microsoft. For this exercise, choose Yes.

7. On the Installation Type screen, select Typical Exchange Server Installation.

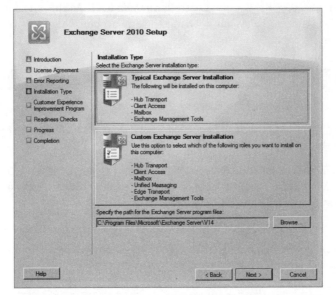

8. The Client Settings screen asks you if your organization has any Outlook 2003 clients. For this exercise, select Yes, and then click Next.

EXERCISE 2.10 *(continued)*

9. On the Configure Client Access Server External Domain screen, put a check mark in the box labeled The Client Access server role will be Internet-facing. Then enter the domain your organization will use for external Client Access servers. For this exercise, enter **mail.mailtask.com**.

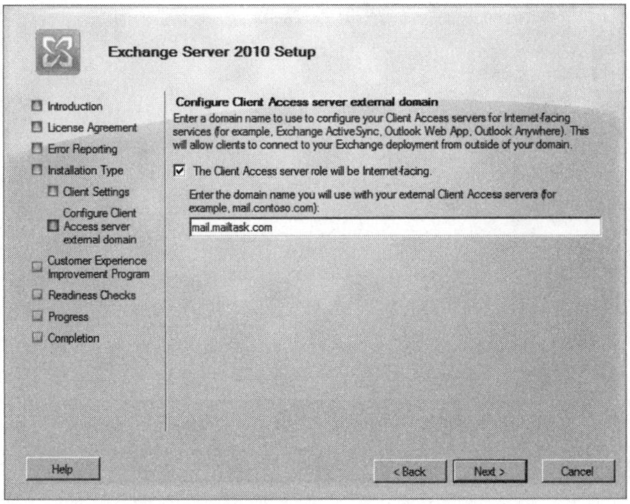

10. The next screen allows you to choose if you want to join the Exchange Customer Experience Improvement Program (CEIP). For this exercise, select the option to join. Each organization will have to determine whether joining is the right choice.

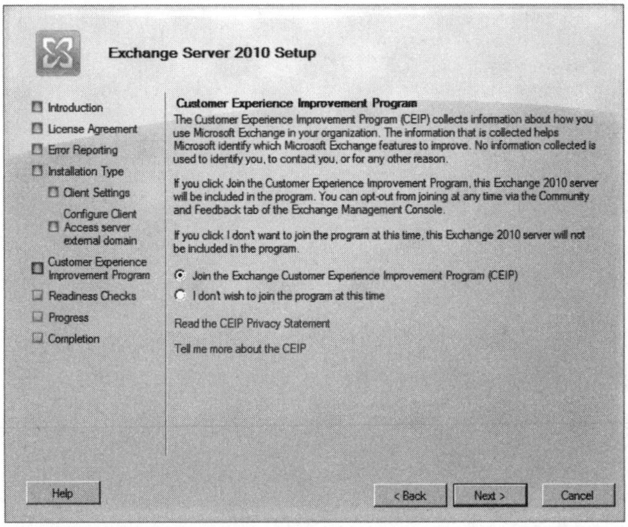

11. On the Readiness Checks screen, click Install after all prerequisites have been verified.

12. The Completion screen updates the installation status in real time and when it completes with no failures, click Finish.

This chapter walked you through the step-by-step process to successfully install Microsoft Exchange Server 2010. After the initial installation is complete, a Post-Installation Tasks console opens. The steps in this console are discussed in the following chapters.

> The previous exercise installed the Exchange program files onto the C: drive. In real-world installations, it is recommended that you install the Exchange program files on a drive that is separate from the operating system page file.

Understanding Role Based Access Control

Role Based Access Control (RBAC) is now provided with a new permissions model in Exchange Server 2010. To modify administrative permissions in Exchange Server 2007, the administrator must modify and manage numerous access control lists (ACLs). This is no longer needed in Exchange Server 2010. This was done to help reduce some of the challenges that ACLs created, such as maintaining ACL modifications when doing an upgrade or unplanned issues when modifying ACLs.

RBAC was designed to provide Exchange administrators with greater control, at both broad and granular levels. This will allow the Exchange professional or administrator to decide what both the end users and other administrators can do. With this increased control, you can closely match the roles you assign users and administrators to the actual responsibilities they hold. In Exchange Server 2007, the permissions applied only to those who managed the Exchange 2007 infrastructure.

You can use RBAC in the following three different ways to assign permissions to users; however, you will probably find yourself using the first two ways more than the third way, which is more advanced:

- Management role groups
- Management role assignment policies
- Direct user role assignment (advanced method)

We will now take a moment to get familiar with the three ways of assigning permissions.

Management Role Groups

The function of the management role groups is to assist you in associating management roles to a group of users. Often times you will have your organization structured with groups of administrators or specialists. Your administrators will have a broad range of tasks and responsibilities or they might be in charge of managing the entire Exchange organization, whereas specialists might be users who don't need a broad range of permissions but would require some level of access. Help desk members would be an example of specialists. The help desk member might need specific Exchange Server rights and management role groups would allow you to give them just enough rights to perform their job without giving them full control.

Role groups consist of the following components or layers:

Role holder   A mailbox that can be added as a member of a role group. When you add a mailbox as a member of a role group, it inherits all the permissions provide by that group.

Management role group   This is where you add and remove members. It's the group to which you assign management roles. This universal security group (USG) contains mailboxes that are members of the role group.

Management role   When a member is assigned this group, it is used to define the tasks that the user can perform.

Management role assignment   This links a management role to a role group. Linking a management role to a role group will give members of the role group the ability to use any cmdlets or parameters that are defined in the management role.

Management role scope   When a role is assigned to a scope, the scope will target the objects that assignment is allowed to manage. This allows you to place restrictions on what members of a role group can manage. Scopes can consist of servers, organizational units, or even filters on server or recipient objects.

When you add a user to a role group, the user is given all of the roles assigned to that particular group. This is the same principle that Active Directory uses, and care must be given when you plan the role groups your organization uses.

Exchange Server 2010 has assignments built into it, but if they are not a fit for your organization's needs, you can change them. Whenever you change the roles that are assigned to role groups, you also need to change the role assignments that link the role groups to roles.

Management Role Assignment Policies

Within the permissions model of Exchange Server 2010 are management role assignment policies. These policies allow for deeper control over what a user may or may not do with specific mailboxes or distribution groups. If a feature is not directly associated with a user, they will not be able to manage it. So when you are creating a role assignment policy, you will have to define everything they can manage.

You could create a role assignment policy, for example, to allow an administrator to change the address or set the display name. Another role assignment policy might be created that would allow the user to set up voicemail or configure inbox rules. By default, every user will have a policy assigned. This of course can be changed to fit your organization's needs, and you can even choose to not assign any policies by default.

Microsoft's end goal here is to allow administrators to have very flexible control over the users. In previous versions of Microsoft Exchange, it was more an all-or-nothing type of permissions model, even though it did allow for some level of control. With Exchange

Server 2010, assigning users to an assignment policy is how you will manage permissions for most users.

Role assignment policies are made up of the following components:

Management role assignment policy   Associates a user with a set of rules that dictate what they can or cannot do with mailboxes or distribution groups. This role assignment policy is linked to the user when their mailbox is created. This can be assigned to end users if needed.

Management role   This is the container for management role entries. A management role entry is a cmdlet script or special permissions that will allow the user to perform tasks. Specific tasks that a user can perform are defined by these roles.

Management role assignment   This is how a role and a role assignment policy are linked together. Providing this link grants the ability to use cmdlets that are defined in the role.

Just like the management role groups, Exchange 2010 has role assignment policies built in. If they do not fit your needs, you can change them.

Direct User Role Assignment

At times you might need to assign permissions or tasks to a single user. This is when you would consider using direct user role assignments. Direct user role assignments will allow you to get very granular with permissions and provide access to a user. This would be the case if no other user in the organization requires these special permissions. If the user leaves or changes jobs, you need to manually remove the assignment permissions and add the permissions to the new employee assigned to these tasks.

Normally you would want to avoid using direct user role assignments because of the administration effort to manage them. It is recommended that you use role groups to assign permissions whenever possible.

You can look at the RBAC permissions model as you would Active Directory (AD) groups and *organizational units (OUs)*. When using AD groups, OUs, and user objects, you would ensure that the least amount of administrative effort is involved to monitor and maintain them. If you assigned all your permissions to a user object, it would become a nightmare to manage. This is why it is better to assign permissions to groups rather than directly to users. RBAC should be thought of the same way when you design and plan your Exchange 2010 environment. If you were to assign all permissions using the direct user role assignments, then you would have to track and maintain which user has what permissions.

RBAC can be intimidating at first glance, but as you dive deeper into the model, it starts to make more sense. It's like AD on steroids. It has been referred to as a triangle of power because the nodes used to make up RBAC.

The nodes form the triangle and the glue holds it together (see Figure 2.7):

- Where (scope)
- What (role)
- Who (role group)
- Glue (role assignment)

FIGURE 2.7   RBAC roles

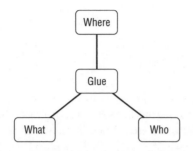

It's worth taking a few minutes to understand what each of these nodes mean and how this triangle helps us to understand RBAC. In a nutshell, you would first create the scope, then the role, and then the role group. And as mentioned, the role assignment is just the glue that holds it all together.

Where (scope) is the first thing you want to work with. You need to determine where the assignment can operate: a group of users, just one OU, maybe in a configuration container. By default, all RBAC roles have a defined scope and it is assigned to a role. When you create a scope, it must be a child of an RBAC role. If you do not define this role then it will inherit the scope of the parent role.

What (role) comes next. This is the definition of what the role is going to be able to do. Exchange Server 2010 comes with 65 built-in roles. Each has its own unique set of tasks it can perform. These 65 roles do not cover every situation you might face, so you might have to create custom roles off of these parent roles.

> When you create custom user roles, keep in mind the following concepts: You use existing custom roles to create child roles. A child role cannot have higher-level rights than its parent role, even when the parent role is also a custom role. You want to always have a get cmdlet for each set/remove cmdlet that you have in the role.

Who (role group) is the node that makes the most sense because it's simply who is going to perform What on Where. The decision you have to make here is whether you want to assign this role to a single person or a group. If you choose to assign the role to a group, you would use a role group, which is really just a universal security group that is being used for RBAC assignments.

Glue (role assignment) is also an AD object, the role assignment. To have a working RBAC definition, you would need to define the Where, What, and Who, which are all AD objects themselves. The role assignment is the glue that binds them all together. While RBAC is similar to managing AD, keep in mind that RBAC roles are not security permissions, so only apply the exact role that you want a user to have. With RBAC roles, the most restrictive rule doesn't necessarily win.

Summary

Before you even start to install the Exchange Server 2010, many items need your time and consideration. Taking the time to prepare your organization properly for the introduction of Exchange Server 2010 will yield positive results regardless of whether this is an upgrade/ coexistence scenario with legacy versions of Exchange or a completely new installation of Exchange Server 2010.

One of the most important phases of an installation is preinstallation. Before starting the actual installation, you must make sure the minimum requirements for Exchange are met. You must obtain the proper licenses to ensure compliance with legal issues. Because Exchange utilizes user accounts from Active Directory, Exchange Server 2010 is tightly integrated with it. Before Exchange server can be installed, you will need to ensure that the required Windows services and components are installed and running. To avoid problems during the setup process, you should use the `dcdiag` tool to test your network's connectivity. Finally, you must prepare the Active Directory forest and domains by running the appropriate commands.

Although installing Exchange Server 2010 is fairly straightforward, you must complete many important tasks correctly beforehand to ensure that the actual installation process will be successful. Planning and analyzing the desired Exchange organization ensures that the correct number of servers and the proper roles are installed where needed. It is just as important to know how to install an Exchange server as it is to know how to plan for the installation—one cannot create success without the other.

Chapter Essentials

Trust but verify.　After you complete the installation of Exchange Server 2010 on each server, take some time to verify that the installation completed successfully by examining the setup logs for errors and verifying that the correct services are installed and running. You can also examine the directory structure created during Exchange setup, check for the Exchange universal security groups in Active Directory, and examine the Event Viewer for indications of how setup really went.

Understand preinstallation `setup.exe` options.　If you are working in a single-domain forest, you may never need to work with the `/PrepareSchema`, `/PrepareAD`, and `/PrepareDomain` commands. Even if this is the case, you should still learn what these powerful setup commands do and what permissions are required in order to use them. Consider the example of a very large, geographically dispersed network where multiple administrators at various levels work together to manage and maintain the network. In this situation, these commands are invaluable tools that can assist you in getting Exchange Server 2010 installed by splitting up the installation tasks according to the appropriate domain group permissions that have been assigned.

Remember the requirements to install Exchange Server 2010.   Exchange Server 2010 can be installed only on a Windows Server 2008 x64 SP2 or a Windows Server 2008 R2 computer. All domain controllers and global catalog servers that the Exchange Server 2010 computer will communicate with must have at least Windows Server 2003 SP1 applied, and the domain and forest functional levels must be at the Windows 2003 native functional level or higher. The hardware and software requirements, detailed previously in this chapter, must also be met to install and operate an Exchange Server 2010 organization successfully.

Understand RBAC.   Role Based Access Control (RBAC) can be very confusing at first glance, so take some time to understand its pieces and how they impact the overall design. Learn how the triangle works and what the glue is that holds it all together. Spend time learning what each node is and what it does for the Exchange environment:

- Where (scope)
- What (role)
- Who (role group)
- Glue (role assignment)

Chapter

3

Configuring Connectors, Routing and Transport, and Connectivity

THE FOLLOWING TOPICS ARE DISCUSSED IN THIS CHAPTER:

- ✓ Configuring Connectors
- ✓ Configuring Message Routing and Transport
- ✓ Configuring Client Access for Exchange 2010

If you are an Exchange veteran, you might think that configuring client connectivity is as simple as enabling the POP3 or IMAP service and just letting Active Directory Domain Services (AD DS) control mail routing. However, you must do more configuring with the addition of Exchange Web Services (EWS) and the Autodiscover service.

The Hub Transport and Edge Transport servers provide email delivery in and out of your Exchange organization. But they also provide security and compliance for messages that route through your Exchange servers. The Client Access servers (CAS) are not only used for connectivity by end users for Outlook, OWA and mobile phones, they also provide organizational information such as free/busy data and the Offline Address Book (OAB) through web services. Outlook Anywhere and now the RPC Client Access service add to the complexity of the CAS server role.

The Microsoft Exchange team does a good job of providing guidance and best practices in the default configuration of Exchange servers. But for most companies, even smaller ones, you will need to configure and customize the default settings of the Hub Transport and Client Access servers for email routing and client connectivity. You need to understand the components of the server roles and the services that they provide to your end users. Only then can you efficiently provide a secure and reliable Exchange environment.

Configuring Connectors

SMTP connectors changed in Exchange 2007 from earlier Exchange versions that used routing group connectors, SMTP connectors, virtual SMTP servers, and X.400 connectors. Exchange 2010 connectors are almost identical (or should we say "very similar") to Exchange 2007 connectors, but there are changes in message routing that we'll explain throughout the first part of this chapter. Both Hub Transport and Edge Transport servers use send connectors and receive connectors for message routing both inside and outside the Exchange organization. Routing messages between Hub Transport servers is based on the Active Directory site topology, which we'll explain in detail later in this chapter. The default configuration for Hub Transport servers will route mail within your Exchange organization but does not ensure external message routing. You need to configure or create new connectors to make this happen.

How you go about creating or modifying your connectors for message routing depends on your organization's policies, connectivity, and Exchange configuration. If you use the Microsoft-recommended configuration that has Edge Transport servers in the perimeter network, you need to use an Edge Subscription to subscribe an Edge Transport server to an Active Directory site, thus allowing replication of recipient and configuration data into an Active Directory Lightweight Directory Services (AD LDS) instance on the Edge Transport server. After you complete the subscription process for an Edge Transport server to an Active Directory site, the following default connectors are created by the Microsoft Exchange EdgeSync service:

- An implicit send connector from all of the current Hub Transport servers in the Active Directory site to the Edge Transport server
- A send connector from the Edge Transport server to all of the Hub Transport servers in the Active Directory site to which the Edge Transport server is subscribed
- A wildcard (*) send connector from the Edge Transport server to the Internet

These connectors then allow full end-to-end message routing in and out of your Exchange organization. Configuring Edge Transport servers is an easy and secure way to create all of your default SMTP connectors. After the defaults are created, you can always create additional connectors or make additional configurations as needed.

Your organization may not choose to utilize Edge Transport servers and opt to use third-party edge appliances or services that handle inbound and outbound filtering. To do this, you will need to create a send connector to route email messages from your Exchange organization to external recipients. You will also need to create receive connectors to allow inbound messages to Exchange from the third-party appliances or external services.

Send connectors for Hub Transport servers are configured for the entire Exchange organization but can be restricted to specific Hub Transport servers. Multiple send connectors can be created for uses such as sending email to the Internet, acting as an alternate send connector to the Internet, or sending email to a specific domain through a smart host. Receive connectors are configured per server. Uses for receive connectors include receiving email from other Hub and Edge Transport servers, receiving email from the Internet, and receiving other email via SMTP.

Configuring Send Connectors

For the purposes of this section and the specific discussion about Hub Transport servers, it is assumed that your Exchange organization does not have an Edge Transport server. In a later section, we discuss the initial configuration that needs to be done for an Edge Transport server. Exercise 3.1 creates a send connector to the Internet for your Hub Transport server.

EXERCISE 3.1

Creating a Send Connector to the Internet with the Exchange Management Console

Follow these steps to create a send connector:

1. Click Start ➤ All Programs ➤ Microsoft Exchange Server 2010 and select Exchange Management Console.

2. Expand the Microsoft Exchange container, expand the Microsoft Exchange On-Prem-
    ises container, expand the Organization Configuration container, and then click the
    Hub Transport node.

3. In the Actions pane, click the New Send Connector link.

4. In the New Send Connector Wizard, type **Internet Send Connector** in the Name
    field and then select Internet from the Select The Intended Use For This Send Con-
    nector drop-down menu. Click Next.

5. On the Address Space page, click the Add button and enter the wildcard address of *.
    Click OK to close the dialog box and return to the Address Space page. Click Next.

6. On the Network Settings page, use the default selection, Use Domain Name System
    (DNS) "MX" records To Route Mail Automatically. Click Next.

7. On the Source Server page, you will be able to select which Hub Transport servers will
    be allowed to use the send connector. Select one Hub Transport server and click Next.

8. The Configuration Summary page is presented with the configuration options chosen.
    Click New to create the send connector.

9. You are then presented with a completion summary of what was configured and
    given the chance to copy the actual PowerShell cmdlet used to create the send
    connector. Click Finish to close the wizard.

The following command is what should be in the completion summary in Exercise 3.1 and can be used from the Exchange Management Shell instead of the EMC (Figure 3.1 shows the results of the EMS command):

```
New-SendConnector -Name 'Internet Send Connector' -Usage 'Internet'
-AddressSpaces 'SMTP:*;1' -IsScopedConnector $false -DNSRoutingEnabled $true
-UseExternalDNSServersEnabled $false -SourceTransportServers 'EX01'
```

FIGURE 3.1   Creating a send connector from the Exchange Management Shell

In the previous exercise, you chose DNS to look up MX records to route email to destination servers. Many organizations use a smart host, which can be a third-party email gateway appliance, to route email to and from the Internet. Later in this chapter, we will configure an Edge Transport server to route email for the Exchange organization. Also, you chose only one Hub Transport server to use the send connector. Depending on your company's connectivity to the Internet, site configuration, and Exchange architecture, you may want a few specified servers using this send connector or all of them. More information on these decisions is included in Chapter 12, "Designing Connectivity and Routing."

You can use the Exchange Management Console (EMC) and the Exchange Management Shell (EMS) to create the send connector quickly. Using the EMC, you can access the send connector's properties either by right-clicking the connector and selecting Properties from the context menu or by clicking the Properties link under the send connector options in the Actions pane on the right side of the EMC. The following four tabs are available on the Internet Send Connector Properties dialog box:

General   On the General tab, shown in Figure 3.2, you have the option to change the friendly name if the connector is being modified. You can specify the fully qualified domain name (FQDN) that the send connector will return in reply to a HELO or EHLO query during an SMTP connection. You can also configure the protocol logging option here as well as configure the maximum message size that the connector will allow. Protocol logging is basically on or off (Verbose or None). When you enable the protocol logs, you can view SMTP conversations that the send connector has with other computers, which can help during troubleshooting. The protocol logs are located in the following directory in a default installation:

```
C:\Program Files\Microsoft\Exchange
Server\V14\TransportRoles\Log\ProtocolLog\SmtpSend\
```

FIGURE 3.2   The General tab of the Internet Send Connector Properties dialog box

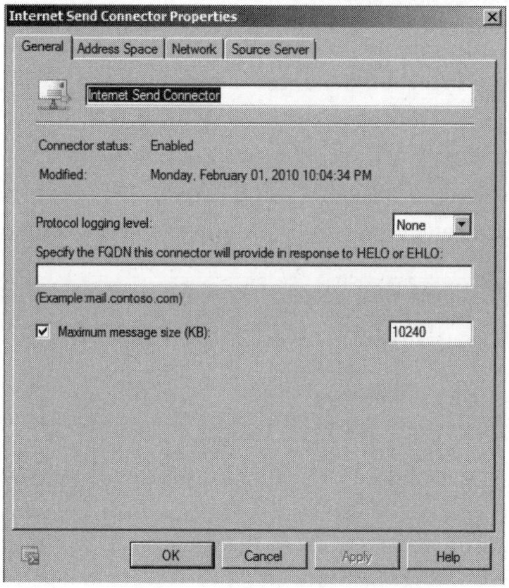

Address Space   On the Address Space tab, shown in Figure 3.3, you can change, add, or delete the address spaces that are used by this send connector.

FIGURE 3.3   The Address Space tab of the Internet Send Connector Properties dialog box

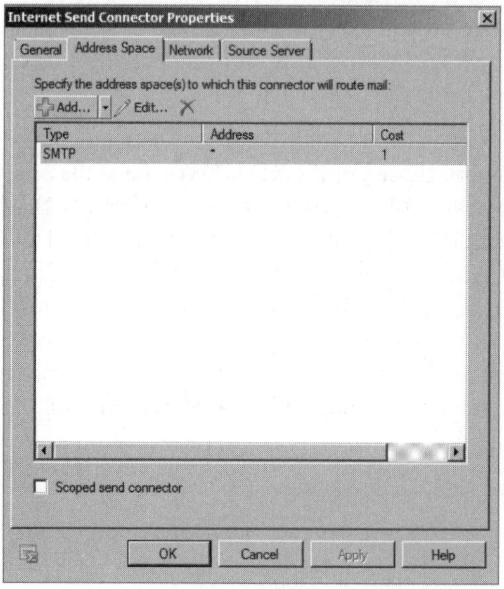

Network   On the Network tab, shown in Figure 3.4, you have several options to change the network configuration of the send connector. The only option that is not directly available during the creation of the send connector is the Enable Domain Security (Mutual Auth TLS) option. This option allows you to configure a send connector to a specific partner's SMTP address space and to attempt to make a connection using Transport Layer Security (TLS) for all messages going out of that connector.

FIGURE 3.4   The Network tab of the Internet Send Connector Properties dialog box

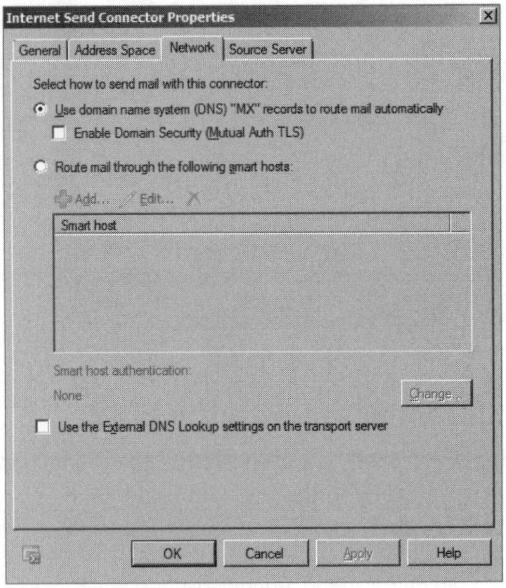

> **NOTE**   Enabling Mutual TLS to a partner address space is not as easy as checking a box. To protect against man-in-the-middle attacks, you'll need to perform several other tasks if you're interested. They include importing a trusted and valid TLS certificate into your Hub or Edge Transport servers, configuring inbound domain and outbound domain security, and testing proper mail flow and TLS protection.

Source Server   The Source Server tab, shown in Figure 3.5, provides no new configuration options but does allow you to change, add, or delete the source servers that should be allowed to send SMTP messages across this send connector.

FIGURE 3.5 The Source Server tab of the Internet Send Connector Properties dialog box

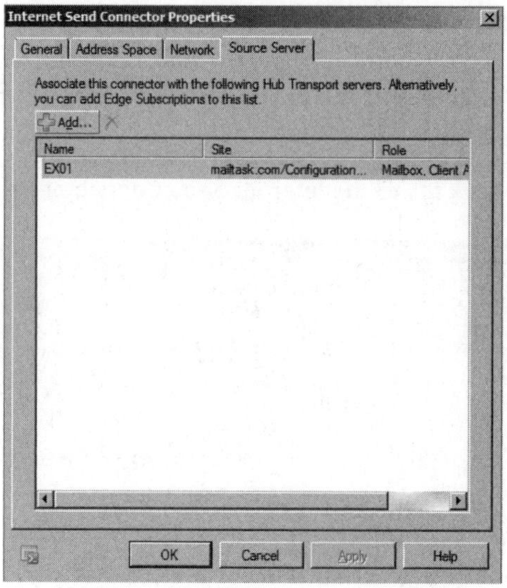

Modifying the Send Connector with the EMS

Using the Exchange Management Shell, you will use the `Set-SendConnector` cmdlet to modify values of send connectors. The following command enables protocol logging and increases the maximum message size:

```
Set-SendConnector -Name 'Internet Send Connector'
-ProtocolLoggingLevel 'Verbose' -MaxMessageSize '25MB'
```

🌐 Real World Scenario

A Real-Life Story

Justin, an Exchange administrator for a major company, one day received a complaint that emails to a certain domain weren't working. A little investigation uncovered that this other domain's DNS was only intermittently responding and they had set the allowed caching time for their DNS records to 0 seconds.

Exchange's ability to create multiple send connectors allowed Justin to create a separate send connector for the failed domain and to set the smart host to relay for that domain to the IP address he had gotten one of the times his DNS query had worked. This flexibility kept vital email flowing during the time it took for Justin to contact administrators for the other company and have them check their DNS settings.

Configuring Receive Connectors

After a default installation of a Hub Transport server role, two connectors are created and configured:

- A default receive connector named Client *servername* accepts email on TCP port 587, which is the standard client port for sending outbound messages from POP3 and IMAP4 clients (such as Windows Live Mail) for SMTP relay. The connector accepts email on all of the local network adapters on the Hub Transport server and accepts inbound messages from all other IP addresses and hosts on the network. It also will accept email from any client IP address, but the client must authenticate to allow relay to external email systems.

- A default receive connector named Default *servername* accepts mail on TCP port 25, which is the standard port for receiving email from other mail transfer agents (MTAs) or SMTP servers. The connector accepts email on all of the local network adapters on the Hub Transport server and accepts inbound messages from all IP addresses, but only from Exchange users, Exchange servers, and Legacy Exchange servers. The connector will not accept anonymous submissions.

You can view the default receive connectors with the Exchange Management Console by selecting Server Configuration folder and then the Hub Transport node, as shown in Figure 3.6.

FIGURE 3.6 The default receive connectors viewed with the Exchange Management Console

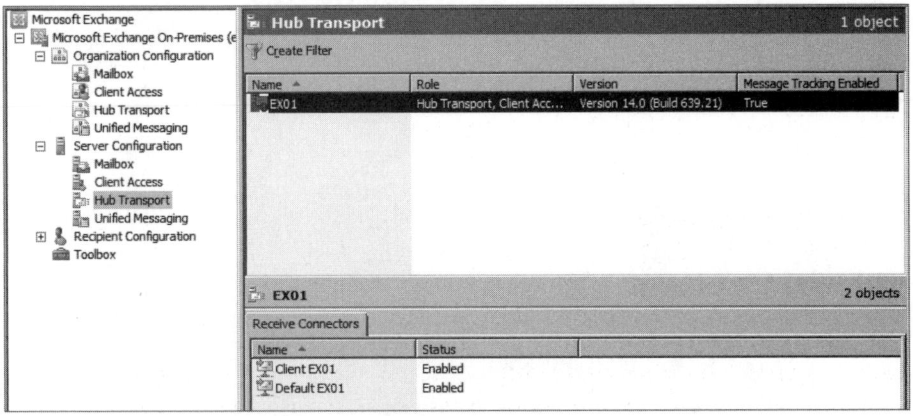

Exercise 3.2 outlines the steps to create a new receive connector. The connector is for an example application server with an IP address of 192.168.1.50.

EXERCISE 3.2

Creating a Receive Connector

Follow these steps to create a receive connector:

1. Click Start ➢ All Programs ➢ Microsoft Exchange Server 2010 and then select Exchange Management Console.

2. Expand the Microsoft Exchange container, expand the Microsoft Exchange On-Premises container, expand the Organization Configuration container, and then click the Hub Transport node.

3. Select the server on which to configure the receive connector. In the Actions pane, click the New Receive Connector link.

4. In the New Receive Connector Wizard, type **CRM Application Receive** as the name and then select the appropriate option from the drop-down menu. In this example, select the Custom option to create a receive connector for receiving SMTP messages from an internal CRM application. Click Next to continue to the Local Network settings page, shown here.

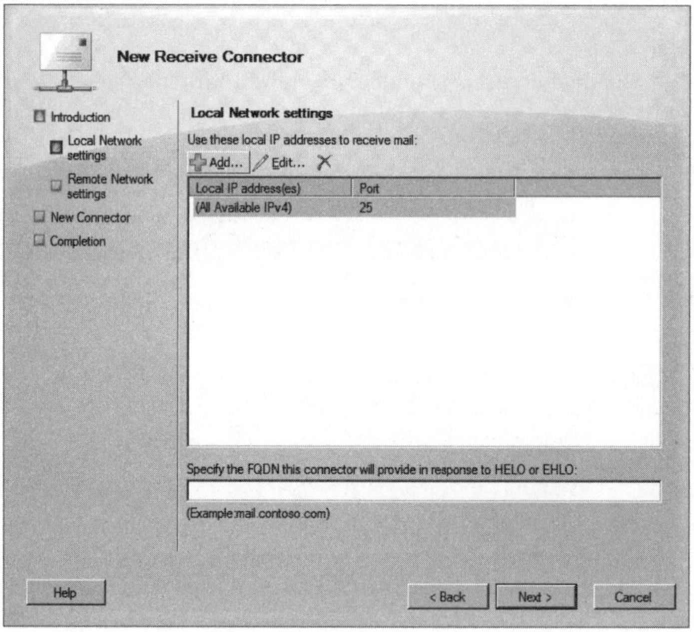

5. On the Local Network Settings page, leave the default selection of All Available IPv4. Click Next to continue to the Remote Network Settings page, shown here.

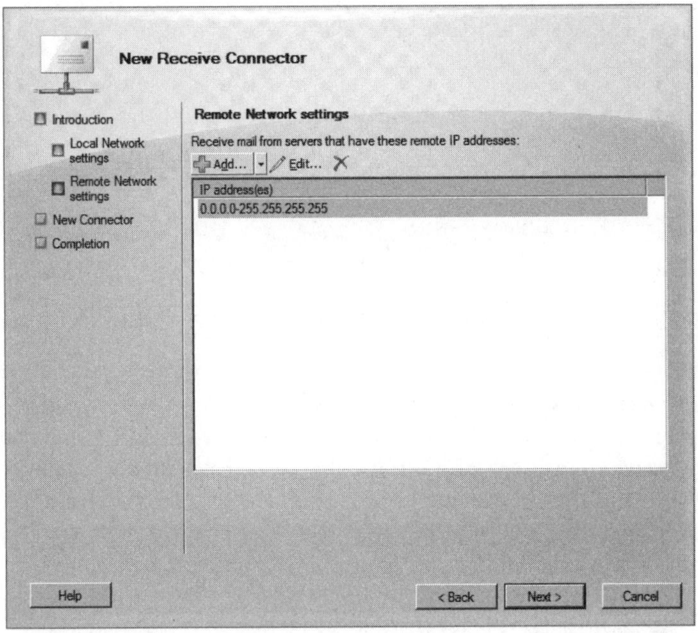

6. On the Remote Network Settings page, delete the default selection of 0.0.0.0-255.255.255.255. Add the IP address 192.168.1.50, then click Next.

7. A Configuration Summary page is presented with the configuration options chosen. Click New to create the receive connector.

8. You are then presented with a completion summary of what was configured and given the chance to copy the actual PowerShell cmdlet used to create the receive connector. Click Finish to close the wizard.

9. Select the new receive connector and click Properties on the Actions pane to bring up the Properties dialog box of the connector.

10. Select the Permission Groups tab and check the box for anonymous users. Click Okay to close the dialog box.

Again, everything the EMC can do, the EMS can usually do, and often with fewer steps. The following command creates a receive connector that accepts messages only from an internal CRM application server that has an IP address of 192.168.1.50:

```
New-ReceiveConnector -Name 'CRM Application Receive Connector'
-Usage Custom -Bindings 0.0.0.0:25
-RemoteIPRanges '192.168.1.50' -Server 'EX01'
-AuthMechanism 'None'
```

Figure 3.7 shows the results of this configuration action.

FIGURE 3.7 Creating a receive connector from the Exchange Management Shell

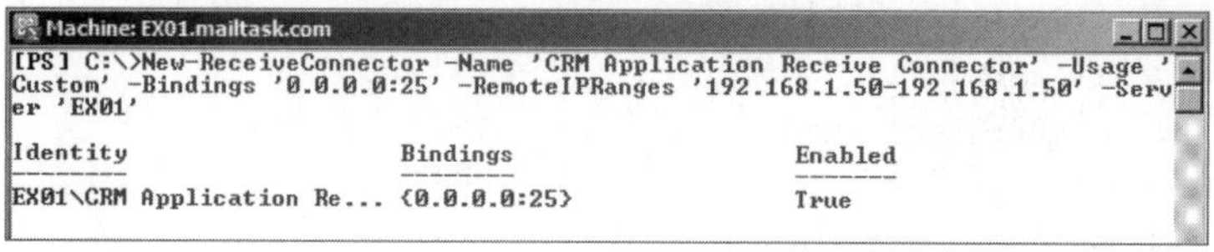

As with send connectors, you can use the Exchange Management Console or the Exchange Management Shell to create the receive connector quickly. Using the EMC, you can access the receive connector's properties either by right-clicking the connector and then selecting the Properties from the context menu or by clicking the Properties link under the receive connector options in the Actions pane on the right side of the EMC. As with send connectors, four tabs are available to configure for receive connectors:

General The General tab of the Default EX01 receive connector properties dialog box is shown in Figure 3.8. This tab provides the ability to change the friendly name of the connector and specify the FQDN that the receive connector will return in reply to a HELO or EHLO query during an SMTP connection. You can also configure the protocol logging option here as well as configure the maximum message size that the connector will allow. Protocol logging is basically on or off (Verbose or None). The protocol logs are located in the following directory in a default installation:

```
C:\Program Files\Microsoft\Exchange
Server\V14\TransportRoles\Log\ProtocolLog\SmtpReceive\
```

Network The Network tab is shown in Figure 3.9. This tab allows you to change the local IP addresses and ports on which the connector will receive SMTP messages and the remote IP addresses that are allowed to send messages through the receive connector.

Authentication The Authentication tab allows you to configure the authentication method to be used on the receive connector. Table 3.1 describes each method available.

On a Hub Transport server, the combination of the local IP address, local TCP port, and remote IP address range must be unique and cannot be duplicated by any other receive connector. You can, however, create the same receive connector on multiple Hub Transport servers.

FIGURE 3.8   The General tab of the receive connector's Properties dialog box

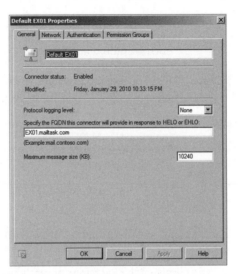

FIGURE 3.9   The Network tab of the receive connector's Properties dialog box

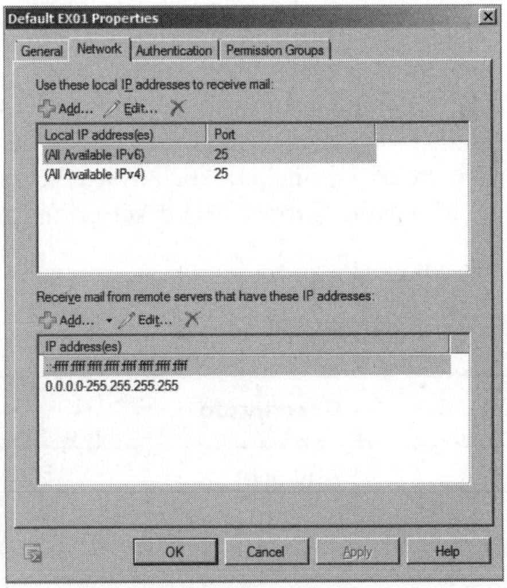

TABLE 3.1   Receive connector authentication methods

Authentication Type	Description
Transport Layer Security (TLS)	Configures the server to advertise STARTTLS when connection attempts are made to remote systems. TLS requires that a server certificate be trusted and installed.
Basic Authentication	Uses standard authentication, which transmits credentials in clear text. Can require TLS to secure credentials.
Exchange Server Authentication	Uses an Exchange authentication method, such as TLS or Kerberos through TLS.
Integrated Windows Authentication	Uses Integrated Windows authentication, which includes NTLM (NT LAN Manager) and Kerberos. This is a good solution if both sides of the connection are Windows-based systems.
Externally Secured	Used when the other end of the connection is secured by some other external means, such as use of a private network or Internet Protocol Security (IPSec). Configuring this option tells Exchange that the connection is secured, even though the Exchange server cannot actually verify this fact. You must also select the Exchange server's permission group on the Permission Groups tab when using this method.
None selected	No authentication configured.

Permission Groups   On the Permission Groups tab, you can select the permission groups associated with this receive connector. Permission groups are predefined sets of permissions that are granted to well-known security principals such as users, computers, and security groups. Table 3.2 outlines the permission groups and description for Hub and Edge Transport servers.

TABLE 3.2   Receive connector permission groups

Permission Groups	Description
Anonymous users	Any user
Exchange users (Hub Transport only)	Authenticated users

TABLE 3.2   Receive connector permission groups *(continued)*

Permission Groups	Description
Exchange servers	Members of the Exchange Servers universal security group
Legacy Exchange servers (Hub only)	Members of the ExchangeLegacyInterop universal security group
Partners	Partner service accounts

In Exercise 3.2, you created a receive connector to receive messages from a CRM application server from the within PowerShell. You selected the Anonymous users permission group after the creation process. Therefore, the receive connector will receive messages from any source. If the messages are being submitted using a known service account, you could consider configuring the Exchange Users option to secure the receive connector somewhat. By comparison, the default receive connectors do have permission groups configured on them. The Client *servername* receive connector is configured with only the Exchange Users permission group as being allowed to send messages through it. The Default *servername* connector is configured to allow the Exchange Users, Exchange Server, and Legacy Exchange Servers permission groups to send messages through it.

Modifying the Receive Connector with the EMS

Using the Exchange Management Shell, you will use the `Set-ReceiveConnector` cmdlet to modify values of receive connectors. The following command modifies the banner that computers will receive when making an SMTP connection to the receive connector. Banners are used to identify the SMTP connector and convey the intended usage and policies of the connector. The command also configures the maximum message size at 25 MB:

```
Set-ReceiveConnector -Name 'CRM Receive Connector'
-Banner '220 Custom CRM Receive Connector' -MaxMessageSize '25MB'
```

Deleting Connectors

You will run into situations when it's necessary to delete connectors because routing topologies or policies change in your Exchange organization. Fortunately, the process of deleting connectors is much simpler than the creation and configuration process for the connector. Login with an administrative account with appropriate rights, then just select the send or receive connector in the Exchange Management Console, right-click it, and select Remove from the context menu. Alternatively, you can click the Remove link under the connector options in the Actions pane on the right side of the Exchange Management Console.

If you're not certain whether you will need the connector any longer but you don't want it to be available for use, you can opt instead to disable it using the same process as discussed earlier, but this time select Disable instead of Remove.

To delete connectors with the Exchange Management Shell, use the `Remove-SendConnector` and `Remove-ReceiveConnector` cmdlets. Disabling connectors is performed using the `Set-SendConnector` and `Set-ReceiveConnector` with the `-Enabled:$False` parameter.

Now that you know how to create the send and receive connectors necessary for mail transport, we will examine both internal and external message routing. These subjects are closely linked because they determine how email is transmitted between servers.

Configuring Message Routing and Transport

In this section, we cover an important fundamental of email—how messages are sent from senders to recipients. With Exchange 2010, internal and external email routing is very similar to Exchange 2007. Hub Transport servers are responsible for all email transport within your Exchange organization. A message sent from an Exchange 2010 user will always be sent to an Exchange 2010 Hub Transport server, even if the recipients are on the same mailbox database (and in some cases, even if the Hub Transport server role is installed on the Mailbox server). The Hub Transport server will then determine the destination of the message, which, depending on the recipients, could be one or more Hub Transport servers, an Edge Transport server to relay to the Internet, or designated partner SMTP servers.

To illustrate Exchange 2010 email routing, Figure 3.10 shows an email sent from an Exchange user, Joel, and the path it will take. Joel sends a message to three people, Brian, Kory, and Erik. Joel, Kory, and Erik have mailboxes in the same Exchange organization, while Brian's mailbox resides in a separate email system.

1. The message originates from Joel's Mailbox server and is sent to a Hub Transport server in the site. The Hub Transport server accepts the message and performs recipient resolution to determine the next hop. In this case, the message will bifurcate (or split) into three messages as the recipients are in three separate destinations.

2. The Hub Transport server sends the message to the Mailbox server where Erik is located for delivery.

3. The Hub Transport server routes the message to a Hub Transport server in the Chicago-Site, which is where Kory's Mailbox server resides.

4. The Hub Transport server in the Chicago-Site sends the message to the Mailbox server for delivery.

5. The Hub Transport server routes the message to the Edge Transport server for delivery to the Internet.

6. The Edge Transport server sends the message over the Internet to Brian's email server.

FIGURE 3.10 An email sent from an Exchange user to multiple recipients

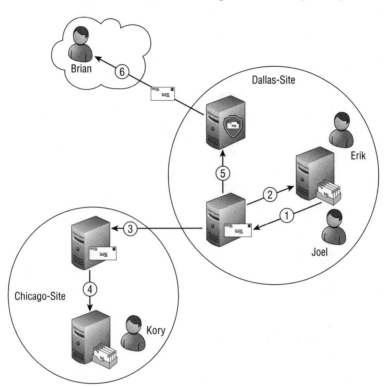

Conversely, email from the Internet will route through your Edge Transport server and then onto a Hub Transport server. From there the Hub Transport server will determine the destination and the next hop, which could be a Mailbox server in the local Active Directory site or another Hub Transport server in a remote Active Directory site.

Let's take the same scenario and go through the route that an email will take if Brian decides to choose Reply All to Joel's message in Figure 3.11.

1. Brian's reply sends the message from his email server to the Edge Transport server.

2. The Edge Transport server accepts the message and routes it to the Hub Transport server in the local Active Directory site. The Hub Transport server performs recipient resolution to determine the next hop. In this case, the message will bifurcate into two messages as the recipients are in two separate destinations.

3. The Hub Transport server sends a single message to the Mailbox server for delivery to Joel and Erik.

4. The Hub Transport server routes the message to a Hub Transport server in the Chicago-Site.

5. The Hub Transport server in the Chicago-Site sends the message to the Mailbox server for delivery to Kory.

FIGURE 3.11   An email sent from an external user to multiple Exchange users

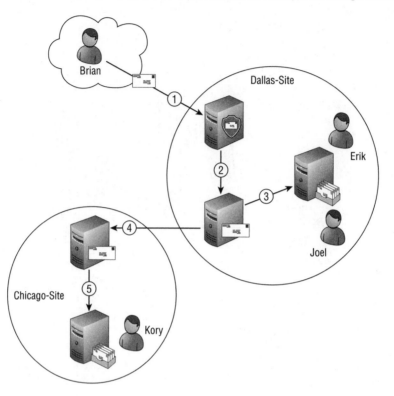

Using Internal Message Routing

Using connectors is especially important when providing coexistence and interoperability with SMTP-based services. However, as mentioned earlier, intra-Exchange 2010 email is controlled by Active Directory sites. In larger environments, Active Directory configuration is usually controlled by an IT group that is separate from the messaging group. In that case, as a messaging professional you need to understand how the Active Directory sites are configured to see how they will affect mail flow and network traffic.

Rather than relaying a message to multiple Active Directory sites, direct delivery from the local Hub Transport server to a destination Hub Transport server in the destination site is the default behavior, as shown in Figure 3.12.

If direct delivery is not possible due to a network or server outage, a back-off occurs and the AD site link configuration is used to determine the closest site to the destination. Then the message is delivered there for later delivery, as shown in Figure 3.13.

Often, no adjustments are needed to the standard AD site configuration. However, if you have dedicated AD sites for Exchange or you need to change the configuration without affecting Active Directory replication, you can set the Exchange cost on the Active Directory site links. This might be used if you wanted to favor one site for queuing over another. The lower the cost, the more likely the link will be used. Here's an example of setting a lower Exchange cost for a site link:

```
Set-AdSiteLink -Identity ChicagoToDallasSiteLink -ExchangeCost 5
```

FIGURE 3.12   Direct delivery of email is always attempted first.

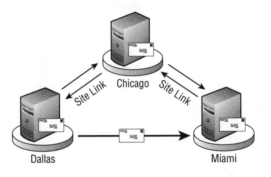

FIGURE 3.13   When direct delivery is not possible, back-off occurs.

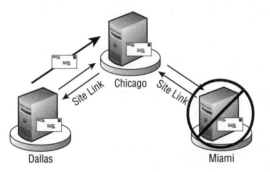

If the Exchange cost is not set, the Active Directory site link cost is used. To remove the Exchange cost and default back to the Active Directory cost, you can run the following command:

```
Set-AdSiteLink -Identity ChicagoToDallasSiteLink -ExchangeCost $null
```

If your network is configured in such a way that it requires all email to travel through a specific site (for bandwidth purposes or company policy), the hub site designation should be used. If a site is designated as a hub, all messages destined for a site on the opposite side of the hub site will first be delivered to a Hub Transport server and then sent to the destination site, if possible. In other words, after the least-cost route is chosen for a message, it is determined if a hub site exists along the path of the message. If it does, the message is first delivered to the hub site.

To set an AD site as a hub site, use the following command:

```
Set-AdSite -Identity Chicago -HubSiteEnabled $true
```

After enabling the Chicago AD site as a hub site, the email delivery would look similar to the model shown in Figure 3.14.

FIGURE 3.14   Delivering email through a hub site

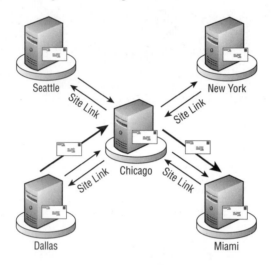

To disable a site as a hub site, run the following command:

```
Set-AdSite -Identity Chicago -HubSiteEnabled $false
```

Using External Message Routing

Earlier in this chapter, we configured a send connector on a Hub Transport server to deliver email to the Internet. This method is acceptable for smaller organizations, but most medium to large companies will utilize a third-party SMTP gateway to send and receive email from the Internet. Microsoft designs the Edge Transport server role for this scenario. Both choices are acceptable, and each will work as long as you ensure that the proper configuration is completed.

> Typically, the Edge Transport server or third-party SMTP gateway device will route external email but also perform antispam filtering and antivirus scanning. The company may use different types of antispam and antivirus protection at the Edge and Hub Transport servers for layered protection. They may also use several Edge Transport servers in different sites and locations for load balancing and redundancy. We discuss this topic more in Chapter 12.

For our purposes here, we'll assume that an Edge Transport server is desired in your Exchange organization; thus, we'll show you how to install, configure, and manage one. Installing the Edge Transport server is really no different from the installations discussed in Chapter 2, "Installing and Configuring the Exchange Server 2010." With this fact in mind, we'll jump right into the configuration and management tasks associated with a freshly installed Edge Transport server, as shown in Figure 3.15.

FIGURE 3.15   The Edge Transport server role viewed from the Exchange Management Console

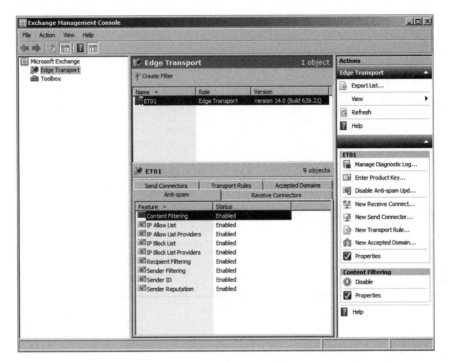

Prerequisites for Installing Edge Transport

For the installation of the Edge Transport role to be completed successfully, you'll need to install the following components before you start the installation:

- The Windows Management Framework that contains Windows PowerShell 2.0 and WinRM 2.0 (Windows Server 2008 R2 already has the Windows Management Framework installed by default; for Windows Server 2008, you must download it from http://support.microsoft.com/kb/968929)

- The .NET Framework 3.5 feature

- The AD DS and AD LDS Remote Server Administration Tool (RSAT) feature

- The Active Directory Lightweight Directory Services (AD LDS) role

Also, you will need to configure a FQDN for your Edge Transport servers, which is not typically done with servers located in the DMZ. Exchange will refuse to install the Edge Transport role if these prerequisite items are not in place. Edge Transport servers can be in a standalone workgroup or be a member of a domain, whether that is one of the corporate domains or a DMZ domain.

Configuring and Managing EdgeSync

The primary role of the Edge Transport server is to route inbound and outbound SMTP messages, checking them for spam and virus characteristics. The Edge Transport server now assumes these roles in organizations where no other third-party software or hardware solution is in place. The following benefits are realized through the use of the Edge Transport server (or a similar solution):

- Reduces load on Hub Transport and Mailbox servers with the filtering of unwanted messages, such as those containing spam or viruses

- Adds extra layer(s) of protection to the Exchange servers located on the internal network

- Prevents Internet connections directly to the Exchange servers located on the internal network

The first step you need to take to start realizing these benefits in your Exchange organization is to configure the EdgeSync service between your Edge Transport servers and your Hub Transport servers. By configuring EdgeSync, you'll install the Active Directory Lightweight Directory Services (AD LDS) role on the Edge Transport server to contain all the pertinent information needed to start filtering both inbound and outbound SMTP traffic. EdgeSync is required because Edge Transport servers are not joined to the domain, but they still need to send connector and user information to perform mail routing and address verification. The following information is replicated to the AD LDS database on the Edge Transport server after you have configured EdgeSync:

- A listing of all internally accepted domains

- A listing of all remote domains

- Any configured message classifications

- Information about internal send connectors that have been configured

- A listing of all valid internal SMTP addresses for the domain, which includes mailbox-enabled users, mail users, mail contacts, mail-enabled groups, and mail-enabled public folders

- The safe and blocked sender lists that have been configured for each of these users

The Edge Transport server is a great defense against undesirable SMTP traffic entering your Exchange organization because of the information it has in the AD LDS database plus the antispam and antivirus capabilities it provides. Even if you already have a third-party solution in place in your perimeter network or DMZ that provides some of these features, there might be a business justification for placing an Edge Transport server (or multiple

Edge Transport servers) in the DMZ between the Exchange organization and the third-party solution so you can take advantage of the Edge Transport server's benefits.

The basic process to enable EdgeSync includes the following steps:

1. Ensure that the required ports on the Internet-to-DMZ and DMZ-to-internal-network firewalls are configured.

2. Ensure that accepted domains for which your Exchange organization will handle mail are configured on a Hub Transport server. We will talk more about accepted domains later in this chapter.

3. Ensure that DNS resolution is functional between the Edge Transport servers in the DMZ and the Hub Transport servers on the internal network.

4. Define all internal Hub Transport servers so that Sender ID does not reject messages from them.

5. Create the Edge Subscription file on an Edge Transport server.

6. Complete the subscription by copying the Edge Subscription file to a Hub Transport server and using the New Edge Subscription Wizard on the Hub Transport server.

We examine each of these steps in the following sections.

 Several enhancements have been introduced to EdgeSync in Exchange 2010. Update-SafeList is no longer required to run as a scheduled task because it is automatically run by the Junk E-Mail Options mailbox assistant. The blocked senders list is now synchronized during recipient synchronization. Synchronization schedules of recipient, configuration, and topology data has also been reduced and are customizable.

Ensuring That Firewall Ports Are Configured for EdgeSync

Edge Transport servers typically reside in a DMZ or perimeter network to protect your internal Exchange servers. Table 3.3 details the port configuration that needs to be in place (at a minimum) to allow your Edge Transport servers to function correctly in the DMZ.

TABLE 3.3   Edge Transport firewall ports

Firewall Location	Rule	Description
Internet to DMZ	Allow port 25 to and from all Internet hosts to and from the Edge Transport servers.	Port 25 is used for SMTP.
Internet to DMZ	Allow port 53 to all Internet hosts from the Edge Transport servers.	Port 53 is required for DNS resolution, which is required to route outbound SMTP messages to Internet hosts properly.

TABLE 3.3   Edge Transport firewall ports *(continued)*

Firewall Location	Rule	Description
Internal to DMZ	Allow port 25 to and from specified Hub Transport servers to and from specified Edge Transport servers.	Port 25 is used for SMTP.
Internal to DMZ	Allow port 50636 from specified Hub Transport servers to specified Edge Transport servers.	Port 50636 is used for Secure Lightweight Directory Access Protocol (SLDAP) replication between Hub Transport servers and the ADAM database located on the Edge Transport servers.
Internal to DMZ	Allow port 3389 from the internal network to the specified Edge Transport servers.	Port 3389 is used for Remote Desktop Protocol (RDP) connections for managing servers remotely.
Internal to DMZ	Allow port 53 from the internal network to the specified Edge Transport servers.	Port 53 is required for DNS resolution, which is required to route messages properly.

Ensuring That DNS Resolution Is working

For Edge Transport servers to operate, DNS resolution between the Edge Transport server and the Hub Transport server must work. From each Edge Transport server, use the Windows nslookup command to check the name of each Hub Transport server to make sure it resolves to the proper IP address. Then from each Hub Transport server, check that the name of each Edge Transport server resolves to the proper IP address.

Defining Internal Hub Transport Servers

Before you can enable EdgeSync, you need to define the list of internal Hub Transport servers that exist in your Exchange organization. This is required so that Sender ID on the Edge Transport server knows which servers are internal to your organization and so that connection filters know they should not reject connections from these internal SMTP servers. This required configuration is one of those tasks that you cannot perform from the Exchange Management Console, so you'll need to use the Set-TransportConfig cmdlet from the Exchange Management Shell. If your Hub Transport servers had IP addresses of 192.168.137.30 and 192.168.137.31, then the command to enter would look like this:

```
Set-TransportConfig -InternalSMTPServers 192.168.137.30, 192.168.137.31
```

There is no feedback provided to let you know that you've done anything right or wrong. However, given that PowerShell is very good about alerting you to syntax errors, you can rest assured that you've gotten the task accomplished.

Creating the Edge Subscription File

To configure the Hub Transport servers to communicate with the Edge Transport servers, you must make sure that the Edge Transport servers are subscribed to the Active Directory site where the Hub Transport servers reside. The subscription process consists of exporting an XML file from the Edge Transport server and then importing that file on one of the Hub Transport servers in the Active Directory site. You create an Edge Subscription file on the Edge Transport server that will be subscribed. When you create this file on the Edge Transport server, it prepares the server to start synchronizing appropriate Active Directory information into the local AD LDS database and provides the authentication information needed by the Hub Transport server to start the EdgeSync process. To create the XML-based subscription file, you once again use an Exchange Management Shell cmdlet, `New-EdgeSubscription`. If you wanted to save the file to the C drive, your entry might look like this:

```
New-EdgeSubscription -FileName "C:\EdgeSubscription.xml"
```

You are presented with a list of items to consider before completing the Edge Subscription file creation process. Note the tasks that are disabled if you continue; you'll be performing them from the Hub Transport server only after EdgeSync is enabled.

The full text is shown here for clarity because it is important to understand the implications of the decision to move forward with creating the Edge Subscription file:

```
Confirm
```

Creating an Edge Subscription makes the configuration of this Edge Transport server ready to be managed via EdgeSync. Any of the following types of objects that were created manually will be deleted: accepted domains; message classifications; remote domains; and Send connectors. Also, the InternalSMTPServers list of the TransportConfig object will be overwritten during the synchronization process. The Exchange Management Shell tasks that manage those types of objects will be locked out on this Edge Transport server. You must manage those objects from inside the organization and allow EdgeSync to update the Edge Transport server. EdgeSync requires that this Edge Transport server is able to resolve the FQDNs of the Hub Transport servers in the Active Directory site to which the Edge Transport server is being subscribed. Those Hub Transport servers must be able to resolve the FQDN of this Edge Transport server. You should complete the Edge Subscription inside the organization in the next "1440" minutes before the bootstrap account expires.

```
[Y] Yes [A] Yes to All [N] No [L] No to All [S] Suspend [?] Help(default is "Y"):
```

If you open the resulting XML file in Notepad, you can see what is inside it, as shown in Figure 3.16. Notice that the file contains both the short and FQDNs of the Edge Transport server; the Hub Transport servers must be able to resolve this name via DNS queries.

FIGURE 3.16 Viewing the Edge Subscription file

Completing the EdgeSync Process

After you create the Edge Subscription file, you need to copy it to the Hub Transport server on which you'll be completing the EdgeSync process. With that task completed, you're ready to complete the EdgeSync process by running the New Edge Subscription Wizard, as detailed in Exercise 3.3.

EXERCISE 3.3

Creating a New Edge Subscription

To create a new Edge Subscription on your Hub Transport server, follow these steps:

1. Click Start ➤ Programs ➤ Microsoft Exchange Server 2010 and then select Exchange Management Console.

2. Expand the Microsoft Exchange container, expand the Microsoft Exchange On-Premises container, expand the Organization Configuration container, and then click the Hub Transport node.

3. Under the Actions pane on the right side, click the New Edge Subscription link. The New Edge Subscription Wizard opens.

4. Select the Active Directory site that the Edge Subscription pertains to from the drop-down list provided, and then use the Browse button to locate the XML file you created on your Edge Transport server and then copied to your Hub Transport server. You should typically leave the selection Automatically Create A Send Connector For This Edge Subscription checked. Click New when you are ready to proceed.

5. After a few seconds, the completion details are presented. Once again, you are informed that the Hub Transport servers must be able to resolve the name of the Edge Transport server in order for EdgeSync to work correctly. Click Finish to close the wizard.

The corresponding Exchange Management Shell cmdlet you could have used to complete the EdgeSync process is `New-EdgeSubscription`. Assuming the filename is as you created it previously and the file was located in `C:\Temp`, your code might look like this:

```
New-EdgeSubscription -FileName 'C:\Temp\EdgeSubscription.xml'
-Site 'Default-First-Site-Name' -CreateInternetSendConnector $true
-CreateInboundSendConnector $true
```

After the wizard has completed, the edge synchronization process should start and begin to synchronize the following configuration data every 3 minutes:

- Hub Transport servers
- Accepted domains

- Message classifications
- Remote domains
- Send connectors
- Internal SMTP servers
- Domain Secure lists

The following recipient information is synchronized every 5 minutes:

- Exchange recipients
- Proxy addresses
- Safe senders, blocked senders, safe recipients
- Per-recipient antispam settings

Topology data, which includes newly subscribed Edge Transport servers or removed subscriptions, is refreshed every 5 minutes. These synchronization times are much improved over Exchange Server 2007, which synchronized configuration data every hour and recipient data every 4 hours. There is a new cmdlet named Set-EdgeSyncServiceConfig to configure the synchronization schedule and logging. Should you need to force synchronization, you can use the Start-EdgeSynchronization cmdlet. Figure 3.17 shows the cmdlet and result for a manual synchronization run from the Hub Transport server.

FIGURE 3.17   Running a manual edge synchronization

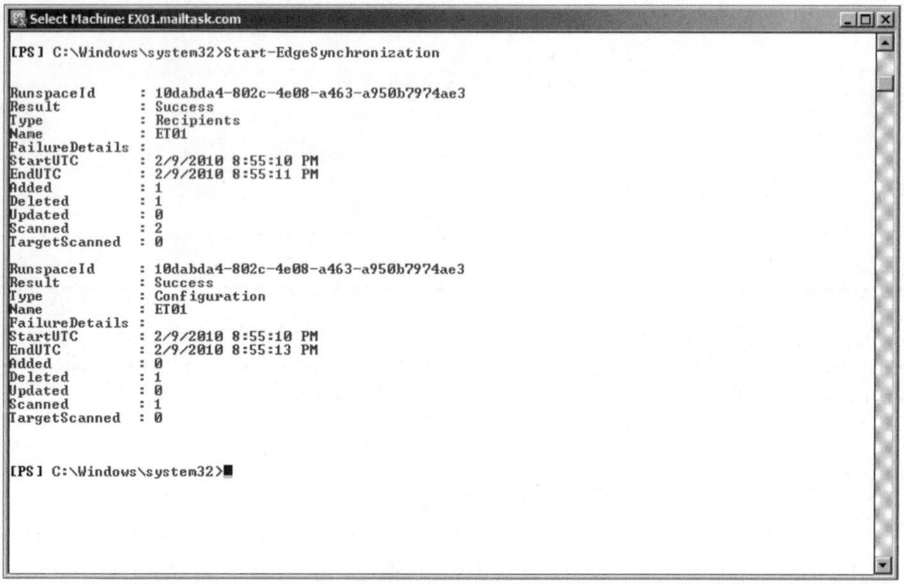

```
Select Machine: EX01.mailtask.com                                    _ □ ×
[PS] C:\Windows\system32>Start-EdgeSynchronization

RunspaceId      : 10dabda4-802c-4e08-a463-a950b7974ae3
Result          : Success
Type            : Recipients
Name            : ET01
FailureDetails  :
StartUTC        : 2/9/2010 8:55:10 PM
EndUTC          : 2/9/2010 8:55:11 PM
Added           : 1
Deleted         : 1
Updated         : 0
Scanned         : 2
TargetScanned   : 0

RunspaceId      : 10dabda4-802c-4e08-a463-a950b7974ae3
Result          : Success
Type            : Configuration
Name            : ET01
FailureDetails  :
StartUTC        : 2/9/2010 8:55:10 PM
EndUTC          : 2/9/2010 8:55:13 PM
Added           : 0
Deleted         : 1
Updated         : 0
Scanned         : 1
TargetScanned   : 0


[PS] C:\Windows\system32>█
```

Moving back to the Edge Transport server, you can verify that synchronization has occurred by examining the accepted domains that are configured on the server, as shown in Figure 3.18.

FIGURE 3.18   Viewing the updated list of accepted domains on the Edge Transport server

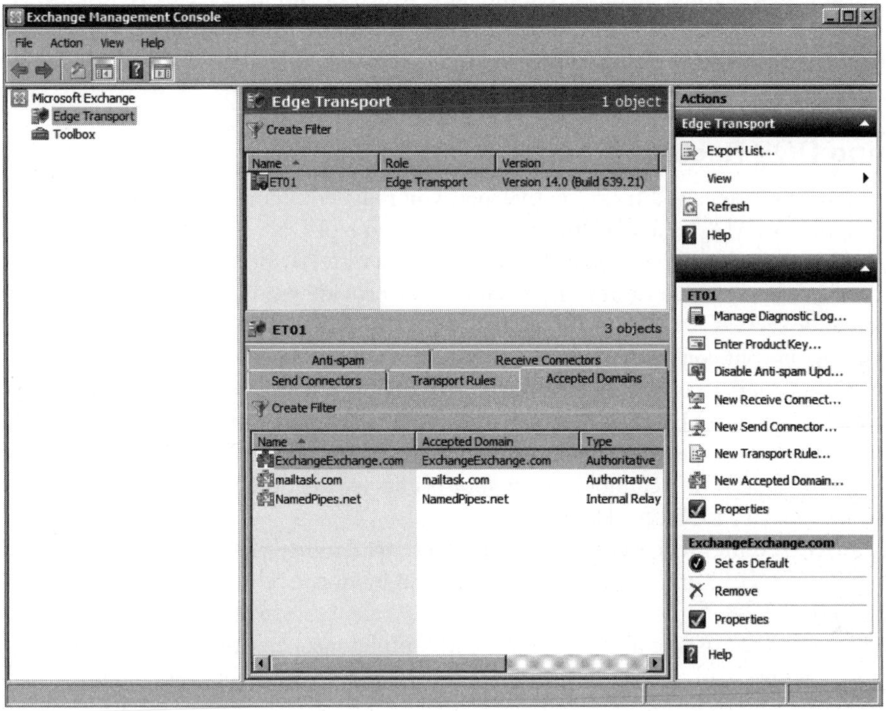

Exchange 2010 antispam filtering can be enabled on both the Edge Transport server role and the Hub Transport server role. You should only configure the antispam filters on the Hub Transport role when there is not an Edge Transport server or third-party gateway that performs antispam filtering. Forefront Protection for Exchange 2010 is a separate software product that will perform antivirus and antispam filtering. Antivirus filtering should typically be performed on both your Edge and Hub Transport servers. Forefront Protection for Exchange 2010 contains many of the same antispam filter agents that are built into the Edge and Hub Transport servers, but it also contains several features not present on Exchange, such as an advanced content filtering agent, a built-in aggregate DNSBL (blocklist), and a new backscatter protection option.

Configuring Transport

So far we've talked about connectors and email routing within Exchange and to the Internet. In the following sections, we discuss message transport features in Exchange 2010. Message transport has changed little since Exchange 2007, but Exchange 2010 adds one important new feature, Shadow Redundancy, which makes message delivery much more reliable without requiring any additional configuration. We will examine how to configure MX records, how to set message size limits, and how to understand and troubleshoot message delivery.

Creating DNS Records

Before email can be received from the Internet, you must configure DNS MX records for your company. An MX (mail exchanger) record is a type of DNS resource record that specifies what servers will be responsible to accept email for a specific domain. Multiple MX records and preference values can be entered to provide redundancy and priority for your Exchange servers.

Depending on your company, you or someone else within your company may be responsible for creating DNS records. Regardless, you will usually create a primary and secondary MX record for a primary Exchange server and secondary Exchange server. The primary MX record will have a lower preference number, and it will be the one other SMTP servers will try to send email to first. If they cannot contact your primary server, the SMTP server will try to contact the secondary MX record and server.

You can also configure load balancing and high availability with Windows Network Load Balancing (NLB) or a hardware network load balancer. This will be discussed in later chapters.

An MX record consists of a domain name, MX preference, and record value. The record value is usually specified as a DNS A resource record and not an IP address. Figure 3.19 shows a sample MX record for the domain mailtask.com.

FIGURE 3.19　DNS MX information for mailtask.com

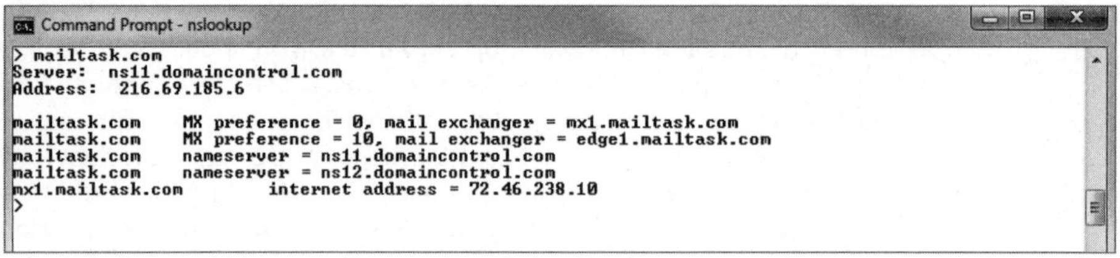

```
> mailtask.com
Server:  ns11.domaincontrol.com
Address:  216.69.185.6

mailtask.com    MX preference = 0, mail exchanger = mx1.mailtask.com
mailtask.com    MX preference = 10, mail exchanger = edge1.mailtask.com
mailtask.com    nameserver = ns11.domaincontrol.com
mailtask.com    nameserver = ns12.domaincontrol.com
mx1.mailtask.com         internet address = 72.46.238.10
>
```

Configuring Accepted Domains

Once DNS records are created to send inbound email to your Edge Transport servers, you must configure the domains that you want to receive email as accepted domains for the Exchange organization. A default installation of Exchange will configure your root

Active Directory domain name as the default accepted domain. There are three types of accepted domains:.

Authoritative domain   All email is delivered to recipients in the Exchange organization or rejected.

Internal relay domain   Email is delivered to recipients in the Exchange organization. If the recipient does not exist in the Exchange organization, the email is relayed to another email server outside of the Exchange organization.

External relay domain   Email is accepted but relayed to another email server outside of the Exchange organization.

You can use both the Exchange Management Console and the Exchange Management Shell to configure accepted domains. Figure 3.20 shows that configuration for accepted domains is found in the Hub Transport node under Organization Configuration in the EMC. To configure accepted domains with the EMS, use the `New-AcceptedDomain` and `Set-AcceptedDomain` cmdlets.

FIGURE 3.20   Accepted domains for the organization in the Exchange Management Console

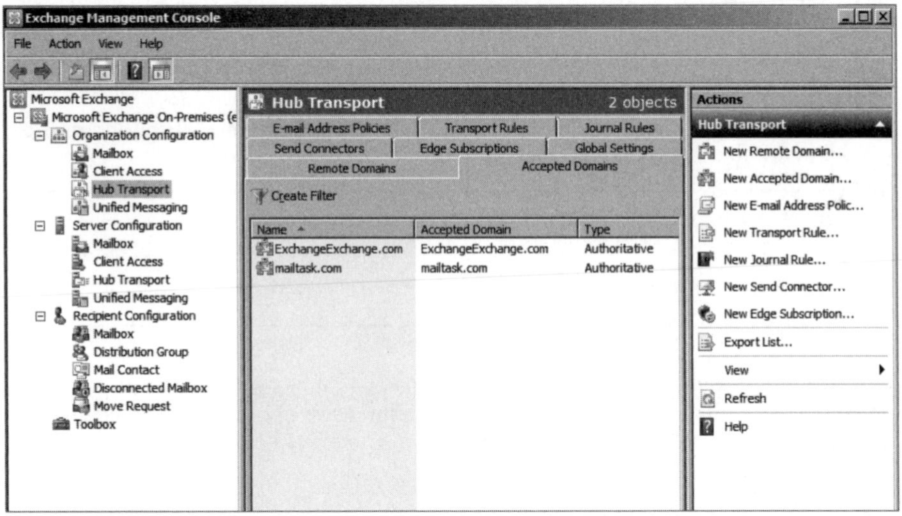

Configuring Message Size Limits

Configuring message size limits for Exchange plays an important role in how email is used within your company and can affect your email service-level agreement (SLA). Configuring smaller message limits might restrict Exchange to a primary message conversation tool, while larger limits might enable users to use Exchange as a collaborative tool for delivering digital documents. Conversely, smaller limits may enable you to meet your message delivery SLA, while larger limits may make it difficult.

When looking at message size limits, you need to look at message scope and the message type. Table 3.5 and Table 3.6 describe both of these topics.

TABLE 3.5 Message scopes

Scope	Description
Organizational limits	Limits defined to all Exchange 2010 and Exchange 2007 servers.
Global limits	Limits defined in Active Directory for Exchange. Carried over from Exchange 2003. Changes to the organizational limits will be reflected in the global limits.
Connector limits	Limits defined on send, receive, and foreign connectors.
Active Directory site links	Limits defined on AD site links used in the least-cost routing path between sites.
Routing group connectors	Limits defined on routing group connectors to Exchange 2003 routing groups.
Server limits	Limits defined on Hub and Edge Transport servers.
User limits	Limits defined to mailboxes, contacts, distribution groups, and public folders.

TABLE 3.6 Message types

Types	Description
Message header size limits	Limits defined by the total size of only the message header fields of the message. The message body and attachments are not considered.
Message size limits	Limits defined by the total size of the message, which includes the header, body, and all attachments.
Attachment size limits	Limits defined to individual attachments of the email message.
Recipient limits	Limits defined to the total number of message recipients in the email message.

You can configure different limits to different scope components and messages will be restricted by the smallest limit if the scope component is traversed or the message type limit is reached. For example, a 50 MB message from an Exchange user will be rejected if the organizational limit is configured at 30 MB. But a 30 MB message will be delivered to the Exchange user even if the Internet send connector is configured at a 25 MB limit. The message does not traverse the Internet send connector and thus is not limited by the connector limit.

In Exercise 3.4, you'll configure message size limits for the default client receive connector and then set the maximum send size for a user named Joel Stidley.

EXERCISE 3.4

Configuring Message Size Limits

To configure message size limits, follow these steps:

1. Click Start ➤ All Programs ➤ Microsoft Exchange Server 2010 and then select Exchange Management Console.

2. Expand the Microsoft Exchange container, expand the Microsoft Exchange On-Premises container, expand the Server Configuration container, and then click the Hub Transport node.

3. Highlight your Hub Transport server and then highlight your default client receive connector.

4. Under the Actions pane, click Properties to bring up the General tab of the client receive connector Properties dialog box.

5. Change the value of the maximum message size (KB) to 50000 (approximately 50 MB).

6. Click OK to save and close the Properties dialog box of the receive connector.

7. Next, open up the Exchange Management Shell by clicking Start ➢ All Programs ➢ Microsoft Exchange Server 2010 and then selecting Exchange Management Shell.

8. Run the following command:

    ```
    Set-Mailbox -Identity JoelStidely -MaxSendSize 50MB
    ```

9. The following command sets the maximum send size to 50 MB for all of your users:

    ```
    Get-Mailbox | Set-Mailbox -MaxSendSize 50MB
    ```

Troubleshooting with Message Queues

Hub and Edge Transport servers store messages in transit in queues on the server. As messages are routed through a transport server, they can sit in a number of different transport queues. Queues are important when troubleshooting message delivery issues. Table 3.7 describes the different types of queues for Exchange 2010 transport servers.

TABLE 3.7   Transport queues

Queue	Description
Submission	Queue used by the categorizer component of the Exchange transport service. It determines recipient information, applies policies, routes messages, and performs content conversion.
Mailbox delivery queue	Queue used for next hop delivery to Mailbox servers. Exists only on Hub Transport servers.
Remote delivery queue	Queue used to hold messages waiting to be delivered to remote servers. These queues group together multiple messages with identical destination domains. Messages can get stuck here if the transport server is unable to reach the destination server.

TABLE 3.7   Transport queues *(continued)*

Queue	Description
Poison message queue	Queue used to contain messages that are detected to be harmful to the Exchange server after a server failure. Messages in this queue are suspended and can be removed or retried for delivery.
Unreachable queue	Queue used for messages that cannot be routed to their destinations.
Shadow Redundancy	Queue used to hold messages that have been delivered to another server supporting Shadow Redundancy. Once the server receives confirmation that the next server has successfully delivered the message, it is removed from the queue.

The poison and unreachable queues should be checked regularly to resolve issues of stuck and suspended messages. You can take action on messages in these queues and other queues such as retrying, removing, resuming, or exporting the messages. You can use the Queue Viewer from the Exchange Toolbox to view and manage the message queues.

Understanding Shadow Redundancy

A new feature in Exchange 2010 named Shadow Redundancy provides message redundancy during message transport. If a Hub Transport server fails and cannot be recovered, messages in its queue could be lost. Shadow Redundancy requires delayed deletion of email messages until the server can verify that the next hop server has successfully delivered the message to its next hop. For transport servers, the message is moved into a Shadow Redundancy queue on the transport server until it receives acknowledgement to delete the message. For Mailbox servers, if the Hub Transport server that it has delivered to fails, the Mailbox server is able to redeliver the message from the sender's mailbox. Shadow Redundancy enables this extra resiliency without any additional configuration. More information about shadow redundancy can be found in Chapter 14, Designing High Availability and Recovery.

Now that we have examined how emails are sent and received between Exchange servers, let's examine how to configure Exchange for users to connect to Exchange 2010.

Configuring Client Access for Exchange Server 2010

The Client Access server role in Exchange 2010 continues to provide client services such as Outlook Web App (OWA, formerly known as Outlook Web Access), Outlook Anywhere, ActiveSync, and availability. Some services available in Exchange 2007 have been removed, such as WebDAV and document access to SharePoint and file shares. New features added include the Exchange Control Panel (ECP), conversation view in OWA, and Remote Procedure Call (RPC) client access.

Exchange Server 2010 provides users with numerous ways to connect to Exchange:

- Various versions of Outlook
- Web browsers
- Third-party clients via POP3 and IMAP4 protocols
- Mobile devices
- Custom applications

You can connect to Exchange in a multitude of ways from anywhere (providing your company policy allows you to do so) and anytime. What types of Exchange objects do you connect to? Including your own mailbox, there are a number of objects and features:

- Built-in mailbox folders such as Inbox and Sent Items
- Custom folders or folders of other users and shared mailboxes
- Calendars and contacts
- Public folders (Yes, they exist!)
- Voicemail and text messaging
- Configuration options for users and groups
- Custom rules for users and the organization

Two important services in accessing Exchange 2010 are the ECP and EWS. ECP not only provides individual mailbox options for customizing rules and out-of-office messages, it now allows users to customize options such as their name, phone number, and group membership of groups they own. Admins in the organization can use ECP to view and manage other users' options as well as complete the following organization tasks:

- Create and modify users, groups, and contacts
- Create and modify administrator and user roles
- Create message delivery reports
- Perform multi-mailbox searches for legal discovery

EWS plays an important role for those times when the configuration options provided by Microsoft don't provide the functionality required by your company. EWS is an application programming interface (API) that can be used to communicate with Exchange via the Client Access servers. As you upgrade or migrate to Exchange 2010, creating EWS solutions and applications is sometimes necessary for your company's custom applications as well as some third-party applications that your company relies on. Your developers can download the EWS API Software Developers Kit at http://msdn.microsoft.com/en-us/exchange.

The Client Access server is accessed directly by web browsers, mobile devices, and other applications from the Internet. In medium to large organizations, the Client Access server sits behind a reverse proxy server such as Microsoft's Internet Security and Acceleration (ISA) server 2006. ISA 2006 is limited in scalability mostly due to its 32-bit architecture. The updated product from Microsoft for medium-sized companies is called Forefront Threat Management Gateway 2010 (TMG). For large companies and deployments, Forefront Unified Access Gateway (UAG) is recommended for network publishing, protection, and secure remote access.

Configuring Client Connectivity with Autodiscover

Configuring the Client Access server really starts with configuring the Autodiscover service. Your users will have a tough time accessing Exchange until you properly configure the Client Access server for connectivity. Exchange 2007 introduced Autodiscover, which allows Outlook 2007 and 2010, Windows Mobile, and other clients to discover configuration information for a specific mailbox. Autodiscover is a web service that resides on the Exchange 2010 Client Access server role. The popular perception of Autodiscover is that it helps Outlook and mobile devices to automatically configure a mail profile when you just enter the user's email address and password, which is correct. However, Autodiscover actually helps Outlook locate a number of different types of Exchange resources, including the following:

- User's home Mailbox server
- Outlook Anywhere URL
- URL (internal or external) for the Offline Address Book
- URL (internal or external) for unified messaging
- URL (internal or external) for EWS, which empowers the Availability service

When a user launches Outlook 2010 for the first time, they are prompted for some basic information (email address or domain/username and password). Outlook 2010 contacts the Autodiscover web service and looks up information such as the home Mailbox server, display name, and URLs for the Availability web service that provides free/busy information and the location of the OAB. If this information is changed, then the Outlook client gets updated information (including the home Mailbox server name) from the Autodiscover service. Outlook will connect to the Autodiscover service upon startup and refresh profile settings every 60 minutes.

When users specify their email address, they should use their default SMTP address. Autodiscover might not work for additional SMTP addresses.

It is important to spend a few minutes talking about EWS. It includes services that were created to access data in the Exchange store programmatically. Previously, many of these functions were spread out into multiple APIs that complicated the task of developers creating software that accessed the Exchange store. What types of operations does EWS enable? Here is a short list:

- Create, copy, move, and delete items
- Create, copy, move, and delete folders
- Create, get, and delete attachments
- Subscribe to notifications
- Synchronize items
- Retrieve user availability and out-of-office information
- Manage delegates

One of the functions of EWS is what is called the *Availability service*. This service is leveraged by both Outlook Web Access and Outlook to retrieve live free/busy information from both Exchange 2010 and legacy mailboxes in not only the local Exchange forest but also in remote forests. Configuring the internal and external URL settings for EWS allows the Autodiscover service to configure clients to use the Availability service properly.

Outlook 2010 is in beta release as of this writing. Features and functionality may differ slightly in the final release product.

Comparing Internal Autodiscover to External Autodiscover

Outlook uses two approaches to locate the Autodiscover service and determine the necessary information. When the Outlook client computer is a member of the Active Directory forest in which the Exchange server exists, Outlook uses Active Directory to locate the Autodiscover service. Figure 3.21 shows the process that Outlook uses to locate resources when the client computer is a member of the Active Directory forest. This is considered the service process for internal clients.

In step 1 of Figure 3.21, Outlook is launched for the first time and there is no Outlook profile for the user account. Outlook contacts Active Directory to find a service connection point (SCP). A *service connection point* is an Active Directory object that can be used to publish and locate network services. The SCP object will provide Outlook with the FQDNs of Client Access servers. Outlook then contacts a Client Access server in its local Active Directory site.

In step 2 in Figure 3.21, the Outlook client queries the Client Access server to retrieve the user's home server. The username and domain name are used to locate the user's home Mailbox server. Outlook also retrieves information about the location of the Availability service and the distribution points for the OAB. From this information, the Outlook profile is created.

In step 3 in Figure 3.21, Outlook connects to the database that contains the user's mailbox using a local Client Access Server.

FIGURE 3.21   The Autodiscover process when a client is in the same Active Directory forest

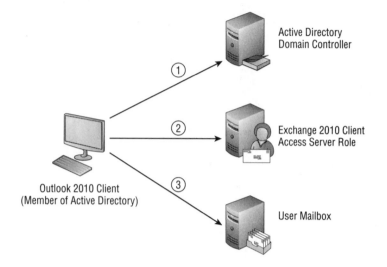

Active Directory
Domain Controller

Exchange 2010 Client
Access Server Role

Outlook 2010 Client
(Member of Active Directory)

User Mailbox

If the Outlook client computer not a member of the Active Directory forest or is outside the corporate network and cannot contact a domain controller, then Outlook 2010 uses the Autodiscover service process for external access. In this approach, DNS is used to locate the Autodiscover service as shown in Figure 3.22. In this example, the user must provide their email address because it cannot be retrieved from Active Directory.

In step 1, Outlook tries to contact an Active Directory domain controller (if the client is a member of the Active Directory). If Active Directory cannot be located or the computer is not a member of the Active Directory forest, the user is presented with the Add New Account dialog box, shown in Figure 3.23. In this dialog box, the user must enter their primary SMTP address, their name, and their account password. The email address is important because the SMTP domain name is used in step 2.

In step 2, the Outlook 2010 client performs a DNS query and uses the SMTP domain name. In our example, the domain name is mailtask.com. Outlook uses the following URLs to try to connect in order to locate the Autodiscover server:

`https://mailtask.com/autodiscover/autodiscover.xml`

`https://autodiscover.mailtask.com/autodiscover/autodiscover.xml`

A DNS Service Location (SRV) record can be created for Autodiscover to point to any hostname—even a host in a different domain. Outlook 2007 requires an update for the feature. For more information about how to use an SRV record, see support.microsoft.com/kb/940881.

FIGURE 3.22 The Autodiscover process when a client is not in the same Active Directory forest

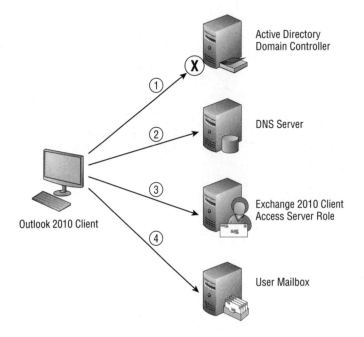

FIGURE 3.23 Providing account information manually to Outlook

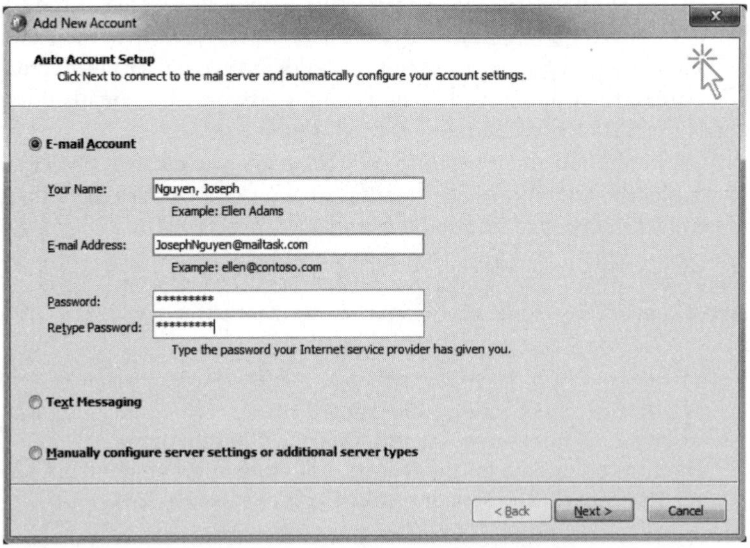

These URLs need to be resolvable in DNS and accessible from outside your network for external clients. If you use the DNS approach for "external" clients on your inside network, you will want to make sure that one of these two URLs is resolvable using your internal DNS.

 You can read more about Autodiscover in the Autodiscover service white paper at technet.microsoft.com/en-us/library/bb332063.aspx. Though written for Exchange 2007, it is still valid for Exchange 2010.

The Client Access server that hosts Autodiscover will be queried in step 3 and return the information needed to configure Outlook. In step 4 Outlook uses the configuration information to connect to the correct client access server and ultimately the Mailbox Server hosting the users mailbox.

Configuring Autodiscover

When an Exchange 2010 Client Access server is installed, a service connection point (SCP) record is created in Active Directory for it. This includes the internal Outlook Anywhere settings, the internal URL for the OAB, and the internal URL for EWS. However, depending on your environment, you will likely need to configure additional settings if, for example, you need to enable Outlook Anywhere (formerly RPC over HTTP) or define external URLs for other web services.

Configuring Autodiscover Virtual Directories

An Autodiscover virtual directory is automatically created on each Exchange 2010 Client Access server. The only way to configure this is through the Exchange Management Shell. The Get-AutoDiscoverVirtualDirectory cmdlet will let you view the Autodiscover virtual directories.

Configuring Outlook Anywhere and Autodiscover

By default, Outlook Anywhere is not enabled on the Client Access servers. To enable Outlook Anywhere, locate each Client Access server in the Server Configuration work center in the Exchange Management Console and select the Enable Outlook Anywhere task in the Actions pane. This launches a wizard that prompts you for the external hostname and the type of authentication, and it gives you the option to use SSL offloading.

If you are using network load balancing, the external hostname will be the FQDN that the clients will use externally. When you have completed the information required by the wizard, click the Enable Outlook Anywhere button in the upper-left corner.

Optionally, you could enable Outlook Anywhere using the Enable-OutlookAnywhere cmdlet. Here is an example:

```
Enable-OutlookAnywhere -Server "EX01"
-ExternalHostname "mail.mailtask.com"
-ExternalAuthenticationMethod "Basic" -SSLOffloading $false
```

After Outlook Anywhere is enabled, you can select the properties of the Client Access server and view the Outlook Anywhere properties of that particular Client Access server. Figure 3.24 shows an example.

FIGURE 3.24   Configuring the external hostname for Outlook Anywhere

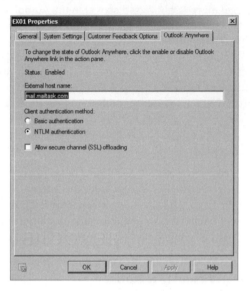

You can retrieve the same information (and more) using the `Get-OutlookAnywhere` cmdlet. When you configure the external hostname for Outlook Anywhere, remember that this is the URL that will be referred to external Outlook clients when Autodiscover is used.

Configuring Offline Address Books and Autodiscover

By default, the Offline Address Book (OAB) distribution points contain only the internal URL used to locate them. You can set these using the graphical user interface by selecting the properties of the OAB virtual directory in the Exchange Management Console. Figure 3.25 shows the URLs tab of the OAB (Default Web Site) virtual directory's Properties dialog box for a Client Access server.

You can also set this parameter using the cmdlet `Set-OABVirtualDirectory`. Here is an example:

```
Set-OABVirtualDirectory "EX01\OAB (Default Web Site)"
-ExternalURL https://mail.mailtask.com/OAB -RequireSSL:$True
```

You can view the configuration of the OAB virtual directory using the `get-OABVirtualDirectory` cmdlet.

The OAB is updated only at 5 a.m. each day by default. If your company creates or modifies mailboxes and groups throughout the day, the OAB will not reflect the change until the next morning. You can configure more frequent updates by accessing the properties of the Default OAB using the Mailbox node under Organization Configuration in the Exchange

Management Console. On the General tab, you can modify the update schedule and specify the Mailbox server that will generate the OAB. On the Distribution tab, shown in Figure 3.26, you can specify which Client Access servers are enabled for web-based distribution and enable or disable public folder distribution of the OAB.

FIGURE 3.25   Configuring the external URL for Offline Address Book distribution

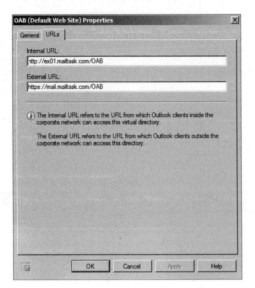

FIGURE 3.26   The Distribution tab of the Default Offline Address Book Properties dialog box

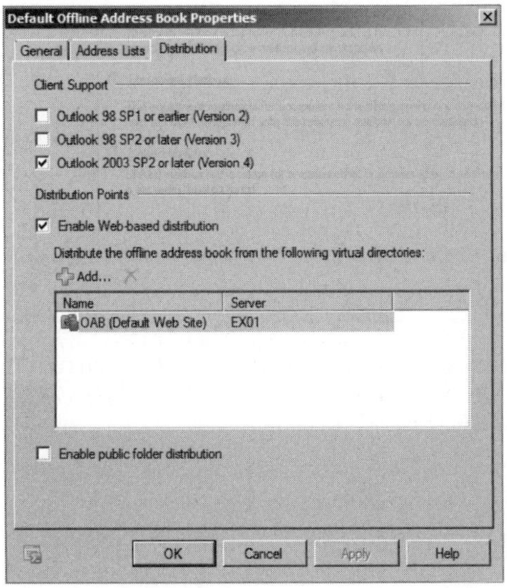

Configuring Web Services and Autodiscover

If remote or external clients need access to custom web services, you should configure the external URL for web services. You can do this only via the Exchange Management Shell. The following cmdlet is an example for setting the external URL for a Client Access server:

```
Set-WebServicesVirtualDirectory "EX01\EWS (Default web site)"
-ExternalUrl "https://mail.mailtask.com/EWS/Exchange.asmx"
-BasicAuthentication:$True
```

To check the configuration of the Web Services virtual directory, you can use the Get-WebServicesVirtualDirectory cmdlet.

Using the Configure External Client Access Domain Wizard

Exchange Server 2010 includes a new wizard in the EMC to automatically configure the external URLs for you. The configuration we just walked through can be used to initially create or modify the external URLs. In Exercise 3.5, you'll use the wizard to modify the external virtual directories.

EXERCISE 3.5

Configure External Client Access Domain Using the Wizard

To modify the external virtual directories, follow these steps:

1. Click Start ➤ Programs ➤ Microsoft Exchange Server 2010 and then select Exchange Management Console.

2. Expand the Microsoft Exchange container, expand the Microsoft Exchange On-Premises container, expand the Server Configuration container, and then click the Client Access node.

3. Select the server on which to configure the virtual directories. Under the Actions pane on the right side, click the Configure External Client Access Domain link.

4. In the Configure External Client Access Domain Wizard, type the domain name for external access and then click the Add button to add in each of your Client Access Servers that you want to modify.

5. Click Configure to complete the changes. Examine the changes and click Finish to close the wizard.

The wizard modifies the external URLs for the following virtual directories:

- ActiveSync
- Outlook Web App
- Offline Address Book
- Exchange Web Services
- Outlook Anywhere

TIP

Microsoft introduced the Exchange Remote Connectivity Analyzer that can remotely test and troubleshoot your connectivity setup for ActiveSync, Autodiscover, Web Services connectivity and more. Domain credentials are required and it is highly recommended that you use a temporary test account when you are using this tool. The tool is located at www.testexchangeconnectivity.com.

Configuring Autodiscover and Secure Sockets Layer

If you have tried to deploy both internal and external URLs already, then by now you are wondering how Secure Sockets Layer is supposed to work if the FQDN of the internal location is different from the external FQDN. After all, if certificates are requested, you usually provide only one name in the certificate-signing request. There is a workaround, however, that allows you to have more than one common name for a Client Access server. This feature is called Subject Alternative Name (SAN) certificates in the Exchange documentation; however, many providers refer to these certificates as Unified Communication Certificates (UCCs). To use the workaround, you have to create the certificate using the New-ExchangeCertificate cmdlet. The command line can be fairly involved. Here is an example:

```
New-ExchangeCertificate -GenerateRequest
-SubjectName "dc=com,dc=mailtask,o=Mail Task,cn=mail.mailtask.com"
-DomainName EX01, EX01.mailtask.com, mail.mailtask.com,
autodiscover.mailtask.com -path c:\certrequest-EX01.txt
```

This cmdlet creates a certificate request with multiple hostnames. In this case, the hostnames include mail.mailtask.com, autodiscover.mailtask.com, EX01, and EX01.mailtask.com.

Exchange server 2010 introduces a new certificate wizard to assist with certificate requests. Exercise 3.6 walks you through the steps to create the new Exchange certificate request.

EXERCISE 3.6

Request a New Certificate with the New Exchange Certificate Wizard

To create a new certificate request, follow these steps:

1. Click Start ➤ All Programs ➤ Microsoft Exchange Server 2010 and then select Exchange Management Console.

2. Expand the Microsoft Exchange container, expand the Microsoft Exchange On-Premises container, expand the Server Configuration container, and then click the Client Access node.

3. Select the server you want to request the certificate. In the Actions pane, click the New Exchange Certificate link.

4. In the New Exchange Certificate wizard, type a friendly name for the certificate, such as mail.mailtask.com, and click Next. The next page asks if you want a wildcard certificate; we'll skip it for this exercise. Click Next.

5. On the Exchange Configuration page, click on the arrows next to Client Access server (Outlook Web App). Then select the Outlook Web App is on the Intranet check box and enter the name of your Client Access server, such as ex01.mailtask.com.

6. Next, select the Outlook Web App is on the Internet check box and enter in the name of the external domain such as mail.mailtask.com.

7. Click on the arrows next to Client Access server (Web Services, Outlook Anywhere, and Autodiscover). Select the Exchange Web Services is Enabled, Outlook Anywhere is Enabled, and Autodiscover used on the Internet check boxes.

8. Type an external domain such as mail.mailtask.com in the External Host Name For Your Organization field. Selecting the Autodiscover used on the Internet check box should automatically add your accepted domains and auto-fill a long URL such as autodiscover.mailtask.com in the Autodiscover URL to use field. Click Next.

9. Review the domains that will be added to the certificate. You can highlight and specify the common name to be used for the certificate here. Click Next.

10. On the Organization and Location page, type the information for your organization. Specify a filename and directory on the server where the certificate request file will be created. For the Certificate Request File Path section, click the Browse button to type in the name and location of the request file. Click Next.

EXERCISE 3.6 *(continued)*

11. On the Certificate Configuration page, click New to create the certificate request file.

12. The wizard will create the request file and a completion page summarizes the tasks completed and the steps that are necessary to complete the certificate request and assign Exchange services to it.

13. Click Finish to close the wizard.

You can now submit the certificate request file to your internal trust certificate authority (CA) or a third-party CA such as Entrust or GoDaddy. Once you receive the issued certificate file, copy it back to the Exchange server where you created the request file and click the Complete Pending Request task in the Exchange Management Console, shown in Figure 3.27.

FIGURE 3.27 Completing the certificate request with the Exchange Management Console

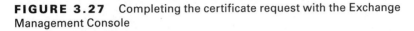

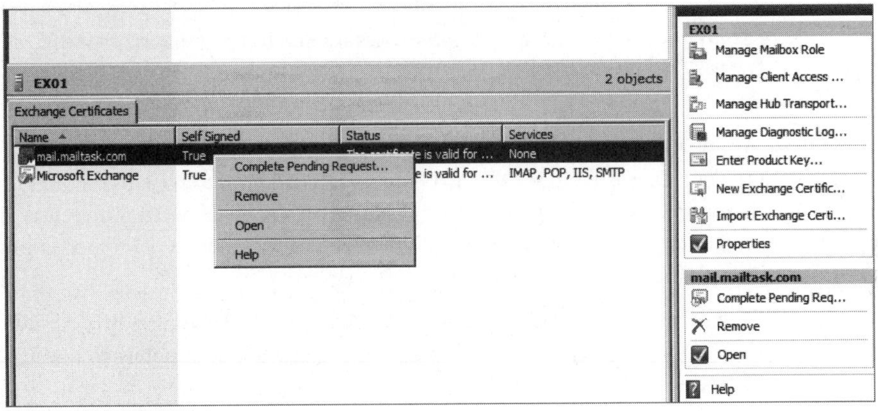

Configuring Client Access

There are several methods for clients to access their email on the Exchange Server. In the following sections, we will examine configuring email access using OWA, RPC, POP3, IMAP4, and ActiveSync.

Configuring and Managing Outlook Web App

Outlook Web App is updated and renamed but maintains its acronym of OWA. OWA is the web interface used to read and send email, check your calendar, and do just about anything you would do in Outlook, but from the convenience of a web browser. New OWA features include a new conversation view, side-by-side calendar view, and chat support via Microsoft Office Communications Server 2007 R2. Another end-user improvement is that OWA supports additional browsers and operating systems. The following operating systems are supported to use the full features of OWA and the Exchange Control Panel:

- On a computer running Windows XP, Windows Server 2003, Windows Vista, Windows Server 2008, Windows 7, and Windows Server 2008 the following are supported:
  - Internet Explorer 7 and later versions
  - Firefox 3.0.1 and later versions
  - Safari 3.1 and later versions
  - Chrome 3.0.195.27 and later versions

- On a computer running Mac OS X the following are supported:
  - Safari 3.1 and later versions
  - Firefox 3.0.1 and later versions
- On a computer running Linux, the following is supported:
  - Firefox 3.0.1 and later versions

 For an updated list of supported browsers see http://go.microsoft.com/fwlink/?LinkID=129362

After installation, OWA is enabled by default on all Client Access servers. Running the Configure External Client Access Domain Wizard (which you used in Exercise 3.5) configures the external URL to access OWA. SSL is required by default on the OWA virtual directory in Internet Information Services (IIS). Several other OWA-related options are available to configure on the OWA (Default Web Site) virtual directory:

General On the General tab of the OWA (Default Web Site) Properties dialog box, shown in Figure 3.28, the date OWA was last modified is shown along with parameters to configure the internal URL and external URL for OWA.

FIGURE 3.28 The General tab of the OWA (Default Web Site) Properties dialog box

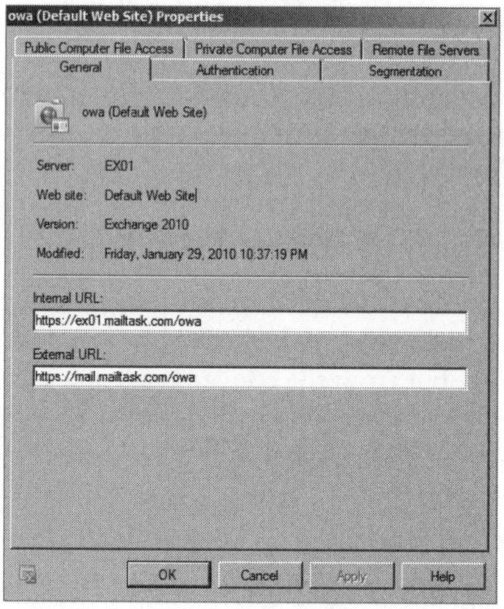

Authentication On the Authentication tab, shown in Figure 3.29, you can change the authentication method used by the OWA website if you desire. By default, OWA in Exchange Server 2010 is configured for forms-based authentication using a self-issued SSL certificate. Self-issued certificates don't offer a seamless experience to users because client computers don't trust them by default and the certificates may not meet your company's policies. Replacing this certificate with one issued by a trusted third-party certificate authority such as Thawte or VeriSign should be a top priority when it comes to configuring OWA. Certificates from these and other similar certificate authority providers are trusted by most computers and browsers and provide security options not available to self-issued certificates such as Extended Validation SSL certificates.

FIGURE 3.29   The Authentication tab of the OWA (Default Web Site) Properties dialog box

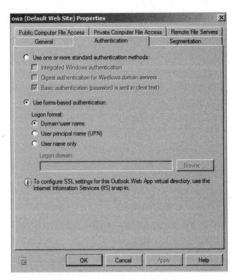

By default, forms-based authentication is configured to use the domain\username format for OWA login. You can change this if desired to either UPN based (user@company.corp) or username based. If you select this method, you must select a default logon domain; only one can be selected. If a default domain is specified, users from other domains can still log on with their domain\username credentials. Users may be confused if they try to log on because the OWA UI will display only a User name field in the logon box instead of a Domain\User field, as shown in Figure 3.30.

On a default installation of a Client Access server, accessing Outlook Web App requires users to enter in the URL of https://*owadomainname*/owa. Users accessing https://*owadomainname* will see the default IIS web page. You should configure redirection to the OWA virtual directory for easy access for your users. Several methods can be deployed to accomplish this, including redirection in the default website to the OWA virtual directory, establishing a new website with the host header and redirecting to the virtual directory, or configuring the default document of the default website with a meta refresh tag to redirect to the OWA virtual directory. You must be careful of the method you deploy when other websites exist on the server. Some of these methods are discussed at technet.microsoft.com/en-us/library/aa998359.aspx.

Segmentation   On the Segmentation tab, shown in Figure 3.31, you can control which features will be available within OWA. If you choose to disable a feature here, it will not be available to any users that log on to the Client Access server. If you want to disable the feature for a select group of users, you'll need to configure an OWA mailbox policy, which is discussed later in this section.

FIGURE 3.30   The Outlook Web Access logon page after the default logon domain is specified

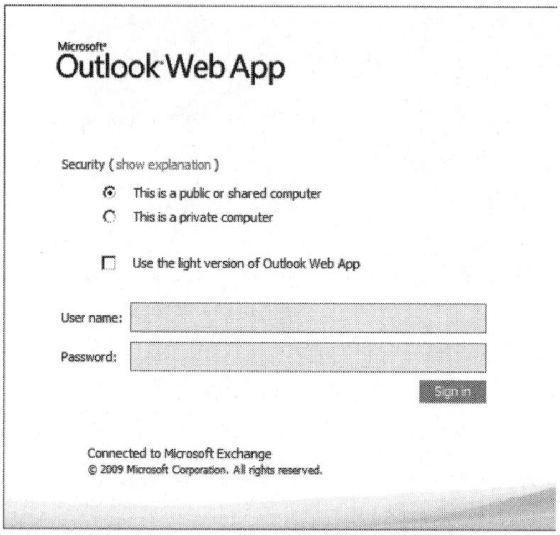

FIGURE 3.31   The Segmentation tab of the OWA (Default Web Site) Properties dialog box

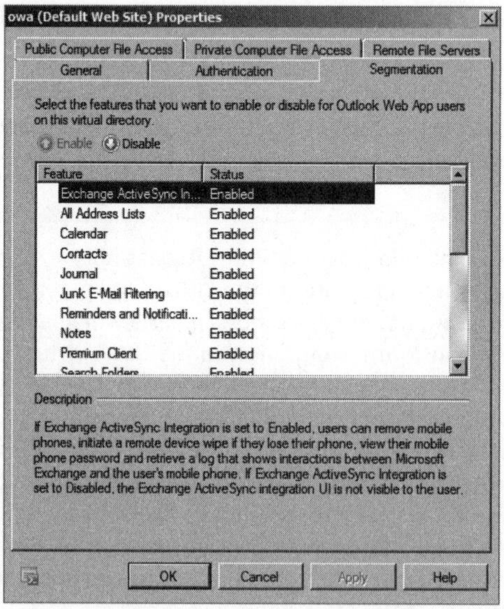

The following OWA options can be disabled or enabled from the Segmentation tab:

Exchange ActiveSync Integration   If disabled, this option hides the Mobile Phones option in OWA.

All Address Lists   When this option is disabled, only the global address list (GAL) is available.

Calendar   If disabled, it hides the user's Calendar folder in OWA. The Calendar folder is still available in Outlook sessions.

Contacts   If disabled, it hides the user's Contacts folder in OWA. The Contacts folder is still available in Outlook sessions.

Journal   If disabled, it hides the user's Journal folder in OWA. The Journal folder is still available in Outlook sessions.

Junk E-Mail Filtering   When this is disabled, users are not able to control or change junk mail settings from OWA. These settings are still available to be changed from Outlook, and any settings in place will work but cannot be changed.

Reminders And Notifications   When this is disabled, users will not get reminders and notifications. Reminders and notifications are not available in OWA Light, which is a simpler version of OWA for browser compatibility and has enhanced accessibility features for blind or low-vision users.

Notes   If disabled, it hides the user's Notes folder in OWA. The Notes folder is still available in Outlook sessions. Notes are read-only in OWA.

Premium Client   When disabled, it allows only OWA Light to be used.

Search Folders   When this is disabled, search folders are not available to users in OWA.

E-Mail Signature   When this is disabled, users cannot manage message signatures in OWA.

Spelling Checker   When this is disabled, spell checking is not available to OWA users. Spell checking is not available in OWA Light and the spell check button is not visible in browsers such as Firefox because they have built-in spell check functionality.

Tasks   If disabled, it hides the user's Tasks folder in OWA. The Tasks folder is still available in Outlook sessions.

Theme Selection   When this is disabled, theme selection is not available. With the release version of Exchange Server 2010, there is only one default theme. Service Pack 1 will bring back themes.

Unified Messaging Integration   If this is disabled, users will not be able to view voice-mail or configure their voicemail options in OWA. This is important because Outlook 2010 relies on OWA to allow users to configure their voice messaging options.

Change Password   When this is disabled, the Change Password option is hidden in OWA.

Rules   If this is disabled, users will not be able to browse or configure their inbox rules.

Public Folders   When this is disabled, public folders are not available to users in OWA. Public folders are not available in OWA Light.

S/MIME   If disabled, it hides the option to download the S/MIME control to read and create signed and encrypted emails. The S/MIME feature is only available with Internet Explorer.

Recover Deleted Items   When this is disabled, OWA users cannot access their Deleted Items folder. The folder is still available in Outlook sessions.

Instant Messaging   If this is disabled, users will not have the instant messaging chat and presence features when OWA is configured with Office Communications Server 2007 R2.

Text Messaging   If this is disabled, users cannot configure text messaging features with mobile phones. This feature is discussed in more detail at the end of the chapter.

Instant messaging and presence information into Outlook Web App requires Office Communications Server (OCS) 2007 R2. Enabling OCS integration requires modification of the web.config file on the Client Access server, installing the OCS 2007 R2 Web Service Provider, and configuring your OCS 2007 servers. More information on how to enable OCS integration can be found at technet.microsoft.com/en-us/library/ee633458.aspx. Exchange Server 2010 Service Pack 1 enables configuration of OCS through EMS.

Public Computer File Access   On the Public Computer File Access tab, shown in Figure 3.32, you have options to control how different file types are handled when accessed via OWA. The settings you make on this tab are applied to OWA sessions in which the user selected This Is A Public Or Shared Computer on the OWA login page.

FIGURE 3.32   The Public Computer File Access tab of the OWA (Default Web Site) Properties dialog box

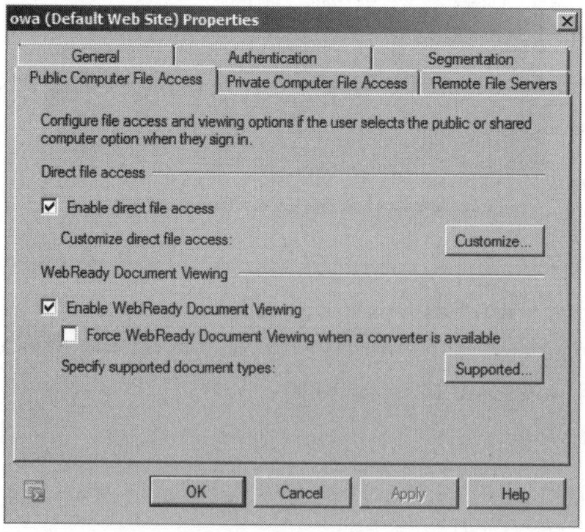

![owa (Default Web Site) Properties dialog box showing the Public Computer File Access tab with Direct file access and WebReady Document Viewing options](image)

In the Direct file access area, you can opt to enable or disable direct file access. These options determine which file types can be opened directly within OWA, which file types can never be opened within OWA, and which file types must be saved first and then opened from the local computer's hard drive. By default, direct file access is enabled, and you'll almost certainly want to leave that setting in place because disabling it will block access to all attachments for OWA users. You may, however, want to customize the allow, block, and force save configurations by clicking the Customize button to open the Direct File Access Settings dialog box, shown in Figure 3.33.

FIGURE 3.33　The Direct File Access Settings dialog box

Direct File Access Settings

Specify how Outlook Web App will handle attachments:

Always Allow

Specify which types of files users can access without saving. The Allow list overrides the Block list and the Force Save list.　[Allow...]

Always Block

Specify which types of files users cannot access. The Block list overrides the Force Save list.　[Block...]

Force Save

Specify which types of files the user must save to disk before opening.　[Force Save...]

Unknown Files

Select how to handle unknown files that are not in the Allow list, Block list, or Force Save list:　[Force Save ▼]

[OK]　[Cancel]

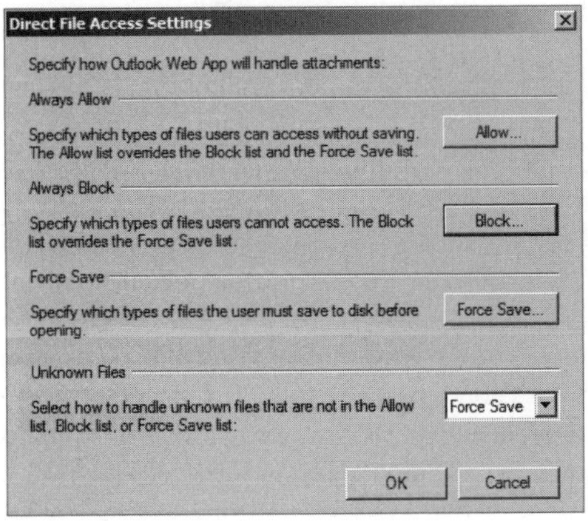

From the Direct File Access Settings dialog box, you can see which file types are always allowed to be opened within OWA, which file types are never allowed to be opened within OWA, which file types must be saved first before they can be opened, and what to do when a file type that hasn't been otherwise accounted for is encountered. Exchange provides many default entries in each section—take time to look through them to make sure they make sense for your organization. When you're finished, click OK to save your changes and close the Direct File Access Settings dialog box.

Certain file types, such as Microsoft Word documents and Adobe Acrobat PDF documents, can be converted to HTML easily. These file types are known as WebReady file types. You can configure OWA to display these file types as HTML documents, thus allowing access to them even on computers that may not have the original applications used to create them installed. This can be a great benefit for computers in public places such as web cafes and public libraries. You can opt to require the use of WebReady display if you like, but it is not enabled by default. Clicking the Supported button on the Public Computer File Access tab of the Properties dialog box opens the WebReady Document Viewing Settings dialog box, shown in Figure 3.34. From here you can change the default settings that Exchange provides.

FIGURE 3.34   The WebReady Document Viewing Settings dialog box

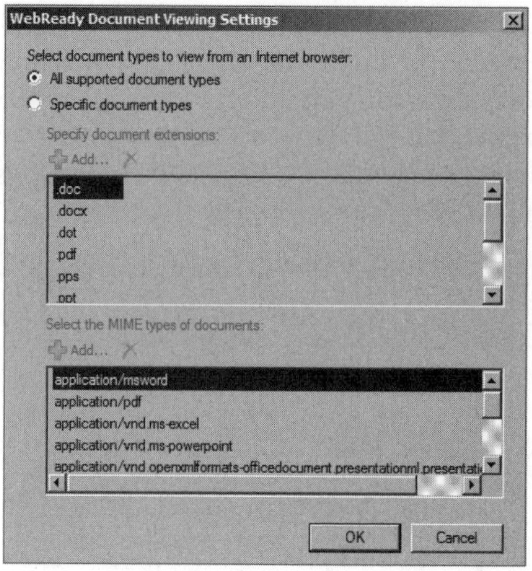

Private Computer File Access   On the Private Computer File Access tab of the OWA (Default Web Site) Properties dialog box, you have the same settings as those on the Public Computer File Access tab. The only difference is that these settings will be applied to OWA sessions that originate from "private" computers as selected by the user on the OWA login page.

> **NOTE**   On the OWA (Default Web Site) Properties dialog box, there is one additional tab named Remote File Servers. As discussed earlier, the features to access remote file shares and internal SharePoint sites were removed in Exchange Server 2010. But the configuration tab in the Exchange Management Console remains in the initial release of Exchange Server 2010. You can configure your internal servers for remote access with the EMC, but the feature will not show up in OWA.

Disabling OWA features was discussed earlier with segmentation for Client Access servers, which affects all users accessing the Client Access server. A new feature in Exchange 2010, OWA mailbox policies, allows Exchange administrators to disable select OWA features for different groups of users. For example, you can create an OWA mailbox policy for users that will deny access to public folders from OWA. Similar to ActiveSync Mailbox policies, you can create multiple OWA mailbox policies to apply different policies to different users. Public and Private Computer File Access settings can also be configured for OWA mailbox policies.

In Exercise 3.7, you'll create a new OWA mailbox policy that removes the ability to change passwords and apply it to a user.

EXERCISE 3.7

Create a New Outlook Web App Mailbox Policy

To create a new OWA mailbox policy, follow these steps:

1. Click Start ➤ All Programs ➤ Microsoft Exchange Server 2010 and then select Exchange Management Console.

2. Expand the Microsoft Exchange container, expand the Microsoft Exchange On-Premises container, expand the Organization Configuration container, and then click the Client Access node.

3. Under the Actions pane on the right side, click the New Outlook Web App Mailbox Policy link. The wizard opens.

4. Enter a policy name, such as OWA Mailbox Policy Restrict Change Password. Next, highlight the Change Password feature and click Disable. Then click New to create the policy.

5. Click Finish to close the New Outlook Web App Mailbox Policy Wizard.

6. In the EMC, expand the Recipient Configuration folder and click the Mailbox node. Highlight a user. Then, under the Actions pane, click Properties.

7. Select the Mailbox Features tab in the user's Properties dialog box.

8. Highlight the Outlook Web App feature and click the Properties button. The Outlook Web App Properties dialog box appears. Select the check box, click Browse to select the OWA mailbox policy you just created, and click OK.

9. Click OK to close the Outlook Web App Properties dialog box and click OK to close the properties dialog box for the user mailbox.

10. Finally, log into OWA with the user's credentials and notice that the ability to change the password is not available.

In the released to manufacturing (RTM) or initial release of Exchange 2010, you may encounter a bug where the Password button is still visible in OWA. When you click the Password button, the following error message is displayed: "This features isn't supported in the light version of Outlook Web App." The ability to change the password is removed but the error message can cause some confusion.

Configuring and Managing the Exchange Control Panel

Another change to Outlook Web App, some may say it's a completely new addition, is the Exchange Control Panel, or ECP. Similar to the options in Exchange 2007 OWA, and accessible via the Options button in Exchange 2010, ECP is a website for end users to manage their personal mailbox settings such as inbox rules, email signatures, and safe senders and recipients. For help desk personal and Exchange admins, ECP can be used to view and manage other users' ECP options as well as perform organization tasks such as creating and modifying new user mailboxes and groups, performing message tracking, and performing discovery searches for legal requests.

 This book, as well as TechNet articles for Exchange 2010, may make references to the Exchange Control Panel as ECP options and/or OWA options. However, users and many administrators may still refer to it as OWA options, since user interface doesn't indicate that it is officially called the Exchange Control Panel.

Users access the Exchange Control Panel by logging into OWA and clicking the Options button on the upper-right side. You can also log into ECP directly by going to https:// domainname/ecp. Features exposed in ECP are based on what options you wish to enable for the Client Access server through segmentation and mailbox policies, as we discussed earlier. Role Based Access Control (RBAC) permissions also determine what features are shown to the user, such as being able to view another user's ECP options or being able to perform message tracking for mailboxes.

The EMC allows you to configure the internal and external URL as well as authentication methods of the ECP (the Authentication tab is shown in Figure 3.35).

Exercise 3.8 shows how an administrator or help desk personnel with proper RBAC permissions can modify the ECP settings of another user.

FIGURE 3.35   The Authentication tab of the ECP (Default Web Site) Properties dialog box

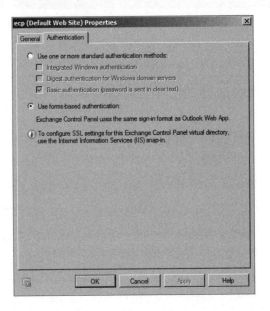

Modify the Automatic Replies (Out of Office) of Another User with Exchange Control Panel

To modify ECP options of another user, follow these steps:

1. Open a browser and log into OWA as an administrator with Organization Administrator permissions.

2. Click the Options button near the upper-right section to access the Exchange Control Panel. From the Select What To Manage drop-down list, choose Another User.

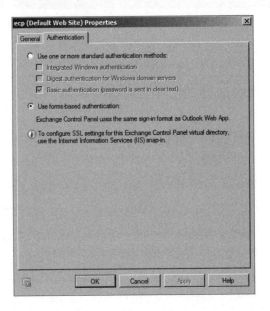

3. A new browser window, Select Mailbox, appears. Highlight a user and click OK.

4. The Select Mailbox window closes and a new window appears that displays the user's ECP options.

5. Click the Organize E-Mail button on the left side. Then click the Send automatic replies button in the middle.

6. Select the button to send automatic replies and type the following sentence for the reply: **I am out of the office and will return next Monday.**

7. Click Save in the lower-right corner of the window to save the settings and close the windows to complete the exercise.

Configuring and Managing Outlook Anywhere

Formerly known as RPC over HTTPS, Outlook Anywhere allows users using Outlook 2003 and above to connect to Exchange 2010 with MAPI over HTTPS to a Client Access server instead of direct MAPI to the Mailbox server. It is designed for users to work outside their network with their Outlook clients without needing to establish a VPN or another remote connection method. In a pure Exchange Server 2010 organization, Outlook Anywhere is fairly simple to configure and maintain. In organizations that still have mailboxes on Exchange Server 2003 or 2007 servers, the configuration and management are more complex but still doable. Configuration of Outlook Anywhere was discussed earlier in this section.

Because Outlook Anywhere runs over HTTPS, it runs securely with SSL. You have the option to configure and enable an SSL certificate on the Client Access server, or you can configure SSL offloading to another server or security appliance in your network. You can also configure it by using the Set-OutlookAnywhere cmdlet with the **-SSLOffloading** parameter.

```
Set-OutlookAnywhere -Identity 'EX01\RPC (Default Web Site)' -SSLOffloading:$True
```

You also have the option to configure Basic authentication or NTLM authentication. Basic authentication will prompt users for their username and password when they open Outlook, while choosing NLTM authentication uses Integrated Windows authentication and will not prompt the user for credentials if they are logged into the Windows computer with their domain credentials. You should use NTLM authentication because it's more seamless for end users and the authentication method will revert to Basic authentication when users aren't using Integrated Windows authentication and must present credentials. Basic authentication must be used when users are traversing older firewalls that don't support NTLM authentication.

Understanding RPC Client Access

A major change in Exchange Server 2010 involves how MAPI clients such as Outlook connect to Exchange. Previously, Outlook used the MAPI protocol over RPC to connect directly to the Mailbox server where the user's mailbox database resided. This method is named RPC Client Access in Exchange 2010.

The change in RPC connectivity was made to consolidate client access to the CAS. It enables Outlook to handle database failovers better and reduces processing and connections to the Mailbox servers. If a mailbox database failover occurs, Outlook clients will reconnect much quicker than Exchange 2007 databases. Also, when Client Access servers are configured in an array, Outlook clients will immediately connect to a new CAS in the array. Configuring Client Access Arrays is discussed in Chapter 7, "Configuring High Availability."

In previous versions of Exchange, Outlook would be referred to and connect to Active Directory global catalog servers for directory information. With Exchange Server 2010, Client Access servers will respond with directory information to Outlook clients. Unfortunately, Outlook clients requesting public folder data will connect to Mailbox servers that host public folders. Figure 3.36 shows an Outlook client connecting to the Client Access server EX01 via RPC. Notice that mail and directory connections use the Client Access server.

A default installation of the Client Access server role will configure the Microsoft Exchange RPC Client Access service. It is a Windows Server service and can be stopped and set to manual startup for troubleshooting purposes. Additional configuration is done with the Set-RpcClientAccess cmdlet.

Outlook 2003, by default, does not enable RPC encryption. This can be an issue as the RPC Client Access service in Exchange 2010 requires encryption by default. If you have a large number of Outlook 2003 users, a manual change is required in the Outlook profile because there doesn't seem to be an easy way to push the change to Outlook. Fortunately, you can disable the encryption requirement on the RPC Client Access settings. The following example disables encryption:

```
Set-RpcClientAccess -Server EX01 -EncyptionRequired $False
```

FIGURE 3.36   Outlook client connectivity

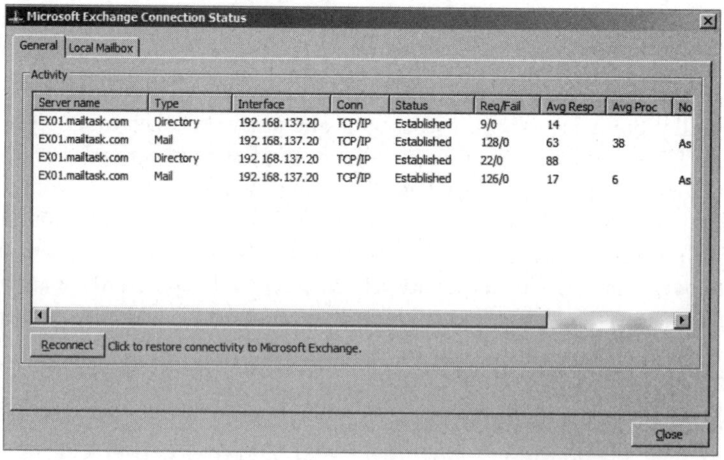

In some scenarios, you may need to block certain versions of Outlook from connecting to Exchange. For example, you may want to keep a particular beta, unpatched version or untested version of Outlook from connecting because you suspect that that version may cause end user problems.. The following example blocks the original version of Outlook 2002 from connecting to the Client Access server through RPC:

```
Set-RpcClientAccess -Server EX01 -BlockedClientVersions "10.0.2627.2625"
```

You must restart the RPC Client Access service for these changes to take effect.

Introducing Exchange Web Services

Exchange Server 2007 introduced Exchange Web Services (EWS), which enabled access to mailboxes and Exchange content programmatically over HTTP. With Exchange Server 2010, Microsoft has further enhanced the API to replace legacy APIs. Older APIs such as MAPI32, CDO, CDOEX, and Exchange WebDAV have been de-emphasized or phased out completely in favor of EWS.

EWS is a virtual directory and configurable in IIS or with the
`Set-WebServicesVirtualDirectory` cmdlet.

> **NOTE** The Microsoft Exchange Web Services Managed API 1.0 is a new resource
> that you can use to access Exchange resources. You can quickly create
> applications to create messages and calendar appointments, search folders,
> and cancel meetings. You can build a custom application to manage room
> resources for your office or create a web application to manage custom
> mailbox properties. Learn more about the EWS Managed API 1.0 at `msdn.`
> `microsoft.com/en-us/library/dd637749(EXCHG.80).aspx`.

With WebDAV deprecated, applications such as Entourage and other email applications for Mac OS X prior to 10.6 cannot fully connect to Exchange. They can connect
to Exchange to send and receive email, but other features, such as calendaring, are broken because they rely on the WebDAV protocol. A new version of Entourage released in
late 2009, aptly named Entourage 2008 Web Services Edition, and the mail application
on OS X 10.6 use the EWS protocol exclusively. They also bring features not previously
available, such as synching tasks and notes, better calendar support, and enhanced
Autodiscover capabilities.

Custom applications and third-party applications should be moving to EWS. Office 2011
for the Mac, currently in beta will replace Entourage, in favor of a Mac version of Outlook.

Supporting POP3 and IMAP4 Clients

POP3 and IMAP4 are two of the most basic email protocols in use. With SMTP, they are
the most straightforward of the email delivery mechanisms, and virtually every email server
available supports them. However, they do have their drawbacks, particularly when used
with Exchange.

For example, if you collect your email with POP3 from your Exchange mailbox, all
email in the mailbox will be marked as read whether or not the message has actually been
read on the client.

The other major issue with POP3 is that it is designed to remove the email from the server
and store it locally. It is easy to make an error in configuration and remove all the email
from the server. Although there are options to leave email on the server, it's easy for users to
overlook them, which can create additional support calls or requests for mailbox restores.

Things are a little better with IMAP4 because the email is actually stored on the server.
However, features are limited compared to the full Outlook client or OWA connecting to
Exchange.

Given that, POP3/IMAP4 access should be the last access protocol of choice. However,
in some settings, such as academic environments or multi-platform organizations, POP3
and IMAP4 clients are popular and must still be supported.

POP3 and IMAP4 are disabled by default in Exchange 2007. You can configure SMTP
for use by POP3/IMAP4 clients using the Exchange Management Console. However, you

may want to look at deploying TLS/SMTP over port 587 because the standard port 25 is often blocked for accessing remote SMTP servers by ISPs and hotels, meaning the POP3/IMAP4 clients will be unable to send email through your server. ISPs and hotels often set up their own SMTP servers, which allow relay but pose a major security concern because mail is sent unencrypted through them.

If you need to track email messages for compliance reasons, force your users who want to use POP3 or IMAP4 to use TLS/SMTP over port 587. Or disable client SMTP receive connectors completely and force your users to use other remote connectivity clients, such as OWA or Outlook Anywhere.

Configuring Exchange Server 2010 to Support POP3 and IMAP4 Clients

Configuring Exchange Server 2010 to support POP3 or IMAP4 clients requires four steps. These include enabling the services and configuring the Client Access servers to support these protocols.

1. Enabling the services

Before clients can connect to the POP3 or IMAP4 services, the services must be enabled and started because they are set to start manually. You can enable POP3 and IMAP4 in two ways. You can change the service in the Services console, shown in Figure 3.37, to Automatic and then start the service.

FIGURE 3.37   Configuring the IMAP4 service

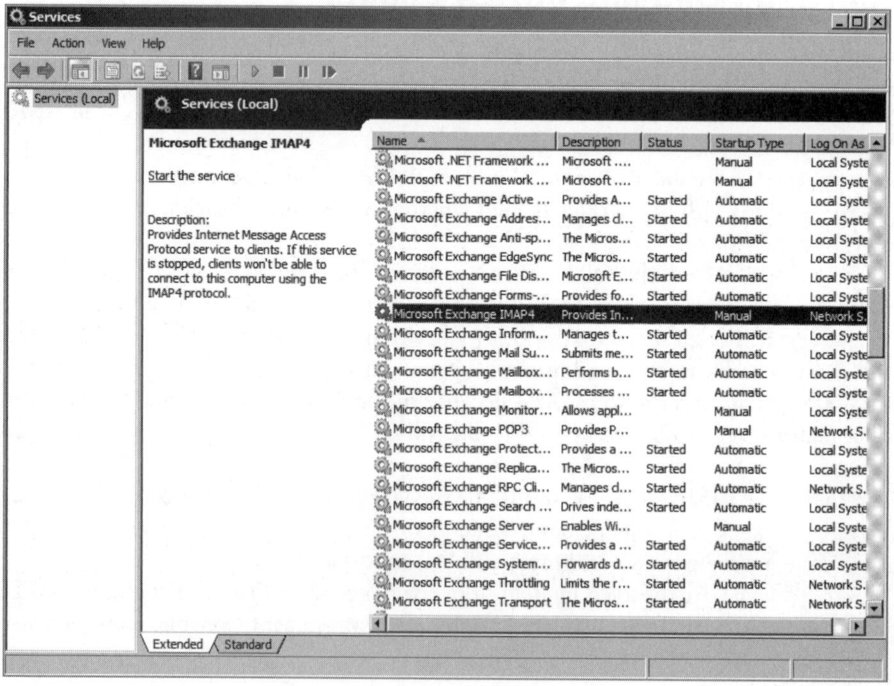

You can also enable the services through the Exchange Management Shell. To enable POP3, use the following command:

```
Set-Service msExchangePOP3 -Startuptype automatic
```

After it is enabled, you need to start the service by entering the following command:

```
Start-Service -Service msExchangePOP3
```

For IMAP4, the procedure is almost identical:

```
Set-Service msExchangeIMAP4 -Startuptype automatic
```

To start the service, you can use the following command:

```
Start-Service msExchangeIMAP4
```

2. Configuring POP3 and IMAP4 servers

   After you have enabled the services, you can configure them using either the Exchange Management Console or the Exchange Management Shell. The default settings may be suitable for you. You can check the current settings using the following cmdlets:

   - For POP3, use `Get-PopSettings`.
   - For IMAP4, use `Get-ImapSettings`.

   The only additional configuration you may want to review is enabling TLS/SSL support, but we won't discuss it here.

 You can find more information about securing POP3 and IMAP4 at the following TechNet location: technet.microsoft.com/en-us/library/aa997149.aspx.

3. Configuring POP3 and IMAP4 mailboxes

   By default, all user accounts are enabled for POP3 and IMAP4 access. Therefore, you may want to review the accounts and disable that functionality for users who will not be accessing Exchange using POP3 or IMAP4. You do this using the `Set-CASMailbox` command.

   For example, to disable POP3 for user BrianTirch@mailtask.com, use the following command:

```
Set-CASMailbox -Identity BrianTirch@mailtask.com -POPEnabled:$false
```

   You can view the status of the mailboxes simply by entering the command `Get-CASMailbox`, which will display all mailboxes in the Exchange organization and whether or not they are enabled.

You can also configure the POP3 and IMAP4 features in the Exchange Management Console in the Mailbox Features tab of the user's Properties dialog box, as shown in Figure 3.38.

4. Configuring a receive connector for use with POP3 and IMAP4

POP3/IMAP4 clients need to have an SMTP connector through which to send their outbound email. That means a receive connector must be configured on a Transport server to accept their messages and allow them to be relayed through the server to the clients. A Hub Transport server is typically used as it is a member of your domain and users can authenticate to the receive connector with their domain credentials.

FIGURE 3.38 Disabling the POP3 feature for a user

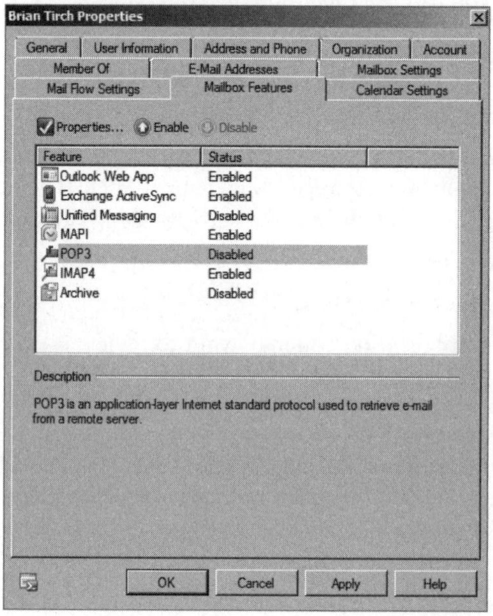

On a default installation of the Hub Transport server, there is already a connector configured that is suitable for use; it is named Client *servername*. You can see this using the Exchange Management Console or by using the Exchange Management Shell command Get-ReceiveConnector.

This default connector should require little configuration. Note that this connector is configured to use port 587, which is the client SMTP submission port, and is also set to use TLS. It uses the certificate that is installed on the Exchange server during installation. If you intend to have clients relay email through the server on this port, then you need to either import the certificate to their machine so that it is trusted or replace the certificate with one from a trusted CA.

If you want to use the standard TCP port 25 to relay email, you can create a new receive connector with port 25, or you can add port 25 to the default client connector, as shown in Figure 3.39. In all cases, Basic authentication needs to be enabled on the connector because it is the only type of authentication that SMTP clients support. You can also use Basic authentication requiring TLS.

Configuring a POP3 or IMAP4 Client

You will no doubt be familiar with the configuration of POP3/IMAP4 clients and SMTP. For Exchange, it is almost the same as any Internet email account you may have configured. For the server address of the POP3, IMAP4, and SMTP servers, you should use a hostname.

FIGURE 3.39   Adding port 25 to the default Client connector

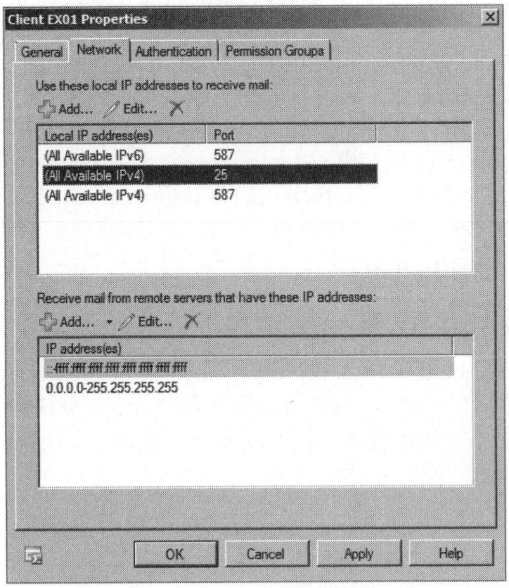

Although you can use an IP address, if you ever need to change the IP address of the server, it is far easier to change a single DNS entry than to try to get many users to update their email client configurations.

What you use for your hostnames is up to you—as long as they resolve correctly on the Internet. You may already have a hostname configured that points to your Exchange server used for MX records. If so, you could use the same hostname in the account settings. Alternatively, if you think you might change the configuration in the future so that the servers are different, you may want to use pop3.domain.com, imap4.domain.com, and smtp.domain.com, with all of them pointing at the same IP address. If you need to change them later, simply adjust the DNS records.

If you are using TLS/SSL for account access, ensure that you change the port setting in the email client to use the alternative port. This is often found in the advanced settings.

Finally, you need to enter credentials. For Exchange, these credentials need to be entered either as *username@domain.local* or *domain\username*.

The choice of authentication format is up to you and what you think will be easiest to support. It is best to decide on one format and then stick to it so it is easier to write documentation and maintain consistency.

Configuring ActiveSync

Microsoft Exchange ActiveSync (EAS) allows synchronization from a mobile device directly to the Exchange server over a network or Internet connection. Initially introduced as an on-demand sync, EAS also supports a Direct Push feature using HTTP or HTTPS, preferably HTTPS. Direct Push enables email to be synchronized with the device as new messages arrive; the mobile device sends a long-lived HTTPS request to the Exchange server, and when a message arrives in the user's inbox, the server notifies the device that a new message must be synchronized. The long HTTPS request, or ping, between the device and Exchange server is defaulted at 15 minutes but is self-configurable if the mobile carrier or network firewalls don't support long HTTPS requests.

Direct Push is enabled on the Exchange server by default but requires that the mobile device have Windows Mobile 5.0 with the Messaging and Security Feature Pack (MSFP) or a more recent version of Windows Mobile, including Windows Phone 7. Non-Windows Mobile devices, such as the iPhone may also support Direct Push, if the software vendor has licensed the EAS technology from Microsoft.

Configuring Exchange to Support ActiveSync

Exchange ActiveSync is enabled by default. This can be confirmed by checking for the presence of a number of elements in the Internet Information Services (IIS) Manager. In the IIS Manager under Default Web Site, check to see whether the virtual directory Microsoft-Server-ActiveSync exists.

As an administrator, you will want to test Windows Mobile for yourself; however, getting a hold of a device with the relevant software may be difficult. Microsoft has released an emulator for Windows Mobile; it was originally designed for developer use but is now available as a stand-alone product. You can install this on your workstation and connect to the Exchange server over your network. At the time of this writing, you can download the emulator from the Microsoft downloads site by searching for "Microsoft Device Emulator 3.0 Standalone Release" at www.microsoft.com/downloads/. Currently, ROM images for the emulator are available for Windows Mobile 5.0, 6.0, 6.1, and 6.5.

You can also check the Exchange-related application pools by right-clicking the MSExchangeSyncAppPool application pool. If Start is available, then EAS is not running. Choose Start to enable the application pool. Figure 3.40 shows application pools and virtual directories for IIS.

Additional configurations of ActiveSync can be made through the Exchange Management Console. Under Server Configuration, choose the Exchange ActiveSync tab. Right-click the virtual directory listed, and choose Properties. You'll see three tabs. The first tab, General, allows you to set the internal and external URLs for ActiveSync. The second tab, Authentication, allows you to control authentication, including whether to use client certificates. The third tab, named Remote File Servers, is not applicable because the feature has been deprecated as it is in OWA.

For Exchange Management Shell configuration, you use several cmdlets:

- `New-ActiveSyncVirtualDirectory` allows you to create a new virtual directory for another website on the same server.

- `Remove-ActiveSyncVirtualDirectory` deletes an existing virtual directory.

- `Set-ActiveSyncVirtualDirectory` allows you to change settings for the ActiveSync virtual directory. This includes settings not available to you through the Exchange Management Console. This command enables basic authentication on a server named EX01:

```
Set-ActiveSyncVirtualDirectory
-Identity "EX01\Microsoft-Server-Activesync"
-BasicAuthEnabled:$true
```

FIGURE 3.40 Viewing the Exchange virtual directories and application pools

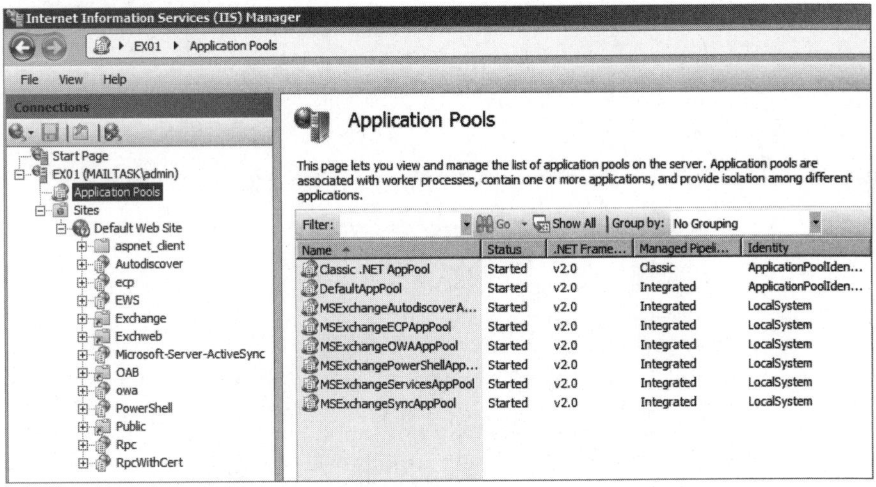

Defining an ActiveSync Mailbox Policy

An ActiveSync Mailbox policy allows you to define specific settings for mobile devices. ActiveSync policies are Exchange organization wide, so you set them in the Client Access node under Organization Configuration in the Exchange Management Console, as shown in Figure 3.41.

Starting with Exchange 2007 SP1 and forward to Exchange 2010, a default ActiveSync policy is created and applied to all users. Multiple ActiveSync policies can be defined with different settings and applied to different groups of users. Some of the settings, such as denying camera usage and unsigned applications, require the Exchange Enterprise Client Access License (ECAL). There are six configuration tabs, and fortunately the Exchange 2010 EMC contains a note on each of the three configuration tabs that require the ECAL.

General You can use the General tab of the ActiveSync policy's Properties dialog box, as shown in Figure 3.42, to modify the name of the policy, allow non-provisionable devices, and configure the refresh interval sent to mobile devices. Allowing non-provisionable devices allows users to configure ActiveSync on mobile devices that may not enforce the policies that you define.

FIGURE 3.41   Viewing ActiveSync policies

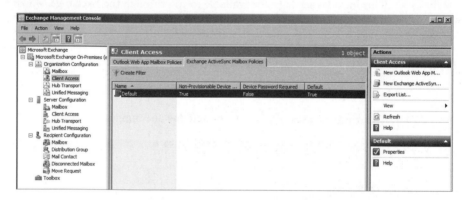

FIGURE 3.42   The General tab of the ActiveSync policy's Properties dialog box

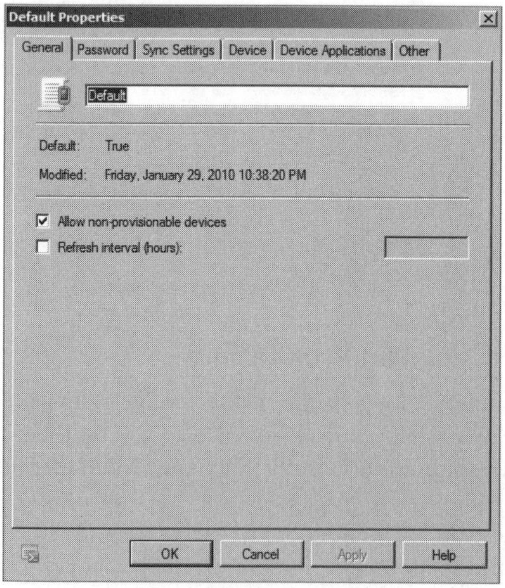

Password The Password tab of the ActiveSync policy Properties dialog box, shown in Figure 3.43, is for configuring the password policy. The settings on this tab are fairly self-explanatory. To take advantage of the remote wipe features of Exchange, you need to require a device password. If you do not, when you attempt to remotely wipe the device, you will be asked to allow enforcement of a password policy. By saying no, you can maintain access to the device. Allow simple password is a policy that allows the user to set a password such as 1234. If you have policies regarding passwords, you may not want to enable that option.

Sync Settings The Sync Settings tab, shown in Figure 3.44, includes options for things such as allowing HTML-formatted email and setting maximum attachment sizes.

FIGURE 3.43 The Password tab of the ActiveSync policy's Properties dialog box

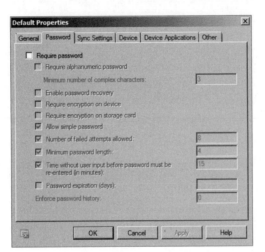

FIGURE 3.44 The Sync Settings tab of the ActiveSync policy's Properties dialog box

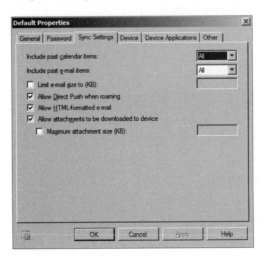

Device, Device Applications, and Other   The last three tabs, Device, Device Applications, and Other, include options such as allowing Bluetooth, allowing unsigned applications, and defining blocked applications. If you want to change any of the default settings, you must have the Exchange ECAL for each of the users for which you will apply the policy. The configuration tabs are shown in Figure 3.45, Figure 3.46, and Figure 3.47.

To create additional ActiveSync policies, select New ActiveSync Policy from the Actions pane in the Exchange Management Console, or run the cmdlet `New-ActiveSyncPolicy` with the required parameters.

FIGURE 3.45   The Device tab of the ActiveSync policy's Properties dialog box

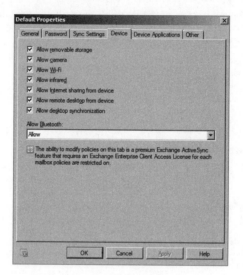

FIGURE 3.46   The Device Applications tab of the ActiveSync policy's Properties dialog box

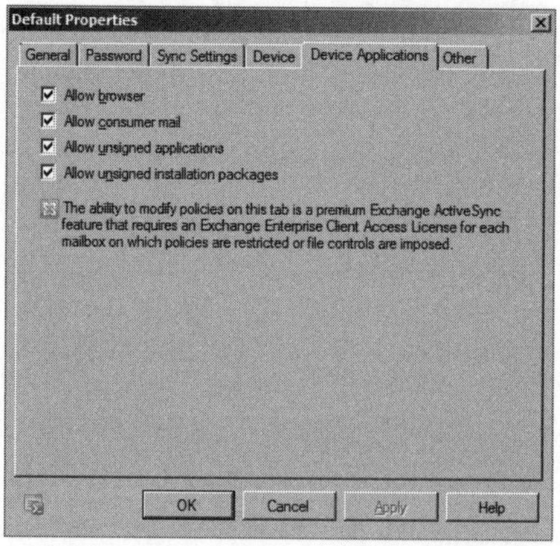

FIGURE 3.47   The Other tab of the ActiveSync policy's Properties dialog box

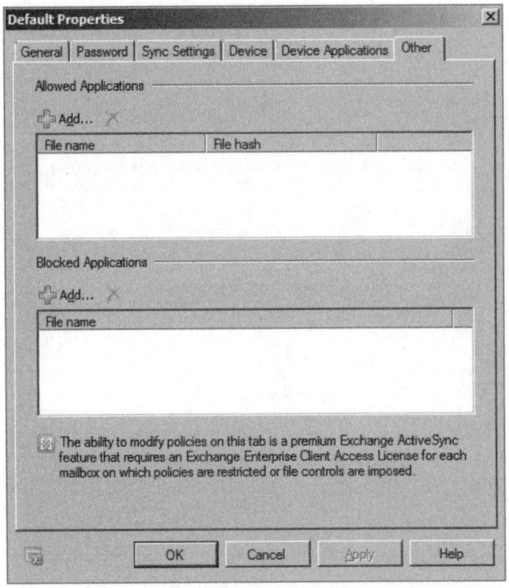

The following command creates a new policy called Sales, with Device Password enabled:

```
New-ActiveSyncMailboxPolicy -Name:"Sales" -DevicePasswordEnabled:$true
```

You can assign a policy to each user as required. To set a policy to a user through the Exchange Management Console, follow the steps in Exercise 3.9.

EXERCISE 3.9

Assigning an ActiveSync Policy to a User

To assign an ActiveSync policy to a user, follow these steps:

1.   Click Start ➢ All Programs ➢ Microsoft Exchange Server 2010 and then select Exchange Management Console.

2.   Expand the Microsoft Exchange container, expand the Microsoft Exchange On-Premises container, expand the Recipient Configuration container, and then click the Mailbox node.

3.   Highlight one or multiple mailboxes. In the Actions pane on the right side, click the Properties link to open the mailbox user's Properties dialog box.

4. Click the Mailbox Features tab, shown here.

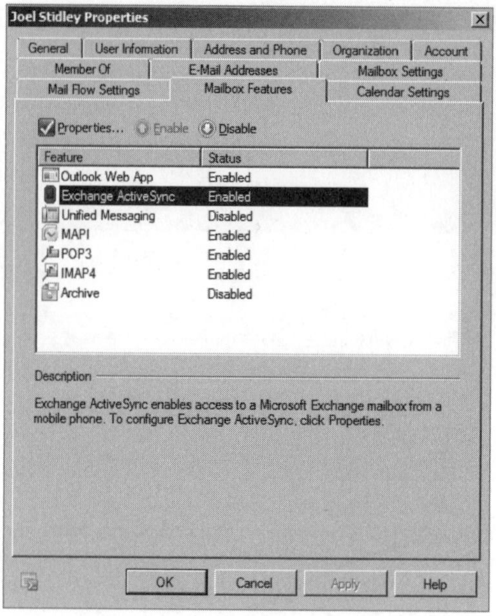

5. Click the Exchange ActiveSync item, and then click the Properties button. The Exchange ActiveSync Properties dialog box opens.

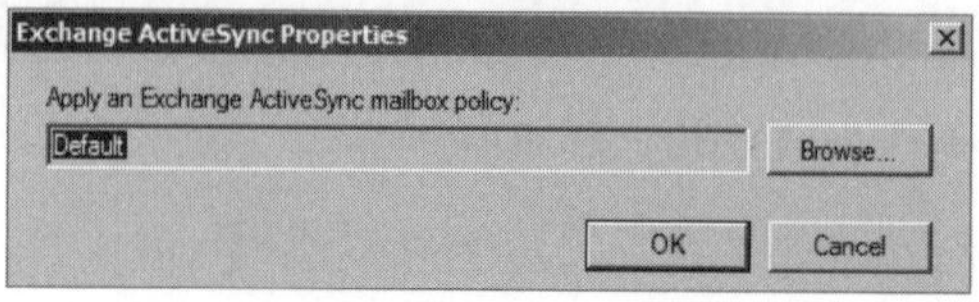

6. Click Browse to locate an ActiveSync Mailbox policy to apply. Select the policy and click OK to close the selection box.

7. Click OK to close the Exchange ActiveSync Properties dialog box.

8. Click OK to close the mailbox user Properties dialog box.

To set the policy through the Exchange Management Shell, use the Set-CASMailbox command. For example, to set a policy named Sales on user Joseph.Nguyen, run the following:

```
Set-CASMailbox Joseph.Nguyen -ActiveSyncMailboxPolicy
(Get-ActiveSyncMailboxPolicy "Sales").Identity
```

If you want to set a policy on all users, which may be a good way to start off, you have to use a combination of commands. The following command sets the Default policy on all users:

```
Get-Mailbox | Set-CASMailbox -ActiveSyncMailboxPolicy
(Get-ActiveSyncMailboxPolicy "Default").Identity
```

> **TIP** Many improvements have been made to the Exchange 2010 console since Exchange 2007. This includes being able to modify mailbox properties of multiple users. In the Mailbox node of the Recipient Configuration folder in the EMC, you can multi-select users with the Ctrl or Shift key and then click the Properties button in the Actions pane. From there, you can modify many mailbox properties, including the ActiveSync mailbox policy, for each of the selected users.

Managing Mobile Phones

As an Exchange administrator, you will probably be told that personnel in the company have lost their mobile phones. Or perhaps a person has been terminated and you're now required to remove email and other Exchange data from their mobile phone. Fortunately, the management of mobile phones is built in to Exchange and can be accomplished in three ways.

First, the end user can manage it through the Exchange Control Panel (ECP). Exchange administrators can turn off this option through segmentation on the Client Access server or OWA mailbox policies. However, if you have lots of remote users, you may want to enable this feature so the users can wipe their devices as soon as they realize they have lost them. Mobile phone management options are accessed via ECP, as shown in Figure 3.48, once the user has logged in.

FIGURE 3.48 Managing a mobile phone via ECP

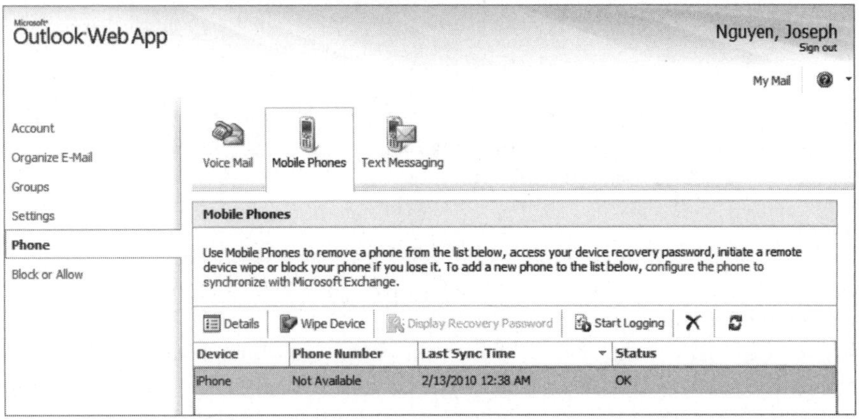

Administrators or help desk personnel can also use the Exchange Control Panel to manage another person's mobile phone. Granular Role Based Access Control (RBAC) permissions can be assigned to manage the mobile phone features of a select group of users.

Second, you can manage the device through the Exchange Management Console. You can manage the device by right-clicking the user in the Mailbox node under Recipients Configuration and choosing Manage Mobile Phone. This runs the Manage Mobile Phone Wizard, shown in Figure 3.49.

FIGURE 3.49 Managing a mobile phone via EMC

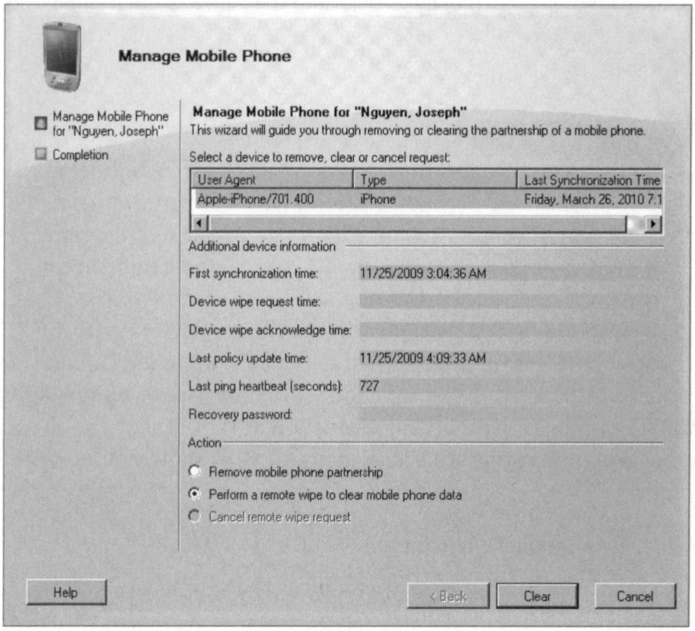

The Manage Mobile Phone task option appears only if there is a mobile device associated with a mailbox.

On the bottom of the Manage Mobile Phone Wizard page, select Perform A remote wipe to clear mobile phone data and then click the Clear button. You can return to this page to confirm that the wipe has taken place.

Finally, you can manage the device through the Exchange Management Shell. A series of commands will allow you to wipe the device. To wipe the device through the Exchange Management Shell, you need to perform the steps outlined in Exercise 3.10.

EXERCISE 3.10

Wiping a Mobile Phone

To wipe data from a supported EAS connected device using the Exchange Management Shell, follow these steps:

1. Get the identity of the device. To get the identity of the device that is used by user Joseph Nguyen, run the following command:

    ```
    Get-ActiveSyncDeviceStatistics -Mailbox "Joseph.Nguyen@mailtask.com"
    | FL Identity
    ```

2. After you have the device ID, you can send the wipe command. To wipe a device with the ID of iPhone§Appl88935ZX5Y, use this command:

    ```
    Clear-ActiveSyncDevice -Identity Joseph.Nguyen@mailtask.com\iPhone§Appl88935ZX5Y
    ```

3. To confirm that the wipe was successful, use the following command:

    ```
    Get-ActiveSyncDeviceStatistics -Mailbox Joseph.Nguyen@mailtask.com
    ```

Using Text Messaging

A new feature introduced in Exchange 2010 is SMS, or text messaging integration. A mobile phone can be used in email, calendar, and voicemail notifications. This phone can be any phone that supports text messaging; it does not have to support ActiveSync or have a partnership with the mailbox user. Configuration of notifications is made in the Exchange Control Panel for the user. Mobile operators in the United States currently include AT&T, Sprint, T-Mobile, and Verizon. After enabling notifications for a mobile phone, the user can set up notification rules to send text messages. The notification rules are essentially inbox rules that will forward messages to the mobile phone.

An additional feature includes the ability to send and receive text messages with Outlook Web App and Outlook 2010 using the mobile phone. After you configure an ActiveSync partnership to include text messaging content, new text messages will be delivered to the mobile phone and then copied to the inbox folder of the user. The user can compose and send a text message with OWA or Outlook 2010. The message is then synchronized to the mobile phone during the next EAS sync and sent out via the mobile phone. Messages that users send may be delayed if EAS sync on the mobile phone is scheduled at specified sync intervals. Configuring EAS sync with Always-up-to-date (AUTD) will send messages more quickly.

This feature requires the user to use Windows Mobile 6.1 phones with an Outlook Mobile update or Windows Mobile 6.5 phones and greater. To update Windows Mobile 6.1 phones with the Outlook Mobile update, configure an ActiveSync mailbox policy with the parameter of AllowMobileOTAUpdate set to $True. The default policy has this parameter set to $True. When the phone is initially configured with an Exchange ActiveSync partnership, the user will receive an email with a link about the Outlook Mobile update. The link should be accessed from the phone and will download and install the update. The installation CAB file for Windows Mobile 6.1 phones can also be found at `https://update.outlook.com/cabs/OutlookLiveSetup.cab`.

Both features require users to configure the text messaging integration via the Exchange Control Panel in the Phone section. Phones from other manufacturers may support the EAS and text messaging integration feature in the future.

Summary

In this chapter, you examined how to configure connectors, email routing, and message transport for Exchange 2010. Although the default configuration of Exchange provides some best practices, you will need to be familiar with all of the configuration options to deploy and maintain your environment in an efficient manner.

The Edge Transport server continues to play an important role to provide security and protection for your Exchange environment. The integration with the Exchange Hub Transport servers and recipient information reduces complexity and management of a third-party gateway solution. Additionally, the Edge Transport servers provide this functionality in a DMZ or perimeter network, which is a requirement in many organizations. Antivirus software like Forefront Protection for Exchange 2010 is still required and recommended to be installed on both the Hub and Edge Transport servers to provide protection from viruses and malware inside and outside the organization.

Outlook 2007 is a pretty user-friendly electronic-messaging client with lots of bells and whistles, such as task and calendaring capabilities and contacts. When released in the summer of 2010, Outlook 2010 and Exchange Server 2010 will provide tighter and enhanced integration with support for new features such as MailTips and conversation view. Outlook 2010 will also rely on the Exchange Control Panel for some end user Exchange customizations. The Exchange service Autodiscover has shown that it can reduce the support burden for Outlook users by reducing the number of calls to the help desk and the confusion surrounding getting an initial Outlook profile configured on a new desktop computer. Further reliance on web services is placed on EWS and the introduction of the Exchange Control Panel.

Remote access to email is now a requirement in most companies. Exchange 2010 provides many options, such as Outlook Anywhere, and introduces new features like text messaging. Users now have full access to their email wherever and whenever they need it, and the security of the network is maintained. Windows Mobile and ActiveSync users can be provided with access to their mailboxes from their mobile devices. They can synchronize their mailboxes from anywhere they can get cell phone or Wi-Fi signals.

Finally, although in some organizations POP3 and IMAP4 clients have been replaced completely by web-browser-based clients or Outlook, many organizations still use POP3 and IMAP4. Scalability and stability have been improved in Exchange 2010 for both protocols.

Chapter Essentials

Understand message routing and transport.   Email routing in Exchange 2010 is similar to routing in Exchange 2007 but has several new enhancements. Get to know what the enhancements are and understand the behavior to optimize routing in Exchange 2010. Also, learn about additional options for message transport to troubleshoot security, performance, and message delivery issues for your Exchange organization.

Understand Client Access connectivity.   The Client Access server functions as the end point to users for OWA, Outlook Anywhere, and IMAP4. When it's configured correctly, users will benefit from the many options to connect to Exchange from your network remotely. With Exchange Server 2010, dependency on the server role has increased with emphasis on web services and is even more critical to your Exchange architecture by taking on the RPC Client Access service. Prior to Exchange 2010, connections from Outlook clients would be disturbed when there were issues with the Mailbox server role. Now you will have to include the Client Access servers when configuring and troubleshooting RPC and MAPI issues.

Know where to go.   The Exchange Management Console has been enhanced with many new options to navigate and get to tasks, but that doesn't mean it won't be difficult to remember later. Take the time as you review the material in this book to think about what types of configuration and management tasks you find yourself performing in each major node of the Exchange Management Console. Becoming familiar with the Exchange Management Shell is still important for some basic tasks and especially important for complex tasks. Many client and transport tasks can be completed only with PowerShell.

Chapter

4

Managing Exchange Server 2010 Mail-Enabled Objects

THE FOLLOWING TOPICS ARE DISCUSSED IN THIS CHAPTER:

- ✓ Creating new mailboxes and understanding their differences

- ✓ Working with move requests

- ✓ Understanding the new Exchange Control Panel

- ✓ Creating distribution groups and their different uses

Most entry-level Exchange administrators start learning how to work with Exchange by adding new users to the organization, moving mailboxes, creating a resource mailbox, or modifying a distribution group. These tasks are at the foundation of managing Exchange and must be well understood to be successful both at the entry level and beyond.

In this chapter we will go over the steps for creating new and existing user mailboxes, creating resource mailboxes, and creating mail-enabled groups and contacts. We'll also discuss the differences among distribution groups, dynamic distribution groups, and public groups. Then you will learn how to move mailboxes by using move requests. Throughout the chapter, there will be times when you are exposed to a new feature of Exchange 2010 called the Exchange Control Panel, when the Exchange Control Panel is a light, web-based version of the Exchange Management Console, or EMC.

Understanding Databases in Exchange Server 2010

Before you begin creating mailboxes and contacts, you need to know more about the databases in Exchange 2010. These databases are used to store an organization's mailboxes or public folders. This is a change from Exchange 2007 and 2003 when they were referred to as data-stores. Exchange Server 2010 also introduces new features to help improve the overall performance of the server and simplify management of an organization's mailboxes. Reporting for public folders was also enhanced. It is now possible to view user-initiated changes to any item in the public folder by running the cmdlet Get-PublicFolderStatistics in the Exchange Management Shell.

Improvements and changes to the store schema have been made as well. These include quarantining rogue mailboxes, transport cutoff of databases with less than 1 GB of drive space available, and thread time-out detection and reporting.

A great deal of thought went in to architecting the Extensible Storage Engine (ESE), the database storage process for Exchange. New ESE functionality helps reduce input/output per second (IOPS) to optimize performance for commodity storage, online defragmentation, and online database scanning. These improvements helped reduce the overall cost of hardware by adding support for additional types of hardware and also improving the server's performance. The reduction of I/O was accomplished by maintaining contiguous data within the database. The page size was also increased to 32 KB; this allows more data to be read and written during each I/O operation, reducing the number of read and write operations required. The use of commodity storage was optimized so now the use of SATA-class hard drives or a JBOD configuration is supported. (SATA stands for Serial Advanced Technology Attachment, and JBOD stands for "just a bunch of disks.") Because disks represent one of the largest costs in an Exchange deployment, these changes help reduce the overall cost by enabling the use of larger and cheaper disks over smaller, faster drives.

Online defragmentation was adjusted from Exchange 2007 so that, by default, it no longer runs just during a specific maintenance period; instead it runs continuously in the background. This constant process takes minimal resources due to small but constant changes versus a large number of changes just once a day, this is similar to defragmenting a computer hard drive just once a month instead of daily; daily defragmentation would take less time to complete compared to preforming it once a month.

Online database scanning examines the database for any physical corruption by scanning each database page for corruption. Online database scanning now has two modes. First, you can run it at the end of a normal maintenance task. The time it takes to run an online database scan can be configured and works best on smaller databases. The default mode is similar to online defragmentation in that it runs continuously in the background. Because the scan is sequential, it generates a lighter load on the storage system. This scan is essential for reporting corrupted data.

Each database and its transaction log files have a separate instance of the ESE process. Changes made to the database are first written to these log files. The transaction logs are truncated, or removed, when the database has been successfully backed up. The database and the current log files represent the current status of the Exchange service. Information about the committed transaction logs is stored in checkpoint files, which reside in the same directory as the log files by default with a naming convention of Enn.chk.

Configuring a database for circular logging will overwrite the transaction logs with new transactions as the transactions are committed to the database. If a database backup is not going to complete for a long period of time or if there is an unusual amount of transaction logs being generated due to mailbox moves or other maintenance, you may want to temporarily enable circular logging to conserve disk space. The major drawback of circular logging is that you can restore only the last full backup. However, without circular logging enabled, the last full backup can be restored along with any of the transaction logs generated after the full backup to recover the lost data. When circular logging is enabled, the transaction logs are not retained and therefore they cannot be used to re-create lost data.

This was just a brief overview of database structure. Next you will learn how to create a database in Exercise 4.1.

EXERCISE 4.1

Creating and Deleting Databases

The following steps walk you through the creation of a new database and then show you how to delete a database:

1. Click Start ➤ Programs ➤ Microsoft Exchange Server 2010 and then select Exchange Management Console.

2. Expand the Microsoft Exchange container, expand the Microsoft Exchange On-Premises container, expand the Organization Configuration container, and then click the Mailbox node.

3. Click the New Mailbox Database link in the Actions pane.

4. On the first page of the New Mailbox Database Wizard, enter the name of the database, **Executives**. Click the Browse button to select a server.

New Mailbox Database

- Introduction
- Set Paths
- New Mailbox Database
- Completion

Introduction
This wizard helps you create a new mailbox database.

Mailbox database name:

Server name:

Browse...

Help   < Back   Move   Cancel

5. The Select Mailbox Database dialog box opens and displays available servers. Select EX01, click OK, and continue to the Set Paths page.

6. On the Set Paths page, verify the database file path and the log folder path. Click Next.

New Mailbox Database

- Introduction
- Set Paths
- New Mailbox Database
- Completion

Set Paths
Enter the file locations for the database.

Database paths

Database file path:
C:\Program Files\Microsoft\Exchange Server\V14\Mailbox\Resources1\Resources.edb

Log folder path:
C:\Program Files\Microsoft\Exchange Server\V14\Mailbox\Resources1

☑ Mount this database

Help   < Back   Next >   Cancel

EXERCISE 4.1 *(continued)*

7. On the Configuration Summary page, click New.

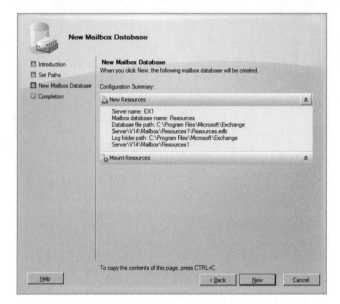

8. On the Completion page, verify that the database was created successfully. Click Finish.

You can now see the newly created database in the middle pane of the EMC. If you need to delete a database, you can do it by right-clicking the database and choosing Remove. You will see a dialog box asking you to confirm the deletion, as shown in Figure 4.1. As you can see in Figure 4.2, once the database has been removed, you will need to browse to the database file's location and delete it to reclaim the storage space.

FIGURE 4.1   Database deletion confirmation dialog box

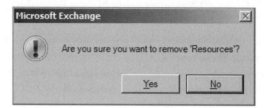

FIGURE 4.2   Database deletion completed dialog box

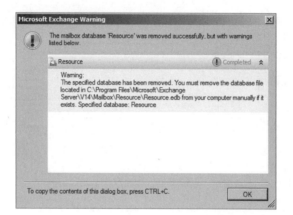

After a database has been created, there may be instances where you need to move the database files from one disk to another. For example, you could be upgrading hardware because the disk is out of drive space on the current drive, or upgrading from a single server with multiple roles to multiple servers with single roles. You will learn how to move a database in Exercise 4.2.

EXERCISE 4.2

Moving Mailbox Databases with the Exchange Management Console

Follow these steps to move a mailbox database by using the EMC:

1.   Click Start ➢ Programs ➢ Microsoft Exchange Server 2010 and then select Exchange Management Console.

2. Expand the Microsoft Exchange container, expand the Microsoft Exchange On-Premises container, expand the Organization Configuration container, and then click the Mailbox node.

3. Start the Move Database Wizard either by highlighting the database in the work pane and then clicking Move Mailbox Database in the Actions pane or by right-clicking the database and choosing Move Database from the context menu.

4. In the Move Database Path Wizard, change the path of the database file to `C:\Program Files\Microsoft\Exchange Server\V14\Mailbox\Resources1\Resources.edb`. Change the log folder path to `C:\Program Files\Microsoft\Exchange Server\V14\Mailbox\Resources1` and then click Move.

5. A dialog box appears stating that the database will have to be temporarily dismounted to be moved. Click Yes.

6. On the Completion page, verify that the move completed successfully, and review the cmdlet that the EMC ran, and then click Finish.

To keep users from connecting to the database while you perform maintenance, you can dismount the database. In Exercise 4.3, you will dismount a database and then mount it.

Dismounting a Database and Mounting a Dismounted Database

The following steps walk you through dismounting and remounting a database:

1. Click Start ➢ Programs ➢ Microsoft Exchange Server 2010 and then select Exchange Management Console.

2. Expand the Microsoft Exchange container, expand the Microsoft Exchange On-Premises container, expand the Organization Configuration container, and then click the Mailbox node.

3. In the Results pane, review the list of databases and their statuses under the Database Management tab.

4. Right-click a mounted database and choose the Dismount Database option.

5. On the confirmation dialog box, click Yes. The time it takes to dismount the database can vary depending on its size and any possible tasks running on it.

6. After the database is dismounted, perform maintenance tasks such as moving the database.

7. After you have completed the tasks on the dismounted database, you will need to mount it before users will have access to their email. Right-click the database that you dismounted and choose Mount Database. The results pane will reflect that the database is now mounted.

Creating Mailboxes

Exchange has four basic types of mailboxes. Each mailbox type has a function that's different from the others. These different types of mailboxes help reduce the management of accounts in an Exchange organization.

User   A *user* is an Active Directory object that typically represents a person who uses the network. Once Exchange is installed and updates the schema, each user in the Active Directory can be mailbox-enabled, mail-enabled, or neither. A *mailbox-enabled user* has an associated mailbox in a mailbox database on an Exchange server. Each user's *mailbox* is a private storage area that allows an individual user to send, receive, and store messages. A user mailbox cannot be used for Resource Scheduling.

Room mailbox   A *room* mailbox is an Active Directory object for room scheduling and is *not* owned by a user. The user account is automatically disabled and normally managed by a person or a group within the organization. Examples of rooms would be conference rooms, training rooms, or even an exercise room. The scheduling of these rooms helps maintain organization within the company so employees know when a resource is available.

Equipment mailbox   An equipment mailbox is an Active Directory object as well. For equipment accounts, the user account is disabled and a designated employee or group manages the schedule of the equipment. You might have equipment accounts for equipment such as projectors for meetings, company cars, or loaner laptops for the road warriors and vacationers with deadlines.

Linked mailbox A *linked* mailbox is an account that is accessed by a principal (user) from another separate but trusted forest. This comes in handy if an organization has many resources and wants to consolidate them into a resource forest.

Exercise 4.4 shows how to create mailboxes using the EMC.

EXERCISE 4.4

Creating a New User with the Exchange Management Console

To use the EMC to create a new user mailbox, follow these steps:

1. Click Start ➤ Programs ➤ Microsoft Exchange Server 2010 and then select Exchange Management Console.

2. Expand the Microsoft Exchange container, expand the Microsoft Exchange On-Premises container, expand the Recipient Configuration container, and then click the Mailbox node.

3. Click New Mailbox in the Actions pane.

4. Select the User Mailbox radio button in the New Mailbox Wizard and click Next.

EXERCISE 4.4 *(continued)*

5.   On the User Type screen that appears, choose New user and click Next.

6.   On the User Information screen, enter the following information: Type **Brian** for the first name, type **Tirch** for the last name, type **btirch** for the user logon name, type **Password01!** for the password and again in the Confirm Password field. Check the box user must change password at next logon. Click Next.

7. On the Mailbox Settings page, type **Btirch** for the alias. Leave the default settings for the managed folder mailbox policy and Exchange ActiveSync mailbox policy. Click Next.

8. The Archive Settings page is used to enable the online archive, leave the default settings and then click Next.

9. On the New Mailbox page, click New to continue.

10. Any errors that are encountered during mailbox creation will be displayed.

The newly created account will be highlighted and displayed in the middle pane.

For creating multiple accounts, you can use the Exchange Management Shell (EMS). You can have it use a pre-created list of accounts. Great care should be used when using PowerShell commands as you can break an Exchange server relatively easily compared to the management console. For more information on the PowerShell commands, see the TechNet article at `technet.microsoft.com/en-us/library/bb691354.aspx`.

In some organizations, not every user account will have a mailbox assigned to it. Also, organizations that have recently deployed Exchange must create mailboxes for their existing Active Directory accounts or a temporary employee or intern may become a full-time employee and need a mailbox. Exercise 4.5 walks you through the steps for creating a mailbox for an existing user.

EXERCISE 4.5

Creating a Mailbox for an Existing Account with the Exchange Management Console

Follow these steps to create a mailbox using the EMC:

1. Click Start ➢ Programs ➢ Microsoft Exchange Server 2010 and then select Exchange Management Console.

2. Expand the Microsoft Exchange container, expand the Microsoft Exchange On-Premises container, expand the Recipient Configuration container, and then click the Mailbox node.

3. Click New Mailbox in the Actions pane on the right side of the Exchange Management Console. You need to make sure you have the Recipient Configuration node expanded and the Mailbox node selected for the New Mailbox link to be available.

4. Select the User Mailbox radio button on the Introduction page of the New Mailbox Wizard and click Next.

5. On the User Type page, select the Existing users radio button and click the Add button.

6. Select the users Jeff, Joseph, Jules, and Wade. Then select Next.

7. These users should now be displayed. Click Next to continue to the Mailbox Settings page.

EXERCISE 4.5 *(continued)*

Note that any settings that you choose will be applied to all of your selected users.

8. On the Mailbox Settings page, leave the check boxes unchecked (the default). Click Next.

Note that an alias will be automatically generated for each new mailbox.

EXERCISE 4.5 *(continued)*

9. On the Completion page, you will see the user accounts you have chosen. Verify that each account has a completed status. Now click Finish.

User Mailbox Properties

Now that you have created new and existing user mailboxes, you can view the properties of these mailboxes. To view the properties of a mailbox in EMC, simply highlight the mailbox, right-click and click Properties. Being familiar with these properties is not only important for your day to day tasks, it is also helpful when preparing to take the certification exam.

The Properties dialog box of a mailbox has some of the same tabs that are are available for a user in the Active Directory management tools. You will see the General tab, which has the alias that you assigned in the first two exercises. You will also notice an option to hide the account from the address list. This useful function can be used for the backup user accounts, an alert account, or maybe that back-door administrator account you created. You wouldn't want some curious user to start sending emails to these accounts or have an executive assistant constantly asking who they are while they update the company directory. You will also see User, Address And Phone, Organization, and Account tabs in the Properties dialog box. These tabs all hold generic information for the selected account. When these tabs are filled in, they will update the global address list accordingly. The Member Of tab is an information tab only.

The other tabs contain sets of settings that can be modified to best suit the needs and policies of an organization.

Mail Flow Settings   This tab has settings for delivery options, message size restrictions, and message delivery restrictions.

Delivery Options   With this option, you can give other users send-on-behalf permissions, set an option for forwarding emails to another user, and set a maximum limit for the amount of email addresses a user can send to in one message. The Delivery Options dialog box is shown in Figure 4.3.

FIGURE 4.3   Delivery Options dialog box

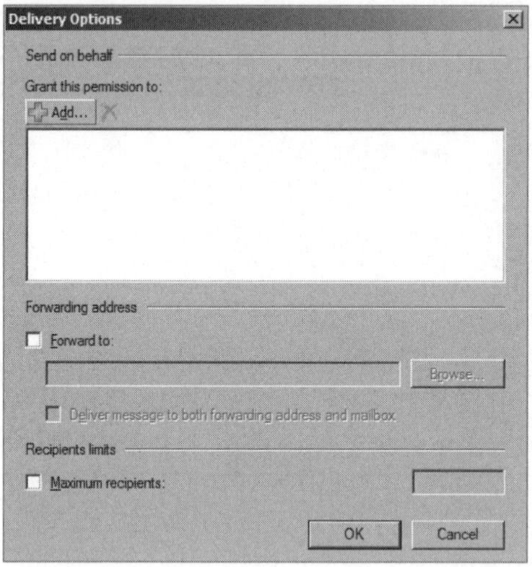

> You can use the Delivery options under the Mail Flow settings tab for forwarding emails. You might need to set up forwarding for a user who is going on vacation for a week and has quotes with clients that have to be approved before they get back. A secretary may have send-on-behalf rights for another employee or an executive to help manage meetings. Using the max recipients setting on a user who sends large attachments to a group of people can help manage the resources of the Exchange server.

Message Size Restriction   Modifying the Message Size Restrictions allows you to override the global settings for a mailbox. The default size is 10 MB. Figure 4.4 shows the settings you can modify for message size restrictions, this can accessed from the Mail Flow Settings tab. You may need to change this setting for a single user to further restrict the message size. For example, you may want to limit task workers from sending large attachments.

FIGURE 4.4   Message Size Restrictions options

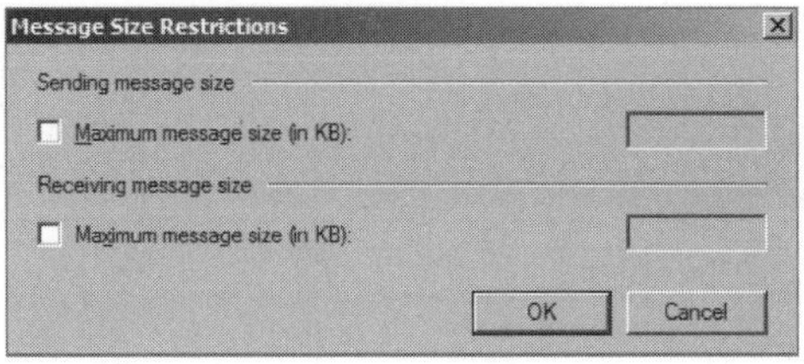

Message Size Restrictions

Sending message size

☐ Maximum message size (in KB): _____

Receiving message size

☐ Maximum message size (in KB): _____

[OK]   [Cancel]

 An engineer is trying to send a 10.7 MB file via email to a client. The client is not able to use an FTP site due to the client's network restrictions. You would have to make the needed changes in Exchange to allow this email to go through. The default message size restriction is 10 MB, changing this setting for the user will allow the email to go through.

Message Delivery Restriction   This option allows you to specify a list of senders from which the opened account can receive messages and a specific list of senders that can't send messages to this recipient. This dialog box is shown in Figure 4.5.

Mailbox Features   This tab has Outlook Web App, Exchange ActiveSync, Unified Messaging, MAPI, POP3, IMAP4, and Archive options. These are shown in Figure 4.6.

FIGURE 4.5   Message Delivery Restrictions configuration choices

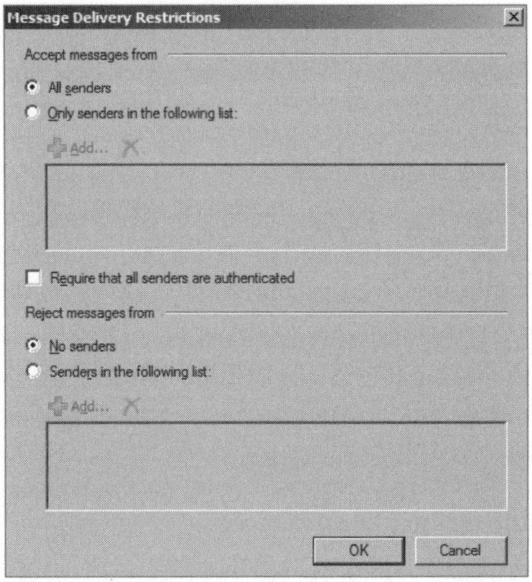

Message Delivery Restrictions

Accept messages from

◉ All senders
○ Only senders in the following list:

➕ Add...   ✕

☐ Require that all senders are authenticated

Reject messages from

◉ No senders
○ Senders in the following list:

➕ Add...   ✕

[OK]   [Cancel]

FIGURE 4.6 The Mailbox Features tab

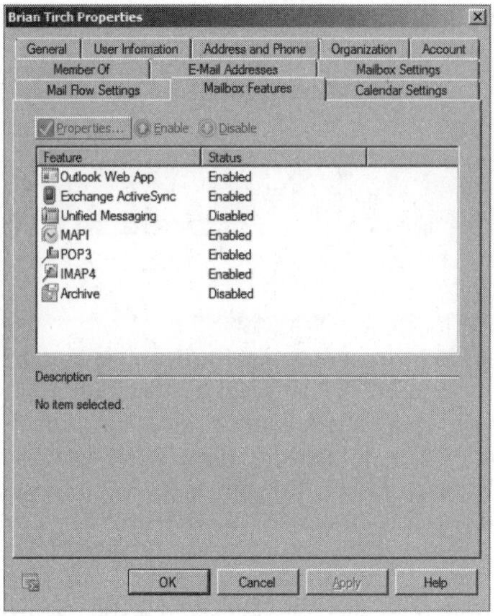

Outlook Web App Within the Outlook Web App properties you can set an Outlook Web App policy. A OWA policy that dictates restrictions for accessing email from a web browser. Modifying an OWA policy will change the features that users will have access to. You can use OWA policies to keep a user from changing their password in OWA, creating public groups, or even updating their contact information.

Exchange ActiveSync Exchange ActiveSync settings enabled is by default. When the ActiveSync setting is disabled, the user won't be able to access their email with a smart phone or PDA. The policy can dictate whether a user has access to remote desktop, Bluetooth capability, allowing Wi-Fi connectivity, forcing encryptions on the device, and idle lock times can be set, just to name a few of the options available. Different users may require different policies. IT staff may need the use of remote desktop access, the CEO wants his phone to be encrypted, and all other users require an idle lock time set. All of these settings can improve security and remote access to the network.

Unified Messaging This option allows the configuration of the unified messaging options such as enabling or disabling Automatic Speech Recognition (ASR), Play on Phone, and missed call notifications. You can also associate the user's mailbox with a different Unified Messaging (UM) mailbox policy which can set the PIN policy. These settings, when configured correctly, can work with VoIP systems, third-party messaging programs, and some multifunction devices.

MAPI This protocol is used by email clients like Microsoft Outlook and it is enabled be default. This can be used in environments when the users are expected to use OWA, POP3, or IMAP4 to connect to their mailbox.

POP3   An organization might require POP3 access for remote or legacy users. Some POP3 clients may require that messages are formatted with a specific format such as text, HTML, HTML and alternative text, enriched text, enriched text and alternative text, TNEF, or best body format. The default setting is to use the protocol default of the best body format. This allows you to override the default formatting of the protocol for a specific user.

IMAP4   Another protocol similar to POP3. This setting allows you to override the default formatting of the email and a different Internet protocol. You have choices for plain text, HTML, HTML and alternative text, enriched text, enriched text with alternative text and TNEF. Older smart phones were unable to read emails in HTML and were unable to convert enriched text correctly, which left plain text as the only way to read the emails. Some clients or users may prefer an older third-party program for email access and only work well with enriched text.

Archive   Creating an online archive as well as enabling Unified Messaging requires an Enterprise Exchange Client Access license. If you have enabled an archive for the mailbox, you can choose the properties of this option to review the configuration of the online archive; otherwise it will be disabled. To enable an online archive you must select the mailbox in EMC and choose Enable Archive from the Actions menu or use Enable-Mailbox cmdlet in EMS.

Calendar Settings   This tab is where you can modify the calendar's default automation settings. The following options are shown in Figure 4.7:

- "Remove meeting forward notifications to the Deleted Items folder" is disabled by default.

- "Remove old meeting requests and responses" is enabled by default. This setting helps keep the inbox from being cluttered with invites, which will slow down searches.

- "Mark new meeting requests as Tentative" is also enabled by default. This will show up in the free/busy scheduling assistant to help alleviate conflicts.

- "Process meeting requests and responses originating outside the Exchange organization" is disabled by default. Enabling this will allow meeting requests from other companies or organizations, like a Novell networked company, to be processed.

FIGURE 4.7   Calendar Settings configuration options

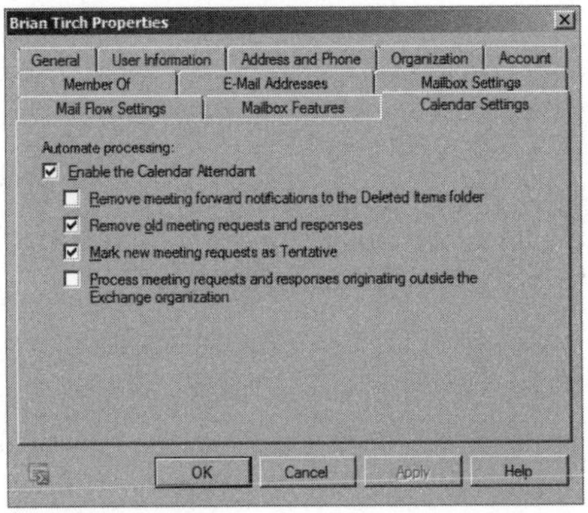

E-Mail Addresses This tab allows you to change the current email address. Figure 4.8 shows how you can add additional email addresses as well. You have to uncheck the Automatically Update E-Mail Addresses Based On E-Mail Address Policy box if you want to change the Set As Reply address. In order for an email address to work, the email domain must be added as an accepted domain. For more information about accepted domains see Chapter 3, "Configuring Connectors, Routing and Transport, and Connectivity."

Mailbox Settings The Mailbox Setting tab on the properties of an Exchange recipient has options for configuring messaging records, federated sharing, role assignments, and storage quotas.

Messaging Records Management This allows you to set a predefined retention policy on the mailbox and folders. This also allows the retention policy to be suspended for a period of time and the ability to enable Litigation hold. Some companies have an email policy that requires email to be saved for a certain amount of time, while others do not allow backups of their emails, as shown in Figure 4.9. You can review more of these settings in Chapter 11, "Deploying the Exchange Server 2010 Infrastructure."

FIGURE 4.8 E-mail addresses of a selected mailbox

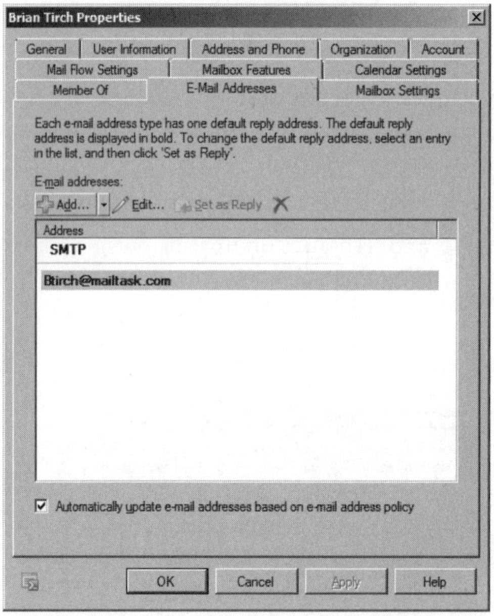

FIGURE 4.9 Options for Messaging Records Management configuration

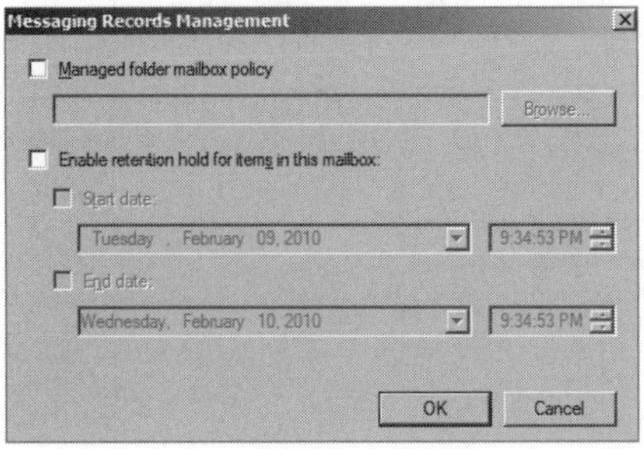

Federated Sharing The Federated Sharing option on the Mailbox Settings tab allows you to assign a sharing policy to the mailbox, as shown in Figure 4.10.You can apply which sharing policy you want the user to have. We will discuss federated sharing policies in Chapter 12, "Designing Connectivity and Routing."

FIGURE 4.10 Federated Sharing setting

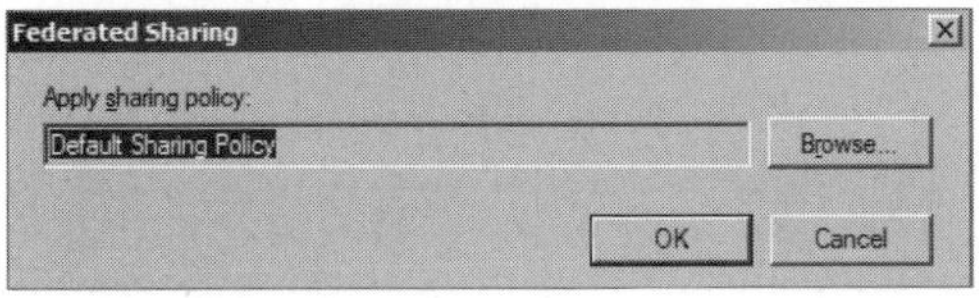

Storage Quotas This option is used to override the global settings for the mailbox size of a user. Some executives may need to have an increased mailbox size to retain all of their attachments, while an intern may have a smaller mailbox size. Figure 4.11 shows the default settings. To change them for a single user, uncheck the use default settings and check each item and type in the new size in KB.

FIGURE 4.11 Modifying a mailbox storage quota

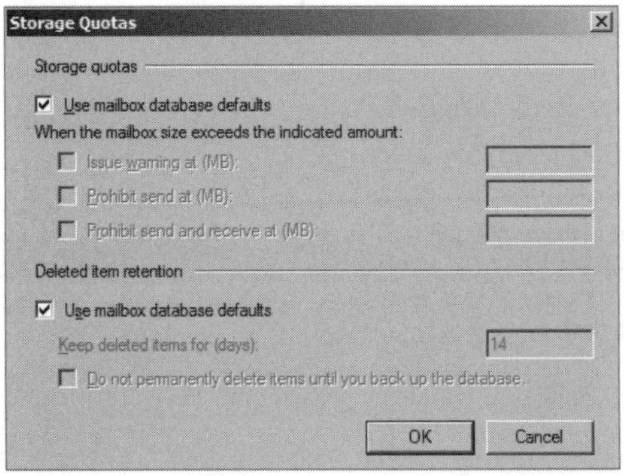

Archive Quota This option can only be set if you have the Exchange Enterprise Client Access Licenses for it. This setting is used to assign a quote for the size of the Online Archive that is offered in Exchange 2010. This will notify the user if their personal archive becomes too large. Figure 4.12 shows the Properties dialog box displayed after clicking on the Archive Quota option on the Mailbox Settings tab of the Mailbox properties.

FIGURE 4.12 Setting the Archive Quota

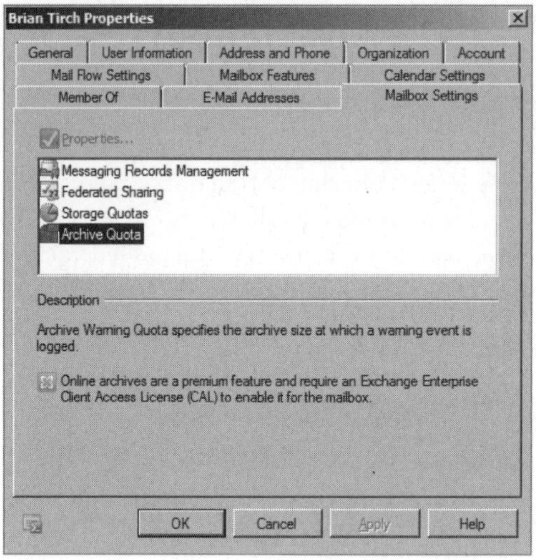

Creating Resource Mailboxes

Now that we have covered creating new and working with existing user mailboxes, we can now discuss resource mailboxes. Resource mailboxes are split up into two different categories: equipment mailboxes and room mailboxes. Creating these resource mailboxes is a necessity for companies. Many companies have multiple resources for their employees to use, such as company cars for traveling to a client or a training site or perhaps two different conference rooms, one with videoconferencing capabilities and the other with only a conference phone. In Exercise 4.6, you learn how to create a room mailbox.

EXERCISE 4.6

Creating Room Mailboxes

To create a room mailbox using the EMC, follow these steps:

1. Click Start ➢ Programs ➢ Microsoft Exchange Server 2010 and then select Exchange Management Console.

2. Expand the Microsoft Exchange container, expand the Microsoft Exchange On-Premises container, expand the Recipient Configuration container, and then click the Mailbox node.

3. Click New Mailbox in the Actions pane. You can also right-click the Mailbox option in the left pane and then choose New Mailbox.

4. Select Room Mailbox and click Next.

5. On the User Type page, you can choose to create a new room or use an existing object in Active Directory (AD). For this exercise, you will assume the room was not created yet and leave New user chosen. Click Next.

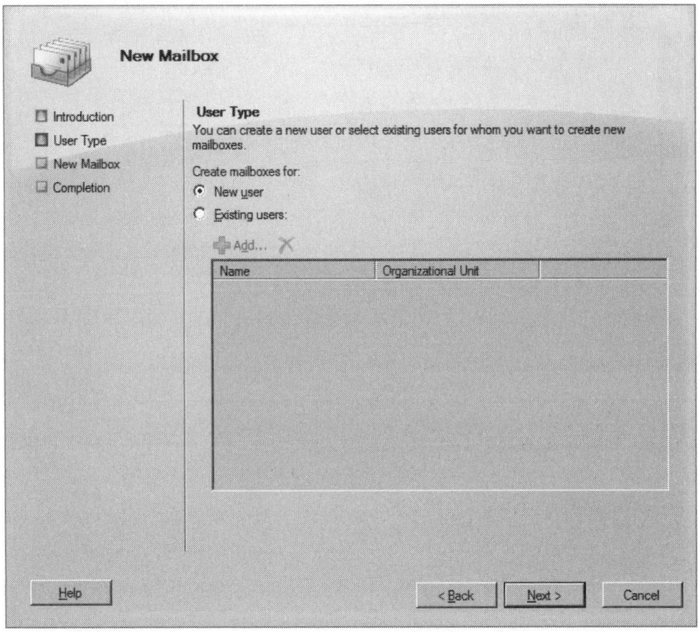

6. On the User Information page, type in the following information:

First Name: Conference

Last Name: **Room 2**

User Logon Name (User Principal Name): **confrm2**

Click Back to make changes or Next to go to the next screen.

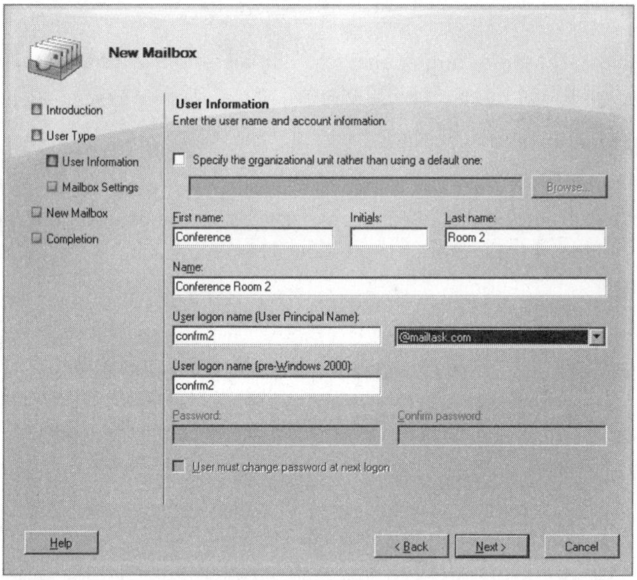

7. Type in an alias for the account. For this exercise just leave the default settings and click Next.

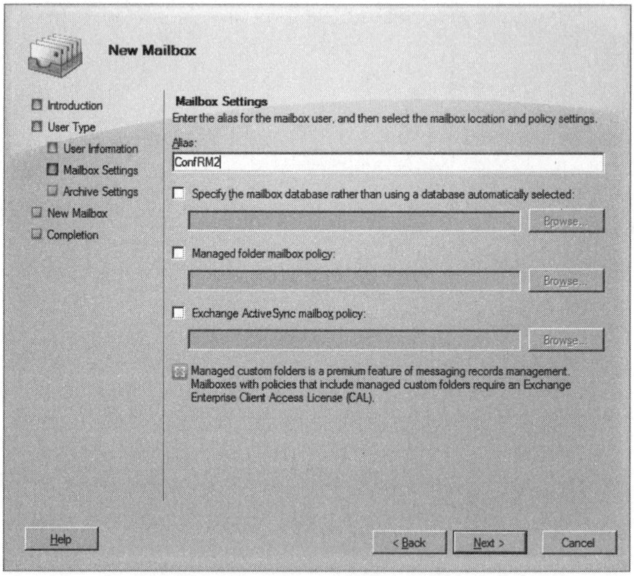

8. Leave the default archive settings and click Next.

9. On the Confirmation page, review the settings and click New if they are correct; otherwise, click Back to make adjustments.

10. If there was an error in the creation of the account, you will be able to view the error and go back to fix it. Click Finish.

At this point, you can create any more room mailboxes that you may need. You can then move on to creating equipment mailboxes. Equipment mailboxes are created the same way as the room mailboxes are created except that you would choose Equipment instead of Room in the New Mailbox wizard.

Modifying Resource Mailbox Properties

After you create a resource mailbox, you need to do some configuration. You may be wondering how to give permissions to the new resource accounts or how the accounts work while the user associated with them is disabled. You could enable the account and then log in as the resource, but that would take more time than just configuring the properties of the mailbox in EMC. You may also wonder why you would create a resource account instead of just a user mailbox with the name of the resource. The resource accounts have more options in which you can configure, including common properties like how they respond to meeting requests and custom properties. For example, a company with maintenance workers may require a company truck or two. One truck might have a lighted sign to warn, notify, or redirect people, and the other truck may have a built-in tool box and four-wheel drive. These two trucks are prime candidates to be represented by two separate equipment mailboxes. Another example would be an organization that has two conference rooms. Conference room A can comfortably seat 12 people; it has a whiteboard, a conference-quality phone, and a videoconferencing device. Conference room B can seat 32 people comfortably and has a projector. Whereas equipment mailboxes would be appropriate for the truck, these two conference rooms would need room mailboxes. Both types contain special or custom properties that cannot be added to a user mailbox.

Resource mailboxes are administrative friendly. You will not have to log in to the resource account and set up multiple rules and the auto attendant as you would need to do with a user's account. You can configure all the settings within the console or via cmdlets in PowerShell. You can set who can and cannot request meetings. You can set the delegates, or users that manage the resource account, all without creating a new Outlook profile.

With Recipient Configuration expanded and the Mailbox node highlighted, you will be able to open the properties of the resource accounts. To modify or view the configured properties, you can right-click the object, double-click the object, or click the link under the Actions pane for properties. In the next section of this chapter, you will be learning about the properties that are specific to resource accounts. If you need to review the other properties, refer to the section "User Mailbox Properties" earlier in this chapter.

There are many options available for configuring resource mailboxes. The Properties dialog of a resource mailbox has five additional tabs compared to a user mailbox. These additional tabs are: Resource General, Resource Information, Resource Policy, Resource In-Policy Requests, and Resource Out-of-Policy Requests. To better understand these settings, we will now consider the settings available on each of these tabs.

Resource General   The Resource General tab, shown in Figure 4.13, contains configuration options that allow you to provide information to your users about the capabilities of the resource. You can add properties such as videoconferencing devices, a fridge, white-board, or a ceiling-mounted projector. The Resource capacity field is used to specify how many people a room or resource can accommodate and accepts only numerical input.

FIGURE 4.13   Setting the resource capacity and custom properties of a resource mailbox

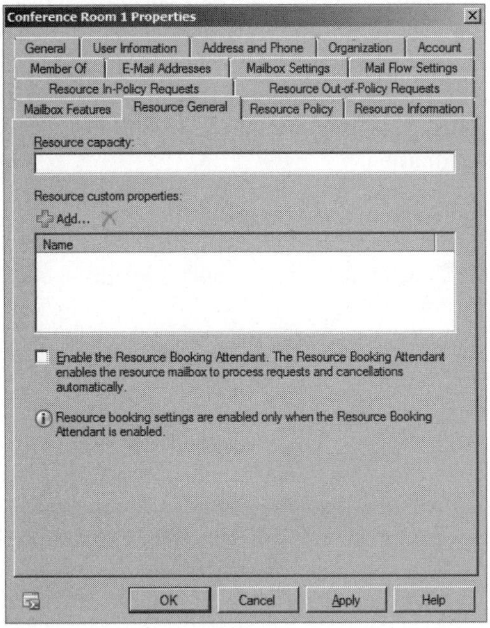

When you view the custom properties of a resource mailbox, you will be able to select any preconfigured settings. For example, you might select audio and video devices to indicate that the room has audio and visual capabilities or conference call to indicate that the room has a conference-call-quality phone. By default, there are no options configured for resource mailboxes to select from, so you'll have to add or configure them yourself from the Exchange Management Shell by using the `Set-ResourceConfig` command. Unfortunately, if you simply use the command in its most basic format, you'll just end up setting the resource custom property to be the last entry you made. If you want to have multiple options available from which to select, you'll have to get more creative—perhaps using code similar to that displayed here, which reads in the current custom properties, adds some custom properties in an array, and then writes the array out:

```
$ResourceConfiguration = Get-ResourceConfig
$ResourceConfiguration.ResourcePropertySchema.Add("Room/AV")
$ResourceConfiguration.ResourcePropertySchema.Add("Room/TV")
$ResourceConfiguration.ResourcePropertySchema.Add("Room/Whiteboard")
$ResourceConfiguration.ResourcePropertySchema.Add("Room/ConferenceCall")
```

```
$ResourceConfiguration.ResourcePropertySchema.Add("Equipment/Projector")
$ResourceConfiguration.ResourcePropertySchema.Add("Equipment/Computer")
Set-ResourceConfig -ResourcePropertySchema $ResourceConfiguration
.ResourcePropertySchema
```

After you create resource custom properties, you can select them by clicking the Add button to open the Select Resource Custom Property dialog box, shown in Figure 4.14. Note that the custom properties will be shown only for the type of resource mailbox being configured, so you won't find the Projector option displayed when working with a conference room based on the PowerShell code used here. The configuration you end up with is limited only by your needs and imagination.

FIGURE 4.14   Selecting custom resource properties

At the bottom of the dialog box, shown previously in Figure 4.13, notice that there is a check box for enabling the resource to process requests and cancellations automatically. If you are familiar with Exchange 2007 or even Exchange 2003, you will recall having to log in to the account to set the auto attendant feature.

Resource Information   The Resource Information tab, shown in Figure 4.15, contains the options for setting what is visible on the resource calendar. These settings help keep the mailbox small and uncluttered. By default, all options are enabled except a custom message for the organizer of the meeting. Removing attachments from meeting invites to a resource will help maintain the mailbox size. Deleting the non-calendar items will help reduce the management needs of the delegates and administrators, making it easier to find invites. You can allow the subject of the requests or private flags being removed for the resource request. You can also customize the response message for the resource to give it a less automated feeling and notify the request was approved or declined due to a conflict. Allowing the delegate/s to manage the requests may be a must to keep immature or competitive employees in check.

FIGURE 4.15 Selecting the information that is visible in a resource's calendar

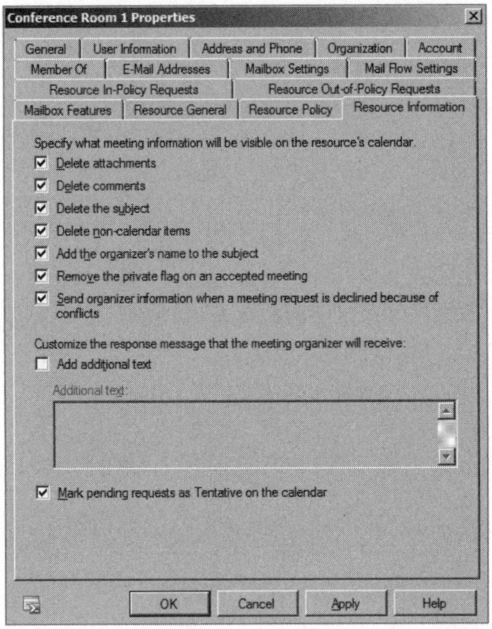

Resource Policy   The Resource Policy tab defines the policy options set for the in-policy and out-of-policy requests. You can view the default settings in Figure 4.16. Here you can set whether conflicting requests and repeating meetings are allowed, if the resource can be scheduled only during business hours, and whether repeating meetings can go beyond the booking window. There are also settings for the booking window in days, the maximum duration allowed for the meeting requests, maximum conflicts allowed (if they are allowed by company policy), and the percentage of conflicts allowed. You will also be able to set the delegates of the account. This alleviates the need to enable the user account in AD and log in as the resource account, saving you time. By default, the delegates will be forwarded all meeting requests.

Resource In-Policy Requests   The Resource In-Policy Requests tab displays the users who can submit meeting requests that will be automatically approved. As you can see in Figure 4.17, you can specify any users that have to be approved by the resource accounts delegates. Interns and entry-level employees of a company would be a great example of users that need to be approved by the delegates of the executive conference room, while the officers of the organization and their administrative assistants are able to submit requests to the resource without a delegate's approval.

FIGURE 4.16   Choosing the policy options of a resource mailbox.

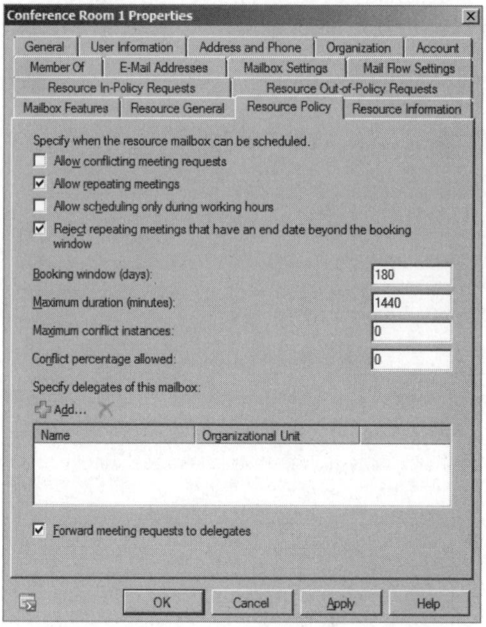

In-Policy Requests

I recall having to set up an In-Policy setting for an engineering firm that required the spare company car being accessible to the construction department. This might be due to various reasons such as normal repairs or due to road conditions. However, some of the other departments wanted access to the same spare company car for its carrying capacity. To avoid a situation where the construction crew would lack transportation, the company car resource was delegated by the construction crew's administrative assistant. The construction department was allowed to request the car at any time without needing their assistant to book it or clear it. This helped them avoid conflicts with the other departments. The delegate was able to decline the other requests or approve them with their knowledge of the construction department's fleet. This reduced the downtime of the construction staff by 10% due to lack of transportation.

FIGURE 4.17   Default settings of the Resource In-Policy Requests options

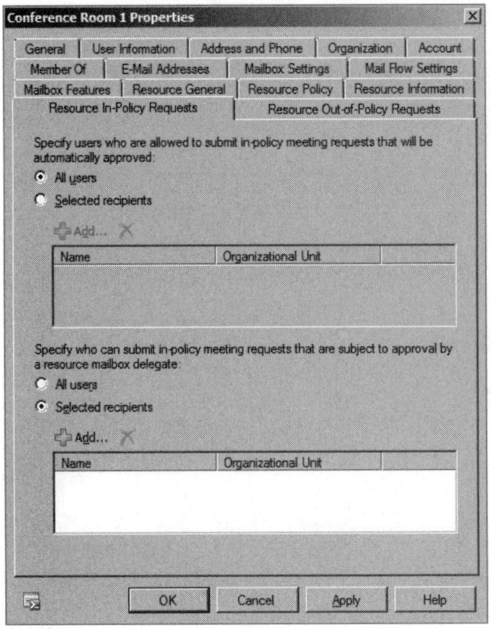

Resource Out-of-Policy Requests   The Resource Out-of-Policy Requests tab is used to allow users to submit requests that fall outside of the defined policy of the resource. Any user that is allowed to submit an out-of-policy request will have to be approved by the delegate of the resource account. This could be anything from the "during business hours only" setting set to not allowing repeating meeting requests past the booking window. You could also give the executives rights to submit requests that conflict with already approved requests for emergency meetings, for example. You can view the options in Figure 4.18.

Real World Scenario

Out-of-Policy Requests

The executive conference room has an Out-of-Policy policy that allows the officers in the company to submit requests that conflict with an already scheduled meeting. Kory has booked the executive conference room for a presentation to fellow staff members. He has it booked from 2 p.m to 4 p.m on Wednesday. Joel received an email from a potential and profitable client on Tuesday, the day before Kory's presentation. We are both executives in the company and have requested the executive conference room for the same time. Joel's meeting is submitted and added in to the schedule. All parties are notified and Kory will have to reschedule his presentation for another day.

FIGURE 4.18 Out-of-Policy Requests tab with no users yet added

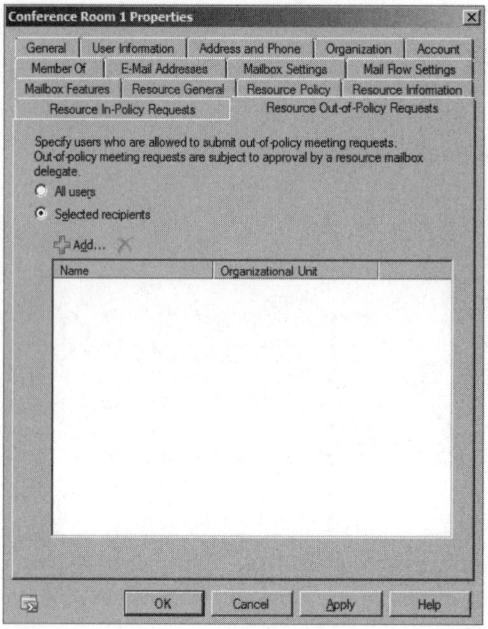

In Exercise 4.7, you will modify a room resource with the following policies:

- The room can have a capacity of 12 people.
- The room is equipped with a videoconferencing device.
- The policy for scheduling the room does not allow repeating meetings.
- The account allows meetings to be scheduled only during working hours.
- The administrative assistants group will be the delegate.
- Interns must have approval from the delegate to schedule a meeting with the resource.
- The officers must be able to schedule a meeting after business hours or even a monthly meeting.

EXERCISE 4.7

Modifying Resource Mailbox Properties with the Exchange Management Console

In this exercise, you will modify the configuration settings for a room resource:

1. Click Start ➤ Programs ➤ Microsoft Exchange Server 2010 and then select Exchange Management Console.

2. Expand the Microsoft Exchange container, expand the Microsoft Exchange On-Premises container, expand the Organization Configuration container, and then click the Hub Transport node.

3. In the results pane, click Conference Room 1. It will have an icon with a small door attached to it.

4. On the Resource General tab, type **12** under Resource Capacity and then click the Add button.

Conference Room 1 Properties					☒
General	User Information	Address and Phone	Organization	Account	
Member Of	E-Mail Addresses	Mailbox Settings	Mail Flow Settings		
Resource In-Policy Requests		Resource Out-of-Policy Requests			
Mailbox Features	Resource General	Resource Policy	Resource Information		

Resource capacity:

`12`

Resource custom properties:

➕ Add... ✕

Name

☐ Enable the Resource Booking Attendant. The Resource Booking Attendant enables the resource mailbox to process requests and cancellations automatically.

ⓘ Resource booking settings are enabled only when the Resource Booking Attendant is enabled.

OK	Cancel	Apply	Help

5. Select the AV custom property and click OK.

Select Resource Custom Property	_ ☐ ☒
File View	
Search: Find Now Clear	

Name ▲
AV
TV
Whiteboard

OK	Cancel

1 object(s) selected.   3 object(s) found.

6. On the Resource Policy tab, clear the Allow repeating meetings check box. Select the Allow scheduling only during working hours check box. Click the Add button to specify the delegates that manage the resource account.

7. Select the user that will manage the resource account.

8. Click the Resource In-Policy Requests tab and add the selected recipients for users that must be approved to schedule a meeting with the resource.

9. On the Resource Out-of-Policy Requests tab, click Add and add the group that will need rights to submit repeating meetings and meetings after normal business hours.

10. When you have completed all of your configuration changes, click Apply.

Configuring Mail-Enabled Groups

A group is an Active Directory object that can contain users and may contain other groups. In the case of security groups, permissions can be assigned to a group and are inherited by all the objects in that group. This makes the group a valuable Windows security construct. Exchange Server 2010 also uses Active Directory groups for another purpose. A group can be made mail-enabled and then populated with other mail-enabled recipients to make a distribution group, a term with which you may be familiar from earlier versions of Exchange Server. A group can contain users, contacts, public folders, and even other groups. When a message is sent to a mail-enabled group, the list of members is extracted and the message is sent to each member of the list individually. Groups are visible in the global address list, or GAL, if they are configured properly to be mail-enabled.

Active Directory Domain Services (AD DS) supports two distinct types of groups. A security group can be assigned permissions and rights and be mail-enabled. A distribution group can be mail-enabled only.

Before we can begin any discussion on creating and managing groups, a discussion on group types and group scopes is necessary. You will need to have a good understanding of how the two different group types work before you can effectively use groups in your Exchange organization:

Security groups   Security groups, as the name implies, are used primarily to configure and assign security settings for user and group objects placed within the group. An administrator can configure the rights and permissions of the group, and these settings will then automatically be applied to all group members without the administrator needing to configure the settings manually on the individual objects. As you can see, this is a benefit from both an administrative point of view (less work to be done) and an accuracy point of view (fewer chances of configuring individual object permissions incorrectly). Security groups can also be mail-enabled, therefore allowing their mailbox-enabled and mail-enabled members to receive all messages that are sent to the security group.

Distribution groups   Distribution groups, as their name implies, are used only for sending messages to a large number of objects without having to select each user, group, or contact manually. You can place all members of a specific department or geographical location into a distribution group and then send one message to the group that will be distributed to all members. Because distribution groups are not access control list (ACL) enabled as security groups are, you cannot assign user rights or permissions to them.

You can change a distribution group into a security group at any time with no loss of functionality. However, changing a security group into a distribution group will result in the rights and permissions that have been configured on that group being lost. You will be warned of this when attempting to make the change.

In Exercise 4.8, you will create a group.

EXERCISE 4.8

Creating a New Distribution Group

To create a new distribution group, follow these steps:

1. Click Start ➤ Programs ➤ Microsoft Exchange Server 2010 and then select Exchange Management Console.

2. Expand the Microsoft Exchange container, expand the Microsoft Exchange On-Premises container, expand the Recipient Configuration container, and then click the Distribution Group node.

3. In the Actions pane, click the New Distribution Group link.

4. In the New Distribution Group Wizard, select the New Group option and click Next to continue to the Group Information page, shown here.

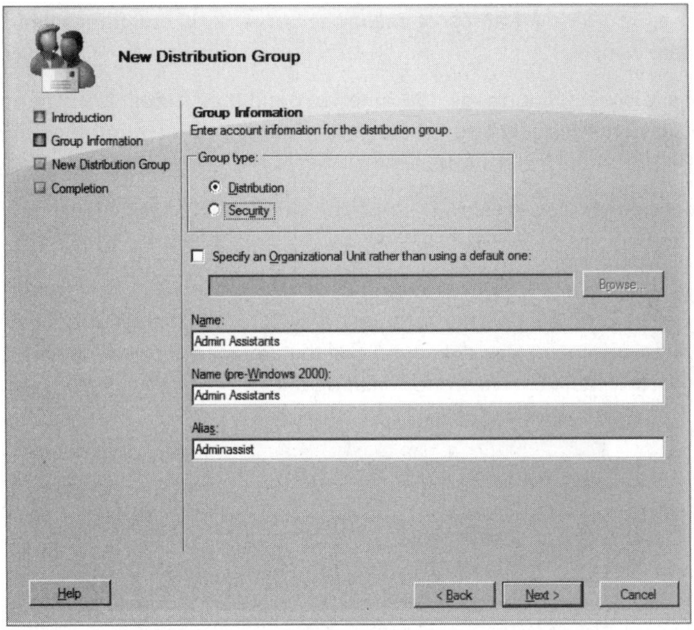

5. On the Group Information page, select Distribution and then select the location within Active Directory where the new group should be created by clicking the Browse button. If you do not choose a new organizational unit (OU) for the group, it will be placed in the default Users OU. You'll also need to supply the group name from which the pre-Windows 2000 name will be automatically created, though you can change this value. Type in the alias for the new group and click Next to continue to the summary page.

EXERCISE 4.8 (continued)

6. On the summary page, review all your configuration entries and click New to create the new distribution group. If you need to change any entries, you can click the Back button.

7. Click Finish.

If you have security groups that already exist in Active Directory but are not mail-enabled, you can perform the steps detailed in Exercise 4.9 to mail-enable those groups.

EXERCISE 4.9

Mail-Enabling an Existing Security Group

Follow these steps to mail-enable an existing security group:

1. Click Start ➢ Programs ➢ Microsoft Exchange Server 2010 and then select Exchange Management Console.

2. Expand the Microsoft Exchange container, expand the Microsoft Exchange On-Premises container, expand the Recipient Configuration container, and then click the Distribution Group node.

3. In the Actions pane, click the New Distribution Group link to start The New Distribution Group Wizard.

4. On the Introduction page, select Existing Groups and then click the Browse button to open the Select Group dialog box, shown here. Note that the security group will need to be universal in scope to be displayed and that you can choose only one group, unlike in the New Mailbox Wizard for existing users.

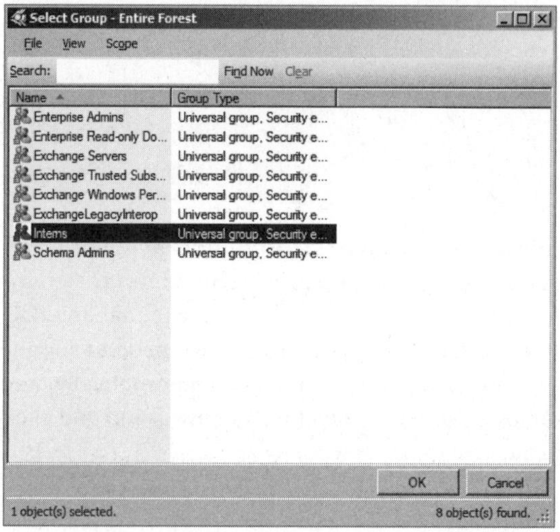

5. From the Select Group dialog box, you will be able to select from a list of the universal security groups in Active Directory that are not mail-enabled. Select a group and click OK to return to the Introduction page. Click OK to go to the Group Information page.

6. On the Group Information page, the only value you'll be able to change is the alias. Click Next to continue to the summary page.

7. On the summary page, review all your configuration entries and click New if you are satisfied. You can click Back to change any of the entries you made. When you click New, the Completion page appears.

8. Click Finish to close the wizard.

Even though every step of the process in Exercise 4.9 discusses distribution groups, by completing the wizard you are mail-enabling only the security group (adding an email address to it). You are not changing the group type from security to distribution, which is something that you can do from the Active Directory Users and Computers console if desired later.

Of course, you can create a new security group using the process outlined in Exercise 4.9 if you want. Managing the security group and its permissions will have to be completed through Active Directory Users and Computers.

Modifying Mail-Enabled Group Properties

It stands to reason that once you have distribution groups in your Exchange organization, you're eventually going to have to manage or modify their configurations. We will go over that now.

Performing Basic Management with the Exchange Management Console

You can manage all distribution groups from the EMC. By expanding Microsoft Exchange and Recipient Configuration, you will be able to select the Distribution Group node. When a distribution group is selected, which you can do in the middle of the console, you'll have specific options that become available on the right side of the console. Of course, all of these options are also available by right-clicking the appropriate mailbox and selecting them from the context menu.

The Disable option is used to remove all messaging attributes from the group object, not to disable the group itself because you can't disable a group in the same way that you would a user account. If you click the Disable link in the EMC, you'll be prompted to consider your action and to confirm that you want to continue. You can accomplish the same effect using the Disable-DistributionGroup cmdlet.

The Remove option causes the Active Directory group account object to be deleted from Active Directory along with the corresponding mail attributes. You can accomplish the same effect using the Remove-DistributionGroup cmdlet.

Managing Group Properties

When you click the last item available for a distribution—that is, Properties—the distribution group's Properties dialog box opens to the General tab. The tabs of the distribution group's Properties dialog box and their configurable items are explained in the following list:

General   The General tab, shown in Figure 4.19, contains some basic identifying information about the distribution. However, you can change only the Display Name field at the top of the tab and the Alias field in the middle of the tab. You can click the Custom Attributes button to open the Custom Attributes dialog box.

FIGURE 4.19   Basic information on the General tab in the Interns Properties dialog box

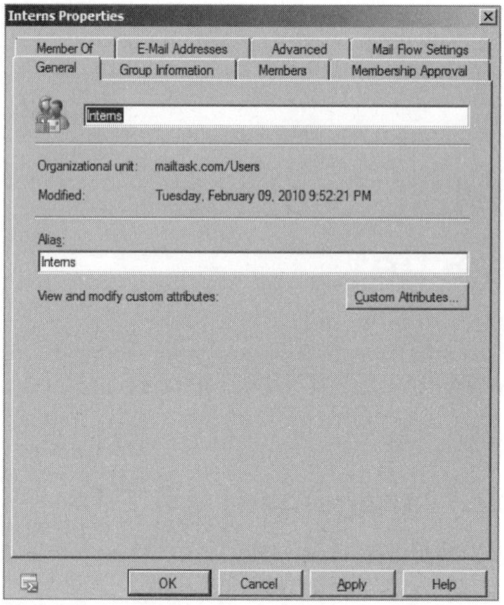

Group Information   The Group Information tab allows you to configure basic information about the distribution group. You can configure the following information on this tab:

- **Name:** Limited to 64 characters

- **Name (pre–Windows 2000):** Limited to 20 characters and cannot contain any of the following characters:

  ! # $ % ^ & - . _ { } | ~

- **Managed By:** A user or security group that can manage the membership of this distribution group using Microsoft Outlook
- **Notes:** Notes about the distribution group that are not displayed

Members   The Members tab, shown in Figure 4.20, is likely where you'll spend the majority of your group configuration time. You can add new members by using the Add button. You can add more than one member at a time. You can remove existing members by using the delete (X) button.

FIGURE 4.20   A newly created group with no members yet

Member Of   The Member Of tab contains read-only information. It lists other groups of which this distribution group is a member. This information is automatically populated as you add this distribution to the Members tab of other distribution groups.

E-Mail Addresses   The E-Mail Addresses tab, shown in Figure 4.21, allows you to add, remove, and edit email addresses assigned to the distribution group. The only type of email address that Exchange Server 2010 supports by default is SMTP, but you can configure custom types, if needed in your organization, by clicking the down arrow next to the Add button. If multiple addresses exist, you can configure one to be the default reply address using the Set As Reply button. Do not forget to uncheck Automatically update e-mail addresses based on e-mail address policy. The Reply As address will default back to the address policy e-mail.

Advanced   The Advanced tab, shown in Figure 4.22, contains some useful configuration options that you'll likely find yourself using more than once for distribution groups.

FIGURE 4.21   E-mail Addresses tab with the email address policy checked

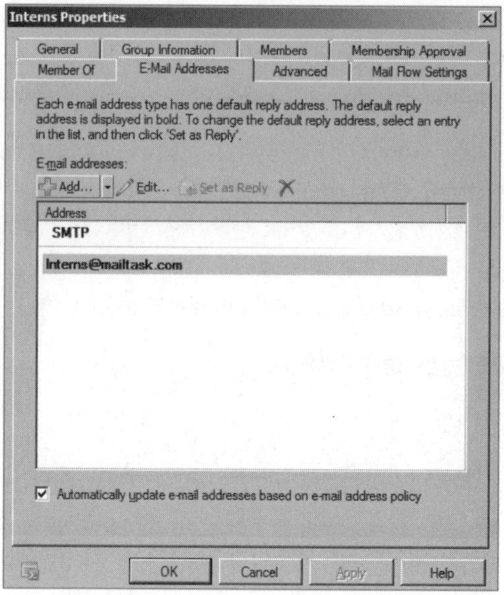

FIGURE 4.22   Default settings of the Advanced tab

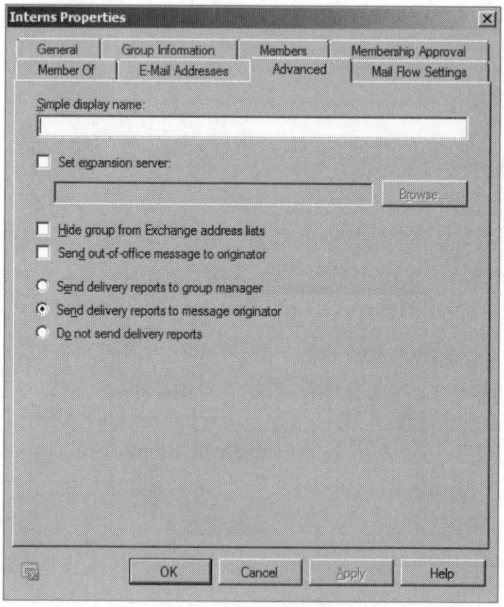

You can configure the following options on the Advanced tab:

Simple Display Name   This option contains only ASCII characters and no Unicode characters. Changes to this will be reflected in how the address list is shown in the global address list.

Set Expansion Server   Whenever a message is sent to a group, the group must be expanded so that the message can be sent to each member of the group. A categorizer performs this expansion. The default choice is Any Server In The Organization. This choice means that the home server of the user sending the message always expands the group. You can also designate a specific server to handle the expansion of the group. The choice of a dedicated expansion server is a good one if you have a large group. In this case, expansion could consume a great amount of server resources, which can compromise performance of busy servers. A max recipient setting can help reduce the impact of expanding a group.

Hide Group From Exchange Address Lists   If you enable this option, the group is not visible in the GAL. You might want to hide mailboxes used for running services or other mailboxes to eliminate questions of what they are for and keep people from sending email to these mailboxes. This will reduce the extra items in the GAL, making it easier for users to find what they are looking for.

Send Out-Of-Office Message To Originator   Users of Outlook clients can configure rules that enable the clients to reply to messages received automatically while the users are away from their office. When this option is enabled, users who send messages to groups can receive those automatic out-of-office messages from members of the list. For particularly large groups, the best practice is to not allow out-of-office messages to be delivered because of the excess network traffic they generate; however, it may be required in some situations to ensure that the sender of the email is aware when a group member is not going to respond to a request.

Send Delivery Reports To Group Manager   If you enable this option, notification is sent to the manager of the group whenever an error occurs during the delivery of a message to the group or to one of its members. Note that this option has no functionality if the group has not been assigned a manager. Enabling this option helps when troubleshooting email issues that occur when messages are sent to groups, especially when a user has created a rule to automatically delete or bounce back messages.

Send Delivery Reports To Message Originator   If you enable this option, error notifications are also sent to the user who sent a message to the group.

Do Not Send Delivery Reports   If you enable this option, error notifications will not be sent.

Mail Flow Settings   The Mail Flow Settings tab, shown in Figure 4.23, allows you to configure specific settings that determine how messages to this distribution group are handled.

When you select the Message Size Restrictions option and click the Properties button, the Message Size Restrictions dialog box opens. From here you can configure distribution-group-specific receive size limits that are applied only to the distribution group and that override those applied at the organizational or SMTP connector level.

When you select the Message Delivery Restrictions option and click the Properties button, the Message Delivery Restrictions dialog box opens. From here you can configure which senders are allowed and which are not allowed to send messages to this distribution group. By default, there are no restrictions configured on the Message Delivery Restrictions dialog box.

FIGURE 4.23   The three options for setting mail flow options

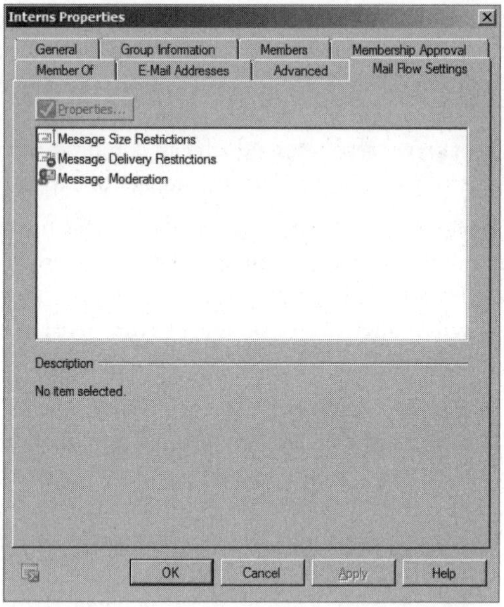

Managing Dynamic Distribution Groups

Dynamic distribution groups were first introduced in Exchange Server 2003 as query-based distribution groups. One of the biggest problems with using static distribution groups in the past was the amount of work and time it took to maintain an accurate and up-to-date group membership. Dynamic distribution groups aim to correct that problem. As the name implies, a dynamic distribution group is a mail-enabled distribution group that has its membership defined by the results of an Lightweight Directory Access Protocol (LDAP) query that is made against the content of Active Directory.

The obvious advantage to using a dynamic distribution group is that it provides a way to configure the membership of a group dynamically from all Exchange recipients based on a configured LDAP query. You can create a query, for example, that might limit the membership of a group to users who are part of the accounting department of your organization. By that same logic, you could also create a dynamic distribution group that specifies membership should be limited to those users, contacts, and distribution groups that are located in a specific building or in a specific geographical area (such as a state or city) within your organization. By being able to create, and change, the queries used to create these groups quickly, you save time and energy over maintaining larger standard distribution groups. Dynamic distribution groups are also much more accurate in their group membership because all the work is done by the results of the query you create.

As you might suspect by now, there is a trade-off to the power and flexibility that dynamic distribution groups provide. This trade-off comes in the form of increased loading on your global catalog servers. Each time an email is sent to a dynamic distribution group, the LDAP query you have configured must be run against the global catalog to determine the membership of the group.

Unlike query-based distributions in Exchange Server 2003, when you create a dynamic distribution group in Exchange Server 2010, you have a fairly small number of object attributes on which you can run queries. These attributes are as follows:

- State or province (from the Address And Phone tab of the object's Properties dialog box)

- Department (from the Organization tab of the object's Properties dialog box)

- Company (from the Organization tab of the object's Properties dialog box)

- Custom attributes 1–15 (from the General tab of the object's Properties dialog box)

Creating Dynamic Distribution Groups with the Exchange Management Console

In the EMC, you will find dynamic distribution groups and their corresponding management options listed in the Microsoft Exchange ➤ Recipient Configuration ➤ Distribution Group node. Creating a dynamic distribution group can be essential in a large company. You can use this type of group to add all users that are from the same office.

This comes in handy when you start adding more users to the organization. Instead of having to join them to the group after they are created, you just have to make sure the informational boxes are filled out. The group will automatically add the new user or users as they are added to Exchange. You could create a dynamic distribution group for a set of external contacts that belong to the same committee, like a large vendor.

Exercise 4.10 outlines the steps for creating a new dynamic distribution group.

EXERCISE 4.10

Creating a New Distribution Group

Follow these steps to create a new dynamic distribution group:

1. Click Start ➤ Programs ➤ Microsoft Exchange Server 2010 and then select Exchange Management Console.

2. Expand the Microsoft Exchange root object, expand the Recipient Configuration folder, and then click the Distribution Group node.

3. In the Actions pane on the right, click the New Dynamic Distribution Group link. The New Dynamic Distribution Group Wizard starts.

4. Enter the name and alias for the new dynamic distribution group, and click Next to continue to the Filter Settings page, shown here.

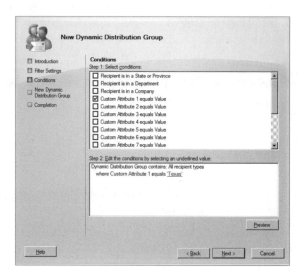

5. On the Filter Settings page, select the scope of the filter, such as a particular organizational unit or an entire Active Directory domain. You can also select which specific types of recipients you want to include, such as just user mailboxes or just mail contacts. Typically, you'll use the default selection to include all recipients. Click Next to continue to the Conditions page.

EXERCISE 4.10 *(continued)*

6. On the Conditions page, select the conditions on which you want to filter in the Step 1 area, such as State. After you've selected a condition, you need to enter a value for it in the Step 2 area of the page. After you've configured your desired conditions, you can click Next to continue to the summary page.

7. On the summary page, review all your configuration entries and click New to create the new dynamic distribution group. If you need to change any entries, you can click the Back button.

8. As always, Exchange displays the PowerShell code it used to perform the preceding actions. Click Finish to close the wizard.

Modifying Dynamic Distribution Groups

It only stands to reason that once you have dynamic distribution groups in your Exchange organization, you're eventually going to have to manage them or modify their configurations.

Using the EMC to Perform Basic Management on Distribution Groups

When a dynamic distribution group is selected in the middle of the console, you'll have specific options that become available on the right side of the console. Of course, all these options are also available by right-clicking the appropriate mailbox and selecting them from the context menu.

Selecting the Remove option causes the Active Directory group object to be deleted from Active Directory along with the corresponding mail attributes. You can accomplish the same effect by using the Remove-DynamicDistributionGroup cmdlet.

Managing Group Properties

When you click the only other item available for a distribution—that is, Properties—the distribution group's Properties dialog box opens to the General tab. Here are the tabs specific to dynamic distribution groups and the configurable items found on each:

Filter   The Filter tab of the dynamic distribution group's Properties dialog box, shown in Figure 4.24, allows you to change the scope of the filter that defines the dynamic distribution group.

Conditions   The Conditions tab, shown in Figure 4.25, allows you to change the filter conditions that define the membership of the dynamic distribution group. These attributes can be the states in which the users are located, a suite in the building they work out of, or even if they are a remote user.

FIGURE 4.24 Filter settings with All recipient types checked

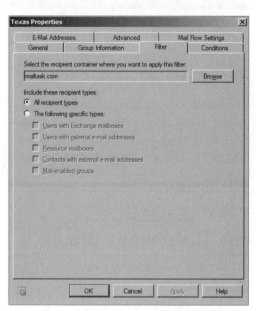

FIGURE 4.25 Custom properties with a custom attribute of Texas selected

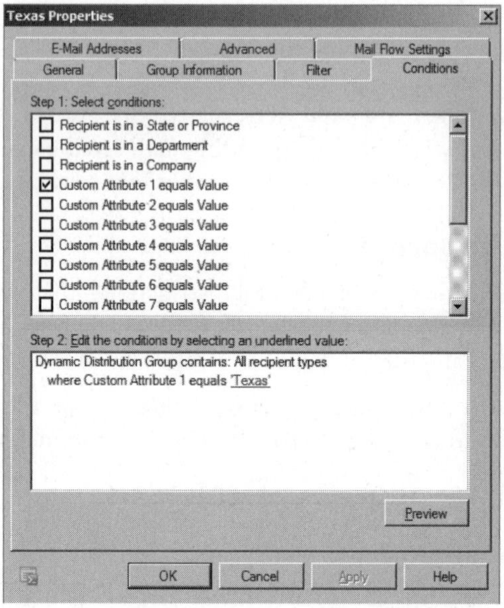

After you've configured a filter scope and the conditions, you'll want to use the Preview button to open the Dynamic Distribution Group Preview dialog box, shown in Figure 4.26. From here, you'll be able to determine how effective your filter and conditions were at getting the recipients you wanted. It's at this time that the importance of maintaining accurate information in Active Directory for all Exchange recipients starts to become very clear to most administrators.

FIGURE 4.26   Preview of a dynamic group with its chosen filter settings

Configuring Mail Contacts

Mail-enabled contacts are commonly created to represent people outside your organization with whom users inside your organization commonly communicate via email. Another common implementation of mail contacts is to provide a means to route messages to mobile phones and pagers from monitoring programs via the Exchange infrastructure. Although you can still create and manage contacts from the Active Directory Users and Computers console, which we'll explore next, you must now create and manage all messaging-related options and functionality from within the EMC or the Exchange Management Shell.

Creating Contacts with the Exchange Management Console

In the EMC, you will find contacts and their corresponding management options listed in the Microsoft Exchange ➢ Microsoft Exchange On-Premises (server name) ➢ Recipient Configuration ➢ Mail Contact node.

The default view is to list all contacts within the organization, although you're initial view may not display them all, depending on how many mailboxes you've configured to be displayed. The default setting limits the view to 1,000 contacts. You can change this by clicking the modify the maximum number of recipients to display link under the mailbox options in the Actions pane on the right side of the EMC.

Other options you have in the Actions pane that appear on the right side of the EMC include creating a new mail contact and creating a new mail user (which you've already examined). If you've selected a contact, then you have the following additional options: Disable, Remove, and Properties. We will examine all these options in the following sections.

Exercise 4.11 outlines the steps for creating a new mail contact.

EXERCISE 4.11

Creating a New Mail Contact

To create a new mail contact, follow these steps:

1. Click Start ➢ Programs ➢ Microsoft Exchange Server 2010 and then select Exchange Management Console.

2. Expand the Microsoft Exchange root object, then expand the Recipient Configuration folder, and then click the Mail Contact node.

3. In the Actions pane on the right, click the New Mail Contact link. The New Mail Contact Wizard starts.

4. Because you want to create a mail contact in this exercise, select the New Contact option and click Next to go to the Contact Information page, shown here.

5. Enter all the required information: first name and last name, display name, alias, and external email address. If you do not want to create the user object in the default Users container of Active Directory, click the Browse button to open the Select Organizational Unit dialog box. After you've correctly entered all the required information, click Next to continue to the summary page.

6. On the summary page, review all your configuration entries and click New if you are satisfied. You can click Back to change any of the entries you made. When you click New, the Completion page appears.

7. As always, Exchange displays the PowerShell code it used to create the mail contact. Click Finish to close the wizard.

If you have contact objects in Active Directory which are not mail-enabled, you can perform the steps detailed in Exercise 4.12 to mail-enable those contacts.

EXERCISE 4.12

Mail-Enabling an Existing Contact

Follow these steps to mail-enable an existing contact:

1. Click Start ➢ Programs ➢ Microsoft Exchange Server 2010 and then select Exchange Management Console.

2. Expand the Microsoft Exchange container, expand the Microsoft Exchange On-Premises container, expand the Recipient Configuration container, and then click the Mail Contact node.

3. In the Actions pane, click the New Mail Contact link. The New Mail Contact Wizard starts.

4. Select the User Mailbox option and click Next to continue to the User Type page.

5. On the Introduction page, select Existing Contact and then click Browse to open the Select Contact dialog box.

6. From the Select Contact dialog box, you will be able to select from a list of the contact objects in Active Directory that are not currently mail-enabled. Select a contact and click OK to return to the Introduction page. Click Next to go to the Contact Information page.

7. On the Contact Information page, you will be able to change only the alias and configure an external address. After you've correctly entered all the required information, click Next to continue to the summary page.

8. On the summary page, review all your configuration entries and click New.

9. Click Finish to close the wizard.

Modifying Mail Contacts

Now that you have mail contacts in your Exchange organization, you'll need to know how to manage them or modify their configurations.

Performing Basic Management with the EMC

When a mail contact is selected, you'll have mail-contact-specific options that become available on the right side of the console. Of course, all of these options are also available by right-clicking the appropriate mailbox and selecting them from the context menu.

The Disable option is actually used to remove all messaging attributes from the mail contact. If you click the Disable link in the EMC, you are prompted to consider your action and whether you want to continue. You can accomplish the same effect using the Disable-MailContact cmdlet.

The Remove option causes the contact object to be deleted from Active Directory. You can accomplish the same by using the Remove-MailContact cmdlet.

Managing Mailbox Properties

When you click the last item available for a mail contact, Properties, the mail contact's Properties dialog box opens to the General tab. We will examine each tab and the configurable items found on each in the following list:

General The General tab of the mail contact's Properties dialog box, shown in Figure 4.27, contains all the information about the mail contact. You have the option to change the Display Name field at the top of the tab and the Alias field at the bottom of the tab. Additionally, you can opt to have the mailbox hidden from view in the GAL, change the MAPI settings, or configure the custom attributes. Hiding the contact from the GAL can help prevent users from sending emails to the wrong email address. Some contacts may only be a forwarder for a smart phone that does not work with Exchange but has its own email address through the service provider.

Contact Information The Contact Information tab has the same basic configuration options mailbox users have and is shown in Figure 4.28. You can configure the following information on this tab:

- The mail contact's first and last names, and initials.
- A name that is displayed within Active Directory. (This setting does not impact the display name in the GAL.)
- A simple display name for the GAL that contains only ASCII characters and no Unicode characters.
- The user's web page URL.
- Notes about the mailbox and user that are not displayed anywhere else.

Address and Phone The Address and Phone tab has the same basic configuration options mailbox users have and is shown in Figure 4.29. From here, you can configure the user's address and contact information, such as their office, home, and mobile phone numbers.

FIGURE 4.27   General tab of a user in the Mailtask.com organization

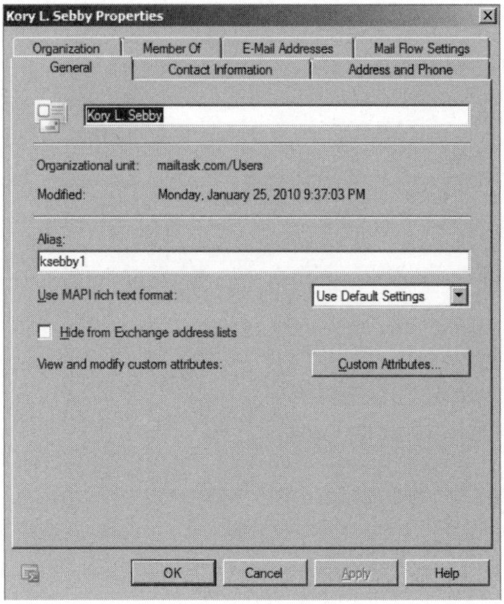

FIGURE 4.28   Contact information of the selected contact in the Mailtask.com organization

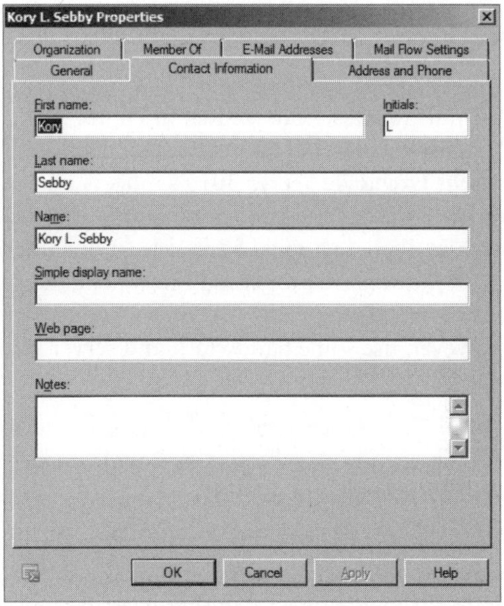

FIGURE 4.29 Empty address and phone information

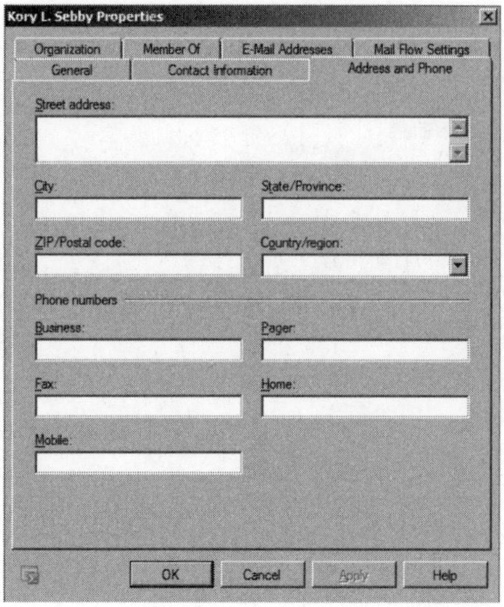

Organization   The Organization tab has the same basic configuration options that mailbox users have. From here you can configure organizational information fields about the mail contact, such as title, company, and manager. The Direct Reports field is not directly configurable but is populated using reverse links from Active Directory user account objects that have the Manager Field configured.

Member Of   The Member Of tab is a view-only listing of all groups that the mail contact is a member of.

E-Mail Addresses   The E-Mail Addresses tab, shown in Figure 4.30, allows you to add, remove, and edit internal and external email addresses assigned to the mail contact. The only type of email address that Exchange Server 2010 supports by default is SMTP, but you can configure custom types if needed in your organization by clicking the down arrow next to the Add button. Each mail contact must have at least one internal and one external email address associated with it to ensure proper mail flow. The internal address acts as a relay and an actual mailbox is not created. This way, the account doesn't take up valuable hard drive space. It will, however, use some bandwidth and server resources to process any emails to the contact.

Mail Flow Settings   The Mail Flow Settings tab of the mail contact's Properties dialog box allows you to configure specific settings that determine how messages to this mail contact are handled, shown for mailbox users in Figure 4.31.

When you select the Message Size Restrictions option and click the Properties button, the Message Size Restrictions dialog box opens. From there you configure specific receive size limits that are applied only to the mail contact and that override those applied at the organizational or SMTP connector level.

FIGURE 4.30 External email address configured as the Set as Reply address with the .com internal relay address

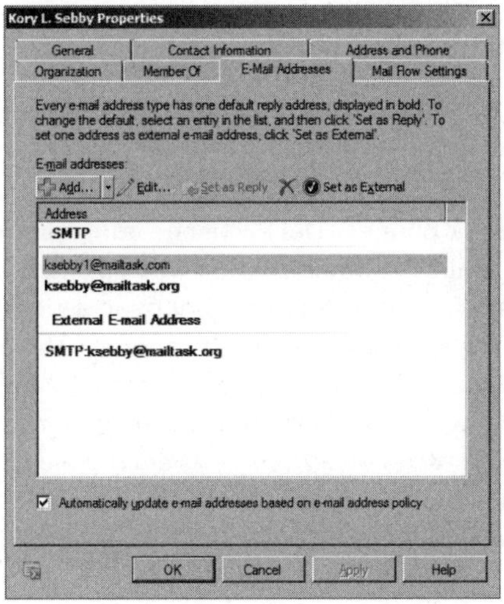

FIGURE 4.31 Displaying the two options available for configuration on the Mail Flow Settings tab

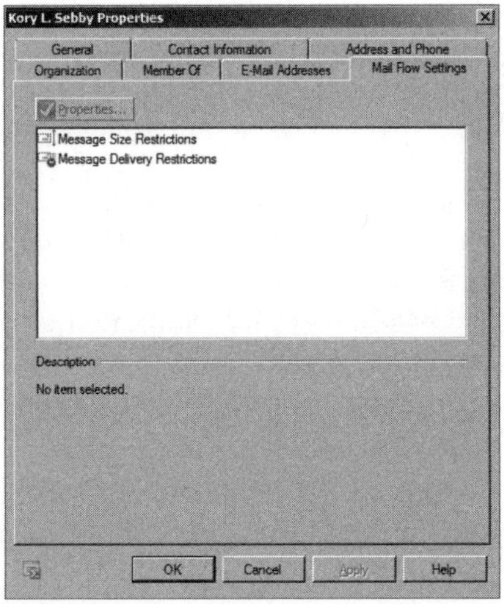

When you select the Message Delivery Restrictions option and click the Properties button, the Message Delivery Restrictions dialog box opens. From here you can configure which senders are allowed and which are not allowed to send messages to this mail contact. By default, there are no restrictions configured on the Message Delivery Restrictions dialog box.

⊕ **Real World Scenario**

Deciding When to Create Mail Contacts

Mail contacts can be a handy tool when you're working with an organization's mobile devices. We once consulted with an organization that migrated from a Novell and POP3 mail service to a Microsoft domain with an Exchange server. They had some executives that required email to reach their phones. The Exchange administrator had to find a way to get email to those phones while the organization came up with the funds to purchase the third-party software. Thankfully, the phone provider had a web-based version of the software that gave the users an email address for the phones. The administrator created a mail contact for each individual with a phone and pointed it to their service provider email address. From there, the web-based program allowed the reply address to be whatever email address they wanted. After everything was set up, the executives were able to receive their company's emails on their phones and reply with that same email address.

Moving Mailboxes

Managing mailboxes is a constant process of adding servers and users, migrating users between databases, and maintaining Exchange database health; therefore, it is essential to understand how to move a mailbox or a group of mailboxes. Most likely you will come up with a plan or method for placing user mailboxes on Exchange servers. Some place them on a specific mailbox server or in specific mailbox databases by department or geographical location or usage. Others place them depending on job role or service-level agreement (SLA) requirements. Regardless, moving mailboxes is simple enough that often entry-level Exchange administrators are tasked with completing the moves, using either the EMC or the EMS. There can be many reasons to moving a mailbox:

- **Organization mergers.** Two organizations may merge in to one and require the least amount of hardware changes. You may have to move mailboxes from one organization to another.

- **Hardware replacement.** A server may need to be replaced with new hardware. With a secondary server already up and running, you can move the mailboxes to the new server.

- **Database size.** You may need to move mailboxes to another database that is housed on a completely different server due to space constraints or load balancing between servers.

- **Corrupted mailboxes.** A mailbox or two may have become corrupted from a hardware failure or infection of some sort. You would want to move corrupted mailboxes to another database to avoid corrupting other mailboxes or from affecting them if you have to dismount the database for additional maintenance.

The most common and familiar method of moving mailboxes is to move them as needed using the GUI, in this case the EMC. There are two different move requests you will see. There is the local move request where you are moving the mailbox from one database to another, whether this is to maintain load balancing, moving the database to the user's new office, or moving it to another database on a newer server. The other type is a remove move request. These are created when a user mailbox is deleted, usually when an employee has been let go and no further emails are being sent to them. To move a mailbox from the EMC, perform the steps outlined in Exercise 4.13.

EXERCISE 4.13

Moving a Mailbox to a Local Database with the Exchange Management Console

Follow these steps to move a mailbox using the EMC:

1. Click Start ➤ Programs ➤ Microsoft Exchange Server 2010 and then select Exchange Management Console.

2. Expand the Microsoft Exchange container, expand the Microsoft Exchange On-Premises container, expand the Recipient Configuration container, and then click the Mailboxes node.

3. Select the mailbox to be moved in the center area of the window.

4. In the Actions pane, click the New Local Move Request link to start the New Local Move Request Wizard.

EXERCISE 4.13 *(continued)*

5. Click Browse to open the Select Mailbox Database dialog. Select the database you want to move the mailbox to and click OK. If you have Mailbox servers, you will see the available databases and which server they are on.

6. On the Move Settings page, you can set whether to ignore corrupted email messages during the move. This will allow you to skip items that are bad and move the mailbox data that is still consistent within the mailbox. If you do not set a limit or the limit is exceeded, the mailbox move will be aborted. Click Next.

7. The Configuration Summary page shows the target database and the amount of corrupted emails to skip before aborting the move. Click New to continue to the completion page.

New Local Move Request

- ☐ Introduction
- ☐ Move Options
- ☐ New Local Move Request
- ☐ Completion

New Local Move Request
The wizard will use the configuration below. Click New to continue.

Configuration Summary:

🖳 Kory Sebby ⊗

　　TargetDatabase: 'Executives'

To copy the contents of this page, press CTRL+C.

[Help]　　　　　　　　[< Back] [New] [Cancel]

8. At the completion page, click Finish.

After you complete a move request, you will notice that the icon in the middle pane of the console has a green arrow. This indicates that the mailbox was moved to another database. If you wish to move the same mailbox, you will have to review the Move Requests node and remove any previous move requests for that specific mailbox.

In the Move Requests node, you will see any recently uncleared requests, as shown in Figure 4.32. If you right-click the request, you can open the properties on it and view the time it was queued, the percentage of the mailbox moved, the date and time the move started, and what the size of the mailbox was during the move. You have to clear the request for the mailbox to be moved again.

In the initial release of Exchange 2010, you were required to delete the online archive before you are able to move the mailbox. This restriction is removed with Exchange 2010 Service Pack 1.

FIGURE 4.32   A move request displaying its current status

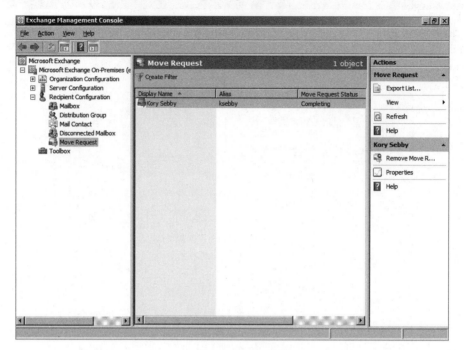

Using the Exchange Control Panel and Outlook Web App

At the beginning of the chapter, we mentioned that Exchange 2010 has made some improvements to Outlook Web App (OWA) and that there is now an administrative interface called the Exchange Control Panel (ECP). Many of the OWA improvements were to give the user more of the full Outlook client look and feel while using a web browser.

If you are familiar with Exchange 2007, you will notice that the first time a user logs in to OWA in Exchange 2010, they too are presented with options to set their time zone and enable the blind and low-vision option. In Figure 4.33, you will notice the changes to the OWA interface. Exchange Server 2010 Service Pack 1 also adds an updated ECP interface with additional features; however much of the functionality covered in this section works the same.

FIGURE 4.33 OWA and the added Favorites folder

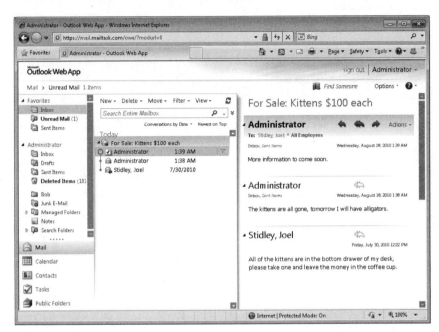

Managing Myself in the Exchange Control Panel

After you click the options link in the upper-right portion of the browser window, you can see the new menus on the left side as well as the new shortcuts, or links, on the far right side. This is shown in Figure 4.34

The Account menu, shown on the left side, is selected by default when you access options in OWA. You can edit your account or contact information. This will replicate within AD. On the right side of the page, you will notice the links shown in Figure 4.34. You can click the Tell people you're on vacation link to access the Automatic Replies setting. Clicking Forward your mail using inbox rules takes you to the Inbox Rules settings page. Clicking Learning how to get direct push e-mail on your mobile phone opens a help page on how to set up a phone to receive direct push email. The Connect Outlook to this account link opens a web page with additional links on how to connect Outlook to your email account. If you want to change your password, you can click the Change your password link. This takes you to the Change Password settings page. If you click Manage Your Organization, the drop-down menu in the top left changes to Organization under the Select what to manage options. You can also choose Learn About Windows PowerShell for a help page with links on how to install Windows PowerShell.

FIGURE 4.34 The new ECP and its layout with menus on the left and additional shortcuts (links) on the right

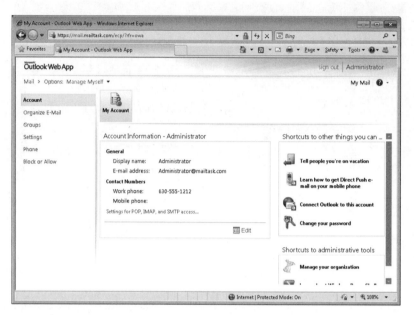

Each tab contains a set of options and configuration settings for your account:

Organize E-Mail By clicking the Organize E-Mail option, you will be able to view, add, edit, and delete your personal e-mail rules. Figure 4.35 and Figure 4.36 show the options for inbox rules.

FIGURE 4.35 Inbox Rules and any current rules that the account has

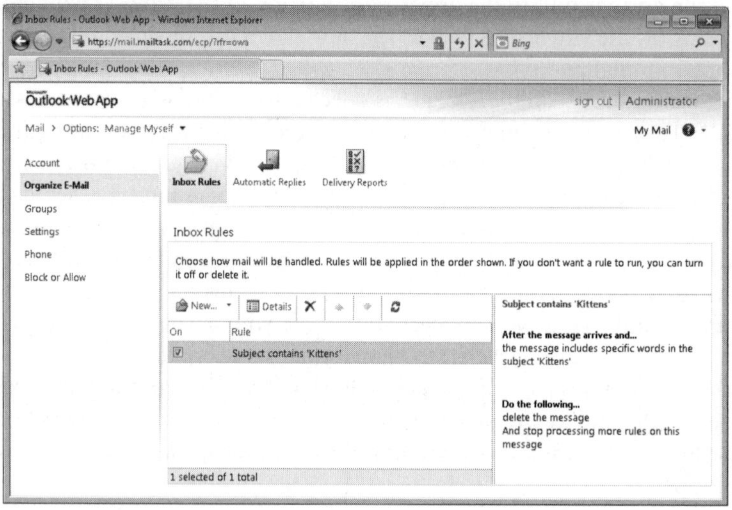

To set up an out of office reply or an automatic reply, you have to click the Automatic Replies tab shown in Figure 4.37 and Figure 4.38. Here you can modify the message sent to your organization and a separate message to those outside of your organization.

FIGURE 4.36   The New Inbox Rule creation page

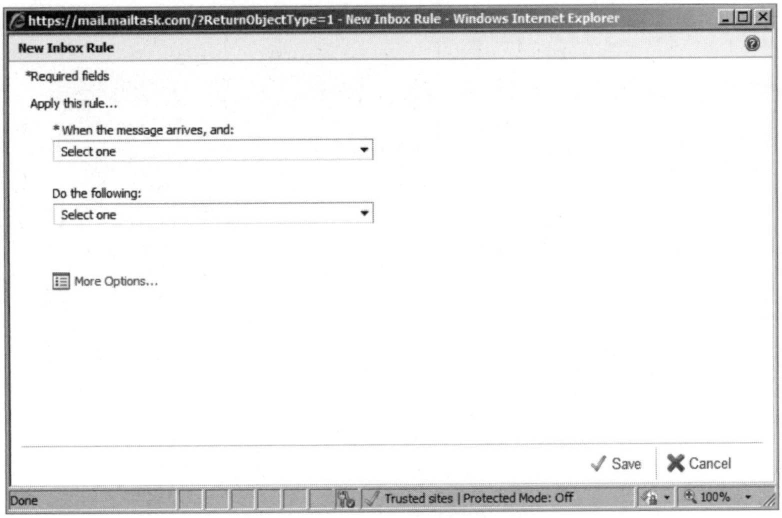

FIGURE 4.37   Currently disabled automatic replies

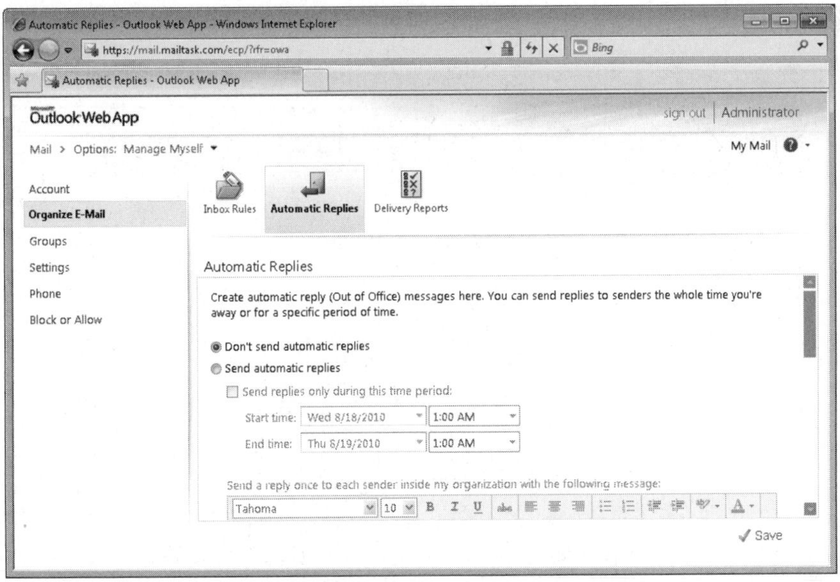

The Delivery Reports tab will display three search fields and a search results pane. This can be seen in Figure 4.39. Using the Delivery Reports field can help you troubleshoot or verify that emails are being received and sent out from the server. You can also see how many times you have sent certain emails. When you run a search, the search results will display anything that fell within your search filters.

FIGURE 4.38 Continued Automatic Replies page

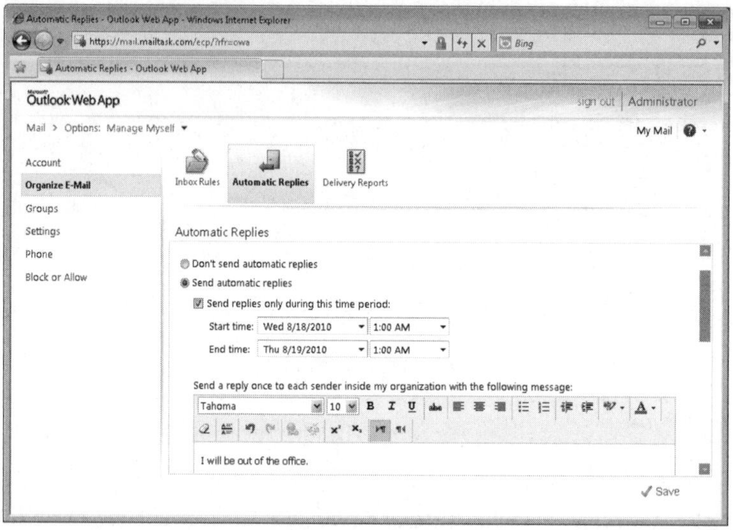

FIGURE 4.39 The Delivery Reports tab and the optional filters to search under

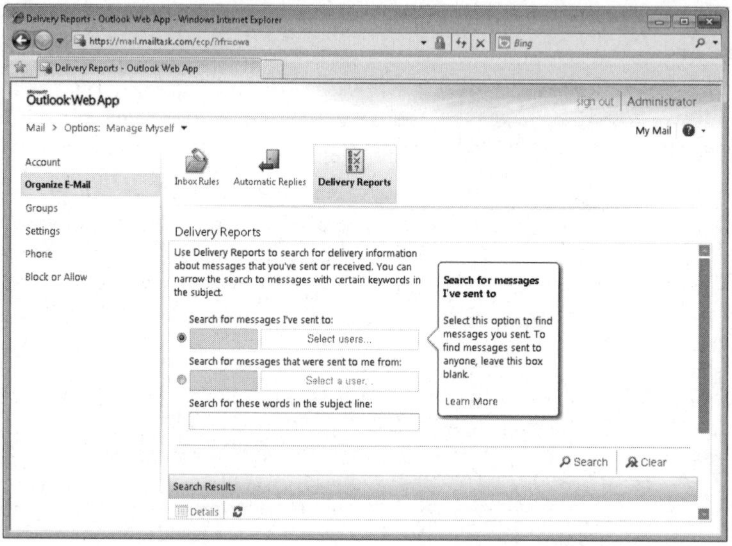

If you double-click a result, you can view specifics on it. You can see this in Figure 4.40. If you need to or would like to send the report to someone, you can do so by clicking E-Mail This Report.

FIGURE 4.40   A displayed report

Groups   The Groups option displays only one tab, Public Groups. Public groups are a bit like your personal distribution groups but you can give permissions to other users to manage them. Other users can also send requests to join these groups, just as you can request to join someone else's group. These groups can be found by using the Search Groups field. When a user creates a public group, they are automatically set as the group's manager. The default settings allow other users to request to be added to the group. You can also give users rights to create these public groups with RBAC, discussed in Chapters 2 and 11. An Exchange administrator has permissions to modify a public group created by another user as long as they are members of the Public Folder Management role group.

To create a group, click the New button in the Public Groups I Own section of the Public Groups tab, shown in Figure 4.41. In the New Group dialog box, you will see fields for a display name, an alias, and a description (Figure 4.42). The alias and display names must be filled in, otherwise the group cannot be created. You must also fill in the Ownership section, and you can have more than owner. You can add additional members further down in the Membership section.

The last option in the New Group dialog box is to configure the way requests are handled. You can choose to have requests automatically accepted, have them be approved by the owner or owners, and automatically rejected. You can also set whether requests to leave the group are accepted or not. This new addition can be very handy. Employees would be able to create a group that can be shared and viewed by the rest of the organization. No longer do they have to contact you to have a new public distribution group created or require assistance with exporting their personal group and having another user import it to their email account. Groups for special projects or events might be handled this way.

FIGURE 4.41 Public groups that the administrator belongs to and owns

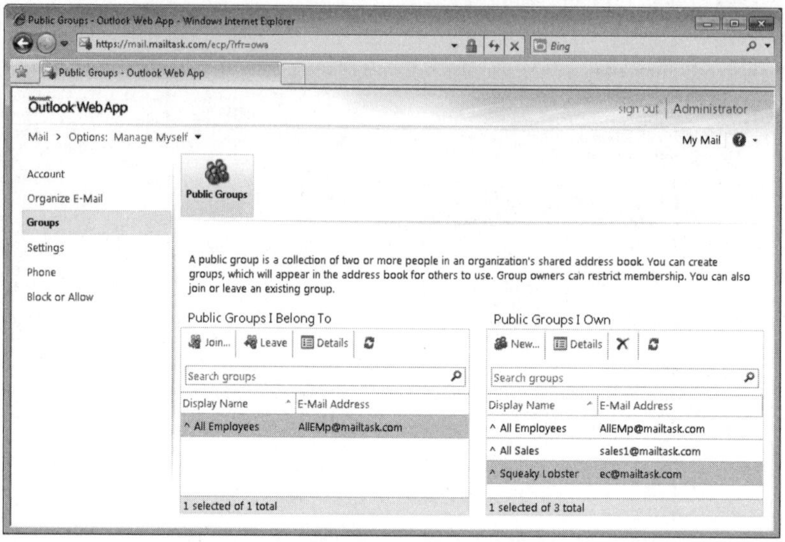

FIGURE 4.42 The New Group dialog box

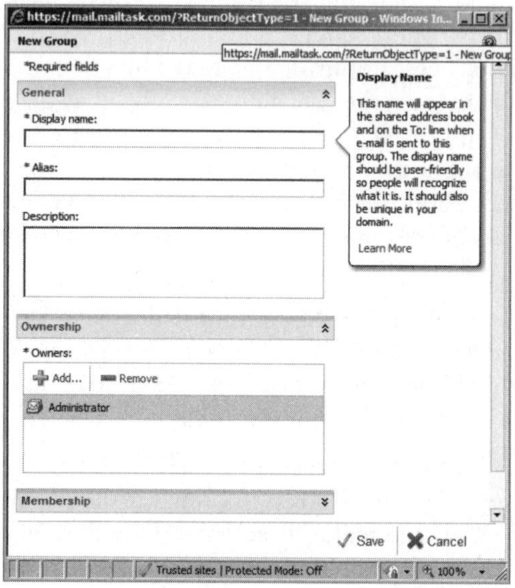

Settings The Settings option gives you access to the Mail, Spelling, Calendar, General, Regional, Password, and S/MIME tabs, as shown in Figure 4.43.

FIGURE 4.43 The tabs for the Settings option

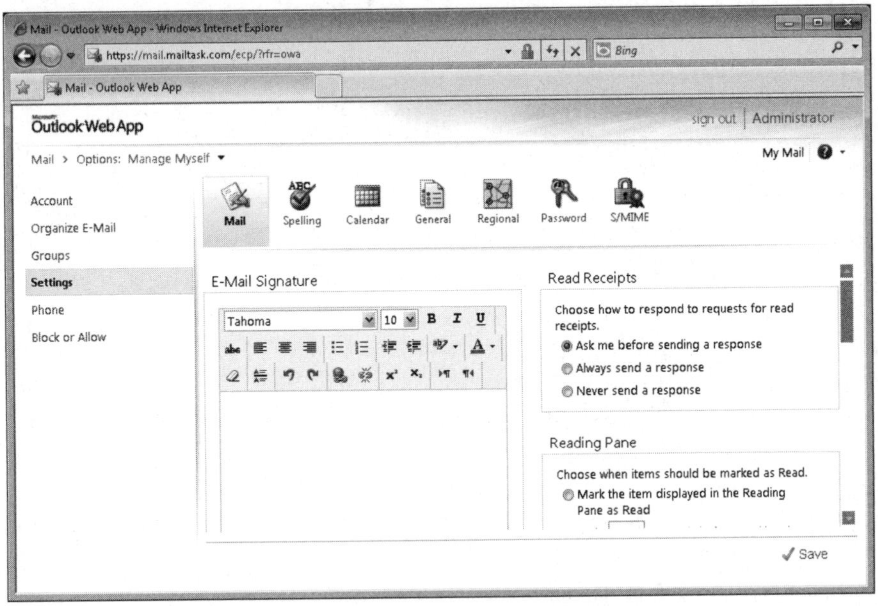

Mail On the Mail tab, you can set up your signature. You can choose the formatting of your emails when they are sent. You can also modify your messaging options and how your account processes read receipts. If you're tired of emails being marked as read when you change from one email to another, you can change the setting for that here as well. This tab is shown in Figure 4.43.

Spelling The options on the Spelling tab are pretty self-explanatory. You have the option of ignoring full uppercase words, words with numbers, and whether to check your spelling before sending an email.

Calendar The Calendar tab, shown in Figure 4.44, contains the appearance options. You can view just a day, a week, or the whole month. You can change the time reminders display and set whether you want to have reminders sent to a personal phone via text messages. There is also a link for troubleshooting your calendar issues.

General The General tab, as shown in Figure 4.45, allows you to modify the way names or email addresses are resolved. You can leave the default, which is the global address list, be the first place to look, or you can set your personal contacts to be the first place to look. You can also enable or disable the blind and low-vision experience setting.

FIGURE 4.44   Calendar options within ECP

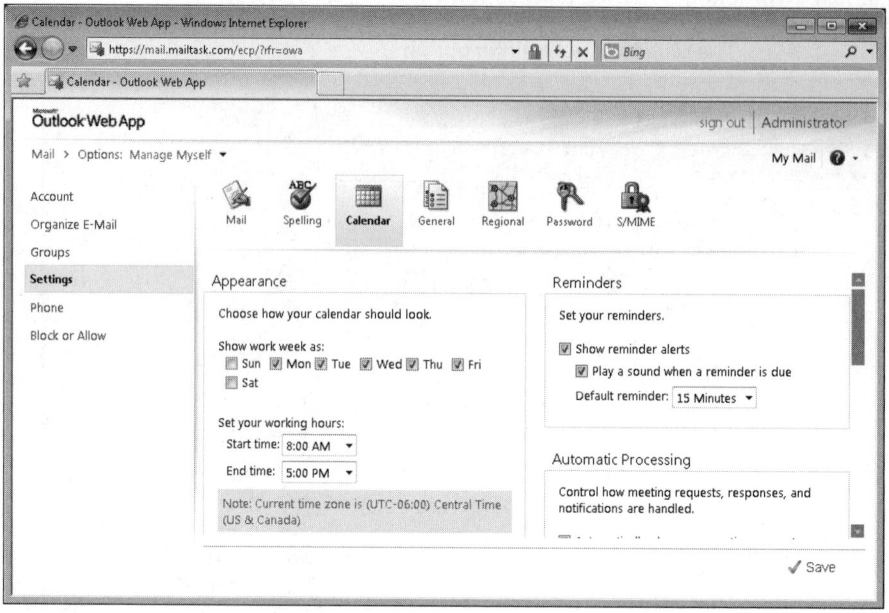

FIGURE 4.45   The default General tab defaults

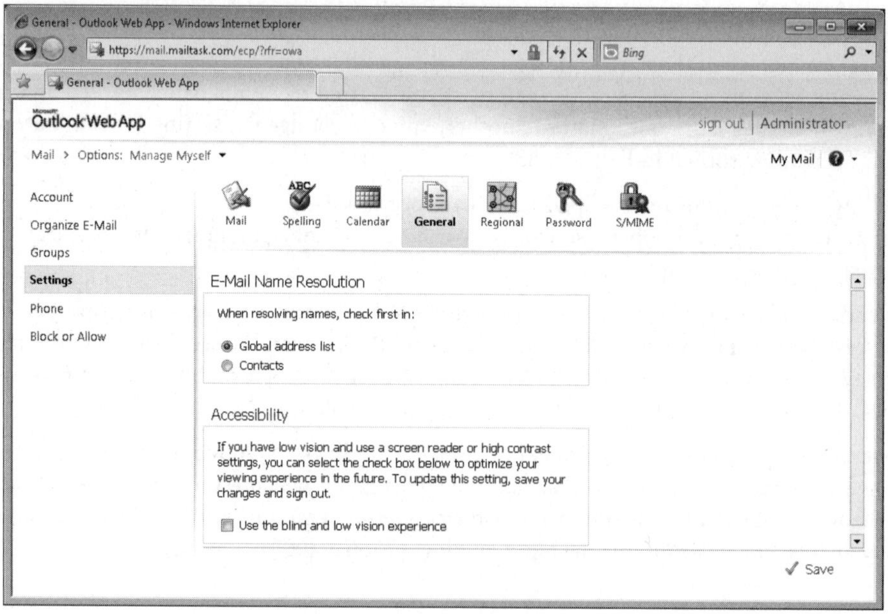

Regional   This tab, of course, has the options for your time zone and language, as shown in Figure 4.46.

FIGURE 4.46   The Regional tab for setting your time zone and language

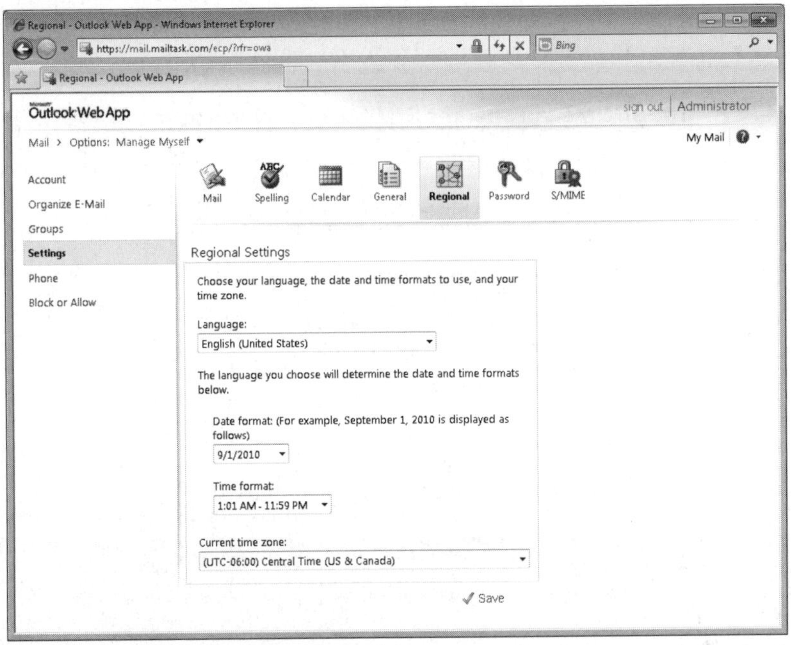

Password   This tab has the only option for changing your password.

S/MIME   On this tab, you can set up S/MIME. If you do not already have it installed, a link will display which will allow you to download it directly from the server. If you do have it installed and it's not working, you can reinstall it via the link displayed, as shown in Figure 4.47. S/MIME stands for Secure/Multipurpose Internet Mail Extensions. Deploying S/MIME requires that a public key infrastructure (PKI) be deployed to allow Exchange to encrypt and authenticate email messages from end to end. This helps protect your data from being read or tampered with during transit. Unfortunately, some clients may not support S/MIME; therefore it can be disabled. S/MIME is covered more in Chapter 6 "Configuring Security and Compliance."

Phone   The Phone option has two tabs to work with. The first tab is Mobile Phones. You can access your device recovery password, remotely wipe your phone in case you lost it or it was stolen, and block the device from receiving emails. If you really need to, you can remove it from the Exchange server. The last option on this tab is a link to help set up your mobile device with Exchange.

The Text Messaging tab, shown in Figure 4.48, allows you to set up text messages sent to a non-smartphone. These will be calendar reminders and other email notifications. These options come in handy when a user loses or needs their smartphone repaired and are using their personal phone.

Block or Allow Just like the option in the EMC User's Properties box, this option allows you to specify who you can receive messages from and send messages to.

FIGURE 4.47 The S/MIME tab after the S/MIME control has been installed

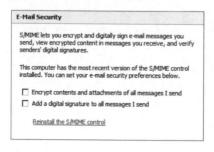

FIGURE 4.48 Text Messaging tab with the status turned off

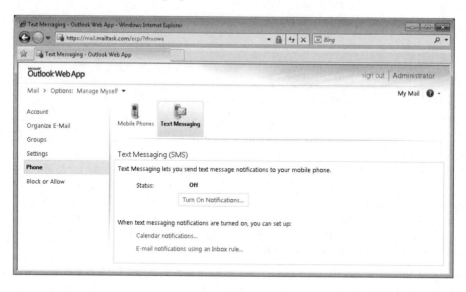

Managing an Organization with the Exchange Control Panel

You can select the organization from the Select what to manage drop-down menu on the Exchange Control Panel window or by clicking Manage Myself and selecting My Organization if SP1 has been deployed. This option allows an account with the appropriate permission to perform some common administrative tasks. As you can see in Figure 4.49, the administrator had additional menu choices: Users & Groups, Roles & Auditing, Mail Control, and Phone & Voice.

FIGURE 4.49   The Users & Groups option and its multiple tabs

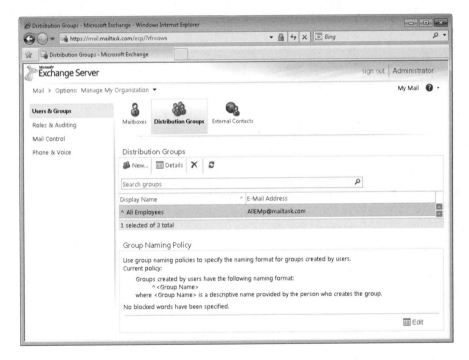

The following list describes the set of options in the tabs:

Users & Groups   Figure 4.49 shows that the tabs that are available for Users & Groups are Mailboxes, Distribution Groups, and External Contacts. In turn, each tab has a set of options to help make management of Exchange 2010 easier and accessible through a web browser.

Mailboxes   The first and default tab is the Mailboxes tab. You cannot create any new mailboxes under this tab. You can modify some settings of already existing mailboxes and see the options available to you, as shown in Figure 4.50.

FIGURE 4.50 The mailbox properties of a user with the E-Mail Options section expanded and the others collapsed

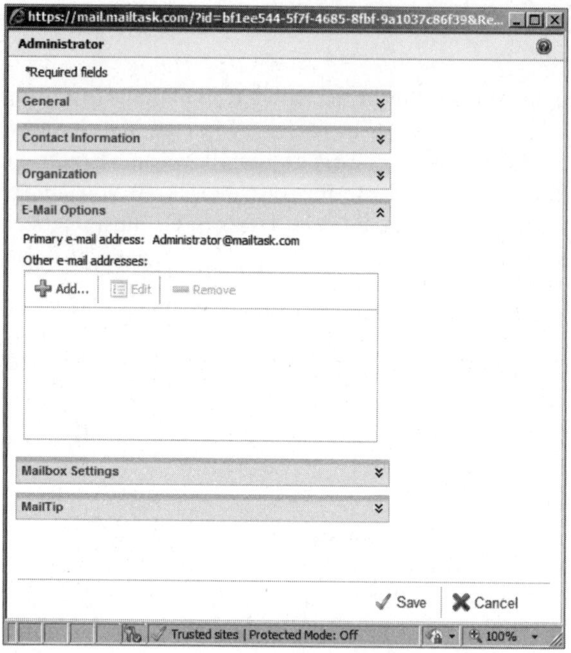

You can modify the contact and user information such as first and last names, contact information, and the organization to which they belong. You can also add additional email addresses for the user. If you have ever made a mistake when creating a username, you will see the usefulness of this tool when you are on vacation and need to quickly fix the mistake. If a new email domain is added to the Exchange organization, you may also need to add a new address.

Distribution Groups Exchange administrators account has access to all of the distribution groups within the organization. They can modify the access employees or users have to groups by accessing the User Roles under Users & Groups in EMC. This is useful for when employees leave the company and were defined as the owner of multiple groups. It could also be that a user created a group that no longer is needed, or they are out of the office and someone else needs to add to the group per a supervisor's request. You can also create new public groups and assign owners and add a list of members. You can review the Distribution Groups tab in Figure 4.51.

External Contacts As seen in Figure 4.52, you can create an external contact much as you can in the EMC without the wizard. The * beside a text box field means it's a mandatory entry.

FIGURE 4.51   The Distribution Groups tab and current groups that are in the organization

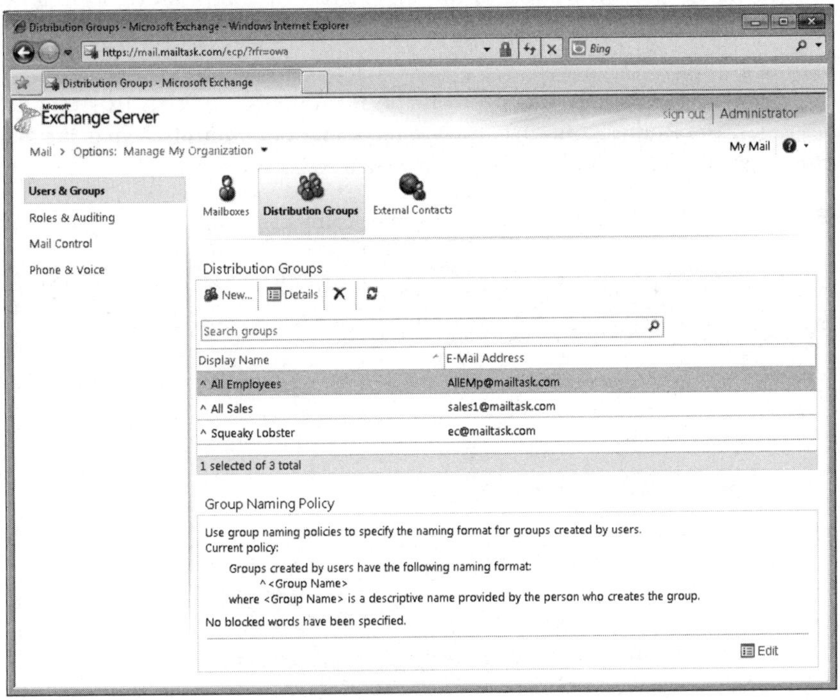

FIGURE 4.52   The organization's external contacts

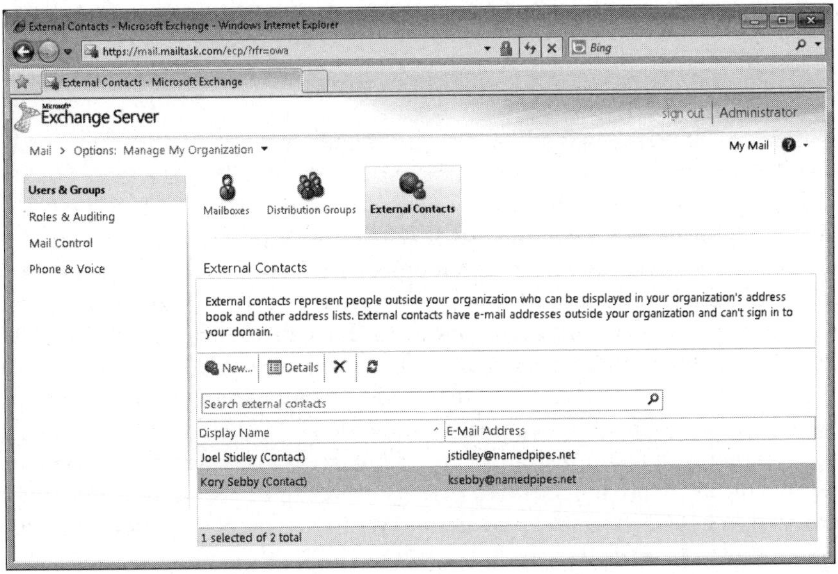

Administrator Roles The Administrator Roles tab gives you access to the roles within AD for Exchange. Double-clicking a role displays a description, what rights it has to the server, and the members of the group (see Figure 4.53). You can also add or remove members from the group.

Figure 4.53 shows that the tabs that are available for Roles & Auditing are Administrator Roles, User Roles, and Auditing. In turn, each tab has a set of options to help make management of Exchange 2010 easier and accessible through a web browser.

FIGURE 4.53 Displayed roles to which users or some assistants can be added

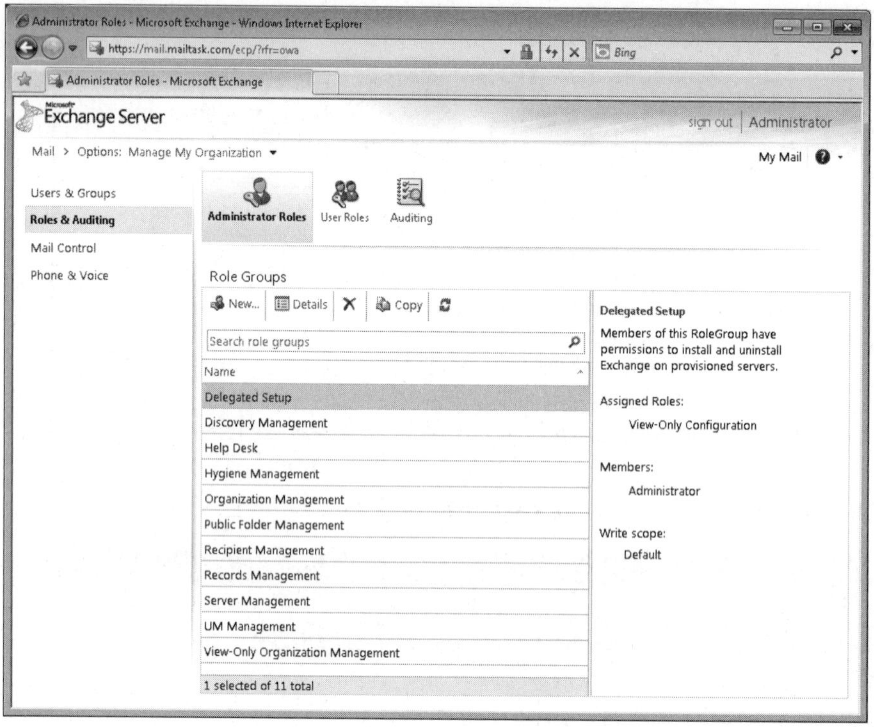

User Roles Figure 4.54 shows the User Roles tab. As you can see, there are some options that can be modified. Users can modify their own first, last, and display names. In addition, they can be allowed to remove themselves from distribution groups. You can give users additional roles with Exchange, such as My Distribution Groups, My Profile Information, and My Contact Information. If you decide to give these roles to the end user, it can help reduce the overall administration effort as users will be able to update basic information without any helpdesk or administrative intervention. Before an administrator can assign users these roles, they must have the Management Role permissions. RBAC management can be accessed by opening the Toolbox within EMC. For more information, please see the Role-Based User Access Control section in Chapter 2.

FIGURE 4.54   The roles in the organization that you can apply to other users

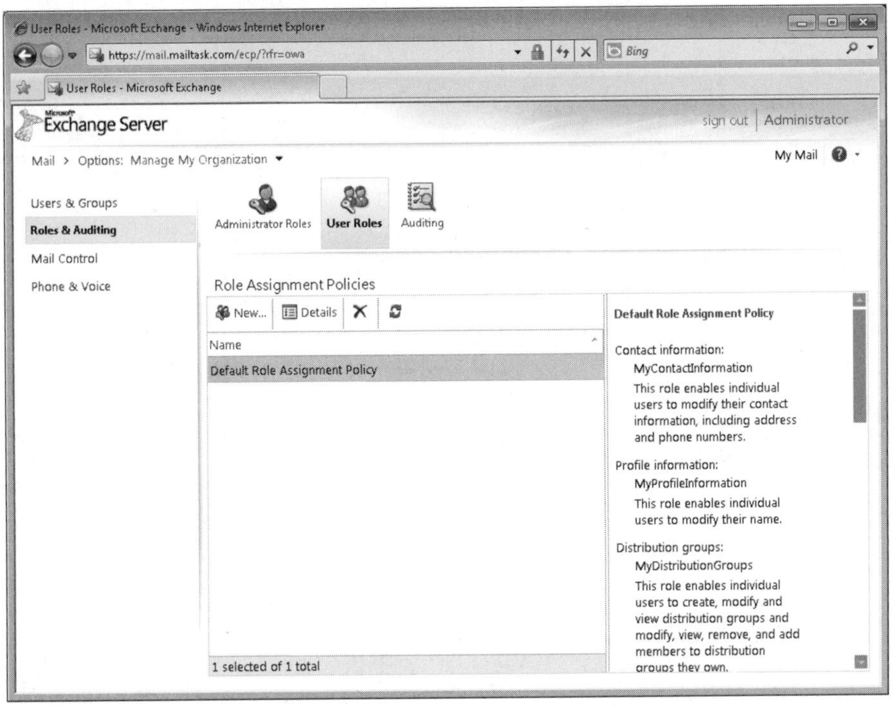

Managing Another User's Inbox with the Exchange Control Panel

The last addition within Exchange Control Panel is the ability to manage another user's inbox. Exchange administrators have access to this by default. However, they can give other users the same permissions using RBAC located in the EMC toolbox under Users & Groups. Just as with the managing myself options, you can change the settings of another user. If your supervisor left for vacation and forgot to set up an out-of-office message, you could set that message for them. In Figure 4.55, you can see the window that appears when you select another user from the drop-down menu. Another Exchange Control Panel will open, taking you directly to the user's options page. Here you can make the needed changes.

FIGURE 4.55 The manage another user search and selection page

Summary

This chapter emphasized the many different configurations and settings that can impact your users and the Exchange organization. Planning ahead and verifying the needs of your organization and its users can help reduce the number of administrative tasks that need to be performed.

Remember the improvements to the databases and the changes to the maintenance tasks that help increase performance and reduce overall downtime. The correct use of these items can reduce the amount of administrative tasks you need to perform because of corrupted mailboxes and database size limits.

Creating mailboxes for users can be simple and straightforward; however, you must pay attention to the needs of the organization and the performance of your server. Forgetting to set a limit on your users' mailboxes or having only one database that contains every mailbox can hinder your server's performance, and that will have an impact on the organization.

The Exchange Control Panel gives the ability to create new groups, modify users' information, and even create new mail-enabled contacts through a web browser.

Chapter Essentials

Understand how to create and manage databases. Make sure you review each of your database settings and their locations. By doing so, you can make management of the databases easier and ensure less downtime and a healthier server. Placing all of your mailboxes into one database may seem easier, but when the database reaches its size limit and your users complain, you will have to create additional databases.

Understand how to create and configuring mailboxes. After creating your mailboxes and configuring them, you will want to take the time to check on your server performance. You may find that you need to change a setting or two or move a mailbox to another database. Checking in with your users periodically can help keep your finger on the performance of the server as well as the needs of the organization.

Understand the benefits of using the Exchange Control Panel. Remember that you do not always have to log in to the EMC. You can use the Exchange Control Panel even when you're out of the office. You can still fix the minor spelling mistakes of an entry-level administrator. You can even manage another user's mailbox if they were having trouble with, for example, a rule deleting incoming emails.

Chapter

5

Configuring and Managing Public Folders

THE FOLLOWING TOPICS ARE DISCUSSED IN THIS CHAPTER:

✓ Creating public folders

✓ Managing and configuring public folders

✓ Public folder replication

Public folders provide a simplified and useful way to share information within groups or organizations. Public folders contain email messages, contacts, calendars, tasks, files, and other content. They are like mailboxes because they can be mail-enabled, allowing them to send and receive email messages. But unlike mailboxes, they are publicly accessible to many users at the same time. Public folders can also be replicated to other Exchange servers with a public folder database in the organization and thus provide redundancy and fault tolerance.

You access public folders using a structured naming system. There is only one MAPI-based public folder hierarchy or tree per organization; therefore, all user folders are included in it. This MAPI folder tree has two subtrees: Default Public Folders (IPM_Subtree) and System Public Folders (Non_IPM_Subtree). The Default Public Folders subtree contains all the user-created content. These folders are created and then nested under the root folder. For instance, a folder named Support might be created in the root of the Default Public Folders subtree for the support department. Nested within the Support folder might be other folders designed to store emails received about specific support cases or a shared contacts folder, which can be utilized for call escalation purposes.

The System folders include Schedule+ Free Busy, Offline Address Book and organizational forms for legacy Outlook clients such as Outlook 2003. Other System folders are created for Exchange configurations.

Each new Exchange server version has provided some enhancements to public folders up to Exchange Server 2007. With the introduction of Exchange 2007, public folders were deemphasized. Therefore, most public folder management functions disappeared from Exchange Management Console and moved to the Exchange Management Shell. As a result, most messaging professionals predicted that Microsoft would replace public folders with SharePoint. But a majority of the public folder management functionalities that were not available with Exchange 2007 Release to Manufacturer were incorporated within the Exchange Management Console in Exchange 2007 SP1 due to a strong demand for the product and negative feedback to Microsoft. This was primarily because public folders are an integral part of Exchange servers and they are fully functional without additional licenses. In addition, most administrators were familiar with managing Exchange and opposed to acquiring the knowledge and skills required to manage SharePoint.

Microsoft SharePoint is a true document management and collaboration tool with document versioning, built-in workflow methodology, and notification of content changes. Using public folders can be described as an easy method to organize and share documents within an organization without the bells and whistles of SharePoint. While the debate goes on,

Microsoft currently supports public folders and will continue to do so in the short term. This explains why we have dedicated a chapter to public folders in this book.

While Exchange 2010 did introduce several enhancements compared to Exchange 2007, it is fair to say that public folders in Exchange 2010 did not benefit from any major improvements or overhaul.

It must be noted that public folders are not installed by default with an Exchange 2010 installation. They are considered optional. Organizations with Outlook 2007 or Outlook 2010 clients do not require public folders for Free Busy and Offline Address Book functionality. These functions are performed by the Autodiscover service, Exchange System Attendant, and Exchange File Distribution Service. However, any pre–Outlook 2007 client will require public folders. It's strongly suggested that organizations continue to use public folders until all their Outlook clients are fully migrated to OL2007 or OL2010.

This chapter provides the information necessary to install, manage, and configure public folders. It explores the different methods to perform these tasks, leveraging the Exchange Management Console, Public Folder Management Console, the Exchange Management Shell (PowerShell), Outlook clients (2007 and 2010), Outlook Web App, and other tools such as ExFolders. The chapter also discusses public folder replication.

Now that you understand what a public folder is, let's begin with creating a public folder database that will serve as the repository for all public folders.

Creating Public Folders

A public folder strategy must be well defined within your organization because it enables ease of administration as well as efficient and streamlined access to information. Several deployment scenarios can be considered based on the amount of public folder usage. A public folder database can be created on the mailbox server or dedicated public folder servers can be deployed.

If you have Exchange Server versions that are prior to 2007, or if you have Exchange clients prior to Outlook 2007 and Entourage clients, you are required to deploy a public folder database for schedule + free busy data, the Offline Address Book and Organizational Forms. The public folder database is created automatically during the setup of the first Exchange 2010 Mailbox server role.

During the installation of a new Exchange 2010 environment, you are prompted during the setup of the first Mailbox server with the following question: Do you have any client computers running Outlook 2003 and earlier or Entourage in your organization?

A yes answer will lead to a public folder database creation. If you answer no, there will not be a public folder database created. You will not be prompted with the question during the installation of a second Mailbox server.

A public folder database can subsequently be created, even if one was not automatically created during the setup of the first Mailbox server role.

Creating a Public Folder Database

A public folder database can be created using either the Exchange Management Console (EMC) or the Exchange Management Shell (EMS).

Using the Exchange Management Console

Let us first explore the EMC. The steps in Exercise 5.1 assume that you have been granted the right permissions (organization management, server management) to create a public folder database.

EXERCISE 5.1

Creating a Public Folder Database

Follow these steps to create a public folder database:

1. Click Start ➤ Programs ➤ Microsoft Exchange 2010 and select Exchange Management Console.

2. Expand the Microsoft Exchange container, expand the Microsoft Exchange On-Premises container, expand the Organization Configuration container, and then click the Mailbox node.

3. In the Actions pane, click New Public Folder Database. You can also right-click Mailbox and select New Public Folder Database.

4. The introduction page of the New Public Folder Database Wizard appears. Enter EX02-PF01 in the Public Folder Database Name field. Then select the server on which the database will be created. You can click Browse and select EX02 and then click OK. Then Click OK. Then click Next

5. On the Set Paths page, select where the database file and the log files will be located. Setup creates a default path. You need to ensure that you have selected the right location for the database file path by typing the location or filename in the text box. Verify that you have selected the right location or enter the location in the Log Folder Path text box.

6. The Mount This Database check box is enabled by default. It's typical to mount the database after creation. There might be circumstances in which a newly created database may not be mounted. In those instances, you will unselect the Mount This Database check box. Click Next.

7. Review your settings on the New Public Folder Database page. After you ensure that your configurations are correct, click New to create the new public folder database. Otherwise, click Back to make changes to your configuration. Clicking Cancel will close the wizard without creating the database.

8. On the Completion page, review the status. Click Finish to close the wizard if the status is completed. If the status is Failed, click Back to make changes to your configuration.

Using the Exchange Management Shell

You can use the EMS to create a public folder database by leveraging the **New-PublicFolderDatabase** cmdlet. You must specify the database name as well as the server name. Other parameters such as the database file name and path and the database log file path are optional. Default values are used if they are not explicitly specified.

After the database is created, you need to run the Mount-Database cmdlet to mount the database.

As an example, use the following command to create a database called Dallas-PF01 on Server EX02 with specific file paths:

```
New-PublicFolderDatabase Dallas-PF02 Server EX02 -EdbFilePath E:\Databases\
PF101\PF101.edb -LogFilePath D:\Logs\PF101
```

Let's now see how to remove a public folder database.

Removing Public Folder Databases

You must carefully weigh the decision to remove any active database from your Exchange organization to avoid the unintended consequences that may cause you several sleepless nights, not to mention your job. When contemplating the removal of a public folder database, you must give additional consideration to the following options:

- A public folder database with data cannot be removed. You must move the data to another public folder database or delete the data first.

- A public folder database cannot be removed if a mailbox database is associated with it. You must associate the mailbox database to another public folder database.

- The last public folder database of an organization cannot be removed if you have Outlook 2003 users or Exchange 2003 servers or previous versions. Furthermore, the last public folder cannot be removed if Offline Address Book (OAB) is configured for public folder distribution. After the last public folder database is removed, only Outlook 2007 or later clients and Outlook Web App can connect to the Exchange organization.

You can remove public folder databases using either the EMC or the EMS. In Exercise 5.2, you will remove a public folder database in the EMC.

EXERCISE 5.2

Removing a Public Folder Database

Follow these steps to remove a public folder database:

1. Click Start ➢ Programs ➢ Microsoft Exchange 2010 and select Exchange Management Console.

2. Expand the Microsoft Exchange container, expand the Microsoft Exchange On-Premises container, expand the Organization Configuration container, and then click the Mailbox node.

3. Click the Database Management tab. On the result pane, select the public folder database that you would like to remove.

EXERCISE 5.2 *(continued)*

4. Click Remove in the Actions pane. You are presented with a message confirming that you want to remove the database. Click Yes.

Whether you remove a public folder database with EMC or EMS, you will receive a warning because removing the public folder database does not remove the actual database files. The files must be manually removed. You need to navigate to the database file location that you specified during creation or to the default file location, *<Exchange Installation Path>\V14\Mailbox\<public folder database name>*, to remove the files.

> Use the `Remove-PublicFolderDatabase` cmdlet in EMS to remove a public folder database.
>
> To remove a public folder database named SalesEngine, you would issue the following command: `Remove-PublicFolderDatabase -Identity "SalesEngine"`. Enter **Y** for yes when a message appears to ask you to confirm your action.

You have learned how to create and remove a public folder database, so you are ready to create public folders that will reside in the database. But before you create the first public folder, it is imperative to have a strategy for public folder hierarchy because of its direct impact on public folder replication and permissions.

Designing a Public Folder Hierarchy

A public folder hierarchy or public folder tree is a list of public folders and their subfolders that are stored in the default public folder stores on the Exchange servers in an Exchange organization. The hierarchy also includes the name of the server on which a copy of each folder resides. Because the public folder hierarchy exists in Active Directory as a separate object, it does not contain any of the actual items in your various public folders. There is one organization-wide public folder hierarchy object.

You must consider *top-level folders* and subfolders when you design your public folder hierarchy for ease of administration and permissions. You want to have a few top-level folders with many nested subfolders. This is called having a deep hierarchy. A public folder hierarchy with many top-level folders and few subfolders is called a wide hierarchy. The deep hierarchy scales and performs better with public folder replication and client actions.

Even though public folder permissions is addressed later in this chapter in the section "Managing Public Folder Permissions," a great public folder hierarchy design helps streamline the process of applying and delegating permission to public folders. As a best practice, public folder permissions are most efficiently administered by leveraging Active Directory groups.

In general, a public folder hierarchy will reflect a company's organizational structure, whether geographic or functional. This means that in a geographic distribution, top-level folders might be labeled NA, East, EMEA, and so forth. Then subfolders might be named HR, Marketing, Support, and Research. In a functional structure, top-level folders are named based on functions, such RD, Sales, HR, or business units.

Once you have a plan in place, you can begin to create and manage public folders.

Creating Public Folders

There are several ways to create public folders in an Exchange 2010 environment: using EMC, EMS, Outlook, and Outlook Web App (OWA). Even though you are able to create public folders in EMC and EMS, you have to use a client such as Outlook or OWA to create the content of public folders.

You must have the right permissions, such as Public Folder Management role, to create a public folder. It is best practice to restrict the right to create a top- level public folder to a group and then manage the group membership as needed. The new Exchange 2010 *Role Based Access Control (RBAC)* is leveraged to that end, and *RBAC* enables you to control what users in your Exchange organization can and cannot do at a granular and broad level. See Chapter 6, "Configuring Security, Compliance, and Policies," for more information.

With EMC, public folders are created using the Public Folder Management Console (PFMC).

Using the Public Folder Management Console

The *Public Folder Management Console (PFMC)* is used for the creation, configuration, and management of public folders. It is designed like EMC with a public folder pane, a result pane, and an Actions pane. In Exercise 5.3, you will create a public folder in the PFMC.

EXERCISE 5.3

Creating a Public Folder in the PFMC

Follow these steps to create public folders using the PFMC:

1. Click Start ➤ Programs ➤ Microsoft Exchange 2010 and select Exchange Management Console.

2. Expand the Microsoft Exchange container, expand the Microsoft Exchange On-Premises container, and then click the Tools node.

3. In the result pane, select Public Folder Management Console. In the Actions pane, select Open Tool.

4. In the public folder tree of the PFMC, navigate to Default Public Folders, and then select the default public folder for a top-level folder or select any other folder as the parent for the new public folder.

5. In the Actions pane, click New Public Folder. The New Public Folder Wizard opens.

6. On the introduction page you must type the name of the new public folder in the Name field. Then verify the path in the grayed-out box. If this box shows a backslash (\), the public folder that you are creating will be a top-level public folder. You cannot change the path unless you close the wizard, select the right public folder as the parent, and start the wizard again.

7. Click New. Then review your selection on the Completion page and click Finish to close the wizard.

Using the EMS to Create a Public Folder

The cmdlet to create a top-level public folder is `New-PublicFolder -Name "Public Folder Name"`. This command creates a top-level folder in the public folder database on the local or closest Mailbox server. Exchange uses site cost to determine the closest server.

Additional parameters such as server name and parent folder name can be specified with the following cmdlet:

```
New-PublicFolder -Name "Public Folder Name" -Path \ParentFolder
 -Server "Server Name"
```

To create a public folder named Sales Engineering in the Sales folder on server E14MB1B, run this command:

```
New-PublicFolder -Name "Sales Engineering" -Path \Sales -Server "EX02"
```

Using Outlook

You can access public folders in Exchange 2010 with Outlook 2010, Outlook 2007, Outlook 2003, and IMAP4 clients. You will learn how to create a public folder using Outlook 2007 in Exercise 5.4.

EXERCISE 5.4

Creating a Public Folder in Outlook

Follow these steps to create public folders using Outlook 2010, Outlook 2007, and Outlook 2003:

1. In Outlook 2007 or 2010, make sure the folder list is displayed. Next, double-click Public Folders in the folder list, or click the plus sign just in front of Public Folders. Notice that the plus sign becomes a minus sign when a folder is expanded to show the folders within it. You've now expanded the top-level folder for public folders, which contains two subfolders: Favorites and All Public Folders. Expand the All Public Folders folder and you'll see that it has at least one subfolder. If your organization uses public folders, you probably have at least one other subfolder here as well.

EXERCIESE 5.4 *(continued)*

2. Right-click the Default Public Folders node. Then select New Public Folder from the context menu to open the new public folder's Properties dialog box. You can also select the parent folder and select New Public Folder from the File menu.

3. This starts the New Public Folder Wizard. In this wizard you are prompted to assign a name to the new public folder.

4. Click New and then the Finish button.

A public folder created in Outlook holds email and posted items, which is the default selection. Email items are messages. Posted items contain a subject and text. You can post an item in a folder designed to hold posts without dealing with messaging attributes such as the item's recipient.

To post an item, click the down arrow near the New icon on the main Outlook window and select Post In This Folder from the drop-down menu. If you wanted to create a public folder to house calendar items, contact items tasks, or notes items, you'd need to select the correct type of public folder contents from the Folder Contains drop-down list.

Using Outlook Web App

Creating a public folder in OWA is somewhat similar to the process that was just covered for Outlook 2007. Exercise 5.5 will show you the steps.

You learned how to create and remove a public folder database using EMC and EMS. Then you learned to create a public folder in EMC, EMS, and also through an Outlook 2007 client and OWA. How do you manage and configure the public folder that you just created? This brings us the next sections, which cover the management and configuration of public folders.

EXERCISE 5.5

Creating a Public Folder in OWA

Follow these steps to create a public folder using OWA:

1. Open Internet Explorer and login to OWA with an administrator account.

2. Select Public Folders in OWA.

3. In the public folder tree, right-click the parent folder or Public Folders to create a top-level folder.

4. Select Create New Folder and then chose the content type of the folder: mail, calendar, contact, task, and notes.

EXERCISE 5.5 *(continued)*

5. Enter the folder name in the empty box with the folder icon. Then enter or click anywhere.

Managing and Configuring Public Folders

We approach the following sections with the same methodology we used with the creation of public folders. The tools used in the previous section, namely EMC, PFMC, and EMS, will be leveraged again. Most public folder management can be performed at the Exchange Server level using EMS, EMC, and PFMC. Some client-specific configuration and management tasks are performed using Outlook or OWA. It must be noted that the entire configuration performed in EMC and PFMC can be performed in EMS.

Public folders can inherit some of their configuration, such as limits, replication, and referrals from the public folder database. Let's first review them. We do not cover general database tasks because they are covered in other chapters, but we do focus on the tasks that pertain to public folders.

Configuring a Public Folder Database

To display the public folder database properties, expand Organization Configuration in the EMC. Then select Mailbox and click the public folder database. In the Actions pane, click Properties. The public folder database properties appear, as shown in Figure 5.1.

FIGURE 5.1   Public folder database properties

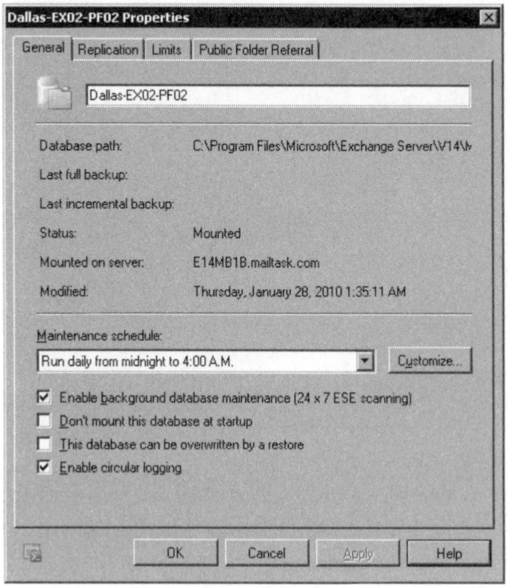

There are four tabs in the Properties dialog box for the public folder database: General, Replication, Limits, and Public Folder Referral.

General   This tab is used to change the name and configure the maintenance schedule of the database. The settings on this tab are similar to the settings for mailbox databases.

Replication   You can configure the database replication interval and the replication time limit and message size limit. By default, the interval is set to "always run" with a time limit of 15 minutes, as shown in Figure 5.2. The time limit can be configured for from 1 minute to 2,147,483,647 minutes. You can also select to customize the replication interval. The replication message size can be set from 1 KB to 2 GB. It is set to 300 KB by default, which means that Exchange sends replication messages of 300 KB in size. Public folder changes that are less than 300 KB are accumulated until they reach 300 KB in size before they are sent to other public folder servers in the form of 300 K email messages. This is extremely important because it could adversely impact replication, especially if you have users posting very large files. You may have to increase the replication message size.

The settings are automatically inherited by the public folders that are created in the database.

FIGURE 5.2   Public folder database replication properties

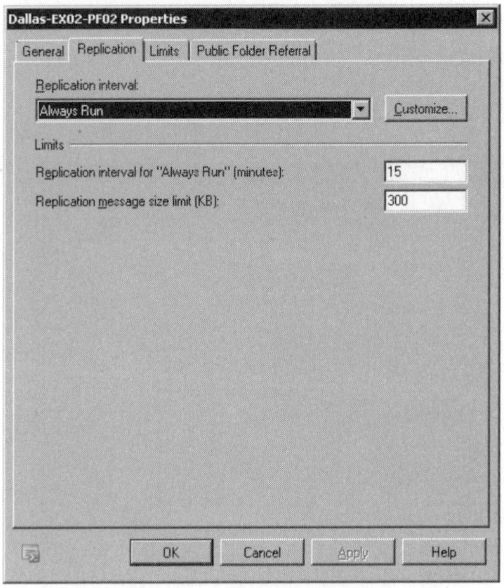

Limits   The Limits tab is where you would set storage limits, warning message intervals, deletion settings, and age limits for the public folders created in the database. These settings, illustrated in Figure 5.3, are inherited by the public folders.

Public Folder Referral   The settings on the *Public Folder Referral* page defines how a public folder replica is accessed by a client application. By default, Use Active Directory Site Costs is checked. This selection clears the custom list and costs. But you have the ability to define a custom list with the corresponding cost.

The cost, which is a number ranging from 1 to 100, is the likelihood of a replica server being used based on a determination by Exchange 2010 routing. Least-cost routing is leveraged. Therefore, the smallest-cost server has the highest likelihood of being used. Consequently, the highest-cost server is less likely to be used. Figure 5.4 shows a default public folder referral configuration. These settings are also inherited by the public folders.

You can use EMS to perform the same configuration. The commands will be provided in the section "Configuring and Managing Public Folders with EMS" later in this chapter.

FIGURE 5.3   Public folder database limits

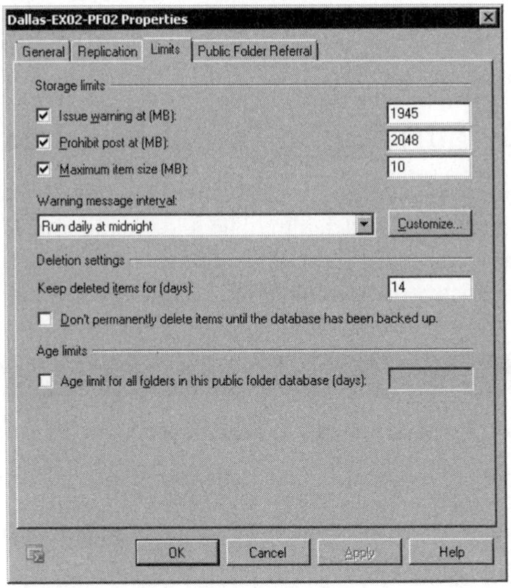

FIGURE 5.4   Public folder database referral

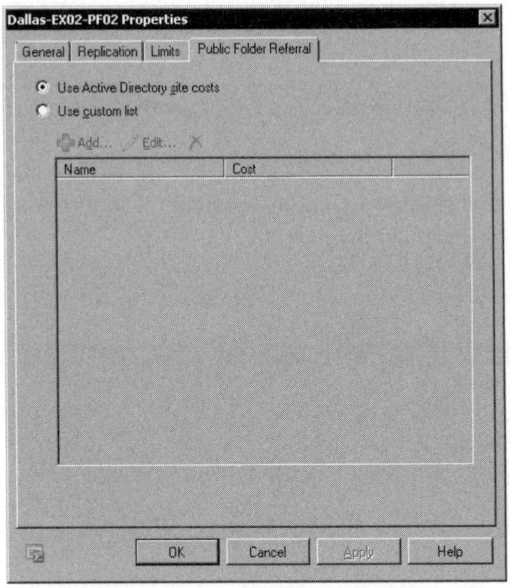

In addition to configuring the public folder database, you may have to change the default public folder database for a mailbox database. This usually occurs in large multisite environments, environments with dedicated public folder servers, or environments with several public folder databases.

Changing the Default Public Folder Database

For clients such as Outlook to view, create, delete, and obtain public folder contents, each mailbox database is configured with a default public folder database. To meet organizational design needs, you may have to associate a mailbox database with another public folder database. Exercise 5.6 will show you how to change the default public folder database.

EXERCISE 5.6

Changing the Default Public Folder Database

Follow these steps to change the default public folder database:

1. Click Start ➤ Programs ➤ Microsoft Exchange 2010 and select Exchange Management Console.

2. Expand the Microsoft Exchange container, expand the Microsoft Exchange On-Premises container, expand the Organization Configuration container, and then click the Mailbox node.

3. In the Details pane, select the mailbox database, and then click properties in the Actions pane under the mailbox database name.

4. In the mailbox database settings, click the Client Settings tab.

5. Click Browse next to the Default Public Folder Database box.

6. In Select Public Folder Database, select the new public folder database from the list of public folder databases and then click OK.

7. Click OK..

With EMS, you will execute the following cmdlet to change the default public folder database:

```
Set-MailboxDatabase -Identity "Mailbox Database Name" -PublicFolderDatabase
"Public Folder database name"
```

To change the default public folder database to EX02-PF03 on mailbox database EX01-MB01, use this command:

```
Set-MailboxDatabase -Identity "EX01-MB01" -PublicFolderDatabase "EX02-PF03"
```

Now that we have completed management and configuration in the EMC, we will cover public folder configuration using PFMC and EMS.

Using PFMC to Configure and Manage Public Folders

In Exchange 2010, you can use the Public Folder Management Console from the EMC tools to perform some public folder management and configuration tasks. But the range of tasks that can be performed is somewhat limited compared to EMS, which offers the bulk of public folder management via cmdlets. To do other tasks, you'll need some other tools, such as Outlook or OWA to manage individual folders.

After the Public Folder Management Console is launched and connected to a public folder server, you can perform these management functions:

- Update the public folder hierarchy
- Add and remove public folders
- *Mail-enable* and *mail-disable* public folders
- View and modify public folder properties
- View and modify *public folder replicas*
- Update public folder content
- Manage Send As permissions for mail-enabled public folders

We will cover the preceding items in detail, but we will cover public folder replication topics such as updating the public folder hierarchy, public folder replicas, and public folder content in the section "Replicating Your Public Folders" later in this chapter.

Figure 5.5, Figure 5.6, and Figure 5.7 show different views of the PFMC.

Upon launching PFMC, you are connected to a public folder database on a mailbox server. You can connect to a different server for management. To do so, click Connect To Server in the Actions pane (see Figure 5.5) and browse to the new server. Select the public folder server to which you need to connect.

Expand the Default Public Folder tree to show the public folders in the environment. You can manage the properties of public folders by selecting a folder in the result pane. This is illustrated in Figure 5.6.

The option to *mail-disable* a public folder is shown in Figure 5.7, as is the option to manage *Send As permissions* for only mail-enabled public folders.

FIGURE 5.5 Public Folder Management Console

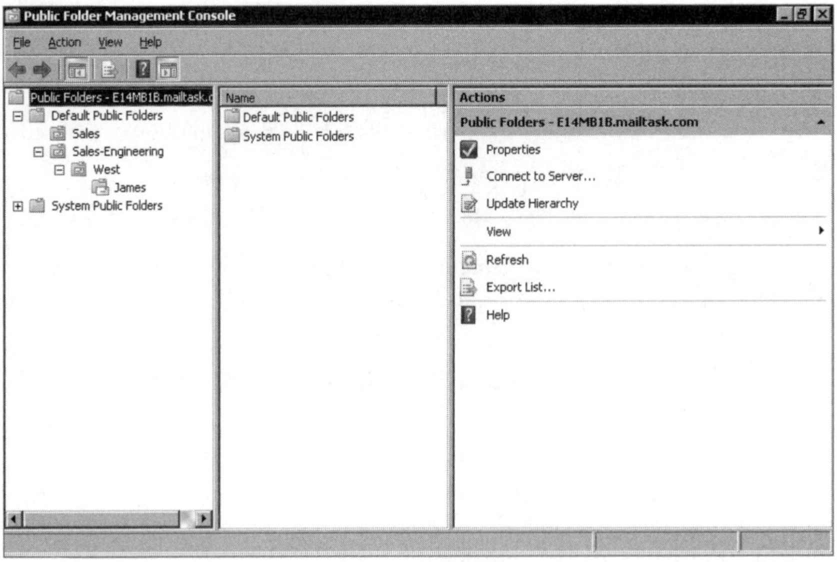

FIGURE 5.6 PFMC result pane

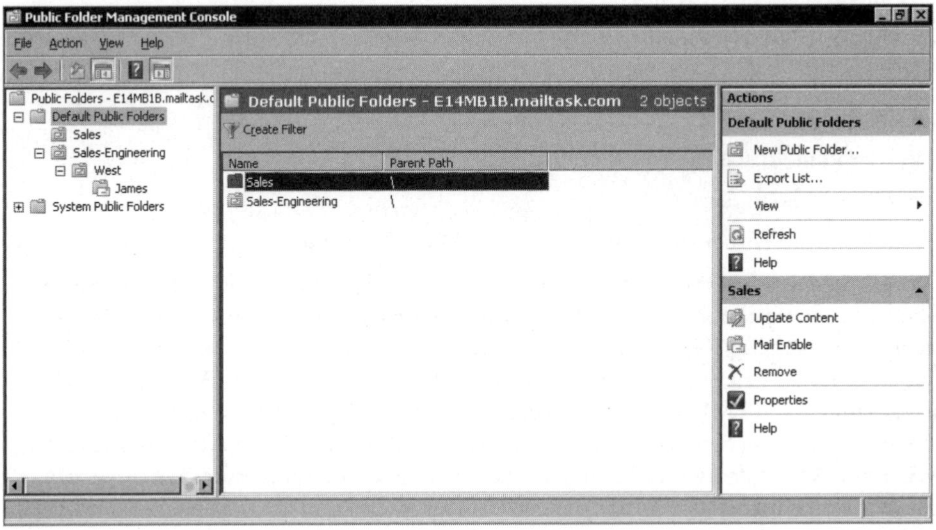

FIGURE 5.7 Mail-enabled public folder Actions pane

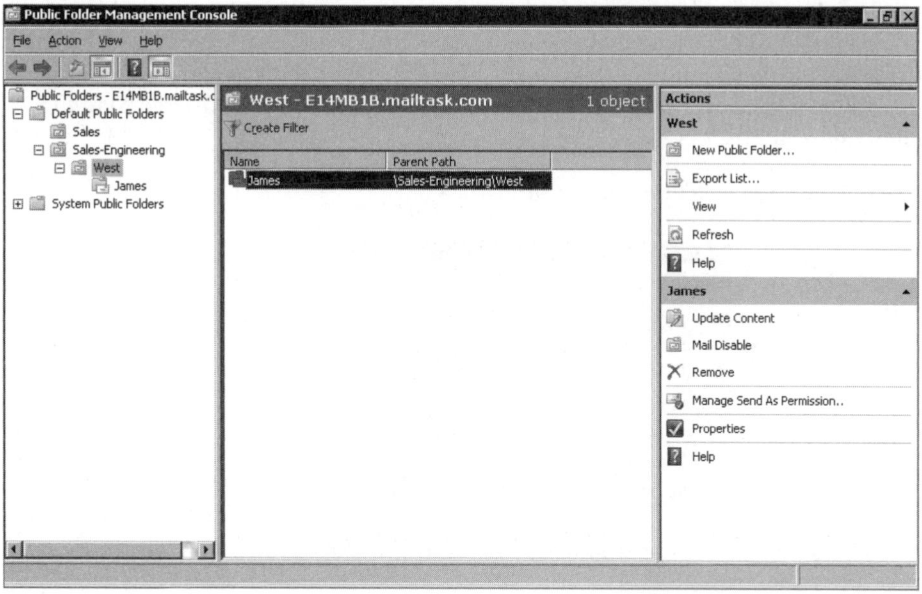

Note that the icon for the mail-enabled public folder *James* shows an envelope in the forefront, compared to the icon of public folders that are not mail enabled.

Both Figure 5.6 and Figure 5.7 show the red X in the Actions pane; you can remove a public folder by clicking it.

🌐 Real World Scenario

Real-World Use of Public Folders

One company runs a revenue-generating operation from public folders. The company has several departments working with public folders. The main order receiving electronic fax is a mail-enabled public folder. A contract group is assigned to monitor new faxes. When a faxed contract is received, it is processed by a member of the contract team. Then a work order is processed and mailed to another public folder for work orders. Another group gets notified and procures the order. The company cannot afford an Exchange outage because it would be unable to process and deliver orders on time. Additionally, the main support email is in another mail-enabled public folder that is monitored by different support groups. Upon receiving an email, the appropriate group uses it to generate a support ticket in the company's support system.

Viewing and Modifying Public Folder Properties

The public folder properties that are displayed depend on whether or not the public folder is mail-enabled. The Properties dialog box of a public folder contains four tabs: General, Statistics, Replication, and Limit (Figure 5.8). There are four additional tabs for a mail-enabled public folder: Exchange General, E-Mail Addresses, Member Of, and Mail Flow Settings (Figure 5.9).

FIGURE 5.8   Public folder properties

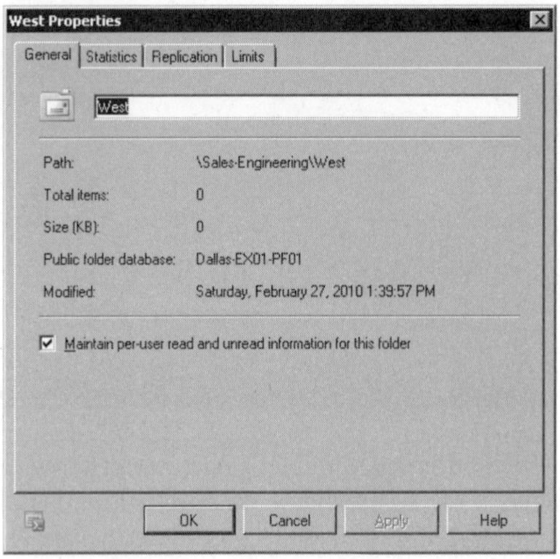

FIGURE 5.9   Mail-enabled public folder properties

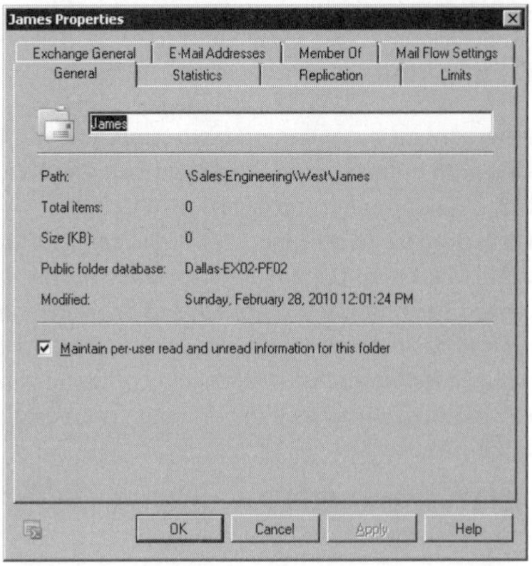

General The General tab, as shown in Figure 5.9, displays general information about the folder such as name, path, total items, size, public folder database, and so forth. Two items can be configured from this tab. First, you can change the name of the public folder by entering the new name in the text box. Second, you can determine whether to enable users to see if a public folder message is read or unread in Outlook by checking the Maintain Per-User Read And Unread Information For This Folder check box.

Statistics The Statistics tab, as the name indicates, provides useful statistics about the folder; namely the number of associated items, total size of associated items, total size of deleted items, owner count , contact count, and the last time the folder was accessed. There are no items to configure in this tab.

Replication In the Replication tab, you can configure the public database for replication, the replication schedule, and the local replica age limit. This will be covered further in the section "Replicating Your Public Folders" later in this chapter.

Limits Tab The Limits tab enables you to configure storage quotas, deleted item retention, and age limits, as illustrated in Figure 5.10.

FIGURE 5.10 Public folder Limits tab

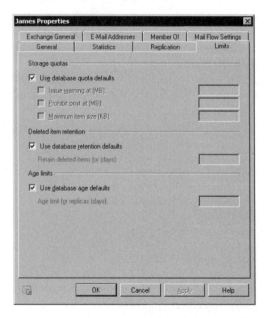

By default, the settings on the Limits are inherited from the public folder database settings. It is best practice to configure these settings at the database level and then modify them as needed for specific public folders:

Storage Quotas In the Storage Quotas section, you can configure Issue Warning to notify the owner that the public folder is reaching its storage limit. The configurable value is between 0 and 2.1TB. You can prohibit posts after the public folder reaches a specific size. The configurable value is between 0 and 2.1TB. And with the Maximum Item Size setting, you can limit the size of items that can be posted into a public folder. The value varies between 0 and 2 GB.

Deleted Item Retention   *Deleted Item Retention* can be configured to determine the number of days that deleted items stay in a public folder. The public folder specific value can be from 0 to 24,855 days.

Age Limit   *Age Limit* is used to configure the age limit for replicas in this public folder. The replicas that exceed the age limit are automatically deleted. The value can be from 0 to 24,855.

The additional configuration tabs to configure a mail-enabled public folder (Exchange General, E-Mail Address, Member Of, and Mail Flow Settings) are similar to that of any other Exchange 2010 mail recipients. Review Chapter 4, "Working with Recipients, Groups and Mailboxes," for additional information.

Selecting Mail-Enable and Mail-Disable Public Folders

Many companies leverage mail-enabled public folders to perform important operational and customer-related functions. These functions vary from receiving customer orders to technical support queues. Public folders are not automatically mail-enabled. To mail-enable a public folder, select the folder in the result pane and click Mail Enable in the Actions pane, as previously illustrated in Figure 5.6.

The mail-enabled folder will have a different icon. Four additional properties tabs will be added (Exchange General, E-Mail Address, Member Of, and Mail Flow Settings). You can modify the new properties as needed.

To mail-disable a public folder, select the mail-enabled folder in the result pane and then click Mail Disable. Click Yes to confirm, as shown in Figure 5.11.

FIGURE 5.11   Mail-disable confirmation message

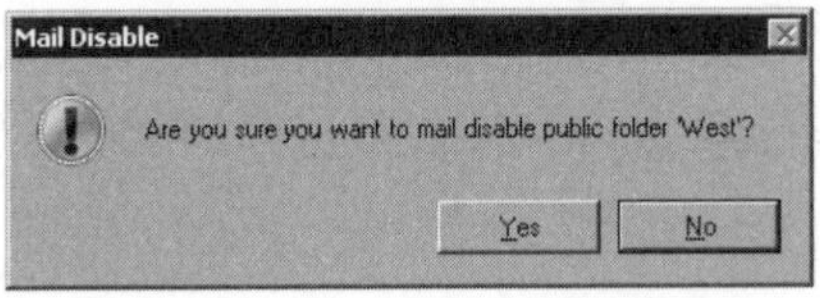

Mail Disable	☒
⚠ Are you sure you want to mail disable public folder 'West'?	
	Yes No

To enable a user or group to send email as or from the mail-enabled public folder, you need to give the user or group Send As rights.

A mail-enabled public folder must have at least the "CreateItems" access right granted to the Anonymous account so that email can be sent to the public folder from the Internet..

Selecting Manage Send As Permission

Select the mail-enabled public folder, then click Manage Send As Permission in the Actions pane, previously shown in Figure 5.7. On the Manage Send As Permissions page, click Add, then select the user or group, as shown in Figure 5.12. Click Manage after you've added the user or group. On the completion page, click Finish.

FIGURE 5.12   Granting users Manage Send As Permission

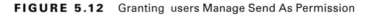

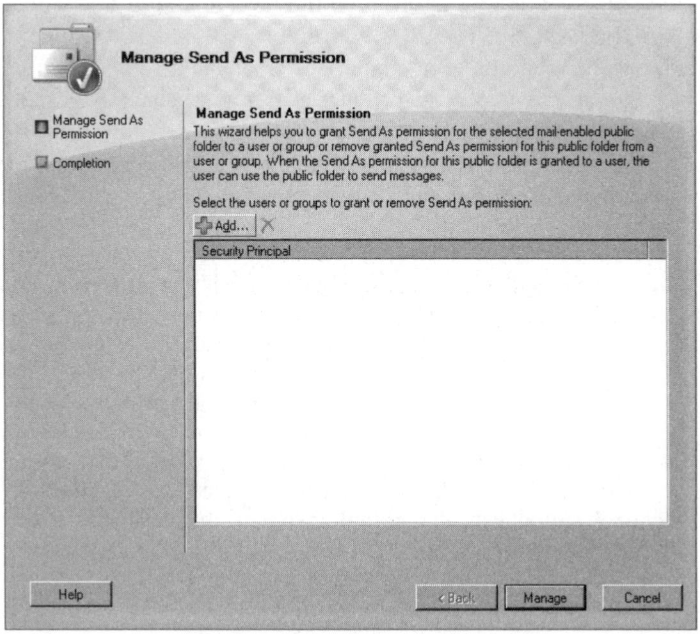

This brings us to the end of the configuration within PFMC. Next we'll explore EMS.

The permissions do not apply automatically until after replication has occurred. You can stop and restart the information store service to force the changes to take effect immediately.

Configuring and Managing Public Folders with EMS

Although the PFMC is good for many common tasks, such as changing folder names and configuring limit and replication schedules, you'll need to use EMS to manage the following tasks:

- Get statistics for public folders
- Suspend and resume public folder replication

- Configure public folder permissions for client users and administrators
- Move public folder content from one public folder database to a new public folder database

We are going to cover these specialized functions of EMS as well as some other basic tasks such as creating, removing public folders and managing public folder properties. To begin, a review of some EMS basics is in order.

As you've seen many times up to this point, EMS is built on the Windows PowerShell technology. Because it is a specialized application of PowerShell, it uses commands with the same format as standard PowerShell cmdlets: Verb-Noun.

By combining the verb and noun, each cmdlet describes the type of operation it performs as well as the object it manipulates. Verbs produce a standard behavior regardless of the object to which they are applied. For example, the `Get` verb will always provide a read-only list of the object's properties, while the `Set` verb will always allow you to modify those properties, even when they vary from object to object.

> In some of the PowerShell examples, you will see a back-tick (`) character at the end of a line. PowerShell uses this character for line termination. It tells the shell that the logical line of input will be continued on the next physical line. This allows you to break up long lines for display and still ensure that they work correctly when you enter them. As a result, the same verbs and nouns tend to be used over and over again; this helps you learn your way around more quickly. Many of the properties are common across multiple objects, so you'll quickly get accustomed to how to use them. The help page for each cmdlet lists all parameters that can be used with that cmdlet.

Performing General Public Folder Tasks

These cmdlets apply to the entire public folder hierarchy at once and provide broad control of your public folder infrastructure:

Get-PublicFolderStatistics   This cmdlet provides a detailed set of statistics about the public folder hierarchy on a given server, such as `Get-PublicFolderStatistics -Server "E14MB1B"`.

Resume-PublicFolderReplication   This cmdlet re-enables all public folder content replication when it has been suspended.

Suspend-PublicFolderReplication   This cmdlet suspends all public folder content replication.

Update-PublicFolderHierarchy   This cmdlet starts the content synchronization process for the public folder hierarchy on the specified server, as in `Update-PublicFolderHierarchy -Server "E14MB1B"`.

Manipulating Individual Public Folders

These cmdlets are designed to work with a specific public folder:

Get-PublicFolder This cmdlet retrieves the properties for the specified public folder. If you don't name a public folder by specifying a value for the -Identity property, it will default to the root public folder. If you need to see system folders, you'll need to set the -Identity property to a value beginning with the string \NON IPM SUBTREE. Here are some examples:

```
Get-PublicFolder-Identity "\Sales\Closed" -Server "EX02"
Get-PublicFolder-Recurse
Get-PublicFolder -Identity \NON IPM SUBTREE -Recurse
```

 By default, the Get-PublicFolder cmdlet returns the values for only a single folder. The -Recurse switch changes the behavior to report on all subfolders as well.

New-PublicFolder This cmdlet creates a new public folder. The -Path property is required and provides the name and location of the new public folder, as in the following example:

```
New-PublicFolder -Identity "\Sales\New" -Server "EX02"
```

Remove-PublicFolder This cmdlet deletes a public folder. The -Path property is required and provides the name and location of the public folder to be deleted:

```
Remove-PublicFolder -Identity "\Sales\Closed" -Server "EX02"
```

 By default, the Remove-PublicFolder cmdlet removes only the named public folder. The -Recurse switch will delete all subfolders as well, which is handy for removing an entire group of folders at once.

Set-PublicFolder This cmdlet allows you to set most of the properties (limits, replicas, replication schedules, and more) for the named public folder, as in this example:

```
Set-PublicFolder -Identity "\Sales\Closed" -Server "EX02"
```

 You cannot use the Set-PublicFolder cmdlet to mail-enable a public folder or to change its mail-related attributes. See the next section, "Manipulating Public Folder Mail Attributes," for the cmdlets to use for these tasks.

Update-PublicFolder   This cmdlet starts the content synchronization process for the named public folder. The -Identity property is required:

```
Update-PublicFolder -Identity "\Sales\Closed"
```

Manipulating Public Folder Mail Attributes

These cmdlets are designed to work with a specific public folder and modify the attributes it receives when it is mail-enabled:

Disable-MailPublicFolder   This cmdlet takes an existing mail-enabled public folder and renders it mail-disabled, as in the following example:

```
Disable-MailPublicFolder -Identity "\Sales\New"
```

Enable-MailPublicFolder   This cmdlet takes an existing public folder and renders it mail-enabled. The optional -HiddenFromAddressListsEnabled switch allows you to hide the folder from your address lists, as follows:

```
Enable-MailPublicFolder-Identity "\Sales\New"
-HiddenFromAddressListsEnabled $true -Server "EX02"
```

 You set the mail-related attributes separately using the Set-MailPublicFolder cmdlet.

Get-MailPublicFolder   This cmdlet retrieves the mail-related properties for the specified public folder. If you don't name a public folder by specifying a value for the -Identity property, it will default to the root public folder:

```
Get-MailPublicFolder -Identity "\Sales\Closed" -Server "EX02"
```

Set-MailPublicFolder   This cmdlet allows you to set the mail-related properties for the named public folder, such as alias, email addresses, send and receive sizes, and permitted and prohibited senders. Here's an example:

```
Set-PublicFolder-Identity "\Sales\Closed" -Server "EX02"
-Alias PostedJobs -PrimarySmtpAddress
"postedjobs@ExchangeExchange.com"
```

 After you configure the mail-related attributes for a public folder, you must still mail-enable them by using the Enable-MailPublicFolder cmdlet.

Managing Public Folder Databases

These cmdlets allow you to manage the public folder databases:

Get-PublicFolderDatabase   This cmdlet provides the functionality used by the Exchange Management Console and allows you to view the properties of existing public folder databases, as in the following example:

```
Get-PublicFolderDatabase -Server "EX02"
```

> The -Identity and -Server parameters are not compatible with each other. Use only one of the three to narrow down your selection.

New-PublicFolderDatabase   This cmdlet allows you to create a new public folder database.

Remove-PublicFolderDatabase   This cmdlet deletes an existing public folder database from the active configuration of the server:

```
Remove-PublicFolderDatabase -Identity "Public Folder Database"
```

> The corresponding EDB file is not deleted by the Remove-PublicFolderDatabase cmdlet; you have to remove it manually from the hard drive.

Set-PublicFolderDatabase   This cmdlet provides the underlying functionality used by the Exchange Management Console to update the properties of existing public folder databases. Here's an example:

```
Set-PublicFolderDatabase -Identity "PublicFolderDatabase"
-Name "New and Improved PF Database"
```

Managing Public Folder Permissions

The cmdlets described in this section allow you to modify and view the permissions on your public folders. Administrative and client permissions are handled through two separate sets of nouns.

Exchange 2010 introduces a new Public Folder Management Role group as part of RBAC, similar to that of Exchange 2007 Public Folder Administrator, which provides a member of that group all the rights necessary to manage public folders.

The Add-RoleGroupMember -Identity "Public Folder Management" -Member Bob cmdlet adds Bob to the Public Folder Management Role group.

The `Add-PublicFolderAdministrativePermission` cmdlet allows you to add administrative permissions to a specified public folder. For example, the command for adding rights for JSmith to the \Sales\Closed public folder might look like this:

```
Add-PublicFolderAdministrativePermission -User "JSmith"
-Identity "\Sales\Closed" -AccessRights
"ViewInformationStore,AdministerInformationStore"
```

Single or multiple access rights can be specified. If multiple access rights are specified, they should be separated by commas. The valid administrative access rights are as follows:

None   Removes all rights to modify public folder attributes

ModifyPublicFolderACL   Adds the right to modify client access permissions for the specified folder

ModifyPublicFolderAdminACL   Adds the right to modify administrator permissions for the specified public folder

ModifyPublicFolderDeletedItemRetention   Adds the right to modify the Public Folder Deleted Item Retention attributes

ModifyPublicFolderExpiry   Adds the right to modify the Public Folder Expiration attributes

ModifyPublicFolderQuotas   Adds the right to modify the Public Folder Quota attributes

ModifyPublicFolderReplicaList   Adds the right to modify the replica list attribute

AdministerInformationStore   Adds the right to modify all other public folder properties included in the other rights

ViewInformationStore   Adds the right to view public folder properties

AllExtendedRights   Adds the right to modify all public folder properties

> You can specify a single access right or list multiple rights at once using the syntax shown in the example for the `Add-PublicFolderAdministrativePermission` cmdlet.

The following cmdlets also work with administrative permissions:

Get-PublicFolderAdministrativePermission   This cmdlet lets you view the administrative permission entries on a given public folder, as in this example:

```
Get-PublicFolderAdministrativePermission -Identity "\Sales\Closed"
```

Remove-PublicFolderAdministrativePermission   This cmdlet lets you remove an administrative permission entry from a given public folder. Here's an example:

```
Remove-PublicFolderAdministrativePermission -User "Joel.Stidley"
 -Identity "\Sales\Closed" -AccessRights "ViewInformationStore".
```

Working with Client Permissions

After you have configured public folders using the cmdlets described in the preceding sections, users and groups can then work with a public folder using their Outlook clients. Once access to a public folder is granted, Exchange recipients access the folder in their Outlook clients while connected to their mailboxes.

If you create a public folder logged in as a domain administrator, then that user account is given the role of Owner. The owner of a public folder has complete control over the folder.

If a user has the appropriate permissions on a public folder, that user can change access permissions on the folder for other users. You can modify them from within the Outlook client using the Permissions tab for a public folder, or you can modify them using EMS.

Which of these you use depends on your security rights. If you are an Exchange user with no extraordinary permissions who is an owner of a public folder, you manage permissions for the folder in Outlook using the Permissions tab for the public folder. If you're an Exchange administrative user, you can use EMS to modify a single public folder or create a PowerShell script to automate administration.

A group named Default includes all Exchange recipients not separately added to the Name list. When the folder is created, this group is automatically given the default role of Author. Note that those given the Author role do not own the folder and cannot create subfolders. Also note that they can edit and delete their own folder items.

There are several predefined roles— including Owner, Publishing Editor, Editor, Publishing Author, Author, Nonediting Author, Contributor, Reviewer, and Custom—each with a different combination of client permissions. Table 5.1 describes these permissions, from the permission with the most capabilities to the permission with the fewest. The word *items* as used in this table refers to the contents of the public folder, such as email messages, forms, documents, and other files. Table 5.2 lists the predefined groupings of permissions according to role. Several of the permissions set the ability to modify all items, only the user's own items, or none of the items in the public folder.

TABLE 5.1 Public folder client permissions

Permission	Description
Create Items	Can create new items in a folder.
Read Items	Can open and view items in a folder.
Create Subfolders	Can create subfolders within a folder.
Folder Owner	Can change permissions in a folder and perform administrative tasks, such as adding rules and installing forms on a folder.
Folder Contact	Receives email notifications relating to a folder. Notifications include replication conflicts, folder design conflicts, and storage limit notifications.

TABLE 5.1   Public folder client permissions *(continued)*

Permission	Description
Folder Visible	Determines whether the folder is visible to the user in the public folder hierarchy.
Edit Items	Can edit (modify) items in a folder.
Delete Items	Can delete items in a folder.

TABLE 5.2   Predefined client roles and their permissions

Role	Create Items	Read Items	Create Subfolders	Folder Owner	Folder Contact	Folder Visible	Edit Items	Delete Items
Owner	Yes	Yes	Yes	Yes	Yes	Yes	All	All
Publishing Editor	Yes	All	Yes	No	No	Yes	All	All
Editor	Yes	All	No	No	No	Yes	All	All
Publishing Author	Yes	Yes	Yes	No	No	Yes	Own	Own
Author	Yes	Yes	No	No	No	Yes	Own	Own
Nonediting Author	Yes	Yes	No	No	No	Yes	None	None
Contributor	Yes	No	No	No	No	Yes	None	None
Reviewer	No	Yes	No	No	No	Yes	None	None
None	No	No	No	No	No	Yes	None	None

You can also assign custom roles that consist of any combination of individual permissions.

When a public folder is created, the following three users are included on the permissions list by default:

The user who created the public folder   This user is automatically assigned the Owner role.

A special user named Default   This user represents all users who have access to the public folder store but aren't explicitly listed in the permissions list. In top-level folders, the Default user is automatically granted the Author role (this can be modified). Below the top-level folders, the Default user automatically inherits the permissions it has at its parent folder.

A special user named Anonymous   The Anonymous user represents all users logged on with Anonymous access. For example, an Exchange server could contain public folders holding promotional information for public viewing. People without user accounts could use a web browser or news reader program and the Anonymous account to access the Exchange server and read the promotional information. Permissions assigned to the Anonymous account are applied to these users.

 Exchange administrators can always designate themselves as the owners of public folders. This is especially important if the recipient who is the owner of a public folder (or all Active Directory accounts that are on the permissions list of that recipient) is deleted.

Client permissions control how users can interact with public folders and their contents. These rights are different from the administrative permissions. The client access rights are as follows:

`ReadItems`   Adds the right to read items within the specified public folder.

`CreateItems`   Adds the right to create items within the specified public folder.

`EditOwnedItems`   Adds the right to edit the items that the user owns in the specified public folder.

`DeleteOwnedItems`   Adds the right to delete items that the user owns in the specified public folder.

`EditAllItems`   Adds the right to edit all items in the specified public folder.

`DeleteAllItems`   Adds the right to delete all items in the specified public folder.

`CreateSubfolders`   Adds the right to create subfolders in the specified public folder.

`FolderOwner`   Sets the user as the owner of the specified public folder. This means the user has the right to view and move the public folder and create subfolders. This does not give the user rights to read, edit, delete, or create items. If the user needs any of these rights, they need to be assigned separately.

`FolderContact`   Sets the user as the contact for the specified public folder.

`FolderVisible`   Allows the user to view the specified public folder, but does not allow the user to read or edit items within the specified public folder.

Unfortunately, there isn't a graphical view of client permissions in EMC or in the PFMC; therefore, a number of cmdlets are used to manage client permissions from within the EMS. The cmdlets are as follows:

Add-PublicFolderClientPermission   This cmdlet lets you add a client permission entry to a given public folder, as in this example:

```
Add-PublicFolderClientPermission -User "JSmith" -Identity
"\Sales\Closed '" -AccessRights "CreateItems"
```

Get-PublicFolderClientPermission   This cmdlet lets you view the client permission entries on a given public folder, as in this example:

```
Get-PublicFolderClientPermission -Identity "\Sales\Closed"
```

Remove-PublicFolderClientPermission   This cmdlet lets you remove a client permission entry from a given public folder. Here's an example:

```
Remove-PublicFolderClientPermission -User "Erik.Gustafson" -Identity "\Sales\
Closed" -AccessRights "CreateItems"
```

To manage Send As permissions, use `Add ADPermission`. The command `Add-ADPermission Support -User mailtask\joe -Extendedrights "Send As"` enables Send As permissions for Joe on the public folder Support.

> The initial release of Exchange 2010 does not provide a console-based management for public folder permissions. Exchange 2010 Service Pack 1 introduces a new GUI-based Managed Settings option for public folders. The new Managed Settings option enables Exchange administrators to manage client permissions and propagate and override settings to subfolders. These console-based functionalities were last available in Exchange 2003 SP2.

Using Additional Scripts for Complicated Tasks

Although the cmdlets described in the preceding sections are certainly great for single-folder operations, performing common operations on entire groups of folders starts getting sticky. Exchange 2010 provides some sample Exchange Management Shell scripts that allow you to perform more complicated server and management tasks that affect groups of folders, as follows:

AddReplicaToPFRecursive.ps1   This script adds the specified server to the replica list for a given public folder and all folders underneath it.

AddUsersToPFRecursive.ps1   This script allows you to grant user permissions to a folder and all folders beneath it.

MoveAllReplicas.ps1   This script finds and replaces a server in the replica list of all public folders, including system folders for a given public folder database.

RemoveReplicaFromPFRecursive.ps1   This script removes the specified server from the replica list for a given public folder and all folders underneath it.

ReplaceReplicaOnPFRecursive.ps1   This script finds and replaces a server in the replica list of a given public folder as well as all subfolders.

ReplaceUserPermissionOnPFRecursive.ps1   This script finds and replaces one user in the permissions on a given public folder and all its subfolders with a second user; the original user permissions are not retained.

ReplaceUserWithUserOnPFRecursive.ps1   This script copies one user's access permissions on a given public folder and all its subfolders to a second user while retaining permissions for the first user.

RemoveUserFromPFRecursive.ps1   This script removes the given user's access permissions from the given public folder and all its subfolders.

You can find these scripts in the Scripts subfolder of the Exchange 2010 installation folder (*<Exchange Installation Path>*\v14\ Server\Scripts). Note that with the default Windows PowerShell configuration, you just can't click these scripts and run them; you must invoke them from within the Exchange Management Shell, usually by navigating to the folder and calling them explicitly.

You have seen how you can use PFMC and EMC to manage public folders. Outlook is another public folder management tool.

Managing Public Folders with Outlook Client

Outlook 2003, 2007, and 2010 clients can be used to access and manage public folders in Exchange 2010. We demonstrated how to create a public folder in Outlook earlier in this chapter.

A newly created public folder appears under the All Public Folders hierarchy.

To manage your new public folder, right-click the folder and select the Properties option from the context menu. This opens the folder's Properties dialog box, shown in Figure 5.13.

Among other things, mailbox owners use the public folder's Properties dialog box to do the following:

- Add a description for other mailbox owners who access the folder

- Make the folder available on the Internet

- Set up a default view of the folder, including grouping by such things as the subject or sender

- Set up administrative rules on folder characteristics, access, and such

- Set permissions for using the folder

The Permissions tab shows the client's permissions that can be modified using cmdlets in EMS or in Outlook, as shown in Figure 5.14.

FIGURE 5.13 Public folder properties in Outlook

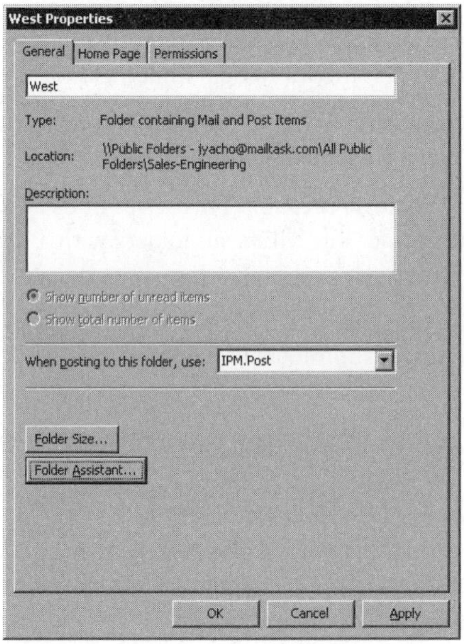

FIGURE 5.14 Public folder permissions in Outlook

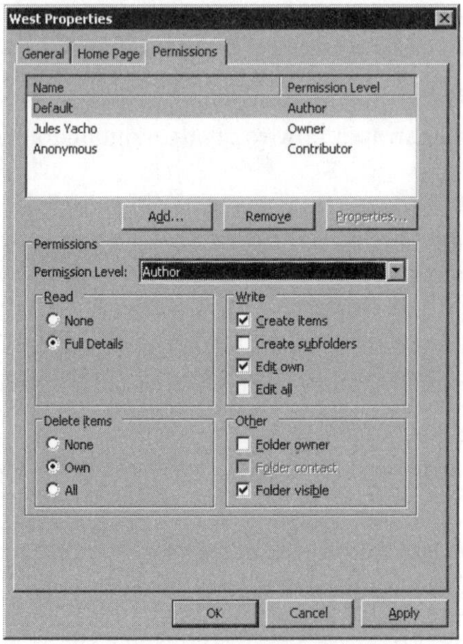

Introduction to ExFolders

In previous versions of Exchange, additional public folder management tools were available. The most frequently used tools were PFDAVAdmin, Pfadmin, and Pfinfo, just to name a few. With Exchange 2010, these tools were discontinued or retired, and that led to the development of a new tool named Exfolders, short for Exchange folders.

ExFolders is actually PFDAVAdmin rewritten to work with Exchange 2010 because PFDAVAdmin uses WebDAV, which has been removed from Exchange 2010. Exfolders uses the same PFDAVAdmin user interface.

You can use PFDAVAdmin to do the following:

- Perform bulk operations on folder properties. In addition, you can do bulk search and removal operations of per-item permissions.

- Apply changes to your list of replicas to a folder and all subfolders without overwriting each folder's replica list (that is, add or remove specific server entries without making each folder's replica list an exact copy of your starting point).

- Export folder permissions on folders, public folder stores, and mailbox stores.

- Export and import public folder replica lists.

Unlike PFDAVAdmin, ExFolders can run only from an Exchange 2010 server, and it can connect only to Exchange 2007 version or higher. ExFolders introduces some new features. In addition to supporting all Exchange folders, private or public, you can do the following:

- Import and export folder properties

- Export item-level properties for all items in a folder

- Have support for the new Exchange 2007/2010 free/busy permissions

- Connect to multiple mailbox stores at same time

The tool is available for download at msExchangeteam.com/files/12/attachments/entry453398.aspx.

Download the tool and navigate around to familiarize yourself. These types of tools are not only administrators' best friend, they also come in pretty handy for troubleshooting purposes.

 NOTE Be sure to check out the readme for more details. While there is no official support for the tool, feel free to comment here or send an email to the owner of the tool, as indicated in the readme files. However, make sure you read the readme first—there are a few known issues, and if you don't run the tool as specified, it will probably crash.

It's now time to expand on public folder replication.

Replicating Your Public Folders

We cannot emphasize enough the importance of public folder replication for your organization. You have to decide whether to take advantage of replicating public folders in your organization or not. It's not a decision that should be made lightly. We would be surprised if you decide not to replicate public folders because of the obvious advantages of resiliency and fault tolerance that replication provides. However, choosing replication would also imply that you have more than one public folder database server in your environment, which carries an extra cost.

Public folder replication is message based and is used to ensure that all public folder databases are synchronized in a multiserver environment.

There are two components to public folder replication: hierarchy replication and content replication.

In an environment with a single Exchange server, the hierarchy or the public folder tree exists and is stored on the Exchange server. In an environment with multiple public folder stores, each Exchange server that has a public folder store has a copy of the public folder hierarchy. Exchange servers work together to ensure that each one has an up-to-date copy of the public folder hierarchy. This process, called public folder hierarchy replication, is automatic. A hierarchy replication is triggered when folder properties such as folder name, replica list, and permissions are modified.

Content replication, on the other hand, has to be configured before the public folder content can replicate. The content replication is induced by adding data to the folder or by sending a message to the public folder. Exchange uses the multi-master replication model for public folders, meaning each copy of a public folder or replica is equal. Each replica can be modified. The changes are then sent to other public folder servers via email messages called system messages. Therefore, public folder replicas can be strategically located to ensure equal load or geographic distribution. Because public folders leverage Active Directory for replication, a sound public folder design must be put in place.

Choosing a Replication Design

If a specific public folder does not exist in the default public folder store, the client is provided with a list of servers where the public folder resides, sorted by distance and based on Active Directory cost. As you can imagine, when many public folders are accessed over a lower-bandwidth network, server and network loads can become very heavy as users access public folders on one or a limited number of Exchange servers. If you need to, you can replicate folders on one Exchange server to other Exchange servers.

When would you want to create replicas of public folders? There are five main circumstances, but perhaps you can think of additional ones:

- **When you need to balance public folder access loads on your Exchange servers.** Having all your users connect to a single server for all their public folder access can quickly result in an overwhelmed server if you have a large number of users or if you have heavy public folder usage.

- **When you have an Exchange server or group of Exchange servers separated from other servers in your organization by low-bandwidth links.** In that case, you may be better off having limited replication traffic over your links and allowing users to connect to local replicas, keeping their traffic on the LAN.

- **When IMAP4 clients see folders only on the Exchange server to which they connect, including public folders.** If you want an IMAP4 client to be able to see a specific public folder, you must create a replica of that folder on the IMAP4 user's Mailbox server.

- **When public folder replication is essential because you are planning to remove an Exchange server from your organization** (like all those Exchange 2003 servers you're migrating away from). If the server you are removing hosts the only replica for a set of public folders and you don't want to lose those folders, you must replicate them to another Exchange server in your organization.

- **When you are coexisting with previous versions of Exchange.** You must have a replica of the public folder on an Exchange 2010 server in order to provide access to the content from within the same Outlook Web App browser window.

With all these considerations, you want to simplify your public folder replication. You want to create replicas for fault tolerance and load balancing. You need to strategically place folder replicas within and across AD sites. You want to ensure that there is not excessive folder replication because it will negatively impact the availability of your network. This can also put undue burden on your server's memory and CPU load.

 Public folders can be deployed on Database Availability Group (DAG) servers, but they do not use continuous replication, unlike mailbox databases. Public folder replication is email based and follows the multimaster replication model. Public folder replication must be explicitly deployed to at least two public folder servers.

Replicating the Hierarchy

As a reminder, a public folder hierarchy or public folder tree is a list of public folders and their subfolders that are stored in the default public folder stores on the Exchange servers in an Exchange organization. The hierarchy also includes the name of the server on which a copy of each folder resides. Because the hierarchy exists in Active Directory as a separate object, it does not contain any of the actual items in your various public folders. There is one organization-wide public folder hierarchy object.

The Public Folder Management Console uses the public folder hierarchy to appropriately display public folder objects in various containers and to retrieve information about public folders, whether that information is stored in the hierarchy or on the server where the public folder physically resides. Email clients such as Outlook and OWA use the hierarchy to list public folders available on all servers in the organization and to access items in a specific folder. The hierarchy includes both default public folders and systems folders.

The public folder hierarchy replicates automatically between public folder servers in the organization. There may be instances where the hierarchy is different among servers. The lack of hierarchy synchronization may indicate that there are replication issues. You can initiate hierarchy synchronization by launching an update of the hierarchy.

When you launch PFMC, select Update Hierarchy in the result pane.

In EMS, you would issue the following command:

```
Update-PublicFolderHierarchy -Server "EX02"
```

The update will initiate replication that might not complete immediately. You can check after a few minutes or hours to see if the hierarchy is synchronized, depending on the number of public folders and subfolders that exist in your organization. There are additional methods to diagnose and troubleshoot replication issues, such as diagnostics logging, message tracking, transport logging, and Active Directory replication monitoring. Refer to Chapter 9, "Monitoring and Reporting," for more information.

Replicating the Content

As previously mentioned, public folder content replication has to be explicitly configured. This starts with the public folder database.

The Replication and Public Folder Referral tabs of the public folder database Properties dialog box should be properly configured, as shown earlier in this chapter in the section "Configuring a Public Folder Database."

In the Replication tab, the default replication interval is 15 minutes, which means that every 15 minutes the system checks for changes and sends replication messages to other public folder servers configured for replicas. A custom schedule can be configured, depending on network topology and server locations.

Public folder referral affects how clients such as Outlook connect to public folder replicas.

After you configure the database for replication and you create public folders, you must configure the public folders for content replication. The folder hierarchy and content have different replication schedules, using monitoring tool you may discover that content has replicated but is still not available because the hierarchy has not yet completed replicating.

Creating Public Folder Replicas

Technically, all copies of a public folder, including the one on the Exchange server where the folder was originally created, are called replicas. There is a good reason for this. After a folder has been replicated, users will place items into it via the replica on their own default public folders server or on the nearest server as calculated using AD site costs. So, no replica of the folder can be considered a master copy. The replicas of a folder update each other on a regular basis, reinforcing the idea that there is no master copy.

You can set up replication of a public folder on either the server that will provide the folder or the server that will hold the new replica of the public folder. You will create a public folder replica in Exercise 5.7.

EXERCISE 5.7

Creating a Public Folder Replica in Exchange Management Console

Follow these steps to create a public folder replica in EMC:

1. Click Start ➤ Programs ➤ Microsoft Exchange 2010 and select Exchange Management Console.

2. Expand the Microsoft Exchange container, expand the Microsoft Exchange On-Premises container, and then click the Tools node.

3. Click on the Public Folder Management Console.

4. In PFMC, expand the default public folder tree. Select the public folder in the result pane and then click Properties in the Actions pane.

5. Select the Replication tab. The Replication tab will list all public folder databases and servers with replicas.

6. Click Add to select a replica server for this folder. Select the replica server from the list and then click OK.

7. By default, Use Public Folder Database Replication Schedule check box is enabled. Clear the check box to create your custom replication schedule. The replication schedule can be set to Never, which indicates that the folder will not replicate. Additional hourly or custom schedules are available.

8. To create a custom schedule, click Customize. You can then select the time to run public folder replication. The replication interval can be set to either 15 minutes or 1 hour. Click OK after setting the replication schedule.

9. Enter the local replica age limit in days. You need to specify a number if you would like to have items in the public folder that have reached the age limit deleted.

10. Click Apply in the folder Properties dialog box and then OK to close it.

You can also create a public folder replica in EMS. Run the following command to create a replica of the public folder called Sales on server EX01 and EX02 using public folder databases EX01-PF01 and Ex02-PF01:

```
Set-PublicFolder "\Sales" -Replicas "EX01\EX01-PF01", "EX02\EX02-PF01"
```

In the event that you encounter public folder replication issues, you may need to temporarily stop the folder content replication process, troubleshoot and resolve the issue, or reconfigure replication. Then restart the replication process. You can only use EMS to suspend and resume replication. The following Suspend-PublicFolderReplication and Resume-PublicFolderReplication cmdlets are used.

These cmdlets will stop or resume all public folder content replication in your organization. The hierarchy replication is not affected by the commands.

Using Tools in the Replication Process

Let's dive deeper into the replication process. For public folder replication to work, Exchange 2010 relies on two important tools, a *change number* and the *replication state table*. Each public folder database maintains a replication state table that contains the following information:

- Information required to update a replica
- Information about the last local update of the replica, with the change number
- Groups of updates to known replicas with their change number set or "CNset"

The following steps describe a replication process and show how the tools are leveraged:

1. You update a public folder in a public folder database on server EX01 by posting a message.

2. The public folder database records the change, assigns a change number, and pushes the update into a replication message.

3. When the replication message reaches the message size limit, the public folder database sends the message to other public folder databases with replicas of the folder. Hierarchy replications and content replications are sent as separate messages.

4. The public folder database on server EX02 receives the replication message and processes it.

5. The public folder database checks the received change numbers against the ones in its replication state table to determine which changes need to be applied and to which folder.

6. The public folder database will update the appropriate folder replicas.

7. The public folder database will record the updates status and change numbers to its replication state table.

The replication process is successfully completed. There may be instances when the replication message does contain information that is inconsistent with the information in the local replication state table. This indicates that the public folder databases are out of sync and they must resynchronize. This process is called backfilling.

Understanding Backfill Events

A *backfill* event occurs when a public folder database verifies that it does not have all the updates for a replica and must obtain the needed updates from another public folder database. This typically happens when the following conditions occur:

- A new folder has been created and the hierarchy has updated but not the content. The database will request content updates from other databases.

- A replication message shows that other replicas have more information than the local replica.

- A new public folder database is created and the hierarchy and replica content must be updated.

The backfill information or missing updates are placed in a backfill array that contains backfill time-outs. The time-outs determine how long each missing update should remain in the array. The time-outs vary from 6 to 48 hours, depending on the type of backfill request and whether the replicas are in the same AD site or a different site.

Additional processes such as status request and response messages are also used to determine whether to issue backfill requests.

A list of servers with replicas is created by Exchange to fulfill backfill requests. A server order is established based on site costs, server availability, and the number of changes. If the first server cannot provide all the required changes, then the next server on the list is used.

The backfill process is heavily leveraged when you remove replicas from databases. The public folder databases ensure that all replicas are in sync before a replica is removed.

Removing a Replica

To remove a replica, navigate to the folder properties in PFMC. Click Properties and select the Replication tab. You will have a list of replicas. Click to select the database and server where the replica should be removed, and then click the red X, as shown in Figure 5.15.

Click Apply and then OK to close the public folder Properties dialog box. Once the backend process ensures that all replicas are in sync, the folder goes from the Pending Delete state to the Delete Now state. The folder is removed from the database during the maintenance window.

FIGURE 5.15   Removing a public folder replica

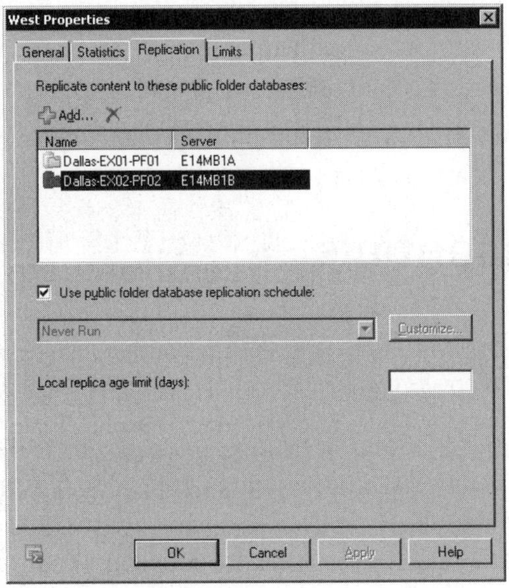

Summary

Public folders are still supported in Exchange 2010. Your environment will determine how much public folder configuration and management you will have to provide. If you have pre–Exchange 2007 servers and pre–Outlook 2007 clients, then you must manage and maintain public folders. Your organization may heavily leverage public folders, which also means that you will continue to support them.

You have several tools at your disposal to be successful. EMC, EMS, PFMC, the Outlook client, OWA, custom scripts, and EXFolders will enable you to perform your administrative duties. EMS enables you to perform far more management and configuration tasks than the graphical user interfaces (EMC and PFMC). This creates an opportunity for you to master the shell commands. These cmdlets also make it easy to do large-scale scripted and bulk management operations.

We would like to leave you with these few points that will help you become successful in managing and configuring public folders:

- Plan your public folder deployment strategy.
- Use a simple hierarchy, more deep than wide.

- Use EMS as much as possible
- Use database settings as much as possible.
- Manage public folder permissions with groups.
- Use a replication strategy for fault tolerance and load balancing.
- Consider your network topology and server architecture in your replication design.

Chapter Essentials

Know which tool to use.   EMS can be your best friend because most public folder management and configuration tasks can be performed within EMS. Take your time to learn PowerShell commands. You can leverage EMC and PFMC for general tasks to create and configure databases and public folders. Client-specific tasks are better achieved within clients such as Outlook and OWA. Furthermore, Outlook is ideal to set client permissions and define the public folder content.

Keep it simple.   Settings and permissions can be inherited. Database-level settings propagate to public folders. Use database-level settings as much as possible while minimizing the use of public-folder-level configurations for limits and replication. Likewise, assign public folder permissions to root or top-level folders as much as possible while configuring subfolder permissions as needed. You need to leverage RBAC to simplify the administration of permissions as well.

To replicate or not.   Public folder replication is a great tool but should be used wisely. You should almost always choose to replicate and deploy a strategy that supports your network infrastructure. The benefits of replication far outweigh the cost of deployment. Replication will not only help you solve latency and client performance issues, it will also provide you with a highly available, redundant, and resilient environment.

Chapter

6

Configuring Security, Compliance, and Policies

THE FOLLOWING TOPICS ARE DISCUSSED IN THIS CHAPTER:

- ✓ Configuring Role Based Access Control
- ✓ Configuring message compliance and records management
- ✓ Configuring transport rules
- ✓ Configuring policies and address lists
- ✓ Configuring antivirus and antispam

Thanks to government regulations, such as the Securities and Exchange Commission regulations and Health Insurance Portability and Accountability Act (HIPAA), we find ourselves in a world with a great number of rules and compliance requirements. Exchange Server 2010 comes with marked improvements and added features to help you get started in this regulated world. The main focus of the Exchange Server 2010 compliance feature set is regulatory compliance, applied in business sectors such as publicly traded companies, financial services companies, and medical companies. The compliance feature set also focuses on protecting private information and providing solutions that ensure that corporate governance principles are being maintained.

The feature set is basically "compliance in transport." Every message in an Exchange organization travels through a Hub Transport server. Even messages sent between mailboxes in the same database and on the same Mailbox server have to travel through a Hub Transport server. This was a deliberate design that allows actions to be applied to every message in an Exchange organization. These actions are what enable you to ensure that your Exchange organization is meeting compliance requirements.

Exchange Server 2010 also features improvements in email retention and email search, making it easier for users to meet regulations on records retention and for organizations to meet legal discovery requirements. Retention policies can be created that allow users to tag emails and folders, specifying how long items should be maintained and when they should be deleted. The addition of Multi-Mailbox Search allows legal and compliance users to perform required searches directly in Exchange without having to purchase additional software or hardware.

The permissions model in Exchange Server 2010 also has some key improvements. Permissions can now be easily assigned based on roles, allowing Exchange administrators to empower members of their help desk and legal department and even end users to manage and use the features they need to efficiently do their jobs.

Other functionality, such as antivirus and antispam, is also extremely important for today's messaging systems. These features ensure that all messages are virus free and as few spam messages as possible are delivered to your users' mailboxes. This chapter goes over each of these topics.

Configuring Role Based Access Control

Microsoft Exchange Server 2010 introduced a new feature called Role Based Access Control (RBAC). RBAC allows administrators to assign granular permissions to end users, help desk personnel, and administrators. It was introduced to allow administrators the ability to assign permissions without having to modify access control lists (ACLs). Modifying ACLs caused several problems because ACL requirements could change through upgrades and because it was difficult to troubleshoot when there were problems caused by ACL modification.

RBAC enables administrators to assign permissions to users based on the roles that they hold within an organization and to assign permissions based on the Exchange commands that those users will be running. For example, if you have administrative assistants at offices in Dallas and Chicago that are responsible for maintaining the office locations and phone numbers of the employees at their locations. You could create a management role that allows them to run the command Set-User but only be able to use the -Office and -Phone parameters. Then, when you assigned the role to those users, you could scope it so that they can modify users only in the Dallas and Chicago organizational units (OUs). When you open a new location in New York, you can easily reuse the same management role and just assign it scoped to the New York OU.

RBAC consists of these basic parts:

Management role   A management role is a collection of role entries that defines what cmdlets, scripts, and permissions users have access to.

Management role group   A management role group is a group that contains users and groups that a management role is assigned to.

Management role assignment   A management role assignment assigns a management role to a role group, giving members of the group the access defined in the management role.

Management role scope   A management role scope defines the objects that the members of a management role group can manage. A management scope can be OUs, servers, or filters based on servers or recipients.

Management role assignment policy   A management role assignment policy is a collection of management roles assigned to a user mailbox. The policy defines what attributes of themselves or their distribution groups they can manage.

RBAC allows administrators to delegate permissions to other members of the organization. It accomplishes this by allowing administrators to define what cmdlets and scripts users are allowed to run and what parameters they can use on those cmdlets and to scope those scripts to run against only specific servers or OUs. The Exchange Control Panel (ECP), and Exchange Management Console (EMC), and Exchange Management Shell (EMS), are all controlled by RBAC. RBAC can be used to give extremely granular permissions, no matter if they are using EMC, the EMS, or the ECP, whichever they prefer.

RBAC also makes it easier to implement a split permissions model, where the Active Directory administrators and Exchange administrators have separate permissions. In a split permissions model, only AD administrators are able to create new security principals, such as users, and only Exchange administrators manage the Exchange attributes on a user. For instructions on implementing a split permissions model, see http://technet.microsoft.com/en-us/library/dd638155.aspx.

RBAC uses management roles, which are collections of role entries. Role entries specify what cmdlets and what parameters for those cmdlets can be run by a user with that role assigned. Management roles are created using the New-ManagementRole command, and role entries are assigned to the management role using the Add-ManagementRoleEntry command. After a role is created, it can be assigned to a user or group using the New-ManagementRoleAssignment command. Management roles are used to grant access to cmdlets, and a user that has been assigned multiple management roles, either directly or through group membership, has access to all of the commands for all of those roles.

Management roles are also assigned to users through role assignment policies. Every user has a single role assignment policy that is assigned to their mailbox. The role assignment policy defines what end users can manage on their own mailboxes and distribution groups. For example, if you wish to allows users to update their phone number or office location or to manage distribution groups that they own, then you assign those permissions through their role assignment policy.

Exercise 6.1, Exercise 6.2, Exercise 6.3, and Exercise 6.4 show you several options for managing RBAC permissions. In Exercise 6.1, you use the ECP to allow users to manage the distribution groups they own and to create new distribution groups.

EXERCISE 6.1

Using the Exchange Control Panel to Allow Users to Edit Distribution Groups

Perform the following steps to allow users to edit distribution groups:

1. Open Internet Explorer and type https://mail.mailtask.com/ecp in the address bar.

2. Login with the Administrator account.

3. From the Select what to manage drop-down list, choose My Organization.

4. In the Users & Groups section, click the User Roles tab. If you have installed Exchange 2010 with Service Pack 1, click on Roles and Auditing on the left and then click the User Roles tab.

5. Double-click Default Role Assignment Policy.

EXERCISE 6.1 *(continued)*

6. Check My Distribution Groups and click Save.

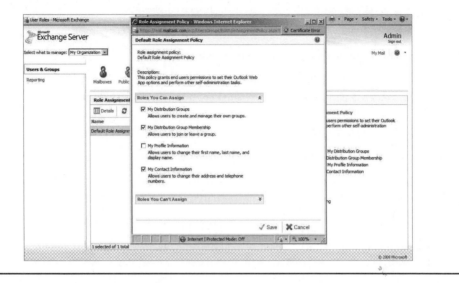

When you activate this option in the previous exercise, it allows users to manage their own distribution groups (DGs) and to create new DGs, which may not be desirable in your company. In Exercise 6.2, you will create a new role assignment policy based on this change that allows users to manage DGs but prevents them from creating new DGs.

EXERCISE 6.2

Creating a Default Management Role Assignment to Prevent Users from Creating Distribution Groups

Perform the following steps to prevent users from creating new DGs:

1. If you have not already done so, log on to EX01 as Administrator. Click Start ➢ Programs ➢ Microsoft Exchange Server 2010 and then select Exchange Management Shell.

2. To create a new management role run:

    ```
    New-ManagementRole –name myCustomRole –parent MyDistributionGroups*
    ```

3. Remove the New-DistributionGroup management role entry by running and confirming the following command:

    ```
    Remove-ManagementRoleEntry myCustomRole\New-DistributionGroup
    ```

EXERCISE 6.2 *(continued)*

4. Get the default role assignment policy with the following command:

```
$assignmentPolicy =
Get-RoleAssignmentPolicy "Default Role Assignment Policy"
```

5. Remove the original distribution group management role:

```
$oldAssignment = Get-ManagementRoleAssignment
-roleassignee $assignmentPolicy.identity -role MyDistributionGroups*

Remove-ManagementRoleAssignment $oldAssignment -confirm:$false
```

6. Add the new management role to the assignment policy:

```
New-ManagementRoleAssignment -name:myCustomAssignment
-role:myCustomRole -policy $assignmentPolicy.identity
```

In Exercise 6.3, you will use the ECP to assign the Discovery Management role to a user. This role allows the user to use Multi-Mailbox Search, which will be discussed later in the chapter. Managing RBAC permissions through the ECP gives you a quick and easy method for assigning permissions to personnel who need access to features like Multi-Mailbox Search.

EXERCISE 6.3

Using the Exchange Control Panel to Assign the Discovery Management Role Group to a User

Follow these steps to give a user the Discovery Management role:

1. Open Internet Explorer and type `https://mail.mailtask.com/ecp` in the address bar.

2. Login with the Administrator account.

3. At the top, choose My Organization.

4. In the Roles & Auditing section, click the Administrator Roles tab.

5. Double-click the Discovery Management role group.

6. Click the Add button and choose the user to which you want to assign the Discovery Management role.

7. Click OK and then Save.

Exchange Server 2010 includes several built-in role groups that can be used to easily assign access to administrators and help desk personnel. For a list of built-in role groups, visit http://technet.microsoft.com/en-us/library/dd351266.aspx. The built-in role groups assign permissions across the entire forest. In Exercise 6.4, you'll see how to view what roles are assigned to a role group and how create new scoped role groups based on the built-in role groups.

EXERCISE 6.4

Assigning a Scoped Help Desk Role Using the Exchange Management Shell

Follow these steps to create a scoped role for help desk users:

1. Click Start ➤ Programs ➤ Microsoft Exchange Server 2010 and then select Exchange Management Shell.

2. To view data in the entire forest run:

   ```
   Set-ADServerSettings -ViewEntireForest $true
   ```

3. To view the management roles assigned to the built-in help desk group, run:

   ```
   Get-ManagementRoleAssignment -RoleAssignee "Help Desk" |
   Get-ManagementRole
   ```

4. Assign the View-Only Recipients role to the Dallas-HelpDesk group.

   ```
   New-ManagementRoleAssignment -Name "Dallas View-Only Recipients"
   -SecurityGroup "Dallas-HelpDesk" -Role "View-Only Recipients"
   ```

5. Create a new scope that allows access to only members of the Dallas OU:

   ```
   New-ManagementScope -Name Dallas -Recipientroot mailtask.com/Dallas
   -RecipientRestrictionFilter {RecipientType -eq "UserMailbox"}
   ```

6. Assign the User Options role to the Dallas-HelpDesk group with the Dallas OU scope:

   ```
   New-ManagementRoleAssignment -Name "Dallas User Options"
   -SecurityGroup "Dallas-HelpDesk" -Role "User Options"
   -CustomRecipientWriteScope Dallas
   ```

Enabling Administrator Audit Logging

After you use RBAC to allow administrators and help desk personnel to make changes in Exchange, it becomes important to log what changes are being made. Exchange 2010 introduced a feature called administrator audit logging that allows you to log commands that are run in Exchange. Administrator audit logging will log all cmdlets run that are not get-* cmdlets, whether they're run from the (EMS), (EMC), or the (ECP). Administrator audit logging stores the logs as messages in a mailbox you create for this purpose.

To enable administrator audit logging, use this command:

```
Set-AdminAuditLogConfig -AdminAuditLogEnabled $true
-AdminAuditLogMailbox adminlog@mailtask.com
```

After you enable audit logging, you'll notice entries from normal users as well as administrators. Some common end user entries will come from new or edited Inbox rules and changes to safe senders and blocked senders. Figure 6.1 shows an audit log entry.

FIGURE 6.1   An example audit log entry

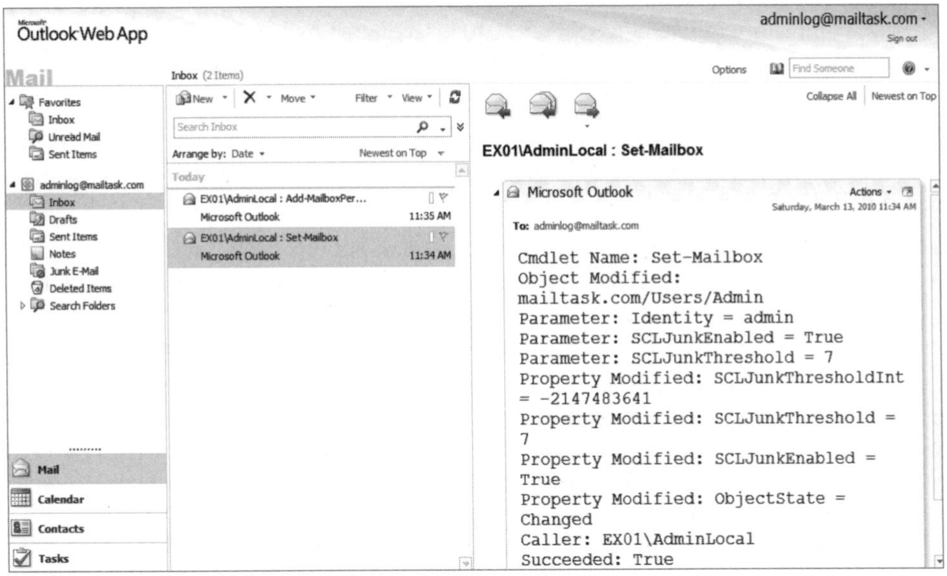

For more information about configuring and using administrator audit logging, see Chapter 9, "Monitoring and Reporting the Exchange Server 2010."

Introducing Message Compliance and Record Management

Corporate compliance requirements are becoming increasingly important across business sectors and geographic locations. In the United States, the market focus has primarily been on regulatory compliance for publicly traded companies and companies operating in regulated sectors, such as healthcare and financial services. In addition to compliance requirements, attention is being focused on protecting private information and on providing solutions that ensure that corporate governance principles are being maintained.

Most compliance-based market attention is focused on the requirements to abide by regulations such as the Health Insurance Portability and Accountability Act (HIPAA), the Sarbanes-Oxley (SOX) Act, the EU Data Protection Act, and California SB 1386. However, the broader demand is driven by the need to maintain controlled access and show both information and process integrity for electronic communications. This section covers the basic compliance feature concepts and how to configure the compliance features offered by Exchange Server 2010.

Message compliance in Exchange Server 2010 is facilitated by messaging records management (MRM). MRM is an Enterprise Client Access License feature set that provides two distinct methods for controlling email retention:

Managed folders Managed folders were introduced in Exchange 2007 and are folders that appear in users' mailboxes and are controlled by the administrator. You can create custom managed folders or work with the default folders.

Retention policies Exchange 2010 introduced retention policies, which use retention tags to apply retention settings to emails. Retention policies allow users to use the default folders or to create custom folders because retention tags can be applied regardless of what folder the message is stored in. This decreases the user impact compared to managed folders.

Exchange MRM depends on users to classify their own messages. Whether you use managed folders or retention policies, one of the keys to successful MRM deployment is categories with effective retention limits so users can correctly designate messages that need to be retained. The other key is effective training and simplification of the categorization process so that users will not have issues determining how to classify a message.

When it comes to planning and deploying MRM, you should consider these key planning points:

- For MRM and messaging policies to be truly effective, you need to prohibit personal folders (.pst) on your network. You cannot control the messages in a personal folder. Because you cannot control them, they present a bit of a hole in any effort to conform to a compliance requirement or in any effort to control messages.

- Apply content settings and policies to default folders. This provides retention actions for message types stored in the default set of user folders. Everyone has these folders, and this is where you can make the most automated impact on messages. If you don't want to delete items from the default folders automatically, you may consider creating a Review And Then Delete folder into which Inbox mail is moved after a given period of time.

- Create any custom-managed folders or retention policies that you might need in order to fulfill any corporate governing body's compliance requirements. With all these settings and mail manipulations in place, how will you know whether they are working? To be best informed, you should develop a tracking plan that monitors how messages are being retained, moved, and dealt with.

- Before implementing any compliance, get buy-in from all of the required stakeholders, like your auditors and legal staff. This way you can make sure you meet the compliance requirements.

Configuring Managed Folders

The Exchange Server 2010 managed folders feature enables you to create message retention folders that better organize and manage email messages. Managed email folders are automatically created in target users' mailboxes. An automated process scans the Inbox and these folders in order to retain, expire, or journal messages based on managed content settings. After you create the managed folders, users choose the retention folder in which a given item should be placed. This is why it is important to preplan the folder names and structure of your managed folders.

Two types of managed folders are available in Exchange Server 2010:

Managed custom folders   Managed custom folders are folders you can create in user mailboxes. They are controlled by the administrator and cannot be renamed, moved, or deleted by the user. They should be given names that reflect their intended purpose—remember that users will decide what goes in these folders. Think like a user, and make the names as short and descriptive as possible.

Managed default folders   Managed default folders are the folders that Exchange creates by default, such as the Sent Items, Deleted Items, and Inbox folders. The administrator and the users can't create new managed default folders or rename managed default folders.

Although you cannot change the name of the default folders, you can create a custom folder with a folder of the same name. For example, you could apply a content setting of Delete After 30 Days to the Inbox of a specific group of users and then create another custom Inbox called Year Inbox. The Year Inbox folder would be created as a type that corresponds to the folder you want to replace. An example would be an Inbox type, and it could be given to users based on a managed mailbox policy. The policy would determine which Inbox folder the users would see: the 30-day one or Year Inbox. The Year Inbox folder would replace the default Inbox folder but would still be named Inbox to the users. In this example, users would always see the standard default folder name Inbox in their mailboxes regardless of whether the mailbox policy specified the 30-day Inbox or Year Inbox folder. In addition, you can specify only one Inbox; you cannot have two instances of any default folders in a user's mailbox.

To create a managed folder, perform the steps outlined in Exercise 6.5 and Exercise 6.6.

EXERCISE 6.5

Creating a Managed Folder Using the Exchange Management Console

To create a managed folder using the EMC, follow these steps:

1. Click Start ➤ Programs ➤ Microsoft Exchange Server 2010 and then select Exchange Management Console.

2. Expand Organizational Configuration and select Mailbox.

3. In the Actions pane to the right, select New Managed Custom Folder or New Managed Default Folder.

4. On the first page of the New Managed Folder wizard, type in a name in the Name field and then select the default folder type of the folder you want to replace with the new managed folder. For some folder types, you will be able to add a message that will be displayed in Outlook or OWA. Click New.

5. On the first page of the New Managed Custom Folder wizard, type in a name for the folder and the Outlook display name. Then type a comment that describes the folder. Click New.

In Exercise 6.6, you create managed folders using the EMS, which requires fewer steps than using the EMC.

EXERCISE 6.6

Creating a Managed Folder Using the Exchange Management Shell

Follow these steps to create a managed folder using the EMS:

1. Click Start ➤ Programs ➤ Microsoft Exchange Server 2010 and then select Exchange Management Shell.

2. To create a managed custom folder, run (make sure to change the parameters enclosed in brackets):

    ```
    New-ManagedFolder -Name <Folder_Name> -FolderName <Folder_Display_Name>
    ```

3. To create a new managed default folder, run:

    ```
    New-ManagedFolder -Name <Folder_Name>
    -DefaultFolderType <Default_Folder_Type>
    ```

Configuring Managed Content Settings

The Exchange Server 2010 MRM managed content settings allow you to control the life span of messages. You can control a message's life span in two ways:

-   By controlling how long a message is retained in a folder before it is moved or deleted.

-   By controlling the journaling or archiving of a message. Message content settings can be applied to both default and user-created custom managed folders.

Each managed folder should have a managed content setting applied to it that defines what should be done with the messages in the folder. Managed content settings can apply to all items in a folder or to specific message types (for example, voicemail messages, email messages, and task items). The managed content settings for a folder specify three retention settings:

-   The period of time a message should be retained in the folder.

-   When the retention period starts. Does it start once a message is placed in x folder, when the message is created, or after the message has been in a folder for x days?

-   What action should be taken at the end of the retention period? Should the message be deleted or moved or placed somewhere else, possibly in an archival system?

As an example, you could create a managed content setting that moves all messages in everyone's Sent Items folder to a custom managed folder called Review & Delete. You could then specify that everything in the Review & Delete folder be deleted after 30 days. To create a new managed content setting, follow the steps outlined in Exercise 6.7 and Exercise 6.8.

EXERCISE 6.7

Creating a Managed Content Setting Using the Exchange Management Console

Follow these steps to manage content settings using the EMC:

1. Click Start ➤ Programs ➤ Microsoft Exchange Server 2010 and then select Exchange Management Console.

2. Expand Organizational Configuration and select Mailbox.

3. Click the Default or Custom Managed Folder tab, and then click the folder to which you want to apply the setting.

4. In the Actions pane to the right, select New Managed Content Setting. This launches the New Managed Content Settings wizard.

5. On the first page of the New Managed Content Settings wizard, type the name of the content setting, select the type of messages you want to change, and then configure the retention periods and actions. Click Next.

6. On the second page of the wizard, configure journaling by selecting a message format for a journaling mailbox. Click Next.

7. On the summary page, verify that all the settings are correct and then click New to create the custom content setting.

In Exercise 6.8, you will create a managed content setting using the EMS, which is faster, although possibly more complex.

EXERCISE 6.8

Creating a Managed Content Setting Using the Exchange Management Shell

Follow these steps to create a managed content setting:

1. Click Start ➤ Programs ➤ Microsoft Exchange Server 2010 and then select Exchange Management Shell.

2. Run (make sure to change the parameters enclosed in brackets):

    ```
    New-ManagedContentSettings -Name <Setting_Name>
    -FolderName <Folder_To_Apply_Setting_TO>
    -MessageClass <Item_Type> -RetentionEnabled $true
    -RetentionAction <Action>
    -AgeLimitForRetention
    <Age_Of_Item_Before_Action_Is_Taken>
    ```

Configuring Managed Folder Mailbox Policies

You can use managed folder mailbox policies to create a group of folders that you can then apply to single user or groups of users. For example, you have salespeople that all need the same folders: 100 Days to Delete, Keep Forever, and Keep for X Years. If you created a policy that had each folder in it, you could simply apply that policy to the sales group and then the salespeople would all have the folders. Otherwise, you would have to add each folder one at a time for every sales user. In this section, first we will cover how to create a managed folder mailbox policy and then we will cover how to apply the policy to a user. To create and apply a managed folder mailbox policy, follow the steps outlined in Exercise 6.9, Exercise 6.10, Exercise 6.11, and Exercise 6.12.

EXERCISE 6.9

Creating a Managed Folder Mailbox Policy Using the Exchange Management Console

Create a managed folder mailbox policy using the EMC:

1. Click Start ➤ Programs ➤ Microsoft Exchange Server 2010 and then select Exchange Management Console.

2. Expand Organizational Configuration and select Mailbox.

EXERCISE 6.9 *(continued)*

3. Open the Exchange Management Console, and click the Mailbox node in the Organization Configuration section. In the Actions pane to the right, select New Managed Folder Mailbox Policy. This will launch the New Managed Folder Mailbox Policy wizard.

4. On the first page of the New Managed Folder Mailbox Policy wizard, enter the name for the policy, click the Add button, and add the folders you want in the policy. After everything is filled out, click New to create the managed folder mailbox policy.

In Exercise 6.10, you will create a managed folder mailbox policy using the EMS instead of the EMC.

EXERCISE 6.10

Creating a Managed Folder Mailbox Policy Using the Exchange Management Shell

Open the Exchange Management Shell and run one of the following commands (make sure to change the parameters enclosed in brackets):

```
New-ManagedFolderMailboxPolicy -Name <Policy_Name>
-ManagedFolderLinks <Folder_Names>
```

In Exercise 6.11, you will assign the policy created in the previous exercise.

EXERCISE 6.11

Applying a Managed Folder Mailbox Policy Using the Exchange Management Console

Use the EMC to apply a managed folder mailbox policy by following these steps:

1. Open the Exchange Management Console and click the Mailbox node in the Recipients Configuration section. In the Actions pane, right-click a user and select Properties. Select the Mailbox Settings tab.

2. On the Mailbox Settings tab, select Messaging Records Management, and in the Messaging Records Management dialog box, check the Managed folder mailbox policy box. Click Browse and choose a Managed Folder Mailbox Policy.

3. Click OK in the Messaging Records Management dialog box and in the user Properties dialog box.

To use the EMS instead of the EMC to assign a managed folder mailbox policy, follow the steps in Exercise 6.12.

EXERCISE 6.12

**Applying a Managed Folder Mailbox Policy
Using Exchange Management Shell**

Apply a managed folder mailbox policy using EMS by following these steps:

1. Click Start ➢ Programs ➢ Microsoft Exchange Server 2010 and then select Exchange Management Shell.

2. Run (make sure to change the parameters enclosed in brackets):

    ```
    Set-Mailbox -Identity <Mailbox_Name>
    -ManagedFolderMailboxPolicy <Managed_folder_Mailbox_Policy_Name>
    ```

Creating and Applying Retention Tags and Retention Policies and Using Archive Mailboxes

Retention policies allow administrators to define how messages will be retained. They are sets of retention tags that get applied to messages. An automated process scans the user's mailbox and processes the messages according to the retention tags applied to them, either archiving or deleting messages once they reach their age limit.

Retention policies in Exchange Server 2010 are made up of three types of retention tags:

Default policy tags (DPTs)   Default policy tags apply to all emails that do not have any other tags applied to them. You can have only one DPT in each retention policy.

Retention policy tags (RPTs)   Retention policy tags apply to untagged items in the default email folders. A retention policy can have one RPT per default email folder, and RPTs can be applied only to the following default folders:

- Deleted Items
- Drafts
- Inbox
- Junk E-mail
- Outbox
- Sent Items
- RSS Feeds
- Sync Issues
- Conversation History

Personal tags   Personal tags are created by the administrator but are assigned to folders or individual emails by the end user using Outlook 2010 or Outlook Web App (OWA).

Personal tags cannot be assigned to folders that have RPTs assigned to them, but they can be assigned to individual emails in folders that have RPTs assigned to them.

Retention tags are composed of two main parts: an age limit and an action that is taken once that age limit is reached. Table 6.1 includes the actions that can be assigned to a retention tag.

TABLE 6.1   Exchange Server 2010 retention tag actions

Retention Tag Action	Description
MoveToArchive	The message is moved to a folder with the same name and in the same relative location in the archive mailbox.
MoveToDeletedItems	The message is moved to the deleted items folder, the same as if a user had deleted the message.
DeleteAndAllowRecovery	The message is moved to the Recoverable Items folder, which was known as the dumpster in previous versions. The user can still recover the email by accessing Recover Deleted Items in Outlook 2010 or OWA.
PermanentlyDelete	The message is purged from the mailbox and is not user recoverable. If a legal hold is in place, the message will still be accessible through Multi-Mailbox Search.
MarkAsPastRetentionLimit	The message is marked as being past the retention limit. OWA and Outlook 2010 will display the message with strikethrough text to inform the user that it is past the retention limit.

As you have probably noticed, one of the possible retention actions is to move the email to the archive mailbox. Archive mailboxes were introduced in Exchange Server 2010 to allow users to store older email in their Exchange mailbox without having it in their primary mailbox. The archive mailbox is accessible only through OWA or Outlook 2010 and does not get downloaded to the Outlook cached mode offline folder file. With Exchange Server 2010 SP1, the archive mailbox can be stored in a separate mailbox database, allowing archive mailboxes to have separate backup options or be stored in separate storage. Figure 6.2 shows how an archive mailbox looks in the navigation pane when viewed in OWA.

To activate an archive mailbox for a user, run the following command:

```
Enable-mailbox <mailboxName> -archive
```

Archive mailboxes can be enabled only for users that do not have managed folder policies assigned to them.

FIGURE 6.2   Archive mailbox in OWA

Exercise 6.13, Exercise 6.14, and Exercise 6.15 demonstrate how to create and apply retention policies and retention tags.

EXERCISE 6.13

Creating Retention Tags Using the Exchange Management Shell

Follow these steps to create a retention tag using the EMS:

1. Click Start ➤ Programs ➤ Microsoft Exchange Server 2010 and then select Exchange Management Shell.

2. To create a default policy tag that deletes items from the Deleted Items folder after 14 days, run:

    ```
    New-RetentionPolicyTag "DeletedItemsFolder"
    -Type "DeletedItems"
    -Comment "Remove messages from Deleted Items after 14 days"
    -RetentionEnabled $true -AgeLimitForRetention 14
    -RetentionAction DeleteAndAllowRecovery
    ```

3. To create a new retention policy tag that archives messages after 2 years, run:

    ```
    New-RetentionPolicyTag "ArchiveAfter2Years" -Type All -Comment "Archive
    untagged messages after 2 years" -RetentionEnabled $true -AgeLimitForRetention
    730 -RetentionAction MoveToArchive
    ```

4. To create a new personal policy tag for permanently deleting items after 14 days, run:

    ```
    New-RetentionPolicyTag "PermanentlyDeleteAfter14Days" -Type Personal
    -Comment "Permanently Delete After 14 Days" -RetentionEnabled $true
    -AgeLimitForRetention 14 -RetentionAction PermanentlyDelete
    ```

In Exercise 6.14, you'll create a retention policy using the retention tags created in the previous exercise.

EXERCISE 6.14

Creating and Applying a Retention Policy Using the Exchange Management Shell

To create and apply a retention tag using the EMS, follow these steps:

1. Click Start ➢ Programs ➢ Microsoft Exchange Server 2010 and then select Exchange Management Shell.

2. To create a retention policy using the tags created in the previous exercise, run:

   ```
   New-RetentionPolicy "GeneralRetentionPolicy"
   -RetentionPolicyTagLinks "DeletedItemsFolder",
   "ArchiveAfter2Years","PermanentlyDeleteAfter14Days"
   ```

3. To apply the retention policy to user Joseph.Nguyen, run:

   ```
   Set-Mailbox Joseph.Nguyen -RetentionPolicy GeneralRetentionPolicy
   ```

In Exercise 6.15, you'll use OWA to apply the personal retention tag created in Exercise 6.13.

EXERCISE 6.15

Apply a Personal Retention Tag Using Outlook Web App

To apply a retention tag in Outlook Web App, follow these steps:

1. Click Start ➢ Programs ➢ Microsoft Exchange Server 2010 and then select Exchange Management Shell.

2. To immediately apply the retention policy created in the last exercise run. More information about the managed folder assistant will be given in the next section, "Scheduling the Managed Folder Assistant.")

   ```
   Start-ManagedFolderAssistant -Mailbox Joseph.Nguyen
   ```

3. Open Internet Explorer and type https://mail.mailtask.com/owa in the address bar.

4. Log on to OWA as Joseph.

5. Create a new folder by right-clicking Inbox and clicking Create New Folder. Name the folder Do Not Keep.

6. Right-click the folder Do Not Keep, click Retention Policy, and select the PermanentlyDeleteAfter14Days retention policy tag.

Scheduling the Managed Folder Assistant

The managed folder assistant is the Exchange Server 2010 function that applies retention policies and managed folder policies and creates managed folders. When the managed folder assistant is run, it will process every mailbox on the server. The assistant can be scheduled to run with a start time and an end time. If it does not complete processing all of the mailboxes on a server in the allotted time, the next time it starts it will continue where it left off. By default, the managed folder assistant runs daily from 01:00 to 09:00.

Be aware that running the managed folder assistant is a resource-intensive process. The process has to read the date on every object in a mailbox, calculate how that date relates to the managed content settings, and then perform the actions in the settings. The managed folder assistant should be run only when the server can tolerate the extra load. It doesn't have to run every night; you should run the assistant just enough to satisfy your compliance obligations.

To schedule the managed folder assistant, perform the steps outlined in Exercise 6.16 and Exercise 6.17.

EXERCISE 6.16

Scheduling the Managed Folder Assistant Using the Exchange Management Console

Use the EMC to schedule the managed folder assistant by following these steps:

1. Click Start ➢ Programs ➢ Microsoft Exchange Server 2010 and then select Exchange Management Console.

2. Expand Organizational Configuration and select Mailbox.

3. Right-click a server on which you want to schedule the assistant to run and select Properties.

4. Click the Messaging Records Management tab, and then click the Customize button and schedule when the assistant should run.

In Exercise 6.17, you will use the EMS to schedule the managed folder assistant.

EXERCISE 6.17

Scheduling the Managed Folder Assistant Using the Exchange Management Shell

Schedule the managed folder assistant using EMS by completing the following steps:

1. Click Start ➤ Programs ➤ Microsoft Exchange Server 2010 and then select Exchange Management Shell.

2. Run (make sure to change the parameters enclosed in brackets):

   ```
   Set-MailboxServer -Identity <Mailbox__Server_Name>
   -ManagedFolderAssistantSchedule <Day_StartTime_Day_StopTime>
   ```

Classifying Message Classifications

The Exchange Server 2010 message classification feature allows administrators to create classifications for users to apply to messages. This allows users to classify messages according to their content or intended purpose. When a user applies a classification in Outlook or OWA, metadata is added to the message. This metadata gives instructions to the recipients and/or to the transport server to help them make decisions about what to do with the messages.

When the recipient opens the message in Outlook or OWA, the classification metadata is used to retrieve and then display a classification message to the recipient. The classification message helps the recipient determine how to treat the message. One of the default classifications is Company Confidential. The Company Confidential classification has a classification message that says, "This message contains sensitive information, the distribution of which should be limited." This will remind the user to not send the message to competitors or people who should not see it in general. Figure 6.3 is an example of what a client would see when viewing a classified message.

FIGURE 6.3 Viewing a classified message in Outlook

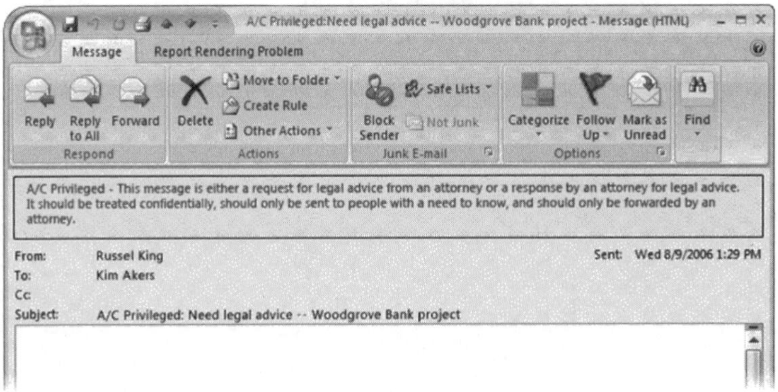

Message classifications can also be applied or acted upon by server-based transport rules. For example, you could have a rule that removes attachments from messages that were deemed inappropriate. After the rule removed the attachment, it could apply another rule that would then tell the user what happened to the message attachment. You could also have a rule that looks for messages with a Company Confidential classification on them, keeps those messages from leaving the company, and then forwards the message to a compliance officer. The compliance officer could then perform any additional steps to find out why an employee tried to forward confidential information.

Exchange Server 2010 ships with a default set of seven classifications as outlined in Table 6.2.

TABLE 6.2   Exchange Server 2010 default classifications

Default Classification	Default Classification Message
A/C Privileged	This message is either a request for legal advice from an attorney or a response by an attorney to a request for legal advice. It should be treated confidentially, should only be sent to people with a need to know, and should only be forwarded by an attorney.
Attachment Removed	An attachment was removed from this email message because the attachment was determined to pose a possible security risk.
Company Confidential	This message contains proprietary information and should be handled confidentially.
Company Internal	This message contains sensitive information that should only be delivered to internal recipients.
Internet Confidential	This message will be transmitted securely to the recipients. Recipients will have full control of the message.
Originator Requested Alternate Recipient Mail	You have received this message because the message originator specified you as an alternate recipient when delivery to the primary recipient fails.
Partner Mail	(No message is displayed for messages marked as Partner Mail.)

You can modify classifications and the classification messages based on your company needs, and you can create new classifications using the EMS command New-MessageClassification. Following is an example of an EMS command that you can use to create a new message classification:

```
New-MessageClassification -Name ContractReview -DisplayName "Contract Review"
```

```
-SenderDescription "This message has been classified as relating to
contract reviews" -RecipientDescription "This message has been
classified as being related to contract review and must be treated
in accordance with company policy"
```

You should be aware of the following several key attributes that each message classification has:

Display name   This attribute defines how the message classification will appear in Outlook and OWA when a user is selecting the classification to apply.

Sender description   This attribute should explain to the sender what this classification is used for.

Recipient description   This attribute should explain to the recipient what the message classification is used for.

Locale   This attribute specifies a culture code to create a locale-specific version of the message classification. If you have a number of locales, you may need to create a number of different classifications to meet the varied needs of these locations.

If you do not want the recipient to know that a message has been classified, you can set the EnableUserDisplay parameter to $false. You can also assign precedence to classifications to help determine in which order classifications should be applied in the event that a message has more than one classification; to do so, use the DisplayPrecedence parameter when using the Set-MessageClassification cmdlet.

Adding Message Classifications in Outlook

You must add classifications manually to Outlook 2007 by creating an XML-based file on the server and making it available to each client computer. The XML file can be generated manually with an EMS script. The script is in a subfolder (named Scripts) of the folder where Exchange is installed on your server. From the folder that has the script, run the following command to create the XML file:

```
.\Export-OutlookClassification.ps1 > c:\exports\Classifications.xml
```

Now that you have the XML file, Classifications.xml, you need to make it available to the client machines. Before Outlook can see this XML-based file, you need to add a Registry key to the computer to turn on this functionality and tell Outlook where the file is stored. But wait, there's more—the Registry key is in the HKEY_Current_User hive, so this has to be added for each user on a given computer. The Registry keys are as follows:

```
[HKEY_CURRENT_USER\Software\Microsoft\Office\12.0\Common\Policy]
"AdminClassificationPath"="c:\Exchange\Classifications.xml"
"EnableClassifications"=dword:00000001
"TrustClassifications"=dword:00000001
```

The AdminClassificationPath key specifies the path from which the client can read the Classifications.xml file. Once the Registry key and the XML-based file are in place on the client computer, Outlook needs to be restarted in order to read the XML file. One last bit of information about classifications: Exchange Server 2010 is a localized server product; almost everything in Exchange can be localized, including the message classification messages. You do this by using the -Locale switch when you create a new classification with the New-MessageClassification EMS command.

Outlook 2010 will also require the message classifications to be added. The process should be the same, except the Registry key will be in the Office\14.0 path instead of Office\12.0.

Configuring Information Rights Management

Information rights management (IRM) is a useful collateral technology that can be used to protect email messages and documents against improper disclosure. IRM embeds usage information in the document so that access restrictions, expiration information, and policy controls travel with the document. Microsoft's implementation of IRM is based on Windows Rights Management Services (RMS), and on the client side, support is built into Office and SharePoint Server. IRM is particularly useful for protecting sensitive content from being improperly forwarded or copied. It also allows for expiration of documents and messages so that they cannot be accessed past a specified date.

Exchange 2010 offers several new IRM configuration options; however, there is no requirement to configure Exchange Server to support RMS (known as Active Directory Rights Management Services—AD RMS—in Windows Server 2008). IRM configuration must be done from the Exchange Management Shell, and the first configuration that must be done is enabling the AD RMS Prelicensing agent. This agent is used to fetch the user licenses on behalf of the client.

Enabling the AD RMS Prelicensing agent is as simple as running the following cmdlet:

```
Set-IRMConfiguration -PreLicensingEnabled $true
```

There are several other IRM options that you can configure in Exchange Server 2010:

Journal report decryption Journaling report decryption allows decrypted copies of rights-protected emails to be attached to the journal report.

Transport decryption Transport decryption allows transport agents to access the message content. For example, a transport rule that blocks emails with certain key words will still be able to access rights-protected email contents to check it against the rule.

Outlook Web App Enabling IRM with OWA allows OWA users to IRM-protect messages and view IRM-protected messages.

Using any of these features requires creating a distribution group, making it the AD RMS super user group in AD RMS, and then adding the Federated Delivery mailbox to that group using the following cmdlet:

```
Add-DistributionGroupMember ADRMSSuperUsers
-Member FederatedEmail.4c1f4d8b-8179-4148-93bf-00a95fa1e042
```

Additionally, after IRM is enabled, as shown in Exercise 6.18, transport rules and Outlook protection rules can be created to apply rights management templates to messages. Outlook protection rules apply AD RMS templates to messages before they are sent from Outlook, and transport rule creation is covered later in this chapter.

EXERCISE 6.18

Enabling and Configuring Information Rights Management

Perform the following steps to enable IRM:

1. Click Start ➤ Programs ➤ Microsoft Exchange Server 2010 and then select Exchange Management Shell.

2. To enable the IRM prelicensing agent, run:

   ```
   Set-IRMConfiguration -PreLicensingEnabled $true
   ```

3. To add the Federated Delivery mailbox to the AD RMS super user group (which needs to have already been created in AD RMS), run:

   ```
   Add-DistributionGroupMember ADRMSSuperUsers
   -Member FederatedEmail.4c1f4d8b-8179-4148-93bf-00a95fa1e042
   ```

4. To create an Outlook protection rule that applies the AD RMS template Legal Communication (which must have already been created in AD RMS) to all messages sent to the legal department, run:

   ```
   New-OutlookProtectionRule -Name "Legal Department Rule"
   -SentTo DL-LegalDepartment -ApplyRightsProtectionTemplate
   "Legal Department Template"
   ```

5. To enable transport decryption, journal report decryption, and Outlook Web App integration, run:

   ```
   Set-IRMConfiguration -TransportDecryptionSetting Mandatory
   -JournalReportEncryptionEnabled $true -OWAEnabled $true
   ```

AD RMS is a powerful tool that provides IRM across several Microsoft products. For more information about installing and configuring AD RMS, see http://technet.microsoft.com/en-us/library/cc771234(WS.10).aspx.

Assigning Legal Holds and Creating Mailbox Journaling Rules

There may be legal and regulatory cases where it becomes necessary to maintain records of emails sent to individuals. In these cases, there are two methods to keep these records: legal holds and journaling. Legal holds are a new feature in Exchange Server 2010 that allow a copy of all items in a mailbox to be maintained in-place. Journaling creates a copy of all emails sent to or from a mailbox, and administrators familiar with journaling in Exchange Server 2007 will find that little has changed.

Legal holds prevent users from deleting emails from their mailboxes. When an email is deleted, it is maintained in the Recoverable Items folder (sometimes called the dumpster). If a user deletes an item from the Recoverable Items folder, it is moved to the Purges folder under the Recoverable Items folder. When an item is changed, the original version is maintained in the Versions folder. Both the Versions and the Purges folders are invisible to the end user and can be retrieved only through Multi-Mailbox Search. Assigning a legal hold to a mailbox requires only a single command:

```
Set-Mailbox Joseph.Nuyen –LitigationHoldEnabled $true
-RetentionComment "This mailbox is under a legal hold"
```

 Although legal holds prevent deleting items from mailboxes, it does not protect the mailbox from being deleted. Administrators will need to ensure that mailboxes protected with legal holds are protected from both manual and automatic deletion.

Journaling is a method for creating a copy of all emails sent to or from a mailbox. After a journal rule is created, any email sent to or from the journaled mailbox is attached to a journal report sent separately to the journaling mailbox. In Exercise 6.19, you will create a journal rule using the EMS.

EXERCISE 6.19

Creating a Journaling Rule Using the Exchange Management Shell

To create a journaling rule using the EMS, follow these steps:

1. Click Start ➢ Programs ➢ Microsoft Exchange Server 2010 and then select Exchange Management Shell.

2. To create a journaling mailbox, run:

   ```
   New-Mailbox JournalingMailbox
   ```

3. Create a journal rule to journal all email sent to or from Joseph Nguyen:

```
New-JournalRule -Name "Joseph.Nguyen Journaling"
-JournalEmailAddress Joseph.Nguyen@mailtask.com
-Recipient JournalingMailbox@mailtask.com -Scope Global -Enabled $true
```

In Exercise 6.20, you will create a journaling rule using the EMC.

Creating a Journaling Rule Using the Exchange Management Console

After creating a mailbox named Journaling, create a journaling rule using the EMC by following these steps:

1. Click Start ➢ Programs ➢ Microsoft Exchange Server 2010 and then select Exchange Management Console.

2. Expand Organizational Configuration and select Hub Transport.

3. Click the Journal Rules tab and click New Journal Rule in the right pane.

4. Type in the rule name, select the mailbox named Journaling, and the mailbox to journal.

5. Click create.

Using Multi-Mailbox Search and Discovery Mailboxes

Many organizations must deal with requirements to perform legal discoveries, whether it's because of a lawsuit or a regulatory requirement. In these cases, Multi-Mailbox Search can be used to perform searches of single mailboxes or large groups of mailboxes. Additionally, when a legal hold is enabled on a mailbox, Multi-Mailbox Search is the only method available to search purged items that are retained because of the legal hold.

Multi-Mailbox Search is accessed through the ECP or through the EMS. It uses the same search syntax and index that users use to search their own mailboxes, making it easy to delegate to nontechnical personnel in an HR or legal department that need access.

Both Exchange search and Multi-Mailbox Search make use of Advanced Query Syntax (AQS). AQS allows you to specify values for specific fields, such as the following:

From:paul@mailtask.com

For a list of search keywords available with AQS, see

msdn.microsoft.com/en-us/library/aa965711(VS.85).aspx

and

technet.microsoft.com/en-us/library/bb232132.aspx#AQS.

The results from a Multi-Mailbox Search are stored in a special type of mailbox called a Discovery mailbox. The following command is used to create a Discovery mailbox:

```
New-mailbox <Name> -Discovery
```

Discovery mailboxes are different from normal mailboxes in a few ways. First, only Discovery mailboxes can be used to store Multi-Mailbox Search results, and when you're performing a Multi-Mailbox Search using the ECP, only Discovery mailboxes are listed when you choose a target to store the results in. Also, Discovery mailboxes have a default storage quota of 50 GB, ensuring that a large amount of data can be stored in them without having to worry about increasing their size. Finally, they're secure by default because they're tied to a disabled Active Directory account, so permissions must be explicitly added to gain access and email delivery to them is disabled.

To perform a Multi-Mailbox Search, a user must be assigned the Mailbox Search role. Also, to view the results of a Multi-Mailbox Search, the user must be given access to the Discovery mailbox in which the results are stored. The default Discovery Management role group gives access to both Multi-Mailbox Search and the default Discovery mailbox, but permission to access additional Discovery mailboxes that are created must be assigned separately. In Exercise 6.21, you will run a Multi-Mailbox Search using the ECP.

EXERCISE 6.21

Perform a Multi-Mailbox Search Using the Exchange Control Panel

To complete this exercise, be sure to have completed Exercise 6.3. To run a Multi-Mailbox Search by following these steps:

1. Open Internet Explorer and log in before you are able to access Multi-Mailbox Search.

2. Click the Mail Control button and the left side to open the Reporting section, and then click the Mailbox Searches tab.

3. Click the New button to open the New Mailbox Search window.

4. In the Keywords box, type your search term—for example, **from: admin@mailtask.com**.

5. Expand Mailboxes To Search, click the Add button, and choose the mailboxes that you want to search.

New Mailbox Search

*Required fields

Keywords   ★

Type words to search for. Separate words with uppercase
AND, OR, or NOT. Use double quotation marks to search for
multi-word phrases. For wildcard searches, place an asterisk
(*) after the word.

from:admin@mailtask.com

☐ Include items that can't be searched

Message types to search: E-mail

Select message types...

Messages To and From Specific E-Mail Addresses   ⩡

Date Range   ⩡

Mailboxes to Search   ★

* Select mailboxes to search:

○ Search all mailboxes

⦿ Search specific mailboxes or the mailboxes of members
    of public groups:

    ✚ Add...   ▬ Remove

    ✉ Admin

                                                        ✓ Save   ✗ Cancel

---

6. Under Search Name and Storage Location, enter the search name **Discovery1**. Then
    click the Browse button and choose the Discovery Search mailbox.

7. The search will now show up in the list of searches in the lower-left portion of
    the Mailbox Searches tab. Once the search is complete, choose it from the list of
    searches to display more details in the right pane.

8. Click the Open button next to the Discovery mailbox name in the Results line to view
    the search results.

Configuring Transport Rules

Transport rules function similarly to Outlook rules, but they are applied to messages during
transport by the Hub and Edge Transport server roles, and they are under complete control
of the administrator. As previously mentioned, every message in an Exchange organization
must travel through a Hub Transport server. Even messages sent to another mailbox on the
same server travel through a Hub Transport server before they are sent right back to the same
Mailbox server. Because this is always the case, this puts the Hub Transport server in a position to perform actions on messages consistently as they pass through.

There is one uniform rule applied throughout the organization with which every Hub Transport server has to work. Transport rules are stored in the Configuration container of Active Directory; therefore, all Hub Transport servers share the same set of transport roles.

Transport rules are great for compliance, and as administrators, we can also use them to have some control over users. The following is a list of some actions you can accomplish using rules:

- You can create ethical walls to limit the interaction of certain groups of users.

- You can filter personal information in emails (SSNs, account numbers, and so on) and prevent it from being sent.

- You can set up message classifications that can be acted upon by transport rules.

- You can use transport rules to add items such as legal disclaimers, notes, and subjects to messages.

- You can forward, copy, and blind copy messages to additional recipients.

- You can create mail flow rules for enforcing encryption and routing policies.

- You can perform message hygiene functions on an Edge Transport server.

You can do a lot more with rules; they are flexible tools for controlling email. The EMC transport rule GUI is similar to the interface used to create rules in Outlook. You can also work with rules in the EMS.

Transport Predicates

Each transport rule contains two components: a predicate and an action. There are two types of *predicates*:

- Conditions specify which email message attributes, headers, recipients, senders, or other parts of the message are used in identifying which messages a rule should act upon. If no condition is applied to a transport rule, the transport rule applies the configured action unless the message matches a configured exception.

- Exceptions specify messages that should be exempt from a transport rule, even if the message matches a transport rule condition. Exceptions are optional.

Table 6.3 lists all the conditions and exceptions available on a Hub Transport server.

TABLE 6.3 Predicates available on a Hub Transport server

Predicate Name (EMC)	Predicate Name (EMS)	Description
Between members of distribution list and distribution list	BetweenMemberOf	Matches email messages that are sent between members of two distribution groups.
From a member of distribution list	FromMemberOf	Matches the email senders that are members of the specified distribution group.

TABLE 6.3   Predicates available on a Hub Transport server *(continued)*

Predicate Name (EMC)	Predicate Name (EMS)	Description
From people	From	Matches the email senders that are mail-enabled Active Directory objects like mailboxes, mail-enabled users, and contacts. If the From address is from outside the Exchange organization, a contact should be created.
From users that are inside or outside the organization	FromScope	Matches email messages that are sent from either inside the Exchange organization or outside the Exchange organization.
Marked with classification	HasClassification	Matches messages that are marked with the specified classification.
Marked with importance	WithImportance	Matches messages that are set to the specified importance.
Sent to a member of distribution list	SentToMemberOf	Matches email messages that are sent to members of the specified distribution group. These recipients can be specified anywhere in the To, carbon copy (Cc), or blind carbon copy (Bcc) fields of the message.
Sent to people	SentTo	Matches email messages that are sent to mailboxes, mail-enabled users, or contacts. These recipients can be specified anywhere in the To, Cc, or Bcc field of the message.
Sent to users inside or outside the organization, or partners	SentToScope	Matches email messages that are sent to either inside the Exchange organization or outside the Exchange organization.
When a message header contains specific words	HeaderContains	Matches messages where the specified message header field contains the specified value.

TABLE 6.3   Predicates available on a Hub Transport server *(continued)*

Predicate Name (EMC)	Predicate Name (EMS)	Description
When any attachment file name matches text patterns	AttachmentNameMatches	Matches messages that contain text patterns in attachment filenames that match a specified regular expression.
When any of the recipients in the Cc field is a member of distribution list	AnyOfCcHeaderMemberOf	Matches messages that are sent to members of a specified distribution group where they are listed in the Cc field of the message.
When any of the recipients in the Cc field is people	AnyOfCcHeader	Matches email messages that are sent to mailboxes, mail-enabled users, or contacts. These recipients must be listed in the Cc field of the message.
When any of the recipients in the To field is a member of distribution list	AnyOfToHeaderMemberOf	Matches messages that are sent to members of a specified distribution group where they are listed in the To field of the message.
When any of the recipients in the To field is people	AnyOfToHeader	Matches email messages that are sent to mailboxes, mail-enabled users, or contacts. These recipients must be listed in the To field of the message.
When any of the recipients in the To or Cc fields are people	AnyOfToCcHeader	Matches email messages that are sent to mailboxes, mail-enabled users, or contacts. These recipients must be listed in the To or Cc field of the message.
When any of the recipients in the To or Cc fields is a member of distribution list	AnyOfToCcHeaderMemberOf	Matches messages that are sent to members of a specified distribution group where they are listed in either the To or Cc field of the message.
When the From address contains specific words	FromAddressContains	Matches messages that contain the specified words in the From field.

TABLE 6.3   Predicates available on a Hub Transport server *(continued)*

Predicate Name (EMC)	Predicate Name (EMS)	Description
When the From address matches text patterns	FromAddressMatches	Matches messages that contain text patterns in the From field that match a specified regular expression.
When the message header matches text patterns	HeaderMatches	Matches messages with a header field that contain text patterns that match a specified regular expression.
When the size of any attachment is greater than or equal to limit	AttachmentSizeOver	Matches messages that contain attachments that are larger than the specified value.
When the Subject field contains specific words	SubjectContains	Matches messages that contain the specified words in the subject field.
When the Subject field matches text patterns	SubjectMatches	Matches messages where text patterns in the Subject field match a specified regular expression.
When the Subject field or the body of the message contains specific words	SubjectOrBodyContains	Matches messages that contain the specified words in the Subject field or in the body.
When the Subject field or the body of the message matches text patterns	SubjectOrBodyMatches	Matches messages where text patterns in the Subject field or body match a specified regular expression.
With a spam confidence level (SCL) rating that is greater or equal to limit	SclOver	Matches messages that have a specified SCL or higher.
When the manager of any sender is people	ManagerIs	Matches messages where the specified user's manager exists in the list of specified addresses.
When the sender is the manager of a recipient	ManagementRelationship	Matches messages where the sender has the specified management relationship with a recipient.

TABLE 6.3   Predicates available on a Hub Transport server *(continued)*

Predicate Name (EMC)	Predicate Name (EMS)	Description
If the sender and recipient's AD Attribute are Evaluation	ADAttributeComparison	Matches messages where the sender's specified Active Directory attribute matches or doesn't match the same attribute of any recipient.
When a recipient's address contains specific words	RecipientAddressContainsWords	Matches messages where a recipient's address contains any of the specified words.
When a recipient's address contains text patterns	RecipientAddressMatchesPatterns	Matches messages where a recipient's address matches a specified regular expression.
When a recipient's properties contains specific words	RecipientAttributeContains	Matches messages where the specified attribute of a recipient contains a specified string.
When a recipient's properties contains text patterns	RecipientAttributeMatches	Matches messages where the specified attribute of a recipient matches a regular expression.
If the message is Message Type	MessageTypeMatches	Matches messages of the specified type.
When the sender's properties contain specific words	SenderAttributeContains	Matches messages where the specified attribute of the sender matches a specified string.
When the sender's properties match text patterns	SenderAttributeMatches	Matches messages where the specified attribute of the sender contains text patterns that match a specified regular expression.
Not marked with a message classification	HasNoClassifications	Matches messages that don't have a message classification.
When an attachment's content contains words	AttachmentContainsWords	Matches messages with attachments that contain a specified string.

TABLE 6.3   Predicates available on an Edge Transport server *(continued)*

Predicate Name (EMC)	Predicate Name (EMS)	Description
When an attachment's content matches text patterns	AttachmentMatchesPatterns	Matches messages with attachments that contain a text pattern that matches a specified regular expression.
When an attachment is unsupported	AttachmentIsUnsupported	Matches messages with attachments that aren't supported.

Because the Edge Transport server does not have direct access to Active Directory and serves a different purpose, it also has different predicates available for transport rules. Table 6.4 lists these predicates.

TABLE 6.4   Predicates available on an Edge Transport server

Predicate Name (EMC)	Predicate Name (EMS)	Description
From users inside or outside the organization	FromScope	Matches email messages that are sent from either inside the Exchange organization or outside the Exchange organization.
When a message header contains specific words	HeaderContains	Matches messages where the specified message header field contains the specified header field value.
When any recipient address contains specific words	AnyOfRecipientAddressContains	Matches messages that contain the specified words in the To, carbon copy (Cc), or blind carbon copy (Bcc) field.
When any recipient address matches text patterns	AnyOfRecipientAddressMatches	Matches messages where text patterns in the To, Cc, or Bcc field match a specified regular expression.
When the From address contains specific words	FromAddressContains	Matches messages that contain the specified words in the From field.

TABLE 6.4   Predicates available on an Edge Transport server *(continued)*

Predicate Name (EMC)	Predicate Name (EMS)	Description
When the From address matches text patterns	FromAddressMatches	Matches messages that contain text patterns in the From field that match a specified regular expression.
When the message header matches text patterns	HeaderMatches	Matches messages where the specified message header field contains text patterns that match a specified regular expression.
When the size of any attachment is greater than or equal to limit	AttachmentSizeOver	Matches messages that contain attachments that are larger than the specified value.
When the Subject field contains specific words	SubjectContains	Matches messages that contain the specified words in the Subject field.
When the Subject field matches text patterns	SubjectMatches	Matches messages where text patterns in the Subject field match a specified regular expression.
When the Subject field or the body of the message contains specific words	SubjectOrBodyContains	Matches messages that contain the specified words in the Subject field or body.
When the Subject field or the body of the message matches text patterns	SubjectOrBodyMatches	Matches messages where text patterns in the Subject field or body contain a specified regular expression.
With a spam confidence level (SCL) rating that is greater than or equal to limit	SclOver	Matches messages that are configured by using the specified SCL.

Transport Actions

The *action* portion of the transport rule specifies what should happen to email messages that match all the predicates defined on the transport rule. Actions modify some aspect of the message or the message's delivery. Every transport rule must have at least one action configured. Actions include the ability to modify the message header or body, add or remove recipients, apply classifications, add disclaimers, bounce the message with a Non-Delivery Report (NDR), or silently drop the message.

Hub Transport servers have the actions listed in Table 6.5.

TABLE 6.5 Available actions on Hub Transport servers

Action Name (EMS)	Action Name (EMS)	Description
Add a recipient in the To field addresses	AddToRecipient	Adds one or more recipients to the To address list of the email message.
Append disclaimer text and fallback to action if unable to apply	ApplyHtmlDisclaimer	Applies an HTML disclaimer to the message.
Apply message classification	ApplyClassification	Applies a message classification to the message.
Blind carbon copy (Bcc) the message to addresses	BlindCopyTo	Adds one or more recipients to the Bcc address list. The original recipients cannot see the additional addresses.
Copy message to addresses	CopyTo	Adds one or more recipients to the Cc field of the message.
Prepend the subject with string	PrependSubject	Prepends a string to the start of the message's subject field.
Redirect message to addresses	RedirectMessage	Redirects the message to one or more recipients that are specified.
Remove header	RemoveHeader	Removes the specified message header field.
Reject the message with status code and response	RejectMessage	Deletes the message and sends a non-delivery report to the sender.
Set header with value	SetHeader	Creates a new or modifies an existing message header field.
Set the spam confidence level to value	SetScl	Sets the spam confidence level (SCL) on a message.

TABLE 6.5 Available actions on Hub Transport servers *(continued)*

Action Name (EMS)	Action Name (EMS)	Description
Delete the message without notifying anyone	DeleteMessage	Deletes the message without sending a notification.
Rights protect message with RMS template	RightsProtectMessage	Applies the specified Rights Management Services (RMS) template to the message. For more information, see "Configuring Transport Protection Rules."
Add the sender's manager as a specific recipient type	AddManagerAsRecipientType	Adds the sender's manager, if defined in the Manager attribute in Active Directory, as the specified recipient type.
Forward the message to addresses for moderation	ModerateMessageByUser	Forwards the message to the specified moderators as an attachment wrapped in an approval request. For more information, see "Understanding Moderated Transport."
Forward the message to the sender's manager for moderation	ModerateMessageByManager	Forwards the message to the sender's manager for moderation, if the Manager attribute is populated in Active Directory. Important: If the sender's Manager attribute isn't populated in Active Directory, the message is delivered to recipients without moderation. This action doesn't require any action properties.

Again, because the Edge Transport role has a different purpose, there are also different actions that can be done on an Edge Transport server, as shown in Table 6.6.

TABLE 6.6   Available actions on Edge Transport servers

Action Name (EMC)	Action Name (EMS)	Description
Add a recipient in the To field addresses	AddToRecipient	Adds one or more recipients to the To address list of the email message.
Blind carbon copy (Bcc) the message to addresses	BlindCopyTo	Adds one or more recipients to the Bcc address list. The original recipients cannot see the additional addresses.
Copy the message to addresses	CopyTo	Adds one or more recipients to the Cc field of the message.
Drop connection	Disconnect	Drops the connection between the sending server and the Edge Transport server. This does not generate a non-delivery report (NDR) message.
Log an event with message	LogEvent	Adds an event into the application log of the local computer.
Prepend the subject with string	PrependSubject	Prepends a string to the start of the message's subject field.
Put the message in spam quarantine mailbox	Quarantine	Quarantine redirects the message to the spam quarantine mailbox that is configured by using the Set-ContentFilterConfig cmdlet.
Redirect the message to addresses	RedirectMessage	Redirects the message to one or more recipients that are specified.
Remove header	RemoveHeader	Removes the specified message header field.
Set header with value	SetHeader	Creates a new or modifies an existing message header field.

TABLE 6.6 Available actions on Edge Transport servers *(continued)*

Action Name (EMC)	Action Name (EMS)	Description
Set the spam confidence level to value	SetScl	Sets the spam confidence level (SCL) on a message.
Reject the message with status code and response	SmtpRejectMessage	Deletes the message and sends a notification to the sender with a specified delivery status notification (DSN) code.
Delete the message without notifying anyone	DeleteMessage	Deletes the message without sending a notification.
Reject the message with status code and response	SmtpRejectMessage	Deletes the email message and sends a notification to the sender. The recipients don't receive the message or notification. This action enables you to specify a specific delivery status notification (DSN) code.

Real World Scenario

A Real-Life Rule Story

One small office deployment had a local administrator who was instructed to prepend *[Contracts]* to the Subject field of every message sent between two specific people. Although the reasoning behind the rule wasn't quite clear, the administrator thought they had it figured out until later in the day when two employees could no longer reply to any messages. None of the messages were being delivered, a Non-Delivery Report was returned saying the Subject field was too long. After looking more closely at the message, the administrator determined the rule was doing exactly what it was configured to do, prepend the text to all messages including ones that already had the text. This wasn't what the local administrator had expected the rule to do. The quick fix was to add an exception to the rule telling it to not add the text if it was already there.

These types of stories demonstrate the power of transport rules and encourage you to plan for all your rules and how they will work. Rules will do what you tell them to do regardless of consequences. With every rule you create, spend some time to figure out what might go wrong and what exceptions you might need.

Working with Transport Rules

You can specify conditions and exceptions using a large number of criteria that allow the rule to match messages according to specific AD objects (such as sender or addressee), patterns of text (either literal or using regular expressions), or other conditions.

Before you configure transport rules, you should consider these few design and planning tips:

- Every Hub Transport server will have to evaluate every rule on every message that passes through it. Rules are cached in RAM. Larger numbers of rules will therefore require larger allocations of RAM on each of the Hub Transport servers.

- The official limit to rules is 1,000 per forest. Note that this rule was based on performance testing and is more of a recommendation than a hard limit. You should monitor server performance and message delivery times to determine the appropriate number of rules for your organization.

- Using regular expressions in rules is very powerful and yet it's easy to make a mistake that causes unexpected behavior. Regular expressions can add to the processing requirements of a rule.

- Transport rules must use universal security groups. This is required because transport rules apply to all Hub Transport servers in the forest; therefore, they need to be accessible in the entire forest. Because Hub Transport uses a recipient cache that refreshes only every 4 hours, changes to members of a group may take several hours to take effect across the organization.

- Test all transport rules in a lab before deploying them into production.

- Hub transport rules are created for the forest, so any transport rule created in the forest is run on all Hub Transport servers in the forest. Edge transport rules have to be created on each individual edge server, which requires more administrative overhead, but they can be used to drop connections at the Edge when necessary.

To create a new Hub Transport rule, follow the steps outlined in Exercise 6.22 and Exercise 6.23.

EXERCISE 6.22

Creating a New Transport Rule Using the Exchange Management Console

To create a new Hub Transport rule using the EMC, follow these steps:

1. Click Start ➢ Programs ➢ Microsoft Exchange Server 2010 and then select Exchange Management Console.

2. Expand Organizational Configuration and select Hub Transport.

3. Click the Transport Rules tab.

EXERCISE 6.22 *(continued)*

4. In the Actions pane, click New Transport Rule and the New Transport Rule wizard will guide you through creating a rule.

5. When you create the rule, you have the option of enabling it. A rule will not do anything until it is enabled, so if you do not enable the rule at the end of the wizard, you can do so later by right-clicking the rule and selecting Enable Rule.

In Exercise 6.23, you create the same transport rule as in Exercise 6.22, except this time you'll use the EMS. Although there are far fewer steps required, using the EMS to create transport rules requires knowing the exact predicates and actions you want to use.

EXERCISE 6.23

Creating a New Transport Rule Using the Exchange Management Shell

1. To create a rule that applies a rights protection template to all messages sent to the legal department, complete the following steps:

2. Click Start ➤ Programs ➤ Microsoft Exchange Server 2010 and then select Exchange Management Shell.

```
New-TransportRule -Name "Legal Department RM"
-SentToMemberOf DL-LegalDepartment
-ApplyRightsProtectionTemplate "Legal Department Template"
```

Managing Policies and Address Lists

The functionality available for controlling and managing a messaging environment is one of the standout features of Exchange 2010. How is it that you are able to customize how email addresses are assigned or how the address lists are laid out? Also, how is it that you can maintain control over content that mobile devices are accessing? In the following sections, we will tackle these questions.

Configuring Email Address Policies

Email address policies assign email addresses to mailboxes and mail-enabled users, contacts, groups, and public folders based on a set of conditions. You can create email policies to assign specific email addresses using criteria such as departments or business units. For instance, your company may want an address of user@exchangeexchange.com assigned to your corporate users; however, your consulting division may require user@namedpipes.net email addresses. This and a lot more can be configured through email policies.

In Exchange Server 2010, the process that creates or modifies a mail-enabled object applies the email address policy. Also, when you make a change to an email policy, you can allow it to run immediately or schedule it to run at a later time. You can also update the email address with the `Update-EmailAdressPolicy` command.

Email address policies are not limited to just assigning basic SMTP email addresses. The following types of addresses are available by default in Exchange 2010:

- Precanned and custom SMTP
- EX (Legacy DN Proxy Address Prefix Display Name)
- X.500
- X.400
- MSMail
- CcMail
- Lotus Notes
- Novell GroupWise
- Exchange Unified Messaging proxy address (EUM proxy address)

Most likely, you will modify the SMTP-based email address policies to create email addresses for users in your company. There are a number of precanned, or premade, SMTP addresses available, as shown in Figure 6.4.

If these precanned options don't meet your needs, you can use variables to create a custom SMTP address policy. Perhaps you want to create an email address based on the first two letters of someone's first name and their last name. In that case, you would enter `%2g%s@mailtask.com` as the custom SMTP address. There are a number of options available for these custom SMTP addresses; Table 6.7 shows the available variables.

FIGURE 6.4 Adding a precanned SMTP email address

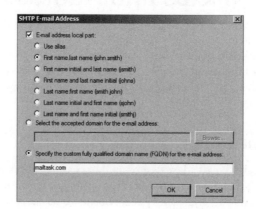

TABLE 6.7 Available variables for custom SMTP addresses

Variable	Value
%g	First name (given name)
%i	Middle initial
%s	Last name (surname)
%d	Display name
%m	Exchange alias
%xs	Uses the first *x* letters of the first name, where *x* is a number
%xg	Uses the first *x* letters of the last name, where *x* is a number

To create a new email address policy, follow the steps outlined in Exercise 6.24 and Exercise 6.25.

EXERCISE 6.24

Creating a New Email Address Policy Using the Exchange Management Console

Follow these steps to create a new email address policy using the EMC:

1. Click Start ➤ Programs ➤ Microsoft Exchange Server 2010 and then select Exchange Management Console.

EXERCISE 6.24 *(continued)*

2. Expand Organizational Configuration and select Hub Transport.

3. Click the E-Mail Address Policy tab.

4. In the Actions pane, click New E-Mail Address Policy.

5. On the first page of the New E-Mail Address Policy wizard, type the name of the policy and select the recipient types that will be affected by the policy, such as Exchange mailboxes, resource mailboxes, external accounts, and more. Click Next.

6. On the second page, select the conditions that must be met by the objects that the policy will apply to. You can apply policies based on state, company, department, and custom attributes 1 through 15. Clicking the Preview button will display a list of objects that will be affected by the conditions. Click Next.

7. On the third page, type the email address that will be applied to the objects that meet the conditions set on the last page. Click the Add button to add addresses. Select how the email address will be formatted. Click Next.

8. On the next page, you are presented with the option of applying the policy immediately or scheduling it to be applied later. After you configure when the policy will be applied, click New.

In Exercise 6.25, you will create a new email address policy with the EMS.

EXERCISE 6.25

Creating a New Email Address Policy Using the Exchange Management Shell

Open the EMS and run the following command (make sure to change the parameters enclosed in brackets):

```
New-EmailAddressPolicy -Name <Policy_Name> -IncludedRecipients
<Who_To_Apply_Policy_To> -EnabledPrimarySMTPAddressTemplate
<Email_Address_To_Apply>
```

Creating Address Lists

An *address list* is a collection of recipient and other AD objects such as groups, contacts, users, and rooms. You can use address lists to organize recipients and resources, making it easier for users to find the recipients and resources they want. Address lists are updated dynamically based on LDAP queries. This is beneficial because objects don't have to be added manually to the lists when they are created in your organizations. The default address list for an organization is called the global address list (GAL). The GAL should contain all the objects in your organization that are Exchange-enabled and not set to be hidden from address lists. There are a number of other default address lists, but none has its own acronym like the GAL. These lists are for the most part self-explanatory:

The All Contacts list   All the Exchange-enabled non-hidden contacts in the Exchange organization

The All Groups list   All the Exchange-enabled non-hidden groups in the Exchange organization

The All Rooms list   All the Exchange-enabled non-hidden rooms in the Exchange organization

The All Users list   All the Exchange-enabled non-hidden users in the Exchange organization

The Public Folders list   All the Exchange-enabled non-hidden public folders in the Exchange organization

The default global address list   All the Exchange-enabled objects in the Exchange organization

In larger environments, the GAL can become unwieldy and difficult to navigate for end users. To alleviate some of this confusion, you can create additional address lists that provide a subset of the objects in it. For example, in a company that has two major divisions that primarily communicate intradivision, you can create an address list for each, allowing the end users to search the local address list for contacts. Of course, end users can also still use the GAL if they need to communicate with others outside of their division.

Address lists are stored on the server and accessed from the server. When Outlook is either disconnected or in cached mode, it does not have access to the server to perform lookups in the GAL. To facilitate this, Exchange also creates an Offline Address Book (OAB). The OAB is downloaded to the Outlook client so that it can use it as a local query source for address book lookups.

Outlook cached mode uses the OAB by default to cut down on network requests over the wire. This has both advantages and disadvantages. The OAB is by default only generated once a night. This means that those who are using the OAB will see address list changes only once a day after they have downloaded the new version. This could lead to users not being able to see any of the changes made to the address lists until they download a new OAB copy. To rectify this problem, you can modify how often the OAB is generated by changing its update schedule properties. The default offline address list automatically includes the default GAL; if additional address lists are created, they must also be added to the OAB.

To create a new address list in the EMC, follow the steps in Exercise 6.26.

EXERCISE 6.26

Creating a New Address List Using the Exchange Management Console

To create a new address list using the EMC, follow these steps:

1. Click Start ➢ Programs ➢ Microsoft Exchange Server 2010 and then select Exchange Management Console.

2. Expand Organizational Configuration and select Mailbox.

3. Click the Address Lists tab.

4. In the Actions pane to the right, click New Address List. The New Address List wizard guides you in creating an address list.

To create a new address list using the EMS instead of the EMC, perform the steps in Exercise 6.27.

Creating a New Address List Using the Exchange Management Shell

Open the EMS and run the following command (make sure to change the parameters enclosed in brackets):

```
New-AddressList -Name <Address_List_Name>
-Container <Where_To_Place_The_Address_List>
-ConditionalCustomAttribute1 <Query>
```

Configuring Mobile Device Policies

Experts agree that the use of mobile devices poses one of the highest risks for divulging confidential information. Because mobile devices are able to synchronize your email and contacts and access SharePoint documents, care needs to be taken to protect your company data. This need has not gone unnoticed. Exchange ActiveSync mailbox policies let you apply a number of settings to a user's or group of users' ActiveSync-capable mobile devices. The settings are there to allow you to have some control over the phones that attach to your organization and how secure they are.

 Not all ActiveSync-capable devices support all of the available policy settings. The policies available can also vary in each version of the device software. Be sure to understand the settings that are available for your user devices and how those devices behave when policies are applied.

Table 6.8 lists some of the available ActiveSync settings.

TABLE 6.8 Common ActiveSync settings

Setting	Description
Allow Nonprovisionable Devices	This allows older Windows mobile devices that do not fully support ActiveSync policies to connect via ActiveSync.

TABLE 6.8 Common ActiveSync settings *(continued)*

Setting	Description
Allow Simple Password	This enables or disables the ability to use passwords based on simple patterns, such as sequential numbers like 5678 (numbers in order) or 0852 (patterns on the phone dial pad).
Alphanumeric Password Required	This requires that a password be more complex and contain at least one nonnumeric character.
Attachments Enabled	If enabled, this setting allows attachments to be downloaded to the mobile device. If your phones are on pay-for-bit data plans, it might be good to disable this setting to help reduce bandwidth costs on the phones.
Device Encryption Enabled	If this setting is enabled, it forces the device to use encryption when communicating with the Exchange servers.
Password Enabled	If this setting is enabled, it forces the device to have a password.
Password Expiration	This setting sets the length of time after which a device password will expire and must be changed.
Password History	This sets how many passwords are saved in order to limit the user from reusing a previous password.
Policy Refresh Interval	This setting defines how frequently the device will connect to the Exchange server and update mobile device policy information.
Maximum Attachment Size	This setting specifies the maximum size of attachments that will be automatically downloaded to the device.
Maximum Failed Password Attempts	This setting specifies how many times an incorrect password can be entered before a device wipe is performed.
Maximum Inactivity Time Lock	This setting specifies the length of time a device can go without user input before the device will be locked and require a password to unlock it.

TABLE 6.8 Common ActiveSync settings *(continued)*

Setting	Description
Minimum Password Length	This setting specifies the minimum required length of a password.
Password Recovery	This enables the device password to be recovered from the server.
UNC File Access	This setting, if enabled, allows the device to access files stored on Universal Naming Convention (UNC) shares on the company network.
WSS File Access	This setting, if enabled, allows the device to access files stored on Microsoft Windows SharePoint Services sites on the company network.

For a list of the available ActiveSync policy settings, see technet.microsoft.com/en-us/library/bb123484.aspx.

To create an ActiveSync mailbox policy, follow the steps outlined in Exercise 6.28 and Exercise 6.29.

EXERCISE 6.28

Creating an ActiveSync Mailbox Policy Using the Exchange Management Console

Follow these steps to create an ActiveSync mailbox policy using the EMC:

1. Click Start ➢ Programs ➢ Microsoft Exchange Server 2010 and then select Exchange Management Console.

2. Expand Organizational Configuration and select Mailbox.

3. Click the Exchange ActiveSync Mailbox Policy tab.

4. In the Actions, click New Exchange ActiveSync Mailbox Policy.

5. On the first page of the New Exchange ActiveSync Mailbox Policy wizard, type the name of the policy and then configure the settings listed in Table 6.8. Click New.

ActiveSync mailbox policies can also be created using the EMS. In many cases, the EMC will be easier to use because the EMS will require finding the name of a setting you want to use. To create an ActiveSync mailbox policy using the EMS, perform Exercise 6.29.

EXERCISE 6.29

Creating an ActiveSync Mailbox Policy Using the Exchange Management Shell

Open the EMS and run the following commands (make sure to change the parameters enclosed in brackets):

```
New-ActiveSyncMaiboxPolicy -Name <Policy_Name>
-DevicePasswordEnabled:$false
-AlphanumericDevicePasswordRequired:$false
```

Configuring Antivirus and Antispam Solutions

The critical components of any email system today always include a comprehensive antivirus and antispam solution. In the following sections, we focus on these two functions of Exchange and how you can configure them.

> **NOTE**
>
> When Exchange is deployed in an enterprise environment, Microsoft recommends using an Edge Transport server to provide the bulk of the antispam and inbound antivirus functions. All of the antispam features are available by default on an Edge Transport server, and therefore most of the antispam documentation you read from Microsoft will be specific to the Edge Transport role.
>
> It is possible to enable all of the antispam features except for the attachment filtering agent on a Hub Transport server; however, this not considered best practice. To enable the antispam features on a single Hub Transport server, you need to run the Install-AntispamAgents.ps1 PowerShell script from the Scripts subfolder where Exchange has been installed, restart the Transport service, and manually exempt all of the internal SMTP servers from connection filtering. You can find more information about this process and its limitations at technet.microsoft.com/en-us/library/bb201691.aspx.

Exchange 2010 offers no built-in antivirus functionality, but it does include a comprehensive set of antispam features. Exchange also does not have an IP block list built in, although there are several third-party companies that offer IP block lists for little to no charge. Microsoft Forefront Protection 2010 for Exchange Server (FPES) offers three important additions to the built-in Exchange functionality. When FPES is installed, it replaces the built-in antispam functionality with the Cloudmark engine, which provides improved antispam detection. FPES also gives access to the Forefront DNS block list, which blocks spam servers based on IP address, blocking spam before it has to be processed. Finally, FPES provides antivirus capability, protecting users from receiving viruses via email. When implementing Exchange, it is important to make sure you have both antivirus and antispam functionality, but it is your decision on whether to use FPES or a third-party antivirus program.

Configuring Exchange Server 2010 Antispam

The following sections describe how to configure the built-in Exchange Server 2010 antispam options. If you have decided to use FPES for Exchange as your antivirus solution, we suggest skipping to the section "Using Forefront Protection 2010 for Exchange Server" and also configuring it for antispam.

Content Filtering

Content filtering in Exchange Server 2010 is really the third generation of the intelligent message filter (IMF) that was introduced in Exchange Server 2003. The content filter works by examining the content of each message passing through the Edge Transport server based on keyword analysis, message size, and other factors. When the analysis has been completed, the message is then assigned a spam confidence level (SCL) value from 0 to 9. A value of 0 means the message has been determined almost certainly *not* to be spam, whereas a value of 9 means the message has been determined almost certainly to be spam.

To configure the Content Filtering options, select the Content Filtering item from the Antispam tab of the Edge Transport options. You can either right-click the Content Filtering item and select Properties from the context menu or click the Properties link in the Actions pane on the right side for the Content Filtering item. Either way, the Content Filtering Properties dialog box opens to the General tab, shown in Figure 6.5.

General   The General tab provides no configurable options but does provide information about the status of content filtering and the last modification date.

FIGURE 6.5   The General tab of the Content Filtering Properties dialog box

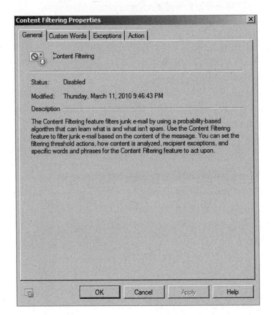

Custom Words   The Custom Words tab, shown in Figure 6.6, allows you to enter a list of words that will modify the default behavior of the content filter. In the top area of this tab, you can enter words that will never be blocked, such as those that might otherwise typically be blocked by the content filter. The bottom half of the tab allows you to enter words that will always be blocked, except if they are also contained in the "always allowed" list.

FIGURE 6.6   The Custom Words tab of the Content Filtering Properties dialog box

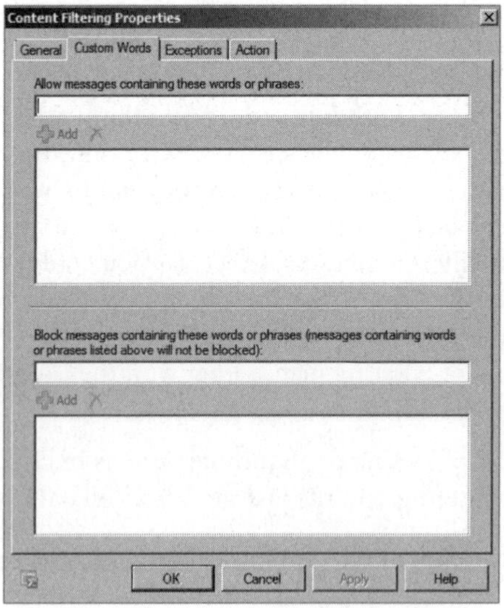

Exceptions   The Exceptions tab, shown in Figure 6.7, allows you to enter a list of email addresses that should always receive messages, even if those messages would have ordinarily been blocked by the content filter. You might want to enter a generic spam email address here to collect these messages, such as spamcollection@mailtask.com. Also, there will likely be one or more users who want to opt out of the content filter completely, so you'll need to enter their email addresses here.

FIGURE 6.7   The Exceptions tab of the Content Filtering Properties dialog box

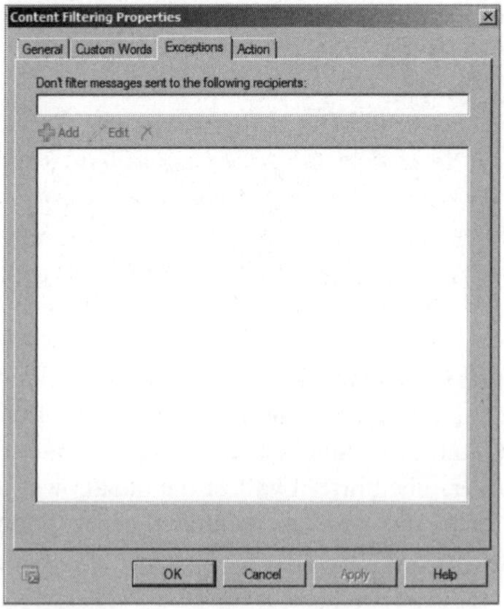

Action The Action tab, shown in Figure 6.8, allows you to configure what the content filter will do when a message has been classified at a certain SCL. You have three options: delete the message (with no NDR), reject the message (with an NDR), or quarantine the message to an internal mailbox. By default, only message rejection is enabled and it has an SCL value of 7. You will want to configure these options to suit your organization's needs and tolerance of spam.

FIGURE 6.8 The Action tab of the Content Filtering Properties dialog box

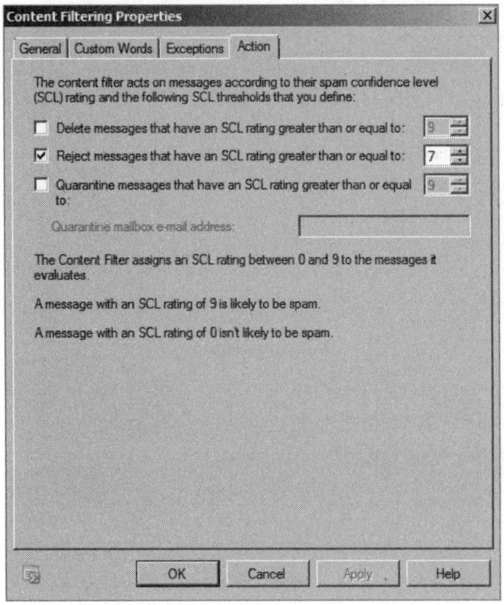

IP Allow Lists

Sometimes you might need to configure one or more IP addresses that are always allowed to send messages that aren't treated as spam. A common implementation of this might be to configure the IP addresses of internal servers that need to send notification email messages, allowing their messages always to be delivered even if they trigger an SCL rating as they pass through the Edge Transport server.

You can manually configure IP addresses to be allowed by opening the Properties dialog box for the IP Allow List item. On the Allowed Addresses tab, shown in Figure 6.9, you'll be able to add IP addresses that are to be allowed or to remove existing entries if they should no longer be allowed to bypass the spam filters.

If you've subscribed to an external service that maintains a verified list of "safe" IP addresses that are known not to send spam, you can configure the IP Allow List Providers item to allow the Edge Transport server to do lookups against that provider upon the receipt of inbound messages. On the Providers tab of the IP Allow List Providers Properties dialog box, shown in Figure 6.10, you can add or remove providers. You can disable or enable providers on the list at any time and change the order as well. You should always put the best or fastest providers highest on the list because Exchange will stop querying other providers once it has matched the IP address of the sending system against an allow provider's list.

FIGURE 6.9   The Allowed Addresses tab of the IP Allow List Properties dialog box

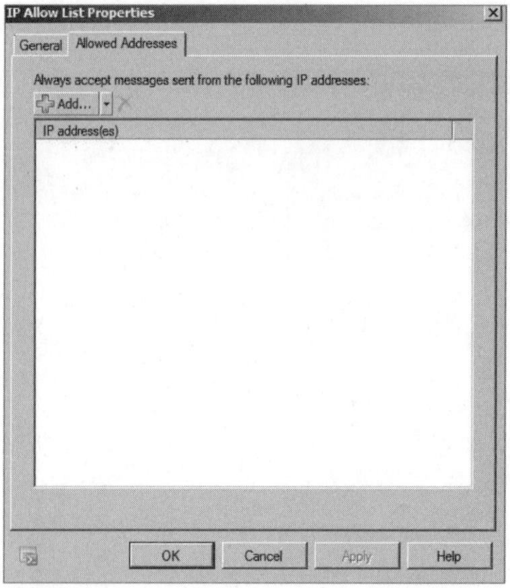

FIGURE 6.10   The Providers tab of the IP Allow List Providers Properties dialog box

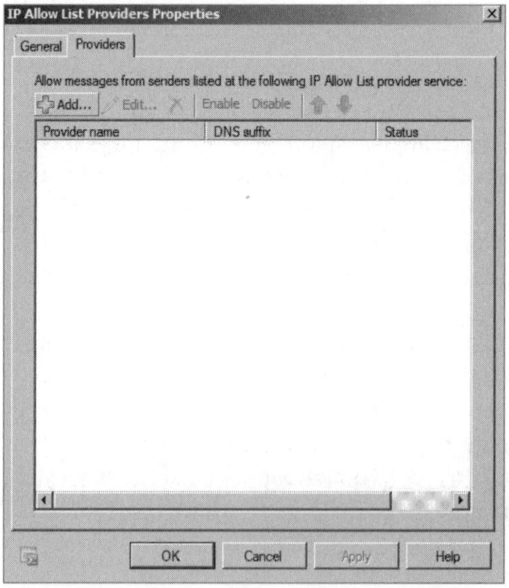

IP Block Lists

Configuring IP addresses to be blocked works the same way as configuring an IP address to be allowed. You can either enter addresses manually from the Blocked Addresses tab of the IP Block List Properties dialog box, shown in Figure 6.11, or configure one or more external services to provide this information to you.

Configuring the IP block list providers options will almost immediately cause a difference in the amount of spam your users receive, so treat this area with the importance it deserves. On the Providers tab of the IP Block List Providers Properties dialog box, shown in Figure 6.12, you can configure one or more providers that the Edge Transport server should consult to determine whether the sending IP address of a received message is a known spammer. Just as with the IP Allow List Providers item, you can add or remove providers as you wish as well as disable, enable, or reorder the providers in the list. Using the best or fastest provider here, as your experience dictates, will provide the best results since the Edge Transport server will stop looking to see whether the IP address belongs to a known spammer once it finds a match.

Some of the most popular block list providers include the following, although you can use any provider you trust:

- Spamhaus can be found at `www.spamhaus.org`
- SpamCop can be found at `www.spamcop.net`
- ABUSEAT CBL can be found at `http://cbl.abuseat.org`
- SORBS can be found at `www.sorbs.net`

Because sometimes you or your users will want or need to get every message sent to them, regardless of its SCL rating, you can configure a list of email addresses on the Exceptions tab of the IP Block List Providers Properties dialog box, as shown in Figure 6.13; the email addresses you configure here will always get messages addressed to them.

FIGURE 6.11   The Blocked Addresses tab of the IP Block List Properties dialog box

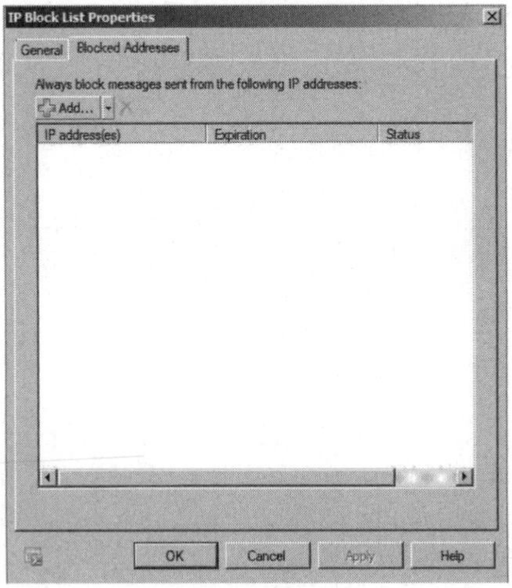

FIGURE 6.12   The Providers tab of the IP Block List Providers Properties dialog box

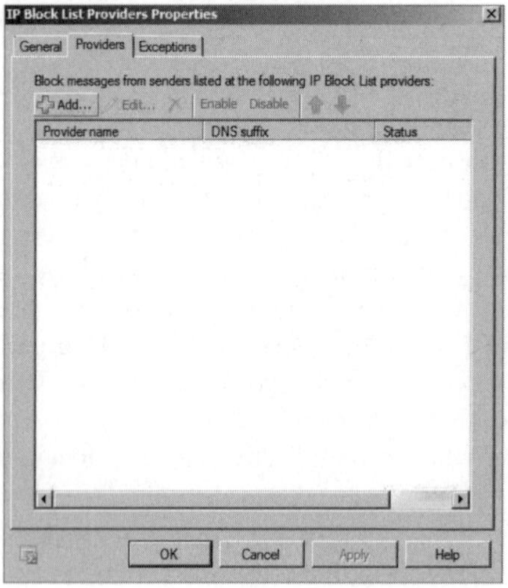

FIGURE 6.13   The Exceptions tab of the IP Block List Providers Properties dialog box

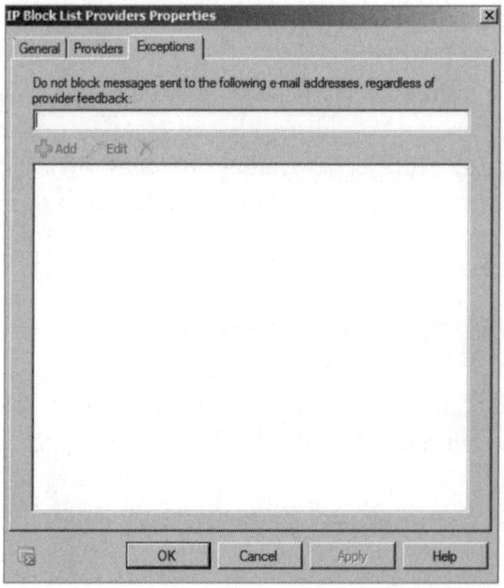

Recipient Filtering

Another powerful spam reduction tool you have available by default in Exchange Server 2010 is recipient filtering. Considering how much email is misaddressed and eventually winds up in the postmaster mailbox, using recipient filtering to block inbound messages to recipients who don't exist in the GAL is a powerful tool. The Blocked Recipients tab of the Recipient

Filtering Properties dialog box, shown in Figure 6.14, allows you to block messages sent to recipients of your choosing and/or those not in the GAL. Take the time at least to enable the GAL-based filtering and you'll save your organization from receiving a lot of spam that might otherwise be delivered.

You can use the option to block additional recipients in situations where you might have some internal email addresses that should never receive mail from the Internet. Typical scenarios for this include compliance reporting, spam and virus reporting, and mail-enabled public folders used for workflow applications.

FIGURE 6.14   The Blocked Recipients tab of the Recipient Filtering Properties dialog box

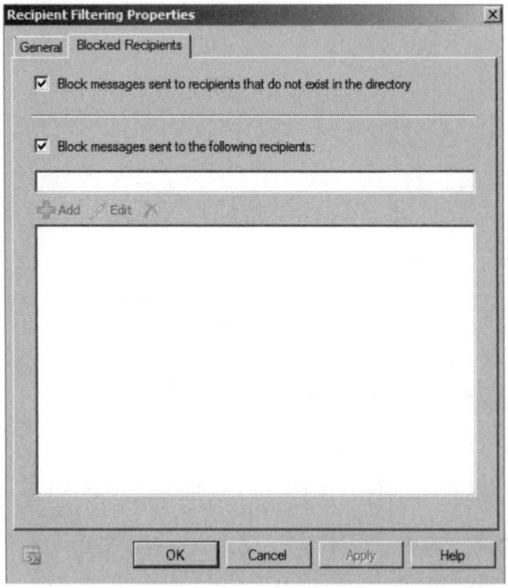

Sender Filtering

Sometimes using an IP block list provider isn't good enough if you need to block certain senders. This can happen when you start getting mail from a new IP address that isn't in the block list provider's database yet but is obviously sending you spam. Alternatively, you might need to block messages from IP addresses that are not sending spam but are otherwise sending messages that your organization has deemed it does not want to receive, such as job offers sent to employees from competing businesses in the area. You can add a list of sender IP addresses to block from the Blocked Senders tab of the Sender Filtering Properties dialog box, as shown in Figure 6.15. Note the option at the bottom of the dialog box to block messages that don't have sender information, since leaving the sender field blank is a common tactic of spammers.

On the Action tab, shown in Figure 6.16, you can configure the desired action to occur if the IP address of the sending system is found in the Blocked Senders listing. Either you can block the message entirely, which is the default setting, or you can opt to adjust the

SCL rating and continue processing the message. Most organizations will likely opt to block the message entirely.

FIGURE 6.15 The Blocked Senders tab of the Sender Filtering Properties dialog box

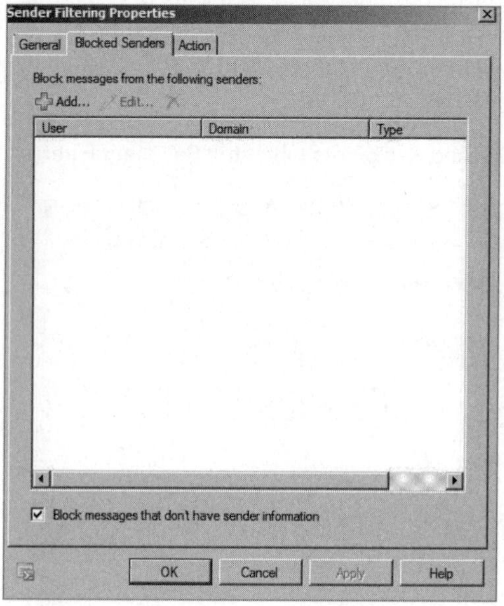

FIGURE 6.16 The Action tab of the Sender Filtering Properties dialog box

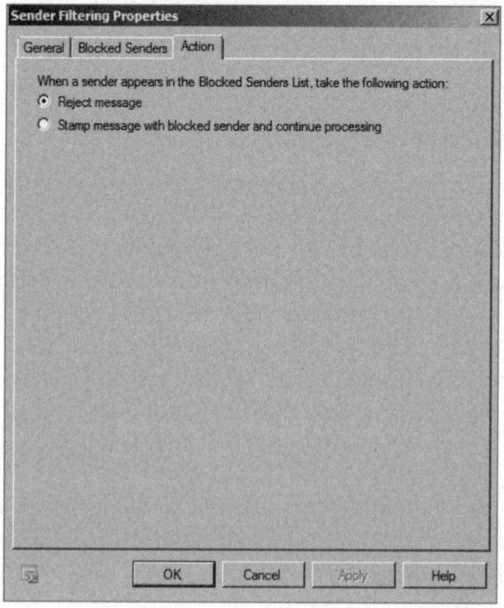

Sender ID

Sender ID is a relatively new method that is being used to fight both spam and phishing email messages. Since it relies on legitimate senders registering their email servers, it cannot be counted on 100 percent of the time in identifying unsolicited email. Many sending systems are not currently participating in Sender ID, even though they are legitimate and valid senders; thus, you should not use Sender ID as an absolute just yet. To that end, the default configuration is to simply note the Sender ID status in the message headers for SCL evaluation and pass the message along for further analysis. You can configure the action that the Edge Transport server should take when a Sender ID check fails on an inbound message from the Action tab of the Sender ID Properties dialog box, as shown in Figure 6.17.

FIGURE 6.17   The Action tab of the Sender ID Properties dialog box

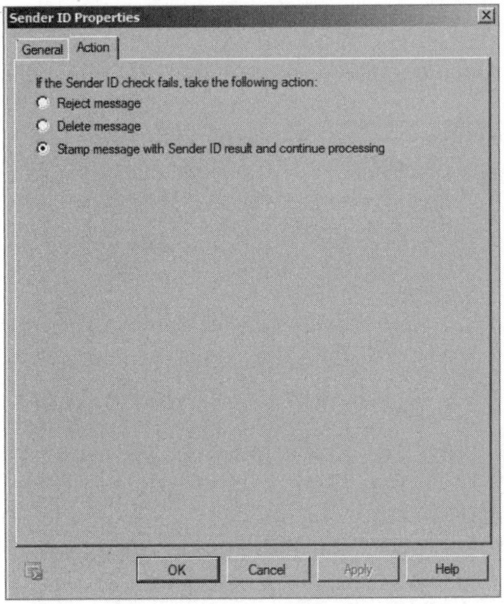

Sender ID Properties

General | Action

If the Sender ID check fails, take the following action:

○ Reject message
○ Delete message
● Stamp message with Sender ID result and continue processing

OK   Cancel   Apply   Help

To find out more about Sender ID and how to publish your Sender ID Sender Policy Framework (SPF) record, visit the Microsoft Sender ID resource center at www.microsoft.com/mscorp/safety/technologies/senderid/default.mspx.

Sender Reputation

The Sender Reputation item is a dynamic method Exchange Server 2010 uses to add (and subsequently remove) sending IP addresses to the IP block list depending on their recent behavior patterns. If a certain IP address does not otherwise appear in any IP block list but has sent a large amount of spam as classified by your Edge Transport servers, then it can be dynamically added to the IP block list for a certain amount of time. Assuming that the IP address does not continue to send spam messages above your SCL ratings, it will automatically be removed from the IP block list after this period of time. Because of its dynamic nature, Sender Reputation can be both a powerful tool and a complex one to use. You could end up putting an IP address on the block list that you did not want to be there, although if the rest of the settings are working correctly (per your organization's needs), then any IP address that the Sender Reputation item adds to the block list is almost certainly there for a good reason.

By default, the Edge Transport server is configured to detect open ports and relays on sending systems. The Sender Confidence tab of the Sender Reputation Properties dialog box, shown in Figure 6.18, allows you to turn off this option, although there is no reason you would ordinarily do this.

FIGURE 6.18   The Sender Confidence tab of the Sender Reputation Properties dialog box

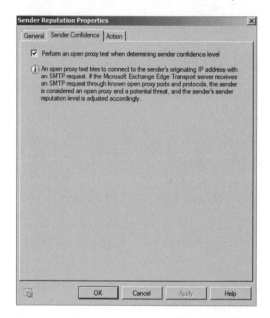

The Action tab, shown in Figure 6.19, allows you to configure the sender reputation level (SRL) value that will result in the sender being added to the IP block list for the number of hours configured. A setting of 0 on the slider indicates that the sender is almost certainly not a spammer, with a less than 1 percent probability of being a spam source. Conversely, a setting of 9 on the slider indicates that the sender is almost certainly a spammer, with a greater than 99 percent probability of being a spam source. The default setting is an SRL of 7, which most organizations will find acceptable. If anything, you will most likely move the slider up to a setting of 8 to decrease the chances of inadvertently adding an acceptable sender to the IP block list.

FIGURE 6.19   The Action tab of the Sender Reputation Properties dialog box

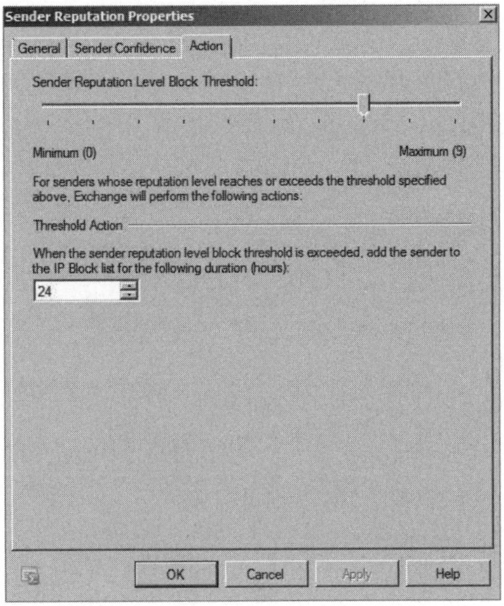

Attachment Filtering

The last antispam agent we'll examine here is the Attachment Filtering agent. Unlike the previous items we've covered, no Exchange Management Console configuration is available for attachment filtering, so warm up your Exchange Management Shell! By default, the Attachment Filter agent is enabled on a newly installed Edge Transport server, but you can check to be sure by issuing the Get-TransportAgent cmdlet from the EMS, as shown in Figure 6.20.

FIGURE 6.20   Checking the status of antispam transport agents

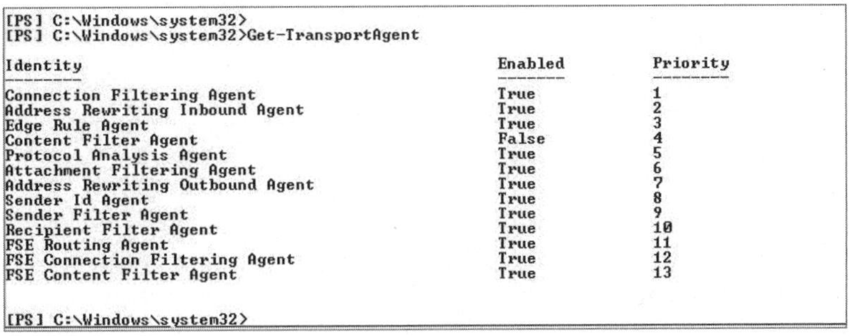

To see the default configuration of the Attachment Filter agent, you will need to use the `Get-AttachmentFilterListConfig` cmdlet. This should return the result shown in Figure 6.21 on a newly installed Edge Transport server.

FIGURE 6.21 Checking the configuration of the Attachment Filter agent

```
[PS] C:\Windows\system32>get-attachmentfilterlistconfig

Name                  : Transport Settings
RejectResponse        : Message rejected due to unacceptable attachments
AdminMessage          : This attachment was removed.
Action                : Strip
ExceptionConnectors   : {}
AttachmentNames       : {ContentType:application/x-msdownload, ContentType:mes
                        sage/partial, ContentType:text/scriptlet, ContentType:
                        application/prg, ContentType:application/msaccess, Con
                        tentType:text/javascript, ContentType:application/x-ja
                        vascript, ContentType:application/javascript, ContentT
                        ype:x-internet-signup, ContentType:application/hta, Fi
                        leName:*.xnk, FileName:*.wsh, FileName:*.wsf, FileName
                        :*.wsc, FileName:*.vbs, FileName:*.vbe...}
AdminDisplayName      :
ExchangeVersion       : 0.1 (8.0.535.0)
DistinguishedName     : CN=Transport Settings,CN=First Organization,CN=Microso
                        ft Exchange,CN=Services,CN=Configuration,CN={72609811-
                        8CD0-443B-88F3-B2903CE01679}
Identity              : Transport Settings
Guid                  : 12a3c708-68eb-4fa7-84ad-6e5330e43960
ObjectCategory        : CN=ms-Exch-Transport-Settings,CN=Schema,CN=Configurati
                        on,CN={72609811-8CD0-443B-88F3-B2903CE01679}
ObjectClass           : {top, container, msExchTransportSettings}
WhenChanged           : 3/12/2010 11:03:13 AM
WhenCreated           : 1/29/2010 10:30:34 PM
WhenChangedUTC        : 3/12/2010 5:03:13 PM
WhenCreatedUTC        : 1/30/2010 4:30:34 AM
OrganizationId        :
OriginatingServer     : localhost
IsValid               : True
```

As you can see, a few file types, such as Access databases, JavaScript files, and VBScript files, are going to be stripped from messages by default. You will likely want to add and/or remove file types of your own. To add new file types to the Attachment Filter agent, you will need to use the `Add-AttachmentFilterEntry` cmdlet. If you wanted to add all attachments with the filename extension of `.pdf`, you would use a command like this:

```
Add-AttachmentFilterEntry -Name *.pdf -Type FileName
```

Because filename extensions can be spoofed, it is advisable also to use a MIME type value to block attachments. For example, you would use the following command to strip all MPEG audio/video files:

```
Add-AttachmentFilterEntry -Name audio/mpeg -Type ContentType
```

You can get a listing of all registered MIME types by visiting www.iana.org/assignments/media-types/.

You can see the results of the commands in Figure 6.22.

Conversely, you can remove a file type from the Attachment Filter agent by using the `Remove-AttachmentFilterEntry` cmdlet. If you wanted to remove the previously added entry for MPEG files, your command would look like this:

```
Remove-AttachmentFilterEntry -Identity ContentType:audio/mpeg
```

FIGURE 6.22   Adding file types to the Attachment Filter agent

```
Machine: ET01 | Scope:                                              _[][X]
[PS] C:\>Add-AttachmentFilterEntry -name *.pdf -type FileName

                Type Name                      Identity
                ---- ----                      --------
            FileName *.pdf                   FileName:*.pdf


[PS] C:\>Add-AttachmentFilterEntry -name audio/mpeg -type ContentType

                Type Name                      Identity
                ---- ----                      --------
         ContentType audio/mpeg             ContentType:audio/mpeg


[PS] C:\>
```

You'll be prompted to confirm your intention, however, as shown in Figure 6.23, when you remove an entry from the list.

FIGURE 6.23   Removing file types from the Attachment Filter agent

```
[PS] C:\>Remove-AttachmentFilterEntry -Identity contenttype:audio/mpeg

Confirm
Are you sure you want to perform this action?
Removing attachment filter entry "contenttype:audio/mpeg".
[Y] Yes  [A] Yes to All  [N] No  [L] No to All  [S] Suspend  [?] Help
(default is "Y"):
[PS] C:\>_
```

If you want an easier way to view the full and current list of file types that are covered by the Attachment Filter agent, you can use the `Get-AttachmentFilterEntry` cmdlet, as shown in Figure 6.24. The information provided here is much easier to read than that provided by the `Get-AttachmentFilterListConfig` cmdlet you saw earlier.

FIGURE 6.24   Viewing file types configured for the Attachment Filter agent

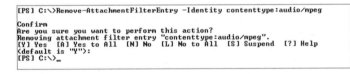

```
[PS] C:\Windows\system32>get-attachmentfilterentry

                Type Name                      Identity
                ---- ----                      --------
         ContentType application/x-msdownload    ContentType:application/x-msdownload
         ContentType message/partial             ContentType:message/partial
         ContentType text/scriptlet              ContentType:text/scriptlet
         ContentType application/prg             ContentType:application/prg
         ContentType application/msaccess        ContentType:application/msaccess
         ContentType text/javascript             ContentType:text/javascript
         ContentType application/x-javascript    ContentType:application/x-javascript
         ContentType application/javascript      ContentType:application/javascript
         ContentType x-internet-signup           ContentType:x-internet-signup
         ContentType application/hta             ContentType:application/hta
            FileName *.xnk                     FileName:*.xnk
            FileName *.wsh                     FileName:*.wsh
            FileName *.wsf                     FileName:*.wsf
            FileName *.wsc                     FileName:*.wsc
            FileName *.vbs                     FileName:*.vbs
            FileName *.vbe                     FileName:*.vbe
            FileName *.vb                      FileName:*.vb
            FileName *.url                     FileName:*.url
            FileName *.shs                     FileName:*.shs
            FileName *.shb                     FileName:*.shb
            FileName *.sct                     FileName:*.sct
            FileName *.scr                     FileName:*.scr
            FileName *.scf                     FileName:*.scf
            FileName *.reg                     FileName:*.reg
            FileName *.prg                     FileName:*.prg
            FileName *.prf                     FileName:*.prf
            FileName *.pif                     FileName:*.pif
            FileName *.pcd                     FileName:*.pcd
```

If you want to change the default behavior or message when attachment stripping occurs, you will need to use the `Set-AttachmentFilterListConfig` cmdlet, which has the following syntax:

```
Set-AttachmentFilterListConfig [-Action <Reject | Strip | SilentDelete>]
[-AdminMessage <String>] [-DomainController <Fqdn>]
[-ExceptionConnectors <MultiValuedProperty>]
[-Instance <AttachmentFilteringConfig>] [-RejectResponse <String>]
```

You can set the `Action` behavior to one of the following options:

- `Reject`, which issues an NDR to the sender and prevents the message and attachment from passing

- `Strip`, which removes the attachment but allows the message to pass through with text indicating that an attachment was stripped

- `SilentDelete`, which deletes the message and sends no NDR to the sender

The `AdminMessage` value specifies the contents of a text file that will be attached to messages to replace a stripped attachment. The default value is "This attachment was removed." However, you might want to customize it to include a contact email address or phone number for the help desk in your organization so that a recipient can get more information about attachment filtering policies. The `RejectResponse` value specifies the message body of NDR messages sent to senders whose attachments have been rejected. The default value of "Message rejected due to unacceptable attachments" is fairly useful, but you might want to customize it also with an externally available contact phone number or email address if a sender needs help determining what attachment types are allowed through your email system. The `RejectResponse` value has a limit of 240 characters, so be sure to check your text before changing the value. You can configure connectors that the Attachment Filter agent should not function on by using the `ExceptionConnectors` value.

The following example command will change the default `Action` behavior to `Reject` and will change the `RejectResponse` value to be more informative:

```
Set-AttachmentFilterListConfig -Action Reject
-RejectResponse "Your message and attachment(s) have not been delivered
to the intended recipient. Please contact the Mail Task Help
Desk at 1-877-555-1234 for more information."
```

Figure 6.25 shows the changes and the verification of the changes using the `Get-AttachmentFilterListConfig` cmdlet.

In Exercise 6.30 and Exercise 6.31, you will enable content filtering and recipient filtering, two of the most important antispam options in Exchange Server 2010.

FIGURE 6.25 Modifying the Attachment Filter agent behavior

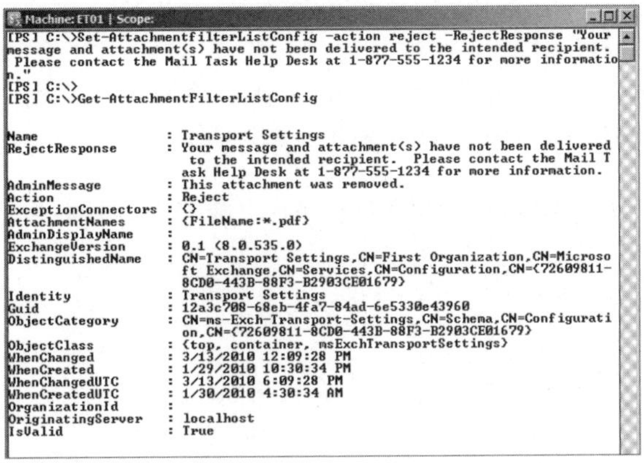

EXERCISE 6.30

Enable Content Filtering and Recipient Filtering Using the Exchange Management Console

To enable content filtering and recipient filtering using the EMC, follow these steps:

1. Log on to ET01 as Administrator.
2. Click Start ➤ Programs ➤ Microsoft Exchange Server 2010 and then select Exchange Management Console.
3. Click Edge Transport in the console tree.
4. Click the Anti-spam tab.
5. Click Content Filtering and Right-click and click Enable.

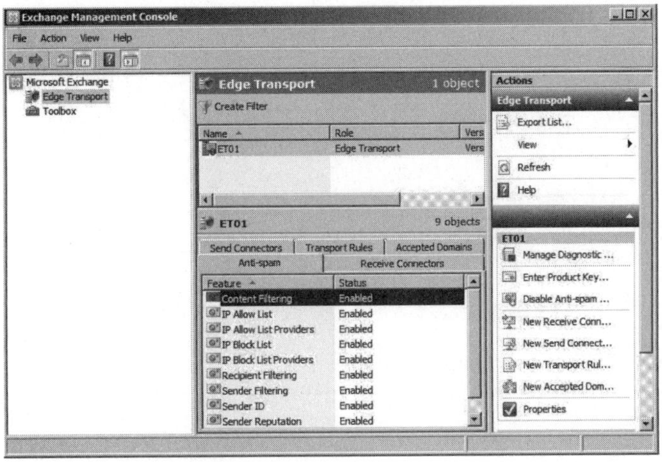

6. In the Actions pane, click Properties.

7. Click the Action tab and enable the Reject messages that have an SCL rating greater than or equal to checkbox and set to the value to 7. Click OK.

8. In Anti-spam tab, click Recipient Filtering. If it is currently disabled, right-click it and choose Enable.

9. In the Actions pane, click Properties.

10. Click the Blocked Recipients tab and enable the Block messages sent to recipients that do not exist in the directory checkbox. Click OK.

11. Restart the MSExchangeTransport service.

In Exercise 6.31, you will enable and configure content filtering and recipient filtering using the EMS. This is a multi-step process, requiring you to first enable the filter and then configure it.

EXERCISE 6.31

Enable Content Filtering and Recipient Filtering Using the Exchange Management Shell

Follow these steps to enable and configure content filtering and recipient filtering using the EMS:

1. Log on to ET01 as Administrator.

2. Click Start ➢ Programs ➢ Microsoft Exchange Server 2010 and then select Exchange Management Shell.

3. To enable content filtering, run:

   ```
   Enable-TransportAgent "Content Filter Agent"
   ```

4. Enable rejection and set the SCL reject threshold to 7 by running the following command:

   ```
   Set-ContentFilterConfig -SCLRejectThreshold 7 -SCLRejectEnabled $true
   ```

5. To enable recipient filtering, run:

   ```
   Enable-TransportAgent "Recipient Filter Agent"
   ```

6. Set the recipient filter to accept only email for recipients in the directory by running the following command:

   ```
   Set-RecipientFilterConfig -RecipientValidationEnabled $true
   ```

Using Forefront Protection 2010 for Exchange Server

The obvious choice for antivirus is Microsoft's own Forefront Security for Exchange. In addition to antivirus options, Forefront Security for Exchange 2010 adds antispam and DNS block list functionality.

You can find and download the Forefront Security for Exchange Server user's guide at go.microsoft.com/fwlink/?LinkID=111583.

Administrators familiar with previous versions of Forefront Security for Exchange Server will find that FPES has had substantial changes in both the interface and the functionality.

FPES can be controlled from the Forefront Management Shell or from the administrator console, the latter of which administrators who have used the System Center line will find repeat.

When Forefront spam filtering is enabled on a Transport server, the built-in Exchange Server spam filtering will be disabled. Forefront's spam filtering can be enabled either during the install or by running the following command in the Forefront Management shell, followed by restarting the transport service:

```
Set-FseSpamFiltering -Enabled $true
```

Policy Management

Configuration from the Forefront administrator console is done from the Policy Management area. The Policy Management area is divided into five smaller areas of administration:

Antimalware   The Antimalware section is where antivirus and antispyware options are configured. The screen will change slightly depending on whether the server is a transport server or a mailbox server, but most of the options will remain the same. The following areas are present on this screen:

General Settings   General Settings is where antivirus and antispyware scanning can be enabled or disabled. In most cases, administrators will want to enable both options.

Engines and Performance   The Engines and Performance sections allows an administrator to choose how many engines will be used when scanning an item. Scanning with more engines increases the chances of detecting a virus but can decrease performance.

Scan Actions   Scan Actions give you the option to either clean or delete infected files, and also the option to quarantine the original files so they can be recovered. If the quarantine option is enabled, you will want to make sure you have adequate disk space to store the quarantined files.

Additional Options   Additional Options offers several fine-tuning options for scanning and performance.

Anti-spam   The Anti-spam area is where antispam settings for transport servers are configured. Many of these options are similar to the antispam options built into Exchange Server 2010, but with additional features.

Connection Filter   The Connection Filter area allows you to configure block and allow lists. It is also where you can enable Forefront DNSBL checking. The Forefront DNSBL is a block list maintained by Microsoft that brings together information from both Microsoft internal teams and external vendors.

Sender ID Filter   Sender ID filtering uses DNS information to ascertain whether the server sending an email is the correct server for the address of the message. Although Sender ID filtering can decrease the amount of spam received, it can also block legitimately forwarded accounts and some email list services, so care is needed when enabling it.

Recipient Filter   Recipient filtering can be used to block emails to certain addresses and to addresses that do not actually exist in an Exchange organization.

Backscatter Filter   The Backscatter filter prevents backscatter, which is receiving Delivery Status Notifications (DSNs) from many locations because a spammer spoofed someone in your organization's email address. The Backscatter filter works by stamping all outgoing emails with a special token and then not accepting DSNs that don't include that token. To work correctly, all servers handing inbound or outbound email must have the same Backscatter key, so it should be generated on one server, exported, and then imported on the rest of the inbound/outbound servers.

Content Filter   The Content Filter section is where the antispam content filter is configured. The *Configure Content Allow Lists* button is where administrators configure senders and recipients that bypass the content filter. The SCL Threshold And Actions section allows administrators to configure the thresholds used for dealing with spam. The lower the suspected spam threshold is (or the higher the certain spam threshold), the more email will be marked as certain spam, which may increase false positives.

Filters   The Filters section is where administrators can configure custom file, keyword, and sender filters.

Online Protection   The Online Protection section is used only when the hosted Forefront Online Protection for Exchange service is purchased.

Global Settings   Global Settings provides three sections. The Scan Options section allows administrators to choose to disable or enable scanning for inbound, outbound, and internal messages. The Engine Options section is used to configure redistribution or proxy options for engine updates. No additional configuration is required to pull updates directly from Microsoft servers.

The final section under Global Settings is the Advanced Options screen. Here administrators can define several options. The most important options are listed here:

Domain names used for identifying internal addresses   This section is used to configure what domain names correspond to internal email addresses, allowing Forefront to differentiate between internal and external email addresses.

Threshold Levels   Threshold levels are used to configure what size emails are allowed and how many levels of nesting are allowed in compressed files. Increasing these thresholds can decrease performance, but it may be necessary for some organizations with large attachments or that send deeply nested compressed attachments.

Intelligent Engine Management   Intelligent Engine Management allows administrators to configure what scanning engines to use and when to have them update. In most cases, the engine management option should be left on Automatic.

> ### Real World Scenario
>
> #### Using Exchange's Built-in Power
>
> As you have seen throughout this chapter, the Edge Transport server provides you with a powerful antispam solution right out of the box. How powerful and effective that solution is, however, will depend on how much time you spend assessing the available options and configuring them in a way that makes the most sense for your organization. If you take the time to evaluate and document your needs thoroughly and then take the time to plan your required configuration, you could get away without even needing to purchase or install an additional antispam product for your Exchange organization. Of particular note are the IP Block List and Content Filtering options. You can use these two areas to block the majority of all spam entering your organization. Whatever path you decide to choose when it comes to spam control, do your organization a favor and take your time. The spam problem will not be going away anytime soon, but you can definitely make a difference to your users if you understand the powerful options Exchange Server 2010 gives you and configure them to their maximum potential.

Monitoring

As with most antivirus applications Forefront has a quarantine area that you'll want to examine and manage periodically. You can find the quarantined file list as well as other important items in the Monitoring area of the administrative console.

Notification   In the Notification area, you have the ability to configure options associated with various notifications that can be enabled or disabled for various events that might occur with Forefront. For each notification, you can also configure the following email-related fields:

- The To address(es) to send notifications to
- The Cc address(es) to send notifications to
- The Bcc address(es) to send notifications to
- The subject text of the notification
- The body text of the notification

Often, virus-laden messages are not sent with a valid return address; it is now common practice not to send notification messages to the sender of antivirus messages because they would most likely not be delivered to the originator of the virus.

As they pertain to viruses, the following notifications are available to configure:

> **Virus Administrators:** Sends alert messages to administrators for all viruses detected on the server. Typically these alerts will be sent to a distribution group containing the mailboxes of all messaging administrators.

> **Virus Sender (Internal):** Sends alert messages to the sender of the message, if the sender is located in your Exchange organization, when a virus has been detected in a message they have sent. The body text of this notification might be customized with information about how to get help with the virus problem.

> **Virus Sender (External):** Sends alert messages to the sender of the message if the sender is not located in your Exchange organization.

> **Virus Recipients (Internal):** Sends alert messages to the recipient of the message, if the recipient is located in your Exchange organization, that the message contained an infected attachment. The body text of this notification might be customized with information about how to contact the help desk for further assistance.

> **Virus Recipients (External):** Sends alert messages to the recipient of the message if the recipient is not located in your Exchange organization.

Incidents   The Incidents area lists virus detections or filter operations for the server. You will likely want to enable the automatic purging of incidents to occur every 30 days or so to keep the database from growing too large. You can also filter the view for items between specific dates and export the information to a text file for archiving or later viewing.

Quarantine   The quarantine area lists all detected files. A copy of the detected file is placed here before a clean, delete, or skip action occurs within Forefront. Over time, the number of items in the quarantine folder will build up, so you might want to enable automatic purging after 30 days or so.

You will be able to release items from quarantine by selecting them and clicking Deliver. Should you not be able to deliver a message and its attachment from the quarantine area, you can save the attachment using the Save button—a task you will likely find yourself performing often for files that wouldn't ordinarily be allowed through but higher-level users will want anyway.

You can also filter the view of the quarantine area or export a list of quarantine items as desired.

In Exercise 6.32, you will enable antispam and antivirus functionality using the Forefront console.

EXERCISE 6.32

Enabling Content Filtering, Forefront DNSBL Checking, and Virus Scanning Using the Forefront Console

Follow these steps to enable antivirus and antispam functionality using the Forefront console:

1. Click Start ➢ Programs ➢ Microsoft Forefront Server Protection and select Forefront Protection for Exchange Server Console.

2. Click the Policy Management button to bring up the Policy Management section.

3. Click Configure below Antispam on the left side of the screen.

4. Make sure Enable Connection filtering and Enable Forefront DNSBL checking are checked.

5. Click Edge Transport under the Antimalware section. Verify that Enable transport antivirus scan and enable transport antispyware scan are checked.

In Exercise 6.33, you will use the Forefront Management Shell to enable antispam and antivirus functionality.

EXERCISE 6.33

Enabling Content Filtering, Forefront DNSBL Checking, and Virus Scanning Using the Forefront Management Shell

To enable antivirus and antispam functionality using the Forefront Management Shell, follow these steps:

1. Click Start ➤ Programs ➤ Microsoft Forefront Server Protection and select Forefront Management Shell.

2. To enable content filtering and the DNS block list, run.

   ```
   Set-FseSpamConnectionFilter -Enabled $true -EnableDnsBlockList $true
   ```

3. Set the SCL threshold to 7 by running the following command:

   ```
   Set-FseSpamContentFilter -Threshold 7
   ```

4. Enable virus scanning by running the following command:

   ```
   Set-FseRealtimeScan -enabled $true
   -EnableVirusScan $true -EnableSpywareScan $true
   ```

Summary

We covered a lot of ground in this chapter, focusing on the basic configuration and management of MRM, rules, and server policies. Every organization that deploys Exchange Server 2010 will have Hub Transport, CAS, and Mailbox servers. This chapter also covered some of the tools available to you to control messages as they travel through an organization and while they are stored in an organization.

We also covered the new permissions and delegation features in Exchange Server 2010. RBAC will allow you to easily delegate access to other members of your organization, and administrator audit logging will help you make sure that those permissions aren't abused. Also, Multi-Mailbox Search will allow your compliance, legal, or HR departments to easily perform any necessary mailbox searches.

For additional security, you should install an antivirus and antispam product on your Edge Transport servers. Forefront Security for Exchange Server is a perfect fit and is fully supported by Microsoft, but you may find other third-party applications that meet your needs as well. You might not even end up using Edge Transport servers at all if your organization already has a functional virus- and spam-control solution in place today.

Chapter Essentials

Understand Role Based Access Control. RBAC is an important new feature in Exchange Server 2010, allowing administrators to delegate permissions to users based on their roles and to control what end users have access to. Understand how to assign permissions to users based on roles and how to control what end users can do using role assignment policies. Also, learn how to monitor that access using administrator audit logging.

Understand MRM. Although managed folders have changed little since Exchange 2007, administrators will find that the new retention policies feature offers increased flexibility and control. Understand how to create retention policies and retention tags and how to assign retention tags to folders and items. Also, take the time to learn how to apply legal holds and use Multi-Mailbox Search so that when you are required to use them, you're ready.

Understand transport rules. Transport rules have changed little since Exchange 2007, but it is important to know how to use them. They provide a lot of flexibility to administrators by allowing them to control messages as they move through the organization. Understand how to create and test transport rules.

Understand policies and address lists. Email address policies, ActiveSync policies, and address lists have changed little since Exchange 2007, but it is important to understand how to use them. Especially when initially rolling out Exchange 2010, it's important to make sure these policies are in place and set correctly so that the email addresses that users see and how they use their devices are consistent.

Understand antivirus and antispam options. The built-in Exchange Server antispam options are practically identical to those in Exchange 2007, but there have been massive improvements in Microsoft Forefront Security for Exchange. Understand how to protect users from spam and viruses entering your organization. Also, make sure you learn the differences between the built-in features and the additional features that Forefront adds.

Know where to go. In this chapter, we've used five different interfaces to configure Exchange: the Exchange Management Console, the Exchange Control Panel, the Exchange Management Shell, the Forefront Protection for Exchange Server Console, and the Forefront Management Shell. Although some configuration items can be accessed through multiple interfaces, there are some configurations that can only be accessed through the management shell. Learn what tasks can be performed where, but also learn where you're most comfortable performing common tasks.

Chapter

7

Configuring High-Availability Solutions for Exchange Server

THE FOLLOWING TOPICS ARE DISCUSSED IN THIS CHAPTER:

✓ High availability for Mailbox servers

✓ High availability for Hub Transport, Client Access, and Edge Transport servers

The term *high availability* (HA) is often thrown into conversations, but few administrators take the time to understand what it really means. Some have been conditioned by numerous articles to think that high availability means the same thing as clustering. Although Microsoft server clustering and network load balancing are highly available platforms for applications, they do not provide high availability by themselves. Every administrator should understand that clustering is only a piece of high availability.

High availability requires strong management processes, proper testing procedures, and well-planned implementation and change control processes. An organization cannot achieve high availability just by implementing clustering technologies. The most important requirement in achieving high availability is implementing a high-availability philosophy or spirit within the organization, where administrators stop, think, evaluate, collaborate, and then decide what to do in the event of a major failure or when changing the configuration of an application or server. Proper change control, for example, is part of that spirit. It is equally important to document, test, and train staff on the high availability solution being used. The documentation should be updated on an annual basis at a minimum, and regular failover testing should be performed.

Introducing High Availability in Exchange Server 2010

In Exchange 2007, there are four options for mailbox availability that combine clustering and replication in different blends. They are *local continuous replication (LCR)*, *single copy cluster (SCC)*, *cluster continuous replication (CCR)*, and *standby continuous replication (SCR)*. Here is a quick review of the key features of each:

LCR Single server, data redundancy, manual failover

SCC Failover cluster, no data redundancy, automatic failover

CCR Failover cluster, data redundancy, automatic failover

SCR Multiple servers, data redundancy, manual failover

Each of these high availability methods provided redundancy for an Exchange server, but they fell short in a number of areas. In Exchange Server 2010, Microsoft enhanced high availability by combining a number of features into a new high availability solution called *database availability groups (DAG)*.

In many aspects, Exchange Server 2010 mailbox high availability has been simplified because there is only one option to configure, whereas Exchange Server 2007 provided four different options and administrators sometimes needed to combine two solutions to provide the appropriate level of redundancy for an Exchange Server environment. The only downside to Exchange Server 2010 high availability is the dependency on Windows Failover Clustering, which means you must purchase Enterprise Edition of Windows Server 2008 or Windows Server 2008 R2 to implement any type of mailbox redundancy. It's possible to use virtualization technology like Microsoft's Hyper-V R2 or VMware, which allows for live migration between hosts without requiring Enterprise Edition software for Exchange, but discussion about virtualization is beyond the scope of this book.

Understanding Database Availability Groups

A DAG is the base component of Exchange 2010 high availability and provides a boundary for mailbox replication, servers, and failovers. A DAG can span Active Directory sites to provide intrasite and intersite redundancy.

When an Exchange Server 2003 or 2007 Mailbox server was configured for high availability, a virtual server was created. In Exchange Server 2003, it was called an Exchange Virtual Server (EVS), and in Exchange Server 2007 the name was changed to Clustered Mailbox Server (CMS). This virtual server is what the Outlook client connected to, and as a failover was initiated and the resource moved to the passive server, the client continued to connect to the same server name. This caused the client to experience an interruption in service and potentially led to support calls. Exchange Server 2010 has changed this behavior, and virtual server names are no longer used for client connections to the Mailbox server.

With Exchange Server 2007, databases that are protected using LCR, CCR, or SCR are required to have only one mailbox database in the storage group. Databases not protected by these replication technologies could have up to five databases in each storage group. With Exchange Server 2010, the concept of storage groups has been removed, and any configuration previously done on the storage group level has been moved to the database objects.

One of the most exciting capabilities added to Exchange Server 2010 is the ability to failover a single mailbox database. In previous versions of Exchange, when a failover was initiated, all databases on the server were moved, causing a momentary outage for every mailbox hosted on the server. Now, an Exchange administrator has the ability to move a single database to another server in the DAG. This new functionality can assist with balancing the load on an Exchange server. The following list shows the Exchange 2010 DAG features:

- A DAG supports up to 16 nodes.
- All Exchange servers must be in the same domain.
- Only servers in the same DAG can be replication partners.
- DAG members can be in different Active Directory sites.

- DAG members must have the same operating system level (Windows Server 2008 or Windows Server 2008 R2).

- DAG members require Windows 2008/2008 R2 Enterprise Edition or Datacenter Edition.

- You cannot install Windows NLB and Windows Failover Cluster on the same server.

- Replication occurs at the database level, allowing for a single database to be moved.

> When creating a DAG using the Exchange Management Console (EMC), there are only a limited number of attributes that can be configured; however, the Exchange Management Shell (EMS) allows all attributes to be configured.

Exercise 7.1 shows how to create a DAG.

EXERCISE 7.1

Creating a Database Availability Group

Follow these steps to create a DAG using the EMC:

1. Log on to EX01 as Administrator.

2. Click Start ➢ Programs ➢ Microsoft Exchange Server 2010 and then select Exchange Management Console.

3. Expand Organizational Configuration and select Mailbox.

4. Click the Database Availability Groups tab.

5. In the Actions pane, click New Database Availability Group.

6. In the New Database Availability Group Wizard, type **DallasDag** in the Database Availability Groups Name field.

7. Select Witness Server and type **EX03.Mailtask.com**.

8. Select Witness Directory and type **C:\FSW**.

9. Click New.

10. Click Finish.

In Exercise 7.1, you successfully created a DAG called DallasDag. However, by itself a DAG is a placeholder, much like a group in Active Directory. As you can see in Figure 7.1, the EMC shows the DAG currently without any members associated with it, and if you look at the directory structure on EX03, you will not find the witness directory. After the first member is added to the DAG, the witness directory gets created and eventually utilized by the DAG as additional members are added. The witness server, also called a file share witness, will be used when an even number of members exists in the cluster and will assist the cluster in determining which node will host a resource in the event of a failure.

FIGURE 7.1   Viewing the DAG in the EMC

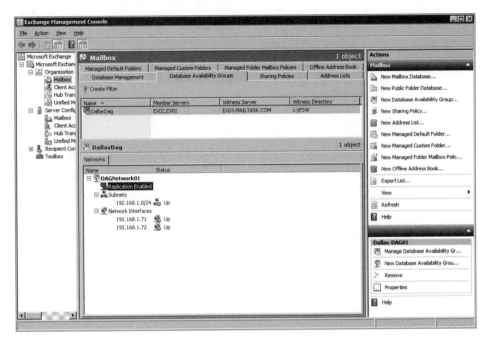

Using Database Availability Group Properties

In Exercise 7.1, you created a new DAG in the EMC called DallasDag that you will use to configure high availability for the Exchange Mailbox servers. A DAG has a number of configurable properties that are available only from the command line (using the EMS). Table 7.1 shows the Windows PowerShell commands that you can use to manage a DAG.

TABLE 7.1:   DAG EMS commands

EMC Cmdlet	Description
New-DatabaseAvailabilityGroup	Creates a new database availability group
Get-DatabaseAvailabilityGroup	Gets a lists of the members and status of the database availability group
Set-DatabaseAvailabilityGroup	Allows you to configure properties of the database availability group: replication port, network compression, etc.
Remove-DatabaseAvailabilityGroup	Deletes a database availability group

TABLE 7.1: DAG EMS commands *(continued)*

EMC Cmdlet	Description
Remove-DatabaseAvailabilityGroupServer	Removes a server from a database availability group
Add-DatabaseAvailabilityGroupServer	Adds a server from a database availability group
Stop-DatabaseAvailabilityGroup	Stops a member of a DAG or an entire site and is used to facilitate a datacenter switchover
Start-DatabaseAvailabilityGroup	Activates Mailbox servers in a recovered datacenter
New-DatabaseAvailabilityGroupNetwork	Creates a network associated with the database availability group
Get-DatabaseAvailabilityGroupNetwork	Displays configuration and network information for a database availability group
Set-DatabaseAvailabilityGroupNetwork	Allows you to configure network properties of a database availability group network
Remove-DatabaseAvailabilityGroupNetwork	Removes a database availability group network
Restore-DatabaseAvailabilityGroup	Activates a database availability group members server in a secondary datacenter

The Set-DatabaseAvailabilityGroup command provides the ability to set a number of important features for a DAG. A list of all parameters can be seen in Table 7.2. By default, when you create a DAG within the EMC, the DAG will be configured to use DHCP and will be automatically assigned an IP address; however, most companies prefer to assign critical applications a static IP address. You can do this from within the EMS only by using the -DatabaseAvailabilityGroupIpAddresses parameter.

Don't be confused by the -AlternateWitnessDirectory and -AlternateWitnessServer parameters because they are used in datacenter switchovers. If you set this property and the current witness server goes offline, the DAG will not utilize the alternate witness information automatically because administrative action is required to bring the alternate witness server online.

The -NetworkEncryption parameter allows you to decide if and when to use encryption for DAG replication. Many organizations today want to secure their environments as much as possible. By default, this option is configured to encrypt only intersubnet replication traffic, but it can be configured to encrypt all traffic, seed only (during a database seed), or disabled. Depending on your company's security needs, you can choose what settings work best for your environment, but we recommend enabling encryption for all traffic for added security.

The -NetworkCompression parameter offers the same configuration options as the -NetworkEncryption parameter offers. By default, compression is only enabled intersubnet and can assist in low-bandwidth environments. Much like encryption, compression puts an additional load on the processor, so an administrator should understand his environment before he chooses to enable compression. The settings available with compression are compress all traffic, seed only (during a database seed), or disabled.

TABLE 7.2 Set-DatabaseAvailabilityGroup parameters

Parameters	Description
-AlternateWitnessDirectory	Allows you to specify an alternate file share witness path
-AlternateWitnessServer	Specifies the alternate file share witness server
-Confirm	Specifies that an acknowledgement is required before the command executes
-DatabaseAvailabilityGroupIpAddresses	Allows you to specify a static Internet Protocol address for the DAG
-DatacenterActivationMode <Off | DagOnly>]	Controls split brain activation scenarios
-DiscoverNetworks	Forces a rediscover of DAG networks
-DomainController	Specifies a domain controller to connect to
-NetworkEncryption <Disabled | Enabled | InterSubnetOnly | SeedOnly>]	Allows you to specify which networks will use encryption
-ReplicationPort	Allows you to specify a port for replication
-WhatIf	Allows you to simulate what action the command would take
-WitnessDirectory	Specifies the directory to the file share witness, i.e., C:\FSW

TABLE 7.2   Set-DatabaseAvailabilityGroup parameters *(continued)*

Parameters	Description
-WitnessServer	Specifies the server to host the file share witness
-NetworkCompression <Disabled | Enabled | InterSubnetOnly | SeedOnly>]	Allows you to specify which networks use network compression

In Exercise 7.2, you will assign a static IP address to a DAG.

EXERCISE 7.2

Assigning a Static IP Address to the DAG

In this exercise, you will assign the DallasDag a static IP address and configure network compression and encryption from within the EMS:

1. Logon to EX01 as Administrator. Click Start ➤ Programs ➤ Microsoft Exchange Server 2010 and then select Exchange Management Shell.

2. Run the following command:

    Get-DatabaseAvailabilityGroup | Format-List

3. Then run this command:

    Set-DatabaseAvailabilityGroup DallasDag
    -DatabaseAvailabilityGroupIpAddresses 192.168.1.77
    -NetworkCompression enabled -NetworkEncryption enabled4.

4. To validate that the IP has been assigned to the DAG, run the following command:

    Get-DatabaseAvailabilityGroup | Format-List

Using Failover Clustering in Exchange Server 2010

Failover Clustering is a technology that allows you to run an instance of software on a single server and have the ability to move that instance between nodes in the cluster without having to restart the application. When deploying Microsoft Exchange Server 2010 HA features, you need to purchase either the Windows Server 2008/2008 R2 Enterprise or the Datacenter Editions because they include Windows Failover Clustering. A controlled failover process maintains the application state in order to reduce the impact on the end users. DAGs uses Windows Failover Clustering and provide heartbeat node management API, and uses the cluster database to provide database mobility to the DAG.

In previous versions of Exchange Server, during installation you were required to make a choice of installing Exchange into a clustered configuration or as a stand-alone server. The only way to change that configuration after you installed Exchange Server was to uninstall and then reinstall Exchange. Exchange 2010 has improved this experience; you no longer have to decide during installation if the Mailbox server is going to be part of a cluster and you have the ability to add and remove the Exchange Server from a DAG without a reinstall Exchange.

> For more detailed information about Windows Server failover clustering and network load balancing, see *MCTS: Windows Server 2008 Applications Infrastructure Configuration Study Guide: Exam 70-643* (Sybex, 2008) or the instructor-led course 6423: "Implementing and Managing Windows Server 2008 Clustering" by Microsoft Learning.

Using Majority Node Set

Microsoft implemented *majority node set (MNS)* quorums in Windows Server 2003 (called Node and File Share Majority quorum in Windows Server 2008 and Windows Server 2008 R2) to address the first two issues. For simplicity, this will be referred to as an MNS cluster. Instead of selecting a shared physical disk to host the quorum, it is possible to select the MNS option to create a server cluster. In an MNS cluster, the quorum data is actually stored on multiple disks across the cluster and a file share is used to help determine cluster quorum. MNS is designed and built to ensure that the stored cluster data remains consistent across the different disks. Since MNS clusters can use locally attached disks, nodes do not require expensive shared disks to maintain clustering information in the quorum. MNS has several unique issues:

- MNS covers only the quorum. It provides a nice geographically dispersed method to handle the quorum. It doesn't provide a method for replicating data that would normally be shared by nodes; it is up to the application or storage vendor to provide this functionality.

- MNS requires a minimum of two nodes and a witness server.

The unique features of MNS dovetail nicely with the new capabilities that Exchange Server 2010 brings to the table.

Employing a Witness Server

To allow for the failure of a node in a majority node set cluster, there must be enough nodes (or votes) online and communicating to constitute more than one half of the number of available votes in order to maintain a quorum. In a two-node implementation, there aren't any extra votes available to allow for failure. The witness server provides the third vote in the cluster to allow for a failure of one of the three, while still allowing the cluster to maintain a quorum.

Microsoft recommends using a Hub Transport server for the witness server, but other types of servers will work just fine as long as they are running the server service and have the Exchange Trusted Subsystem group added to the local Administrators group. If you currently have a clustered file server, it provides a perfect place for the witness server while providing redundancy for the witness.

In previous versions of Exchange Server, an administrator would install Windows Failover Clustering and make the appropriate configuration changes to the cluster before Exchange Server was installed. Microsoft has simplified this task for us and will install Windows Failover Clustering when Exchange Server is added to the DAG. All members of the DAG must be running the same server operating system, Windows Server 2008 or Windows Server 2008 R2.

In Exercise 7.3, you will add a Mailbox server to a DAG.

EXERCISE 7.3

Adding a Mailbox Server to a DAG

In this exercise, you will add EX02 to the DallasDag and validate that the components of the DAG are created and functioning properly:

1. On EX01, click Start ➢ Programs ➢ Microsoft Exchange Server 2010 and then select Exchange Management Console.

2. Run the following command:

   Add-DatabaseAvailabilityGroupServer DallasDag -MailboxServer EX02

   This command installs Windows Failover Clustering.

3. Run Get-DatabaseAvailabilityGroup | Format-List and verify that EX02 has been successfully added to DallasDag.

```
Machine: EX01.Mailtask.com
[PS] C:\Windows\system32>Get-DatabaseAvailabilityGroup | fl

RunspaceId                                : c59dd689-a35e-492d-beb8-dc95011846e5
Name                                      : DallasDag
Servers                                   : {EX02}
WitnessServer                             : EX03.MAILTASK.COM
WitnessDirectory                          : c:\FSW
AlternateWitnessServer                    :
AlternateWitnessDirectory                 :
NetworkCompression                        : InterSubnetOnly
NetworkEncryption                         : InterSubnetOnly
DatacenterActivationMode                  : Off
StoppedMailboxServers                     : {}
StartedMailboxServers                     : {}
DatabaseAvailabilityGroupIpv4Addresses    : {192.168.1.77}
OperationalServers                        :
PrimaryActiveManager                      :
ThirdPartyReplication                     : Disabled
ReplicationPort                           : 0
NetworkNames                              : {}
AdminDisplayName                          :
ExchangeVersion                           : 0.10 (14.0.100.0)
DistinguishedName                         : CN=DallasDag,CN=Database Availability Groups,CN=Exchange Administrative Group
                                            {FYD1BOHP23SPDLT},CN=Administrative Groups,CN=Mailtask,CN=Microsoft Exchange,C
                                            N=Services,CN=Configuration,DC=Mailtask,DC=com
Identity                                  : DallasDag
Guid                                      : 4923ecc2-b429-4dd3-95de-0d00d33dde0f
ObjectCategory                            : Mailtask.com/Configuration/Schema/ms-Exch-MDB-Availability-Group
ObjectClass                               : {top, msExchMDBAvailabilityGroup}
WhenChanged                               : 2/21/2010 11:10:24 PM
WhenCreated                               : 2/21/2010 10:35:29 PM
WhenChangedUTC                            : 2/22/2010 4:10:24 AM
WhenCreatedUTC                            : 2/22/2010 3:35:29 AM
OrganizationId                            :
OriginatingServer                         : EX01.Mailtask.com
IsValid                                   : True
```

4. Logon to EX02 and click Start ➢ Programs ➢ Administrative Tools ➢ Active Directory Users and Computers.

5. Expand Mailtask.com and select the Computers container.

6. Verify that there is a computer object named DallasDag. This cluster name object (CNO) is created when the first server is added into the DAG.

7. Click Start ➢ Programs ➢ Administrative Tools ➢ Failover Cluster Manager.

8. In the console tree, click DallasDag.Mailtask.com.

9. In the Summary of Cluster section, verify that the Quorum Configuration is Node and File Share Majority.

10. Verify that EX02 is currently assigned to the cluster.

11. Expand Cluster Core Resources and verify the IP address associated with DallasDag.

12. Expand Nodes and Networks to review the settings.

13. To validate the witness server, click Start, and in the search box, type **\\EX03**. Then press Enter.

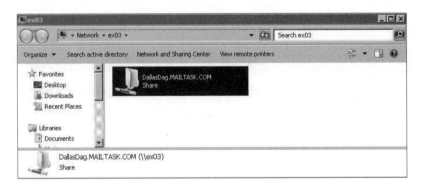

14. Click DallasDag.Mailtask.com and review the access denied error message. Click Close.

15. Log on to EX03.

16. Click Start, and in the search line type **C:\FSW** and then press Enter.

17. Right-click the FSW folder and click Properties.

18. Click the Sharing tab.

19. Click Advanced Sharing.

20. Click Permissions.

EXERCISE 7.3 *(continued)*

21. Verify that only the computer object for DallasDag has access to this share.

In Exercise 7.4, you will use EMC to add server EX01 to the DAG named DallasDag.

EXERCISE 7.4

Adding EX01 to a DAG Using the Exchange Management Console

Follow these steps to use the EMC to add an Exchange Server to an existing DAG:

1. Log on to EX01 as Administrator.

2. Click Start ➢ Programs ➢ Microsoft Exchange Server 2010 and then select Exchange Management Console.

3. Expand Organizational Configuration and select the Mailbox node.

4. Click the Database Availability Group tab.

5. Right-click DallasDag and then click Manage Database Availability Group Membership.

6. Click Add.

7. Select EX01 and then click OK.

8. Click Manage.

9. Click Finish on the completion page.

10. Log on to EX03 as Administrator.

11. Click Start ➢ Computer ➢ Local Disk C and then the FSW folder.

12. Verify that there are two files: VerifyShareWriteAccess and Witness.

Managing a Database Availability Group

After an administrator has created a DAG and added the appropriate number of Exchange servers to it, the task of managing this new infrastructure is key to providing end users with an optimal experience. One task that should be done before deploying any Exchange server is to use the storage calculator to properly size the servers. You can find the Exchange Mailbox Server Role calculator at http://msexchangeteam.com/archive/2009/11/09/453117.aspx. This tool will provide guidelines to assist with the number of databases that should be deployed and the required server parameters. The calculator configures Exchange for a worst case scenario and should be used as a guide. Since every deployment of Exchange is different, you should also use tools like Exchange Load Generator to validate your configuration (http://www.microsoft.com/downloads/details.aspx?familyid=CF464BE7-7E52-48CD-B852-CCFC915B29EF&displaylang=en.)

In each of the last few versions of Exchange Server, Microsoft has increased the number of databases that can be hosted on a Mailbox server. Exchange 2010 now supports up to 100 mounted databases for Enterprise Edition and five databases for Standard Edition per Mailbox server. As you will find out in the upcoming exercises, Exchange 2010 replicates at the database level between identified DAG members, and each replicated copy of a database counts toward the 100 database limit. However, an Exchange server can host over 200 replica copies but can only mount 100 databases. You should design your mailbox infrastructure using the 100 database maximum.

Microsoft refers to each instance of a database as a copy. If you install a single Exchange server that hosts a single database, that server hosts one copy of that database. It does not matter if the copy is active or passive. An active copy of a database is used to designate the Mailbox server that is actively hosting the copy of the database that is being used. The passive copy is the standby version of the database that receives regular updates from the active copy.

In Table 7.3, there are three Exchange servers that are members of the same DAG and have been configured to replicate a number of databases between each server. The server EX01 has been configured to be the active host for DB1 and created a copy of the database on EX02 only. Not all members of the DAG are required to replicate between each server, and the number of database copies that you require will be dictated by the failure tolerance you are willing to accept.

TABLE 7.3   Scenario for a three-copy configuration

EX01	EX02	EX03
DB1 Active	DB1 Passive	No copy
DB2 Passive	DB2 Active	DB2 Passive
DB3 Passive	DB3 Passive	DB3 Active

In this configuration, if there is an outage of EX01, there is a copy on EX02 that will become active and users will see little to no difference when the failure occurs. At that point, EX02 is hosting DB1 and DB2, as seen in Table 7.4. If EX02 fails, all users on DB1 will experience an outage because there is no additional copy of the database on EX03.

TABLE 7.4   A three-copy configuration after an EX01 failure

EX02	EX03
DB1 Active	No copy
DB2 Active	DB2 Passive
DB3 Passive	DB3 Active

A simple solution would be to create an additional copy on EX03, and Microsoft recommends the use of three copies of the data, depending on the storage configuration that you decide to utilize. Remember that every copy of the database requires the appropriate amount of storage for each server, and you can have up to 16 nodes in a single DAG. Deciding the number of database copies that should be deployed really comes down to your company service-level agreement (SLA) requirements. In the previous scenario, if the second outage occurs on EX03, then users do not experience an outage and two copies of the data can sustain a multinode failure if you are lucky enough that the right nodes fail.

When you are using Exchange 2010 high availability, each server requires the same drive paths available for storing the database. This means that if you created a mailbox database on

EX01 located in D:\Data\ExchangeDB01 and store the logs in D:\Exchange\Data\LogsDB01, all servers that host a copy must have the same drive path available. You do not have to create the path on the secondary servers as they will be created during the copy process.

In Exercise 7.5, you will create a mailbox database copy in the DallasDag.

EXERCISE 7.5

Creating a Database Copy in the Exchange Management Console and Replicating It

Follow these steps to create a new mailbox database called DallasDagDB01 and configure the database to replicate to EX02:

1.   Log on to EX01 as Administrator.

2.   Click Start ➢ Programs ➢ Microsoft Exchange Server 2010 and then select Exchange Management Console.

3.   In the console tree, expand Organizational Configuration and select Mailbox.

4.   Click the Database Management tab.

5.   In the Actions pane, click New Mailbox Database.

6.   In the New Mailbox Database Wizard, type **DallasDagdb01**.

EXERCISE 7.5 *(continued)*

7. Click Browse, select EX01, and then click OK.

8. Leave the default path for the logs and database and then click Next.

9. On the Configuration Summary page, click New.

10. On the Completion page, click Finish.

11. Verify that the DallasDagDB01 database is mounted.

12. In the Work pane, right-click the database and click Add Mailbox Database Copy.

13. In the Add Mailbox Database Copy Wizard, click the Browse button, select EX02, and click OK.

14. Click Add.

15. On the Completion Summary page, click Finish.

16. Verify that there are now two copies of the database, one mounted on EX01 and one healthy copy on EX02.

Managing Database Copies

In Exercise 7.5, you created the first highly available Exchange database. There are a number of concepts that must be understood to help manage database copies, many of which are only available from the EMS. These concepts are seeding, log truncation, database switch-over, and monitoring database copies.

Seeding a Database Copy

The process of creating a database copy or updating an unhealthy copy of the database is known as seeding. One improvement that has been made to Exchange 2010 is the ability to seed a database from another passive copy. This feature reduces WAN replication for a multi-site deployment or allows an administrator to reduce the load on an active server when creating a new database. In this chapter's exercises, the current configuration has EX01 and EX02 as members of DallasDag. For example, suppose you add two servers located in Virginia named VA01 and VA02 to the DallasDag and create a database copy from EX01 to VA01. If another copy is created on VA02, VA01 should be specified as the source server to reduce the seed replication traffic across the WAN. However, each passive copy will receive new updates over the WAN link from the active database, as seen in Figure 7.2. When you're determining the number of copies to have in remote datacenters, the bandwidth must be planned properly.

FIGURE 7.2   DAG replication over a WAN

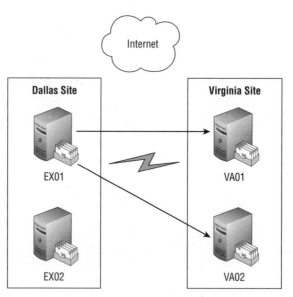

The two commands that you will use to seed a database for the first time or update an unhealthy copy will be `Add-MailboxDatabaseCopy` and `Update-MailboxDatabaseCopy`. In the previous exercise, you used the EMC to create a new database copy, which calls the `Add-MailboxDatabaseCopy` command. In the next exercise, you will break the healthy copy and utilize the `Update-MailboxDatabaseCopy` to resolve the issue. This reseed could also be done from within the EMC, but it is better to get familiar with the management shell commands associated with Exchange because this will help you better understand the process.

In Exercise 7.7, you will work with an unhealthy copy of a mailbox database.

EXERCISE 7.6

Updating an Unhealthy Database Copy from the Exchange Management Shell

In this exercise, you will modify the healthy copy of a mailbox database so it becomes unhealthy and reseed/update the copy to resolve the issue:

1. Log on to EX02 as Administrator.

2. Click Start ➢ Programs ➢ Microsoft Exchange Server 2010 and then select Exchange Management Console.

3. In the navigation tree, expand Microsoft Exchange On-Premises and then Server Configuration and then click Mailbox.

4. In the upper portion of the result pane, click EX02.

5. In the lower portion of the Results pane, right-click the database copy and click Suspend Database Copy.

6. Type a comment in the pane that appears and then click Yes.

7. Minimize the EMC.

8. Open Windows Explorer, then browse `C:\Program Files\Microsoft\Exchange Server\V14\Mailbox\DallasDagDB01`. Right-click dallasdagdb01.edb, click Rename, and then type **dallasdagdb01.old**.

9. Maximize the EMC, right-click the database copy, and click Resume Database Copy.

10. The database copy should now have a copy status of Failed and Suspended.

11. Click Start ➢ Programs ➢ Microsoft Exchange Server 2010 and then select Exchange Management Shell.

12. Run the following command:

    ```
    Update-Mailboxdatabasecopy dallasdagdb01\EX02 –SourceServer EX01
      –DeleteExistingFiles
    ```

13. After the command completes, maximize the EMC, select EX02 from the Server menu, and click Refresh from the Actions pane. The database copy should now have a copy status of Healthy.

Using Log Truncation

In the exercise lab environment, there are now two copies of the database. Replay lag time can delay the logs from being written to the database, but what happens to the transaction log files? You have the capability to configure the truncation time for the log files after they have been replayed into the database. This does not mean that after the log is written it will be deleted; you are telling the system to allow this log to be deleted by a backup or circular logging. The default setting for log truncation is 0, which is disabled.

FIGURE 7.3   Using Get-MailboxDatabase to retrieve recovery settings

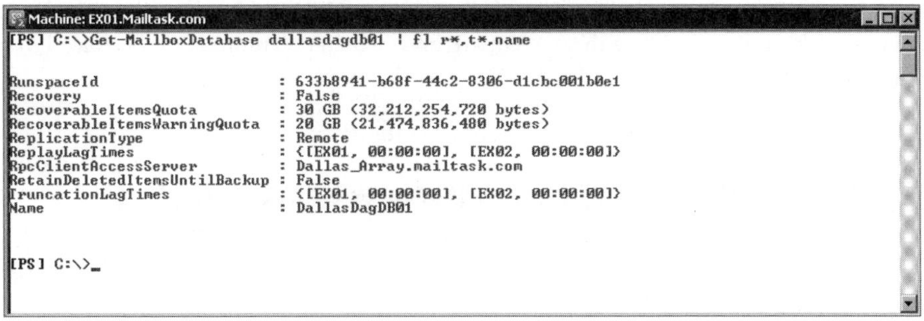

```
Machine: EX01.Mailtask.com                                              _ □ X
[PS] C:\>Get-MailboxDatabase dallasdagdb01 | fl r*,t*,name

RunspaceId                    : 633b8941-b68f-44c2-8306-d1cbc001b0e1
Recovery                      : False
RecoverableItemsQuota         : 30 GB (32,212,254,720 bytes)
RecoverableItemsWarningQuota  : 20 GB (21,474,836,480 bytes)
ReplicationType               : Remote
ReplayLagTimes                : {[EX01, 00:00:00], [EX02, 00:00:00]}
RpcClientAccessServer         : Dallas_Array.mailtask.com
RetainDeletedItemsUntilBackup : False
TruncationLagTimes            : {[EX01, 00:00:00], [EX02, 00:00:00]}
Name                          : DallasDagDB01


[PS] C:\>_
```

Before log truncation can occur, the following requirements must be met:

- The log must have been backed up or circular logging enabled.
- The log must be below the checkpoint depth.
- If there is more than one copy, all copies must have replayed the log.

If you are using a lag database copy, then some additional requirements must be met:

- The log must be below the checkpoint depth.
- The log file needs to be older than replay lag plus truncation lag time.
- The log must be first truncated on the active database copy.

Suspending, Resuming, and Switching Over Database Copies

Some of the most common tasks an Exchange administrator will perform when managing a DAG are related to suspending, resuming, and moving database copies. When you moved the databases between servers in previous versions of Exchange, the term *failover* was always used, even when there was not a failure. In Exchange 2010, the correct term is *switchover*. A switchover is the act of mounting a passive database copy when no failure occurs, and the database is moved by an administrator. The term *failover* is used when an event occurs that causes a disruption in service that results in the unplanned activation of a database copy on another server. You might ask why we believe these are common tasks; most administrators will need to patch their servers at least on a monthly basis, and the proper steps to patch a server will consist of suspending database replications, switching active database copies to other servers, and resuming the replication after the patching for that server is completed.

Configuring *AutoDatabaseMountDial*

Microsoft has implemented controls to handle the behavior in the case of an active Mailbox server failing. Exchange databases have an attribute that can be used to control unscheduled failures. We can use the Set-MailboxServer command to configure this attribute and the Get-MailboxServer command to view the current settings, which default to good BestAvailability and can be seen in Figure 7.4.

FIGURE 7.4   Getting the AutoBaseMountDial settings

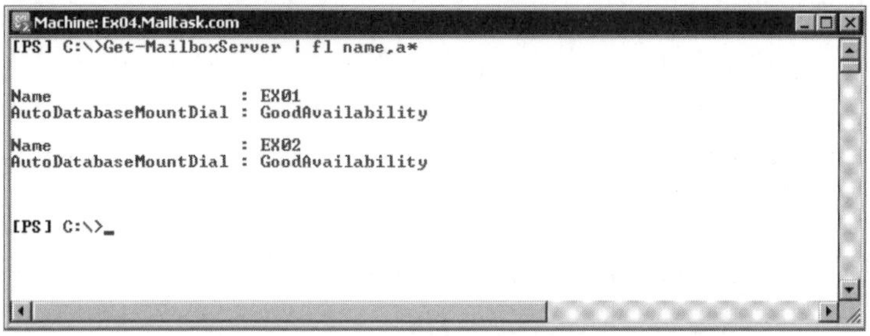

```
Machine: Ex04.Mailtask.com
[PS] C:\>Get-MailboxServer | fl name,a*


Name                : EX01
AutoDatabaseMountDial : GoodAvailability

Name                : EX02
AutoDatabaseMountDial : GoodAvailability


[PS] C:\>_
```

The attribute, AutoDatabaseMountDial, has three possible values:

Lossless   When AutoDatabaseMountDial is set to Lossless, the passive node waits for the failed node to come back online before its databases are mounted. In this mode, it is vital that there is no loss of messages. For the process to succeed, the failed node must come back online with all logs available. When the unscheduled outage occurs, the passive node becomes the active node, and the information store is brought online using standard clustering technologies. The new active node then checks to see whether all the databases can be mounted without any lost data. If it is possible to mount the databases without any lost data, then the information store will mount the databases and make sure the mailbox is available to clients. If the databases cannot be mounted without lost data, then the active node will look to the other node and try to copy logs from it to bring itself fully up-to-date. If the failed server comes back online with all its logs available, then this process will eventually update the active node. If the failed node comes back online and its logs are not available, then the database will not mount. In this environment, it is possible for the Exchange administrator to mount the databases manually.

GoodAvailability   When AutoDatabaseMountDial is set to Good Availability, the database will mount automatically if there are six or fewer logs in the copy queue.

Best Availability   It allows automatic recovery even if replication has some latency. In case of a failure, the new active node might be slightly behind the state of the old active node after the failover and some data loss is experienced. The database copy will mount if there are less than or equal to 12 logs in the copy queue.

The Lossless AutoDatabaseMountDial setting can result in long outages. In some cases, it does not make sense to use Lossless because the downtime will cause major impacts on organizational production.

In Exercise 7.7, you will practice some common administration tasks related to a DAG.

EXERCISE 7.7

Suspending, Resuming, and Switching Over Database Copies

This exercise will show you how to perform a server switchover. This allows you to move multiple databases hosted on a single server at once:

1. Log on to EX02 as Administrator.

2. Click Start ➤ Programs ➤ Microsoft Exchange Server 2010 and then select Exchange Management Console.

3. In the console tree, expand Microsoft Exchange On-Premises, expand Server Configuration, and then click Mailbox.

4. In the upper portion of the result pane, click EX02 and then under the Database Copies tab, right-click the healthy copy of DallasDagDB01, and click Suspend Database Copy.

Mailbox						3 objects

Database Management | Database Availability Groups | Sharing Policies | Address Lists | Managed Default Folders | Managed Custom Folders | Managed Folder Mailbox Policies | Offline Address Book

Create Filter

Name ▲	Database File Path	Log Folder Path		Mounted	Servers
DallasDagDB01	C:\Program Files\Microsof...	C:\Program Files\Microsoft\Exchange Server\V14\Mailbox\DallasDagDB01		Mounted	EX01, EX02
DallasEx01DB1	C:\Data\dallasex01db1\D...	C:\Data\dallasex01db1log		Mounted	EX01
DallasPF	C:\Program Files\Microsof...	C:\Program Files\Microsoft\Exchange Server\V14\Mailbox\Public Folder Datab...		Mounted	EX01

DallasDagDB01						2 objects

Database Copies

Database ▲	Mailbox Server	Copy Status	Copy Queue Length	Replay Queue Length	Activation Preference
DallasDagDB01	EX01	Mounted	0	0	1
DallasDagD	EX01 / Suspend Database Copy	Healthy	0	0	2
	Activate Database Copy...				
	Remove				
	Properties				
	Help				

5. Type a comment in the window that appears and click Yes.

6. The lower portion of the result pane now shows the database copy status as Suspended.

EXERCISE 7.7 (continued)

7. Right-click the suspended database and click Resume Database Copy.

8. On the Comment page, click Yes. The database will resynchronize and become healthy. The time this takes depends on how many log files will need to be replayed. You might need to click the refresh button to get the screen to update to show a healthy status.

9. Once the database has a copy status of Healthy, right-click it and choose Activate Database Copy.

10. On the Active Database Copy dialog box, click the drop-down menu and review the available options. Select None and then click OK.

11. The database should now report being mounted on EX02. You might notice some logs now on EX01 in the replay queue due to the switchover.

12. In the console tree, expand Microsoft Exchange On-Premises, then Server Configuration, and then click Mailbox.

13. Click EX02 in the server list.

14. In the Actions pane, click Switchover Server.

15. In the Switchover server database copies dialog box, select Use the specified server as the target for switchover, select EX01, and click OK.

16. Verify that the database copy from EX02 is now reporting Healthy and EX01 is once again the active copy.

Monitoring Database Copies

Microsoft Exchange Server has become a very reliable product over the years, and in many cases, once a system is configured it can be left alone and will continue to run without issue. However, as administrators, we know that anything can happen, from hardware failures to third-party software causing issues for a server. The ability to monitor database copies is critical so that you can react to whatever issues arise. A great way to monitor an Exchange system is with Microsoft System Center Operations Manager 2007 R2, which provides in-depth monitoring and alerting capabilities. You can find out more information about Microsoft System Center Operations Manager at the following location:

www.microsoft.com/systemcenter/operationsmanager/en/us/default.aspx

If you do not have any monitoring tool installed in your environment, there are a number of built-in PowerShell commands and scripts that can provide an administrator with information about the status of the database copies. The first command we would like to introduce is `Get-MailboxDatabaseCopyStatus`, which gives you a detailed view of the health of the database copies. In Figure 7.5, you can see the results of running the `Get-MailboxDatabaseCopyStatus -ConnectionStatus | Format-List`. The two properties that should stand out immediately are the context index state and the status, which should both currently be healthy. By adding the `-ConnectionStatus` parameter, the `IncomingLog CopyingNetwork` properties will be retrieved and provide additional information as to what network is being used to copy the log file to the server.

FIGURE 7.5 Viewing the database copy status

```
Machine: EX02.Mailtask.com
[PS] C:\>Get-MailboxDatabaseCopyStatus -ConnectionStatus | fl

RunspaceId                           : e1b5dc1a-9801-479d-83a2-09408a1416f9
Identity                             : DallasDagDB01\EX02
Name                                 : DallasDagDB01\EX02
DatabaseName                         : DallasDagDB01
Status                               : Mounted
MailboxServer                        : EX02
ActiveDatabaseCopy                   : ex02
ActivationSuspended                  : False
ActionInitiator                      : Administrator
ErrorMessage                         :
ErrorEventId                         :
ExtendedErrorInfo                    :
SuspendComment                       :
SinglePageRestore                    : 0
ContentIndexState                    : Healthy
CopyQueueLength                      : 0
ReplayQueueLength                    : 0
LatestAvailableLogTime               :
LastCopyNotificationedLogTime        :
LastCopiedLogTime                    :
LastInspectedLogTime                 :
LastReplayedLogTime                  :
LastLogGenerated                     : 0
LastLogCopyNotified                  : 0
LastLogCopied                        : 0
LastLogInspected                     : 0
LastLogReplayed                      : 0
LatestFullBackupTime                 :
LatestIncrementalBackupTime          :
LatestDifferentialBackupTime         :
LatestCopyBackupTime                 :
SnapshotBackup                       :
SnapshotLatestFullBackup             :
SnapshotLatestIncrementalBackup      :
SnapshotLatestDifferentialBackup     :
SnapshotLatestCopyBackup             :
LogReplayQueueIncreasing             : False
LogCopyQueueIncreasing               : False
OutstandingDumpsterRequests          : {}
OutgoingConnections                  : {{EX01,DAGNetwork01}}
IncomingLogCopyingNetwork            :
SeedingNetwork                       :
ActiveCopy                           : True
```

In Exercise 7.8, you will use the `Get-MailboxDatabaseCopyStatus` command to monitor the health of your DAG replication.

EXERCISE 7.8

Monitoring a DAG with `Get-MailboxDatabaseCopyStatus`

Follow these steps to use the `Get-MailboxDatabaseCopyStatus` command to validate the replication health of the DallasDag:

1. Log on to EX01 as Administrator.

2. Click Start ➢ Programs ➢ Microsoft Exchange Server 2010 and then select Exchange Management Shell.

3. Run the following command:

   `Get-MailboxDatabaseCopyStatus -ConnectionStatus | Format-List`

4. Review the data that is returned on the screen.

The next command is the `Test-ReplicationHealth` command, which will run 15 tests against the specified DAG member to make sure the required services, roles, and features are functioning properly. As administrator, you can write a custom script that calls this command and emails a copy of the result. You can use Task Scheduler to run the command at a desired interval to validate all components of a DAG member are functional.

The `Test-ReplicationHealth` command runs the following tests:

- Checks if the cluster service is healthy

- Checks if the Microsoft Exchange Replication service is running

- Checks that Active Manager is running and has a valid role

- Checks that the Tasks RPC Listener is running and is responding to remote requests

- Checks that the TCP Listener is running and is responding to requests

- Verifies that the members of a database availability group are up and running

- Checks that the networks are healthy

- Checks if any database copies are in the Suspended state

- Checks if any database copies are in the Failed state

- Checks if any database copies are in the Initializing state

- Checks if any database copies are in the DisconnectedAndHealthy state

- Verifies that log copying and inspection for the database copy is keeping up with log generation on the source server

- Verifies that log replay is keeping up with log copying and inspection

Figure 7.6 shows some sample output.

In Exercise 7.9, you will use the Test-ReplicationHealth cmdlet to monitor the status of the DallasDag.

EXERCISE 7.9

Monitoring a DAG with the Test-ReplicationHealth cmdlet

This exercise will show you how to monitor your DAG with the Test-ReplicationHealth cmdlet to validate key components of the DallasDag:

1. Log on to EX01 as Administrator.

2. Click Start ➢ Programs ➢ Microsoft Exchange Server 2010 and then select Exchange Management Shell.

3. Run Test-ReplicationHealth.

4. Run Test-ReplicationHealth | Format-List.

Microsoft has provided a number of scripts for administrators that are by default located in C:\Program Files\Microsoft\Exchange Server\V14\Scripts. There are two scripts in particular that can help an administrator monitor a DAG: CollectReplicationMetrics.ps1 and CollectOverMetrics.ps1. The CollectReplicationMetrics.ps1 script is a real-time monitor that will actively collect information about the DAG for a specified interval and produce a report. The script takes in the parameters outlined in Table 7.5.

FIGURE 7.6   Viewing the results of `Test-ReplicationHealth`

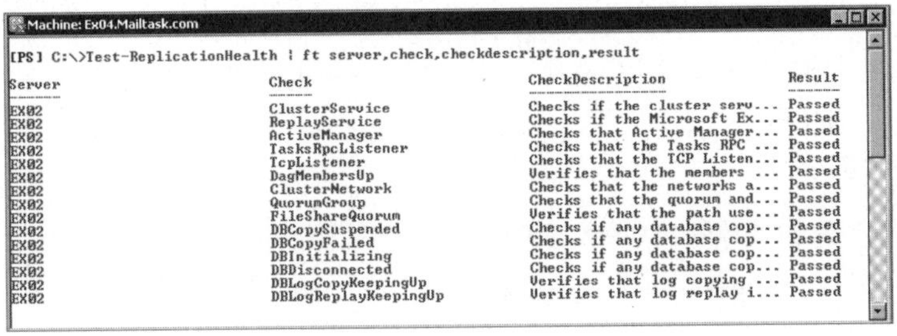

TABLE 7.5   Parameters for the `CollectReplicationMetrics.ps1` script

Parameter	Description
DagName	The name of the DAG you want to monitor
DatabaseName	List of databases on which you want to report
ReportAlias	An email alias to which you want a copy of the report sent
TemporaryDataPath	Location where you want temporary files to be stored. The default is %SystemDrive%\Temp\CollectReplicationMetrics\ <ScriptStartTime>
ReportPath	A folder where you want the report file placed
Duration	The length of time you want the script to run. Specified in D.HH:MM:SS (for example, 1.04:05:30)
Frequency	Specifies the frequency of the samples taken. The default is 10 seconds
Verbose	Shows the task on the screen after it completes.
ProcessOnly	Specifies that data has already been collected and only processing is required.

In Figure 7.7, you can see the output after running the `CollectReplicationMetrics.ps1` script. The script breaks the output into two sections, one for the database and one for the servers. The information that is provided can assist an administrator to provide data to show the amount of downtime that has occurred. The output on the script also generates two CSV files that stores the raw data.

FIGURE 7.7 Collecting replication metrics

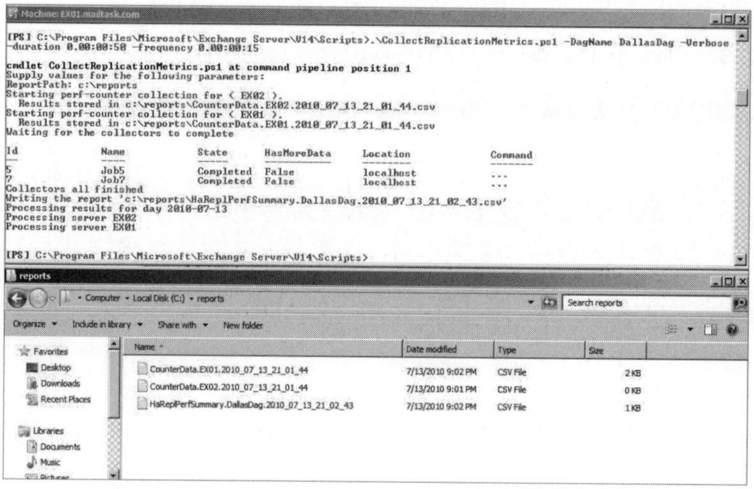

The database report provides a list of the following information:

- ServerName
- DatabaseName
- HoursMounted
- MinutesUnavailable
- MinutesResynchronizing
- MinutesFailed
- MinutesSuspended
- MinutesFailedSuspended
- MinutesDisconnected
- AverageLogGenerationRate
- PeakLogGenerationRate
- AverageLogReplayRate
- PeakLogReplayRate
- OutofCriteriaSeconds
- AverageOutofCriteriaSeconds

The server report provides a list of the following information:

- ServerName
- HoursMeasured
- HoursUnavailable

- AverageMountedMinutes
- AverageLogReplayRate
- PeakLogReplayRate

In Exercise 7.10, you will use the CollectReplicationMetrics.ps1 script to gather statistical data for the DallasDag.

EXERCISE 7.10

Monitoring a DAG with the CollectReplicationMetrics.ps1 Script

This exercise will show you how to use the CollectReplicationMetrics.ps1 script to provide real-time statistics for the DallasDag.

1. Log on to EX01 as Administrator.

2. Create a new folder called Reports located at C:\Reports

3. Click Start ➢ Programs ➢ Microsoft Exchange Server 2010 and then select Exchange Management Shell.

4. Run the following command to change to the scripts directory:

   cd "C:\Program Files\Microsoft\Exchange Server\V14\Scripts"

5. Run the following command:

   ./CollectReplicationMetrics.ps1 -DagName DallasDag
   -Verbose -Duration 0.00:00:50 -ReportPath C:\Reports -Frequency 0.00:00:15

6. Browse to the Reports folder located at C:\Reports and view the three files with Excel (or other editor):

The second script is `CollectOverMetrics.ps1`, and it's also located in the scripts directory. This script can easily produce a nice HTML report of any database outages that have occurred for a specified time period. When launching the script, if you do not specify a start or end date, the script will be configured to use the last 24 hours to collect data. An administrator can open the EMS and run the command `./CollectOverMetrics.ps1 -DatabaseAvailabilityGroup Dallasdag -GenerateHTMLReport -ShowHTMLReport` to produce a report similar to the one in Figure 7.8.

FIGURE 7.8 Output from the `CollectOverMetrics.ps1` script

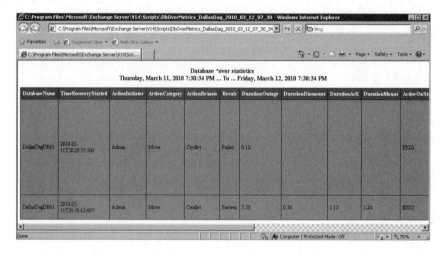

Table 7.6 shows a list of the input parameters that you can use to configure the script.

TABLE 7.6 Parameters for the script

Parameters	Description
DatabaseAvailabilityGroup	The name of the DAG you want to monitor
Database	List of databases you want to report on
TemporaryDataPath	Location where you want temporary files to be stored. The default is %SystemDrive%\Temp\CollectOverMetrics\ <ScriptStartTime>.
StartTime	The date and time to start
EndTime	The date and time to stop collecting data
ReportPath	A folder where you want the report file to be placed
ReportAlias	An email alias that you want a copy of the report sent to

TABLE 7.6   Parameters for the script *(continued)*

Parameters	Description
IncludeApplogs	Use this parameter if you want events in the app log to be collected, merged, and processed. By default, the following are included: MSExchangeIS, MSExchangeIS Mailbox Store, and MSExchangeRepl.
AppLogProvider	Use this parameter if you want specific app log events to be collected. If this parameter is used, the parameter *Include-AppLogs* won't be included. You will then need to explicitly specify what event providers you want to use.
AnalyzeOnly	Use this parameter if the data has already been collected and only processing needs to occur.
MergedXmlFile	Configure this parameter if you want to merge all collected information into an XML file.
GenerateHtmlReport	Converts the output into an HTML file
ShowHtmlReport	After the report is generated, this will launch a web browser and display the report,

In Exercise 7.11, you will use the `CollectOverMetrics.ps1` script to create an HTML report for the DallasDag.

EXERCISE 7.11

Monitoring a DAG with the `CollectOvermetrics.ps1` Script

The following exercise will show you how to create an HTML report using the `CollectOverMetrics.ps1` script to show historical data about DallasDag:

1. Log on to EX01 as Administrator.

2. Click Start ➢ Programs ➢ Microsoft Exchange Server 2010 and then select Exchange Management Shell.

3. Run the following command:

   ```
   cd "C:\Program Files\Microsoft\Exchange Server\V14\Scripts"
   ```

4. Run the following command:

   ```
   ./CollectOverMetrics.ps1 -DatabaseAvailabilityGroup DallasDag
    -GenerateHTMLReport -ShowHTMLReport
   ```

In the next section, you will look at providing high availability to other Microsoft Exchange 2010 roles.

Availability for Client Access, Hub Transport, and Edge Transport Roles

Failover clustering is not an option to provide HA services for the non-Mailbox server roles. To provide your Exchange organization with Hub Transport services, you need a single Hub Transport in each Active Directory site with a Mailbox server. To provide for redundancy, two or more Hub Transport servers should be configured in each site. There is no additional configuration required. When you are providing highly available Client Access services, there are two options: DNS round-robin or NLB—and really only one if you want true redundancy: Network Load Balancing (NLB).

For inbound email delivery with Edge or Hub Transport servers, the typical way to provide redundancy is to use an MX record for each of the email servers accessible for email delivery. MX records are weighted records in DNS that point to the email servers responsible for receiving mail for a domain. MX records with a lower weighting will be attempted before higher-weighted records. Records that have the same weight will be load-balanced. Since using MX records to provide this redundancy is part of the way SMTP was designed, this configuration is often sufficient. In some instances, however, NLB is also leveraged to distribute SMTP load.

The next section discusses using NLB for CAS and SMTP servers.

 You can find more information about MX records and how they are used in RFC 2821.

Client Access Server Arrays

One of the major changes with Exchange 2010 is related to the MAPI endpoint. In all previous versions of Exchange, the Outlook client (using MAPI) would connect directly to an Exchange Mailbox server. With Exchange 2010, the Outlook client connects to an Exchange server running the CAS role. The Client Access server will be the new MAPI endpoint for all connections except public folder access, which will go directly to the Mailbox server. A common issue that users experience when they are running Outlook 2003 is related to the default configuration requiring encryption to be enabled on the Outlook client or the connections will fail. When a user opens Outlook today, a number of items occur but the main one is the connection from the client directly to the Mailbox server to retrieve their mail via MAPI-RPC, as shown in Figure 7.9.

FIGURE 7.9 How clients connected prior to Exchange Server 2010

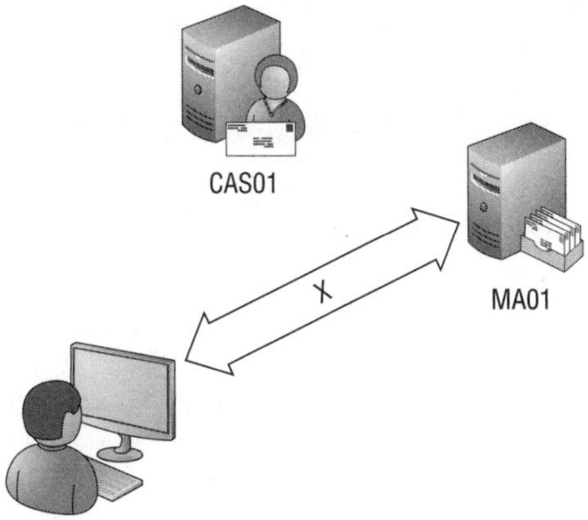

One of the issues with this configuration, even when using an Exchange Server 2007 SCC or CCR cluster, is that during a failover, the client connection point will be disrupted, even if only for a few moments. This means that clients are making a direct connection to the Mailbox server, which is limited to approximately 60,000 connections to the information store.

As Microsoft's Exchange product group looked at how they could better scale Exchange Server 2010, one of the new techniques was to move the client connection endpoint to the CAS instead of the Mailbox server. This allows for the following two things to happen:

1. During a database move/failover, the client endpoint does not go down and makes the move seamless to the user.

2. If you near the port limit, you just add an additional CAS to the RPC Client Access array.

Determining the MAPI Endpoint

At first glance, you may think the MAPI endpoint is configured per user, but that is not the case. To find out what your RPC client endpoint is, you need to run the command `Get-MailboxDatabase <Database Name>" | Format-List Name,Rpc*` . The output of this command will show the RpcClientAccessServer associated with each database. By default, there are no CAS arrays configured; the name of a random CAS in the same AD site will be directly associated with each database. In Figure 7.10, you can see the settings after running this command:

```
Get-MailboxDatabase | Format-List Name,Rpc*
```

In Exercise 7.12, you will create a mailbox database copy from the Exchange Management Console.

FIGURE 7.10   RpcClientAccessServer

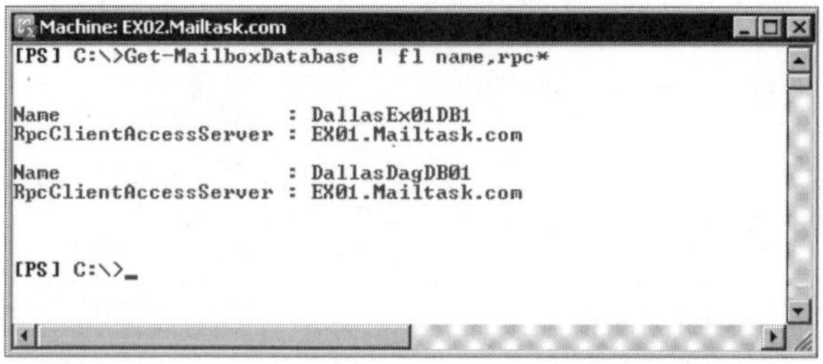

EXERCISE 7.12

Creating a Database Copy in the Exchange Management Console

The following exercise will show you how to create a copy of a mailbox database from the EMC:

1. Log on to EX02 as Administrator.

2. Click Start ➢ Programs ➢ Microsoft Exchange Server 2010 and then select Exchange Management Console.

3. In the console tree, expand Microsoft Exchange On-Premises, then Organization Configuration, and then click Mailbox.

4. In the upper portion of the result pane, click the Database Management tab.

5. In the Actions pane, click New Mailbox Database.

6. In the New Mailbox Database Wizard, type **DallasDagdb02**.

7. Click the Browse button under the server name field and select EX02.

8. On the Set Paths page, leave the default path for the logs and database and click Next.

EXERCISE 7.12 *(continued)*

9. On the Configuration Summary page, click New.

10. On the Completion page, click Finish.

11. In the lower portion of the result pane, verify that DallasDagDB02 has a copy status of Mounted.

12. Click Start ➢ Programs ➢ Microsoft Exchange Server 2010 and then select Exchange Management Shell.

13. Run Get-Mailboxdatabase | fl Name,Rpc*.

As you can tell, by default Exchange 2010 does not provide redundancy for the RpcClientAccessServer component. In the current configuration, if EX02 fails, then any database that is configured to use EX02 as the RpcClientAccessServer endpoint will fail to connect to their mailbox even if there was a mounted copy of the database on another server. The RpcClientAccessServer attribute does not get dynamically updated when the databases are moved. Later in this chapter, you will create an RpcClientAccessServer array, which can be used to provide redundancy for the RpcClientAccessServer component.

In Exercise 7.13, you will use Outlook to set up a profile to the Exchange Server and view the current RPC settings.

EXERCISE 7.13

Setting Up an Outlook Profile

Follow these steps to set up an Outlook profile and view the RPC settings, which will show the MAPI endpoint that is currently configured:

1. Log on to EX01 as Administrator.

2. Click Start ➢ Programs ➢ Microsoft Exchange Server 2010 and then select Exchange Management Console.

3. In the console tree, expand Microsoft Exchange On-Premises, then Recipient Configuration, and then click Mailbox.

4. Verify that you have created a mailbox to use in this lab.

5. Log out as Administrator and then log on to EX01 as Jodie Tirch or the account that you have created. Logon locally rights must be granted to the user account that is used.

6. Click Start ➢ All Programs ➢ Microsoft Office ➢ Outlook 2007. If you have not created a profile, you will be prompted to do so. If you have already created a profile, skip to step 11.

7. On the Outlook startup page, click Next.

8. On the Email Accounts page, leave the default of Yes and click Next.

9. On the Auto Account Setup page, enter the name of the account and the email address and click Next. Since the machine is domain joined, this information should auto-populate for you.

> Your Name: Jodie Tirch
>
> E-mail Address: Jodie.Tirch@mailtask.com

10. On the Configuring page, click Finish.

11. Once the Outlook profile opens, Click Tools ➢ Account Settings.

12. On the Account Settings window, click Change.

13. Verify that the Microsoft Exchange server is the CAS FQDN and not the Mailbox server. Since we have the CAS role installed on our Mailbox servers, this may show up as EX01 or EX02, which can be misleading.

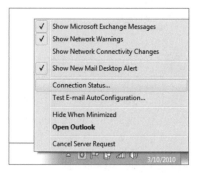

14. To close the Microsoft Exchange Settings page, click Cancel.

15. On the Account Settings page, click Close.

16. Hold down the Ctrl key, right-click the Outlook icon in the system tray, then click Connection Status.

17. Verify that EX01.Mailtask.com is listed in the Server name column.

Server name	Type	Interface	Conn	Status	Req/Fail	Avg Resp	Avg Proc	No
EX01.Mailtask.com	Directory	Local Area...	TCP/IP	Established	12/0	6		
EX01.Mailtask.com	Mail	Local Area...	TCP/IP	Established	155/0	13	7	As
EX01.Mailtask.com	Directory	Local Area...	TCP/IP	Established	7/0	2		
EX01.Mailtask.com	Directory	Local Area...	TCP/IP	Established	6/0	0		
EX01.Mailtask.com	Mail	Local Area...	TCP/IP	Established	181/0	4	1	As
EX01.Mailtask.com	Directory	Local Area...	TCP/IP	Established	6/0	5		

Microsoft Exchange Connection Status

General | Local Mailbox

Activity

Reconnect   Click to restore connectivity to Microsoft Exchange.

Close

18. Review the connections and click Close.

In Exercise 7.13, you saw that all the Directory and Mail connections were going to EX01. This is a bit misleading since the CAS role and Mailbox role are on the same server. In Exercise 7.17, you will see the MAPI endpoint move from EX01 to a client access array.

How Does a Client Access Server Array Work?

On each CAS, there is a new service that runs called MSExchangeRPC. The executable that spawns this service is `Microsoft.Exchange.RpcClientAccess.Service.exe`, and it listens on port 6001 for an HTTP connection and uses dynamic ports by default for TCP/IP connections. In Exercise 7.18, you will configure a scoped port to use for TCP/IP connections.

By default, when you install Exchange 2010, the files that are associated with this service will be located in `C:\Program Files\Microsoft\Exchange Server\V14\Bin`.

When connections are made to the CAS by a MAPI client, the CAS creates a channel to the Mailbox server to retrieve the mailbox data. The CAS then creates a maximum of 100 RPC connections to the Mailbox server. This connection limit drastically reduces the number of connections to the information store and allows an Exchange Mailbox server to increase the number of users it can host because the server is less likely to hit the hard-coded 60,000 connection limit, as shown in Figure 7.11.

FIGURE 7.11 Client MAPI connections

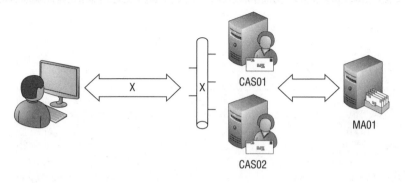

Encrypting the Client Access Server Array

As briefly mentioned in the Introduction, by default Exchange requires the client to connect with encryption enabled. This is not set on each database but on each RPC server and can be found with the following command:

```
Get-RpcClientAccess | fl server,encrypt*
```

After running the Get-RpcClientAccess command, you can see that each CAS and Mailbox server has encryption configuration. You may ask why the Mailbox server would still require encryption settings if all the client connections are directed to the CAS. You may recall that we stated previously that clients still connect directly to the Mailbox server for public folder access. In Exercise 7.14, you will use Outlook to validate the current encryption settings that are configured.

EXERCISE 7.14

Checking Outlook Encryption Settings

Follow these steps to check the Outlook encryption settings:

1. Log on to EX01 as Jodie.Tirch.

2. Click Start ➢ All Programs ➢ Microsoft Office ➢ Outlook 2007.

3. Click Tools ➢ Accounts Settings.

4. Select the profile and click Change.

5. Click More Settings.

6. Select the Security tab. Outlook 2007 and higher has encryption enabled by default, however, Office Outlook 2003 does not have it enabled by default. Therefore on Outlook 2003 clients this needs to be manually configured.

7. Click OK to close the Microsoft Exchange settings.

8. Click Cancel to close the Email Account Wizard.

9. Click Close to close Account settings page.

10. Log Off EX01.

If you manage an environment with Outlook 2003 users, you have a number of options to enable the encryption settings, or you can disable encryption on the Exchange server. It is recommend that you leave encryption enabled because it provides a more secure environment. The encryption setting affects both MAPI users and Outlook Anywhere connections.

If you have Outlook 2003 users, you have the following options to adjust the encryptions configuration:

- Use Group Policy to configure the client computers.

- Disable encryptions on the Exchange servers with `Get-RpcClientAccess |` `Set-RpcClientAccess -EncryptionRequired:$false`.

- Manually configure the client computers.

Configuring a Client Access Server Array

Now that you have a basic understanding of how a Client Access server array functions, you can configure the first Client Access server array. You can use NLB or a hardware load balancer from a company like F5 or Citrix for the Client Access server array because either is supported. However, you cannot install NLB on a DAG member because mixing Failover Clustering and Network Load Balancing is not supported. Therefore you need to deploy a third-party load balancing solution for that configuration. To allow us to use the built in Windows load balancing in the next exercises, we created two additional servers, EX03 and EX04.

The DNS entry for the array should not use a DNS name that is available on the public DNS servers, as it only needs to be resolvable on the internal network. To follow best practices, do not use an FQDN that matches your current Outlook Anywhere configuration. That configuration will work, but it will increase the time it takes to connects to your mailbox.

In Exercise 7.15, you will create a new Client Access array that will be used by MAPI connections.

Creating a Client Access Server Array

The following exercise will show you how to create a new client access array that will be used to provide high availability to MAPI connections:

1. Log on to EX01 as Administrator.

2. Click Start ➢ Programs ➢ Microsoft Exchange Server 2010 and then select Exchange Management Shell.

3. Run Get-ClientAccessArray to validate that an array is not already created. Minimize the EMS.

4. Open the DNS administration tools by clicking Start ➢ Administrative Tools ➢ DNS.

5. Expand EX01, then expand Forward Lookup Zone, and then click on Mailtask.com.

6. Right–click the zone Mailtask.com and click New Host.

7. In the Name field, type **Dallas_Array**, and in the IP Address field, type **192.168.1.76**. Click Add Host.

8. On the Success dialog, click OK.

9. To close the new host menu, click Done.

10. Maximize the EMS window and run the following command: Nslookup Dallas_ Array to verify name resolution.

11. Run Get–AdSite and note the site name.

12. Run the following command:

    New-ClientAccessArray -Name Dallas_Array.mailtask.com
    -Fqdn Dallas_Array.mailtask.com -Site Dallas_AD_Site

In Exercise 7.15, you created a Client Access server array named Dallas_Array; however, at this time the array is not functional, nor have we configured any databases to use the new array. Once an array has been created, all new mailbox databases will be associated with the array by default. Quite often administrators ask why the member's parameter shows all the CAS when they may not be a part of the NLB response to the MAPI requests. When you run the `Get-ClientAccessArray` command, the members property only shows what CAS are in the Active Directory site that is associated with the Client Access server array. When the load balance is created, only the members of the load balance will respond to MAPI requests.

Installing and Configuring Network Load Balancing

Many organizations have applications that are critical to daily operations, such as databases, messaging systems, and file/print services. There are some places where technologies such as Network Load Balancing (NLB) are more appropriate than using server clustering to achieve high availability for those applications.

Email is often considered a mission-critical application, and it must be running 24 hours a day, 7 days a week. In addition, network email services need the ability to scale performance to handle large volumes of traffic without creating unwanted delays. Network load-balanced clusters enable you to manage a group of independent servers as a single system for higher availability, easier manageability, and greater scalability.

Windows includes NLB functionality that is a fully distributed, software-based solution and does not require any specialized hardware or network components. Even better, there aren't any additional licensing costs associated with using NLB. All members of the Windows Server family have NLB built into their operating systems at no additional cost.

There are a number of scenarios when it is recommended to deploy hardware load balancers over Windows Network Load Balancing. We have listed three of them:

- If you have a deployment that requires you to scale to more than 10 CAS in a load balance
- If you intend to deploy Microsoft Office Communications Server, which is only supported with a hardware load balancer
- If you combine the CAS role and Mailbox role on the same server and want to create an RPC array and a DAG

 NOTE   NLB is also available from third parties and, in some cases, provides additional features such as the ability to ensure that a specific server is functioning properly before allowing access to it. The principles are the same for all sorts of NLB solutions.

Exchange Server 2010 is somewhat limited when it comes to where NLB can be used. The Edge Transport server role and the Client Access server role can both use NLB and are fully supported for NLB.

As the name suggests, an NLB cluster uses the network to provide load balancing and redundancy. It is able to accomplish this using a virtual IP address and a virtual media access control address that is shared between all nodes in the cluster. Client connections are all made to this virtual IP address. When an incoming packet is addressed to the virtual IP address, all the NLB nodes receive it, but only the appropriate node responds.

When a client request arrives, all hosts simultaneously perform a calculation in order to determine which node should handle the request. The chosen node then accepts and responds to the client request and the other cluster nodes discard it. If the NLB driver decides it is supposed to process the packet and the packet meets the port rules for the NLB cluster, then it passes the packet to the TCP/IP layer and through the rest of the network model. If all nodes are configured identically, the same percentage of client requests will be load-balanced to each node; however, this can be customized to match server capabilities. All nodes synchronize their data about which node should respond to each request and which nodes are active members of the cluster.

One feature of NLB that you need to know when working with Exchange 2010 is creating port rules. Port rules specify how requests to a specific port range are sent to the NLB cluster. This allows you to specify which nodes will receive traffic for specific TCP/IP ports. For an example of how this might be used, suppose you have an NLB cluster consisting of four servers and it needs to load-balance the OWA and POP3 connections. OWA, which runs on TCP ports 80 and 443, can be limited to use only three of the NLB nodes, and POP3 can be set to run only on two nodes of the NLB cluster. This will help reduce the number of nodes the POP3 services will impact when under load.

One drawback with Windows Server NLB is that it is not natively capable of looking into the individual nodes and testing to see whether an application or service is running properly. If an application or service (such as the World Wide Web Publishing Service) fails, NLB will continue to include the node in the NLB cluster and some connections will fail.

In Exercise 7.16, you will install Windows Network Load Balancing and create a Windows Network Load Balancing cluster that will respond to the MAPI requests.

EXERCISE 7.16

Creating an NLB Cluster to Respond to MAPI Requests

The following exercise will show you how to install Windows Network Load Balancing and create an NLB cluster that will be used for the Client Access array:

1. Log on to EX03 as Administrator.

2. Click Start ➢ Administrative Tools ➢ Server Manager.

3. Select Features in the console tree, then click Add Features.

4. In the Add Features Wizard, select Network Load Balancing and click Next.

5. Click Install on the Confirm Installation Services page.

6. Click Close after the installation completes successfully.

7. Repeat steps 1 through 6 on EX04.

EXERCISE 7.16 *(continued)*

8. Launch NLB Manager by clicking Start ➢ Administrative Tools ➢ Network Load Balancing Manager.

9. In Network Load Balancing Manager, click Cluster ➢ New.

10. In the New Cluster: Connect dialog box, type the IP address or hostname of the CAS (EX03) and click Connect.

11. On the New Cluster Wizard, click Next.

12. On the New Cluster: Host Parameters page, click Next.

13. Click Add to add the virtual IP for the cluster. This should match the IP used to create the DNS record for the array.

14. Enter the IP associated with the array and click OK.

15. On the Cluster Parameters page, click Next.

16. On the next Cluster Parameters page, verify that the following information is entered and then click Next:

IP Address: 192.168.1.76

Full Internet Name: Dallas_Array.mailtask.com

Cluster Operation Mode: Multicast

17. On the Port Rules page, click Finish.

18. Verify that EX03 is listed and the computer icon is green.

EXERCISE 7.16 *(continued)*

19. Right-click Dallas_Array.mailtask.com and click Add Host To Cluster.

20. On the Add Host to Cluster page, type **EX04** in the Host field and click Connect. After the host appears, click Next.

21. On the Add Host to Cluster: Host Parameters screen, click Next.

22. Click Finish on the Port Rules page.

23. Verify that both EX03 and EX04 are converged and green.

We are now only one step away from allowing the users to have redundancy with MAPI connections and providing additional scalability to the Exchange environment. So far we have created a Client Access server array, configured Network Load Balancing, and created the appropriate DNS records. The last step we need to complete is the association of the mailbox database with the Client Array. To do this last step, we will need to use the Set-MailboxDatabase command. Any database in the same Active Directory site can be configured to use the Client Access server array at the MAPI endpoint. We are not limited to configuring Client Access arrays only for DAG databases.

In Exercise 7.17, you will associate the new Client Access array NLB to each database.

EXERCISE 7.17

Associating a Client Access Array with a Database

Follow these steps to associate a Client Access array with a mailbox database:

1. Log on to EX03 as Administrator.

2. Click Start ➤ Programs ➤ Microsoft Exchange Server 2010 and then select Exchange Management Shell.

3. Run the following command:

    ```
    Get-MailboxDatabase | Set-MailboxDatabase -RpcClientAccessServer Dallas_Array
    .mailtask.com
    ```

4. Validate the array association by running this command:

    ```
    Get-MailboxDatabase | Format-List name,rpc*
    ```

    ```
    Machine: EX02.Mailtask.com                                    _ □ X
    [PS] C:\>Get-MailboxDatabase | fl name,rpc*

    Name                   : DallasEx01DB1
    RpcClientAccessServer  : Dallas_Array.Mailtask.com

    Name                   : DallasDagDB01
    RpcClientAccessServer  : Dallas_Array.Mailtask.com

    Name                   : DallasDagDB02
    RpcClientAccessServer  : Dallas_Array.Mailtask.com


    [PS] C:\>_
    ```

5. Log on to EX01 as Jodie.

6. Launch Outlook by clicking Start ➤ All Program Files ➤ Microsoft Office ➤ Outlook 2007.

7. To speed up the configuration process, we are going to run a repair on the Outlook profile. Click Tools ➤ Account Settings.

8. On the Account Settings page, select the E-Mail tab and click Repair.

EXERCISE 7.17 *(continued)*

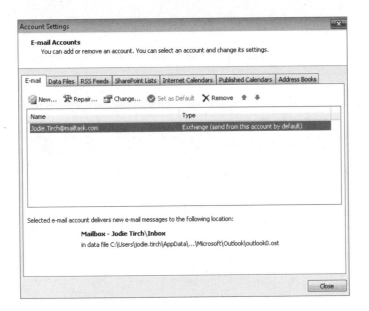

9. On the Repair E-Mail Account screen, click Next.

10. When prompted to restart Outlook, click OK and then click Finish.

11. Click Close on the Account Settings page.

12. Close Outlook and wait at least 20 seconds.

13. Launch Outlook by clicking Start ➢ All Program Files ➢ Microsoft Office ➢ Outlook 2007. When prompted to restart Outlook, click OK.

14. Launch Outlook by clicking Start ➢ All Program Files ➢ Microsoft Office ➢ Outlook 2007.

15. When Outlook opens, it may be set to work offline. In the lower-right portion of the screen, click the Offline button, then click Work Offline.

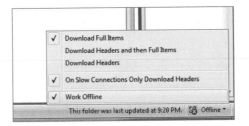

16. Click Tools ➢ Account Settings.

17. In the Account Settings dialog, click Change. The Mailbox server name is the new Client Access array.

18. Click Cancel on the Change E-Mail Account page and then click Close on the Account Settings page.

19. Hold down the Ctrl key, right-click the Outlook icon in the system tray, and click Connection Status.

20. Verify that all connections besides the public folder are connecting to the Client Access array.

In Exercise 7.17, you performed a repair on the profile to speed up the update process for the Outlook clients; however, this attribute will automatically get updated by the Autodiscover process.

Scoping the MAPI Ports

By default, when you open your Outlook client it attempts to make a connection to the RPC port (135) on the server and negotiate a dynamic port above 1024 for usage. If there are no firewalls between the clients and servers, the default behavior will work. However, in many scenarios there are firewalls between the client network and servers. Many organizations want to reduce the number of ports required to be open on the firewalls and do not want to open port 135 and 1024 through 65, 535. A few simple modifications to the CAS registry can reduce the number of ports that are required to be open on the firewall.

To scope the RPC and NSPI/RFR ports, you must make two modifications which are listed below. The first is a modification to the registry on the CAS and the second is a modification to the Microsoft.Exchange.Addressbook.Config file. Please note that in Exchange 2010 SP1, the Address Book change has been moved to the registry instead of the config file.

- MAPI, which is a registry key change on the CAS HKLM\SYSTEM\CurrentControlSet\Services\MSExchangeRPC

- Exchange 2010 SP1

  - Address book registry change HKEY_LOCAL_MACHINE\SYSTEM\CurrentControlSet\Services\MSExchangeAB\Parameters\ RpcTcpPort

- Exchange 2010 RTM

  - Address Book (NSPI) and Referral Service (RFR), which are modified in the configuration file Microsoft.Exchange.Addressbook.Service.exe.config

If you choose to scope the MAPI configuration, you can reduce the number of ports required by clients to connect to the RPC Client Access array to three ports, one for each of the following settings: RPC (Port 135), MAPI, and Address Book.

In Exercise 7.18, you will configure the RPC Client Access array to use port 135, 50,000, and 50,001 instead of the dynamic port range.

EXERCISE 7.18

Scoping RPC Client Access Ports

The following exercise will show you how to reduce the number of ports required to communicate to the Client Access server array based on Exchange 2010 SP1. If you have Exchange 2010 RTM, the steps are slightly different:

1. Log on EX03 as Administrator.

2. Click Start, type **Regedit**, and then click the Registry Editor icon.

EXERCISE 7.18 *(continued)*

3. Expand HKLM\SYSTEM\CurrentControlSet\Services\MSExchangeRPC.

4. Right-click the MSExchangeRPC key and select New Key.

5. For the new key, type **ParametersSystem**.

6. Right-click the ParametersSystem key and create a new Dword with the name TCP/IP Port and decimal value of 50000.

7. Expand HKLM\SYSTEM\CurrentControlSet\Services\MSExchangeAB.

8. Right-click the MSExchangeAB key and select New Key.

9. For the new key, type **Parameters.**

10. Right-click the Parameters key and create a new String with the name RpcTcpPort and value of 50,001.

11. Click Start ➢ Administrative Tools ➢ Services.

12. Right-click Microsoft Exchange RPC Client Access Service and click Restart.

13. Right-click Microsoft Exchange Address Book Service and click Restart.

14. Click Start, type **Cmd**, and press Enter.

15. Type **NetStat -na** and locate 50,000 and 50,001 in the list.

```
Administrator: Command Prompt                                        _ □ ×

C:\>netstat -na

Active Connections

  Proto  Local Address          Foreign Address        State
  TCP    0.0.0.0:25             0.0.0.0:0              LISTENING
  TCP    0.0.0.0:80             0.0.0.0:0              LISTENING
  TCP    0.0.0.0:135            0.0.0.0:0              LISTENING
  TCP    0.0.0.0:443            0.0.0.0:0              LISTENING
  TCP    0.0.0.0:445            0.0.0.0:0              LISTENING
  TCP    0.0.0.0:587            0.0.0.0:0              LISTENING
  TCP    0.0.0.0:593            0.0.0.0:0              LISTENING
  TCP    0.0.0.0:808            0.0.0.0:0              LISTENING
  TCP    0.0.0.0:3389           0.0.0.0:0              LISTENING
  TCP    0.0.0.0:6001           0.0.0.0:0              LISTENING
  TCP    0.0.0.0:6002           0.0.0.0:0              LISTENING
  TCP    0.0.0.0:6004           0.0.0.0:0              LISTENING
  TCP    0.0.0.0:6005           0.0.0.0:0              LISTENING
  TCP    0.0.0.0:6006           0.0.0.0:0              LISTENING
  TCP    0.0.0.0:6007           0.0.0.0:0              LISTENING
  TCP    0.0.0.0:47001          0.0.0.0:0              LISTENING
  TCP    0.0.0.0:50000          0.0.0.0:0              LISTENING
  TCP    0.0.0.0:50001          0.0.0.0:0              LISTENING
  TCP    0.0.0.0:57150          0.0.0.0:0              LISTENING
  TCP    0.0.0.0:57154          0.0.0.0:0              LISTENING
  TCP    0.0.0.0:57176          0.0.0.0:0              LISTENING
  TCP    0.0.0.0:57189          0.0.0.0:0              LISTENING
  TCP    0.0.0.0:57226          0.0.0.0:0              LISTENING
  TCP    0.0.0.0:57232          0.0.0.0:0              LISTENING
  TCP    0.0.0.0:57237          0.0.0.0:0              LISTENING
```

16. Repeat steps 2 through 15 on EX04.

17. Log on to EX01.

18. Click Start ➢ All Program Files➢ Microsoft Office ➢ Outlook 2007.

19. Click Start, and in the search bar type **CMD**. Press Enter.

20. Type **Netstat –na** and look for connections to 192.168.1.76 on ports 135 and 50,000.

In Exercise 7.18, you did not make any changes to the Mailbox server hosting the public folder role. If you choose to scope the MAPI ports, you will also need to modify the registry on each Mailbox server that hosts a public folder. Because the ports are scoped for the Client Access server array, the NLB cluster can be configured to only load-balance three ports: 50,000, 50,001, and 135.

Using DNS Round-Robin

DNS round-robin may sound like something complicated, but in reality it is very simple to set up. When you create multiple DNS host record entries with the same name, the DNS server will alternate responding to queries with each of the different IP addresses. For example, you could create a host record entry for owa.mailtask.com with an IP address of 192.168.2.50 and another host record entry for owa.exchangeexchange.com with an IP address of 192.168.2.51. Each time owa.mailtask.com is requested from the DNS, the response would alternate between the two IP addresses and thus load-balance between the two addresses. If the two servers providing services for owa.mailtask.com were overloaded, another server could be configured and another owa.mailtask.com host record with an IP of 192.168.2.52 could be added. What happens is that the first client receives the first address; the second client, the second address; the third client, the third address; the fourth client receives the first address; and they continue to loop in this manner. Thus by using DNS round-robin, it is possible to spread the load among multiple servers.

Can you spot a problem with using round-robin DNS for high availability? There are several. One is that it is completely unable to handle a down server. In the event that one of the servers fails, the address will continue to be given to clients (unless DNS is modified), and a portion of the clients will use the address of the unavailable server and will fail to connect. Another problem is that, if multiple clients share the same local DNS server, as in a LAN environment, all of those clients will use the same IP address that is cached by the local DNS server; if most of the clients are from the same location, the load will be very unbalanced across the servers.

Summary

Exchange Server 2010 has taken some great strides toward filling of the holes from previous versions of Exchange. Database availability groups provide the capability to span multiple Active Directory sites and provide local and remote failovers for Microsoft Exchange databases without the requirement of third-party tools is a major improvement to Exchange 2010.

Microsoft has also provided administrators with the ability to create Client Access server arrays that provide redundancy for MAPI connections from Outlook clients to Exchange. This not only provides redundancy for MAPI connections, but it also reduces the load on the Mailbox server, which allows for increased scalability of Exchange 2010.

As you saw throughout this chapter, with the new high availability features in Exchange 2010, there is no doubt that Microsoft has made dramatic improvements that will help administrators produce a better end user experience.

Chapter Essentials

Embrace the Shell.   There are a number of monitoring and management features that can be done only from the EMS. Do not be afraid to learn how to govern your Exchange servers from the command line.

The DAG is your friend.   Exchange Server 2010 has provided Exchange administrators with the ability to create multinode, multisite redundant Exchange servers easily. It's important to understand the basic management options and how to properly manage the DAG so you can produce a stable, highly available Exchange infrastructure.

High Availability for MAPI.   Exchange Server 2010 has a new method for highly available MAPI endpoints with the new RPC Client Access arrays. They allow administrators to utilize a load balancer, which could be software or hardware based; this provides a redundant endpoint for MAPI clients, and allows Exchange 2010 to increase its scalability easily.

MAPI port scoping.   By default, a MAPI connection will use random ports to make connections to your Exchange servers, but with minimal configuration changes, an administrator can reduce the number of ports down to three. Port scoping is commonly used in environments that have a number of firewalls and want to reduce the number of ports that are allowed through the firewall.

Chapter

8

Disaster Recovery Operations for Exchange Server

THE FOLLOWING TOPICS ARE DISCUSSED IN THIS CHAPTER:

- ✓ Configuring disaster recovery
- ✓ Configuring backups
- ✓ Recovering messaging data
- ✓ Backing up and recovering server roles

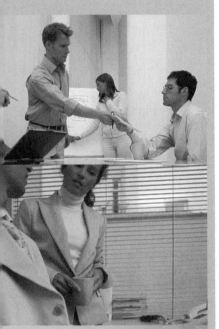

Messaging services are critical to the operation of many organizations. The failure of such a business-critical service could result in the loss of productivity and earnings. Even if a small part of the Exchange organization is not available, it could significantly impact your company. Once the Exchange Server 2010 infrastructure is installed and configured, the disaster recovery plan designed along with the infrastructure should be put into place. A proper, basic disaster recovery plan should cover how to back up the mailbox data, and configuration and how to restore these items.

Once the plan is in place, you can broaden it to encompass handling the loss of an entire datacenter or the offices from which users connect. This plan should be well documented and practiced so that in the event of a disaster you are able to make the best decisions in a limited time frame. To be able to create and execute a disaster recovery plan, you need to understand and practice backup and recovery.

What Is Disaster Recovery?

Disaster recovery means different things to different people, and it is applied differently at different companies, depending on administrator experience and company requirements. For the purpose of this chapter, *disaster recovery* means recovering from the loss of any Exchange server data or Exchange server. This can be limited to the loss of a single email message or it can encompass the loss of an entire datacenter. To create a disaster recovery plan properly, you need to plan for any possible disaster situation and protect against that eventuality.

You need to keep backups for a number of reasons, such as data loss, hardware failure, site loss, and compliance. Data seems to have a way of becoming corrupted, lost, or needed after it has been deleted. Although you may never experience one of these situations, it is best to be prepared for them just in case.

To plan properly for a disaster involving Exchange Server 2010, you need to consider the following circumstances:

- You should understand the kinds of disasters from which you might need to recover, including the loss of a single mail item, a mailbox, a server, a datacenter, or your only office location.

- You should understand how Exchange relies on Active Directory and whether there is a plan in place to protect Active Directory.

- You should understand how Exchange relies on Active Directory's directory service for both server configuration and user setting and configuration data.

- You should know how to establish a service-level agreement (SLA). If you are proposing no more than 5 hours of downtime a year, you will plan differently than if you were offering guaranteed uptime only during business hours.

- You should understand the Extensible Storage Engine (ESE) database technology that Exchange uses to store data. The ESE's database is a transaction-based database that writes data to a log file before the data is committed to the database.

- You should know what backup technology is available to your organization and how your choices will affect your backup implementations. Different companies have different budgets, requirements, and needs for backup that will affect what you use to backup your system.

- You should understand the backup technologies in Exchange and how they can solve some of your backup needs.

You need to have backups of your Exchange server's configuration, the Exchange databases, and Active Directory recipient information. You then need to have a plan to rebuild your servers and recover your Exchange databases. This chapter will cover how to use Exchange Server 2010, Windows backup technologies, and the Exchange Management Shell (EMS) to back up everything you need. It will also cover how to restore those backups.

Avoiding Disasters and Reacting to Them

The best way of dealing with something that you fear, or with which you might be uncomfortable, is to prepare adequately with the right knowledge and tools. Fear tends to subside as knowledge and experience grow. This chapter will empower you to understand the tools and features available in Exchange Server 2010 to deal with disasters. Exchange Server 2010 offers a number of technologies that help you avoid data obstacles or easily overcome them quickly.

Avoiding Data Loss

The first step to avoiding data loss is to design your Exchange server hardware and disk systems to be as redundant as possible. You have many different choices and methods for accomplishing a good redundancy plan. The absolute best hardware configuration varies with budget and usage but also changes over time as new technology becomes available. Also, choosing the latest technology can often result in a steep learning curve, causing undue frustration and the possibility of data loss while you learn how to use it. The following are some recommendations for designing highly redundant hardware solutions:

- Purchase the highest-quality hardware your budget will allow and as much redundancy as you can afford. This includes hardware with more than one processor, separate memory buses, redundant-network connections, and hardware that has the ability to autocorrect or to run even with hardware errors.

- Consider the support agreement that comes with the hardware. Find out how soon parts can be shipped or whether parts can be stored on-site to fix a problem. Find out within how many hours (4, 8, 24, 38, 72, or more) a support issue will be fixed after it is reported.

- Know how quickly the hardware can be replaced. With blade server technology and servers booting and running entirely from a SAN, you could install your Exchange server on blade hardware and have a hot-swappable spare blade available that, in the event of a hardware failure, automatically replaces the server.

- Make sure your operating system is always stored on mirrored disks and that it has the adequate I/O performance.

- Make sure your database and transaction logs are redundant. This might be a RAID solution, where the loss of a disk does not mean the loss of all your data. It could also mean that your data is stored on a SAN or NAS solution where the entire disk subsystem replicates to another site. This may also mean using a database availability group (DAG) to provide redundancy by having up to 16 copies of databases in separate locations.

- Even the best hardware can fail. It is important to monitor your hardware for any signs of failure.

- Place your hardware in a datacenter with redundancy. This includes redundant Internet service providers with separate lines, battery- or flywheel- and generator-based power backups with sufficient fuel, and redundant cooling systems.

Exchange Server 2010 has a number of new and improved availability technologies that can help you almost completely avoid the need to recover your data in the event of a hardware failure or data loss situation. DAGs allow you to have a near real-time replica of your Exchange database on separate hardware. For more information about DAGs, see Chapter 7, "Configuring High-Availability Solutions for Exchange Server."

Reacting to Disasters

How you react to a disaster can affect the amount of downtime and the loss of productivity your organization could experience. Reacting effectively and efficiently is possible when you know and practice your disaster recovery procedure. Exchange Server 2010 offers a number of new and improved tools to help you react to a disaster quickly and efficiently:

Dial-tone recovery   This recovery method was an option in previous versions of Exchange and continues to be an excellent tool for recovery. Dial-tone recovery can be likened to restoring the "dial tone" of your email service—the ability to send and receive email without historical email data. This allows quick recovery from a lost Exchange database by mounting an empty database. The users will then be able to send and receive email. It will further allow users to get back up and running while you work to recover and/or restore the Exchange database. After the data is recovered or restored, it can be migrated back into the users' mailboxes in the background.

Database portability   Databases can be moved to or mounted on any Exchange Server 2010 server in an organization. If one Mailbox server fails but you still have access to your Exchange databases, you could quickly mount the databases on a new server and run the `Set-Mailbox -database` EMS command to point your users to the new location.

Deleted item retention   When a user deletes an item, it appears deleted to them. However, a copy of the deleted item is kept in the mailbox database for a specified period of time, which allows the item to be recovered quickly and easily if it was deleted unintentionally.

Deleted mailbox retention   When a mailbox is deleted, it appears deleted to the user. However, the mailbox is kept in the mailbox database in a disconnected state for a specified period of time, which allows the mailbox to be recovered if it was deleted unintentionally

Setup /mode:RecoverServer   Almost all the configuration information for your Exchange Server 2010 servers is stored in Active Directory. In the event of a server loss, you can quickly reinstall Exchange on a server with the same settings by running `Setup /mode:RecoverServer` and applying all the configuration information stored in Active Directory to the new server.

> Setup /mode:RecoverServer will not work on an Edge Transport server because the Edge Transport server is not a member of the Active Directory domain. It will also not recover any of the modifications made to IIS on a Client Access Server. In addition, any local configuration settings applied to any server role in areas such as the Registry or XML configuration files will not be recovered. Exchange Server 2010 includes two scripts, ImportEdgeConfig.ps1 and ExportEdgeConfig.ps1, that you can run on Edge servers to back up and restore their settings.

Database technology   The Exchange database is designed to alert you to problems and recover from failure. For example, before a disk fails, you will receive -1018 error messages that indicate possible errors in the disk subsystem. After a database has failed, you can use Exchange-provided tools, such as the Disaster Recovery Analyzer, ISInteg, , and New-MailboxRepairRequest that can repair most errors in the database. If you need to recover from a point-in-time backup, you can apply all the transaction logs since that backup and recovery almost to the point of failure.

Understanding these tools and knowing which one is best for any given situation will allow you to react quickly, correctly, and efficiently in the event that a disaster does happen. That said, sometimes you might not have enough experience to judge properly what needs to be done. To assist, numerous consulting companies specialize in dealing with disasters. We mention this only to give you all the tools you need to deal most effectively with a disaster.

Configuring Backups

By far the most important information to backup is your Exchange database. The Exchange database holds all of the email, calendaring, contact, and task data associated with the users' mailboxes stored in it. The importance of the database makes it the focus of most disaster recovery plans. Exchange Server 2010 offers one built-in method to back up your Exchange database: Volume Shadow Copy Service (VSS).

VSS was introduced in Exchange 2003, and a great deal of development time has been invested and improvements have been implemented with Exchange Server 2010. The VSS backup engine pauses all write operations to the Exchange database and log files, prepares the backup for the snapshot, and then takes a snapshot of the database. It takes only a few seconds to take a snapshot, and then the database resumes.

In addition to choosing a backup technology and software product, you need to consider a number of variables when designing your backup process. A proper backup plan needs to back up all needed information and data while minimizing the impact to users. When needed, those backups are then used to return your systems to full working order or to get data that is not available online. When you create your backup plan, keep in mind the following variables:

- Consider the duration of time that your backups will take to complete and the time allocated to restore them. You should have an established expectation with your company of how long a database can be down—20 minutes, 2 hours, 2 days, or something else. Once you know that, you should then determine how much data you could restore in that given amount of time. That size should be your maximum database size.

- Consider the required resources needed for a backup and what you will need to accomplish with those resources. Exchange runs an online maintenance process by default at night that checks the database for errors and fragmentation. You should be aware of when this process runs and how it might compete with your backups, if they happen to run at the same time because this can overburden a server. A backup can be a very CPU- and I/O-intensive operation, so it is not recommended that you run it during times of high user load on the server. Watch the system CPU, I/O load, and network bandwidth to determine the best window of time in which to perform your Exchange backups.

- Define recovery point objectives. Recovery point objectives should cover the expected and minimum data losses that your company can tolerate, including how much data you must recover. If the loss of more than one day's worth of data is not acceptable, you will need a different backup scheme than if the loss of no more than one hour of data is acceptable.

- Consider the backup hardware you have and how it helps you support the recovery requirements. Older, slower tape technology might limit what you can offer in the form of recovery point objectives. Newer disk- or optical-based backup technology might allow faster and more consistant backup and restore operations.

- Consider the backup applications you are using. Different software can support different backup types and media, which might allow for faster or more efficient backups and restores.

- Consider your use of single item retention (which is discussed later in this chapter), DAG, and database copies with lagged replay or truncation lag times. For example, if you have three database copies, then you can sustain the loss of two database servers without any loss of data. If you add in a fourth database copy with a replay lag time of 14 days, which means that the database data is kept at a constant 14 days old and logs are played into the database to keep it at that age, then you can restore to any point in time in the past 14 days by replaying a subset of the logs. This may substantially reduce your need to keep frequent backups.

- You should consider having a copy of your data off-site in some format; you need to determine what the mandated business requirements are and do your best to satisfy those needs. In addition to business requirements, you need to determine whether any government or regulatory agency policy might require a specific data retention policy for your company. With this information in mind, you then need to create a media rotation policy. A typical media rotation schedule will be based on tape devices and will require a number of tapes.

  Table 8.1 shows an example of a tape rotation schedule for a company that makes a log file backup every day of the week and then a full backup every week, month, and year. The full backups are rotated as needed. This is only an example; the needs of your organization might be very different.

TABLE 8.1   Tape rotation schedule

Tape Name	Tape Usage
Weekly Even	This tape is used every day except Friday of an even week to back up the log files.
Weekly Odd	This tape is used every day except Friday of an odd week to back up the log files.
Friday 1–5	These tapes are Friday full-backup tapes numbered 1 through 5 to cover every week of a month.
Monthly 1–12	These tapes are monthly month-end tapes numbered 1 through 12, so you will have one for each month of the year.
Yearly 1–7	These tapes are yearly year-end tapes numbered 1 through 7, so you will have one for the end of each year for seven years.

After considering the previous points, you need to determine the best backup type to use to backup your Exchange databases. Each backup type has inherent advantages and disadvantages that should be considered. An Exchange Server 2010 backup created using Windows Server Backup only supports full and copy backups. If you're using another backup product, such as Microsoft Data Protection Manager, you may also be able to perform incremental and differential backups. The following are the types of backups normally used:

Full backup   A full backup is a complete backup that captures all the data in a given location. Log files older than the checkpoint at the time of the backup are deleted after the backup completes. Perform a full backup on a daily basis to ensure that log files do not build up and consume all the space in the log file drive. The full backup is the simplest backup with which to work because it requires only a single backup set for both backup and restore. It takes the longest to complete because it captures all the data.

Copy backup   A copy backup is the same as a full backup except that log files are not deleted at the completion of the backup. You can perform a copy backup to capture a specific point in time. Copy backups should be used before performing maintenance on the database.

Incremental backup   An incremental backup is a change-only backup that archives only the transaction log files created since the last full or incremental backup. Log files older than the checkpoint are deleted after the backup is complete. You cannot perform an incremental backup when circular logging is enabled because circular logging limits and reuses log files. An incremental backup can be used to support a short data loss window by allowing you to perform backups on an hourly or more frequent basis, and these backups do not take very long to complete or have major user impact. The downside is that you need to have the last full backup and all the incremental backups since that full backup to restore the database fully.

Differential backup   A differential backup is a change-only backup that archives only the transaction log files created since the last full or incremental backup. The difference between an incremental and a differential backup is that the differential backup does not delete the log files after it completes a backup. Incremental and differential backups are the smallest backup files and take the shortest time to complete.

Ideally, your backups should be run in a given window of time at night when your servers have the fewest users connected. You should capture all your Exchange databases and any server data you might need to restore your servers.

Using Replication-Based Backup

With Exchange Server 2010, it may be possible to meet your backup needs without creating separate backups but to instead secure your data using database availability groups. For example, if your business requirements dictate having only two weeks of Exchange mailbox backups, you could design your backups as follows:

1. Create a four-server DAG and place each server in separate cabinets, such that a single outage would not eliminate all database copies.

2. Identify a single server in the DAG to store lagged copies of your mailbox databases. This server will need enough space to store two weeks of transaction log files for all databases.

3. Block database activation on the lagged server using `Set-MailboxServer -DatabaseCopyAutoActibationPolicy blocked`.

4. Set the mailbox copies on the lagged server to have a two-week lag using the command `Set-MailboxDatabaseCopy DB1\LaggedServer -ReplayLagTime 14.00:00:00`

5. If you will not be using another backup solution, then you will need to set all mailbox databases to use circular logging using the following command: `Set-MailboxDatabase -CircularLoggingEnabled $true`. Without this command, transaction logs would be stored indefinitely on all database servers and eventually fill your transaction log storage.

If you use replication-based backup, then a point-in-time restore can be accomplished by copying the lagged database and the transaction logs for that database up to the desired point in time to a recovery database. Replication-based backups do not offer the same options and security as a separate backup product that allows backups to be written to tape and stored indefinitely, but combined with the new single-item recovery features discussed in the section "Recovering Messaging Data" later in this chapter, it may meet the backup requirements for some organizations.

Creating, Modifying, and Performing Backup Jobs

At the core of any Exchange backup plan is backing up the mailbox database. You can rebuild any server role if it comes down to it, but you cannot rebuild your mailbox data without a proper mailbox.

To use Windows Server Backup to back up your Exchange databases, you will first need to install it. In Windows Server 2008, Windows Server Backup is a feature you can add.

Exercise 8.1 outlines the basic steps to create, modify, and schedule a backup job using Windows Server Backup on a Windows Server 2008 computer.

EXERCISE 8.1

Backing Up the Exchange Server Mailbox Database with Windows Server Backup on Windows Server 2008 R2

Follow these steps to back up the mailbox database:

1. Open Windows Server Backup and click Backup Once.

EXERCISE 8.1 *(continued)*

2. Choose Different Options, which will allow you to specify your backup options, and then click Next.

3. Choose Custom and click Next. Then click Add Items and in the Select Items dialog box select the path to your database and log files, and then click OK to return to the wizard.

4. Click Advanced Settings, and in the Advanced Settings dialog box, choose the VSS Settings tab. Choose VSS full Backup to perform a full backup and then click OK. On the wizard page, click Next.

5. On the next screen, choose whether you want to save to a local drive other than where your database is stored or to a network drive. Click Next, specify the path to save the backup, and then click Next.

6. Click Backup to begin the backup.

   To schedule a backup, you use the same steps, except with an additional screen to specify the scheduled time.

Monitoring and Validating Backup Jobs

You should never consider a backup valid unless you have tested it and verified that there is restorable data in it. It is good practice to schedule time to restore a backup at least once a month. In the meantime, you can perform a number of tasks to feel more confident that your backups are running properly.

The Windows Server Backup utility writes backup confirmations and errors to a backup log file and to the Windows Server event log. You should check both the backup log file and the server event logs on a daily basis. Almost every backup application should have some sort of logging, regardless of whether you are using Windows Server Backup or a third-party application; you should still expect to see a backup log file in addition to the event log entries. When monitoring and validating your backup job, you should do the following:

- Make sure there are no error messages in the log indicating that there was an error in the backup process. Any error messages should give you enough information to begin to determine what went wrong.

- Make sure the backup that completed was the backup you had configured to run. If you back up the wrong data, it is as useless as though you had not run a backup at all.

- Verify that the size of the backup is close to the size of the data you are backing up.

The Exchange backup engine writes a number of events to the application event log. These indicate when a backup started, when it completed, the log files that successfully purged, the backup type used, and more. Look for events with a source of "ESE" or "ESE backup". You need to research ESE and ESE backup errors or warning events to determine whether a problem has occurred. If a problem has occurred, then you need to fix it.

🌐 Real World Scenario

Test Your Backups

An Exchange Expert shares his story:

"I worked with a school district that would faithfully backup all its student records. The IT staff scheduled a full backup every night, and the backup operator would take a copy home with her at night and rotate the copy at home into the backup schedule. There were three backup sets in rotation.

"Then one day, one of the drives in the server died and we needed to recover from backup. Up until that failure, the backups had never been tested. When we went to restore the backups, it became apparent that over the course of time the backup media had become worn out. Therefore, the backups were useless; there was nothing to restore.

"We had to send the backup media away to a data recovery company that was able to extract data in a clean room with special tools. Thankfully, they were successful and returned the data to us. The recovery process took three days and cost about $3,000. This story underscores how important it is to monitor that your backups are complete and valid. It is also shows how important it is to test the restore process to ensure that the backups contain restorable data. Had we ever tested a restore, we would have realized the media was damaged and would have been able to replace it with fresh media, and we could have avoided learning this costly lesson."

Repairing a Damaged Exchange Database

Repairing an Exchange database can be a complex, frustrating, and time-consuming process. The Exchange database repair process begins by determining the problem with the database. You can usually find an error message in the application event log that will be generated when you try to mount the database. Armed with the error message, you can then follow one of two paths. You can search the Microsoft support site and the Internet to find more information about the problem, or you can contact someone who is experienced in disaster recovery. The cost to have a Microsoft professional will vary depending on your service contract with Microsoft. However, the cost may be a very small price to pay to have a trained Microsoft professional walk you through the database repair process.

After determining which path to take, whether you are contacting Microsoft or going it alone, your next step is to start the database repair process. After the database has been repaired, you then get to see whether the repair was successful by attempting to mount the database. At this point, you are presented with either success or another error in the application event log, and you get to continue the repair process. Knowing which commands and utilities to run and how long they will take to run is key to having a successful database repair.

If a recent backup is available, restoring the backup may be preferred over repairing the database because when you recover from a backup, you get a known good database at the end of the recovery process. When you repair a database, you are unsure what, if any, data was lost, and there is a chance that other errors will crop up later.

Understanding the Exchange Database Structure

The Exchange database is referred to as the ESE database, and it stores all the user data and almost all the configuration data used by Exchange Server 2010. There are databases on the Edge Transport server, the Hub Transport server, and the Mailbox server.

At one time the ESE database, also known as the Joint Engine Technology (JET) database, was a single B-tree database product inside Microsoft. It then diverged into a number of different databases as different product groups wanted to use the JET database. These product groups had different needs and requirements and wanted to do different things with the JET code. The JET databases we use now was once called JET Blue and JET Red. Simply put, Blue was for Exchange and Red was for Microsoft Access. When Active Directory came about, the Windows Server Active Directory team borrowed some resources from the Exchange team that had already implemented an X.400 directory structure in Exchange. Windows NT Server had already used the JET database for a number of features, such as DHCP and WINS, and the Exchange team was very comfortable with the JET database, so it was decided that JET would be the database for Active Directory.

The ESE Exchange databases on the Edge Transport, Hub Transport, and Mailbox servers consist of the same database with a few minor configuration differences. Regardless of the server roles, databases consist of a number of files. The main files are as follows:

The Exchange database file (.edb)   The EDB file is the file where all the data is stored. It has a size limit of 16 TB based on the ESE database design, but the actual database size limit that you enforce should be much smaller. This allows time for backups and restores to complete without disrupting business and within time limits specified in your SLAs.

The temporary database (Tmp.edb)   The temporary database is used to process transactions as they are being committed to the EDB file.

The checkpoint file (Exx.chk)   The E00.chk file maintains the checkpoint for the database. This checkpoint file keeps track of the last-committed transaction log file. If you are ever forced to perform a recovery, this file contains the point at which the replaying of transaction logs must start. The *00* after the E is the designation for the database.

Transaction log files All changes made to the Exchange database are first committed to memory and then to transaction log files. Once the server has time, the log files are applied to the EDB file. The total number of transaction log files created depends on the transaction load on the server. There are three types of transaction logs:

Working log file (Exx.log) This file is the current transaction log being written for the database. Once the log file reaches 1 MB in size, it is renamed and a new E00.log file is created. The *00* after the E is the designation for the database.

Transaction log (Exxhhhhhhhh.log) These are the main transaction logs. They are numbered sequentially starting with E0000000001. Transaction log files are created and named based on an E followed by a two-character sequence, which is then followed by a hexadecimal number from 1 to 0x7FFFFFFF, allowing for a total of 2,147,483,647 log files in the log stream. The *00* after the E is the designation for the database.

Reserved log files (Exxres00001.jrs and Exxres00002.jrs) These are the reserved log files. In the event that the disk runs out of space, then the last transactions are written to these log files while the database dismounts. The **xx** after the E is the designation for the database.

Using the Recovery Tools

Exchange Server 2010 includes two main command-line tools and two GUI wrappers for those tools to repair and work with your Exchange databases. The two tools, ESEUtil and ISInteg, are the main tools for working with the Exchange database:

ESEUtil The Exchange Server Database Utility (ESEUtil.exe) is a command-line tool that you can use to repair, view, and modify an Exchange database at the page level. ESEUtil is located in the Bin directory under your Exchange installation. In the past, ESEUtil could be used to work only with mailbox and public folder databases. To perform most of its operations, ESEUtil will create a new temporary database and write all the fixed information to that new database. It is recommended that you have 1.2 times as much free space as there is data in your Exchange database before performing ESEUtil operations. You can determine the size of your database by looking for event ID 1221 in your event log and subtracting the white space reported from the total file size. For example, if your database is 45 GB and the 1221 event for the database says that you have 12 GB of white space in the database, then your database is 33 GB and you should be sure that you have approximately 40 GB of free space to perform ESEUtil operations on the Exchange database.

You can load ESEUtil with a number of switches; you can see them by running eseutil /? from a command prompt. The following list gives a brief explanation of the switches:

/P Repair Repairs a corrupt offline database by discarding any pages that cannot be fixed. In repair mode, the ESEUtil tool fixes individual tables but does not maintain the relationships between tables. Use the ISInteg tool to check and fix links between tables in the repaired database.

/R Recovery   Replays transaction log files to restore a database to internal consistency.

/G Integrity   Verifies the page-level and ESE-level logical integrity of the database. Does not verify the integrity at the application level. You can verify application-level logical integrity with the ISInteg tool.

/M File Dump   Displays headers of database files, transaction log files, and checkpoint files. Also displays database page header information and database space allocation and metadata.

/K Checksum   Verifies checksums on all pages in the database, log files, and checkpoint files.

/C Restore   Allows you to run hard recovery on a database restored from a streaming backup. It also allows you to view some of the `Restore.env` file.

/Y Copy File   Copies large files much faster on the same volume than the normal Windows copy routine. It copies larger blocks at a time to accomplish the greater speed. You can use this switch to copy more than just Exchange files.

ISInteg   The Information Store Integrity Checker (`ISInteg.exe`) finds and eliminates errors from the Exchange database at the application level. The ISInteg tool works at the logical schema level, and it can recover data that ESEUtil cannot. This is because data that is valid for the ESEUtil tool at the physical schema level can be invalid at the logical schema level. ISInteg is most often used after running the ESEUtil repair operation. The ISInteg tool repairs information, relationships, and index tables between pages in the database at the application level.

In Exchange 2010 with Service Pack 1, ISInteg is no longer a separate executable, rather it's functionality has been moved into two new commands: New-MailboxRepairRequest and New-PublicFolderDatabaseRepairRequest. These commands are run against a mounted database and can repair logical corruption in a single mailbox or the entire database, fix corrupt search folders, and fix aggregate counts. You can only have one database-level repair request and up to 100 active mailbox-level requests running per server. After submitting a new repair request, you can monitor the results using Event Viewer. The events are logged under the MSExchangeIS Mailbox Store source. The following event IDs are logged on the Mailbox server containing the active database:

- 10047 – A mailbox-level repair request started.
- 10048 – The repair request successfully completed.
- 10050 – The mailbox repair request task skipped a mailbox.
- 10059 – A database-level repair request started.
- 10062 – A corruption was detected.
- 10064 – A Public Folder repair request started.

Recovering Messaging Data

The simplest way to recover deleted messaging data is with Exchange Server 2010's message retention and mailbox retention features. These features basically provide a repository, called the dumpster, which retains every deleted message and mailbox for a given period of time. At the end of that period, the dumpster will be emptied. Message and mailbox retention settings can be configured on a per-database basis as well as a per-user basis, the latter of which is useful if, for example, your board of directors has different retention requirements than your sales force. Per-user mailbox retention settings will always override per-database settings, which makes it simple to mix and match settings to serve your end users better. If a message or mailbox is deleted and it is no longer in the retention dumpster, then the recovery process becomes much more involved.

Exchange 2010 also introduces several new options that make it easier to recover data. For example, you can enable Single Item Recovery per-mailbox. In previous versions of Exchange, if a user opened their deleted item recovery (also known as the dumpster) and removed a message, that message was no longer stored in Exchange. With Exchange 2010, if you run `Set-Mailbox -SingleItemRecoveryEnabled $true` on a mailbox then those mail items will be stored in a folder named Purges in the dumpster for the remainder of the retention window. Messages stored in the Purges folder are only recoverable via Multi-Mailbox Search, discussed in Chapter 6, "Configuring Security, Compliance, and Policies."

Recovering messages or mailboxes that are no longer in the retention dumpster involves first restoring the database to a recovery database (RDB) or a test server. After you do that, you can export the message or mailbox to a Personal Folder file (PST), or in the case of mounting to an RDB, you can attach the mailbox to a user account. Although performing this process may provide you with needed practice performing restore operations, it can be time consuming and just plain annoying.

Recovering Messages with Deleted Items Retention

To a user, an email message appears to be gone once it's deleted and emptied from the Deleted Items folder. Similarly, when a user deletes an item while holding down the Shift key, the item instantly appears to be gone from the folder from which it was deleted. Although both actions will place the message in the server retention dumpster, a Shift+Delete will bypass the Deleted Items folder.

Exercise 8.2 illustrates how to recover deleted items from the OWA client.

EXERCISE 8.2

Recovering Deleted Items in Outlook Web Access

Follow these steps to recover a deleted item from within Outlook Web Access:

1. Open Internet Explorer and type https://mail.mailtask.com/owa in the address bar.

2. Log on as Administrator.

3. Right-click on the Deleted Items folder and choose Recover Deleted Items.

4. Choose the items you want to recover and then click the recover button, which looks like a small envelope with an arrow above it, at the top of the screen.

Exercise 8.3 illustrates how to recover deleted items from the Outlook client.

Recovering Deleted Items in Outlook

Follow these steps to recover a deleted item from within Outlook:

1. Open Outlook, and then click the Folder ribbon and then click Recover Deleted Items.

2. On the Recover Deleted Items dialog box, select the items you want to recover and click the Recover Selected Items button.

Recovering Deleted Mailboxes with Deleted Mailbox Retention

Exchange Server 2010's deleted mailbox retention feature is meant to primarily safeguard against accidentally deleting a mailbox. This can happen, for example, when someone is let go from a company and it is determined that some content is still needed from the mailbox after it has been deleted. Deleted mailbox retention will hold a mailbox until the mailbox retention period for that mailbox database has lapsed and a full Exchange backup has completed, assuming the Don't permanently delete items until this database has been backed up setting is enabled. If you need to remove a deleted mailbox immediately, you can purge the mailbox from the database.

Exercise 8.4 illustrates how to recover a deleted mailbox using the Exchange Management Console (EMC).

EXERCISE 8.4

Recovering a Deleted Mailbox Using the Exchange Management Console

Follow these steps to recover a deleted mailbox using the EMC:

1. Click Start ➢ Programs ➢ Microsoft Exchange Server 2010 and then select Exchange Management Console.

2. Expand Organizational Configuration and Recipient Configuration and then click the Disconnected Mailbox node.

3. In the Contents pane, all the disconnected mailboxes on the selected server are listed.

4. Select the mailbox you want to recover and then, in the Actions pane, click Connect to Server to start the Connect Mailbox wizard.

5. Follow the instructions to reconnect the disconnected mailbox in the Connect Mailbox wizard.

Exercise 8.5 illustrates how to recover a deleted mailbox using EMS.

EXERCISE 8.5

Recovering a Deleted Mailbox Using the Exchange Management Shell

Follow these steps to recover a deleted mailbox using the EMS:

1. Click Start ➢ Programs ➢ Microsoft Exchange Server 2010 and then select Exchange Management Shell.

2. To find all the disconnected mailboxes on a given server, you need to run the Get-MailboxStatistics command piped to a where statement that searches for mailboxes that don't have DisconnectDate set to null. To do this, run:

```
Get-MailboxStatistics -Server <server> |
where { $_.DisconnectDate -ne $null } |
  select DisplayName,DisconnectDate
```

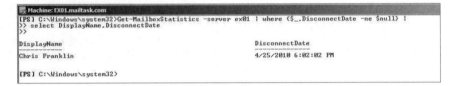

3. To reconnect a disconnected mailbox where the user object is still in Active Directory, run:

```
Connect-Mailbox -Database <Mailbox_Database>
-Identity <Deleted_Mailbox>
```

Recovering Mailbox Databases

Recovering an Exchange Server 2010 mailbox database is a somewhat simple process; it is by no means as complicated as attempting to repair an Exchange database. Before you start to restore a database, it helps to understand why you are restoring it. Different restoration needs will require a different restoration process and will be approached differently. The following reasons might motivate you to restore an Exchange database from backup:

- A hardware or site failure to the point that your Exchange server needs to be rebuilt. Once the server is rebuilt, mailbox databases are restored to the server so that it can serve data to users and receive email.

- A minor system failure—including power, hard disk, software, or hardware—that caused the Exchange database to be corrupted. It is usually simpler in this case to restore from backup and replay the log files into the restored database than it is to attempt to repair the database.

- Something was deleted from the mailbox database after the point in time in which it might be in the retention dumpsters.

After you've determined the business requirements for the backup, then you can determine the best approach to restoring the data. You will approach recovering a single mailbox or mail item differently than you would approach restoring 10 servers in a datacenter that was down for a number of days because of some failure. The following are some situations and some different approaches you might take:

- A request was accepted by your manager to provide an employee that left the company in good standing two months ago with a copy of her contacts. In this case, you would need to find a backup taken before this employee left the company and restore it to a recovery database (RDB). Once the restore is complete, you could export the mailbox contents to a PST using the Export-Mailbox or New-MailboxExportRequest if Service Pack 1 has been deployed.

- A SAN failure during business hours caused a loss of one of the five databases on the Exchange server and only streaming tape backup is available. In this situation, the first step is to create a dial-tone database so users can resume sending and receiving email. Then recovery from the most recent backup can begin to the RDB. That backup might be in the form of a full backup or in the form of a full backup plus a number of incremental backups. After the restored database is mounted to the RDB and all recovered log files have been played into the database, the Database Recovery Management tool can be used to swap the dial-tone and restored databases and then merge the two databases.

- An Exchange server in your organization has failed, and a restore process will take longer than the business mandates. In this situation, a dial-tone database can be created on another Exchange server in the organization and the Move-Mailbox -ConfigurationOnly cmdlet can be used to redirect all your users to the new databases. This process allows users to send and receive email and continue working. In the background, all of the data can be restored into an RDB on the new server. Then the recovered and dial-tone databases can be merged.

As these examples illustrate, you need to approach each situation a little bit differently. Although the approaches might have been slightly different, a few key concepts and technologies stand out. Understanding these concepts will allow you to create better disaster recovery plans and to deal skillfully with the situations that confront you. The key concepts and technologies that will help you the most with an Exchange database restore revolve around reducing user impact as much as possible. The goal is to create a manual level of functionality quickly for the users to give you the time to deal with the overall situation properly. Although most of these have been mentioned briefly already, the technologies and concepts that make this possible are as follows:

RDB   The RDB is a special database on an Exchange server that allows you to mount a database that is not connected to any user accounts or that might have come from another Exchange server in the same organization. Once a database is mounted in an RDB, mailboxes can be linked to users and moved to a production database or extracted and merged into an existing user's mailbox.

You cannot restore an Exchange database from a different Exchange organization or a different version of Exchange to an RDB. You can, however, mount Exchange Server 2010 databases from the same Exchange Server 2010 organization to a RDB.

Dial tone   The goal in any disaster situation is to recover as much functionality as possible as quickly as possible. The dial tone allows you to recover quickly from the loss of an Exchange database by mounting an empty database that will allow users to send and receive email.

The basics of a mailbox recovery are to restore mail service using a dial tone as quickly as possible, recover as much previously stored mail data as possible, and make that data available to your users. Before you can start your recovery, you should have the following in place:

- A server in position with enough disk space to hold the restored database and all the log files that you might need to restore.
- A safe copy of database and transaction files made prior to attempting to repair or restore over them, just in case they are needed later to recover from a mistake made during the repair or recover.
- The most recent backups that are relevant to the situation.

Now let's look at one of the situations shown at the beginning of this section, where you lose a single database on a server. In Exercise 8.6, you will see how to recover an Exchange database.

EXERCISE 8.6

Recovering an Exchange Database

Follow these steps to recover an Exchange database:

1. Click Start ➤ Programs ➤ Microsoft Exchange Server 2010 and then select Exchange Management Shell.

2. Create a new database to use as a dial-tone database by running the following command:

   ```
   New-MailboxDatabase -Name DialToneDB -EDBFilePath c:\exchange\DialToneDB\
   DialToneDB.edb
   ```

3. Move the affected users to the dial-tone database with the following command:

   ```
   Get-Mailbox -Database Database1 | Set-Mailbox -Database DialToneDB
   ```

4. Mount the dial-tone database by entering the following command:

   ```
   Mount-Database -Identity DialToneDB
   ```

5. Create a recovery database by entering the following command:

   ```
   New-MailboxDatabase -Recovery -Name Recovery1 -Server MailboxServer
   ```

6. Restore your backup into the recovery database, and copy the log files from the failed database to the recovery database log folder.

7. Mount and dismount the recovery database using the following commands:

   ```
   Mount-Database Recovery1
   Dismount-Database Recovery1
   ```

8. Copy the database and log files for the recovery database to a safe location.

The following steps will cause a service interruption as users are given access to their original mailboxes:

9. Dismount the dial-tone database with the following command:

   ```
   Dismount-Database DialToneDB
   ```

10. Move the database and log files from the dial-tone database folder into the recovery database folder.

11. Open Windows Explorer and then move the recovery database and log files from the safe location to the dial-tone directory.

12. Mount the recovered database to restore user access to their original mailbox with the following command:

    ```
    Mount-Database DialToneDB
    ```

13. With the following command, recover the data from the recovery database, which now contains the email data that was saved while users were using the dial-tone database:

    ```
    Get-mailbox -Database DialToneDB | Restore-Mailbox -RecoveryDatabase Recovery1
    ```

14. Dismount and remove the recovery mailbox database using the following commands:

    ```
    Dismount-Database Recovery1
    Remove-MailboxDatabase Recovery1
    ```

Backing Up and Recovering a Mailbox Server Configuration

Mailbox server recovery is a two-part process. Part one is recovering the server back to a usable state. Part two is recovering the mailbox database. Now that we've covered recovering mailboxes, we can address the mailbox configuration.

Almost all configuration data for the Mailbox server is stored in Active Directory. As long as Active Directory is present and properly backed up, the Mailbox server configuration will also be backed up. To restore the Mailbox server, all that needs to be done is to build a new server with the same name and then run `Setup /Mode:RecoverServer`. Once that is done, the Mailbox server is configured for use. As discussed previously, the mailbox and public folder data will still need to be recovered.

Backing Up and Recovering Server Roles

Along with backup and restoring mailbox data, it is important to back up and restore the other Exchange Server 2010 roles. The following are some of the concerns when dealing with other server roles:

- The Client Access Server IIS Metabase is no longer synced with Active Directory, so you have to back up the IIS Metabase along with the system state on a Client Access Server.

- Edge Transport server configuration is not stored in Active Directory but can be backed up into XML files with included PowerShell scripts.

- Messages in transit may still be in the Transport server's queue database, which is an ESE database.

- The unified messaging custom audio files do not even have to be stored on an Exchange server. They just have to be accessible to the Unified Messaging server via a UNC path.

- Local configuration information on each server role is stored in the Registry and in local files.

Backing Up and Recovering a Client Access Server

The Client Access Server has a very basic backup process, unless you've done any customizations that are not stored in Active Directory. Modifications to a Client Access Server, such as changes to the `Web.config`, `Microsoft.Exchange.Imap4.Exe.Config`, `Microsoft.Exchange.Pop3.Exe.Config`, or OWA files, constitute customizations that will need to be captured in order to be restored.

If the Client Access Server was not modified, then all of the essential information needed to recover it is stored in Active Directory. If this is the case, the restore procedure is first to build a new server with the same name and OS configuration as the previous server and then to run `Setup /Mode:RecoverServer`. All settings stored in Active Directory will be applied to the server.

If there are modifications applied to your Client Access Server, you should be aware of what they are and what kind of backup will be required for each modification. The following list includes some of the modifications on the Client Access Server that will need to be backed up:

IIS settings   The IIS Metabase stores configuration data for all the websites and web services on the Client Access Server. Changes made to the IIS Metabase are not synchronized with Active Directory; they are stored locally only on the CAS where the changes were made. To back up the IIS Metabase, you should perform a system state backup of the Exchange server.

web.config   The `web.config` file holds settings for the websites and web services on the Client Access server. If these are modified, you need to document the modifications so they can be reapplied to a server, or you should back them up with a file-level backup application.

Web pages   For any web pages (for example, ASP or HTML files) that were modified, you need to document the modifications so they can be reapplied to a server, or you should back them up with a file-level backup application.

Installing an Exchange service pack or rollup hotfix might change the web pages, requiring that you reapply your web page modifications. If you have modified web pages, you should apply them to a test machine before applying them in production to see what is modified and how it affects any customizations you might have made.

POP3 and IMAP4 settings   You can modify POP3 and IMAP4 configurations by modifying settings in XML files. You need to document these XML file modifications so they can be reapplied to a server, or you should back them up with a file-level backup application.

Windows Registry settings   You can set some custom Registry settings on a Client Access Server. You need to document these settings so they can be reapplied to a server, or you should back them up with a system state backup.

If your Client Access Server has been modified, you can recover it as shown in the section "Reacting to Disasters" at the beginning of this chapter by running `Setup / Mode:RecoverServer`. Once you've done that, you will need to reapply all the modifications. How you reapply those will depend on how you backed up the modifications.

Backing Up and Recovering a Hub Transport Server

The Hub Transport server is the easiest role to recover because almost all of the configuration settings for the Hub Transport server are stored in Active Directory. As long as your Active Directory is present and backed up, then your Hub Transport server is also backed up. To restore your Hub Transport server, all you have to do is build a new server with the same name and then run `Setup /Mode:RecoverServer`. After you've done that, your Hub Transport server is set up and ready to go again.

A few things are not captured and restored in a recovery scenario, but for the most part they are not key to the functionality of the Hub Transport server. These items and how they might impact the Hub Transport server are as follows:

The message queue database   Data in the message queue database is transient information that exists in the database only while a message is in transport on the server or while messages are in a retry queue. A salvaged queue database can be mounted on any Hub Transport server in the organization, or messages can be extracted from the database via the EMS by using the command `Export-Message`. Keep in mind that the data you might recover could be minimal. You can find the message queue database in the `\Exchange server\V14\ TransportRoles\data\Queue` folder. Exchange 2010 introduces the shadow redundancy queue, which stores messages on an Exchange server until the next hop has confirmed that it has successfully passed the email on. This means that messages in transport inside your Exchange organization are on two different servers until they are delivered or handed off to an outside organization, limiting the amount of data that is lost if a transport server fails.

Windows Registry settings   You could set custom Registry settings on a Hub Transport server. You need to document these settings so they can be reapplied to a server, or you can back them up so they can be reapplied.

The message tracking logs   Each Hub Transport server has message tracking logs that hold a record of all the actions taken for every message that the server touched. The message tracking logs can be useful for performing diagnostic and forensic operations in an Exchange organization. If this data is valuable, then you should back it up on a regular basis with a file-level backup utility. You can find the message tracking logs in the `\Exchange Server\ TransportRoles\Logs` folder.

Backing Up and Recovering an Edge Transport Server

Unlike all the other Exchange Server 2010 server roles, the Edge Transport server role does not store configuration data in Active Directory. The Edge Transport server role uses Active Directory Lightweight Directory Services (AD LDS) to store configuration data. This database is a static copy of Active Directory and is not replicated to any other server. This means you cannot recover an Edge Transport server as simply as running the `Setup /Mode:RecoverServer` command. This also means that if you have more than one Edge Transport server, you must back up the configuration data for each server.

To recover the Edge Transport server, Microsoft included with Exchange Server 2010 two EMS scripts that back up and restore all of the Edge Transport server configuration data using XML files. You can back up and restore the Edge Transport server configuration by using the following scripts in the EMS:

ExportEdgeConfig.ps1   This script exports all configuration data from an Edge Transport server and stores that data in an XML file.

ImportEdgeConfig.ps1   This script imports all configuration data stored in the XML file that is created by the **ExportEdgeConfig.ps1** script and applies those settings to a new Edge Transport server.

The default location of the folder in which you can find these scripts is `C:\Program Files\Microsoft\Exchange Server\V14\Scripts`. The script exports the critical configuration information stored on an Edge Transport server out to an XML file. Once this XML file is created, it should be copied off the server and backed up.

An added benefit of this XML file backup process is what is called the *cloned configuration process*. It allows you to configure one Edge Transport server and then clone the configuration to other Edge Transport servers.

 For more detailed information about the ExportEdgeConfig.ps1 script, see the topic "Configure Edge Transport Server Using Cloned Configuration" at http://technet.microsoft.com/en-us/library/aa996008.aspx.

To capture the configuration of an Edge Transport server, run the ExportEdgeConfig.ps1 script. Running this script extracts the Edge Transport server configuration and places it in an XML file that can be backed up for later use. To reapply the XML backup to a newly installed Edge Transport server with the same server name, run the ImportEdgeConfig.ps1 script. Running this script will apply all the settings in the XML file to your Edge Transport server. After the settings have been applied, you need to initiate EdgeSync to populate the local configuration database. Your Edge Transport server should now be restored and ready to go.

Exercise 8.7 provides a basic outline of the steps that you take to back up an Edge Transport server.

EXERCISE 8.7

Backing Up an Edge Transport Server

To back up an Edge Transport server, use the following steps:

1.   Log on to ET01

2.   Click Start ➤ Programs ➤ Microsoft Exchange Server 2010 and then select Exchange Management Shell.

3.   Run the following:

```
.\ExportEdgeConfig.ps1-CloneConfigData:"<Path_and_FileName_Of_XML_File>"
```

4.   Place the XML file on a secure server in a location that is backed up.

Exercise 8.8 gives the steps that you take to restore an Edge Transport server.

EXERCISE 8.8

Restoring an Edge Transport Server

To restore the configuration on an Edge Transport server, follow these steps:

1. Perform a fresh install of an Exchange Server 2010 Edge Transport server, giving the server the same name as the server you are replacing.

2. Place the XML backup file on the Edge Transport server that you want to restore.

3. On the Edge Transport server you want to restore, run the following EMS command:

   ```
   .\ImportEdgeConfig.ps1 -CloneConfigData
   "C:\CloneConfigData.xml" -isImport:$true
   ```

4. Once your server has been configured with the restored settings, you need to repopulate the AD LDS database by running the EdgeSync process to import all the user objects from Active Directory.

Summary

Disaster recovery for Exchange Server 2010 is an involved and complex concept that includes numerous levels of protection and different methods for recovery and restoration. With the multiple server roles in Exchange 2010, each server role requires different elements that must be considered when creating a backup and recovery plan.

The best way to deal with a disaster is to prevent it before it happens, with redundant and reliable hardware, diligent monitoring, excellent planning, and knowledge. If a disaster cannot be prevented and you must cope with one, the best way to deal with it is to have well-documented and well-practiced procedures in place. Even with the best disaster prevention plans, you still need to have good, verified backups.

Chapter Essentials

Avoid disasters.   Exchange Server 2010 introduces several new features, including Shadow Redundancy and DAG, which make it easier to create a resilient infrastructure. You should design an infrastructure that is likely to withstand the most common problems so that you hopefully never have to recover from a disaster.

Create and test backups.   It's important that you test your ability to restore from your backups. No matter how good your backup plan is or which option you decide to use, your backups are useless if you can't restore from them.

Know how to use the Exchange Server 2010 tools.   It's important to know how to use the Exchange tools, such as ESEUtil and `setup /mode:RecoverServer`, before you have a disaster. That way, during a disaster, you're working on restoring service and data instead of becoming familiar with the tools.

Have a disaster recovery plan, and don't hesitate to seek help during a disaster.   Your business processes and data are at their most vulnerable during a disaster. It's important for you to have plans for what to do if you experience a disaster. Also, know when to stop and ask for help so that you don't inadvertently make the problem worse.

Chapter
9

Monitoring and Reporting with Exchange Server 2010

THE FOLLOWING TOPICS ARE DISCUSSED IN THIS CHAPTER:

✓ Monitoring databases

✓ Performing message tracking

✓ Monitoring client connectivity

✓ Creating server reports

✓ Creating usage reports

Monitoring a server many times falls into the same category as configuring security in that you only think about it when you need it. When you do think about it, you realize that it was not set up properly or you have failed to learn how to use it to your advantage. This can lead to frustration when it comes time to troubleshoot issues, and can make it seem that you, as the Exchange Server administrator, are not being proactive when it comes to preventing email or server issues. This chapter will show you how to make monitoring your Exchange servers simple and effective.

You'll want to monitor your Exchange servers to keep track of trends, both healthy or unhealthy ones. In addition, you will likely be required to produce data for reports on the status of the Exchange infrastructure and determine when problems occur and how to remedy them quickly. Whatever your circumstances, you'll need to have some monitoring and reporting skills in your toolset.

Monitoring Databases

Databases are the lifeline of the Exchange server, and as such they should be high on your list when it comes to monitoring. So how do you go about successfully monitoring the Exchange database? Let's start at disk space. Why? Exchange databases need disk space, and if they run out, they will stop functioning.

One reason to monitor disk space is that Exchange keeps a log of every single event that occurs on its database; these logs are called transaction logs. If transaction logs are not properly maintained, they can become very large and simply bring down the server.

When the Exchange store detects that the disk space is below 1 GB, it will cut off all transport delivery to the database. It does this to prevent the disk from running out of free space. If the disk runs out of free space, the database cannot be mounted or debugged. This self-protecting feature is great, but it should not be the only protection you use. When the Exchange store determines that the disk or database is getting low on free space, it produces the following events on the server:

- 10014 indicates low disk space on the log.

- 10015 indicates low disk space on the database.

You can use many third-party applications to monitor the Exchange server for critical events, and you may also use *Windows Performance Monitor*. Windows Performance Logs and Alerts has been around since the days of Windows NT, but very few administrators use it because early versions had a steep learning curve and took too long to set up. Many of the third-party tools you pay to use utilize the same performance counters that Windows Performance Monitor was built to analyze. So why not take advantage of the free tools that Microsoft provides? It's one way that you can cut costs while still getting the job done.

In Exercise 9.1, you will use Windows Performance Monitor to view the status of the disk free space.

EXERCISE 9.1

Monitoring Disk Free Space

Follow these steps to view the disk free space using Windows Performance Monitor:

1. Click Start ➤ Programs ➤ Microsoft Exchange Server 2010 and then select Exchange Management Console.

2. Expand the Microsoft Exchange container, expand the Microsoft Exchange On-Premises container, and then click the Toolbox node.

3. In the Details pane, click Performance Monitor.

4. The Performance Monitor window appears. Expand Performance Logs and Alerts, Monitoring Tools, and then Performance Monitor.

EXERCISE 9.1 *(continued)*

5. In the Details pane, click the green plus sign to add a counter. The Add Counters dialog box opens.

6. In the Available counters box, expand LogicalDisk by clicking the plus sign to the right of it select % Free Space. Then choose <All instances>.

7. Now click the Add button. The counter appears in the Added counters box on the right.

8.   Click OK.

9.   In the Details pane, select the Change Graph Type drop-down box and choose Report.

10.   The right Details pane now shows the disk free space on all drives.

In addition to using Windows Performance Monitor, you can use Windows 2008 Server Manager, which has *disk quotas* to also help monitor disk space and control disk usage if necessary.

Disk quotas were originally introduced in Windows 2000 and have evolved over the years. Of course, new versions have new improvements and changes to how they are implemented. You might have used disk quotas in the past or at least taken a look at it. If so, you might be cautious of using them because most administrators cringe at the thought of capping or limiting the use of disk space. But recent changes warrant that we should revisit them and see if they will provide any benefit to monitoring Exchange server disk space.

Before you can use disk quotas, you need to install both the File Server role and File Server Resource Manager service on Windows 2008 Server, which you will do in the next two exercises. Normally, you can install both when you install File Services, but many times the File Server role is already installed, and therefore it will be installed as a separate exercise, Exercise 9.2.

EXERCISE 9.2

Installing the File Server Role

Follow these steps to install the File Server role on Windows 2008 Server:

1. Click Start ➤ Programs ➤ Administrative Tools ➤ Server Manager.

2. In the Console tree, choose Roles and select Add Roles in the right reading pane.

3. Click Next on the Before You Begin page.

4. Put a check mark in the File Services box and click Next.

EXERCISE 9.2 *(continued)*

5. Select Next on the Introduction To File Services page.

6. Select Next on the Select Role Services page.

7. On the Confirm Installation Selections page, choose Install.

In Exercise 9.3, you will install the File Server Resource Manager service.

EXERCISE 9.3

Installing the File Server Resource Manager Service

Follow these steps to install the File Server Resource Manager feature in Windows 2008:

1. Click Start ➤ Programs ➤ Administrative Tools ➤ Server Manager.

2. In the Console tree, choose Roles. Select Add Role Service in the right reading pane.

3. In the Add Role Services Wizard, put a check mark in the File Server Resource Manager box on the Select Role Services page and click Next.

4. On the Configure Storage Usage Monitoring screen, select the drives you want to monitor.

5. On the Set Report Options page, click Next.

6. On the Confirm Installation Selections page, click Install.

7. On the Installation Results screen, click Close.

After the installation of Server Resource Manager is complete, it will allow an administrator to configure quota's for disk management. Both hard quotas, which actually prevent users from adding more files, and soft quotas, which only generate events and warnings, can be used to monitor disk free space.

Care must be taken when using hard quotas on disk space. For example, let's say it's your organization's busy time of the year. Many orders and documents are generated during this time and they take up disk space. If you implement hard quotas on a disk and users try to save files to that disk after the quota has been met, they will be denied. This might easily result in the help desk being swamped with service tickets and management becoming upset. This kind of situation can impact production and cause the company to lose business, so it's best to use soft quotas.

When you use soft quotas, you are given advanced warning that disk free space is low but users can continue to save files to the disk until it runs out of free space. Proper planning is needed to allow sufficient time to acquire additional disk space after receiving warnings.

Exercise 9.4 will walk you through configuring a soft quota to monitor the disk free space.

EXERCISE 9.4

Configuring Soft Disk Quotas

Follow these steps to configure soft disk quotas to monitor disk free space:

1. Click Start ➢ Programs ➢ Administrative Tools ➢ File Server Resource Manager.

2. In the Console tree, expand Quota Management.

3. Right-click Quotas and choose Create Quota.

4. In the Create Quota dialog box, click the Browse button next to the Quota Path text box, click Browse. In the Browse For Folder dialog box, select the local disk where you want to create the quota, and then click OK to return to the Create Quota dialog box.

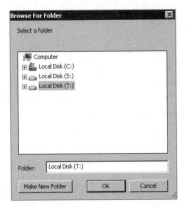

5. In the Quota Properties section, choose Monitor 200 GB Volume Usage and click Create.

Creating custom quotas is also an option and can be easily done. The Define Custom Quota Properties button, shown in Figure 9.1 right above the Custom Properties button, allows you to make changes to fit your needs. These quotas can then be used to send emails and generate event log warnings. If you have many quotas to enforce, consider using quota templates. Using templates will allow you to just make changes to the template, which will then make changes to all quotas that are using the template.

FIGURE 9.1 Defining custom quotas

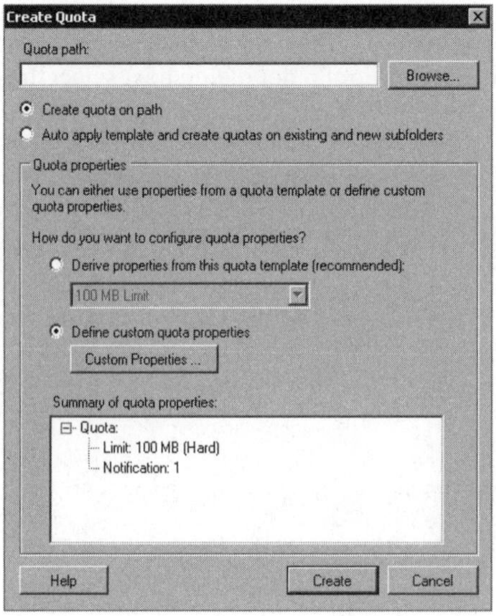

Don't let monitoring your Exchange server be the item that you put on the back burner. It's best to not wait until after the Exchange server has been deployed into production. Plan ahead and do some testing to determine the right monitoring solution for your organization. If you take some time during the planning stages of your Exchange Server deployment, it will pay off in the long run.

Performing Message Tracking

Eventually it will happen—message flow in your Exchange organization will stop working correctly. It might be a dismounted database, a problem with DNS, a problem with the network, or a variety of other possibilities. Regardless of what the problem is, examining the Exchange message queues will most likely be the first step in troubleshooting the problem. In the following sections of this chapter, we'll examine the queues found on an Exchange Server 2010 Hub Transport server and show how you can interact with them. We'll also spend some time examining how to configure and use the message tracking functionality of Exchange Server 2010.

The message tracking tool has been a staple for Exchange administrators for some time, and its usefulness is not likely to change anytime soon. To access the message tracking interface, simply go to the Exchange Management Console Toolbox and double-click the Message Tracking item. The first time you run the message tracking tool, you'll be prompted to check for updates. After you've done this and you are using the tool itself, you'll have an interface to work with like that shown in Figure 9.2. Note how the actual `Get-MessageTrackingLog` cmdlet that will be used to perform the tracking action is already displayed and changes as you select parameters.

FIGURE 9.2   Viewing the message tracking interface

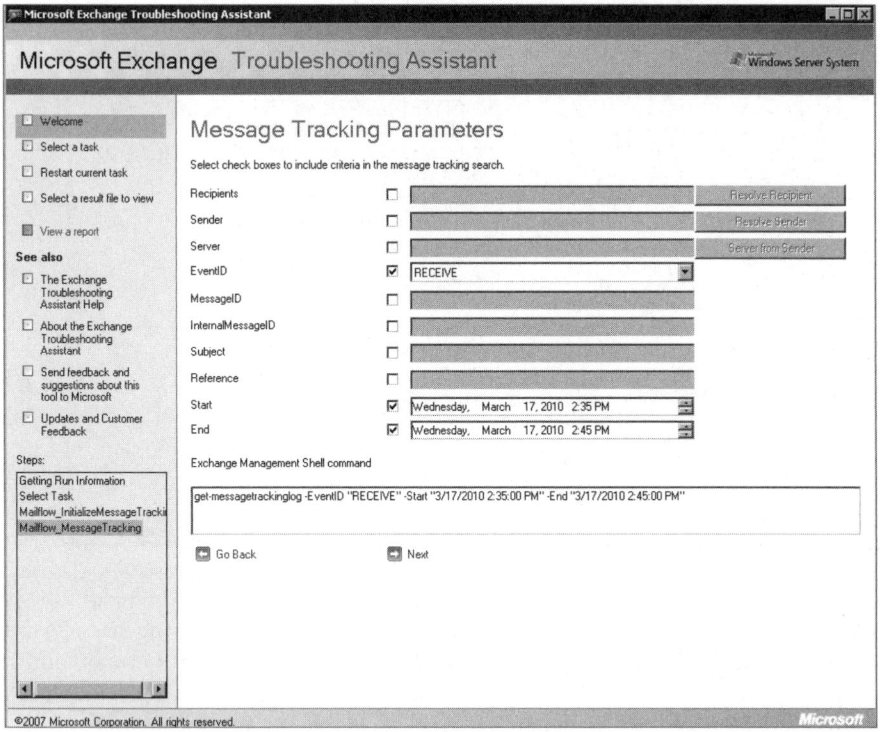

Reviewing Message Tracking

The actual process to use message tracking hasn't really changed much from Exchange Server 2003, so administrators with experience using it there should be able to jump right into it in Exchange Server 2010. Even if you haven't had a lot of experience with tracking messages, the interface is simple and purpose-built, so you can get right to work.

As an example, if you wanted to check the delivery status of all messages sent from Kelly Gustafson (kgustafson@mailtask.com) to Alex Carpenter (acarpenter@mailtask.com), you might configure the message tracking parameters as shown in Figure 9.3.

The corresponding cmdlet to execute this search is

```
Get-MessageTrackingLog -Recipients:acarpenter@mailtask.com –Sender
"kgustafson@mailtask.com" -EventID "DELIVER"
```

FIGURE 9.3 Configuring message tracking parameters

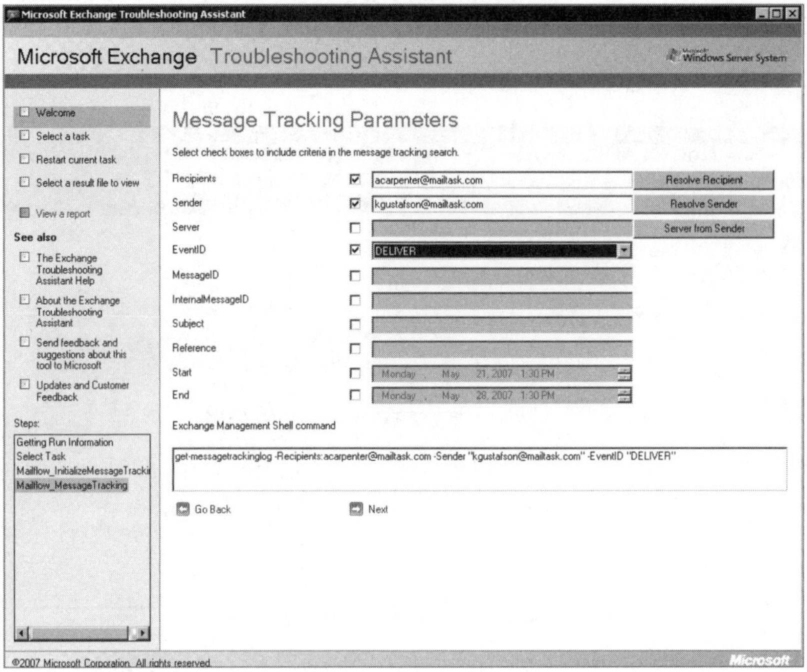

The EventID field is searchable and is often the piece of information you're looking for when it comes to determining the final status of a specific message. Was the message that Jim claimed to never have received really delivered? You can answer that question and many others through message tracking. The EventID field has the following values, each of which will tell you the exact status of that particular line in the tracking logs:

BADMAIL: The message could not be delivered or returned to sender.

DELIVER: The message was delivered to the recipient's mailbox.

DEFER: The delivery of the message was delayed.

DSN: A delivery status notification was generated for the message.

EXPAND: The membership of a distribution was expanded to determine the final recipients of the message.

FAIL: Delivery of the message has failed permanently.

POISONMESSAGE: The message was put into or removed from the poison message queue.

RECEIVE: The message was received and committed to the database.

REDIRECT: The message was redirected to another recipient.

RESOLVE: The message's recipient was resolved to a different email address.

SEND: The message was sent using SMTP to a different server.

SUBMIT: The message was submitted to the Hub Transport server from a Mailbox server or Edge Transport server.

TRANSFER: The recipients of the message were moved to a forked message because of recipient limits or conversion of the message content.

Note that the DELIVER status in the EventID field is your confirmation that a message was actually delivered to a recipient's mailbox—no matter what they try to tell you!

Configuring Message Tracking

Figure 9.4 shows that the actual message tracking logs are located (in a default installation) at

`C:\Program Files\Microsoft\Exchange Server\TransportRoles\Logs\MessageTracking`

The logs are formatted as comma-separated-value (CSV) files, so you can open them in any text editor. You can even import them into Microsoft Excel for advanced sorting and grouping if you want, although you'll most commonly access the logs using the message tracking interface.

FIGURE 9.4   Locating the message tracking logs

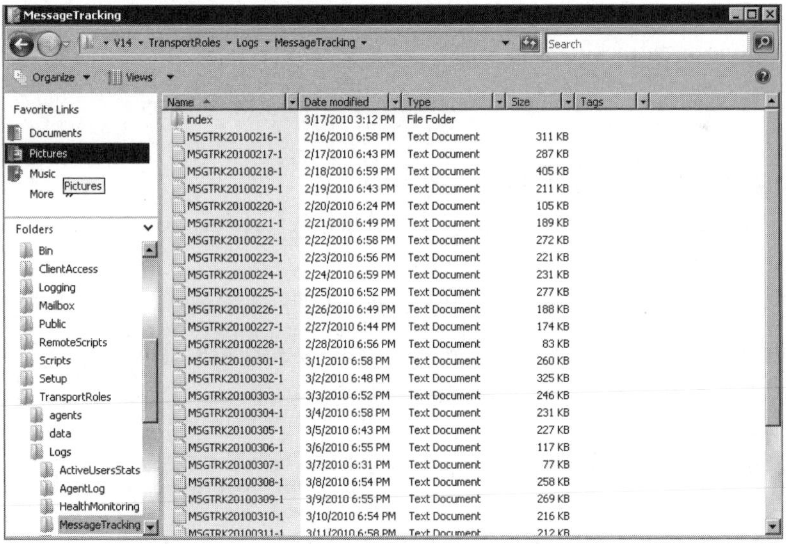

MessageTracking					
Name ▲	Date modified	Type	Size	Tags	
index	3/17/2010 3:12 PM	File Folder			
MSGTRK20100216-1	2/16/2010 6:58 PM	Text Document	311 KB		
MSGTRK20100217-1	2/17/2010 6:43 PM	Text Document	287 KB		
MSGTRK20100218-1	2/18/2010 6:59 PM	Text Document	405 KB		
MSGTRK20100219-1	2/19/2010 6:43 PM	Text Document	211 KB		
MSGTRK20100220-1	2/20/2010 6:24 PM	Text Document	105 KB		
MSGTRK20100221-1	2/21/2010 6:49 PM	Text Document	189 KB		
MSGTRK20100222-1	2/22/2010 6:58 PM	Text Document	272 KB		
MSGTRK20100223-1	2/23/2010 6:56 PM	Text Document	221 KB		
MSGTRK20100224-1	2/24/2010 6:59 PM	Text Document	231 KB		
MSGTRK20100225-1	2/25/2010 6:52 PM	Text Document	277 KB		
MSGTRK20100226-1	2/26/2010 6:49 PM	Text Document	188 KB		
MSGTRK20100227-1	2/27/2010 6:44 PM	Text Document	174 KB		
MSGTRK20100228-1	2/28/2010 6:56 PM	Text Document	83 KB		
MSGTRK20100301-1	3/1/2010 6:58 PM	Text Document	260 KB		
MSGTRK20100302-1	3/2/2010 6:48 PM	Text Document	325 KB		
MSGTRK20100303-1	3/3/2010 6:52 PM	Text Document	246 KB		
MSGTRK20100304-1	3/4/2010 6:58 PM	Text Document	231 KB		
MSGTRK20100305-1	3/5/2010 6:43 PM	Text Document	227 KB		
MSGTRK20100306-1	3/6/2010 6:55 PM	Text Document	117 KB		
MSGTRK20100307-1	3/7/2010 6:31 PM	Text Document	77 KB		
MSGTRK20100308-1	3/8/2010 6:54 PM	Text Document	258 KB		
MSGTRK20100309-1	3/9/2010 6:55 PM	Text Document	269 KB		
MSGTRK20100310-1	3/10/2010 6:54 PM	Text Document	216 KB		
MSGTRK20100311-1	3/11/2010 6:58 PM	Text Document	212 KB		

You may want to perform a few configuration actions for tracking logs (we'll discuss these in the following sections):

- Disabling or enabling message tracking on a server
- Changing the tracking log location

- Changing the tracking log maximum size
- Changing the tracking log directory maximum size
- Changing the tracking log maximum age
- Disabling or enabling message subject logging

Disabling or Enabling Message Tracking on a Server

By default, message tracking is enabled on all Edge Transport, Hub Transport, and Mailbox servers. You can disable (or enable) message tracking by using the following commands for Edge Transport and Hub Transport servers:

- To disable message tracking, use

  ```
  Set-TransportServer servername -MessageTrackingLogEnabled$false
  ```

- To enable message tracking, use

  ```
  Set-TransportServer servername -MessageTrackingLogEnabled$true
  ```

You can disable (or enable) message tracking by using the following commands for Mailbox servers:

- To disable message tracking, use

  ```
  Set-MailboxServer servername -MessageTrackingLogEnabled$false
  ```

- To enable message tracking, use

  ```
  Set-MailboxServer servername -MessageTrackingLogEnabled$true
  ```

Changing the Tracking Log Location

To change the location of the tracking logs from their default location, you can use the following commands:

- For Hub Transport and Edge Transport servers, use

  ```
  Set-TransportServer servername -MessageTrackingLogPath "T:\Message Tracking"
  ```

- For Mailbox servers, use

  ```
  Set-MailboxServer servername -MessageTrackingLogPath "T:\Message Tracking"
  ```

Changing the Tracking Log Maximum Size

To change the maximum size of each individual tracking log, you can use the following commands:

- For Hub Transport and Edge Transport servers, use

  ```
  Set-TransportServer servername -MessageTrackingLogMaxFileSize 15MB
  ```

- For Mailbox servers, use

```
Set-MailboxServer servername -MessageTrackingLogMaxFileSize 15MB
```

By default, each message tracking log created has a maximum size of 10 MB. You can use values in bytes (B), kilobytes (KB), megabytes (MB), gigabytes (GB), or terabytes (TB) when you configure the maximum size of each message tracking log.

Changing the Tracking Log Directory Maximum Size

To change the maximum size of the folder that contains the message tracking logs, you can use the following commands:

- For Hub Transport and Edge Transport servers, use

```
Set-TransportServer servername -MessageTrackingLogMaxDirectorySize 5GB
```

- For Mailbox servers, use

```
Set-TransportServer servername -MessageTrackingLogMaxDirectorySize 5GB
```

Changing the Tracking Log Maximum Age

To change the message tracking log age, you can use the following commands:

- For Hub Transport and Edge Transport servers, use

```
Set-TransportServer servername -MessageTrackingLogMaxAge 45.00:00:00
```

- For Mailbox servers, use

```
Set-MailboxServer servername -MessageTrackingLogMaxAge 45.00:00:00
```

The value entered has a format of dd.hh:mm:ss, where d = days, h = hours, m = minutes, and s = seconds. If the value is set to 00:00:00, Exchange will not automatically prune tracking logs because of age.

Disabling or Enabling Message Subject Logging

By default, message subject logging is enabled, but you can disable or enable it if you want. You can disable (or enable) subject logging by using the following commands for Edge Transport and Hub Transport servers:

- To disable subject logging, use

```
Set-TransportServer servername -MessageTrackingLogSubjectLoggingEnabled $false
```

- To enable message tracking, use

```
Set-TransportServer servername -MessageTrackingLogSubjectLoggingEnabled $true
```

You can disable (or enable) message tracking by using the following commands for Mailbox servers:

- To disable message tracking, use

  ```
  Set-MailboxServer servername -MessageTrackingLogSubjectLoggingEnabled $false
  ```

- To enable message tracking, use

  ```
  Set-MailboxServer servername -MessageTrackingLogSubjectLoggingEnabled $true
  ```

Using the Routing Log Viewer

Exchange 2010 does not rely on link-state routing as in previous versions. Therefore, the tools used to troubleshoot Exchange 2003 Server message routing no longer works. The Routing Log Viewer, designed to view routing information, was added into the Exchange Management Console Toolbox in Exchange 2007 Service Pack 1.

The Routing Log Viewer allows the administrator to open routing logs to view how the local Hub Transport or the Edge Transport server has identified message routing information from Active Directory. This is useful for a few very important reasons. First, an administrator can use this information to determine what path a message will take and determine if any routing adjustments need to be made. The second benefit is that previous versions of the log files can also be parsed to see how, or if, routing has changed over time. Last, log files from multiple servers can be opened to establish any differences existing between servers.

The Routing Log Viewer is launched through the Toolbox in the Exchange Management Console just like the other mail flow tools. After you launch the Routing Log Viewer, open a log file, as shown in Figure 9.5.

FIGURE 9.5   Opening routing table log files

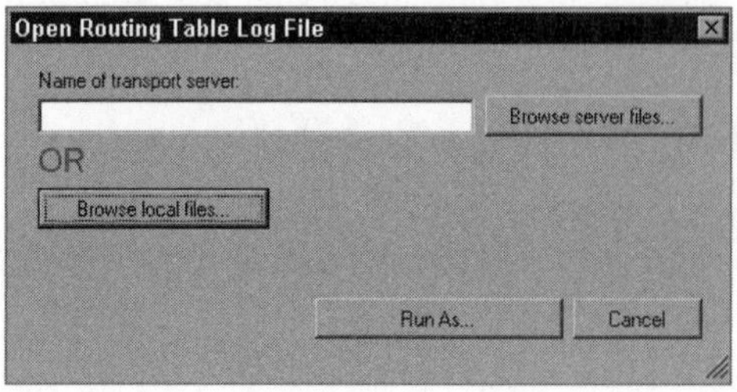

After you open the log file, you are presented with a window with four tabs: Active Directory Sites & Routing Groups, Servers, Send Connectors, and Address Spaces. The Active Directory Sites & Routing Groups tab, as shown in Figure 9.6, shows what the Hub Transport server has discovered about Active Directory sites and any routing group connectors. The Servers tab lists all the Exchange servers in the organization, in what site they are located, the cost to send to the servers from the local server, databases hosted on each the server, and other details. The Send Connectors tab lists all of the connectors in the Exchange organization along with details about each connector, including costs and address spaces. The last tab, the Address Spaces tab, lists all of the address spaces in the Exchange organization as well as details about their cost and an ordered list of each of the address space connectors.

FIGURE 9.6 Viewing the Active Directory Sites & Routing Groups tab

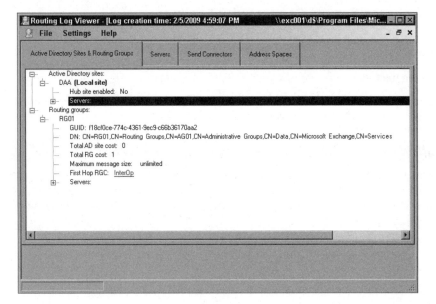

Monitoring Client Connectivity

Although testing internally is extremely important, testing from outside the network is also a good tool to aid in troubleshooting. The Exchange support team designed a tool that can perform a wide variety of client connectivity tests. The tool, called the Exchange Remote Connectivity Analyzer, is at www.testexchangeconnectivity.com.

Before the Exchange support team set up this wonderful tool for performing connectivity tests, testing consisted of an administrator checking connectivity using several user accounts and several different methods. With the release of the Exchange Remote Connectivity Analyzer, features such as Exchange ActiveSync, Autodiscover, Outlook Anywhere and inbound email all can be tested using this tool.

The Exchange Remote Connectivity Analyzer is not only a very effective tool during an Exchange deployment, it can be used to troubleshoot any issues that might come up after the server has been deployed for production. For example, suppose you get a help desk ticket regarding one of the Exchange services not working. This could be a problem to verify or troubleshoot if it involves only one user. Many times it's difficult to understand just where we should start troubleshooting. We highly recommend that you bookmark this site and make full use of it for any deployments or future troubleshooting.

Exercise 9.5 will demonstrate the use of the Exchange Remote Connectivity Analyzer.

EXERCISE 9.5

Using Exchange Remote Connectivity Analyzer

Follow these steps to test the connectivity of Outlook Anywhere:

1. Open a web browser and enter **https://www.testexchangeconnectivity.com** in the location bar.

2. On the Select the test you want to run page, select Outlook Anywhere (RPC over HTTP) under the Microsoft Office Outlook Connectivity Tests line, and then click Next.

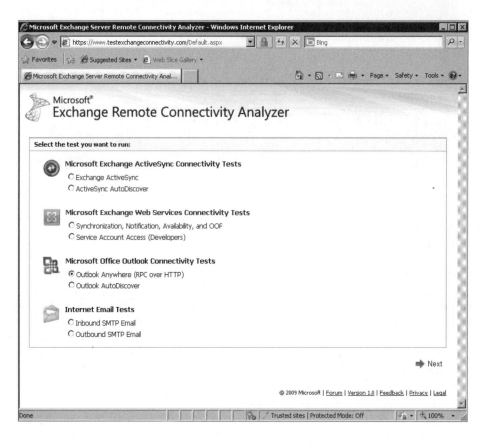

3. In the Outlook Anywhere (RPC over HTTP) dialog box, fill in the appropriate information for your organization, accept the use agreement, and enter the verification code. Then click Perform Test.

Outlook Anywhere (RPC over HTTP)

Email Address:

egustafson@mailtask.com

Domain\Username (or UPN):

mailtask\egustafson

Password:

••••••

Confirm Password:

••••••

◉ Use Autodiscover to detect settings

◯ Manually Specify Server Settings

RPC Proxy Server:

Exchange Server:

Mutual Authentication Principal Name:

RPC Proxy Authentication Method:

Ntlm ▾

☑ I understand that I must use the credentials of a working account from my Exchange domain to be able to test connectivity to it remotely; I acknowledge that I am responsible for the management and security of this account.

Verification

AASRNB

↻

🔊

Enter the verification code from the left:

AASRNB

Notice

The Remote Connectivity Analyzer is a web based tool that's designed to help IT administrators to troubleshoot connectivity issues with their Exchange Server deployments. It allows administrators to test connectivity to their Exchange domains remotely from outside of their organizations internal networks. In order to use this tool, you must enter the credentials of a working account from the Exchange domain to be tested. **To avoid the potential risk of working credentials being exploited and therefore compromising the security of your Exchange environment, we strongly recommend that you create a test account for the purpose of using this tool, and delete this account immediately after you have completed the connectivity testing.**

⬅ Previous ➡ Perform Test

Reviewing these external results can save an administrator a lot of time troubleshooting and deploying Exchange and subsequently can reduce the costs associated. There are other ways to test an Exchange deployment, one of which is using test cmdlets.

Using the Test Cmdlets to Test Functionality

Rather than leave you to your own devices, Microsoft has developed 17 cmdlets to provide a wide range of tests. Many of these cmdlets are used to gather information on the health of the Exchange environment. Understanding these powerful tools will allow you to get the information you need to pinpoint potential issues.

The cmdlets are as follows:

Test-ActiveSyncConnectivity   Tests a full simulated synchronization using Exchange ActiveSync.

Test-EdgeSynchronization   This is run against a Hub Transport server to test its ability to synchronize with an Edge Transport server.

Test-ExchangeSearch   Tests whether search indexes are being updated.

Test-ImapConnectivity   Tests connectivity to a Client Access Server via the IMAP4 protocol and returns the results.

Test-IPAllowListProvider   Tests an IP address to determine if it is listed on a configured safe list provider.

Test-IPBlockListProvider   Tests the configuration of the specified IP Block List provider.

Test-Mailflow   Tests email transportation to a specific server, between two servers, or to external addresses.

Test-MAPIConnectivity   Tests connectivity to Active Directory and to a mailbox. If the server parameter is specified, connectivity to the system mailbox on the server specified is tested.

Test-OutlookWebServices   Performs a series of tests against a Client Access Server role to verify that the Autodiscover settings are properly configured.

Test-OwaConnectivity   Tests the configuration of the Exchange virtual directories.

Test-PopConnectivity   Tests connectivity to a Client Access Server via the POP3 protocol and returns the results.

Test-ReplicationHealth   Tests the health of all replication types, status of cluster services, and replay status to provide a comprehensive status.

Test-SenderId   Tests an IP address to determine if it is valid for a given SMTP domain.

Test-ServiceHealth   Tests to determine whether the required services that are set to start automatically are started.

Test-SystemHealth   Tests to see how the current Exchange configuration adheres to best practices.

Test-UMConnectivity   Tests basic unified messaging connectivity or full end-to-end unified messaging connectivity.

Test-WebServicesConnectivity   Tests to determine if Outlook Anywhere is functioning properly.

The moral of the story is that testing your Exchange Server deployment is a must; it provides valuable feedback to ensure that your Exchange organization is set up properly. If you fail to test your Exchange deployment, rest assured your users will let you know what is not working. Any administrator's goal should be to have a properly configured Exchange environment before releasing it to production; testing user connectivity will verify that it is.

Creating Server Reports

To get a good handle on what is going on in your Exchange environment, you will need to be able to report overall usage. This information will allow you to trend how the environment is changing in response to company needs and equip you with the information required to identify changes that may be necessary to implement in response to those changing needs. The following sections cover some of the common types of server and usage reports you might be asked to prepare.

Creating Health Reports

Creating a server health report in Exchange Server 2010 is an easy task thanks to the Exchange Best Practices Analyzer (ExBPA), now a built-in tool. You can find the ExBPA in the Toolbox node of the Exchange Management Console. To create a health report using the ExBPA, follow the steps outlined in Exercise 9.6.

EXERCISE 9.6

Creating a Health Report

Here's how to use the ExBPA to create a health report:

1. Click Start ➤ Programs ➤ Microsoft Exchange Server 2010, and then select Exchange Management Console.

2. Expand the Microsoft Exchange container, expand the Microsoft Exchange On-Premises container, and then click the Toolbox node.

3. In the Details pane, click the Best Practices Analyzer item. The Exchange Best Practices Analyzer opens.

4. Click the Select options for a new scan link. The Connect To Active Directory page opens.

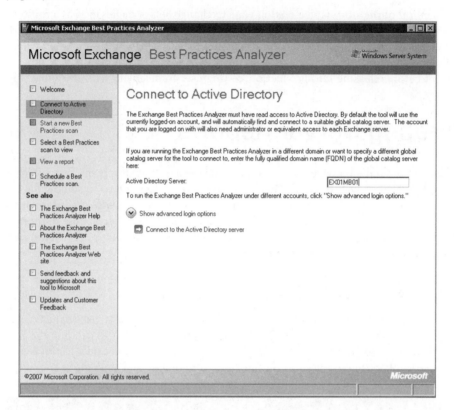

5. Type the name of a global catalog server that the ExBPA should connect to, and then click the Connect to the Active Directory server link. After a brief connectivity check, the Start a new Best Practices scan page will appear, as shown here.

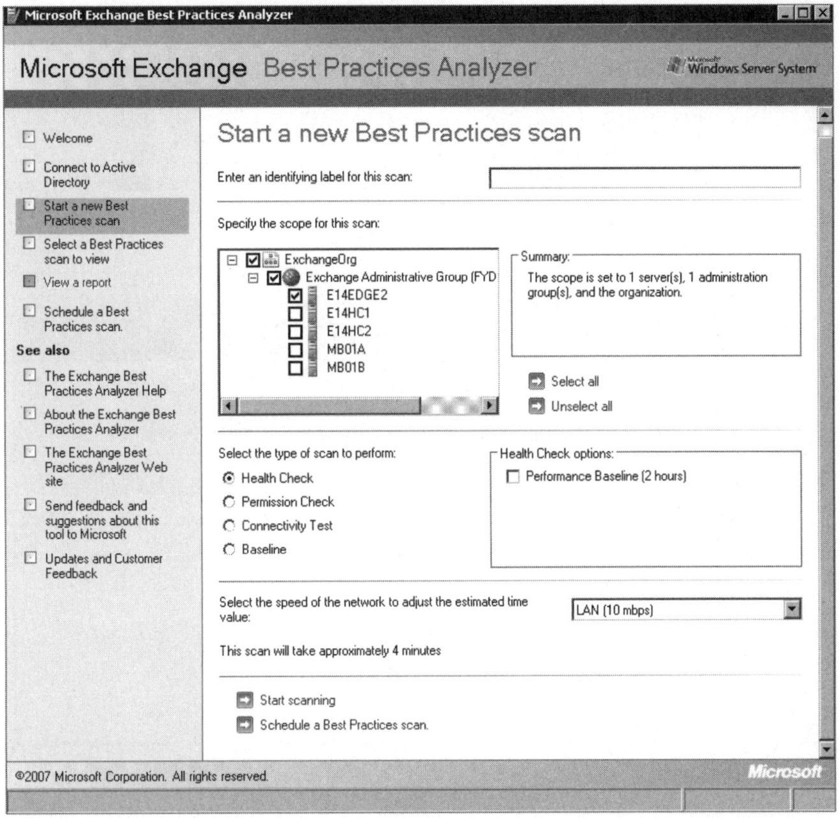

6. On the Start a new Best Practices scan page, select the Health Check option and choose one or more Exchange servers on which to perform the health check. To make it easier to locate this ExBPA report later, you can give it a friendly label. After entering all selections, click the Start scanning link at the bottom of the page.

7. A health check takes about 2 minutes per server to complete. After the check is completed, you are presented with the option to view the report. Click the View a report link to open the report, shown here.

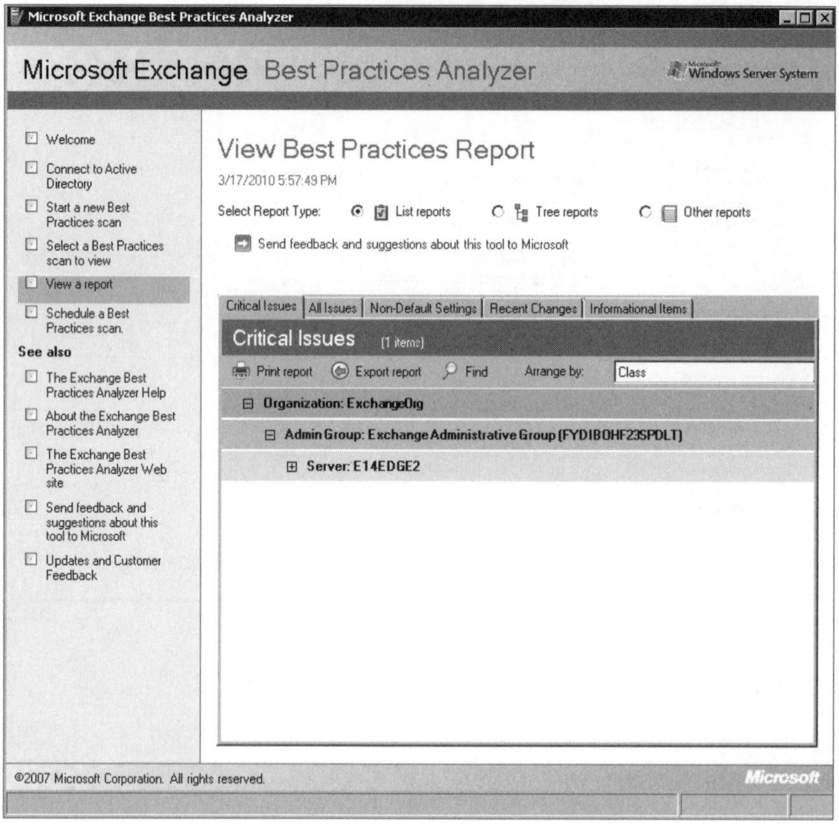

8. The first tab is the Critical Issues tab, and that's where you'll want to start focusing your efforts if anything is listed there.

9. You can also print or export the ExBPA report to HTML, CSV, or XML. Exporting to HTML or CSV will export only the currently selected tab; exporting to XML will result in the entire scan report being exported.

10. Alternatively, you will have the ability to revisit scans later by returning to the Welcome page of the ExBPA and clicking the Select A Best Practices Scan To View link. A listing of all past scans will be made available, as shown here.

11. To view a previous scan report, click it to expand a list of options. You can view a report from the scan, export the scan as an XML file, delete the scan, or label it to make it easily identifiable.

Creating Availability Reports

To get true, usable availability reports on Exchange Server 2010 R2, you'll need to use another application, such as System Center Operations Manager (SCOM) 2007 with the Exchange Server 2010 Management Pack (MP). SCOM includes many reports on the Exchange environment. Table 9.1 lists the available reports in SCOM with the Exchange Server 2010 MP. The reports are divided into three columns; the first column lists the service availability reports, the second column list metrics reports, and the third column lists antispam reports.

TABLE 9.1   System Center Operations Manager reports for Exchange Server 2010

Service Availability	Metrics	Antispam
Service Availability Summary	Client Performance	Attached File Filter
Mailbox Service Availability	Mailbox Count	Connection Filter
Mailflow Local Service Availability	RPC and Database Performance	Recipient Filter
Mailflow Remote Service Availability	Unified Messaging Call Summary	Sender ID
Outlook Web Access External Service Availability	Unified Messaging Message Summary	Sender Filter
Outlook Web Access Internal Service Availability		Content Filter
ActiveSync Internal Availability		Protocol Analysis
Unified Messaging Local Voice Service Availability		
Unified Messaging Local Fax Service Availability		
Unified Messaging Remote Voice Service Availability		

Working with SCOM is beyond the scope of the book, but if your organization has more than two or three Exchange servers, you should take the time to explore how SCOM or another third-party monitoring tool could help you monitor Exchange, Active Directory, and many other key Microsoft products and services.

⊕ Real World Scenario

Using SCOM to Achieve a Higher Class of Service

Although Exchange 2010 offers a number of monitoring capabilities, it doesn't offer enough tools to meet the needs of many larger organizations. In addition, automated monitoring and alerting is often called for because of the critical role that Exchange has in most organizations. To meet these requirements, you should consider implementing SCOM.

It's not just an Exchange-only benefit; SCOM can monitor and report on almost any current Microsoft product as well as many non-Microsoft products. SCOM offers management packs for Exchange, SQL Server, Windows, network load balancing, Active Directory, HP storage arrays, Windows Software Update Services (WSUS), SharePoint Services, Forefront for Exchange, File Replication Service (FRS), and many others.

SCOM is not necessarily inexpensive, and it does require some training to be able to implement and manage it properly, but if you spend the time and effort to deploy and customize it to your organization's needs, it will pay off over time with quicker failure recovery, detailed performance reporting, and improved application availability. So if you're looking for better monitoring and reporting, get to know SCOM to see the benefits it can bring your organization.

Creating Usage Reports

Of the many usage reports, most of them will involve users and/or mailboxes. You'll want to know how many mailboxes are located in a certain database, storage group, or server. You'll want to know which users are using the most space in the mailbox database so that you ensure that the appropriate quotas are set. This type of information will also be helpful when it comes to planning for server migrations or decommissioning.

The general *cmdlet* you can use to get information about mailboxes is the `Get-Mailbox` cmdlet. When run from the Exchange Management Console just like that, the cmdlet will return a small subset of data fields from what's really available to you.

If you use the cmdlet `Get-Mailbox | Export-CSV` *c:\mailboxes.csv*, you'll get a CSV file, and in that there will likely be more information than you'll need or want. Again, by using the `Select-Object` cmdlet to filter the information that is exported to the CSV file, you can get a much more usable report. The following is a list of the properties available for reporting:

AcceptMessagesOnlyFrom	CustomAttribute7
AcceptMessagesOnlyFromDLMembers	CustomAttribute8
AddressListMembership	CustomAttribute9
Alias	CustomAttribute10
AntispamBypassEnabled	CustomAttribute11
CustomAttribute1	CustomAttribute12
CustomAttribute2	CustomAttribute13
CustomAttribute3	CustomAttribute14
CustomAttribute4	CustomAttribute15
CustomAttribute5	Database
CustomAttribute6	DeletedItemFlags

DeliverToMailboxAndForward

DisplayName

DistinguishedName

EmailAddresses

EmailAddressPolicyEnabled

EndDateForRetentionHold

ExchangeGuid

ExchangeSecurityDescriptor

ExchangeUserAccountControl

ExchangeVersion

Extensions

ExternalOofOptions

ForwardingAddress

GrantSendOnBehalfTo

Guid

HiddenFromAddressListsEnabled

Identity

IsLinked

IsMailboxEnabled

IsResource

IsShared

IssueWarningQuota

IsValid

Languages

LegacyExchangeDN

LinkedMasterAccount

ManagedFolderMailboxPolicy

MaxBlockedSenders

MaxReceiveSize

MaxSafeSenders

MaxSendSize

Name

ObjectCategory

ObjectClass

Office

OfflineAddressBook

OrganizationalUnit

OriginatingServer

PoliciesExcluded

PoliciesIncluded

PrimarySmtpAddress

ProhibitSendQuota

ProhibitSendReceiveQuota

ProtocolSettings

RecipientLimits

RecipientType

RecipientTypeDetail

RejectMessagesFrom

RejectMessagesFromDL-Members

RequireSenderAuthenticationEnabled

ResourceCapacity

ResourceCustom

ResourceType

RetainDeletedItemsFor

RetainDeletedItemsUntilBackup

RetentionHoldEnabled

RulesQuota

SamAccountName

SCLDeleteEnabled

SCLDeleteThreshold

SCLJunkEnabled

SCLJunkThreshold

SCLQuarantineEnabled

SCLQuarantineThreshold

SCLRejectEnabled

SCLRejectThreshold

ServerLegacyDN

ServerName

SimpleDisplayName

StartDateForRetentionHold

UMDtmfMap

UMEnabled

UseDatabaseQuotaDefaults

UseDatabaseRetentionDefaults

UserAccountControl

UserPrincipalName

WhenChanged

WhenCreated

WindowsEmailAddress

A useful report on mailboxes might use the following cmdlet:

```
Get-Mailbox | Select-Object Name,SamAccountName,*Quota,
Database | Export-CSV c:\mailboxes.csv
```

You may have noticed that this report does not include the size of the mailboxes. For that information, you'll have to leverage the `Get-MailboxStatistics` cmdlet. Here is one example of using it:

```
Get-Mailbox | Get-MailboxStatistics | Select-Object
DisplayName,TotalItemSize,ItemCount,StorageLimitStatus
| Export-CSV c:\mailboxes.csv
```

The following list shows the report fields available when you use the `Get-MailboxStatistics` cmdlet:

AssociatedItemCount	LastLogonTime
Database	LegacyDN
DatabaseName	MailboxGuid
DeletedItemCount	ObjectClass
DisconnectDate	OriginatingServer
DisplayName	ServerName
Identity	StorageGroupName
IsValid	StorageLimitStatus
ItemCount	TotalDeletedItemSize
LastLoggedOnUserAccount	TotalItemSize
LastLogoffTime	

You can create quick, useful reports on the status of all Exchange databases and queues on a server by using the Exchange Management Shell (EMS). To create a report that shows all the information about all mailbox databases on a server, use the `Get-MailboxDatabase | Export-CSV c:\mailboxdb.csv` cmdlet and specify your own location and name for the output file. The following information is available:

AdminDisplayName	EventHistoryRetentionPeriod
AdministrativeGroup	ExchangeLegacyDN
AllowFileRestore	ExchangeVersion
BackupInProgress	Guid
CopyEdbFilePath	HasLocalCopy
DatabaseCreated	Identity
DeletedItemRetention	IndexEnabled
Description	IssueWarningQuota
DistinguishedName	IsValid
EdbFilePath	JournalRecipient

LastFullBackup	OriginatingServer
LastIncrementalBackup	ProhibitSendQuota
MailboxRetention	ProhibitSendReceiveQuota
MaintenanceSchedule	PublicFolderDatabase
MinAdminVersion	QuotaNotificationSchedule
MountAtStartup	Recovery
Mounted	RetainDeletedItemsUntilBackup
Name	Server
ObjectCategory	ServerName
ObjectClass	StorageGroup
OfflineAddressBook	StorageGroupName
Organization	WhenChanged
OriginalDatabase	WhenCreated

More than likely, however, this much information is more than you'll really need to create the report you want. To create a report that contains just the specific fields of data in which you're interested, you can use a cmdlet similar to the following:

```
Get-MailboxDatabase | Select-Object Name,Server,StorageGroup,
Mounted,*Quota* | Export-CSV c:\mailboxdb.csv
```

The output from this more structured cmdlet will be much less and will be easier to work with. You can use any of the available fields listed for the Select-Object cmdlet.

To create a report showing all the public folder databases on a server, you can use the Get-PublicFolderDatabase | Export-CSV c:\publicfolderdb.csv cmdlet, specifying your own location and name for the output file. The following list shows the properties available from the Get-PublicFolderDatabase cmdlet:

AdminDisplayName	FirstInstance
AdministrativeGroup	Guid
Alias	HasLocalCopy
AllowFileRestore	Identity
BackupInProgress	IssueWarningQuota
CopyEdbFilePath	IsValid
DatabaseCreated	ItemRetentionPeriod
DeletedItemRetention	LastFullBackup
Description	LastIncrementalBackup
DistinguishedName	MaintenanceSchedule
EdbFilePath	MaxItemSize
EventHistoryRetentionPeriod	MinAdminVersion
ExchangeLegacyDN	MountAtStartup
ExchangeVersion	Mounted

Name	ReplicationPeriod
ObjectCategory	ReplicationSchedule
ObjectClass	RetainDeletedItemsUntilBackup
Organization	Server
OriginatingServer	ServerName
ProhibitPostQuota	StorageGroup
PublicFolderHierarchy	StorageGroupName
PublicFolderReferralServerList	UseCustomReferralServerList
QuotaNotificationSchedule	WhenChanged
ReplicationMessageSize	WhenCreated

To create a report detailing the current status of all the queues on the server, you can use the Get-Queue | Export-CSV *c:\queues.csv* cmdlet. The following list shows the report fields available:

DeliveryType	NextHopConnector
Identity	NextHopDomain
IsValid	NextRetryTime
LastError	ObjectState
LastRetryTime	Status
MessageCount	

Using Administrator Audit Logging

Exchange 2010 brings a new, much needed feature called administrator audit logging. This feature allows administrators to *audit* all actions performed by both users and administrators. With it, you can find out who is logging into other user's mailboxes. All actions performed in the console, shell or ECP will be logged. Things like Get cmdlets will not be logged, and this makes sense because that would generate a large number of log files each day.

By default, administrator audit logging is not enabled, and there are several things that you need to accomplish before this feature becomes available. Complete the following actions to ensure that the auditing works correctly:

- Configure a dedicated mailbox for storing the audit logs. You want to tightly control access to this mailbox.
- Enable the audit feature and confirm its status.
- Configure the audit agents so they send logs to the mailbox you set up for auditing.
- Determine cmdlets to be audited.
- Define the audit parameters.

The first step is to set up a mailbox for the audit logs to be sent to. This can be a normal user mailbox, or you could create one with the name Audit, which is what we recommend so you don't have trouble down the road if the user leaves the company. You will need the name of this mailbox when you complete the steps that follow.

Now you should confirm that administrator audit logging is not already enabled.

You can confirm the status of administrator audit logging by running the following cmdlet, as shown in Figure 9.7:

```
Get-AdminAuditLogConfig | fl
```

FIGURE 9.7 Confirming that administrator auditing is enabled

Use this cmdlet to configure the auditing agent:

```
Set-AdminAuditLogConfig –AdminAuditlogMailbox "Auditmailtask.com"
```

After you finish configuring the auditing agent, you need to determine what cmdlets to audit. The following cmdlet will audit two of the more common cmdlets, *mailbox* and *transport*. Notice the use of the wildcards, which allow you to audit all changes to a feature:

```
Set-AdminAuditLogConfig –AdminAuditLogCmdlets *mailbox*, *transport*
```

In the same way you audit cmdlets, you can select the parameters of your choice. The following cmdlet will audit the parameters database and server:

```
Set-AdminAuditLogConfig –AdminAuditLogParameters database, *address*
```

To enable administrator logging, run this cmdlet:

```
Set-AdminAuditLogConfig –AdminAuditLogEnabled $true
```

To test your setup, in Exercise 9.7 you will create a new mailbox from the Exchange Management Console.

EXERCISE 9.7

Creating a New Mailbox

Follow these steps to create a new mailbox to test the administrator audit logging feature:

1. Click Start ➢ Programs ➢ Microsoft Exchange Server 2010, and then select Exchange Management Console.

EXERCISE 9.7 *(continued)*

2. Expand the Microsoft Exchange container, expand the Microsoft Exchange On-Premises container, expand the Recipient Configuration container, and then click the Mailbox node.

3. Right-click Mailbox and select New Mailbox.

4. On the first page of the New Mailbox Wizard, choose User Mailbox and click Next.

5. On the User Type screen, choose New User and click Next.

6. On the User Information screen, type the user information and click Next.

7. On the Mailbox Settings screen, click Next.

8. On the Archive Settings screen, click Don't create an archive and click Next.

9. Click New to create the mailbox.

10. Audit logs will be sent to that mailbox with configuration and audit information.

It's highly recommended that you utilize the administrator audit logging feature as it will create an audit trail that can be used to troubleshoot an issue or provide proof of activity in an Exchange organization.

Summary

In this chapter, we briefly covered some of the most common monitoring and reporting tools that Exchange Server 2010 offers you. As is often said in management circles, you can't manage what you can't measure. That axiom holds true for every aspect of system administration—if you don't know what's going on with your servers or applications, you can't effectively manage or troubleshoot them.

Chapter Essentials

Practice performance monitoring. Using the performance counters effectively is not something you can just start doing on your first try. To get effective results out of your performance monitoring, you need to do it often and you need to take the time to understand what each counter is telling you. We covered some of the more specific counters relevant to Exchange Server 2010, but dozens of other counters are important to the Windows

Server operating system as well. After all, if your server is not performing well, it stands to reason that Exchange won't be performing well. Take some time to learn which counters are pertinent to your organization, and make it a point to take performance measurements on a schedule to get an accurate indication of how your servers are performing.

Learn the PowerShell commands. Almost every configuration or management action you perform from the Exchange Management Console will present you with the PowerShell code that was used to perform the action. Take advantage of this information and learn how to use the Exchange Management Shell to your advantage.

Know where to go. Take the time as you review the material in this book to think about what types of configuration and management tasks you find yourself performing in each major node of the Exchange Management Console.

Messaging Professional's Guide to Exchange Server 2010

PART

III

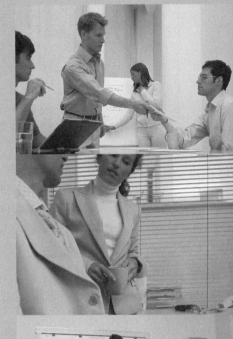

Chapter

10

Planning the Exchange Server 2010 Migration and Infrastructure

THE FOLLOWING TOPICS ARE DISCUSSED IN THIS CHAPTER:

✓ Understanding the messaging professional's job role

✓ Using a framework for deploying Exchange Server 2010

✓ Preparing Exchange Server 2010 for deployment

✓ Planning namespaces

✓ Planning your migration and coexistence

The messaging professional spends a lot of time thinking about and working on the overall design and health of the Exchange environment. This includes controlling change in the environment, evaluating and deploying new features, and deploying new versions of the software.

This chapter discusses the messaging professional's job role. You'll also get a basic understanding of the Microsoft Operations Framework (MOF) and ITIL process of deploying Exchange server. The chapter concludes by covering the design and deployment guidelines for Exchange 2010.

Understanding the Messaging Professional's Job Role

Depending on the size of an organization, the messaging professional's job role can vary. In small to medium-sized companies, the messaging professional can be directly responsible for both the implementation and management of the Exchange server. In larger, enterprise-sized companies, the functions are split up into several parts. One group of administrators might design the messaging environment and another group might provide tiered support for the messaging administration groups.

When you work in your environment, you many not fall directly into just one of the roles that are defined for Exchange professionals. Keep in mind that Microsoft writes exams based on a job profile and a certain minimum level of expertise. To see what is recommended for Exam 70-663, visit the exam's web page:

```
http://www.microsoft.com/learning/en/us/exam.aspx?id=70-663
```

The end goal of a messaging professional is to provide a messaging infrastructure that meets the needs of the business. If you already fill this role in your company, continue to hone and improve your skills both from the technical and the business perspective. If you are reaching out for this position, spend the time learning how things work and when and why they should work. This will help you apply your skills to new opportunities.

Using a Framework for Deploying Exchange Server 2010

Many IT professionals who regularly perform solution deployments and migrations adopt a methodology for completing the work. Adopting such a framework is a repeatable process for deployments; however, if you are concerned with doing only a single Exchange deployment, it still can prove beneficial. The benefits of following an established framework include being able to use an established process that has been tested, being able to use templates provided for project plans, and spending more time focused on executing the project rather than developing a project framework. MOF is a freely available framework provided by Microsoft that includes job aids and project plans that can help you get started developing your deployment project. Microsoft also has Infrastructure Planning and Design guides developed that closely follow MOF and provide detailed guidance around specific technologies.

MOF 4.0 is broken into three phases: Plan, Deliver, and Operate, with an additional operational layer named Manage.

The first phase, the Plan phase, involves creating an IT strategy for the entire company that all IT projects would follow. For example, the business decision makers may decide that the IT strategy should include deploying a global messaging environment and that it should include mobile access for employees in all of the offices as well as for the mobile workforce. These decision makers may also assign a budget to this project.

The second phase, Deliver, is where the strategy is executed. This phase can be broken in four categories with a total of nine general steps:

Envision

1. Envision: Identify all of the business and technical requirements.
2. Assess: Identify the configuration and limitations of the current environment.
3. Evaluate potential solutions and designs.
4. Build a proof of concept. Test the design in a lab environment to prove key design elements.
5. Create a design. With information gathered from the previous steps, create a final design.

Project Planning

6. Develop the deployment plan and obtain buyoff from project stakeholders.

Build/Stabilize

7. Implement a pilot. After the pilot, adjust the plan and design as needed.

Deploy

8.   Deploy. Begin the production deployment.

9.   Post-implementation review. Review the results of the project and determine if it meets all business requirements. Determine if any changes still need to be made.

Once the messaging solution has been deployed, the third phase, the Operate phase, takes over. This is where the solution is continually maintained. The teams responsible for this monitor the solution to be sure that it is meeting service-level agreements. They also proactively apply service packs and other updates to address problems that occur. If an incident occurs, a team will also remediate the problem and restore services.

The Manage layer involves peripheral processes that touch all phases of MOF. These processes include governance, risk management, compliance, change management, and process improvement. Although you may see these processes as impediments to completing your work, they are put in place to police or govern other processes to ensure a consistent level of service for everyone. If these processes were not in place, different groups within the IT department might not adhere to the same standards. The Network department may properly notify users of changes and fully document network changes, but the team responsible for managing Active Directory (AD) may feel they do not need to follow the same standard. This usually works until a team has an extended outage that was caused by poor planning.

Although this book is not specifically written as a guide for following these processes, it is key that a messaging professional understand why these processes are important and how to follow them. Especially when you work in enterprise environments, understanding these processes will help you to work better within the established confines.

For more information about MOF, visit `http://www.microsoft.com/mof`. Another framework that is similar and perhaps broader than MOF is ITIL. You can find out more information about ITIL by visiting `http://www.itil-officialsite.com/AboutITIL/WhatisITIL.asp`.

Preparing Exchange Server 2010 for Deployment

Exchange Server is by definition reliant on the infrastructure that it runs on. If there are bottlenecks or inefficiencies in the environment, they will show up in the performance of Exchange and may be difficult to pinpoint. The following sections cover the requirements for successfully preparing the infrastructure for an Exchange deployment.

Satisfying DNS Requirements

Exchange relies on DNS in three main ways. The first way is that Exchange relies on Active Directory Domain Services (AD DS) to function, and AD DS leverages DNS for locating services like domain controllers and global catalogs within defined AD sites. The second way Exchange relies on DNS is for email delivery in that DNS is used to deliver outbound SMTP email. The third way is that Exchange clients like Outlook, Outlook Web App (OWA), and Entourage all use DNS to connect to Exchange.

Setting up DNS to support AD is fairly straightforward. Either the Windows Server DNS is used or a third-party DNS server that supports SRV records is used. The DNS server built into Windows Server provides features for secure dynamic updates. This feature requires a host to authenticate before it is able to add or modify DNS records. A unique feature to the Windows DNS server is that it can replicate the DNS zones using AD replication. This greatly simplifies the traditional DNS zone transfer configuration, as replications happen automatically.

Exchange uses DNS to determine how to deliver email messages to external SMTP servers, and this generates at least one DNS query for every domain to which an email message is sent. If there are other applications using the same DNS servers as the Exchange transport servers, this can lead to slow response times if the DNS servers are not properly sized. You should closely monitor the DNS servers to ensure that they are responding to queries. You may need to add dedicated DNS servers just for email delivery in large environments.

Planning the Site Topology

In an enterprise environment, deciding where to place Exchange servers and the peripheral services is an important and nontrivial task. As a basic review, you need to meet the following AD requirements:

- The schema master must be running at least Windows Server 2003 Standard with Service Pack 1 (SP1); however, because support for SP1 has been retired, at a minimum Windows Server 2003 Standard Edition with Service Pack 2 (SP2) should be deployed. Also, because Windows Server 2003 is in extended support, it may be prudent to upgrade all domain controllers to Windows Server 2008 or Windows Server 2008 R2.

- At least one global catalog server must be present in each AD site where Exchange will be installed. As with the schema master, the global catalog must be running at least Windows Server 2003 Standard with SP1; however, a newer version is recommended.

For more information about the Microsoft support policy for Windows Server versions, see http://support.microsoft.com/gp/lifeselectserv/en-us.

Exchange relies heavily on AD, therefore it is important to ensure that Exchange has appropriate connectivity to AD and global catalog servers have enough resources to respond to Exchange queries. In large environments or environments that include client machines or remote access servers that perform authentication against AD, it may be better to segregate the domain controllers used for Exchange by putting Exchange in a separate AD site, as shown in Figure 10.1. This will reduce the likelihood that other applications will consume resources on the domain controllers used by Exchange and be able to affect the performance of Exchange.

FIGURE 10.1   Separating Exchange in a dedicated AD site

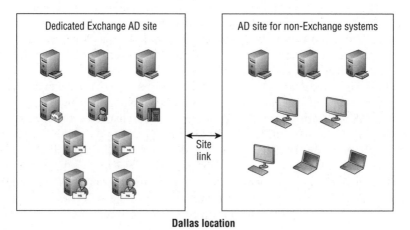

Dallas location

It is also recommended that if you use an x86 version of Windows Server for your global catalog servers, you have a domain controller with at least one processor core for every four processor cores in the Mailbox servers in that AD site. For example, if there are two Mailbox servers with 16 processor cores each, you would need a minimum of one global catalog with eight processor cores. If you use the x64 version of Windows Server for your global catalog servers, you should have a domain controller with at least one processor core for every eight processor cores in the Mailbox servers in that AD site. For example, if there are two Mailbox servers with 16 processor cores each, you would need a minimum of one global catalog with four processor cores. The AD site configuration cannot be designed with just client authentication in mind because the design affects how email is routed through the Exchange organization. For more information about how to configure AD for Exchange routing, see Chapter 12, "Designing Routing and Client Connectivity."

Defining Deployment Locations

Defining where to put Exchange servers will vary for each environment. There are three general configurations that are chosen for deploying Exchange Server: centralized, regional, and distributed.

The simplest deployment is one that has all of the Exchange servers at a centralized location, as shown in Figure 10.2. This deployment is usually acceptable when there is a centralized messaging department and the client computers have connectivity to access their email at the central site. The drawback of this deployment is that every client must make a connection to the centralized site for email, and adequate bandwidth must be provided to accommodate each active client. The bandwidth required for clients depends on the protocol being used (MAPI, Outlook Anywhere, POP3, IMAP, HTTP) as well as the activities the user is doing with the client. For example, the amount of email sent and received by the client, the size of the offline address book (OAB), and the number of public folder items read and posted all affect the amount of bandwidth needed.

It can be difficult to accurately estimate the bandwidth required; however, at the following location some guidance has been given for previous versions of Exchange Server that helps to provide a baseline for estimating network requirements for Outlook:

`http://msexchangeteam.com/archive/2008/04/10/448668.aspx`

Because each environment varies, you should verify any estimate by examining actual network usage. The centralized model shown in Figure 10.2 has become more viable with the reduction of bandwidth required for Outlook configured in Exchange cached mode. When determining the network requirements for any of the deployment options, be sure to complete a full audit of all network traffic. In most cases, additional communication needs to occur over the same network connections that Exchange uses. These systems can include be a VoIP system, instant messaging traffic, AD replication, or other corporate systems.

FIGURE 10.2   A centralized deployment

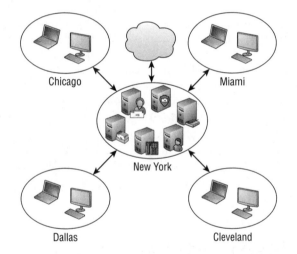

There are reasons to choose other deployment types. A centralized deployment option isn't usually acceptable for companies with clients on multiple continents because connectivity between continents is usually expensive and has high latency. In these cases, a regional deployment may be chosen. This type of deployment locates Exchange servers in regions that are well connected. As shown in Figure 10.3, a regional deployment may have several locations with Exchange servers deployed to reduce latency and bandwidth costs. Using a regional deployment can also help segregate Exchange servers when multiple departments or business units manage Exchange. This type of deployment requires trained resources at more locations than a centralized deployment and may require more maintenance activities to keep all security and application updates applied.

FIGURE 10.3 A regional deployment

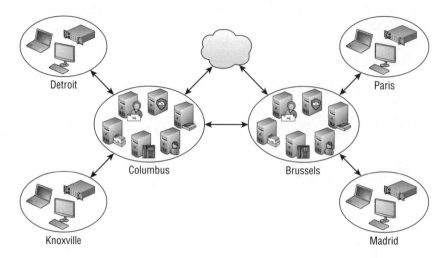

A fully distributed deployment locates Exchange servers in a location closest to the users, as shown in Figure 10.4. In environments where email is mostly sent among users in the same site, less bandwidth is required between sites because most of the email is kept within the site, and in the event of network connectivity failure to other sites, the local users may continue to send and receive email to other local users. A fully distributed deployment usually results in additional Exchange servers over a centralized or regional deployment, which means there will be more servers to administer and update. This may require more people to manage and it requires that each of the locations is adequately equipped with power, bandwidth, smart hands support, and ability to back up and facilitate a restore of server data. When servers are located at remote sites with limited IT staff, it is often difficult to maintain a high level of control over the environmental conditions and maintenance of the server.

Planning Namespaces

A namespace is a logical structure commonly represented by one or more domain names in DNS. This namespace is often reflective of the deployment type selected (described in the previous section). First, it affects planning of the Client Access Server (CAS) deployments and how clients will connect to them. However, it also affects the design and deployment of the Hub Transport and Edge Transport roles. When defining the namespace of a new deployment, it is good to review the requirements for the namespace to ensure that the namespace chosen falls within the supported guidelines. One guideline has to do with a single label domain (SLD), which is a DNS domain that does not have a suffix such as .com or .org and does not include a period in the name, such as Sybex or Mailtask. Some companies create an AD DS domain that matches their previous NT domain NETBIOS name, and others choose to deploy new SLDs. Starting with Windows Server 2008 R2, an SLD can no longer be created—if you have an SLD, you might consider migrating or renaming to a traditional namespace to prevent issues in the future. Exchange Server 2010 does support SLDs; however, this is not a recommended configuration because future Exchange versions may be unsupported in that configuration.

FIGURE 10.4 A distributed deployment

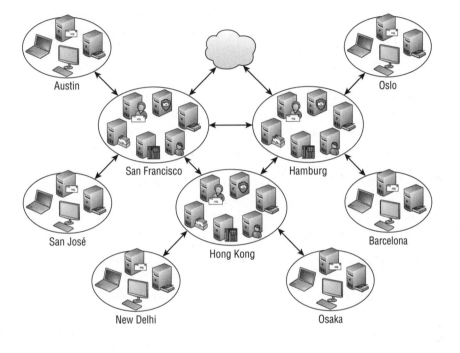

 You can review the Microsoft namespace supportability statement for Exchange 2010 at http://msexchangeteam.com/ archive/2009/10/27/452969.aspx.

Planning the Active Directory Forest

In many cases, AD will already be in place well before you decide to deploy Exchange. You may, however, want to modify the design of AD to support a large or complicated environment. When starting with a brand-new design, you should apply the Keep It Super Simple (KISS) method, which means you try to keep the design as simple as possible and only add complexity if there are no simple alternatives. This methodology keeps the solution easy to deploy and the solution has fewer parts to break and troubleshoot. There are three types of forest deployments: single, multiple, and resource forest.

Single forest topology   The simplest design is a single forest with a single domain. All user accounts and Exchange servers reside in that single domain. There are, however, reasons that might cause you to consider using multiple domains within the forest. One example might be that you have multiple IT departments that autonomously manage different business units or geographic regions. Giving the IT department management rights over only its domain will keep the IT department from making changes that might affect other departments. Only one Exchange organization can exist in an AD forest; therefore Exchange would need to be managed centrally or at least cooperatively.

Cross-forest (multiple forest) topology   A multiple forest implementation can include up to one Exchange organization in each forest and usually includes trusts being created to facilitate cross-forest accessibility. Since an Exchange organization cannot span two forests, additional tools are required to share address lists and public folder information. Multi-forest configurations are common in environments where two large companies merge but each continues to manage its infrastructure separately. This topology requires the use of tools like Microsoft Forefront Identity Manager to synchronize account information between the forests.

Resource forest topology   A resource forest deployment has at least one forest where the user accounts reside and another forest where the Exchange servers, distribution lists, mailboxes, and public folders reside. In this scenario, the administration of the accounts is kept separate from the Exchange organization. In the resource forest, the user accounts of the mailboxes are disabled and associated to user accounts in the account forest.

There are a number of factors that might make this configuration a viable option:

- When Exchange administration is outsourced to a service provider. This keeps the outsourcing forest and the company forests separate.

- When Exchange requires AD configuration that is not compatible with the account forest.

- When trying to reduce the size of the account forest's replication traffic. Installing Exchange in a separate forest keeps the Exchange object information out of the account domain, thus reducing the amount of data that must be replicated and maintained in the account domain.

Forest Functional Levels

The forest functional level controls the behavior and controls some of the features and functionality of the forest. Exchange 2010 requires a minimum forest functionality of Windows Server 2003; this requires that each of the domains in the forest have at least the same domain functional level. The version of Windows Server that the DCs run directly affects which forest and domain functional levels can be set.

The forest functional levels are as follows:

- Windows 2000 native
- Windows Server 2003

- Windows Server 2008
- Windows Server 2008 R2

The domain functional levels are as follows.

- Windows 2000 native
- Windows Server 2003
- Windows Server 2008
- Windows Server 2008 R2

 For more information about AD functional levels, visit the following location:

`http://technet.microsoft.com/en-us/library/understanding-active-directory-functional-levels(WS.10).aspx`

Satisfying Schema Requirements

Before you install the first Exchange Server 2010 server in your organization, you must prepare AD and your domains. This creates the required schema and objects in AD to define the configuration of Exchange and Exchange objects that are part of the organization. AD uses the schema to define a set of rules that define AD and any objects it contains. The schema controls things like naming structures, data types, object types, and so forth. To run the /PrepareSchema command, you must belong to the Schema Admins and Enterprise Admins security groups. In addition, you must belong to the local Administrators group on the server on which Exchange will be installed. If you are not a member of these groups, the appropriate administrator will have to run the /PrepareSchema command before you can install Exchange Server 2010.

Planning Your Migration and Coexistence

Exchange 2010 natively supports coexistence with Exchange 2003 and Exchange 2007. If the Exchange organization includes any previous Exchange versions, they must be removed. If Exchange 2000 is in the environment, you must upgrade to either Exchange 2003 or Exchange 2007 before embarking on the Exchange 2010 deployment. The upgrade from Exchange 2000 to Exchange 2003 is fairly straightforward, and in most cases an in-place upgrade can be performed. If Exchange 2000 is currently deployed, it is usually best to migrate from Exchange 2000 to Exchange 2003 rather than from Exchange 2000 to Exchange 2007 and then to Exchange 2010.

Using the Exchange Deployment Assistant

A new tool released for Exchange 2010 is the Exchange Server Deployment Assistant (ExDeploy). This wizard-driven tool, shown in Figure 10.5, will ask questions about your deployment and create a custom deployment checklist for your deployment. This should be used to scope and then validate your deployment plan. The tool can be found at the following location:

http://technet.microsoft.com/en-us/exdeploy2010/

FIGURE 10.5   Using ExDeploy to plan your deployment

Two other invaluable tools that you can use in preparing for a deployment is the Microsoft Exchange Best Practices Analyzer (ExBPA) and the Microsoft Exchange Pre-Deployment Analyzer (ExPDA). ExBPA has been available for a number of years, and most Exchange administrators have become very familiar with its functionality. Using ExBPA on the currently deployed Exchange environment can help pinpoint any configuration issues that need to be corrected before a deployment should be attempted.

The new tool, ExPDA, which is based on ExBPA, will perform a readiness scan of the Exchange environment and provide a detailed report of any issues that have been identified that might impede or prevent a successful Exchange 2010 deployment.

Using the Exchange Deployment Assistant, ExBPA, and ExPDA along with a good understanding of the deployment process can greatly reduce the possibility of running into issues during the deployment.

Planning Coexistence with Exchange Server 2003

Exchange 2003 uses several logical boundaries that Exchange 2007 and Exchange 2010 no longer maintain. Exchange 2003 has the concept of administrative groups that are used for organizing and delegating permissions to Exchange objects. Starting with Exchange 2007, administrative groups are no longer boundaries for management. To support coexistence with Exchange 2003, all Exchange 2010 servers exist within a single administrative group named Exchange Administrative Group (FYDIBOHF23SPDLT). This administrative group will be visible in the Exchange 2003 management tools, but it will not be found anywhere within the Exchange 2010 management tools.

Another boundary used in Exchange 2003 that does not exist within Exchange 2010 is the routing group. To support coexistence with Exchange 2003, all Exchange 2010 servers are placed in a single routing group named Exchange Routing Group (DWBGZMFD01QNBJR). During setup of the first Exchange 2010 Hub Transport server, a routing group connector is created and an Exchange 2003 server is chosen as a Bridgehead to enable message transport between the Exchange 2003 routing group and the routing group created for the Exchange 2010 servers.

Do not move any of the Exchange 2010 servers out of the Exchange Routing Group (DWBGZMFD01QNBJR) or the Exchange Administrative Group (FYDIBOHF23SPDLT).

During the coexistence phase, it is important to always manage the Exchange Server configuration using the management tools for the version of Exchange Server or object being modified. It's not possible to use message tracking between Exchange 2003 and Exchange 2010. To track a message that is sent through both versions, you must track it twice to obtain the entire message route, once in each system.

For more information about management console interoperability, be sure to read "Exchange Management Console Interoperability" in the Exchange Server 2010 help file or online at http://technet.microsoft.com/en-us/library/dd638174.aspx.

When you're migrating from Exchange 2003 to Exchange 2010 and there is a possibility that you would want to deploy an Exchange 2007 server into the environment in the future, you must deploy and maintain at least one Exchange 2007 server into the organization before deploying your first Exchange 2010 server.

Planning Coexistence with Exchange Server 2007

The changes from Exchange 2007 to Exchange 2010 are not as drastic as they are from Exchange 2003 to Exchange 2010. Neither Exchange 2007 nor Exchange 2010 uses the legacy Exchange 2003 administrative or routing groups for management. They both use AD sites to define the routing topology. However, despite their similarities, an Exchange 2010 Mailbox server can only communicate with Exchange 2010 Hub Transport servers. Likewise, an Exchange 2007 Mailbox server can only communicate with an Exchange

2007 Hub Transport server. Therefore, every Mailbox server requires a Hub Transport server running the same version of Exchange in the same site. This is covered in more detail in Chapter 12.

Planning Coexistence with Third-Party Email Systems

Exchange 2010 does not have any natively supported third-party coexistence options. Exchange 2003 provides native Lotus Notes and Novell GroupWise connectors. To provide any native interoperability with GroupWise, you must maintain an Exchange 2003 server in the environment.

There aren't any native connectors within Exchange 2007, but with the Exchange Transporter Suite for Lotus Domino, you can migrate users, groups, personal address lists, mailboxes, personal mail archives, and applications from Lotus Domino 5, 6, 7, and 9 to Exchange 2007. This suite also provides tools to migrate data from POP3 and IMAP4 servers into Exchange 2007. The Transporter Suite is not supported with Exchange 2010, so you are required to maintain at least one Exchange 2007 server in the environment to act as a bridge.

If you cannot maintain an older version of Exchange in the environment to provide these services, or perhaps additional features are needed, it may be worthwhile to investigate third-party tools.

NOTE   For a list of the independent software vendors working with Microsoft for Exchange 2010 migration tools, see http://www.microsoft.com/ exchange/2010/en/us/independent-software-vendors.aspx#migration.

Upgrading from Previous Versions of Exchange

Many organizations considering upgrading to Exchange 2010 will already be running Exchange 2003 or Exchange 2007. Upgrading from either of these versions cannot be done with an in-place upgrade and thus requires a swing migration to a new set of servers. All previous versions of Exchange must be removed from the environment before a migration begins. In general, the process for upgrading Exchange within the same forest is as follows:

Upgrade legacy servers.   Ensure that all Exchange 2003 servers in the organization have Exchange Server 2003 Service Pack 2 installed and that all servers running previous versions of Exchange Server have been removed. Also, in an Exchange 2007 environment, upgrade all Exchange 2007 servers to at least Exchange Server 2007 Service Pack 2 (SP2); however, only the CAS and Unified Messaging (UM) servers are required to have at least SP2 installed.

Prepare Exchange environment.   In an Exchange 2003 environment with multiple routing groups, link-state routing should be disabled. Exchange 2010 does not use or propagate link-state updates used by Exchange 2003; rather, it uses the queue at point of failure method to perform routing. Also, in an Exchange 2003 environment, to ensure that the Recipient Update Service (RUS) continues to function after the first Exchange 2010 server is deployed, additional permissions must be granted. This is done manually by using the `/PrepareLegacyExchangePermissions` switch for Setup or is automatically done by the Exchange 2010 setup process if the domain that contains Exchange 2003 is accessible and the user account has the appropriate permissions. If it's not done already, you must set the Exchange 2003 organization to native mode. If Exchange 2007 has already been deployed, setup will also make any required AD modifications.

Define a migration namespace.   A second namespace is needed to allow access for OWA, Outlook Anywhere, POP3, IMAP4, and Exchange ActiveSync for the legacy Exchange servers during the coexistence period. For example, if clients currently use the fully qualified name of mail.mailtask.com to access their email, an additional namespace such as legacy.mailtask.com will be needed to support the migration and coexistence process. In order for this namespace to work, new SSL certificates will need to be created that also include this new namespace. When migrating from Exchange 2003, at least one Exchange 2003 front-end server is required to provide coexistence.

1. Deploy Exchange 2010 servers to each site. Starting with the Internet-accessible sites, deploy Exchange 2010 CAS servers to the current namespace and configure the legacy servers for the legacy namespace, like legacy.mailtask.com. For more information on this process, see Chapter 13, "Designing Security and Compliance." Next, to enable mail delivery, deploy the Hub Transport servers in the site along with any required Edge Transport servers.

2. Migrate inbound and outbound email routing to use Exchange 2010 servers. After the Internet-accessible sites have Exchange 2010 servers deployed, you can migrate MX records to point to the new transport servers, modify and send connectors to send email out using the new Exchange 2010 servers, and move UM endpoints to the new UM servers.

3. Move mailboxes and public folders to Exchange Server 2010 servers. As Mailbox servers are deployed, public folder replicas can be added and mailboxes moved to the new servers. As the migration progresses, the public folder replicas can be removed from the legacy servers.

4. Upgrade custom LDAP filters to OPATH filters (Exchange 2003 only). Exchange 2003 and earlier versions use LDAP filters to define email address policies, address lists, and distribution groups. Exchange 2007 and higher use OPATH filters.

Remove the legacy Exchange servers.   Verify that all legacy servers are no longer needed, and then decommission the legacy Exchange servers. Once this is completed, there is no supported way of reintroducing legacy Exchange servers into the organization.

This process should be performed starting with the sites that are Internet-facing so that all Internet-based services are moved onto Exchange 2010 first. After the Internet-facing sites have been migrated, the non-Internet sites can be migrated. However, before just performing a one-to-one migration from the legacy servers, take time to analyze the options Exchange 2010 provides along with new hardware to consolidate and streamline the Exchange deployment design.

Planning Public Folder Coexistence and Migration

If you need to maintain public folders from Exchange 2003 to support Outlook 2003 clients because of legacy applications, or because you are still using them, the migration process is pretty straightforward. To provide access to needed public folders, replicas need to be available in the appropriate locations. This is particularly important if you have OWA users that must access public folders during the coexistence. As a rule, if a mailbox is on Exchange 2003, a replica of the public folder must exist on an Exchange 2003 server to be viewable in OWA. However, if the mailbox is on Exchange 2010, the public folder can be on an Exchange 2003 or Exchange 2010 server and still be viewable in OWA.

Maintaining Free/Busy During Coexistence

Exchange Server 2003 and earlier provides free/busy information, and the distribution of offline address books is done through the use of public folders—in particular, system folders. Starting with Exchange 2007 and continuing in Exchange 2010, the Availability service is leveraged by newer versions of Outlook and OWA. To properly maintain free/busy information during coexistence, it is important to understand the clients that the users will be leveraging to view free/busy information.

Ideally, as an Exchange administrator you would prefer that all of the users be able to leverage the latest version of Outlook to connect to your newly deployed Exchange servers. Unfortunately this doesn't always happen. If you must continue to support Outlook 2003 clients, you must also maintain the system folders that contain the free/busy information because Outlook 2003 does not use the Availability service. Table 10.1 summarizes how coexistence is achieved for free/busy when migrating from Exchange 2003 to Exchange 2010.

TABLE 10.1   Free/busy access during coexistence

Requestor Mailbox	Client	Requested Mailbox	Free/Busy Access
Exchange 2010 or Exchange 2007	Outlook 2010 or 2007	Exchange 2010 or Exchange 2007	The Availability service reads information from target mailbox.
Exchange 2010 or Exchange 2007	Outlook 2010 or 2007	Exchange 2003	The Availability service reads information from target public folders from the target server's OWA/public virtual directory.
Exchange 2010 or Exchange 2007	Outlook 2003	Exchange 2010 or Exchange 2007	Outlook retrieves free/busy information from public folders.
Exchange 2010 or Exchange 2007	Outlook 2003	Exchange 2003	Outlook retrieves free/busy information from public folders.

TABLE 10.1   Free/busy access during coexistence *(continued)*

Requestor Mailbox	Client	Requested Mailbox	Free/Busy Access
Exchange 2010 or Exchange 2007	Outlook Web App	Exchange 2010 or Exchange 2007	The Availability service reads information from target mailbox.
Exchange 2010 or Exchange 2007	Outlook Web App	Exchange 2003	The Availability service reads information from target public folders from the target servers' OWA/public virtual directory.
Exchange 2003	Any client	Exchange 2010 or Exchange 2007	Client retrieves free/busy information from public folders.

To provide free/busy information during the migration from Exchange 2003 to Exchange 2010, you must maintain the system folders until all of the mailboxes have been moved to Exchange 2010 and all clients have been upgraded to at least Outlook 2007. Also keep in mind that some third-party products that provide mobile access or calendaring information may rely on free/busy information being available. Before you remove these public folders, you should verify that these products will continue to function.

If you need to maintain the free/busy system public folders upon migrating to Exchange 2010 Mailbox servers, you should follow the public folder coexistence and migration process in the next section.

Migrating Public Folder Data

Migrating public folders is a straightforward process when migrating either from Exchange 2003 or Exchange 2007. Although not required if public folder referrals are enabled on the routing group connector, you should retain public folder content on Exchange Server 2003 servers as needed until mailboxes have been moved to Exchange Server 2010 to ensure access to the content by Exchange Server 2003 OWA users.

In Exercise 10.1, you will use the AddReplicaToPFRecursive.ps1 script to add replicas to the new Exchange 2010 public folder server.

EXERCISE 10.1

Migrating Public Folders

The following steps walk you through using the AddReplicaToPFRecursive.ps1 script to add replicas to a new Exchange 2010 public folder server, much as you would do when migrating to Exchange 2010 from Exchange 2003:

- Click Start ➤ Programs ➤ Microsoft Exchange Server 2010 and then select Exchange Management Shell.

EXERCISE 10.1 *(continued)*

- Run the following commands:

```
cd 'C:\Program Files\Microsoft\Exchange Server\v14\Scripts'
.\AddReplicaToPFRecursive.ps1 -Server EX01
-TopPublicFolder \ -ServerToAdd EX02
.\AddReplicaToPFRecursive.ps1 -TopPublicFolder
"\NON_IPM_Subtree\OFFLINE ADDRESS BOOK" -ServerToAdd EX02
.\AddReplicaToPFRecursive.ps1 -Server EX01
-TopPublicFolder "\NON_IPM_Subtree\EFORMS REGISTRY" -ServerToAdd EX02
.\AddReplicaToPFRecursive.ps1 -TopPublicFolder
"\NON_IPM_Subtree\SCHEDULE+ FREE BUSY" -ServerToAdd EX02
```

The amount of time it takes to replicate the data to the new server will depend on the amount of data that needs to be replicated. After all of the mailboxes have been moved to Exchange 2010 and all of the content has replicated, the public folder replicas can be removed from the original servers by using the `RemoveReplicaFromPFRecursive.ps1` script.

Additional information on planning public folders and determining alternatives to public folders can be found in Chapter 11, "Designing and Deploying Mailbox Services."

Migrating Offline Address Books

Another feature from Exchange Server 2003 and earlier that relies on public folders is the Offline Address Books (OAB) feature. However, starting with Exchange Server 2007, OABs also can be distributed using HTTP and Background Intelligent Transfer Service (BITS) to Outlook 2007 and newer clients from CAS servers. Primarily, this new method eliminates the need for public folders, but because of its use of BITS to transfer the data, it provides a more flexible distribution model. As in previous versions of Exchange, the client OAB types are selected and a Mailbox server is configured as the generation server; however, when an Exchange 2010 Mailbox server is configured as the generation server, you can also add the CAS servers that will be used to distribute the OAB, as shown in Figure 10.6. If you choose to generate version 2 or version 3 OABs, you will also need to enable public folder distribution.

When you install Exchange Server 2010 into an existing Exchange Server 2003 organization, the Offline Address Book will continue to be generated by the Exchange 2003 server until it is manually moved.

To begin benefiting from web-based distribution, you can assign an Exchange 2010 server to generate the OAB. However, you also need to continue to distribute the OAB to public folders until all mailboxes have been moved to Exchange 2010 and the clients have been upgraded. After all mailboxes have been moved to Exchange Server 2010, public folder distribution can be disabled.

In Exercise 10.2, you will move the OAB generation server from one Mailbox server to another using EMC.

FIGURE 10.6   OAB distribution properties

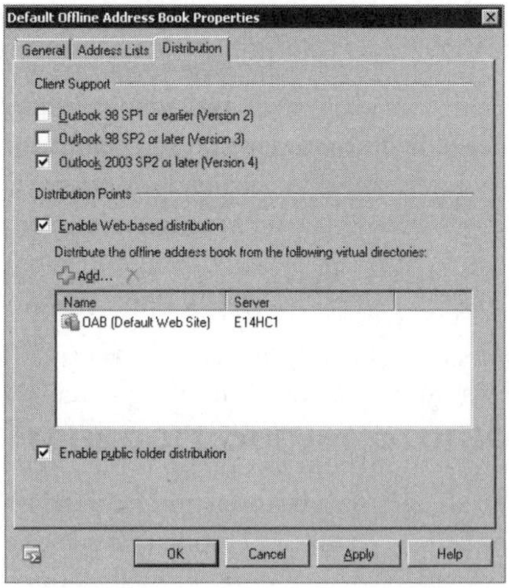

EXERCISE 10.2

Moving the OAB Generation Server

The following steps walk you through moving the OAB generation server from one Mailbox server to another, just as you would do when migrating to Exchange 2010 from Exchange 2003:

1. Click Start ➤ Programs ➤ Microsoft Exchange Server 2010 and then select Exchange Management Console.

2. Expand the Microsoft Exchange container, expand the Microsoft Exchange On-Premises container, expand the Organization Configuration container, and then click the Mailbox node.

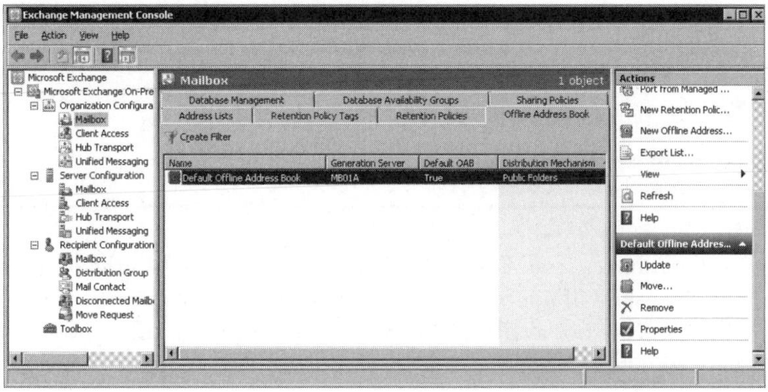

3. In the Content pane, click the Offline Address Book tab, click Default Offline Address Book, and then click Move in the Actions pane.

4. On the first page of the Move Offline Address Book Wizard, click the Browse button.

5. On the Select Mailbox Server dialog box, select EX02 and then click OK.

6. Click Move.

As with all Exchange administrative tasks, this can all be done from within EMS, which can be especially helpful when a number of OABs need to be moved from server to server. For example, to move all the OABs from EX01 to EX02 you would run the following command:

```
Get-OfflineAddressBook -Server EX01 | Move-OfflineAddressBook -Server EX02
```

Migrating Mailboxes to Exchange 2010

Moving mailboxes from Exchange 2003 or Exchange 2007 servers to Exchange 2010 involves creating local move requests. Whether the mailbox is being moved from Exchange 2003 or Exchange 2007, the local move request must be created from an Exchange 2010 server. If you are moving a mailbox from Exchange 2007, however, the mailbox can be moved online, allowing the user to stay connected to the mailbox while the contents are being moved. Table 10.2 summarizes the supported scenarios for online mailbox moves.

TABLE 10.2   Supported online mailbox moves

Moving From	Moving To	Online Moves
Exchange 2010	Exchange 2010	Yes
Exchange 2007 SP2	Exchange 2010	Yes
Exchange 2003 SP2	Exchange 2010	No
Exchange 2010	Exchange 2007 SP2	No
Exchange 2010	Exchange 2003 SP2	No

When moving mailboxes from Exchange 2003 to Exchange 2010, the process is done offline, meaning the user will not be able to access their mailbox during the move process. Because the mailboxes are not available during the move process, these moves should be scheduled to happen outside of business hours or during a maintenance window.

When a mailbox used for resource scheduling is moved from Exchange 2003 to Exchange 2010, the mailbox is converted to a shared mailbox. To take advantage of the advanced resource scheduling features of Exchange 2010, you must manually convert the mailbox to a room or an equipment mailbox. For example, suppose you have a ConferenceRm1 shared mailbox that has been moved to an Exchange 2010 Mailbox server and needs to be converted to a room mailbox. To do this, you can run `Set-Mailbox ConferenceRm1 -Type Room`.

> Moving mailboxes generates a large number of transaction logs on the destination server. Be sure to monitor free space on the Mailbox servers, especially during periods when mailboxes are being moved.

Configuring the Recipient Update Service

The Recipient Update Service fills a major role in Exchange 2003 because it ensures that all Exchange objects have the appropriate properties to work properly. This includes applying email address policies (creating email addresses) and adding objects to the right address lists. In Exchange 2010 as well as 2007, the RUS is no longer used for these tasks because its functionality is now enforced within the Exchange tasks. Because of the change in behavior, there are a number of things that must be kept in mind during the migration.

For the RUS to continue to function, it must have a target Exchange 2003 to run against. For organizations with multiple domains, an Exchange 2003 server is required in each domain to perform RUS functionality until all mailboxes have been moved to Exchange 2010. This is especially important if the environment is performing directory synchronization or using third-party applications to provision users that rely on the RUS to function properly.

Recipient Policies

In Exchange Server 2010, email address policies are applied when a change is made to a recipient object, unlike in Exchange 2003, where a policy change could be made and then not applied, or even if the changes were applied, they might not have been applied as expected due to problems with the RUS. When a mailbox is moved from Exchange 2003 to Exchange 2010, the policy will automatically be applied, which in some cases can cause changes to the email addresses. To minimize the potential for confusion, email address policies should be reviewed and applied if needed prior to moving mailboxes to Exchange Server 2010. To avoid any potential confusion relating to email address changes during the migration, many seasoned migration experts suggest clearing the Automatically Update E-Mail Addresses Based On E-Mail Address Policy option on moved mailboxes until after the move is completed so that any email address changes can be done independently from the move.

Another behavior change in Exchange 2010 and Exchange 2007 from Exchange 2003 is that the recipient policy is now separated into two features: email address policies and accepted domains. When AD is prepared for Exchange 2010, the recipient policies are evaluated and configured for use by Exchange 2010. Before running PrepareAD, be sure to evaluate the Exchange 2003 recipient policies to ensure that all authoritative domains are listed in a recipient policy and marked as authoritative. For more information, see "Exchange 2007 PrepareAD Could Interfere with Exchange 2003 Mailflow When E-Mail Address Space Is Ambiguously Nonauthoritative" at the following location:

```
http://msexchangeteam.com/archive/2008/09/05/449764.aspx
```

Converting LDAP Filters to OPATH Filters

LDAP filters are used to define distribution groups, address lists, and email address policies in Exchange 2003. However, OPATH filters in Exchange 2010 and Exchange 2007 replace the legacy LDAP filters. Exchange 2010 supports the use of LDAP filters migrated from Exchange 2003 or earlier versions, but to edit these LDAP filters from an Exchange 2010 server, the LDAP filters must be upgraded to the OPATH filter syntax.

You can determine if an object needs to be updated in two ways. The first method you can use is to attempt to modify the object using the EMC. If it has not been upgraded, you will receive an error similar to the one shown in Figure 10.7.

FIGURE 10.7 Error received when trying to modify a legacy LDAP filtered object

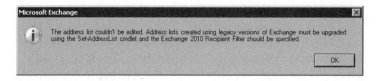

Another way to determine if the object needs to be upgraded is to use the EMS to retrieve the object details. For example, to determine which email address policies require upgrading, you can run `Get-EmailAddressPolicy | Format-List Name, *RecipientFilter*, ExchangeVersion`. If the email address policy is blank, or if `RecipientFilterType` has a value of `Legacy` or `ExchangeVersion` has a value of `0.0 (6.5.6200.0)`, the object needs to be upgraded with the OPATH syntax.

You can also determine which address lists need to be upgraded using the `Get-AddressList` and `Get-GlobalAddressList` cmdlets.

To upgrade any custom LDAP filters created, you must determine the desired results of the LDAP filter and then re-create the results with an OPATH filter. To upgrade the object, use the corresponding `Set-` cmdlet to apply the OPATH filter with the `-RecipientFilter` parameter.

In addition to any custom address lists, dynamic distribution groups, and recipient policies, in most environments the following default address lists will also need to be upgraded:

- All Users
- All Groups
- All Contacts
- Public Folders
- Default Global Address List

Because these five address lists have known LDAP filters, upgrading them with appropriate OPATH filters can be done using the following script:

```
Set-AddressList "All Users" -IncludedRecipients MailboxUsers
Set-AddressList "All Groups" -IncludedRecipients MailGroups
Set-AddressList "All Contacts" -IncludedRecipients MailContacts
Set-AddressList "PublicFolders" -RecipientFilter
{ RecipientType -eq 'PublicFolder' }
Set-GlobalAddressList "Default Global Address List"
-RecipientFilter {(Alias -ne $null -and (ObjectClass
-eq 'user' -or ObjectClass -eq 'contact' -or ObjectClass
-eq 'msExchSystemMailbox' -or ObjectClass -eq
'msExchDynamicDistributionList' -or ObjectClass -eq 'group' -or ObjectClass -eq
'publicFolder'))}
```

Also available is the LDAP-to-OPATH conversion script that has been published by the Microsoft Exchange product group. You can read about the script in the article "Need Help Converting Your LDAP Filters to OPATH?" at the following location:

```
http://msexchangeteam.com/archive/2007/03/12/436983.aspx
```

Planning Unified Messaging Server Coexistence

If you have Exchange 2007 UM already deployed, you can deploy the first Exchange 2010 UM server and then add it to an existing UM dial plan that contains Exchange 2007 UM servers. The second step is to configure each IP gateway to send incoming calls to the new Exchange 2010 UM servers.

This configuration allows the incoming call to be received from the Exchange 2010 UM server and then processed if the UM-enabled mailbox resides on an Exchange 2010 Mailbox server. However, if the user's mailbox is located on an Exchange 2007 Mailbox server, the incoming call is redirected to be processed by an Exchange 2007 UM server within the same UM dial plan. When all UM-enabled mailboxes have been migrated to Exchange 2010, the Exchange 2007 UM servers can be removed from the UM dial plan and then uninstalled.

Removing Legacy Exchange Servers

As you deploy new Exchange 2010 servers in each site and move resources, you can decommission the legacy servers in each site. When removing Exchange 2007 servers, remove them in the following order to ensure that any required functionality is maintained:

1. Mailbox servers. After all mailboxes, public folders, and OABs have been moved to Exchange 2010, the Mailbox server can be decommissioned.

2. Unified Messaging servers. After all UM-enabled mailboxes have been moved to Exchange 2010, these servers can be removed.

3. Hub Transport servers. After all connectors have been moved to Exchange 2010, these servers can then be removed.

4. Client Access servers. After all other servers have been removed from the site, these servers can be removed.

> For more information on removing the last Exchange 2003 server from the environment, see "How to Remove the Last Legacy Exchange Server from an Organization" at `http://technet.microsoft.com/en-us/library/bb288905(EXCHG.80).aspx`.

🌐 Real World Scenario

Deploying Exchange 2010 in a Legacy Environment

Deploying Exchange 2010 into an Exchange 2003 environment can be a challenging task. Over the years, different administrators and professionals that have worked on the messaging environment have come and gone and best practices have gone in and out of vogue. It is too easy to assume that the system in place is correctly configured or that all issues have already been discovered.

During one Exchange migration, it was discovered that at one time there had been two Exchange servers with the same name deployed into different sites. Although one of the servers had been removed, the server object was still in the directory. Doing a thorough discovery of the environment and reviewing the Exchange Best Practices Analyzer and the Exchange Pre-Deployment Analyzer may have provided details about this problem before it was discovered during the migration.

Although not all problems can be caught in advance, spend an adequate amount of time gathering information about the environment. Be sure to compare the information gathered about the environment with what is expected to see if there are any gaps. By doing this, you will save hours of frustration and lost user productivity.

After you deploy Exchange 2010 into each site and resources are migrated off the legacy servers, you need to ensure that you have migrated everything before you finalize the shutdown of the last servers. Use the following checklist before deciding to remove the last legacy server from your organization:

1. Verify that all third-party applications have been migrated.

2. Verify that all mailboxes and public folders have been migrated.

3. Move the public folder hierarchy to the Exchange 2010 administrative group.

4. Verify that all OABs have been moved to Exchange 2010.

5. Verify that all connectors have been moved to Exchange 2010 and that messages are following a known path.

6. Verify that clients are able to connect via supported protocols and that they are leveraging the correct servers. For example, check Exchange ActiveSync, Autodiscover, EWS, OWA, Outlook Anywhere, and others.

7. Delete public folder stores from Exchange 2003 servers.

8. Delete routing group connectors.

9. Remove legacy recipient policies that are no longer needed, such as, for example, those policies used for Mailbox Manager settings.

10. Delete the RUS domain instance.

11. Uninstall Exchange 2003 from the last Exchange 2003 server.

12. Delete the RUS enterprise instance.

Summary

Before you even start to install the first Exchange Server 2010 server, many items need your time and consideration. Taking the time to design, and prepare your organization properly for, the introduction of Exchange Server 2010 will yield positive results, regardless of whether this is an upgrade/coexistence scenario with legacy versions of Exchange or a completely new installation of Exchange Server 2010.

When introducing a new version of Exchange into an established environment, there are a lot of things that can go wrong. To reduce complications and to ensure that the right expectations are set and then met, use an operational framework like MOF or ITIL. These frameworks will help create a process that is repeatable and can be tracked.

Exchange is tightly integrated with AD, and as such requires that certain levels of service are met within the infrastructure. As part of the deployment process, audit the name resolution configuration, define a suitable namespace, and plan a site topology that meets the needs of the business.

Most environments that Exchange 2010 will be deployed into already have a messaging system deployed. Exchange 2010 will natively coexist with only Exchange 2003 and Exchange 2007. All older versions of Exchange must be removed. Also, if there are third-party email systems in place, these may require that older versions of Exchange are maintained or that other products and services be purchased to provide that coexistence. Exchange 2010 can coexist with Exchange 2003 and Exchange 2007, but you must plan to maintain public folders, free/busy information, Offline Address Books, and other services during the coexistence period.

Chapter Essentials

Follow a process.   When making changes like deploying a new version of Exchange, you need an operational framework to define the process. These frameworks, among other things, help set and meet expectations for the deployment.

Define the topology.   Exchange Server 2010 requires that the infrastructure be configured in a certain way. There is flexibility in the options available to allow for small and large organizations to deploy a workable Exchange solution. Be sure to review the DNS, AD, and namespace requirements for Exchange to best understand any changes that need to be made for a successful deployment.

Understand coexistence options.   Many Exchange 2010 deployments will be upgrades from either Exchange 2003 or Exchange 2007. The migration path from Exchange 2003 to Exchange 2010 differs slightly from the path from Exchange 2007 to Exchange 2010. Understand the overall steps in the coexistence and migration process.

Chapter

11

Designing and Deploying Mailbox Services

THE FOLLOWING TOPICS ARE DISCUSSED IN THIS CHAPTER:

✓ Designing the Mailbox server role

✓ Deploying the Mailbox server role

The Mailbox server role is a core component of the Exchange infrastructure, and it requires a great deal of planning to ensure that the configuration meets the needs of the users and will continue into the near future. Exchange 2010 introduces some welcome improvements that help reduce the cost and complexity of designing and deploying Mailbox servers.

Designing Mailbox Services

Although properly designing other server roles is an important aspect of a properly sized Exchange environment, the Mailbox server design tends to be the most difficult and expensive. In both Exchange 2007 and Exchange 2010, a number of improvements have been made to Mailbox servers that reduce the cost of the storage that is needed to support large mailboxes and reduce the services provided by the servers.

Understanding the Exchange Storage Structure

Before we get to some of the details of deploying the Mailbox server role, we'll discuss the Exchange storage structure and provide some important fundamentals.

Reviewing Exchange Databases

Mailbox servers contain databases that hold either mailbox or public folder data. Within these databases reside all the messages and other content items that exist within both the email and public folder items of the organization. Each database in Exchange Server 2010 consists of a single *rich-text (EDB)* file. By default, Exchange Server 2010 creates the first database for you.

In Exchange 2000 Server and Exchange Server 2003, the database is made up of two files: a streaming media file (.stm) that contains email received in Multipurpose Internet Mail Extensions (MIME) format and the familiar Extensible Storage Engine, or ESE (.edb), and B-tree database file that stores MAPI-formatted messages. Exchange Server 2007 and Exchange Server 2010 use only a single ESE file that stores all messages in MAPI format and only converts to and from Internet formats when needed.

Reviewing Exchange Databases and Related Files

Exchange Server 2010 Enterprise Edition allows up to 100 databases to be mounted on a single server. Exchange Server 2010 Standard Edition allows for up to five databases to be mounted.

Each database is a single instance of the Extensible Storage Engine (ESE) and has a single set of transaction log files. Whenever a transaction occurs on the database, the change is recorded in memory and then to a transaction log file . Data is written to these log files sequentially as transactions occur. Later, regular database maintenance routines commit changes in the logs to the database files. As a result, the most current state of an Exchange service is represented by the EDB file along with all of the current log files.

Checkpoint files are used to keep track of the transaction logs that are committed to the database. The checkpoint file ensures that transactions cannot be committed to a database more than once. Checkpoint files are named `Exx.chk` and normally reside in the same directories as the transaction log files. Transaction logs that have been committed to the database are cleared during a database backup. You can see the checkpoint file, log files, and other database files in Figure 11.1.

FIGURE 11.1 Mailbox database files

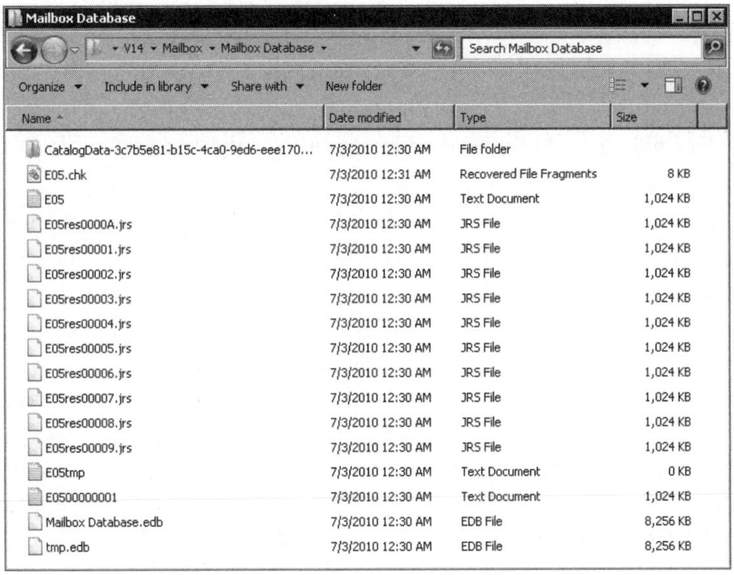
Mailbox Database
V14 ▸ Mailbox ▸ Mailbox Database
Search Mailbox Database
Organize
Include in library
Share with
New folder
Name
Date modified
Type
Size
CatalogData-3c7b5e81-b15c-4ca0-9ed6-eee170... 7/3/2010 12:30 AM File folder
E05.chk 7/3/2010 12:31 AM Recovered File Fragments 8 KB
E05 7/3/2010 12:30 AM Text Document 1,024 KB
E05res0000A.jrs 7/3/2010 12:30 AM JRS File 1,024 KB
E05res00001.jrs 7/3/2010 12:30 AM JRS File 1,024 KB
E05res00002.jrs 7/3/2010 12:30 AM JRS File 1,024 KB
E05res00003.jrs 7/3/2010 12:30 AM JRS File 1,024 KB
E05res00004.jrs 7/3/2010 12:30 AM JRS File 1,024 KB
E05res00005.jrs 7/3/2010 12:30 AM JRS File 1,024 KB
E05res00006.jrs 7/3/2010 12:30 AM JRS File 1,024 KB
E05res00007.jrs 7/3/2010 12:30 AM JRS File 1,024 KB
E05res00008.jrs 7/3/2010 12:30 AM JRS File 1,024 KB
E05res00009.jrs 7/3/2010 12:30 AM JRS File 1,024 KB
E05tmp 7/3/2010 12:30 AM Text Document 0 KB
E0500000001 7/3/2010 12:30 AM Text Document 1,024 KB
Mailbox Database.edb 7/3/2010 12:30 AM EDB File 8,256 KB
tmp.edb 7/3/2010 12:30 AM EDB File 8,256 KB

TIP

Using multiple databases allows you to plan your organization's data storage by classifying various types of data or assigning separate databases to different types of users.

The function of each type of file shown in Figure 11.1 is as follows:

Exx.chk   The checkpoint file is named with the log file prefix, such as E00 for the first database, E01 for the second database, and so on. The checkpoint file contains a record of which logs have been committed to the Exchange database and which transaction logs still remain to be committed.

Exx.log   This file is the active transaction log (the file to which data is actively being written) for the database indicated by the number. When this transaction log contains 1,024 KB of changes or is closed, it will be renamed with the next sequential number for the database. A new Exx.log file will then be created, and transactions will be written to it until the file reaches the maximum size or otherwise closed.

Exxhhhhhhhh.log   These are older transaction log files and are named with the log prefix, such as E01, followed by an eight-character hexadecimal number. Thus, you would have E0100000001.log as the first log file for the second database on the server. The numbers 1 through 0 and the letters *A* through *F* are used in the hexadecimal numbering system. The file size will always be 1,024 KB.

Exxres00001.jrs and Exxres00002.jrs   These two files are reserve transaction log files and serve only as emergency storage if the volume the logs are located on becomes full. If the volume does become full, the transactions currently being processed are written to disk and the databases on that volume are dismounted. By having two reserved transaction logs, Exchange can reduce the possibility that transactions are lost during this process. These files will always be 1,024 KB.

Exxtmp.log   This file serves as the transaction log file for the Tmp.edb workspace. This file will never be larger than 1,024 KB.

name.edb   This file is the B-tree database file. In Figure 11.1, it was named Mailbox Database, but you will see different names in your organization over time for each mailbox and public folder database file.

Tmp.edb   This file is a temporary workspace for processing active transactions. This file is typically only a few megabytes in size and will be deleted automatically when all databases are dismounted or the Microsoft Exchange information store process has stopped.

Database transactions are always first committed to the transaction logs and then written into the actual database file. Transaction log files are typically read or written sequentially, whereas database access is almost always random. By placing the transaction logs on one physical volume and the database files on another physical volume, you'll improve recoverability of the database because a single disk failure will not cause loss of both sets of files.

In Exchange 2010, the database schema, or the layout of the data in the database, has been overhauled to reduce the I/O requirements. In all previous versions of Exchange, each database has an attachment, a folder, a mailbox, and a message table where information is stored for all of the mailboxes in the database. Also, every folder in every mailbox has a separate table that stores the contents of the folder. This design provides single instance storage, where messages and attachments that existed in multiple mailboxes in the same database need to be stored only once. This single instance storage reduces the storage space required and was particularly beneficial when Exchange servers had only a few expensive 2 GB SCSI disk drives to store all the messaging data.

Over the years, the amount of data and how people use messaging services has increased the size and storage I/O requirements for mailboxes. As a result, the cost of the storage systems which will be able to meet these needs had become the major concern with most Exchange Server 2003 deployments. Thankfully, the storage improvements in Exchange 2007 and Exchange 2010 have reduced the need for expensive high-speed storage area network (SAN) storage. These changes improve performance while removing the single instance storage feature.

Reviewing Storage Technology

We will do a brief review of storage technology so you can better understand the storage choices available for your Exchange servers. Fibre Channel (FC) disks provide very high performance with good density and are usually reserved for deployment in a SAN; therefore, an FC deployment can be more expensive than other options. Serial Attached SCSI (SAS) is similar in performance to FC, but it is usually used in less-expensive SAN-based storage or for direct attached disks. Serial Advanced Technology Attachments (SATA) disks provide a higher density at a lower cost than the other storage options, but this sort of disk does not perform as well for random read and write operations. Each of the disk drive technologies with spinning media reads and writes data continuously faster than it is able to read and write data randomly. Solid state drives (SSDs) do not use spinning media and are not limited in this fashion; however, because SSDs have a much higher cost per gigabyte, using them for database storage is usually cost prohibitive.

Exchange 2010 introduces an updated database schema that is optimized to perform well on lower-cost storage technologies. Rather than attempting to minimize the database size using single instance storage and trying to write data tightly within the database file, the new schema attempts to store data contiguously. Storing data within the database contiguously along with making performance adjustments such as gap coalescing, on-demand view updates, write smoothing, and improved caching tunes the storage I/O to net a significant reduction in the I/O requirements compared to all previous versions of Exchange.

Determining Mailbox Server Hardware Requirements

Determining the hardware required for a Mailbox server isn't as simple as looking at a chart and picking the correct configuration. Each Exchange user will have different messaging patterns, so each deployment is unique in that way. The hardware-sizing process is as follows:

1. Identifying the Exchange usage profile
2. Creating a configuration
3. Validating the configuration

Identifying the Exchange Usage Profile

Identify the usage patterns of the users that will be deployed on Exchange 2010. You can use tools such as the Exchange Profile Analyzer (EPA) along with performance metric gathering tools like Performance Monitor to create the profile information. The user usage profile is a compilation of information such as the average number and size of email messages sent and received each day, the average and maximum size of each mailbox, and the type and version of client software used.

The EPA tool is used to analyze an Exchange server that is already in production. If you are upgrading from a previous version to Exchange 2010, you can run EPA against the current legacy Exchange servers to gather information about your Exchange users. EPA gathers the following statistics for each scanned mailbox:

- Number of email messages received per day

- Number of email messages sent per day

- Number of items in the mailbox

- Number of inbox rules

- Sizes of items

To run EPA, you need a user account with permissions to open each of the mailboxes you will scan with the tool. Because EPA opens each mailbox and scans the contents to create the detailed report, the scan is time consuming and resource intensive. You will likely not be able to run EPA against all mailboxes in your enterprise. However, you should run it against a number of mailboxes to obtain a representative average of your users. In an environment with 10,000 mailboxes, you would not just use EPA to report against the largest 20 mailboxes because this would no doubt result in an average profile heavier than the actual average for your environment.

You may, however, choose to create multiple profiles that represent the various departments within your environment. You may create an average profile for users in the engineering, operations, accounting, marketing, information technology, and other departments because each set of users will no doubt use Exchange differently. Each of those profiles can then be used as an input into the configuration tools.

After EPA completes a scan, it will create a report similar to the one shown in Figure 11.2.

Along with the EPA information, other aspects of the usage profile can be gathered using a performance monitoring tool like Performance Monitor. To determine the average CPU, memory, and I/O operations per second (IOPS) required per mailbox, you monitor the currently deployed legacy Exchange servers. Although you can expect that these averages will change when the users are migrated to Exchange 2010, this will provide a baseline for you to compare usage metrics during the configuration validation and after deployment.

If you do not have Exchange server currently deployed and you plan to move to Exchange 2010 from another messaging system, this usage information cannot be calculated the same way. That doesn't necessarily mean that it cannot be gathered. Third parties make reporting tools for some messaging systems that can gather information that is similar to the information reported by EPA and thus provide you with the information you need.

FIGURE 11.2 Viewing an Exchange Profile Analyzer report

Microsoft Exchange Server Profile Analyzer
Microsoft Exchange Server Profile Analyzer
Windows Server System
Welcome
Connect to Active Directory
Configuration
Status
View a report
About
View Profile Analyzer Report...
Aggregate of mailbox size:
avg: 43,592.75
min: 35,083.00
max: 63,018.00
Total count: 4
Total size: 174,371.00
Rules
Folder Hierarchy
Folder Size
Aggregates of folder size across all folders:
avg: 3,790.67
min: 0
max: 38,835.00
Size of various system folders:
inbox: 107,503.00
deleteditems: 6,344.00
outbox: 0
sentitems: 60,469.00
©2007 Microsoft Corporation. All rights reserved.
Microsoft

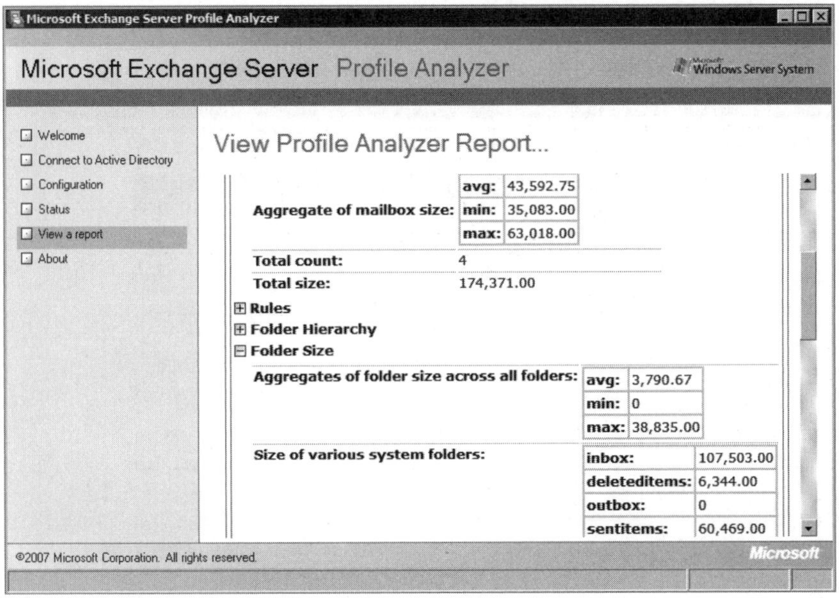

Creating a Configuration

Create an Exchange configuration using the Exchange 2010 Mailbox Server Role Requirements Calculator and vendor-specific sizing tools. Using the profile information gathered in the first step, you can adjust the tools to estimate a configuration for your environment.

NOTE You can download the latest Exchange 2010 Mailbox Server Role Requirements Calculator from the Exchange product team blog at `http://msexchangeteam.com/archive/2009/11/09/453117.aspx`.

The Exchange 2010 Mailbox Server Role Requirements Calculator is a spreadsheet-based tool created and supported by the Microsoft Exchange product group that generates a Mailbox server configuration. On the Input tab, as shown in Figure 11.3 of the tool, you are required to provide details about the users and environment.

After you have added your information to the Input tab, other tabs provide information about the suggested configuration. The Storage Design tab provides selections to pick the disk types and sizes that you will use in your configuration. As shown in Figure 11.4, the Role Requirements tab displays information about the number of servers and database copies. The Logical Unit Number (LUN) Requirements tab displays information on how the LUNs should be sized. The Backup Requirements tab displays information about the how backups should be configured in the environment.

FIGURE 11.3 Exchange 2010 Mailbox Server Role Requirements Calculator

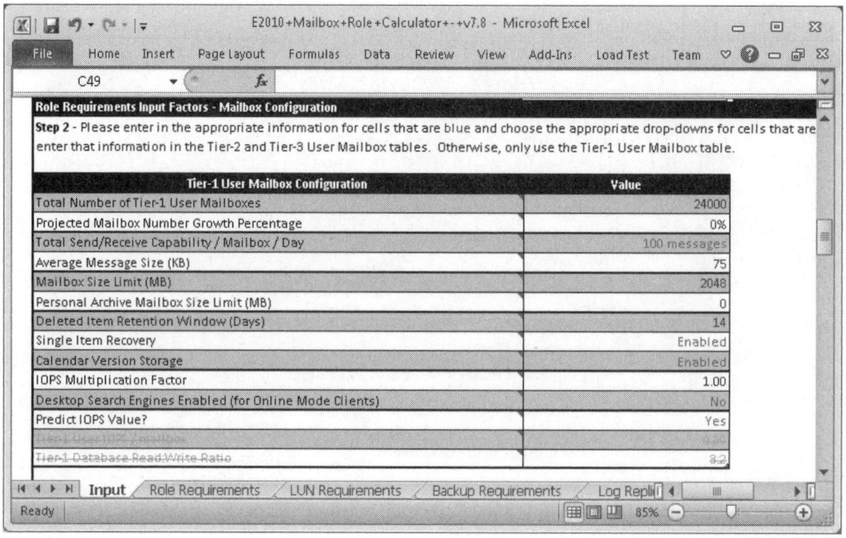

FIGURE 11.4 Role Requirements tab

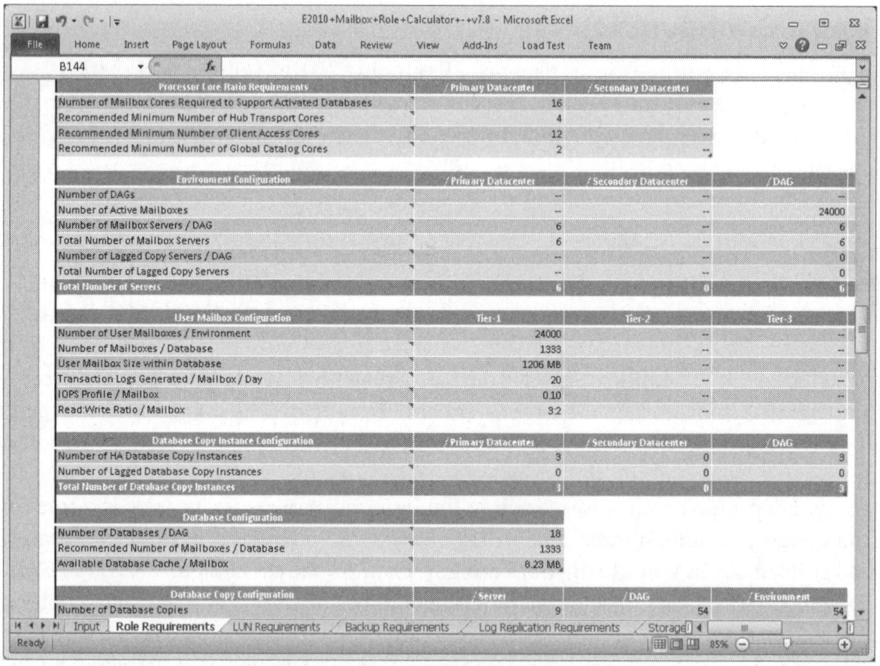

Many hardware vendors also have tools that create Exchange configurations using their hardware. If your hardware vendor has such a tool, you can use both the vendor tool and the Exchange 2010 Mailbox Server Role Requirements Calculator and compare the suggested configurations to create a configuration based on both solutions.

Validating the Configuration

Rather than just hoping that the configurations that you have created work as expected, you can test to validate that the configuration will work in your environment before you deploy the servers. Tools such as Jetstress and Exchange Load Generator are available to simulate load against the Exchange Server hardware that has been chosen to validate performance before Exchange is put into production. Any needed configuration adjustments can be made based on the test results.

Using Jetstress

Jetstress is a tool that simulates the storage I/O generated by the Exchange databases. This tool can perform three types of tests: performance, database backup, and soft recovery. The performance configuration tests a specific mailbox usage profile or it can perform a throughput test. The throughput test should be used to test storage reliability and to determine the storage performance limits. The database backup and soft recovery modes allow storage performance testing. Running Jetstress does not require Exchange to be installed on the server. It only requires that you copy ese.dll, eseperf.dll, eseperf.ini, and eseperf.hxx from the Exchange installation files.

Figure 11.5 shows the configuration of a performance test based on a mailbox profile. After defining a test profile, you must define the length of time the test will run, the output location for the test results, and the disk configuration. The disk configuration defines the number and the location of the database and transaction log files that will be used to complete the test. If you have previously used Jetstress in this configuration, you will have the option to attach or restore previously used test databases, or you can create new databases for this test.

Once the test has been configured, the test will run for the duration selected. At the end of the test, several files will be place in the output folder. There will be an XML file with raw data from the test, a copy of the application event log from the duration of the test, a copy of the system event log from the duration of the test, and most notable, an HTML report summarizing the results. The detailed results should be reviewed by the group or person responsible for maintaining the storage systems.

Using Exchange Load Generator

Exchange Load Generator is a tool used to simulate client activities against a configured set of Exchange servers prior to deploying the solution in production. Exchange Load Generator can simulate Outlook in cached Exchange mode and online mode, and it can simulate POP3 clients, IMAP4 clients, Exchange ActiveSync clients, and Outlook Web App (OWA) clients. As with Jetstress, you can configure and customize user profiles that will simulate sending and receiving email messages, deleting messages, and creating appointments. As with any testing tool, the closer you can tune the tests to mimic your production environment, the closer the test results will mirror it. If you are simulating over several thousand client connections,

Exchange Load Generator can coordinate multiple client machines to add additional client connections.

FIGURE 11.5 Configuring an Exchange mailbox profile in Jetstress

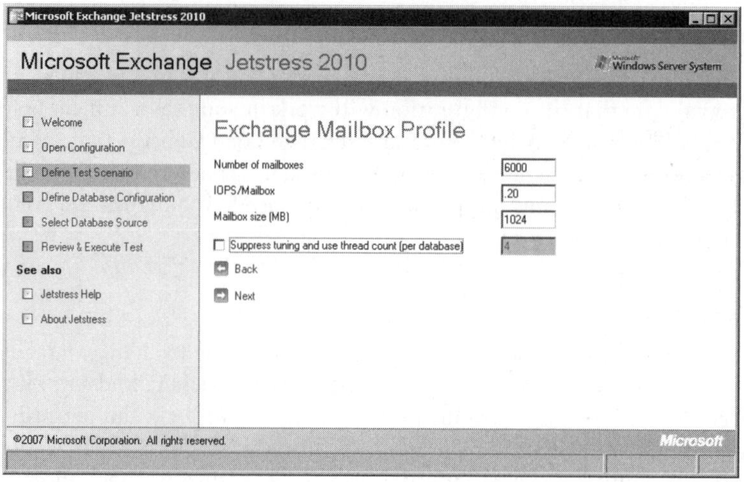

Because Exchange Load Generator simulates client connectivity, the tool creates mailboxes, distribution groups, and contacts to set up the test environment. Exchange Load Generator should be used in a test environment that is isolated from the production environment.

To determine the effects of the tests, Exchange Load Generator provides performance counters that can be gathered on the client machines. To get detailed views of the tests, however, you should also capture performance metrics from the Exchange servers using a tool like Performance Monitor.

After you have validated the performance of your hardware, you can deploy the solution into production.

Determining Whether to Deploy Public Folders

Public folders have been de-emphasized since the introduction of Exchange 2007. This means that although public folders are supported, you should not expect any new functionality to be created around their use. You should also expect that in a future version of Exchange, public folders will be discontinued. Because public folders are supported, you can continue to use them inside your organization; however, careful consideration should be given when deploying a new use for public folders. Table 11.1 summarizes the key uses for public folders and when other solutions should be considered.

In many cases, Microsoft SharePoint can be considered as an option for sharing documents and for developing custom intranet or workflow applications. SharePoint provides a much richer platform for document sharing because it includes document locking and versioning, and with the introduction of SharePoint 2010, it now includes the Office Web Apps to allow viewing and editing of documents directly within the site.

Some companies use public folders by creating custom Outlook forms that can be published and then used for workflow applications, time sheets, and so on. If you are already using such a solution, it will continue to work with Exchange 2010. If not, you should consider using InfoPath and SharePoint to create the solution.

SharePoint can be used for shared calendars and contacts. Email sent to distribution lists can be archived by creating a shared mailbox, a public folder, or an email-enabled SharePoint library. A discussion forum can be created in a public folder or by using SharePoint.

TABLE 11.1   Deciding when to use public folders

Use	Already Deployed	New Deployment
Intranet applications	Consider SharePoint	Consider SharePoint
Shared documents	Consider SharePoint	Deploy SharePoint
Shared calendars and contacts	No requirement to move	Use shared mailboxes, public folders, or SharePoint
Forum	No requirement to move	Use SharePoint or public folders
Email archive	No requirement to move	Use shared mailboxes, public folders, or SharePoint
Organizational forms	No requirement to move	Use InfoPath and/or SharePoint

Defining Naming Conventions

Naming conventions can be used to bring order and predictability to a messaging environment. Having a naming standard for servers, connectors, address lists, public folders, mailboxes, distribution lists, databases, contacts, database availability groups, and all other objects within the environment reduces confusion when supporting the environment. Even in smaller environments, naming standards help to improve the overall management experience. The next several sections discuss options for defining naming standards for different parts of the environment.

Selecting Server Names

When standards are created and followed, server locations and roles can be made apparent, thus allowing new employees or temporary workers to spend less time learning or looking up information. Many large companies will use a couple of different attributes to create a server name, such as the location, server role, department, or customer that owns the server and a number to provide for multiple servers with the same function at the same location. Although Exchange 2010 does not require it, if you need to support Windows Internet Naming Service (WINS) in your environment, be sure to keep server names at 15 or fewer characters.

The location could be the name of the city (or the abbreviation) or the local airport code. Location identifiers such as postal codes or telephone area codes tend to change more often than the city name, so transient identifiers should be avoided. If there is a possibility of having multiple locations in the same city or multiple cities with similar logical abbreviations, a tie breaker should be included. For example, a company that will be deploying servers in many locations may choose the following standard:

< first two letters of the city name><two-letter state or province abbreviation> <single-number tie breaker><server role><three-letter tie breaker>

For a multiple-role Exchange server located in the first location in Dallas, Texas, the server name would be DATX1EXC001. For a database availability group (DAG) member server in the same location, the name would be DATX1MBX001A, and the second DAG member would be DATX1MBX001B. Using letters to differentiate DAG members helps to easily identity all of the members of a DAG. Table 11.2 includes some suggested server role abbreviations.

TABLE 11.2 Exchange-related server name abbreviations

Role	Two-Letter Abbreviation	Three-Letter Abbreviation
Client Access	CA	CAS
Edge Transport	ET	EDG
Hub Transport	HT	HUB
Mailbox	MB	MBX
Multiple roles	EX	EXC
Unified Messaging	UM	UMS

Selecting Database Names

Exchange 2010 requires that all database names in the organization be unique. When databases are deployed within a DAG, databases copies can be created on all of the members of the DAG. You may choose to name databases based on the contents, the location of the primary copy, or the mailbox limits assigned. Here are some examples of database names:

- DAG001MB001
- DATX1DAG01MB001
- DATX1DAG02MBAAA
- DATX1EXC001MB01
- MIAMI-MB001

Defining Usernames

Defining username and display name conventions is important for several reasons. First, users find other users in the global address book by using display names. Some companies prefer to list employees with the last name (surname) first in the address list. Proponents of this method say that this works better for the following reasons:

- First names are often shortened and difficult to find. For example, Michael may be listed as Mike in the address list, making it slightly more complicated to find.
- There are often more people with a common first name than people with a common last name. Sorting by last name makes sorting through the list of people easier.

Others feel that it is far easier to find people using their first name. By default, display names are created with the first name followed by the last name, which makes this the easier option. When there are duplicates, display names can be modified to designate which John Smith works in which department to make it easier for users to distinguish them in the address list.

Dealing with email addresses and login names can be a little more complicated. A common naming convention that includes a combination of first initial and last name or first initial, middle initial, and last name will help avoid many possible username issues when users have the same first or last name. If the naming convention is to use the first initial and the last name, both Jim Smith and John Smith would assume that their user name and alias might be jsmith. The solution might be to use the first two letters of their first names so that their aliases would be jismith and josmith. If there is another Jeff or another John or maybe a Jesse or Joan, another standard would be needed. To alleviate this potential problem, you may choose to use numbers to provide a tie breaker. The first alias in the example would be jsmith01 and the second jsmith02; this allows up to 99 user accounts with same name first initial and last name.

Rather than following a strict naming convention that treats all as equal, you may choose to not have a ridged naming convention. You may choose email addresses and logon names with a nonstandard combination of the first, middle, and last name. Using this method would allow Jeff Smith to use jeffs, jeffsmith, jesmith, jeffsmi, or some other amalgamation of letters depending on which alias is available. One reason this nonstandard convention works is that an outside user cannot just guess that Jeff Smith's alias is jsmith. This can reduce unsolicited email. This also works in some situations because it is flexible and generally fair to all users.

In Exchange 2010 SP1, the New Mailbox Wizard no longer requires a mailbox alias to be manually assigned. The wizard will derive the alias from the other information you entered.

Provisioning Mailboxes

After deciding on the naming convention for the mailboxes, the next important decision to make is how to provision mailboxes. You can find the steps for creating mailboxes and mailbox databases in Chapter 4, "Managing Exchange Server 2010 Mail-Enabled Objects."

Rather than putting all mailboxes in a single database, creating multiple databases has the following benefits:

- A single database failure will impact fewer mailboxes because mailboxes are in multiple databases.

- A database restore is faster because each database is smaller.

- Databases can be used to organize mailboxes.

- Databases can be used to define mailbox limits rather than applying limits directly to each mailbox.

Creating multiple mailbox databases reduces the size of each database, and as a result, the time needed to back up and restore each database. This will reduce the time it takes to return missing data to the affected users. Having more and smaller databases also reduces the number of mailboxes in each database, meaning that a problem affecting a single mailbox will affect fewer users.

 For more information about working with Exchange mail-enabled objects, see Chapter 4, "Managing Exchange Server 2010 Mail-Enabled Objects." For more information about configuring address lists, see Chapter 6, "Configuring Security, Compliance, and Policies."

🌐 Real World Scenario

Organizing Mailboxes for Special Users

In every company it is expected that a certain group of people (for example, executives) will never have any problems with anything. At first blush, you may choose to place all of these important users' mailboxes in a single mailbox database with multiple copies and thereby be able to make sure the mailboxes are always online. There is, however, another way to look at providing the best service to these users, and that is to randomly assign these mailboxes across the available databases, thereby affecting fewer users in the case of a failure. Managing the rapid recovery of only one or two of these special users is far easier than having to restore 100 mailboxes if the special user database goes offline.

Many Exchange administrators will suggest separating mailboxes in databases based on size, service levels, or user location to organize them. Organizing mailboxes this way can simplify capacity planning because the distribution of mailboxes follows a known pattern. When all mailboxes with the same service-level agreement (SLA) are hosted in the same database, you can easily identify the SLA and size limits for each mailbox. For example, Mailtask has 25,000 mailboxes. There are 100 mailboxes with 5 GB limits and an SLA that allows for only 4 hours of unplanned downtime each year for the company executives. These mailboxes are distributed in five mailbox databases, each with three high availability copies and one lagged copy within the DAG. The remaining 24,900 mailboxes have a limit of 500 MB and an SLA that allows for up to 32 hours of downtime a year. These mailboxes are deployed with only two highly available copies and are backed up using backup software. If the mailboxes were not separated into different databases, it would be difficult to provide the two distinct levels of service.

Deploying the Mailbox Server Role

Once you make the decisions about the design and the standards that will be used, you can deploy the Mailbox server.

Installation Prerequisites

Installing the Exchange Mailbox role is similar to installing the other server roles. The minimum requirements for installing the Exchange roles are summarized in Table 11.3.

TABLE 11.3   Minimum Exchange Server hardware requirements

Component	Requirement
Disk space	At least 1.2 GB available on the installation drive. A minimum of 200 MB of available disk space is required on the system drive. Additional storage separate from the system and program drives should be used to store the databases.
File format	The system partition and partitions that store Exchange binary files, transaction log files, database files, and any other Exchange files should be formatted with NTFS.
Memory	A minimum of 2 GB of RAM is recommended; additional memory as needed.
Processor	Must have x64 architecture-based computer with Intel processor that supports Intel 64 architecture (formerly known as Intel EM64T) or AMD processor that supports the AMD64 platform. Intel Itanium IA64 processors are not supported.
Screen resolution	The screen resolution used to perform the installation should be at least 800x600 pixels to allow you to properly view the installation and management tools.

The software requirements for the Exchange Server computers again depend on the role that will be installed on the server; however, there are a number of common requirements that must be met. The software requirements for the Exchange Mailbox server role are as follows:

- A 64-bit version of Windows Server 2008 Standard Edition with Service Pack 2 or higher, including Windows Server 2008 R2 Standard Edition.

- Microsoft .NET Framework 3.5 SP1

- Windows PowerShell 2.0

- Windows Remote Management

- Microsoft Filter Pack (Version 1.0 is required for the initial release of Exchange 2010; however, version 2.0 is required when deploying Exchange 2010 SP1.)

Windows Server 2008 R2 includes the .NET Framework, Windows PowerShell 2.0, and Windows Remote Management as native features that just need to be enabled. On Windows Server 2008, these components need to be downloaded and installed. When deploying Exchange on either Windows Server 2008 or Windows Server 2008 R2, you will need to enable additional features. If using the Exchange 2010 SP1 installation media, setup has an option to automatically install the prerequisites, as shown in Figure 11.6.

FIGURE 11.6   Enabling Exchange setup to automatically install prerequisites

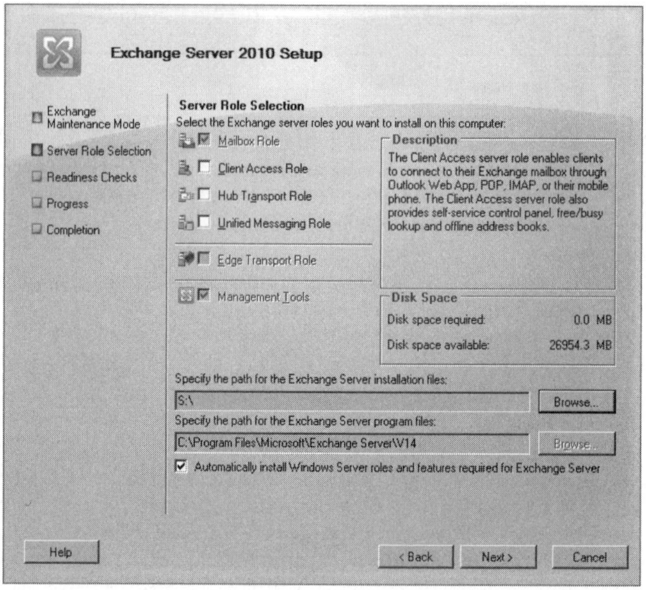

Additional information about manually installing the operating system components can be found at Exchange 2010 Prerequisites: Exchange 2010 Help at http://technet.microsoft.com/en-us/library/bb691354.aspx.

Sizing Mailbox Server Hardware

Determining how to size a Mailbox server is predominantly based on the mailbox count and the user profile. This profile includes the number, type, and size of messages sent and received and can also include the average storage I/O requirements.

Determining Memory Requirements

The basic requirement for a Mailbox server is 4 GB of RAM if there are 20 or fewer database copies hosted on the server; for every 10 additional database copies, another 2 GB of RAM is required. In any case, additional memory is recommended to provide RAM for the mailbox database cache, which is used to cache database I/O operations. Having ample mailbox database cache will minimize the required storage I/O. Sizing this cache is one of the more complicated Exchange sizing tasks.

A simple way to estimate the mailbox database cache requirements is to multiply the number of mailbox copies and the average I/O calculated for each mailbox and then multiply that number by 50 MB/IOP (for example, 2,500 mailboxes × .180 IOPS/mailbox × 50 MB/IOPS = 22,500 MB).

 If you do not have the exact IOPS requirements, see the Estimated IOPS Per Mailbox Based On Message Activity And Mailbox Database Cache table at http://technet.microsoft.com/en-us/library/ee832793.aspx.

After you determine the amount of mailbox database cache you need, you must determine the amount of total physical memory required. Using Table 11.4, you can see that to provide 22,500 MB of cache for the preceding example, the physical server should have 32,522 GB of memory to provide 24.4 GB of mailbox database cache.

TABLE 11.4 Exchange mailbox database cache

Physical Memory (GB)	Mailbox Role Only: Mailbox Database Cache (GB)	Multiple Role: Mailbox Database Cache (GB)
4	1	Not Supported
8	3.6	2
16	10.4	8
24	17.6	14
32	24.4	20
48	39.2	32

TABLE 11.4   Exchange mailbox database cache *(continued)*

Physical Memory (GB)	Mailbox Role Only: Mailbox Database Cache (GB)	Multiple Role: Mailbox Database Cache (GB)
64	53.6	44
96	82.4	68
128	111.2	92

For more information about sizing memory for Exchange 2010, see http://technet.microsoft.com/en-us/library/dd346700.aspx.

Determining Storage Requirements

The Mailbox Server Role Requirements Calculator applies the fundamental sizing concepts, but it is also important to understand these concepts. One is that the data stored on disk is not the sum of the amount of data that Outlook says is stored inside all of the mailboxes in the database because there is overhead that must be accounted for. To estimate the maximum size a mailbox would consume on disk, you add the mailbox limit, the white space, and the dumpster size.

Database white space is the transient data in the mailbox that may take up space on disk but is quickly deleted. White space is estimated to be the total of the messages sent and received each day. A user profile that sends and receives 100 messages a day with an average size of 100 KB each would have an estimated white space of about 10 MB for each mailbox.

The size of the mailbox dumpster depends on the configuration. Simple deleted item retention is estimated by multiplying the average size of messages sent and received each day by the length of the retention period. However, if you enable Single Item Recovery, an additional 1.2 percent of the mailbox size needs to be added to the size on disk. And if calendar version logging is enabled as the default, you must also add an additional 5.8 percent of the mailbox size.

For example, if a mailbox has a 2,048 MB limit and has roughly 10 MB of changes each day, a 21-day retention window, and Single Item Recovery disabled, the dumpster size would be roughly 210 MB plus 119 MB (2,048 MB mailbox limit × 5.8 percent) for leaving calendar version logging enabled. The maximum size for the 2,048 MB mailbox in this scenario would be roughly 2,387 MB (2,048 MB mailbox limit + 10 MB white space + 329 MB dumpster) on disk. To ensure that you do not run out of space, be sure to add additional space for growth and about 20 percent of additional space as a buffer.

Determining the Database Size

The primary factor for determining the maximum database size should be based on meeting the SLA. Sizing the database based on an SLA will ensure that in case of a database failure, the database can be restored and the service level can be met. If the failed database has multiple healthy copies within the DAG, the recovery is automatic and instantaneous. However, you need to keep in mind that the failed database will need to be reseeded. If the database is not highly available, manual recovery needs to be completed using database repair tools or from a backup copy. For example, if the SLA requires that an outage must not last more than 4 hours, you must be able to repair or restore the database from backup within the SLA. If you can repair or restore 100 GB each hour from a backup, the database should be smaller than 400 GB to be able to meet the SLA. In a DAG with at least two copies of each database, the product documentation does not recommended databases being larger than 2 TB.

When the maximum database size is decided, the number of mailboxes in each database can be determined with a simple calculation. For example, if a maximum database size has been determined to be 500 GB to meet SLAs, each database can have 209 (500 GB maximum database size/2,387 MB mailbox size = 209 mailboxes) of the 2,048 MB mailboxes mentioned earlier.

Sizing Transaction Logs Storage

Transaction log files record all of the changes made to the database. As the transaction log is filled, it will close when it reaches 1 MB in size or when it is closed by the Information Store process. The number of transaction logs generated depends on the number and size of changes made to the database. By default, these transaction logs will continue to accumulate until they are truncated after a successful full or incremental backup. If you have deployed a backup-less environment—an environment with enough highly available copies and no need for long-term retention—circular logging should be enabled to keep transaction logs from building up. When continuous replication circular logging (CRCL) is enabled for a database in a DAG, the transaction log files are truncated after the data has been replicated to each DAG member with a copy of the database.

In cases where circular logging is not enabled, you provide storage space for the transaction logs that will be generated between successful backups. Using your identified user profile along with the information in Table 11.5, you can estimate the number of transaction log files that will be generated depending on the number and size of the messages.

TABLE 11.5   Estimated number of transaction log files generated per day

Messages Sent and Received per Day	Transaction Logs Created (75 KB Average Message Size)	Transaction Logs Created (100 KB Average Message Size)	Transaction Logs Created (150 KB Average Message Size)	Transaction Logs Created (300 KB Average Message Size)
50	10	13	19	38
100	20	26	38	76

TABLE 11.5 Estimated number of transaction log files generated per day *(continued)*

Messages Sent and Received per Day	Transaction Logs Created (75 KB Average Message Size)	Transaction Logs Created (100 KB Average Message Size)	Transaction Logs Created (150 KB Average Message Size)	Transaction Logs Created (300 KB Average Message Size)
150	30	40	57	114
200	40	53	76	152
250	50	66	95	190
300	60	79	114	228
350	70	92	133	266
400	80	105	152	304
450	90	119	171	342
500	100	132	190	380

You need to estimate the storage needed between *successful* backups because if a backup does not complete and truncate the transaction logs, the logs will continue to accumulate until the next successful backup completes. Depending on the reliability of your backups, you may need to allow enough space to sustain several failed backups as well as additional space for mailbox moves and variations in message traffic.

For a Mailbox server with a database with 400 mailboxes that send and receive an average of 100 messages each day with an average size of 75 KB, each mailbox will generate around 20 transaction logs. Because each transaction log is 1 MB, each database will need roughly 8 GB of storage to store one day's worth of transaction logs to support normal mailbox usage (8 GB = 400 mailboxes × 20 transaction log files/mailbox × 1 MB). A full backup is run every other day; to sustain two backup failures, enough space is needed for three days' worth of transaction logs, which is about 24 GB of storage space.

Also, additional space is needed to store transaction logs generated from mailbox moves. When a mailbox is moved between databases, transaction log files are generated for all data that is inserted into the new database. If you plan to move 5 of the 1,024 MB mailboxes each day, you will need to have an additional 25 GB of transaction log storage for the three days' capacity needed.

As an example, suppose you have a database that generates 8 GB of transaction logs each day during normal mailbox use and 5 GB of transaction logs for mailbox moves. During three days of use, the transaction log storage is 47 GB—3 days × (8 GB transaction logs for normal mailbox usage + 5 GB transaction logs for mailbox moves) + 20 percent for growth. Of course, each environment is different, so be sure to use information that you have gathered from your environment to perform your own sizing.

Determining the Disk Layout

Now that you have determined the storage size and I/O requirements, you can determine how to lay out the database and transaction log disks. There are a number of supported ways to design the storage for the transaction log files and the database files. The design strategy you use should be based on your performance and backup requirements. These basic storage design options are as follows:

Volume Shadow Copy Service (VSS)   This configuration stores the database and its transaction log files on the same LUN or disk. This strategy should only be used for databases in a DAG that has two or more database copies and doesn't use a hardware-based VSS solution because this does not provide hardware isolation between the transaction log and database storage to protect against a single LUN failure. This is beneficial because fewer LUNs are easier to manage and the databases are separated to ensure that one database cannot affect the performance of another database.

Two LUNs/database   This configuration stores the database and the transaction log files are stored on separate LUNs or disks. This is used when VSS clones are made or when redundancy is critical. It allows hardware-based VSS to be completed at a database level, providing single database backup and restoration. This strategy will often use more than the available number of drive letters; therefore, volume mount points must be used. It also requires a large number of LUNs and may exceed storage array maximums. This strategy also separates databases to ensure that one database cannot affect the performance of another database.

Two LUNs/backup set   This configuration stores all of the databases to be backed up during the same backup window on a single LUN or disk and the corresponding transaction log files on a separate LUN or disk. This strategy reduces the number of LUNs. However, if a single LUN failure occurs, multiple databases are affected.

Deploying Public Folders

In environments where public folders are heavily used, using dedicated Mailbox servers to host public folders is recommended. This allows dedicated processor, memory, and disk resources to host and replicate public folders, reducing the likelihood of resource contention.

Deploying fewer larger public folder databases rather than having many small public folder databases scales well, reduces the amount of replication traffic that must occur, and requires fewer servers that need to be managed and monitored.

Also important is the hierarchy of the public folders. Due to how replication works, it is better to have more nested folders than more folders at the root. When deploying the hierarchy, you must consider the permissions that will be granted on the folders. Your goal should be to simplify administration and reduce complexity as much as possible when assigning permissions. To do this, try to position the folders that will have the least restrictive permissions toward the top of the hierarchy and folders that require more restrictive permissions toward the bottom. To reduce the possibility of performance issues, create fewer than 250 folders in any one folder. A common practice is to create root folders for each business unit, region, or department and allow project and other folders to be created below those root folders.

To understand where public folder replicas need to be placed, it is important to know how clients find and access public folder replicas. When a user utilizes Outlook or OWA to connect to a public folder, the following occurs:

1. The default public folder database for the user's account is always the initial target for all requests. If a replica of the public folder is available, Exchange Server directs the client to the default public folder.

2. If a replica of the public folder is not in the user's default public folder database, Exchange Server redirects the client to the least-cost Active Directory site that does have a replica. The Active Directory site must include a computer that is running Exchange 2010 or Exchange 2007.

3. If no computer running Exchange 2010 or Exchange 2007 has a copy of the public folder contents, Exchange redirects the client to a computer running Exchange 2003 with a public folder replica, using the routing group connector(s) cost. However, public folder referrals must be enabled on the routing group connector.

4. If no public folder replica exists on the local Active Directory site, on a remote Active Directory site, or on a computer running Exchange Server 2003, the client cannot access the contents of the requested public folder.

As you can see, configuring public folder replicas requires that you understand the AD site topology along with the locations from which public folder data is accessed. The primary goal for deploying replicas should be to strike a balance of fewer replicas while still providing adequate access and redundancy.

 For more information about creating and managing public folders, see Chapter 5.

Summary

The Mailbox server role is the core of the messaging system. The database schema for Exchange 2010 has been reengineered to provide support for large mailboxes on less-expensive storage.

To create a Mailbox server design, you must first understand the user mailboxes that will be hosted on the new server. To do this, you can use tools like Exchange Profile Analyzer and Performance Monitor. The user profile that you create will be used to run configuration tools like the Exchange 2010 Mailbox Server Role Requirements Calculator. These tools will generate a configuration based on your input. You can also size hardware based on the knowledge these tools use to determine the amount of storage and memory and the processors you need.

Because not every environment works with a configuration based on these tools due to variations on how they use the messaging system, you should validate your configuration using tools like Exchange Load Generator and Jetstress.

Deploying the Mailbox server role requires installing prerequisite software, updates, roles, and role services. Exchange 2010 SP1 simplifies the installation of the required roles and role services.

Chapter Essentials

Know how to gather user profile information.   Understand that Exchange Profile Analyzer (EPA) gathers information about users' mailboxes. This information is used as input to various sizing tools.

Know how to use the sizing validation tools.   Exchange Load Generator and Jetstress are tools used to test and validate that the hardware performs as expected. These tools cannot be used in a production environment.

Chapter

12

Designing Routing and Client Connectivity

THE FOLLOWING TOPICS ARE DISCUSSED IN THIS CHAPTER:

- ✓ Designing message routing and transport

- ✓ Planning an Exchange Server 2010 routing design

- ✓ Deploying an Exchange Server 2010 infrastructure

- ✓ Designing client access and connectivity

- ✓ Planning and deploying the Exchange 2010 Client Access server role

- ✓ Planning Client Access load balancing

- ✓ Upgrading and coexistence with Exchange 2003 or 2007

At the core of the Exchange Server 2010 messaging system is the functionality of routing a message from its source to its intended destination and, we might add, in the most efficient manner. Given the increased volume of electronic communication sent and received today, as well as the complexity involved in today's messaging systems, it is imperative to design and deploy an Exchange-routed messaging infrastructure in such a way that it mitigates hardware failure, message loss, message delays, and loops. Each design, however, would differ based on each organization's specific business and technical needs as well as existing infrastructure.

As described in Chapter 3, "Configuring Connectors, Routing and Transport, and Connectivity," Exchange Server 2010 builds upon the Exchange Server 2007 implementation of transport and email routing, providing new transport and routing functionality such as shadow redundancy, moderated transport, and end-to-end message latency as well as component latency and federated delivery, to mention but a few.

In addition, routing a message between Exchange servers is only part of the equation. The type of clients generating the email messages and connecting to the Exchange servers and their method of connection form another aspect of the messaging infrastructure. Proper consideration and planning must be given to client access and connectivity to the Exchange Server 2010 messaging system. In Exchange Server 2010, processing of all client connections, MAPI and non-MAPI and with the exception of access to public folders, now occurs on the Client Access server role. This is a major architectural change over previous versions of Exchange Server, providing better scalability and performance improvements.

This chapter provides an overview of key features of Exchange 2010 transport and routing as well as design guidelines and deployment considerations. It also covers specific guidelines and general recommendations to be considered when designing client access and connectivity to the Exchange 2010 messaging infrastructure.

Getting to Know Exchange 2010 Server Transport and Routing Features

The overall transport architecture in Exchange 2010 is not significantly different from that of Exchange 2007. Exchange transport is still implemented on two roles, the Hub Transport server role and the Edge Transport server role. This separation of transport functionality from mailbox functionality provides a significant architectural change from versions of Exchange

Server prior to Exchange 2007. It was an answer to an enterprise customer requests for ease and flexibility of deployment. The Edge Transport role is typically deployed in a perimeter network and provides inbound and outbound message routing to external organizations as well as a slew of message hygiene operations. The Hub Transport server, on the other hand, is deployed inside the Active Directory (AD) forest and provides message routing and delivery between Active Directory sites and local delivery to mailboxes. To facilitate secure movement of some data, such as for recipient filtering and safe senders, Hub Transport servers can synchronize data with Edge Transport servers via EdgeSync (Edge Synchronization) and securely move data from the AD to Active Directory Lightweight Directory Service (AD LDS) on the Edge Server role.

The design goal of Exchange 2010 transport, however, is significant and worth mentioning. Exchange 2010 is aimed at increasing transport availability and making the overall administrative experience easier, hence the introduction of some of the features mentioned at the outset. Also noteworthy is the reduction in hardware and operations costs as well as the input/output per second (IOPS) improvements achieved in the mail.que database and transport dumpster. Exchange 2010 development also introduced a unique transport architecture for deployment in Microsoft datacenters hosting multitenant, service environments. This cloud-based service provides customers with a much needed choice. They can opt for simply a hosted service or enable coexistence and routing between the cloud and on-premises environment, thus providing much needed flexibility and scalability.

The following sections summarize some key transport features and functionality affecting routing design introduced in Exchange 2010. Many of these new features only function within the realm of Exchange 2010, and the timing as to the use of some features may depend on your coexistence requirements. We give an example when we discuss moderation in a later section.

What Is Shadow Redundancy?

This is a phenomenal feature aimed at addressing message loss during message transit. Based on the SMTP mechanism, a sending server relinquishes ownership of a message once a receiving SMTP server responds with a "250 2.6.0 Message Queued for Delivery" status message. In Exchange 2007 and earlier versions of Exchange, the message cannot be resent if the receiving server experiences some sort of catastrophic failure, in which case the message is lost.

With shadow redundancy in Exchange 2010, the sending server maintains a copy of the message even after it is accepted by the receiving server, thus providing a previous hop redundancy. After the receiving server successfully delivers the message, it sends a discard notification to the sending server, which then deletes its shadow copy out of the shadow queue. For shadow redundancy to occur, both servers must support and advertise the XSHADOW verb an SMTP extension. In Exchange 2010, the shadow queue is exposed in the queue view as well as from the management shell. Figure 12.1 shows the shadow queue viewed from the Queue Viewer.

FIGURE 12.1 The Queue Viewer showing the shadow queue

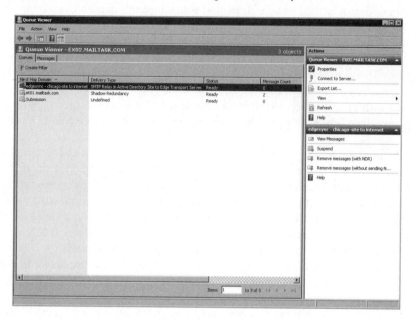

The concept of shadow redundancy also applies when messages are submitted from the Mailbox server to the Hub Transport server for delivery. Messages in the users' Sent Items folder can be used as shadow copies and be resent if there is a failure of the Hub Transport server role. This feature is called Redundant Mail Submission, and when used in conjunction with the transport dumpster, it provides recoverability and fault tolerance.

Another subtle but important feature introduced along the lines of message redundancy is delayed acknowledgement. This is used if the receiving server supports shadow redundancy and the sending server does not. To ensure that message ownership is retained for a few more seconds by the sending (non-Exchange) server, the receiving Exchange 2010 server delays the acknowledgement response while it attempts to deliver the message to the next hop. If a failure occurs, the sending server never got an acknowledgment; it resends the message for delivery.

> **TIP** In Exchange 2010 Service Pack 1 (SP1) release, some enhancements delayed acknowledgement feature. If there is a significant backlog of messages not yet delivered within the default 30-second window when message delivery is attempted by the receiving hub server, after a certain threshold, these messages would be automatically rerouted to another Hub Transport server in the AD site if one exists. A shadow message would then be maintained on the Hub Transport server that performs the message reroute.

In Exercise 12.1, you'll test shadow redundancy by connecting to an Exchange 2010 server using the Telnet utility and use the Exchange Management Shell (EMS) to view the shadow queue.

EXERCISE 12.1

Viewing the Shadow Message Queue and Message

Follow these steps to test shadow redundancy:

1. Click Start ➤ All Programs ➤ Microsoft Exchange Server 2010 and select Exchange Management Shell.

2. Run Get-TransportConfig | Format-List Shadow* (confirm that shadow redundancy is enabled).

3. Open a command prompt and type **telnet EX02 25**.

4. Type **EHLO** and check for the XSHADOW verb.

5. Using a client of your choice (Outlook or Outlook Web App), send a test message from erik@mailtask.com to Internet user joeuser@yahoo.com.

6. Click Start ➤ Programs ➤ Microsoft Exchange Server 2010 and then select Exchange Management Shell.

7. Run Get-Queue (notice the shadow queue).

8. Run Get-Queue -Identity <QueueName> | Get-Message, where <QueueName> is the name of the shadow queue.

Understanding Transport Service and the Mail.que ESE Database

Much administrative time and effort is spent repairing or recovering a transport database when a corruption of the database occurs. A transport database corruption could prevent the transport service from starting, hence the mail.que database could effectively become a single point of failure. In Exchange 2010, if the transport service encounters an error during startup when attempting to mount the transport database, either the transport service would delete the existing database and log files, create a new mail.que database, mount it and start up successfully or it would move the existing database and log files to a separate directory and create a new database to start up with. The type of action taken can be configured, including the legacy behavior of keeping the service stopped and logging an exception in the event log. The resiliency of the transport service reduces much downtime. Additionally, significant Extensible Storage Engine (ESE) database improvements have been made to the transport database, reducing IOPS per message and thus increasing message throughput.

Understanding Moderated Transport

New to Exchange 2010 is the approval framework, which forms the basis for several new features in transport. These include moderated distribution groups and recipients, group membership approval, and moderated transport rules. Now administrators have the ability to specify a moderation recipient for a mailbox recipient or distribution group. All messages sent to a mailbox recipient or distribution group is sent to the moderation recipient for approval or rejection. Moderation also applies to distribution group membership, whereby the owner can configure a moderator before users can join or leave a distribution group. Even transport rule actions now allow for moderation when messages meet defined transport rule conditions. These have been features long asked for by Exchange customers.

Here are some caveats to be aware of when implementing moderated recipients in a coexistence scenario:

Mailboxes   Exchange 2007 does not support enabling mailboxes for moderation only. Exchange 2010 Mailbox servers do. Hence, when coexisting with Exchange 2007, if a mailbox is moved to Exchange 2010 and enabled for moderation, it must not be moved back to Exchange 2007.

Distribution groups and dynamic distribution groups   If messages to a distribution group or dynamic distribution group are moderated, for it to work correctly, the distribution group must be expanded by an Exchange 2010 Hub Transport server. By default, there is no expansion server set on distribution groups or dynamic distribution groups. Hence, if Exchange 2007 Hub servers still exist within the AD site, they may be used to expand messages to moderated groups. It is recommended that you implement moderation after all your hub servers have been upgraded to Exchange 2010.

Mail contacts and mail users   The target address is the external email address specified on these recipients. You may want to hold off enabling these recipients for moderation since you cannot control messages for these recipients to pass through Exchange 2010 Hub servers.

Measuring End-To-End Message Latency

In legacy versions of Exchange server, there was no easy way to determine the volume of messages passing through the messaging system. In addition, it was almost impossible to determine the latency of a message from entry into the organization until delivery to the destination mailbox. Exchange 2010 now provides the ability to measure per-message delivery latency and per-message component latency. Thus, administrators can quickly identify potential bottlenecks in message delivery. It is also helpful in studying message trends. This information is persisted within the message tracking logs and performance monitor log.

Integrating Cross-Premises Message Routing

Exchange 2010 provides the ability for companies to scale their existing on-premises Exchange infrastructure to integrate with additional hosted services in the cloud hosted at Microsoft datacenters. In some cases, an institution may choose to deploy the majority of its user mailboxes in the cloud while maintaining select few executive mailboxes on-premises. In this scenario, seamless cross-premises message routing can be configured. More information on Exchange Hosted Services can be found at the following location:

```
http://www.microsoft.com/online/exchange-hosted-services.mspx
```

Understanding Version-Based Routing

Although Exchange 2010 can be introduced into an existing Exchange 2007 environment, due to the transport architectural changes introduced in Exchange 2010, proper design consideration must be given to placement of Hub Transport servers because this could impact message routing. Given the architectural changes, Exchange 2010 Hub Transport servers cannot accept mail or deliver mail to Exchange 2007 Mailbox role servers and vice versa, hence the introduction of version-based routing, which is the ability to use an Exchange server's version information to make routing decisions.

For example, in Figure 12.2 a message originating from Joel cannot be delivered from an Exchange 2007 Hub Transport server directly to an Exchange 2010 Mailbox server, it must be relayed to an Exchange 2010 Hub Transport server, which will then perform a MAPI delivery to the destination Exchange 2010 Mailbox server where Erik's mailbox resides.

Therefore, when designing for routing in an environment where Exchange 2010 will coexist with Exchange 2007, ensure that for each Exchange 2010 Mailbox server deployed, there exists at least one Exchange 2010 Hub Transport server or messages will not be delivered.

FIGURE 12.2 Versioned routing

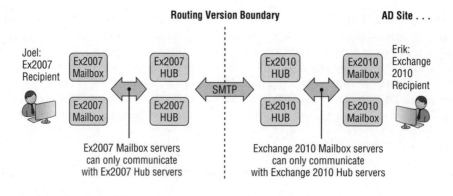

Ex2007 Mailbox servers can only communicate with Ex2007 Hub servers

Exchange 2010 Mailbox servers can only communicate with Exchange 2010 Hub servers

Improvements in Edge Synchronization

The Edge Synchronization feature introduced in Exchange 2007 allowed secure and encrypted replication of configuration and recipient information from the Active Directory to the Active Directory Lightweight Directory Services (ADLDS) on the Edge Transport server in the perimeter network. Exchange 2007 EdgeSync always replicated the entire configuration and recipient information each time edge synchronization occurs. For large organizations with an extensive AD topology, this can impact network utilization. Exchange 2010 provides the ability to perform incremental updates. After the initial full synchronization, subsequent updates are incremental, thus reducing network utilization. If Exchange 2010 is coexisting with Exchange 2007, incremental updates will only be available between the Exchange 2010 Hub and Exchange 2010 Edge Transport servers. Full synchronization would continue to be performed with Exchange 2007 Hub servers.

Planning Exchange Server 2010 Routing

A successful deployment of an Exchange 2010 routed messaging environment begins with a thorough understanding of the current infrastructure, current messaging trends, and future projected growth requirements. Even where a previous messaging infrastructure does not already exist, consideration must be given to server hardware requirements, Exchange server role placements, Active Directory topology, network topology, and understanding Exchange 2010 routing components as well as current messages routing. These, among other specific business and technical requirements, are key design elements that must be considered. A proper routing design and implementation project must include planning, testing, deployment, and maintenance phases. The following sections discuss the dependencies for an Exchange 2010 message routing design.

Understanding Exchange 2010 Server Role Dependencies

The Exchange 2010 Hub Transport and Edge Transport roles are primarily responsible for message routing. Their placement, capacity, and configuration are important in a routing design. We'll now review the key dependencies for both transport roles.

Placing the Hub Transport Server Role

At the very core of message routing is the Hub Transport server role. Placement of this server role is an important consideration in routing design. As with Exchange 2007, every message sent or received in the organization must be processed by the Hub Transport server, even a message a user sends to him- or herself. The categorizer component on the Hub Transport server is responsible for making routing decisions based on the message recipients and other message details. At least one Hub Transport server must exist in each Active Directory site where a Mailbox server role exists. Although the Hub Transport server is primarily used for message routing within the Exchange organization, it can be configured to route and receive messages to and from the Internet. This is accomplished by configuring a send connector for outbound message flow and configuring either the existing default receive connector or a new receive connector with anonymous access permissions to receive mail from the Internet. However, it is a best practice to implement an Edge Transport server role for message hygiene as well as for protecting access to your internal Active Directory infrastructure.

When designing the placement of Hub Transport servers, consideration must be giving to the following:

Active Directory topology   It is important when designing Hub Transport server placements to determine if the existing or future AD topology consists of single or multiple AD sites or if multiple forests would be involved. This influences the message routing, as we discuss in the section "Planning Active Directory Site-Based Routing" later in the chapter.

Server capacity requirements and load balancing   Hardware sizing for the Hub Transport server and Edge Transport server may differ considerably from any other server role. Proper planning and review of statistical data, including messaging trends such as total emails sent/ received daily is essential for proper sizing. Load balancing is achieved by adding more Hub Transport server roles into the Active Directory site. Hardware sizing is discussed in "Defining Transport Server Hardware" later in this chapter.

Permissions and administration   With the introduction of Role Based Access Control as the new permissions model in Exchange 2010, it is easier to delegate administration of Exchange servers by role or function. For example, while preventing organization-wide transport server administration, a junior admin could be granted permissions to manage distribution groups or message tracking across transport servers in the organization.

Secure email transmission   By default, a self-signed certificate is installed during deployment of each Exchange server role. Hence, all traffic between Hub Transport servers is encrypted by using Transport Layer Security (TLS) with self-signed certificates. In addition, traffic between Edge Transport servers and Hub Transport servers is authenticated and encrypted. However, unlike with Exchange 2007, TLS can now be disabled on Hub Transport servers to enable data compression over wide area network (WAN) optimization devices. Disabling TLS, however, is not recommended except when absolutely necessary to meet business or technical requirements. For example, in Figure 12.3, where the Chicago and Seattle sites are separated by a WAN and a WAN optimizer is used to conserve bandwidth, TLS can be disabled only on the receive connectors of the Hub Transport servers in the Chicago and Seattle sites. Thus, a message across the WAN optimizer is unencrypted. However, Exchange costs and routing must be designed in such a way that messages are not routed directly from Seattle to Miami or Dallas sites and vice versa.

FIGURE 12.3 Disabling TLS across a WAN

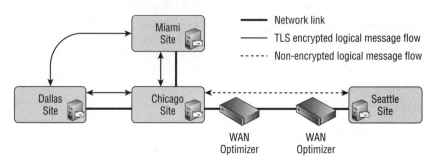

Placing the Edge Transport Server Role

Placement of this server role is typically in the perimeter network where access to the internal servers is protected by a firewall. The Edge Transport server acts as a smart host and relay server for messages sent to and received from the Internet. In addition, it provides message protection and hygiene features such as antispam, antivirus, and the processing of configured transport rules. To provide secure communication and data transfer with the Hub Transport server inside the Exchange organization, it is recommended to configure an edge subscription that automatically provisions the required send connectors, enabling message flow out of and into the Exchange organization.

In the design of this server role, as with the Hub Transport role, consider the current message trends, such as percentage of spam and valid messages received per day. If multiple Edge Transport servers will be deployed, then deployment must include a mechanism for ensuring the same configuration on all Edge servers by configuring Edge Synchronization and running custom setup scripts. It is important to keep in mind that in multi-AD site environments, one or more Edge Transport servers can be subscribed to a single Active Directory site. The converse, however, is not true. You cannot subscribe a single Edge Transport server to more than one Active Directory site.

In complex deployment scenarios where a large number of Edge Transport servers are deployed and ease of administration is a requirement, a separate Active Directory forest can be created in the perimeter network to manage the Edge Transport servers.

As an alternative to using Edge Transport servers for antispam and antivirus scanning, some organizations may opt for Exchange Hosted Filtering (EHF). This online managed service does not require the organization to install or deploy any software or hardware on-premises. The only requirement is a change in the accepted domain's MX record, routing all inbound mail through the EHF network for filtering. Likewise, all outbound Internet mail is smart hosted through the EHF for virus scanning and policy enforcement. Depending on the business requirements, this can be an economical alternative to hosting Edge Transport server's on-premises. Other Microsoft Exchange-hosted services include Hosted Archive, Hosted Encryption, and Hosted Continuity.

Understanding Active Directory Dependencies and Routing

As with its immediate predecessor, Exchange 2010 is tightly integrated with the Windows Active Directory. Site link costs associated with an AD site can affect message routing. Therefore, the AD topology and design become key dependencies when designing Exchange 2010 routing.

If the AD infrastructure is already deployed prior to designing the Exchange 2010 deployment, then it must be assessed to ensure that it meets the requirements for Exchange to be deployed on top of the existing infrastructure. The Active Directory forest functional level must be Windows 2003 native mode or higher. Additionally, domain controllers and global catalog servers can be either 32-bit or 64-bit Windows 2003 SP2 or 2008 servers.

If, on the other hand, the design of Exchange 2010 includes the AD topology design, then due consideration should be given to the use of 64-bit servers to increase directory service performance. Also, consider deploying Windows 2008 SP2 or R2 servers on your domain controllers as well as your Exchange servers. A 4:1 ratio of Exchange Server processors to global catalog server processors of similar model and speeds is the general recommendation. As a general rule of thumb, it is recommended to install Exchange 2010 on member servers rather than domain controllers due to security and performance reasons.

Planning a Basic Active Directory Topology

In its most simple form, an AD topology will consist of a single AD forest, an AD site, a domain, and global catalog server. For Exchange 2010 routing, one Hub Transport server must exist in every AD site where an Exchange 2010 Mailbox server role is deployed. For redundancy and load balancing, additional Hub Transport role servers can be deployed as needed. If no Edge Transport server is deployed in a perimeter network and antispam features are desired, they can be implemented by running the `Install-AntispamAgents.ps1` script. Figure 12.4 shows the Mailtask.com AD domain with a single AD site in Chicago. The Exchange 2010 server EX01 has all roles installed. For small organizations, this basic topology is often sufficient to meet their business and technical requirements; however deploying an Edge Transport server or other SMTP gateway in the DMZ is recommended.

FIGURE 12.4   Basic AD topology

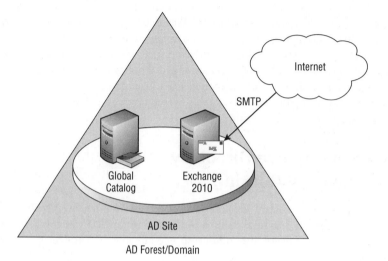

Planning Active Directory Site-Based Routing

Midsize to large organizations may have AD topologies that span multiple sites. The dynamics of Exchange 2010 routing changes and may depend on several factors, such as if there is a technical requirement to route all messages via a hub site. As far as Exchange 2010 message routing goes, the AD site represents not only the routing boundary for Hub Transport server roles but also the service discovery boundary for other Exchange roles. So if multiple AD sites exist with mailbox recipients in them, the Hub Transport server must relay messages to a Hub Transport server existing in the remote AD site for delivery to the mailbox recipient. Exchange 2010 attempts a direct connection to a Hub Transport server in the AD site where the mailbox recipient exists. If a hub site is configured and the AD site cost is identical, then the message would be routed through a Hub Transport server in the hub site before being routed to its destination. If no hub site is configured, then route selection is purely based on AD site cost or Exchange cost if configured. In general, the following factors related to the Active Directory affect the eventual route a message takes:

AD site membership determination   Exchange 2010 is an AD site-aware application and uses site membership to determine, among other things, which Hub Transport servers are located in the AD site. Since each AD site is associated with a particular subnet, the IP address of the Exchange 2010 automatically determines which site it belongs to. The Active Directory Topology Service on the Exchange server periodically checks and updates the site membership information stored in the Active Directory. During message routing to a remote AD site, the next hop will be `SMTPRelayToRemoteADSite`, with DNS resolving the AD site to a list of Hub Transport servers existing in the remote site.

IP site links design consideration   While the design of AD sites generally reflects the physical network layout, IP site links represent the logical path between AD sites and may or may not closely match the physical network layout depending on the transport protocol used. Every AD site is associated with an IP site link, and the cost configured can affect how messages are routed in the environment. Exchange 2010 will use site links only when determining the least-cost path. By default, it always attempts a direct delivery to a Hub Transport server in the remote AD site.

Hub site design consideration   Sometimes business and technical specifications require an override of the existing default message routing pattern such that all messages are routed through an interim site before delivery to their ultimate destination. Exchange 2010 routing can be designed to meet this requirement. Hub sites can alter the existing least-cost route, forcing messages to be routed through a specific AD site. It is best to analyze the existing environment for least-cost routing before implementing a hub site. This can be done by examining the routing logs to determine the current message route into and out of the organization and the desired AD site. Careful planning is required before you implement a hub site to avoid message loops, delays in message delivery, and possible undeliverables due to invalid routes.

Configuring an AD site as a hub site is relatively easy, as shown in Exercise 12.2. However, the implications of changing the message route must be carefully thought out. In Exercise 12.2, you will create a hub site in Chicago.

EXERCISE 12.2

Making the Chicago Site a Hub Site

Follow these steps to make the Chicago site a hub site:

1. Click Start ➤ All Programs ➤ Microsoft Exchange Server 2010 and select Exchange Management Shell.

2. Run Set-AdSite "Chicago-Site" -HubSiteEnabled $true.

3. Force AD replication between AD sites.

4. Next, using the Outlook client or Outlook Web App, send a test message from Joel in the Dallas site to Erik in the Miami site.

5. Track the message from source to destination by running the cmdlet Get-MessagetrackingLog -Sender joel@mailtask.com -MessageSubject "Hub Site Enabled".

EXERCISE 12.2 *(continued)*

6. The route that the message took is shown here.

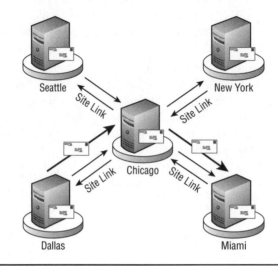

Configuring DNS

To ensure a successful Exchange 2010 deployment and message routing, DNS must be configured properly in the environment. All Exchange 2010 servers, including the Hub Transport role, must be able to perform a successful name resolution (NetBIOS and DNS name) both internally and outside the organization. Each computer in the AD domain has both a fully qualified domain name (FQDN) and a NetBIOS name. The FQDN consists of one or more subdomains separated by a dot (period) and is terminated by a top-level domain name. Also, each computer has a primary DNS suffix and can have additional DNS suffixes. Careful planning must be done when deploying Exchange 2010 in a disjoint name space environment.

> **NOTE** The Internal and External DNS lookup settings configurable on the transport server settings override the network interface DNS configuration.

The DNS suffix for the Edge Transport server role must be manually configured prior to Exchange 2010 installation. For Internet domain MX resolution, reverse name lookups, and mail routing, the external network interface on the Edge Transport server must be configured to use a public DNS server. For inbound internal name resolution, the internal network interface must be configured to use a DNS server in the perimeter network that can resolve the names of the Hub Transport servers. Alternatively, host files can be created, although that's not recommended for larger deployments.

> ### ⊕ Real World Scenario
>
> #### The Importance of Proper DNS Configuration
>
> The importance of DNS configuration to message routing can never be overemphasized. In some cases, the root cause of a routing problem may be seemingly unrelated to a routing change and could be due to other underlying factors. Consider what can happen as described in the following scenario.
>
> **Problem**   A customer recently introduced Exchange 2010 into the existing Exchange 2003 messaging environment and has yet to move all mailboxes to Exchange 2010. It has been reported that a user whose mailbox is on an Exchange 2003 server sends a meeting request to a resource mailbox on Exchange 2010 and the meeting is not auto-accepted but remains as tentative. There is no response sent back to the Exchange 2003 user indicating that the message was accepted.
>
> **Root Cause and Resolution**   The cause of the issue was due to a mail routing configuration. Two IP addresses were bound to the network adapter configured on the Exchange 2010 Hub Transport server. While one was an internal IP address, the other was an external or public IP. Both IP addresses were registered in DNS for the Hub Transport server. When the client on 2003 sends a meeting request, sometimes the request uses the external IP address and causes the meeting to show as if it came from an external recipient. Removing the external IP address or preventing it from registering in DNS for the Hub Transport server resolved meeting requests from Exchange 2003 users to the resource mailbox.
>
> **Take Away**   Carefully consider the implications of your DNS and network configuration.

Understanding Complex Active Directory Topologies

With many industry acquisitions and mergers, it is becoming fairly common to design and deploy Exchange 2010 into more complex Active Directory environments. They may consist of multiple AD domains and in some cases multiple forests where companies may require complete isolation. Some organizations may want to isolate the Exchange servers in a separate forest different from the AD forest that hosts the user accounts. Routing in complex environments can fall into any of the following categories:

Multi-domain topology   This applies to and is not limited to deployment of Exchange servers in domains with disjoint namespaces.

Cross-forest topology   This applies to topologies with multiple Exchange forests where Microsoft Forefront Identity Manager, Identity Integration Server (MIIS), or GALSync is used to synchronize the global address lists. Each forest has its own installation of Exchange.

Resource forest topology   This applies to topologies where users are deployed in an account forest separate from the resource forest that hosts the Exchange 2010 servers.

Migrating and Coexistence Considerations

During the routing design phase of an Exchange 2010 messaging environment, it is important to determine not only whether a messaging system already exists in the environment but what type of messaging system is in use and how its message routing is configured. While some customers would want to deploy Exchange 2010 into an existing non-Exchange environment (Lotus Domino, say), the majority of customers seek to upgrade their existing Exchange infrastructure.

It is important to note that there is no direct server upgrade path to Exchange 2010 from an existing Exchange legacy server installation. Exchange 2010, however, would have to be deployed on new hardware into an existing Exchange legacy environment, after which mailboxes can be transitioned from the legacy servers to the Exchange 2010 servers.

Exchange 2010 can be deployed only into an existing Exchange 2003 and/or Exchange 2007 legacy environment. Exchange 2010 cannot coexist with Exchange 2003 SP1 or earlier versions of Exchange. The minimum legacy server version must be Exchange 2003 SP2 or later. Any existing Exchange 2003 and/or 2007 servers must be upgraded to Service Pack 2. Hence, Exchange 2010 cannot be deployed into an existing Exchange 2000 environment. It is recommended that the organization first be upgraded to Exchange 2003 SP2 before upgrading to Exchange 2010.

The following Exchange topologies are supported for deployment and/or coexistence with Exchange 2010:

- Pure Exchange 2010 installation (Greenfield)

- Mixed Exchange 2010 and Exchange 2007 Service Pack 2

- Mixed Exchange 2010 and Exchange 2003 Service Pack 2

- Mixed Exchange 2010, Exchange 2007 Service Pack 2, and Exchange 2003 Service Pack 2

 If due to some specific business or technical justification a customer with Exchange 2007 SP1 cannot upgrade to SP2 but wants to deploy Exchange 2010 into the same organization, they must create a separate Active Directory site and install the Exchange 2010 servers into that site.

Defining Transport Server Hardware

Designing Exchange 2010 routing does not stop with Active Directory and network planning. After the infrastructure and placement of transport servers comes hardware and capacity design considerations. Transport servers should be able to route messages efficiently from source to destination. Hardware requirements become extremely important when making business decisions such as whether to reuse existing hardware or purchase new hardware. Most companies make hardware budget considerations once every couple of years, and these decisions can have a considerable impact on Exchange 2010 performance.

There are several factors to consider when planning the size of the transport server hardware. Sizing for the Hub Transport server may differ from sizing for the Edge Transport server, notably, among other things, if the Hub Transport server role will coexist with another Exchange 2010 server role. The Edge Transport server role, of course, cannot coexist with any other server role. Other factors include the total number of messages processed by the transport servers daily, especially at peak periods; the maximum allowable size limit of messages flowing through the transport servers; what type of transport agents and rules are enabled; and what antivirus, antispam, and/or third-party agents are used.

Understanding Transport Server Storage

The aforementioned factors have an impact on the storage design of the transport server since we commit messages to the transport ESE database and write to the transaction log and several others. These logs include message tracking logs and connectivity logs, both of which are enabled by default on a transport server role, and protocol logs and agent logs.

With the improvements in the storage engine organizations comes the option to utilize low-cost storage solutions such as SATA DAS and JBOD (RAID-less). This can significantly reduce the cost of deploying Exchange 2010 and at the same time enable an increase in the mailbox storage capacity of the end users.

Planning Edge Transport Servers

Messages are committed to the transport ESE database (mail.que) while in transit and do not persist indefinitely, but it is best to plan for a worst case scenario. At the very minimum, 4 GB of drive space must exist on the drive housing the mail.que database and logs, otherwise transport goes into back pressure, which is a transport monitoring feature introduced in Exchange 2007 to mitigate complete server service unavailability. The mail.que database size may be estimated by multiplying the average message size received over a 24-hour period by the maximum queue, which in some cases could be about a million messages.

Since message tracking and connectivity logs are enabled by default, it is best to study the current log generation rate and determine how many days' worth of logs to retain before being moved to an alternate storage or discarded.

Unlike with the message tracking logs, which are manually purged, circular logging is enabled by default for transaction log generation, so not much disk space needs be considered. Transaction logs can therefore be placed on the same disk as the server operating system.

Overall, after estimating the mail database and transaction and other log sizes, it is recommended to factor in a 20 percent overhead to allow for growth.

Planning Hub Transport Servers

All the factors considered for the Edge Transport server role also apply to the Hub Transport server role and may vary depending on message throughput, log generation, and additional server roles or applications installed. However, a significant difference is the planning for the transport dumpster, which exists only on the Hub Transport server role.

The transport dumpster is designed to help protect against data loss by maintaining a queue of all recent email messages sent to users whose mailboxes were protected by a cluster. In the event of a failure, the hub resends all the messages in the transport dumpster. The transport dumpster is used for replicated mailbox databases only.

Hence, the Hub Transport server storage must be designed with enough capacity to hold email messages long enough for the messages in all mailbox databases in the AD site to be recovered in the event of a loss.

Defining the Processor and Memory Requirements

Exchange 2010 supports both the Intel Extended Memory 64 processors and AMD64. It does not however support Itanium-based processors. The requirements for the specific transport server roles as well as multiple server roles installed with the Hub role are as follows:

Edge Transport server   Processor utilization on the Edge Transport server depends on message rate, average message size, number of enabled transport agents, antivirus configuration, and third-party applications. Two x processor cores are recommended for a typical deployment, with a maximum of 12 x processor cores. Midsize to large business with a higher message rate may consider 4 x processor cores.

Hub Transport server   Complete categorization of messages occurs on the Hub Transport server; hence, processor utilization on the Hub Transport server depends not only on the factors mentioned above for the Edge server but on the ratio of Mailbox servers to hub servers in the AD site. Four x processor cores are recommended in midsize to large organizations where Hub Transport servers may be deployed with several Mailbox servers and thousands of mailboxes. Eight processor core servers are recommended when antispam and antivirus features are enabled on the Hub Transport server.

Multiple server roles   As shown in Table 12.1 and Table 12.2, the recommendation for a computer with any combination of Hub, CAS, or Mailbox roles installed would be to size the server the same way you would size a Mailbox server role, taking into consideration the number of mailboxes on the server.

TABLE 12.1   Processor configuration on transport servers

Exchange 2010 Server Role	Minimum	Recommended	Maximum
Edge Transport	1 x processor core	4 x processor cores	12 x processor cores
Hub Transport	1 x processor core	4 x processor cores	12 x processor cores
Multiple roles (HT/CAS/MB)	2 x processor cores	8 x processor cores	24 x processor cores

TABLE 12.2   Memory configuration on transport servers

Exchange 2010 Server Role	Minimum per Sever	Maximum per Server	Recommended
Edge Transport	4 GB	16 GB	4 GB min; 8 GB max
Hub Transport	4 GB	16 GB	4 GB min; 8 GB max
Multiple roles (HT/CAS/MB)	8 GB	64 GB	8 GB + 2-10 MB per mailbox

Planning the Number of Transport Servers

At this point you have an idea or projection of the message rate and size your servers would be expected to handle. You also have made decisions regarding processor, memory, and disk configurations you would be deploying. Armed with this information and depending on the hardware you chose, you can calculate how many individual servers you would need to deploy and what roles to deploy. Every messaging environment would be different based on business and technical requirements.

However, keep in mind that for redundancy, it is best to deploy at least two Hub Transport servers in your AD site as well as two Edge Transport servers in your perimeter network to allow for outages (due to upgrades) or service interruptions.

All of the Exchange 2010 server roles with the exception of Unified Messaging are supported when run in a virtual environment, even in production. Using a virtual environment is also an effective means of testing your design before deployment. However, the virtualization platform must be based on either Microsoft hypervisor technology or one approved by Microsoft. This can provide huge cost savings, but you must consider the potential performance tradeoffs if deploying large mailboxes.

Use the following link to determine which virtualization platform Microsoft tests and supports: http://www.windowsservercatalog.com/svvp .aspx?svvppage=svvpwizard.htm.

Deploying the Exchange Server 2010 Infrastructure

After the design and planning phase, you are now ready to deploy Exchange 2010 servers. An important point to note is that Exchange 2010 server roles are deployed alphabetically by name, meaning the order would be Client Access, Hub Transport, Mailbox, and Unified

Messaging server roles. The Client Access server role must be the first role deployed into your new or existing infrastructure. The Edge role is installed into the perimeter network so it can be deployed after the Hub role is installed and configured.

 In an effort to reduce deployment complexity, Microsoft has released the Exchange Server Deployment Assistant tool. With this tool, you are asked a few questions related to your intended deployment and provided with customized instructions to review and follow prior to and during your deployment. These instructions consist of prerequisites and requirements, much of which you may have already covered in your planning phase. This tool essentially can prove to be a validation of your design and planning. You can access the tool using the following link: http://technet.microsoft.com/en-us/exdeploy2010/default.aspx#Home.

In the following sections, we review the deployment of the Exchange 2010 server into various environments, concentrating on the Hub Transport server role and the Edge Transport role deployment. We also make reference to the Exchange Server Deployment Assistant when deploying the Hub Transport server.

Deploying a New Exchange Installation (Greenfield)

Deployment into a Greenfield environment is typically straightforward because you don't have to consider any coexistence requirements with other Exchange versions. However, as discussed in the section "Getting to Know Exchange 2010 Server Transport and Routing Features" earlier in this chapter, several factors may influence the final design and deployment. With the exception of the Edge Transport server role, Exchange 2010 roles can be combined on the same hardware depending on available resources. In its simplest form, although not recommended, this may consist of a single server with all roles installed as well as the antispam and antivirus agents enabled and deployed into a single Active Directory site.

A small-scale business may choose to deploy a configuration similar to that in Figure 12.5, which would consist of one server running all Exchange roles and an Edge Transport server in a perimeter network.

This configuration does not take into consideration server and service redundancy and high availability. The configuration in Figure 12.6, however, illustrates a typical Greenfield deployment with high availability factored in. Although the server roles have been separated, the Hub Transport role and CAS role could be combined and a CAS array configured. For the Unified Messaging role, redundancy can be achieved by installing additional servers into the same dial plan.

Let us now walk through a simple Greenfield deployment using the deployment assistant. The deployment steps assume you are deploying a highly available Greenfield design in which each server role is deployed on separate hardware. You must first consider the questions highlighted by the deployment assistant when you select the New Installation of Exchange 2010 option. The answers to the questions in Figure 12.7 validate your predeployment plans and affect the configuration of your servers in the later deployment phases. For example, additional configuration steps would be required as shown by the deployment assistant if you answer yes to "Are you running a disjoint namespace?"

FIGURE 12.5   Simple Greenfield design

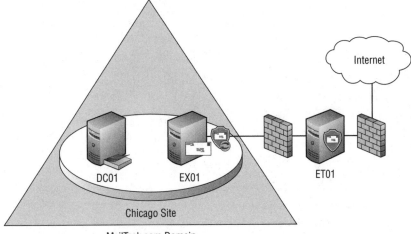

Before you continue with the deployment assistant, Microsoft recommends that you run the Exchange Pre-Deployment Analyzer (ExPDA), which scans your AD environment making sure Exchange 2010 can be deployed. This scan ensures that you have met the following requirements:

- Directory servers:
    - Schema master. Typically the first domain controller installed into the AD forest has this role. It must be a 32-bit or 64-bit edition of Windows 2003, Windows 2008 SP2, or Windows 2008 R2.
    - Global catalog server. This is typically the same as the first domain controller installed into the AD forest. Same as requirements for schema master.
    - Active Directory forest.
    - Domain controller. Same as requirements for global catalog server.
- Operating system: Only 64-bit Standard or Enterprise editions of Windows 2008 SP2 or Windows 2008 R2.
- Operating system components: .NET Framework 3.5 SP1 and Internet Information Services (IIS) must be installed.
- Windows Management Framework: Windows PowerShell V2.0 and Windows Remote Management 2.0 must be installed.

FIGURE 12.6 A highly available Greenfield design

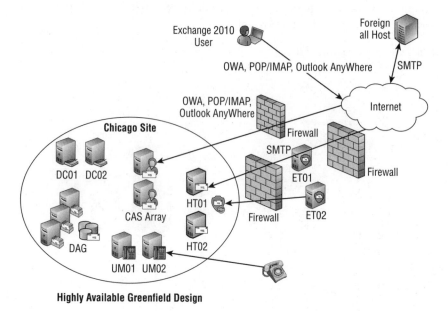

Highly Available Greenfield Design

FIGURE 12.7 Exchange Server Deployment Assistant questions

	Yes	No
❅ 1. Are you planing to deploy Internet-protocol (HTTPS, IMAP, POP) clients?	○ Yes	⦿ No
❅ 2. Are you running a disjointed namespace?	○ Yes	⦿ No
❅ 3. Are you planning to use public folders in Exchange 2010?	○ Yes	⦿ No
❅ 4. Are you planning to deploy an Edge Transport server role?	○ Yes	⦿ No
❅ 5. Are you planning to deploy a Unified Messaging server role?	○ Yes	⦿ No

Continuing with the deployment assistant, you would next install the Client Access server role by running setup.exe from your Exchange 2010 installation media and following the installation prompts. If you do not have Outlook 2003 clients because this is a new installation, then you can disregard turning off the RPC encryption requirement at the end of the installation. After the CAS is installed, import and enable your Subject Alternative Name (SAN) certificate, enable Outlook Anywhere if that is desired, and configure your OAB and Web Services virtual directories.

After you successfully install the Client Access server role, you would proceed to install and configure the Hub Transport server role. You have the option of installing the Hub Transport role on the same hardware as the CAS role just deployed, as shown in Figure 12.8, or installing the Hub role on separate hardware, in which case you only select the Hub Transport role, as shown in Figure 12.9.

With the Client Access and Hub Transport roles deployed, the next step would be to deploy the Mailbox role (not shown), configure public folders if desired, and finally, install the Edge Transport role, assuming you are not deploying a Unified Messaging role.

The Edge role is installed on separate hardware in the perimeter network. During setup, as shown in Figure 12.10, you must select a custom installation and choose the Edge Transport server role.

FIGURE 12.8   Installing Hub/CAS on the same hardware

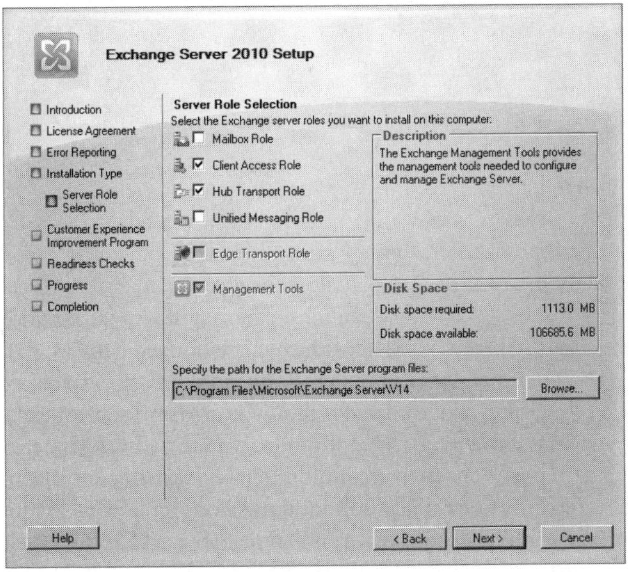

FIGURE 12.9   Installing Hub on dedicated hardware

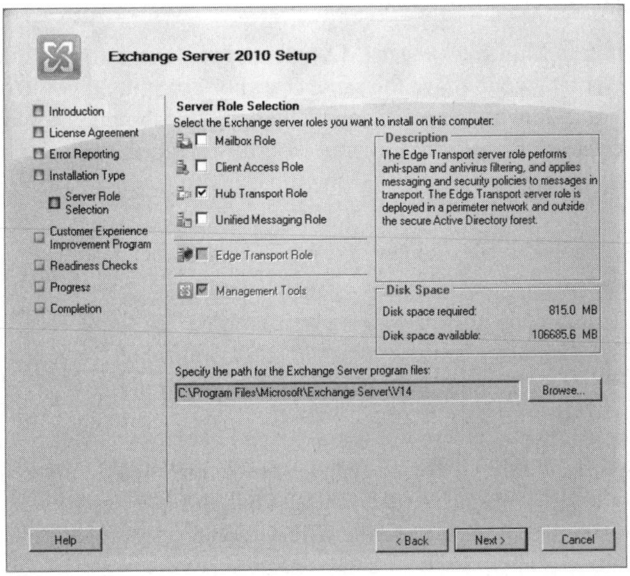

FIGURE 12.10 Installing the Edge role

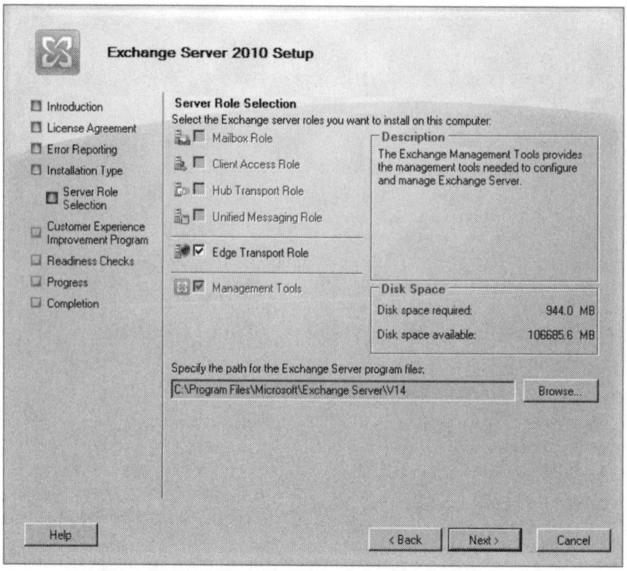

After the Hub and Edge roles have been deployed, the following transport server post-deployment tasks are recommended:

Configure-edge subscription See the steps outlined in the section in Chapter 3 on configuring and managing EdgeSync.

Configure accepted domains See the steps outlined in the section in Chapter 3 on configuring accepted domains.

MX records Configure Mail Exchanger (MX) records to point to the IP address of the Edge servers. Both servers would have the same cost. For example, if you would be responsible for both the mailtask.com and ExchangeExchange.com domains, configure your MX records to resemble the configuration shown in Figure 12.11.

FIGURE 12.11 MX record configuration

```
mailtask.com       mail exchanger = 10 ET01.mailtask.com.
mailtask.com       mail exchanger = 10 ET02.mailtask.com.
ExchangeExchange.com       mail exchanger = 10 ET01.ExchangeExchange.com.
ExchangeExchange.com       mail exchanger = 10 ET02.ExchangeExchange.com.
```

Configure Internet mail flow (optional) Note that an implicit send connector already exists in transport and is not visible in the management tools. This send connector is computed based on your Active Directory site topology and enables your Hub Transport servers to communicate with each other. After the edge subscription is configured, additional send and receive connectors are configured between the Hub and Edge servers. Hence, unless explicitly required, you do not need to configure additional connectors.

After you deploy your transport servers, it is necessary to verify the installation by performing a few post-installation tasks as outlined in Exercise 12.3.

EXERCISE 12.3

Transport Server Post-installation Tasks

Verify the installation and services status as well as perform the following post-installation tasks:

1. Click Start ➢ All Programs ➢ Microsoft Exchange Server 2010 and then select Exchange Management Shell.

2. Run `Get-ExchangeServer <EX01>` and verify installation of the role(s).

3. Run `Get-Service MSExch*` to ensure that the services are running.

4. Run `Get-AcceptedDomain` and note the default accepted domain already configured.

5. Add a new accepted domain called ExchangeExchange.com.

6. Click Start ➢ All Programs ➢ Microsoft Exchange Server 2010 and then select Exchange Management Console.

7. Expand the Microsoft Exchange container, expand the Microsoft Exchange On-Premises container, expand the Organization Configuration container, and then click the Hub Transport node.

8. In the Details pane, select the Accepted Domains tab.

9. Right-click anywhere in the area and click New Accepted Domain.

   Type **ExchangeExchange** for the name and **ExchangeExchange.com** for the accepted domain and then select the Authoritative Domain option. Click OK.

10. Click Finish.

11. Run `Start-Edgesynchronization` to update this information on the Edge Transport server role.

12. Run `Get-AcceptedDomain` on the Edge Transport server to verify that the new accepted domain has been replicated to the Edge server. If your MX records have been updated, you can send an inbound test message to verify mail delivery.

Upgrading and Coexistence with Exchange Server 2003

Quite a few Exchange deployments fall into either an upgrade or a coexistence scenario. These would consist of organizations that never upgraded to Exchange Server 2007. As was the case for a few deployments in Exchange 2007, some organizations may choose to deploy an Exchange 2010 Edge Transport server in the perimeter network while not immediately upgrading their internal AD infrastructure. This gives them an added layer of antispam protection in addition to the Exchange 2003 Intelligent message filter. In deployments where the Exchange 2010 was introduced in the perimeter network without upgrading the internal Exchange 2003 environment, send and receive connectors typically are manually created on the Edge Transport server to control mail flow in and out of the organization. However, not all features of Edge Transport are available with this configuration. Figure 12.12 shows a sample routing topology where Exchange 2010 is deployed into an existing Exchange 2003 environment.

Before you perform an upgrade, you must determine if all user mailboxes will be moved to Exchange 2010 or if there will be a period of consistence. Additionally, you need to review the current messaging topology for any special routing configuration, such as SMTP connectors for specific domains or partners with custom permissions or other settings. If multiple routing groups exist in Exchange 2003, then you should modify the Registry to suppress minor link-state updates on all the Exchange 2003 servers.

In Exercise 12.4, you will create the SuppressStateChanges Registry key to suppress minor link-state updates on all the Exchange 2003 servers. This is because Exchange 2007 and Exchange 2010 do not understand or support the use of these updates.

FIGURE 12.12   Coexisting with Exchange 2003

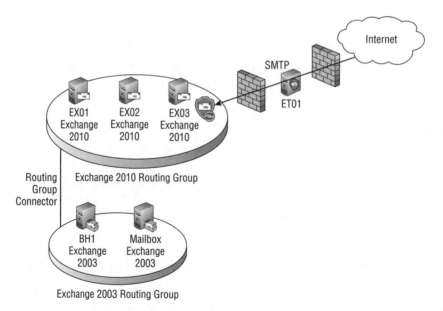

EXERCISE 12.4

Disabling Link-State Updates

Follow these steps to disable link-state updates on an Exchange 2003 server:

1. Click Start ➤ Run and type **regedt32**.

2. Expand until you get to SYSTEM\CurrentControlSet\Services\RESvc\Parameters.

3. Create a REG_DWORD value called SuppressStateChanges and set it to 1.

As discussed previously in the section "Deploying a New Exchange Installation (Greenfield)," it is recommend that you run the ExPDA tool to scan your AD environment to make sure Exchange 2010 can be deployed based on your existing AD topology and hardware.

As you deploy Exchange 2010, consider which Exchange 2003 routing group would be the last to be decommissioned. Plan to deploy Exchange 2010 tool to connect directly to this routing group. You must install the Client Access server role before deploying the Hub Transport role.

During a deployment of Exchange 2010 into the existing Exchange 2003 environment, setup creates the Active Directory universal security group ExchangeLegacyInterop. Adequate permissions are granted to this group to enable the Exchange 2003 servers to route mail to the Exchange 2010 server. For messages to be routed to and from the Exchange 2003 environment, setup prompts you to create a routing group connector between the Exchange 2003 and an Exchange 2010 server, as shown in Figure 12.13. You are required to select an Exchange 2003 server, as shown in Figure 12.14. This is required to enable mail flow between both versions of Exchange.

FIGURE 12.13   Configuring mail flow settings with Exchange 2003 during setup

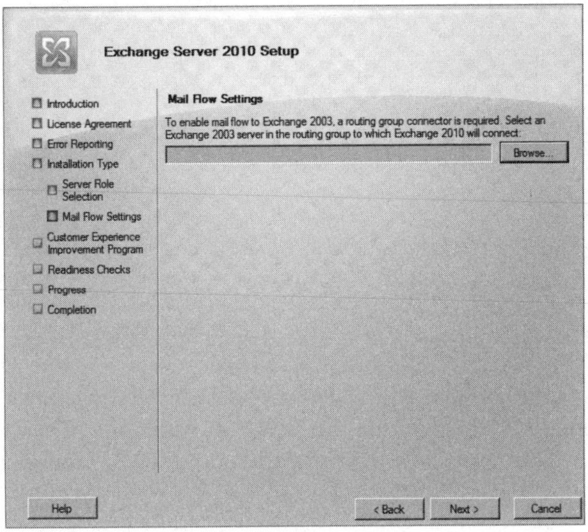

Finally, deploy the Edge Transport server after the Hub Transport server deployment is complete. Deployment steps as well as transport post-deployment tasks are identical to the Greenfield deployment.

Upgrading and Coexistence with Exchange Server 2007

The actual server deployment will not differ greatly from that of the Greenfield deployment. Organizations upgrading from Exchange 2007 with multiple AD sites need to carefully plan their deployment, upgrading the Internet-facing AD sites first. The recommended upgrade order is to deploy the CAS server roles before the transport server roles. If both Exchange 2003 and 2007 servers already exist in the environment, you are not prompted to select an Exchange 2003 routing group to directly connect to. This would have already been done during the deployment of the first Exchange 2007 Hub server into the Exchange 2003 environment. Figure 12.15 shows a typical topology where Exchange 2010 coexists with Exchange 2003 and Exchange 2007. The Exchange 2010 Hub Transport server would be deployed into the same DWBGZMFD01QNBJR routing group as the existing Exchange 2007 servers.

FIGURE 12.14 Choosing an Exchange 2003 server

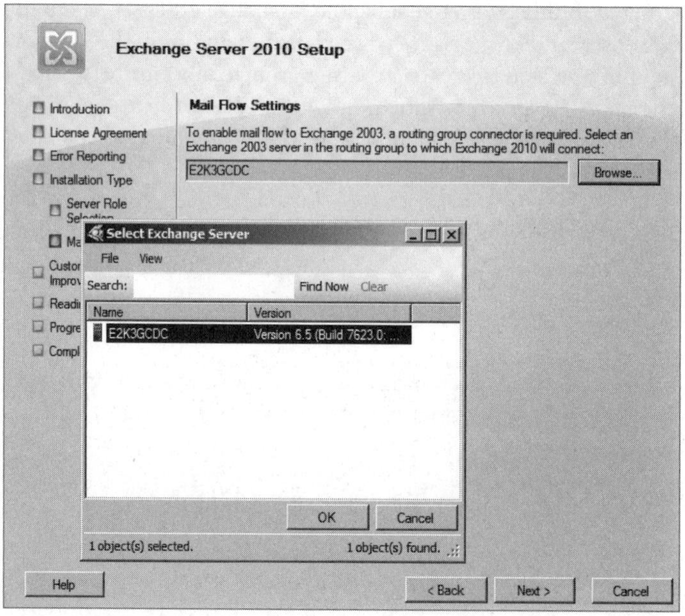

As discussed previously in the section "Deploying a New Exchange Installation (Greenfield)," we recommend that you run the ExPDA to scan your AD environment, making sure Exchange 2010 can be deployed based on your existing AD topology and hardware.

Before Exchange 2010 can be deployed into an existing Exchange 2007 environment, each Exchange 2007 server must be running Exchange 2007 Service Pack 2 or later.

FIGURE 12.15   Coexistence with Exchange 2003/2007

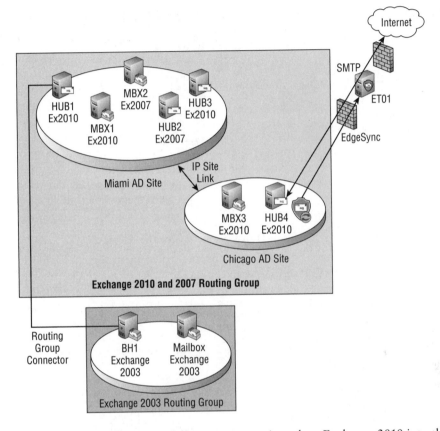

Based on Figure 12.15, use the following steps to introduce Exchange 2010 into this messaging environment:

1. Deploy the first Exchange 2010 Hub Transport into the existing Exchange 2007 site.

    When the Exchange 2010 Hub Transport is deployed, it immediately assumes edge synchronization responsibilities with the Exchange 2007 Edge Transport server, but all mail flow to the Internet would be routed through the Exchange 2007 server. As alluded to in the section "Improvements in Edge Synchronization" earlier in this chapter, only full synchronization of configuration and recipient data takes place between the Exchange 2010 Hub Transport and Exchange 2007 Edge Transport servers. This is shown in Figure 12.16. If you are replacing all the existing Exchange 2007 servers in the site, then proceed to deploy all the Exchange 2010 Hub Transport servers that would replace the Exchange 2007 Hub Transport servers.

FIGURE 12.16 Deploying Exchange 2010 into an Internet-facing site

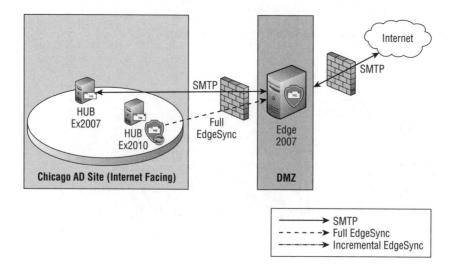

2. Resubscribe Exchange 2007 Edge Transport servers to the AD site.

   After all planned Exchange 2010 Hub Transport replacement servers have been deployed into the site, resubscribe the Exchange 2007 servers in the perimeter network to the AD site again. As shown in Figure 12.17, the Exchange 2010 Hub Transport server now takes over both edge synchronization and mail flow responsibilities.

FIGURE 12.17 Resubscribe the Exchange 2007 Edge Transport to the site

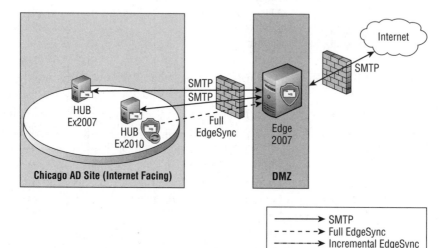

3. Introduce the Exchange 2010 Edge Transport server into the perimeter network.

Figure 12.18 shows what happens after deploying an Exchange 2010 Edge Transport server and configuring a new edge subscription. This enables incremental updates with the Exchange 2010 Edge Transport server. All Hub Transport servers can route mail to either an Exchange 2007 Edge Transport or Exchange 2010 Edge Transport and vice versa. The Exchange 2010 Hub Transport servers continues to handle edge synchronization responsibilities.

FIGURE 12.18   Deploy the Exchange 2010 Edge Transport into the perimeter network

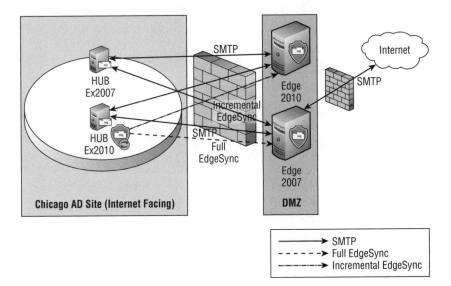

4. Allow for a version-based routing phase.

If the Mailbox servers have not been upgraded and user mailboxes are still on Exchange 2007, then you must ensure that there is an Exchange 2007 Hub Transport server in the AD site. If for some reason the Exchange 2007 Hub Transport servers become unavailable, mail flow will fail because the Exchange 2010 Hub Transport servers will not deliver to the Exchange 2007 Mailbox servers. Refer to the detailed discussion in the section "Understanding Version-Based Routing" earlier in this chapter.

5. Decommission the Exchange 2007 Edge Transport server.

As shown in Figure 12.19, you can finally decommission the Exchange 2007 Edge Transport server. This would allow for the Exchange 2010 Edge Transport server to perform both routing and mail flow functions.

FIGURE 12.19 Decommission the Exchange 2007 Edge

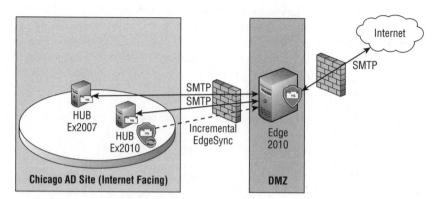

🌐 **Real World Scenario**

Synchronizing System Time

One of the key requirements of a routing design is to have at least one Hub Transport server in every AD site where a Mailbox server is deployed. It is important, however, to ensure that the time on the Hub Transport server is synchronized with the time on the domain controllers in that site. If there is a time delta greater than 5 minutes, Exchange authentication may fail, resulting in messages being queued and ultimately returned with an NDR.

Take Away: Each Exchange server's computer time should match that of the domain controllers in the Active Directory site.

Exchange 2010 Client Access and Connectivity

As client communication methods become diverse and available on many devices, Exchange inboxes and other data is now accessible from a wide variety of platforms and technologies. Chapter 3 introduced you to the various features and connectivity methods available for clients to access the Exchange 2010 server. As you recall, a significant architectural change made in Exchange 2010 is the consolidation of MAPI mailbox access paths to a middle tier (MoMT) housed on the CAS server role. With the introduction of the Exchange RPC Client Access service and the Exchange Address Book service on the CAS role, client requests are now processed by the CAS role with the exception of MAPI access to public folders, which goes directly to the Mailbox server role.

Connectivity to the Client Access server role can originate from at least three sources: internal clients within the Active Directory, external clients connecting from the Internet, or connections from other Client Access servers attempting to proxy client requests. Figure 12.20 shows a summary of the different clients connecting to the CAS role and the access methods used.

FIGURE 12.20   Client Access architecture in Exchange 2010

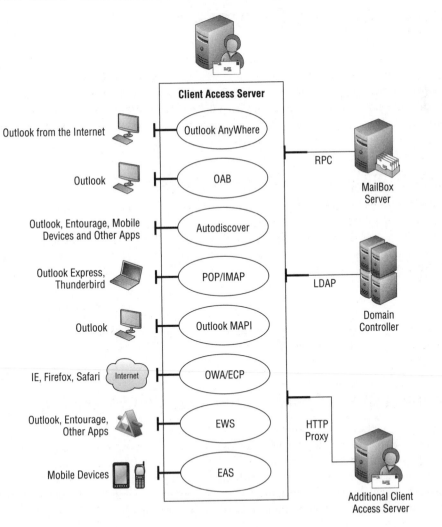

This architectural shift to process MAPI on the middle tier is a huge benefit for scalability of client connections and performance. An advantage is that it provides better client experience in load balancing and failover scenarios with minimal impact on the client and significantly higher number of concurrent connections per server. However, whether you are designing a CAS role for deployment into an existing or new Exchange environment, several factors must be considered. In the following sections, we'll review the design considerations when planning and deploying the Exchange 2010 Client Access server role.

Deploying Exchange Server 2010 Client Access Servers

When planning Exchange 2010 CAS server deployment, it is important to review the existing messaging infrastructure if one exists as well as determine what type of clients will be supported to access the CAS server and how. With this in mind, other client access methods not used may be disabled for performance and security reasons. It is also important to have a good idea of the total number of clients connecting to the CAS role because this relates directly to memory consumption on the CAS role.

Understanding Active Directory Topology

As a general rule of thumb, you must deploy a Client Access server into any Active Directory site where a Mailbox server role exists. If Exchange 2010 is deployed in multiple Active Directory sites, consideration must be given to which AD sites are accessible from the Internet. Upgrade or deploy Exchange 2010 CAS servers to this Internet-facing AD site first before the internal AD sites. This is important to allow Client Access proxying to legacy Exchange CAS servers.

NOTE Installing a Client Access server role into a perimeter network or DMZ is not supported.

Planning Client Access Namespace and Proxying

A namespace is the domain name used by clients to access the Client Access server role or CAS array. After reviewing your AD topology, as a general rule, it is recommended that each AD site with an Internet-facing CAS role or array should have a unique namespace. Namespaces can be simple such as Mail.Mailtask.com, which has a single namespace to multi-AD sites in different geographical regions, with each region having an Internet-facing AD site such as NorthAmerica.Mail.Mailtask.com, for example.

Deciding on the namespace to be used is extremely important because it affects what URLs the (OWA), POP/IMAP, and Outlook Anywhere clients would use to connect to the CAS server. Also affected is the DNS configuration as well as the type of digital certificate deployed.

The CAS server can be configured to proxy client connections to an internal Client Access server in a different AD site. This can be very helpful if your namespace decision is to configure just one Internet-facing AD site while you have user mailboxes in multiple AD sites that are not Internet-facing. This proxying is automatic and occurs using the RPC protocol between the CAS servers. Exchange 2010 also proxies requests to an Exchange 2007 CAS server, thus allowing for coexistence.

As you plan your Exchange 2010 CAS design, it is important to note that the Exchange 2010 CAS server supports proxying for OWA, Exchange ActiveSync, and Exchange Web Services (EWS). On the Internet-facing CAS servers, the ExternalURL setting for these services' virtual directories is configured to match the namespace registered in DNS and the authentication set to Integrated Windows Authentication. Internal non-Internet-facing CAS servers would have the ExternalURLs set to null. Table 12.3 shows the configuration on both the Internet-facing and non- Internet-facing CAS servers.

TABLE 12.3   InternalURLs and ExternalURLs

Internet-facing Client Access server

Exchange 2010 Service	InternalURL Setting	ExternalURL Setting
Outlook Web App	`https://<computername>/OWA`	`https://www.contoso.com/OWA`
Exchange ActiveSync	`https://<computername>/` `Microsoft-Server-ActiveSync`	`https://www.contoso.com/` `Microsoft-Server-ActiveSync`
Exchange Web Services	`https://<computername>/EWS`	`https://www.contoso.com/EWS`
Availability service	`https://<computername>/AS`	`https://www.contoso.com/AS`

Non-Internet-facing Client Access server

Exchange 2010 Service	InternalURL Setting	ExternalURL Setting
Outlook Web App	`https://<computername>/OWA`	`$N$Null`
Exchange ActiveSync	`https://<computername>/` `Microsoft-Server-ActiveSync`	`$N$Null`
Exchange Web Services	`https://<computername>/EWS`	`$Null`
Availability service	`https://<computername>/AS`	`$Null`

For only the OWA service, Exchange 2010 allows redirection when a client connects to an Internet-facing CAS server which is existing in a different AD site than where the mailbox resides. In this scenario, the Internet-facing CAS server simply returns a web page with the URL of the CAS server in the same AD site where its mailbox resides. The client would have to manually click on the link to be redirected to the appropriate CAS server in the same AD site where the mailbox exits.

> You can disable redirection for the Outlook Web App, forcing it to use proxying by running the following cmdlet: Set-OwaVirtualDirectory "Owa (EX01)"> -RedirectToOptimalOWAServer $False.

Planning Client Access Load Balancing

With the CAS server now the single connection point for all clients, it is important to include load balancing to allow for scalability and performance. A group of CAS servers can be configured in a CAS array, if one CAS server goes down for any reason; the client is redirected to another CAS server in the array. Also, rather than pointing the Mailbox server role to one specific CAS server, it is configured to point to the FQDN of the CAS array.

When designing for the CAS array it is important to note that the AD site is the effective boundary for the CAS array. In other words, you cannot join CAS servers in multiple AD sites to the same CAS array. There can be only one CAS array for each AD site. In addition, it is not supported nor recommended to mix different Exchange Server versions in the same CAS array. For example, you cannot mix Exchange 2007 and Exchange 2010 CAS servers in the same load balanced array.

Deciding on Software or Hardware Load Balancing

The choice of which type of load balancing solution to use would depend on a variety of factors. However, it is important to understand the limitations of each. Hardware load balancing devices, although more ideal than Windows network load balancing (NLB), are typically quite expensive! For small organizations, hardware budget constraints may prevent this from being an option. Software load balancing such as NLB adds no additional cost to the planning but comes with several limitations:

Co-located Exchange Server roles   If the CAS server role is installed on a Mailbox server role that is already a member of a DAG, then NLB will not work. This is because NLB is incompatible with the Windows failover clustering feature.

Scalability   Serious performance issues result when more than eight CAS servers are added to a CAS array using NLB.

Port flooding   May occur and likely to result in network outages.

Affinity   NLB maps a connecting client IP to a specific CAS server in the array and would fail over based on the connecting IP. This becomes a limitation if the client's source IP pool is small; multiple clients are accessing the load balancer from the same IP address or clients are connecting via a reverse proxy solutions such as Microsoft Forefront Threat Management Gateway (TMG), ISA, or UAG devices. This is a limitation of WNLB.

Because WNLB has an affinity for IP addresses, failure of a particular service or protocol may not be detected, so the client's connections will continue to the failed CAS server in the array.

Additionally, hardware load balancing offers more options for affinity than WNLB and the affinity set for each service or protocol may vary.

Restricting the MAPI Client Version

The Exchange 2010 RPC Client Access service requires RPC encryption by default. Outlook 2007 and Outlook 2010 client versions are compatible because they also support RPC encryption by default. This provides a more secure server/client communication. Legacy MAPI clients such as Outlook 2003 and earlier do not support RPC encryption by default. Hence, you must factor into your design your MAPI client version. The three options available are upgrading your existing clients to a newer version, disabling RPC encryption on the RPC Client Access service to allow your existing legacy clients to connect, or finally, configuring your legacy Outlook clients for RPC encryption. To bulk-configure your Outlook 2003 clients to use RPC encryption, you can roll out a group policy object (GPO), forcing them to use it.

 To configure a single Outlook 2003 client to use RPC encryption to access Exchange 2010, in the Outlook client security settings, select Encrypt Data Between Microsoft Office Outlook And Microsoft Exchange Server. To change the default encryption configuration of the RPC Client Access service, you can run the following PowerShell cmdlet: `Set-RpcClientAccess -Server <Exchange_server_name> -EncryptionRequired $False`.

Encrypting Client Access Security

Exchange 2010 uses Secure Sockets Layer (SSL) to secure data between the client and server. By default, all client services and protocols are encrypted using SSL with the exception of POP3 and IMAP4 clients. However, both protocols can be configured to require SSL. A digital self-signed certificate is created during installation, however it is recommended to purchase, install, and enable trusted third-party certificates. Sever-to-server communication in Exchange 2010 is also secure.

Also by default, the communication between the Client Access server and other server roles, including domain controllers and global catalog servers, is encrypted.

Choosing Hardware and Sizing

There are a variety of factors to consider when choosing hardware and sizing for a CAS server role, especially considering the expanded role of the CAS server. The most important, though, are processor and memory. The rate of consumption of these resources is directly related to the number of clients connecting to the CAS server and the protocols or services being processed.

For the Exchange 2010 CAS server with no other roles installed, 4 gigabytes (GB) of RAM is sufficient with 8 GB RAM recommended. With so many server models having multi-core processors, this represents 1 GB per processor core. A total of 8 processor cores is recommended with a maximum of 12. Consider increasing to 2 GB per processor core if most of your clients will be using Outlook Anywhere. This is essentially due to the memory footprint created when processing RPC over HTTP connections.

The ratio of CAS servers to Mailbox servers is also a factor to consider. Remember that at least one CAS server must be deployed in every AD site where a Mailbox server role is deployed. However, it is recommended that for every four Mailbox server processor cores, you deploy one CAS server processor core. In other words, if you have two Mailbox servers with four processor cores each, then you should deploy one CAS server with two processor cores.

Performance degradation may occur on the CAS server as a result of thread and connection exhaustion. The issue stems from the re-architecture of process execution in IIS7. For security reasons, concurrent executing client requests to the server by design are limited to 12 for each processor. It is easy to exhaust this limit. Hence, Microsoft recommends configuring 36 threads per processor and setting the MaxConnections value to 2000 on CAS servers in proxying environments. For more information on this resource exhaustion, see the knowledge base article at the following location: http://support.microsoft.com/?kbid=821268.

Deploying the Exchange Server 2010 Client Access Server Role

The CAS server role should be the first role to be deployed in any environment, whether the Greenfield or Exchange 2010 environment is coexisting with a legacy Exchange version. As mentioned earlier in this chapter, careful planning is required to ensure that clients are not impacted during the deployment. The Greenfield deployment steps for the Client Access server here are identical to the deployment steps mentioned in the section "Deploying a New Exchange Installation (Greenfield)" earlier in this chapter because there are no legacy version prerequisites needed. The actual deployment, however, would vary depending on the organization's budget as well as technical and business requirements. Depending on your design, the first deployment may be just a single CAS server or it could be an entire CAS array. Deployment into an existing Exchange 2003 or 2007 environment, on the other hand, requires even more careful thought. The Exchange Server Deployment Assistant and ExPDA are tools that can guide you through specific deployment scenarios. In the following sections, we consider some upgrade-specific deployment steps, concentrating on the Client Access server role.

Upgrading and Coexistence with Exchange Server 2007

In a single-AD-site environment, the Exchange 2010 CAS server is deployed into the site after meeting the deployment requirements. However, in multi-AD-site environments, not all AD sites may be Internet facing or have access to the Internet. Exchange 2010, hence, must be deployed from outside in, meaning that Exchange 2010 must be introduced into the Internet-facing AD sites before it's introduced into the non-Internet-facing AD sites. It is recommended that you deploy one site at a time. If you have more than one Internet-facing AD site, the first sites to be deployed should be those responsible for handling the external Autodiscover service requests. Depending on your topology and design, the first deployment may be just a single CAS server or a CAS array.

The upgrade process may include the following steps:

1. Installing Exchange 2010 on new hardware into the Internet-facing AD site. The new CAS servers will handle the front-end protocols and proxy requests to mailboxes on Exchange 2007.

2. Configuring the installed CAS servers. This may include configuration of a CAS array and configuration of Outlook Anywhere, OWA settings, and ActiveSync settings, depending on your organization's needs.

3. If Exchange 2010 is coexisting with Exchange 2007, creating legacy hostnames to be associated with Exchange 2007. This step is not necessary if all mailboxes would be immediately moved to Exchange 2010.

4. Procuring Subject Alternative Name (SAN or UCC) or wildcard certificate, depending on your need and installation on the Exchange 2010 CAS server. Be aware that Windows Mobile 5.0 devices do not support the use of wildcard certificates.

5. Associating your current namespace to your Exchange 2010 deployment.

6. Moving mailboxes to Exchange 2010.

7. Validating and testing all client connections and Internet protocol usage.

8. Decommissioning the Exchange 2007 servers.

Upgrading to Exchange Server 2010 Outlook Web App

When Exchange 2010 CAS is deployed in the Internet-facing AD site, Exchange 2007 users connecting to their mailboxes using OWA will connect to the Exchange 2010 CAS server. The connection will be redirected to an Exchange 2007 CAS server within the AD site or proxied to an Exchange 2007 CAS server if the mailbox is in a different AD site. For this redirection and proxy to work, both CAS server versions must have external FQDNs and the desired namespace associated with the Exchange 2010 CAS server. All users will access their mailboxes using the Exchange 2010 CAS server URL and redirection will take place, providing a single sign-on experience. After mailboxes have been moved to Exchange 2010 Mailbox servers, then users would use OWA to connect to their mailboxes directly on Exchange 2010.

Upgrading to Exchange Server 2010 ActiveSync

With the CAS servers deployment completed and the Exchange ActiveSync settings configured, users connecting to their mailboxes on Exchange 2007 using Windows Mobile 5 and Windows Mobile 6 devices will be redirected by the Exchange 2010 CAS server to an Exchange 2007 CAS server. If the hostnames are already configured on Exchange 2010, then Windows Mobile users would not need to manually reconfigure their devices. After mailboxes are moved to Exchange 2010, Windows Mobile clients would be prompted to perform a full synchronization of their data. If the organization transitioned to using a new namespace, then Windows Mobile clients will have to manually reconfigure their devices. Windows Mobile 6.1 or later devices will be automatically reconfigured , by finding the new URL using the Autodiscover service.

Upgrading to Exchange Server 2010 Outlook Anywhere

With the deployment of Exchange 2010 CAS servers, if Outlook Anywhere is being used it needs to be configured on at least one Exchange 2010 CAS server. If the Autodiscover service is already configured, then Outlook 2007 and later clients will use Autodiscover to obtain configuration information that will be used to automatically reconfigure their client settings when an Exchange 2010 CAS server is introduced in the AD site or when their mailboxes are moved from Exchange 2007 to Exchange 2010.

You may use the Test-OutlookConnectivity cmdlet to test end-to-end Outlook client connectivity. You may also use the Exchange Remote Connectivity Analyzer (ExRCA) available at https://www .testexchangeconnectivity.com.

Upgrading to Exchange Server 2010 Exchange Web Services

If Autodiscover has been configured on the deployed Exchange 2010 CAS server, then Exchange Web Services (EWS) clients that use Autodiscover will be automatically reconfigured through the Autodiscover service. EWS clients that use hardcoded URLs to access their

Exchange 2007 mailbox will have to be manually reconfigured since they would fail to connect when the URL is pointed to Exchange 2010.

Finally, after upgrade and tests are completed, the legacy Exchange 2007 servers should be decommissioned in the following order:

1. Mailbox server
2. Unified Messaging server
3. Hub Transport server
4. Client Access server
5. Edge Transport server

Upgrading and Coexistence with Exchange Server 2003

The steps to upgrade from Exchange 2003 are identical to the steps to upgrade from Exchange 2007. In the Exchange 2003 organization, an Exchange 2003 front-end server is required to support the upgrade. For OWA redirection to work, you must configure one Outlook Web Access 2003 URL. Keep in mind that the type of page rendered to the user, whether a user sees the OWA client of Exchange 2003 or the OWA client of Exchange 2010, depends on the location of the user's mailbox. If the user's mailbox is located on an Exchange 2003 back-end server and the Client Access server is running Exchange 2010, the user will see Exchange 2003 Outlook Web Access.

Finally, after upgrade and tests are completed, the legacy Exchange 2003 servers should be decommissioned in the following order:

1. Mailbox server
2. SMTP server
3. Front-end server

Proxying POP3 and IMAP4 Clients

When an Exchange 2010 CAS server is deployed and configured in an AD site, POP3 and IMAP4 client commands are proxied from the Exchange 2010 CAS server to a random Exchange 2007 CAS server in the same site if the mailbox resides on an Exchange 2007 server. The same is true if the mailbox resides on an Exchange 2003 back-end server. The way POP3/IMAP4 service discovery works is much the same as the Exchange 2003 front-end/back-end topology where POP3/IMAP4 commands were proxied from the front end to the back end. The Exchange 2010 CAS server can take POP3/IMAP4 protocol commands issued by clients and route them to either a CAS server in the existing site, another AD site, or an Exchange 2003 back-end server when configured.

In the following sections, we'll consider the different scenarios under which POP3/IMAP4 commands could be proxied.

In order for POP3/IMAP4 commands to be proxied, the following parameters must be configured:

InternalConnectionSettings/ExternalConnectionSettings   This parameter specifies the hostname or FQDN, port number, and encryption type POP3/IMAP4 clients will use to connect when located within the corporate network and outside the corporate network, respectively. This information is also used by the CAS server to connect a remote CAS server to service client requests.

ProxyTargetPort   This parameter is used by the Exchange 2010 CAS server when proxying commands to an Exchange 2003 server. This must be a valid TCP port and must match the port specified on the Exchange 2003 POP3/IMAP4 virtual servers.

LoginType   This parameter specifies the login type used for authentication in order to proxy commands. The login type for the POP3/IMAP4 protocol on the Exchange 2010 CAS server must match the login time of the destination Exchange 2007 CAS server or Exchange 2003 back-end server.

Proxying Exchange 2010 Cross-Site Proxy

Consider the topology in Figure 12.21. Kori's mailbox resides on an Exchange 2010 server in the Miami site. The Exchange 2010 CAS server in the Chicago site is the Internet-facing CAS server. When Kory attempts to access his mailbox using POP3, the commands are proxied from the CAS server in the Chicago site to the CAS server in the Miami site and he is able to access his mailbox. You can test this by following the steps outlined in Exercise 12.5.

FIGURE 12.21   Cross-site POP3/IMAP4 command proxy

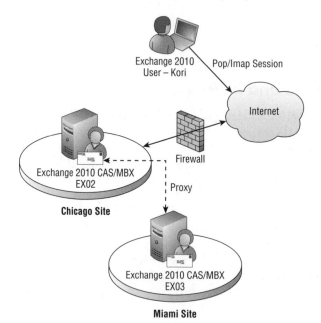

EXERCISE 12.5

POP3/IMAP4 Cross-site Command Proxy

Follow these steps to configure POP3/IMAP4 redirection in a multi-AD-site environment:

1. Configure a POP3 client to connect to Kori's mailbox. Use the EX02 CAS server in the Chicago site.

2. Enable POP3 logging on both the EX02 CAS server in the Chicago site and the EX03 CAS server in the Miami site.

3. Send a test message to another mailbox in either the Miami or Chicago site.

4. Review POP3 logs.

Proxying Exchange Server 2010 to Exchange 2003 POP3/IMAP4

Exchange 2010 supports proxying POP3/IMAP4 commands to legacy Exchange 2003 back-end servers. The Exchange 2003 servers must minimally have Service Pack 2 installed. This is described in Figure 12.22. Keep in mind that by default, the login type for POP3/IMAP4 on Exchange 2003 is set to PlainTextLogin.

FIGURE 12.22   Exchange 2010 to 2003 POP3/IMAP4 command proxy

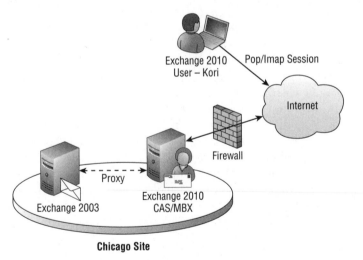

Chicago Site

Proxying Exchange Server 2010 to Legacy Exchange 2007/2003

Exchange 2010 supports proxying POP3/IMAP4 commands to legacy environments consisting of Exchange 2003 and Exchange 2007. In this scenario, the Exchange 2007 CAS server must support the same port and encryption type as the Exchange 2010 CAS.

Proxying Exchange ActiveSync Coexistence for Exchange 2003

Exchange 2010 supports proxying ActiveSync communications to Exchange 2003. To enable this functionality, you must enable Windows authentication on the Microsoft-Server-ActiveSync virtual directory on the Exchange back end. To do this, install and configure the Exchange 2003 hotfix on the back-end server; it is located at `http://support.microsoft.com/?kbid=937031`.

Summary

In this chapter, we reviewed the new transport features available in Exchange 2010 and how they affect message routing. Features such as shadow redundancy, moderation, cross-premises delivery, and versioned routing can indeed have an impact on the routing topology. We examined critical and noncritical design dependencies essential to planning and deploying routing and client access in an Exchange Server messaging environment.

While the Hub Transport and Edge Transport server roles continue to form the basic components of message routing, we can never underestimate the importance of a well-thought-out AD topology or a careful analysis of an existing AD topology. Keep in mind that besides the AD topology, several other factors discussed can affect transport and Client Access server performance.

As with any Exchange deployment, it is necessary to decide when and if certain features would be implemented and how they can impact routing or client access. For example, we discussed message moderation and distribution groups. If the Exchange 2010 deployment is coexisting with the Exchange 2007 environment, it may be helpful to delay configuration of distribution group moderation until all the Exchange 2007 Hub Transport servers have been decommissioned. An alternative to this approach, however, may be to configure an expansion server for any distribution group configured for moderation. This may require additional administrative effort and is a decision left up to each organization.

Moreover, adequate hardware sizing for Client Access servers is critical to mitigating client access problems. It is critical as you research the existing messaging topology to determine what type of clients would be connecting and the average frequency as well as future projected load. If you're implementing new client access methods such as Outlook Anywhere, determine whether your existing hardware can handle the increased client requests. Also keep in mind that if you're using Outlook 2003 or older clients and connecting to Exchange 2010 CAS, encryption must be disabled on the Client Access server or the clients must be configured for encryption.

Finally, POP3 and IMAP4 protocol usage continues to increase for some organizations. Microsoft has made many improvements in the use of these protocols in Exchange 2010. It is important to deploy and configure Client Access servers to properly handle these requests depending on the existing messaging topology.

Chapter Essentials

Understand message routing and transport. The overall transport and routing architecture in Exchange 2010 has not changed from that of Exchange 2007. Significant feature improvements have been made in Exchange 2010 SP1. Understand and become familiar with how messages are routed in both Greenfield and coexistence messaging topologies. Become familiar with the new features introduced in Exchange 2010 transport and how they affect message routing. Get to know how to introduce Exchange 2010 Edge Transport servers into an existing Exchange 2007 environment as well as how to deploy and manage multiple Exchange 2010 Edge Transport servers.

Understand client access. Significant architectural changes have been made in the Exchange 2010 Client Access server, it being the end point for clients connecting using OWA, Outlook Anywhere, ActiveSync, EWS, POP3, and IMAP4. Understand that Outlook still connects to the Mailbox database directly for access to public folders. Plan on upgrading your existing infrastructure from outside in! Upgrade the Internet-facing AD sites before the non-Internet-facing sites. Become familiar with client connectivity behavior when upgrading to Exchange 2010.

Chapter

13

Designing Security and Compliance

THE FOLLOWING TOPICS ARE DISCUSSED IN THIS CHAPTER:

- ✓ Designing messaging security and compliance
- ✓ Planning Exchange permissions models
- ✓ Designing message hygiene
- ✓ Designing client access security
- ✓ Designing message archival and discovery

In most cases, email is the fastest, easiest, and cheapest way for one person to send information and documents to any number of other people. This has made email critical to practically every company that exists, but it also means that your organization's email messages need to be protected and rules need to be put in place that protect your organization from having messages sent that shouldn't have been.

Exchange Server 2010 includes many features that can protect your email and organization, including encryption between partner organizations, encryption during client downloads, and message compliance features to protect documents from being opened by people other than the intended recipient. Each of these features requires planning, design, and end-user communication before they're implemented. You need to understand how to design these features and what factors will affect your company's decisions on how to design your Exchange security and compliance.

Designing Messaging Security and Compliance

When you design your Exchange Server 2010 infrastructure, it is important to make sure that your email messages are secure. Exchange veterans will be familiar with many of the options available for securing email. Exchange Server 2010 continues to support Secure/Multipurpose Internet Mail Extensions (S/MIME), which allows your employees to perform certificate-based email signing and encryption from Outlook Web Access (OWA). Exchange 2010 has also seen little change in send and receive connectors from 2007, so the same security settings that were used in 2007 still apply. Exchange 2010 also continues to support journaling rules, allowing you to journal a copy of every email sent or received from a mailbox.

In addition to having features that have changed little, Exchange 2010 has seen major improvements to messaging security, many of which are focused around integration with Active Directory Rights Management Services (AD RMS). With AD RMS integration, you can now create Outlook protection rules and create transport rules to apply RMS templates. Depending on your organization's requirements, you may use some or all of these features.

Supporting S/MIME

Exchange Server 2010 supports using S/MIME from OWA. S/MIME allows users to sign, encrypt, and decrypt emails sent or received using OWA. When implementing S/MIME, it is important to remember that the S/MIME control that users must install is supported only in OWA Premium using Internet Explorer 7 or Internet Explorer 8. Although enabling S/MIME is easy, requiring only that you run the command `Set-OWAVirtualDirectory -SMimeEnabled $true`, there are decisions that you must make when you design your S/MIME implementation.

The most important decision is how you will assign certificates for S/MIME use. Because S/MIME is certificate based, everyone sending and receiving S/MIME-encrypted emails needs to have certificates assigned to them. To allow widespread use of S/MIME in your organization, you will need to set up a public key infrastructure (PKI). You can set up a PKI by creating a domain-joined certificate authority (CA). This CA would provide keys to your users, but because only your users would have access to it, you would only be able to use S/MIME to send emails internally and to partners that you provide your CA's public certificate to. You could also use an outside CA to provide certificates for some or all of your users. Using a well-known outside CA would allow you to use your certificates to communicate with practically anyone but could also incur significant costs.

There are also several S/MIME options that you can control through the Registry on your CAS servers. Usually the default Registry settings are adequate, but it may be beneficial to change a few of them. For example, you may want to enable Copy Recipient Headers, which includes a copy of the To, Cc, and Bcc headers in the signed portion of the email, allowing receivers to verify that the headers were not tampered with. You could also enable Always Sign, which will force recipients to sign all emails sent using OWA with the S/MIME control. For a full list of S/MIME Registry settings and their values, see `http://technet.microsoft .com/en-us/library/bb738151.aspx`.

S/MIME is useful for having end users sign outgoing email. It can also be useful for when people need to encrypt emails they send to specific individuals in other organizations. When you need to offer the ability to control emails sent to others in the organization, or in other trusted organizations that you can set up federation with, it may be beneficial to look at using AD RMS, discussed in the section "Planning AD RMS Integration" later in this chapter.

Planning Secure Internal Receive Connectors

When you design your Exchange send and receive connectors, there are several options that allow you to maintain their security. By default, the Exchange 2010 receive connectors are secured by requiring users to authenticate before sending emails, only allowing users to send emails from addresses for which they have permissions, and by requiring Secure Sockets Layer (SSL) or Transport Layer Security (TLS) connections. Of course, it's important to make sure these settings work. For example, if you can use telnet to connect to the Simple Mail Transfer Protocol (SMTP) port and send an email in plain text, the SSL/TLS requirement isn't working, possibly because you haven't imported a certificate. It's also important to make sure you don't purposefully bypass these settings without a good reason.

Many server applications that require sending email are unable to do SMTP authentication or unable to connect using SSL or TLS. For these applications, you may need to remove the requirement to use SSL/TLS, or you may need to allow anonymous relay. Although it would be simple to decrease the security on the default client receive connectors, the better solution is to create a separate receive connector without those requirements and allow connections to that receive connector from only specified Internet Protocol (IP) addresses. Although this requires more maintenance, requiring you to edit the receive connector on each hub transport server every time you need to allow a different server to relay, it is much more secure. For more information on creating and configuring receive connectors, see Chapter 3, "Configuring Connectors, Routing and Transport, and Connectivity."

Because the default receive connectors in Exchange 2010 require users to authenticate before sending emails, and only allows them to send emails from addresses for which they have permissions, users usually trust emails sent from inside the organization to be authentic. Because this is the case, it's important to take steps to protect your organization from spoofed addresses. If possible, creating a transport rule on your Exchange Edge Transport server that rejects emails with a From or Reply-To address inside your organization complements the security on your receive connectors. To learn how to create a transport rule, see Chapter 6, "Configuring Security, Compliance, and Policies."

Securing Interorganization Email

Exchange 2010 adds support for a new feature called opportunistic TLS. By default, Exchange 2010 creates a self-signed TLS certificate and supports sending and receiving email using TLS when it can be negotiated. This means that when two Exchange 2010 organizations communicate, the communication is automatically secured using TLS.

Although opportunistic TLS protects the email from packet sniffing, it doesn't protect against man-in-the-middle attacks. If your organization has partners that you routinely send confidential email to, you should consider configuring Mutual Auth TLS. Mutual Auth TLS allows your Edge Transport server to verify that the Edge server for the other organization is really from that organization. This requires that both of your organizations have TLS certificates on the Edge Transport server that the other organization trusts, and it requires you to configure your Edge Transport server to require domain security when connecting to the other organization's domain. For information about configuring Mutual Auth TLS, see Chapter 3, "Configuring Connectors, Routing and Transport, and Connectivity."

Planning AD RMS Integration

AD RMS allows an organization to specify encryption and permissions on emails and documents that are sent. AD RMS templates can be assigned using Outlook protection rules, which run on the client side, or transport rules, which will apply the AD RMS template as it passes through a Hub Transport server.

There are really two parts to AD RMS integration. The first step is to install AD RMS and configure AD RMS templates. Depending on your AD RMS implementation, this may be done by the Exchange administrator, another system administrator, or a security department. When AD RMS is ready and templates are installed, the AD RMS Prelicensing agent can be installed and Outlook protection rules and transport rules can be created to apply the AD RMS templates. For information about enabling AD RMS integration, see Chapter 6.

AD RMS allows you to apply information rights management (IRM) templates using Outlook, OWA, and transport rules. IRM templates can control whether or not emails can be forwarded, can encrypt information, or can be used to provide other restrictions. AD RMS is useful both for allowing users to control emails and for automatically applying IRM templates defined by the organization. It can be used only between members of the organization or with other organizations with which you have established a federated trust. More information about federation can be found at `http://technet.microsoft .com/en-us/library/cc771425(WS.10).aspx`.

Using Transport Rules

Transport rules are one of the most flexible and powerful tools when addressing security and compliance in Exchange 2010. They are rules that run on the transport servers and can perform actions, such as blocking, redirecting, or appending information based on the properties of the message. Here are some examples of transport rules that organizations may implement:

Ethical firewall   A newspaper wanting to appear unbiased could create a transport rule to block emails between the Authors group and the Ad Sales group unless the subject line begins with *Personal*.

RMS templates   Email to or from the legal department could be stamped with an RMS template for attorney-client privileged communication.

Compliance   Emails sent between certain groups, or emails sent to the domain of a competitor, could be Bcc'd to the company's compliance department.

Blocking known bad emails   During a phishing or virus attack, transport rules can be created to block incoming or outgoing emails matching certain criteria or to specific addresses.

There are many more functions that transport rules can be used to accomplish. It is important to identify business requirements that may benefit from transport rules, test them thoroughly, and then implement them. It is also worth considering who will need access to create and modify transport rules. For example, some companies may want to have their IT's security group modify transport rules so they can react quickly during attacks. For detailed information on the abilities of transport rules and how to create them, see Chapter 6.

Planning Exchange Permissions Models

Exchange Server 2010 offers several areas where permissions must be configured:

- Mailbox permissions
- Distribution group permissions
- Public folder permissions
- Administrative permissions
- Help desk and other role permissions
- End-user permissions

Real World Scenario

Dynamically Created Transport Rules

As you have seen, transport rules can be powerful and flexible. In some cases, it may even be worthwhile to schedule the scripted creation of transport rules.

Chris, an Exchange administrator at a major southern university, was dealing with the problem of students responding to phishing attacks. Not only did the compromised accounts represent a chance for attackers to gain personal information, but the compromised accounts would be used to send out spam and phishing attacks from the university's email systems. These outgoing emails would cause the university's mail systems to get blacklisted, preventing normal mail flow from the university and impacting business operations.

To combat this problem, Chris devised a plan to scan outgoing emails for spam. He enabled outgoing spam confidence level (SCL) stamping on the Edge servers, and then wrote a PowerShell script to look at outgoing email logs. The script ran every 5 minutes and would find all outgoing emails with high SCLs. Based on the number of emails with a high SCL from a single address, it would send a notification to IT's security team and, if the number was high enough, remove those messages from the queue and create a transport rule to block further emails.

This script successfully caught a number of compromised accounts, protecting the university's email reputation and allowing the university's security department to react quickly to compromised accounts. The one false positive they had, a mass email by the university's president, was identified and resolved almost immediately. This story shows both the power and flexibility of scripting and transport rules and the need to closely monitor the actions taken by such scripts.

For each of these areas, there are design decisions that must be made about how to assign permissions, who assigns permissions, and under what circumstances permissions are granted. In many cases, these permissions can be controlled using Role Based Access Control (RBAC), which is discussed in Chapter 6, but some permissions are also controlled using other methods, as the following list shows:

Mailbox permissions   For most user mailboxes, permissions will never need to be assigned other than folder permissions at the client level, but for resource mailboxes, and for some users, it may be necessary to assign permissions, such as Full Access or Send As, to users. For many organizations, using security groups to define resource mailbox access can greatly simplify granting and tracking those permissions. Depending on the organizational structure, you might create a security group for each resource mailbox created, or you might use pre-created groups that are based on department to grant access to resource mailboxes. Either way, using security groups can prevent leaving orphaned security identifiers in the permissions lists when users are deleted, and it can make it easier for help desk personnel to grant access because all they have to do is add people to the appropriate groups. In fact, if you choose to mail-enable the groups that are used, you could even push the permissions management for resource mailboxes to the end-user level and allow them to modify the group membership using the software they're already familiar with, Outlook and OWA. Additionally, using security groups simplifies seeing what permissions a user has and revoking those permissions when necessary. Even if only one person is in a group, the ease with which group membership can be identified and reassigned makes using groups worthwhile.

Distribution group permissions   Exchange 2010 introduced the ability to manage distribution group permissions, including moderators and managers, directly from OWA. If your organization is comfortable allowing managers of distribution groups to add and remove other managers, this can decrease the IT overhead required to support distribution groups. If not, or if you want to allow your help desk employees to modify distribution groups for those end users uncomfortable with doing it themselves, you may need to edit the default RBAC roles to accommodate those decisions.

Public folder permissions   Exchange veterans will find that public folders are virtually unchanged from Exchange 2007. When creating public folders, you will need to make sure that the top-level permissions are restricted so that users are unable to cause problems in subfolders that they shouldn't have access to. You should also consider using security groups for public folder permissions, for the same reasons as described previously for mailbox permissions.

Administrative permissions   Every organization running Exchange has domain administrators and Exchange administrators. Active Directory (AD) is used by many services, including Exchange, so changes made to AD must be carefully controlled, and the number of domain administrators should be limited. Exchange stores sensitive information, and problems in Exchange can cause lost or compromised emails, leading to lost productivity or compromised information, so the number of Exchange administrators should be kept to a minimum. For small organizations, these groups may be the same people, but for large organizations it may make sense to separate the Exchange Administrator and the Domain Administrator permissions.

It is up to the organization to identify what level of separation of duties is appropriate based on its size and layout. When considering this decision, it is important to make sure that at least two administrators are assigned to each duty. Having only a single person administering AD or Exchange puts the organization at risk of problems if that person becomes unavailable. In some cases, it may even be beneficial to set up two-person integrity (TPI) for some actions. TPI means that two people must be present to perform an action and can be accomplished by setting up a dedicated account for protected actions and then giving two people half of the password. For information on implementing these split-permissions, see http://technet .microsoft.com/en-us/library/dd638106.aspx.

Help desk and other role permissions   Although the ability to grant role-based access has been possible in previous Exchange versions by using AD permissions and security groups, the introduction of RBAC features in Exchange 2010 provides flexibility in setting granular access to the Exchange infrastructure based on user roles. For any role in your organization, whether it is your help desk, legal department, or administrative assistant, it's important to fully plan out what permissions those users should have, and what objects those permissions should apply to, before using RBAC to assign those permissions. For example, your organization may decide that help desk employees should be able to add and remove permissions for resource mailboxes but not for other mailboxes. You could do this by placing resource mailboxes in a separate organizational unit than user mailboxes and then creating an RBAC role and assignment that provides them with those scoped permissions. The same applies to giving administrative assistants the ability to create mailboxes for new employees at their site or controlling what mailboxes your legal department can perform multi-mailbox searches against. Any time RBAC is used to assign roles, the permissions assigned, and the scope of those permissions, needs to be carefully decided upon. This may involve assigning the built-in RBAC roles or creating your own to meet your needs.

End-user permissions   It is important to examine the default role assignment policy to make sure that end users are provided with only the permissions they should have. For example, your organization may want to allow users to create distribution groups at will, or your organization may want to restrict creating distribution groups to avoid Active Directory clutter. For information about editing the default role assignment policy, see Chapter 6.

Exercise 13.1 provides some suggestions on how to apply Exchange permissions.

EXERCISE 13.1

Considering Permissions

When you implement Exchange 2010, assigning permissions is an important step. This exercise will help you determine what permissions should be assigned.

1. Identify which users will need additional access in Exchange. This may include help desk employees, your legal department, or employees responsible for provisioning new users.

2. Identify what permissions those users will need. Help desk employees may need the ability to view Exchange attributes, while the legal department may need the ability to perform multi-mailbox searches. The built-in RBAC roles provide a good starting place when looking at sets of permissions for particular roles.

3. Consider the scope of these permissions. Will these users need access only to users at specific locations or in specific departments?

4. Identify users to test these permissions and apply the permissions to them. If your organization spans several sites, it may be useful to test the permissions at the same site as the Exchange administrators before assigning them to other sites.

5. Train users to use the Exchange tools and permissions that you are assigning, and then assign those permissions to all of the identified users.

Designing Message Hygiene

It is important to protect your users from spam, phishing emails, and viruses. In the following sections, we focus on designing your Exchange infrastructure using Microsoft's Forefront Protection for Exchange Server (FPES), although it is possible to use other third-party products to achieve this functionality. No matter what product is used, it is vital to make sure your anti-spam and antivirus engines are kept consistently up-to-date. For information about configuring these options, see Chapter 6.

Configuring FPES for Virus Protection

FPES provides antivirus scanning using several engines, and it can provide scanning on transport servers and on Mailbox servers. Using FPES with multiple engines, each of which receives updates frequently, provides protection against the multitude of new viruses entering the wild daily. It's important to remember that the first FPES server in an organization to scan a message stamps that message so that other FPES servers do not waste resources rescanning it. This means that you should use the same engines used across all FPES servers so that your virus protection is consistent across the organization. Figure 13.1 illustrates where scanning takes place.

FIGURE 13.1   FPES virus scanning during mail flow

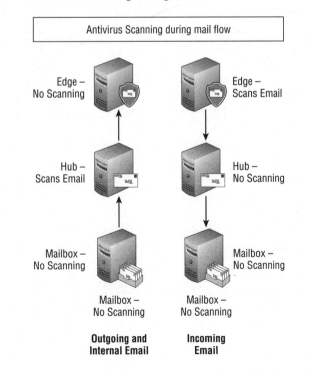

Antivirus Scanning during mail flow

Edge – No Scanning

Edge – Scans Email

Hub – Scans Email

Hub – No Scanning

Mailbox – No Scanning

Mailbox – No Scanning

Mailbox – No Scanning

Mailbox – No Scanning

Outgoing and Internal Email

Incoming Email

You can use FPES to scan messages during transport or while they are on the Mailbox servers. The following sections discuss virus scanning on each of those servers.

Transport Scanning

When FPES is installed and configured on an Exchange transport server, it will scan messages as they move through the transport server. For maximum protection, it is recommended that FPES be configured to scan all messages and to use the maximum number of engines that the server can handle based on load. After enabling FPES, it is important to monitor the transport servers to verify that FPES is not configured to use too many engines, which may overload the transport server's hardware. The FPES installation on the Edge servers will scan incoming emails, and the FPES installation on the Hub servers will scan outgoing and internal emails, so it is important to consider load on each of them separately.

In addition to performing virus scans, FPES can be used to filter emails and attachments based on criteria. File scanning can be based on multiple criteria, including file type (which ignores the filename extension and instead uses headers to accurately identify file types), filenames (which can be used to filter files based on name or filename extension), or a combination of the two. Preventing the sending of file types that can transmit viruses via email can help to decrease the likelihood of virus infections occurring by email. Depending on your organization's requirements and how you normally send and receive documents, you may want to block only executable files, or you may want to also block file types such as Microsoft Office files.

When configuring FPES on the transport servers, it's important to configure your quarantine options. You can separately enable quarantining for virus, spyware, corrupted compressed files, file filter, and on scan time-out. Corrupted compressed files and scan time-out files are the options most likely to cause false positives, so quarantining those instead of deleting them is recommended. If you have the disk space available, you may want to quarantine virus and spyware files in case there is a false positive and they need to be recovered. You will also need to set the quarantine purge times to make sure old quarantined files are removed. When enabling these settings, it is important to monitor disk space to make sure quarantined files do not consume all available disk space. It may also be useful to review why files are being blocked or quarantined. Figure 13.2 shows the interface used to review quarantined files in FPES.

Mailbox Scanning

FPES can also be installed on Mailbox servers. By default, FPES installed on a Mailbox server will not scan incoming or outgoing emails, instead leaving that responsibility up to the Edge and Hub servers. FPES will perform on-access scans of emails that have not been previously scanned. Primarily, this may include emails imported from an Outlook Personal Store (PST) or emails delivered before FPES was installed on your transport servers. FPES on Mailbox servers can also be used to scan emails delivered during a virus outbreak, which can be vital if virus-contaminated emails were delivered before the transport servers received engine updates to catch the virus. Although installing FPES on mailbox servers is not required to provide virus and spyware protection, it can be beneficial, especially during a virus outbreak.

FIGURE 13.2   Quarantined files in FPES

FPES installed on mailbox servers can also perform scheduled scans. The decision to perform scheduled scans on mailbox servers will be based primarily on two factors: whether or not the mailbox server has the extra capacity necessary to perform the scans, and your organization's overall antivirus capabilities, such as workstation-based scanning. Combined with transport scanning and separate workstation protection, scheduled scans on mailbox servers outside of a virus outbreak may not be necessary.

If your organization decides not to schedule scans on mailbox servers, you should still consider scheduling scans on public folder databases. Because public folders can be used to transfer information between members of an organization, bypassing transport scans, they represent a potential vector for virus infections. Scheduled scans for public folder databases are recommended to prevent them from being used to spread viruses.

Configuring FPES for Spam and Phishing Protection

Exchange and FPES on an Edge server provide protection against incoming spam and phishing emails. There are several options that can be configured independently to protect your organization from spam and phishing emails:

Spam confidence levels Exchange and FPES allow you to configure actions based on the SCL of emails. When an email enters the organization, FPES stamps the email with an SCL from –1 to 9, with higher emails more likely to be spam. FPES considers emails with an SCL of at least 5 likely to be spam but allows you to choose your own cutoff between suspected spam and certain spam. For suspected spam, FPES allows you to choose to either quarantine the emails or to spam the header and continue. For certain spam, FPES allows you to either quarantine or reject the emails. There are several ways you can combine these settings based on your organization's requirements:

Stamp header If you choose options to stamp the header of suspected spam, then you can configure spam options on a per-mailbox level. Although this allows you to use set-mailbox to customize spam actions for deletion, rejection, and sending spam to the junk folder per user, there is no built-in ability for users to customize those values. Stamping the header and continuing is also the only way to send spam emails to user junk email folders. Although using junk email folders increases storage requirements, it also makes it easier for end users to retrieve emails marked as spam.

Stamping the header can either be used for all incoming spam, to allow all actions to be customized per-mailbox, or it can be used only for suspected spam with a separate action used for certain spam. If your organization has enough storage space, the safest and most user-friendly method for filtering spam is to only stamp headers and to set all mailboxes to filter suspected spam to their junk folders.

Quarantine Quarantining suspected spam is a safe way to make sure suspected spam is maintained in case it is a false positive and needs to be delivered. The downside to using the quarantine option is that it can be time consuming to recover quarantined emails and there is no notification that the spam was quarantined.

Reject The Reject option for certain spam allows the Edge server to reject the email during the SMTP communication. This option allows the sender to know that the suspected spam was rejected, and if it's a legitimate sender, they can then take steps to resend the email in a way that is less likely to be tagged as spam.

Delete The Delete option for certain spam deletes the spam without any notification to the sender. Because this option can cause senders to not realize that their email was not delivered, this option is not suggested.

When you configure your spam confidence levels (SCLs), it is important to test the settings to make sure the thresholds you have chosen are neither so high that too much spam enters the organization or so low that you have excessive false positives. You should also monitor end-user feedback and Exchange statistics to ensure that the threshold originally chosen continues to be the best option. For information on choosing SCLs to block, see Exercise 13.2.

Choosing SCLs

When you implement FPES for spam blocking, deciding on the SCLs to block is one of the most important decisions you will make. The following steps provide a method to choose the SCL ratings to take action against:

1. Decide on an action to take against spam.

    The recommended actions are to either reject the spam or to stamp it and set SCL junk thresholds for users to send spam to their junk folders.

2. To enable one of these options, start by filtering email with an SCL of 9. Depending on your choice in step 1, you will do one of the following:

    -   Set FPES to reject certain spam, and set suspected spam to stamp the header of emails with an SCL from 5 to 8.

    -   Set FPES to stamp the header of suspected emails with an SCL from 5 to 9, and use `set-organizationconfig -SCLJunkThreshold 9` from the EMS of an Exchange server in your organization to send email with an SCL of 9 to the junk mail folder of users.

3. Assess the amount of spam that is received. There are several methods you can use to gather information:

    -   Provide a method for users to report spam, including the headers, to assess what SCL spam is marked with.

    -   Use the command `Get-FseSpamReport` to view information about how many messages are marked with each SCL.

    ```
    Administrator: Forefront Management Shell                              _□x
    PS C:\Program Files (x86)\Microsoft Forefront Protection for Exchange Server> Ge
    t-FseSpamReport -Starttime (get-date).addhours(-12) -Endtime (get-date) : select
     *scl*

    MessagesMarkedSclNegative1 :  937
    MessagesMarkedScl0         :  10878
    MessagesMarkedScl1         :  0
    MessagesMarkedScl2         :  0
    MessagesMarkedScl3         :  0
    MessagesMarkedScl4         :  0
    MessagesMarkedScl5         :  0
    MessagesMarkedScl6         :  0
    MessagesMarkedScl7         :  0
    MessagesMarkedScl8         :  24
    MessagesMarkedScl9         :  2265
    ```

    -   Use the command `Get-FSESpamAgentLog` to view information about emails marked with SCLs, including sender, recipient, and message ID. This information can be combined with message tracking logs to provide even more information.

4. Based on the SCLs marked on spam messages that continue to get through, adjust your spam settings. Monitoring spam is a process that must be performed periodically to protect your organization from spam and to prevent false positives.

Sender ID   Sender ID is a method for identifying what servers are authorized to send email from a specific domain. For example, if mailtask.com has the outgoing email server edge.mailtask.com, their domain name server (DNS) records would indicate that edge.mailtask.com is a legitimate sender for @mailtask.com addresses, and any other server is not legitimate.

Once Sender ID filtering is enabled, Exchange will query DNS for every email it receives to see if the sending server for each email is allowed for the domain the email is from. If the domain has specified legitimate servers and the sending server is not one of them, FPES can stamp the message's header, reject the message, or delete the message. Rejecting the message tells the sender that the message was rejected, allowing the sender to correct the problem and resend the message. Deleting the message can cause problems because it may cause legitimate emails to be deleted with no end-user notification, so that action is not recommended. Stamping the message's header allows you to take other actions against the message. For example, you could create a transport rule to check the header and if the message failed the Sender ID check, prepend the words *Suspected Spam:* to the message header.

Although Sender ID uses the sending domain's published information to verify the validity of the sending server, there are some scenarios in which this can cause false positives. If a user has an account at an outside host set to forward emails to their account in the Exchange organization, those forwarded emails could fail the Sender ID check because the sending server that Exchange sees wouldn't be the original sending server. Also, some Listserv servers may cause false positives for the same reason. If either of these scenarios is likely, it may be safer to stamp the message instead of rejecting it.

For more information about Sender ID, including how to set up your own Sender ID DNS entries, visit `http://www.microsoft.com/mscorp/safety/technologies/senderid/default.mspx`.

Whether you choose to configure Sender ID filtering or not, setting your own SenderID entries can be helpful to both your organization and others. For other organizations that use Sender ID filtering, it will prevent them from receiving spam from spammers spoofing your organization's domain. This helps other organizations filter spam and keeps them from thinking that your organization sends spam.

Sender reputation level   One of the antispam options in Exchange 2010 is to use sender reputation level (SRL) filtering. SRL filtering tracks the SCLs stamped on emails received from each IP address and checks the sending IP to see if it is an open proxy. This information is combined to assign the IP address an SRL. If the SRL exceeds a configured threshold, then the IP address is blocked for a specified amount of time. Although SRL filtering can decrease the amount of spam received, it can be confusing for end users when a false positive occurs because an address may be blocked on one Edge Transport server and not another. If SRL filtering is enabled, it should be thoroughly tested at the threshold chosen to ensure that false positives are not occurring.

User communication   During any antispam or antivirus deployment, it is important to thoroughly communicate everything with the end users. Users should be told what is being implemented, how it's being implemented, and what to do if they notice a problem, such as not receiving email or email being improperly marked as spam. It's also a good idea to set your rejection messages to provide information on how to contact your help desk if an email is improperly rejected.

Designing Client Access Security

When designing client access security, organizations will look at the following features:

- ActiveSync policies
- ActiveSync device access rules
- OWA segmentation
- Client encryption

Although implementation of ActiveSync policies/device rules and OWA segmentation will be largely dependent on organization-specific security requirements, all organizations should enable client encryption to protect user email and credentials.

Designing ActiveSync Policies

Exchange Server 2010 includes many ActiveSync policies that can be applied to users. For a full list of ActiveSync policies and how to configure them, see Chapter 6. When you design your ActiveSync policy, it's important to decide which settings you need to configure to meet your business needs. Here are some general policies you should consider setting:

Password Enabled   This setting enables the mobile phone password, increasing the device security if the phone is lost.

Password Expiration   This setting allows you to specify a length of time after which the device password should expire.

Password History   This setting specifies the number of past passwords to store and not allow the user to reuse.

Maximum Failed Password Attempts   This setting specifies how many times a user can get the password wrong before the phone performs a data wipe.

Minimum Password Length   This setting specifies the minimum password length.

Require Device Encryption   This setting specifies whether device encryption is required.

Require Storage Card Encryption   This setting enables encryption on the storage card.

There may be additional settings, such as disabling the device camera or preventing unsigned application installation, which would be beneficial depending on your organization's security requirements. Exercise 13.3 provides a framework for deciding on how to implement ActiveSync policies.

EXERCISE 13.3

Deciding on ActiveSync Policies

When implementing ActiveSync policies, it is important to consider what policies to implement and for whom to implement them. This exercise provides guidance on what steps to take when making those decisions.

1. Examine the complete list of ActiveSync policies.

   The full list of ActiveSync policies is included in Chapter 6. Pay particular attention to the general security policies listed in the section in this chapter, "Designing ActiveSync Policies."

2. Group users based on the policies they should receive. For example, you may group users as follows:

   - Users with confidential information, such as R&D or your legal department: These users would require additional security, such as encrypted devices and strong passwords.

   - Executives: Executives may require the same security settings as users with confidential information but be unhappy with short time-outs.

   - General: General users without confidential information may not require long or complex passwords.

3. After policies and groups have been identified, identify users from each group to pilot these settings with. Assign policies to these pilot users and obtain feedback on the settings assigned.

4. After testing is complete, communicate with the entire organization about ActiveSync policies and assign the policies to all users. Continue to allow feedback to address any issues or concerns from members of the organization.

For organizations requiring more control over their Windows Mobile devices than Exchange provides, Microsoft has created Microsoft System Center Mobile Device Manager (MDM). For information about the additional controls that MDM provides, see http://www.microsoft.com/windowsmobile/en-us/business/solutions/enterprise/mobile-device-manager.mspx. If your organization will have a combination of owned devices and personal devices contacting Exchange, it may be beneficial to use both MDM and ActiveSync policies.

Using ActiveSync Device Access Rules

Exchange Server 2010 offers the ability to control what ActiveSync devices are allowed to synchronize with your Exchange server. Not all devices support all ActiveSync policies, so depending on your security requirements, you may want to block some devices, such as devices that don't support encryption. You could also use device access rules to block devices that are not owned or approved by your organization. If you do have such business requirements, you can set three settings for devices:

Allow   This setting is applied to devices that your organization has confirmed to meet your requirements, allowing them to synchronize with your server.

Block   This setting is applied to devices that your organization has confirmed do not meet your requirements, preventing them from synchronizing with your server.

Quarantine   The Quarantine option is for blocking devices that have not been tested by your organization. By activating the Quarantine option, you can notify the Exchange administrator when an untested device attempts to synchronize, allowing the administrator to contact the device owner for testing.

Exchange 2010 SP1 adds the ability to view quarantined devices and control quarantine settings through the Exchange Control Panel (ECP), making it easier for Exchange administrators to control ActiveSync quarantining. As with any policy, it's important to thoroughly test the devices and settings before activating them.

Using OWA Segmentation

Using `New-OWAMailboxPolicy` and `Set-CASMailbox` or the Exchange Management Console (EWC), you can specify what segments of OWA users have access to. OWA segmentation is useful for controlling what features and information users have access to when they are connecting to Exchange from a web browser, which may be at an insecure location. For example, you could disable password changes from OWA and force users to change their password from only secure machines.

Your organization may also have business reasons to prevent some users from accessing some OWA features. For example, if your organization is a school with students or has a set of workers that don't need to use calendaring or public folder functionality, it may be beneficial to hide those features from them. Restricting users to only the OWA features they need access to simplifies the OWA interface and can reduce support costs.

Encrypting Client Communication

For client access, it is important to encrypt client communication. This protects your user information, including passwords and information contained in emails. When setting up client encryption, it is necessary to obtain a certificate for the Client Access server and enable encryption for POP, IMAP, and OWA.

Designing Message Archival and Discovery

Message archival and discovery includes the following areas:

- Admin audit logging
- Message tracking
- Single Item Recovery, journaling, and legal hold
- Retaining deleted mailboxes
- Message records management
- Multi-Mailbox Search

Each of these areas of message archival and discovery needs to be examined to have a comprehensive archival and discovery plan. Although some areas, such as enabling journaling or legal holds, may not actually take place until there is an incident that requires it, such as litigation, these areas still need to be planned out well in advance of any such incident.

Understanding Admin Audit Logging

Admin audit logging allows you to keep a log of commands that are run. This provides information about which people with administrative access are using that access for, which may be necessary to record for compliance reasons or for internal auditing. For information about enabling and configuring admin audit logging, see Chapter 9, "Monitoring and Reporting with Exchange Server 2010."

Admin audit logging works by sending the logs as emails to an Exchange mailbox anytime a logged action is performed. When enabling admin audit logging, it is possible to set what commands are logged. Also, admin audit logging will not audit Get- commands because the logs for those would grow quickly. You will need to consider what commands you need to audit. Depending on your needs, you may want to audit only per-mailbox commands, or you may want to audit all commands, including those that affect the entire organization.

When enabling admin audit logging, it is important to consider your needs for retention of these records. If the records also need to be maintained in a system outside of Exchange, you may need to set up the logging mailbox to forward its messages to an outside address or set up an automatic process to download the messages from the mailbox. If you want to control how long the logs are stored in Exchange, you can assign a retention policy to the mailbox.

You will also need to consider what to do with these records based on why you are enabling these logs. If you are enabling the logging for compliance or regulatory reasons, it may be necessary to provide access to the logging mailbox for your compliance officers. Alternatively, if they're being enabled for auditing what Exchange administrators and help desk employees are doing, it may be an IT employee that is reviewing the logs, or you may decide not to review the logs unless there is an incident that needs to be investigated.

Admin audit logging is important for logging what actions are performed by Exchange administrators and help desk employees, but how those logs are used will be strongly defined by your organization's security policies and any regulations requiring auditing. Also, in the event that an administrator account is compromised, the logs can be invaluable for identifying what the account is used for.

Working with Message Tracking Logs

One of the most important logs, both for troubleshooting mail delivery problems and for compliance records, is the message tracking log. By default, each transport server keeps a log of all messages it transports, up to 250 MB or 30 days, whichever is less. If your organization uses a third-party logging application capable of indexing and searching comma-separated logs, you should consider shipping the message tracking logs to the server. If your organization does not have a logging server available, you should consider increasing the amount of space that your transport servers will use for logging.

When considering increasing the size of message tracking logs, one of the primary considerations is making sure the logs do not consume all available disk space on the servers. If the message tracking logs do consume all available disk space, then mail flow can be negatively impacted. Once disk space is considered, the reasons message tracking logs are needed should also be considered. If message tracking logs are only required for troubleshooting, then keeping logs for one week will generally be sufficient. If there are any legal or regulatory compliance reasons to retain message tracking logs, your compliance or legal department may ask that records be retained for a longer time period. A requirement for an extremely long retention period may require storing the logs off of the transport servers, either by using another product for log processing or by scheduling a script to copy message tracking logs to a file server. If you do retain message tracking logs on the transport server, storing them on separate disks than the Exchange and operating system install may improve performance and mitigate the risk of server problems caused by logs filling up the disk.

Reviewing Single Item Recovery, Journaling, and Legal Hold

In 2008, the White House admitted that it had lost tapes containing email backups from 2003, costing millions of dollars for employees and contractors to scour workstations and tapes for the missing emails. Depending on the legal and regulatory requirements of your company, it may be necessary to protect records from deletion. Even in the absence of such requirements, if your organization is ever subpoenaed, then you will be required to retain the records you currently have, and not preserving those records could results in costly fines and penalties.

Exchange veterans will be familiar with mailbox journaling, a method for retaining mailbox records that involves two steps:

- Create a mailbox to use for journaling.

- Create a journal rule that specifies the mailbox from which you want to capture all new mail (both received mail and sent mail), and the mailbox in which you want to save the information.

Although Exchange Server 2010 retains the ability to perform journaling, it also introduces two new features that administrators can use to retain emails. The first feature, Single Item Recovery, is useful for short-term retention of all emails in a mailbox. The second new feature, legal holds, is used for long-term retention of all information currently in a mailbox and all new information that enters a mailbox. In this section, we examine the pros and cons of each method and how to combine them to meet your organization's needs. For information about enabling journaling or legal holds, see Chapter 6.

Single Item Recovery Single Item Recovery is used to retain all information in a mailbox for a set period of time. It is enabled on a per-mailbox basis, and combined with the RetainDeletedItemsFor setting on a mailbox, specifies how long mail is retained after being deleted before it is purged from the mail store. Single Item Recovery protects items from being purged from the dumpster by the end user and instead moves items the user attempts to purge into the hidden Recoverable Items\Purges folder. Once a user attempts to purge an item, it is only recoverable via Multi-Mailbox Search.

Depending on the amount of mail store available, administrators may want to enable Single Item Recovery only for employees of some departments or for all employees, possibly with longer retention times for employees of certain departments. Single Item Recovery is a preemptive setting for use before an incident occurs requiring that email be retained. Because it is used preemptively, it is usually set to retain email only for short periods of time because retaining all deleted emails for an extended period of time can require a significant amount of storage.

Journaling Journaling is a tool used to retain all new mail sent to or from a mailbox. Generally, an Exchange administrator will receive a request to retain email sent to or from a specific user, either for compliance reasons or because of pending litigation. Once the request is received, the administrator creates a journal mailbox and sets up a journal rule targeting the user's mailbox. Once the journal rule is in place, any new mail that is sent or received is also attached to a journal report and sent to the journal mailbox.

Journal rules can be easily used to retain information for a single person or a group of people, and since the journal mailbox is a separate mailbox, there is no concern that the journaled mail will be lost when a user leaves. Using journaling for retention has two main disadvantages. Journaling doubles the amount of space required per user because it creates a separate copy of the email. Also, journaling does not retain information currently stored in the mailbox. To retain information currently in the mailbox, the administrator will need to copy the data out using `export-mailbox` or Multi-Mailbox Search. If `export-mailbox` is used, the email can be exported directly to the journal mailbox so that all mail is in a single location. `Export-Mailbox` does not export messages that were retained because of Single Item Recovery, so mailboxes with Single Item Recovery will require a multi-mailbox search to save their current email. Since multi-mailbox search can save email only to discovery mailboxes, if the organization wishes to retain all email in the journal mailbox, the administrator will then have to export the mail from the discovery mailbox to the journal mailbox. Although journaling makes it easy to retain future emails, it can be complicated to save current emails and requires significant additional space.

Legal hold   To address the difficulties of journaling, Exchange Server 2010 introduces legal holds. The legal hold feature works the same way that Single Item Recovery does, by preventing users from purging items from their mailbox. Once a legal hold is enabled on a mailbox, any retention limits are ignored and all email is retained until the legal hold is removed. Because the emails are retained in the current mailbox, legal hold overcomes the disadvantages that journaling has because activating a legal hold does not duplicate emails and it retains all current and future emails in a single step.

The main disadvantage to using the legal hold feature is that it will require changes to an organization's identity management procedures. Because the email, retained as a result of enabling a legal hold, is kept in the user's mailbox, care must be taken not to delete a user account that is under a legal hold. This may require employee training, a change of automated systems, or moving legal hold mailboxes to a protected organizational unit when a legal hold is activated. Also, once a user under a legal hold leaves the organization, it may be necessary to hide the account from the global address list and change the email address to avoid confusion.

Although the legal hold feature will often be the preferred method for retaining emails, the difficulties surrounding account deletion may cause some organizations to use journaling until those difficulties can be overcome. No matter which method is used, Exchange administrators should carefully consider preemptively enabling Single Item Recovery to protect the organization from having important emails deleted before notification of litigation is received.

Retaining Deleted Mailboxes

When an individual leaves the organization, it is important to identify what should be done with that user's mailbox. Retaining the user's email may be required by company policy, and in many cases there are laws requiring that these records be maintained. There are a couple of options for retaining emails, including keeping the associated user account, leaving the mailbox disconnected in the database, and archiving the mailbox to another location. In this section, we examine the factors that go into deciding how to retain mailboxes.

Retaining user accounts   One method for retaining a user's email after they leave the organization is to leave the user's account in AD. Leaving the user's account in AD makes it easy to reenable the account if the user returns to the organization. It can also make it easy to search the account's mailbox using a multi-mailbox search if it is necessary. If you decide to retain the user's account, it is important to make sure the account is disabled, is removed from the

Global Address List (GAL), is removed from distribution lists (to prevent confusing bounces to senders), and has mail delivery turned off. It is also important to find a way to record when disabled accounts should be removed from AD because keeping unneeded AD accounts for too long will cause AD clutter and unnecessarily consume Exchange storage space.

Keeping disconnected mailboxes   The easiest method for keeping a mailbox is to leave it in a disconnected state in the Exchange database. Once an AD account is deleted, mailboxes are retained in the mailbox database for a time that is configurable on a per-database basis using `Set-MailboxDatabase -MailboxRetention`. Because these mailboxes are not associated with AD accounts, it is not possible to search them via multi-mailbox search without first reconnecting them to an AD account. It is also not possible to move a disconnected mailbox to another database, which may be required for a future Exchange upgrade or if hardware is being decommissioned. Finally, because the location of a disconnected mailbox is not stored, it can be time consuming to scan all of the databases in an organization to find a particular disconnected mailbox.

Mailbox archival   The final method for retaining a mailbox after a user leaves is to store the email in another location. This may mean that you export the email to a personal store file to save in another location, or it may involve using a third-party product to archive the email. Although archiving the email to another location makes it easy to locate later and avoids the problems associated with leaving it in Exchange, it does make it more difficult to search the contents of the mailbox.

Many organizations will find themselves using a combination of these methods to retain emails after employees leave. For example, an organization that stores email for only 90 days may disable the user account for 45 days, making it easy to search the mailbox immediately after the employee departs, and then retain the disconnected mailbox for an additional 45 days. On the other hand, a government organization that is required to retain records for seven years may leave the account disabled for one year and then archive it to another location for six years.

It is also important to make sure you accommodate any one-off requirements that may affect how individual mailboxes should be retained. For example, if your organization uses the seven-year plan but there is ongoing litigation that may require searching a mailbox after the first year has passed, it would be prudent to make sure the mailbox is retained until that litigation is resolved.

Introducing Message Records Management

For many organizations, there are laws and regulations that require that certain emails be kept for specific periods of times. Exchange's message records management (MRM) technology provides a framework to provide your users with the ability to specify how long emails should be retained, making it easier for your users to comply with the regulations that affect them.

Exchange Server 2010 introduces retention policies as the newest MRM technology. Although Exchange 2010 continues to support managed folders, which were introduced in

Exchange 2007, retention policies offer more functionality than managed folders and are the technology we focus on when we examine the design and implementation of MRM. Retention policies allow users to assign retention tags to folders and allow administrators to assign retention tags to the default folders, such as the Inbox or the Junk E-mail folder. Retention tags are used to specify how long emails should be kept before they are archived or deleted, allowing users to create folders based on regulatory requirements, and allowing administrators to specify how long items like junk mail should be retained.

When planning an MRM implementation, it is important to remember that MRM is based on end-user classification of emails. This means that user input, training, and communication are vital at each step of an MRM implementation. We will examine MRM implementation as a six-step process:

1. Requirements gathering

2. Pilot program

3. Training

4. Nonexpiration (learning) implementation

5. Full implementation

6. Monitoring

Although large organizations or organizations where different departments may operate under different regulatory requirement may want to approach MRM in a phased implementation, these general steps will apply to all organizations. For information on creating retention tags and policies, see Chapter 6.

1. Requirements gathering

   The first step to a successful MRM implementation is requirements gathering. During this phase, Exchange administrators should gather the following information:

   - Regulatory requirements

   - Legal or compliance department preferences

   - Company and departmental regulations on records keeping

   - Current end-user practices

   Gathering information on current end-user practices may be difficult, but understanding what users are currently doing will allow the Exchange administrators to train users on how those methods will change, and it will also allow the administrators to discuss how to retain records that are currently being retained. This may also give some insight to the Exchange administrators on the increase in disk space that will be required to retain future records and to bring current records, such as those saved in (PST) files, back into the Exchange mailbox store.

2. Pilot program

   Once the requirements have been gathered, the Exchange administrators should create retention tags and one or more retention policies. Then, the Exchange administrators will need to identify a group with which to pilot those retention policies. If users are reluctant to participate in the pilot program, it may be advantageous to explain that MRM will not only make it easier for them to classify and retain their own messages, it will also require increasing their storage quota and giving them an archive mailbox.

The pilot program will require thorough communication with the pilot group to identify what retention tags and policies need to be added, changed, or removed. Depending on the size of the organization, it may make sense to start with a small pilot group and then increase its size over time once the initial issues are addresses.

3. Training

Once the pilot program has resulted in retention policies that the Exchange administrators are comfortable deploying, the end users must be trained. This will include both training end users on how to use retention tags and making sure users are familiar with regulatory and company regulations on email retention.

4. Nonexpiration (learning) implementation

Once end users have been trained, the Exchange administrators should increase quota sizes, activate archive mailboxes, and apply the retention policies with email expiration disabled. This will give users time to become familiar with the retention tags that are available and apply them to their emails. Users should also be encouraged to upload PST files into their archive mailboxes during this time. Depending on the number of users, this implementation may need to be phased because the first run of the Managed Folder Assistant on a mailbox after MRM is enabled will consume additional server resources.

5. Full implementation

Once users are comfortable with using retention tags, which may take two to three weeks, the Exchange administrators can enable email expiration. Also, the Active Directory administrators should roll out group policies that disable writing to PST files, which will prevent users from trying to use PST files instead of the archive mailboxes.

6. Monitoring

Once MRM has been fully implemented, it is important to monitor system performance. This will include verifying that the Managed Folder Assistant is completing during its scheduled time and ensuring that the resources consumed by the Managed Folder Assistant are not causing a performance impact on the Exchange mailbox servers. The Exchange administrators will also need to monitor storage capacity since MRM will increase storage requirements.

On the end-user side, the company's compliance department will need to perform audits to confirm that MRM is being properly used, and new employees will need to be trained in company policies and retention tag usage.

Implementing MRM is a long, time-consuming process, and it is likely that there will be internal resistance as people disagree about which retention tags should be used or complain about having to change their current methods of records retention. Despite the difficulty of implementing MRM, the advantages in terms of records retention and demonstrating regulatory compliance are likely to be well worth the effort.

Performing Multi-Mailbox Searches

Now that we have covered how to retain records, it is important to examine how to search those records. When assigning multi-mailbox search permissions, you need to determine who needs to perform searches, who should be able to search, and how the results will be stored. For information about assigning search permissions using RBAC or for information about performing searches, see Chapter 6. Exercise 6.3 in Chapter 6 provides instructions on assigning the Discovery Management role group to a user.

There are multiple people in any organization that may need to perform searches. If Single Item Recovery is enabled, IT employees may be asked to perform a search to recover accidentally purged items. Members of the legal department may need to perform searches to discover information on pending litigation. Depending on the size of the legal department, there may be individuals dedicated to discovery and other members assigned to simply review the data found in the searches, or the entire legal department may need to perform searches. Finally, there may be other departments, such as compliance departments, that need to perform searches as part of internal investigations or audits.

Once the searchers have been identified, it is necessary to identify the mailboxes that will be subject to searches by each group. For example, when giving IT employees access to perform searches for data recovery, you may wish to give help desk employees access to most users but reserve searches of critical mailboxes to only specific Exchange administrators. If the organization is using the legal hold feature, it may be desirable to give legal department members access only to search mailboxes in an organizational unit reserved for accounts under legal hold. These decisions represent a profound impact on email security and should be carefully considered.

Finally, where search results should be stored has to be decided. Exchange requires that searches be placed in discovery mailboxes, but it is up to the organization to decide how to organize its discovery mailboxes. The users in the legal department may have preferences on how search results are organized for their department. They may prefer to use a discovery mailbox for the entire department, or they may prefer creating a separate discovery mailbox for each case or each person searched. How long to maintain these search results, which in some cases may be mandated by law, may also factor into how the discovery mailboxes are organized. This decision will primarily be based on the preferences of the legal department, but it may also be influenced by mailbox- and database-sizing requirements.

Of course, there are third-party products that can be used instead of using the Multi-Mailbox Search functionality built into Exchange. When looking at a third-party product, consider the following aspects:

Ease of end-user use Some search products work by storing older emails in the search tool instead of in Exchange. The products may work by storing a stub in Exchange that users can use to access the email in the search tool. Such tools may make it difficult for users to access or search older emails.

Combined search If your organization is required to search multiple areas, such as Exchange, SharePoint, and file shares, then being able to perform those searches from a single product may be easier than using Multi-Mailbox Search combined with other searching methods for the other areas.

Summary

In this chapter, you examined how to design your implementation of the security and compliance features in Exchange 2010. For many features, the out-of-the-box setup may meet your requirements, but for most organizations, at least some customization will be necessary.

Exchange 2010's introduction of the Single Item Recovery and legal hold features provide the ability to protect your organization from the impact that deleted emails may have. When these features are combined with the new Multi-Mailbox Search, it's easier than ever to retain and find the email necessary for compliance and litigation purposes. That said, these new features are useless if their implementation isn't properly planned well before an incident happens that requires their use.

Combined with FPES, Exchange 2010 offers excellent protection against viruses and spam. It's important to plan the implementation and test the values chosen to make sure they provide the correct level of protection. It's also important to communicate with users so that when a false positive happens, they know what to do.

It's important to carefully consider your permissions models when implementing Exchange 2010. Permissions for departments and users must be examined to define what access is appropriate and what is not.

Finally, messaging security and compliance, through transport encryption and transport rules, can be vital to securing your Exchange system. When confidential information is sent between your organization and another partner, TLS can protect that information from man-in-the-middle attacks. Transport rules provide the power and flexibility to control and monitor email communication as it happens.

Chapter Essentials

Understand messaging security and compliance.   Email is most vulnerable as it is transported outside your organization. Understand how to secure interorganization email. Also understand how to secure receive connectors so that emails sent internally to your organization are authenticated. Finally, understand how to enable S/MIME so that users can encrypt and sign their emails.

Understand Exchange permissions models.   Exchange permissions apply at every level of the Exchange organization. It's important to understand the permissions that apply to mailboxes and distribution groups. It's also important to examine the permissions assigned through RBAC, whether they are for help desk employees or other departments.

Understand message hygiene.   When implementing FPES and Exchange 2010, you should understand how to implement and test antivirus and antispam functionality. It is also necessary to design a communications plan for letting users know what is being implemented and what to do if they have problems.

Understand client access security. The most important aspect of client access security is enabling POP3, IMAP, and OWA using encryption. Depending on your organization's requirements, you may also want to take advantage of the increased security of ActiveSync policies and device rules.

Understand message archival and security. Exchange 2010 introduces Multi-Mailbox search, legal holds, and Single Item recovery. Understand how to use each of these to create a comprehensive plan for retaining and searching email for compliance and litigation purposes. Also understand how to facilitate end-user message classification and retention using retention policies and tags.

Designing High Availability and Recovery

THE FOLLOWING TOPICS ARE DISCUSSED IN THIS CHAPTER:

✓ Overview of high availability

✓ Designing and deploying Exchange High Availability

✓ Designing and Deploying Exchange Backup and Recovery

Exchange 2010 provides significant improvements in the areas of high availability and recovery. Mailbox server availability has been overhauled with new availability options and a simplified, yet flexible, installation process.

Going hand in hand with high availability is backup and recovery. The obvious goal would be to provide a stable solution that never requires recovery, but you still must plan for issues that may result in the need for a recovery.

High Availability Overview

Many organizations go through a process called risk management or risk identification where they list everything that could possibly go wrong or that would cause Exchange Server 2010 services to be unavailable. For example, an organization may list disk failure as a possible risk and then take steps to mitigate that risk by using Redundant Array of Inexpensive Disks (RAID) controllers and configuring all disks in fault-tolerant arrays. Another organization may list systemboard failure as a risk and then decide to implement a server clustering solution to mitigate that risk.

In a nutshell, high availability is an achievement reached when the infrastructure is well designed, well planned, and well tested and the implemented processes, software, and fault-tolerant hardware are focused on supplying and maintaining application availability.

As a high-level example, consider messaging in an organization. A poor implementation of Exchange is usually slapped together by purchasing a server that the administrator thinks is about the right size and installing Exchange Server 2010 on it. Messaging clients are installed on network-connected desktops and profiles are created. The Exchange server might even be configured successfully to connect to the Internet. It is possible to install an Exchange messaging environment within a week or even overnight in some cases. It is easy to do it fast and complete the install, however, important details within may be missed.

By contrast, in a high-availability environment, the deployment of messaging must be properly designed and implemented. Administrators research organizational messaging requirements. Users are brought into discussions with administrators and managers. Messaging is considered a possible solution for many company ills. Research may go on for an extended period while consultants are brought in to help build and review designs. Vendors are brought in to discuss how their products (antivirus and content management solutions, for example) will keep the messaging environment available and not waste messaging resources processing spam and spreading viruses. Potential third-party software is tested and approved after a large investment of administrator and end-user time. Hardware is sized and evaluated based on performance requirements and expected loads. Hardware is also sized and tested for disaster recovery and to meet service-level agreements (SLAs) for both performance and time for recovery in the event of a disaster. Hardware that's selected will often contain fault-tolerant components such as redundant memory, drives, network connections, cooling fans, power supplies, and so on.

A high-availability environment will incorporate a significant amount of design, planning, and testing. It will often, but not always, include additional features such as server clustering, which decreases downtime by enabling rolling upgrades and allowing for a pre-planned response to failures. A top-notch high-availability messaging environment will also consider the messaging client software and potential configurations that lead to increased availability for users. For example, Outlook 2003 and later offers a cache mode configuration that allows users to create new messages, respond to existing email in their inboxes, and manage their calendars (among many other tasks) without having to maintain a constant connection to the Exchange server. Exchange cached mode allows users to continue working with locally stored data even though the Exchange server might be down for a short time, and it also allows for more efficient use of bandwidth.

All critical business systems have to be analyzed to understand the cost incurred when they are unavailable. If there is a significant cost, then the organization should take steps to minimize downtime. Taking this view to the extreme, the goal is really to provide continuous availability (CA) of applications and resources for the organization. Doesn't everyone want Exchange to always be available for processing messaging traffic and helping the people in the organization collaborate? Of course we want applications and their entire environment to continue running forever. We strive for continuous availability, and we often settle for high availability.

Unfortunately, hardware eventually fails and software too can cause failures. Don't forget that high availability includes not just the hardware and software solution but also the backup/restore solution and failover processing. Most high-availability experts will also add that a true high-availability environment includes a well-documented development, test, and production-migration process for any changes made in production environments. All in all, there is much to take into account to achieve high availability, but you can achieve high levels of application availability through well-designed, -planned, -tested, and -implemented processes, software, and hardware.

In Exchange Server 2010, you can use Network Load Balancing (NLB) for the Edge Transport server role and for the CAS role. NLB helps keep the applications available to your users. The same can be said for failover clustering; however, you need to take into account the unavailability of email during the actual failover of your application in the event of hardware or software failures. Sometimes, failover is a matter of seconds; in other cases, it can be several minutes. In all cases, a clustering solution will drive down unavailability significantly and increase the uptime of applications run on your servers. For any application or system to be highly available, the parts need to be designed around availability, and the individual parts need to be tested before being put into production. For example, if you are using third-party products with your Exchange environment, you may find that they are a weak link that results in the loss of availability. Implementing a cluster will not necessarily result in high availability if there are problems with other portions of the entire solution.

This bit of background should not detract from the great features provided for high availability in Exchange 2010; rather, the purpose of this discussion is to provide a frame of reference as the Exchange-specific high-availability features are discussed. High availability is so much more than just placing a couple of servers together in a cluster.

Exchange 2010 includes many new and enhanced features that increase availability. Database availability groups (DAG) and CAS arrays are both designed to increase the reliability and availability of Exchange Server 2010 services.

 To review the basic high-availability features of Exchange 2010, see Chapter 7, "Configuring High-Availability Solutions for Exchange Server."

Designing and Deploying Exchange 2010 High Availability

As discussed in the previous section of this chapter, high availability is not something that is a feature or piece of hardware or software that is installed. Rather, it is an achievement, an achievement that takes thought, planning, and careful execution. To attain high availability, you must make sure each area of the Exchange design meets certain standards. The following sections cover each of these main areas and discuss what you must consider outside the basic deployment steps as covered in Part II of this book.

Designing and Deploying High Availability for Exchange Infrastructure

Exchange relies on the infrastructure much like a building relies on its foundation. If the foundation fails, the building comes crumbling down. As you design a highly available Exchange deployment, you must first evaluate the infrastructure to ensure that it is solid.

Exchange builds on top of the foundation of Active Directory Domain Services (AD DS) and is completely dependent on the performance and availability of AD DS. To provide high availability for AD DS, the server hardware needs to be redundant and also needs to provide enough resources for the Exchange servers in the event of a failure. Because AD DS relies on Domain Name Service (DNS) to function, DNS also needs to be made redundant by adding multiple DNS servers into the environment.

Facility Resiliency

Both the site and the datacenter need to be examined to ensure that they meet the resiliency needs of the solution. Does the facility have redundant power feeds from the power company? Does the facility have redundant cooling? Is the site in a location prone to issues? Because all other components rely on the availability of the facility resources, the facility resources are of the utmost importance.

Network Resiliency

Unfortunately, Internet connections, routing and switching equipment, network adapters, and network cables can all fail. Resiliency can be provided for each of these failure points. Network adapter teaming can be configured on each of the servers, redundant routers and switches can be deployed to protect against failures, and multiple Internet connections can be acquired to provide redundancy.

Server and Storage Hardware Resiliency

The servers on which the infrastructure and Exchange run also need to provide the proper level of redundancy. This is often accomplished by purchasing server-class hardware with multiple power supplies, RAID-protected local storage, redundant storage and network adapters, and other resilient features.

High availability can be achieved only if appropriate management processes are put into place. These processes include change management, preventative maintenance, and proactive updates. Change management provides structure for documenting, introducing, and validating change in the environment. The goal of this structure is to minimize the number and impact of the changes made to the environment, which should result in predictable changes.

The application of security updates to all portions of the environment is a change that should be managed. When security updates are released, they should be fully tested and then deployed through the change management process. Other updates, such as cumulative updates and service packs for Exchange, should also be proactively tested, evaluated, and deployed.

Designing and Deploying High Availability for Mailbox Servers

The Mailbox servers are the most stateful servers in an Exchange deployment because they include mailbox information. With the introduction of DAGs, the importance of any one server can be significantly reduced. A DAG is a collection of servers that provides continuous replication and availability for databases, as shown in Figure 14.1. You can have up to 16 servers and 16 copies of a database in a DAG.

Exchange Server does not use Windows Failover Clustering to handle database failover. Instead, it uses Active Manager to manage that process. It does, however, use the Windows Failover Clustering feature and therefore requires an Enterprise version of Windows Server. A DAG has the following characteristics:

- All DAG members must have the same operating system version.

- A DAG can have up to 16 members.

- A DAG with 16 members can have up to 16 copies of a database.

- A server is added to a DAG after the Mailbox server role is installed. Also, a Mailbox server already hosting active mailbox databases can be added to a DAG.

- Failover occurs per mailbox database, not for an entire server. A single database can be moved between servers in the DAG without affecting other databases.

- A DAG member can host only one copy of each database.

- The database and transaction log files must be stored in the same path on all DAG members. For example, if Database 1 is stored on `S:\DB\Database 1\` on MB01A, it will be stored in `D:\DB\Database 1\` on all other members hosting copies of Database 1.

- Only DAG members can host database copies; database copies cannot be replicated to Mailbox servers that aren't in the same DAG.

- Not all databases need to have the same number of copies. In a 16-node DAG, one database can be configured to have 16 copies while other databases can be configured to not be redundant or to have varying number of copies.

- A DAG can maintain 1 active copy on an Exchange server and up to 15 passive copies of that database on the same number of Exchange servers in the DAG. As changes are made on the active database copy, asynchronous log shipping is used to maintain the copies.

FIGURE 14.1   In a DAG, the transaction logs are replicated from the active database copy to the passive copies.

Database Availability Group

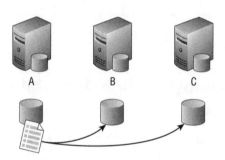

Databases created on a DAG member are not automatically redundant. Only a single copy is created; additional copies need to be manually configured.

For information on how to create and manage DAGs and database copies, see Chapter 7.

Before this transaction log shipping process can start, the database copy must first be seeded. Seeding creates a baseline copy of the database on a DAG member so that it can begin maintaining a passive copy of the database. Seeding can be accomplished automatically when a new database is created, by manually copying the offline database, by using the Update Database Copy Wizard, or by using the `Update-MailboxDatabaseCopy` cmdlet.

After the database is seeded, the continuous replication process keeps the passive copies of the database in sync with the following process:

1. On the server with the active database, a transaction log is written and then closed.

2. The Microsoft Exchange Replication service replicates the closed transaction log to all servers hosting passive copies of the database.

3. The Log Inspector examines the transaction logs for the following:

   - Verifies the physical integrity of the transaction log.

   - Verifies that transaction log header generation is not higher than the highest generation for the current database copy.

   - Verifies that the transaction log header matches the generation specified by the filename.

   - Verifies that the transaction log file signature in the header matches the log file.

4. The Log Inspector places the transaction log into the database's transaction log directory on the target server and the information store inspects the transaction log files and then applies them to the database copy.

This transaction log shipping occurs over TCP sockets. You can view the current TCP port used for replication by running:

```
Get-DatabaseAvailabilityGroup-Status | Format-List
```

The default TCP port used for replication is 64327. You can change the TCP port using the Set-DatabaseAvailabilityGroup-ReplicationPort cmdlet and manually creating a Windows Firewall exception. After the configuration change is made, the Microsoft Exchange Replication service needs to be restarted on each node in the DAG.

A DAG is a Windows failover cluster and requires that quorum be maintained. Quorum is achieved when a majority of the DAG members agree on the status of the cluster. This keeps a single member from being isolated by a network failure and attempting to take control of the clustered resources. In DAGs with an even number of members, a witness server (previously called the file share witness) is required to break any voting ties. For example, if there are four DAG members and members A and B believe that C and D are down and members C and D believe A and B are down, neither group can seize control of the cluster as neither has a majority of the members in agreement. In these cases, the witness server is required to obtain a majority. The witness server is a server with a file share that stores the cluster configuration. Figure 14.2 shows how quorum can be maintained even with two members offline because quorum is achieved with members A and B with the witness server.

The witness server cannot be a member of the domain but must be in the same Active Directory forest as the DAG members. The Exchange documentation recommends using a Hub Transport server in the same site as the witness server. An alternate witness server can also be configured; however, this is used to specify the witness server located in the secondary datacenter when the DAG spans two datacenters.

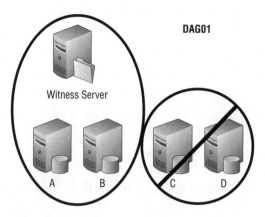

Quorum is just the first step because if quorum is not achieved, none of the databases can come online. The databases still need to have copies available on the operational servers to be online, so not only do you need to plan to achieve quorum—databases must be placed on multiple DAG members to provide redundancy.

Continuous replication   block mode was introduced in Exchange 2010 Service Pack 1 (SP1), this reduces the exposure of data loss during a failover by replicating all logs writes to the passive database copies in parallel to writing them locally. Enabling and disabling block mode is done automatically by the log copy process. Block mode will automatically become active when continuous replication file mode is up-to-date with the database copies. The replication transport is the same when block mode is enabled or disabled. When block mode is disabled, the traditional file mode replication method is used.

Active Manager and Activation Preference

Exchange 2010 has a new component called Active Manager, which is a component of the Microsoft Exchange Replication service (`MSExchangeRepl.exe`). Active Manager monitors the databases and copies of the databases. It runs on all Mailbox servers that are members of a DAG. This component is broken up into two pieces: the Primary Active Manager (PAM) and the Standby Active Manager (SAM). The server that hosts the PAM role will be the server that currently hosts the cluster group resource. To see which member is acting as the PAM, you can run:

```
Get-DatabaseAvailabilityGroup <DAG name> -Status | Format-List
```

As you can see in Figure 14.3, MB01A is currently acting as the PAM.

FIGURE 14.3   Viewing the PAM

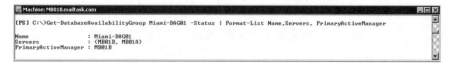

The PAM is responsible for deciding which copies of the database are active and which copies are passive, but it also receives topology change notifications so it can react to failures. The server that hosts the PAM will also take on the responsibilities of the SAM; in this case, it is MB01A. The SAM monitors the status of the local database copies and the information store. The SAM does not make any decisions on where database copies will be mounted in the case of a failure; it only reports that information to the server hosting the PAM role. It does not update any database information. The SAM also reports which mailbox server is hosting the active database copy to some additional Exchange components such as the Hub Transport and RPC Client Access service.

A database created on MB01B is assigned an activation preference of 1 and the database copy on MB01A is given the preference of 2. You can view the active preference using the `Get-MailboxDatabase` command or view the setting in the Exchange Management Console (EMC). What does this preference do? The activation preference does not dictate which database copy will be brought online unless there is a tie between two different database copies after Active Manager looks for a validated server to host the new active copy. Active Manager will compare the health of the content index, the length of the log copy queue, and the log replay queue to determine which server should host the new active copy of the database. If there is more than one server that meets all the criteria, the activation preference breaks the tie. For a full list of what is compared by Active Manager, see the TechNet article at `http://technet.microsoft.com/en-us/library/dd776123.aspx`.

Database Copy Auto Activation Policy

You may want to limit which servers can host an active database in the event of a failure. This could keep a database from activating at a secondary datacenter or on a server on which you are performing maintenance. Microsoft has provided the ability to configure database activation policies on the Mailbox servers to assist administrators from preventing unwanted activations. You can use the `Get-MailboxServer` command to view the current settings. You can see in Figure 14.4 that the servers are set to the default setting of Unrestricted.

FIGURE 14.4   Viewing the activation policy

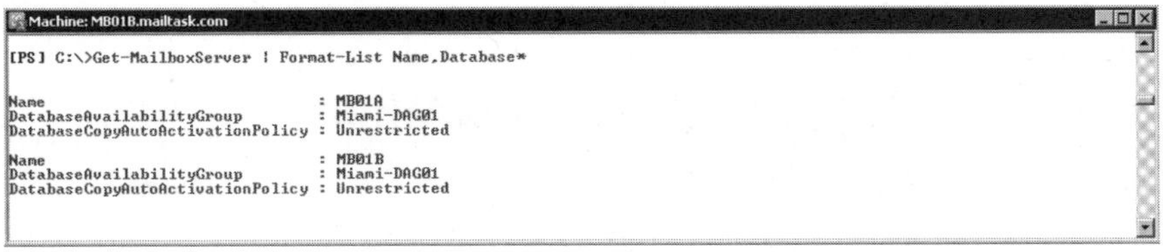

```
Machine: MB01B.mailtask.com                                                    _ □ ×

[PS] C:\>Get-MailboxServer | Format-List Name,Database*


Name                           : MB01A
DatabaseAvailabilityGroup      : Miami-DAG01
DatabaseCopyAutoActivationPolicy : Unrestricted
Name                           : MB01B
DatabaseAvailabilityGroup      : Miami-DAG01
DatabaseCopyAutoActivationPolicy : Unrestricted
```

There are three policies that can be configured with the `Set-MailboxServer` command:

Blocked   No database can be automatically active on this server.

IntrasiteOnly   This prevents database failovers from activating database copies that are not in the same Active Directory site.

Unrestricted   This is the default setting on the servers and allows any server in the DAG to be selected in the event of a failure.

Maximum Active Databases

Exchange 2010 has improved I/O performance drastically, which allows administrators to increase the scalability of their servers. As more users are added to Mailbox servers, there may be greater potential for server degradation, or if an Exchange server has been improperly sized, mounting too many databases on a single server could affect the user's experience. Exchange 2010 provides us with the capability to configure the maximum number of databases that can be active on a mailbox server. When configuring this property, you need to take into account your current number of database copies and failure tolerance.

If a failure occurs and a server reaches the configured threshold for the maximum number of databases on each node, the failed database will not mount on any server and your users could experience an outage. If you have multiple copies of the database and a server has not reached its maximum database limit, the database copy will be mounted. You can use the Set-MailboxServer command to configure the maximum number of databases allowed to mount on a server and view the current settings with the Get-MailboxServer command. By default, this value is set to null, which means there is not a limit, as shown in Figure 14.5.

Exchange Server 2010 Service Pack 1 includes the StartDagServerMaintenance.ps1 script that you can use to take a DAG member out of service. The script moves active databases off of the specified DAG member and blocks databases from activating. It also ensures that all the PAM is moved to another member, and blocked from moving back. The StopDagServerMaintenance.ps1 script is used to remove the blocks and allow databases to be activated on that member.

FIGURE 14.5 Getting the maximum number of active database settings

Designing and Deploying High Availability for Client Access Servers

For a highly available CAS deployment, multiple CAS servers need to be deployed within a site; however, there is no integrated mechanism that provides the redundancy. To provide the redundancy, the CAS servers need to be configured identically and network load balancing is used to load-balance and provide failover of client connections and other CAS servers. Table 14.1 summarizes the services that need to be load-balanced.

TABLE 14.1 Client Access service load-balancing requirements

Client Access Service	Protocol	Ports	Persistence
RPC Client Access	RPC	RPC Ports	Source IP
POP3	POP3	110/994	
IMAP4	IMAP4	143/993	
Exchange ActiveSync	HTTP	80/443	Source IP
Outlook Anywhere	HTTP	80/443	Source IP
Outlook Web App	HTTP	80/443	Cookie or Source IP

Choosing a Load Balancer Type

The CAS servers can be load-balanced a number of ways. Windows Server includes the Network Load Balancing (NLB) feature, which can be used to provide simple load balancing. However, it lacks built-in service health checking and only offers source IP affinity, which can lead to uneven load distribution across the load-balanced cluster when multiple clients are connecting from a single IP address, as often occurs when connecting across the Internet behind a firewall. NLB also cannot be combined with Windows Failover Clustering and thus cannot be used when collocating CAS on a DAG member server.

Another load-balancing option might be an application firewall like Microsoft Threat Management Gateway (TMG). TMG provides more complicated affinity rules and health checking as well as other features that NLB cannot provide, such as Secure Sockets Layer (SSL) offloading. However, be aware that TMG is not able to load-balance the RPC Client Access connections, and thus an additional load-balancing technology is needed if you chose TMG.

A variety of hardware load balancers are available in a number of formats. As you might expect, hardware load balancers are available as hardware appliances that you can purchase and install. Also, a number of top-tier hardware vendors now offer lower-cost or even free versions of their hardware appliances that can be run as a virtual machine. Regardless of the format in which these are delivered, there is a large variance in the capabilities of these devices. When you are evaluating hardware load balancers, be sure to read any documentation available for configuring the product for Exchange 2010.

 For information on Client Access arrays, please read Chapter 7.

Designing and Deploying High Availability for Transport Servers

As mentioned in Chapter 12, "Designing Routing and Client Connectivity," a number of transport availability improvements have been introduced in Exchange 2010. Most notable are the forms of shadow redundancy that provide protection for email messages while they are in transit.

🌐 **Real World Scenario**

Deploying Exchange Server 2010 with Hardware Load Balancers

You will need to configure each hardware load balancer differently to support Exchange, and not all hardware load balancers will support deploying Exchange 2010. Be sure to check with the vendor before purchasing a hardware load balancer to make sure they support all the features you are deploying. For an overview of the deployment process, see the following white papers:

- Deploying L65 with Microsoft Exchange Server 2010:

  http://www.f5.com/pdf/deployment-guides/f5-exchange-2010-dg.pdf

- Citrix NetScaler Deployment Guide for Microsoft Exchange 2010:

  http://community.citrix.com/download/attachments/37847055/NetScaler_Exchange2010.pdf

This list has just two examples, but there are numerous capable hardware load balancers available on the market that may work for your Exchange deployment.

To provide Hub Transport redundancy in a single site, multiple Hub Transport servers need to be deployed in the site. Unlike the CAS server, no external configuration needs to be done to provide load balancing; Exchange handles load balancing across the available Hub Transport servers in the site and attempts to use another Hub Transport server if the first one fails.

To better understand how shadow redundancy works within the Exchange organization, it is best to consider an example of a message being successfully delivered to an external SMTP server, as illustrated in Figure 14.6.

1. Hub1 delivers the email message to Edge1:

    a. Hub1 opens an SMTP session with Edge1.

    b. Edge1 advertises shadow redundancy support.

    c. Hub1 notifies Edge1 to track discard status.

    d. Hub1 sends the message to Edge1.

   e. Edge1 acknowledges receipt of the message and registers Hub1 to receive discard information for the message.

   f. Hub1 moves the sent message to the shadow queue and marks Edge1 as the primary server. Hub1 becomes the shadow server.

2. Edge1 delivers the message to the next hop:

   a. Edge1 sends the message to SMTP1, a third-party email server.

   b. SMTP1 acknowledges receipt of the email message.

   c. Edge1 updates the discard status for the message as delivery complete.

3. Hub1 queries Edge1 for discard status:

   a. At end of each SMTP session with Edge1, Hub1 queries Edge1 for the discard status on messages previously sent. If Hub1 has not sent any other messages to Edge1, it will open an SMTP session with Edge1 to query for the discard status after 5 minutes and will failover after three request failures or 15 minutes. You can configure this time using `Set-TransportConfig` with the `ShadowHeartbeatTimeoutInterval` parameter. The number of retries can be configured by running `Set-TransportConfig -ShadowHeartbeatRetryCount`.

   b. Edge1 checks the local discard status and sends back the list of messages registered to Hub1 that have been delivered and then removes the discard information.

   c. Hub1 deletes the delivered messages from its shadow queue.

FIGURE 14.6 Shadow redundancy inside the Exchange organization with a successful delivery

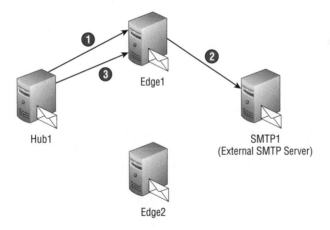

If the message is not successfully delivered to the external SMTP server, the process, as shown in Figure 14.7, is as follows:

1. Hub1 delivers the email message to Edge1:

   a. Hub1 opens an SMTP session with Edge1.

   b. Edge1 advertises shadow redundancy support.

    c.   Hub1 notifies Edge1 to track discard status.

    d.   Hub1 sends the message to Edge1.

    e.   Edge1 acknowledges receipt of the message and registers Hub1 to receive discard information for the message.

    f.   Hub1 moves the sent message to the shadow queue and marks Edge1 as the primary server. Hub1 becomes the shadow server.

2.   Edge1 fails before it is able to deliver the email message to the next hop.

3.   When Hub1 queries Edge1 for discard status and cannot contact Edge1, Hub1 resumes the primary role and resubmits the messages in the shadow queue to another available transport server, Edge2.

4.   The resubmitted messages are delivered to Edge2, and the workflow starts from step 1.

FIGURE 14.7   Shadow redundancy inside the Exchange organization with a failure during delivery

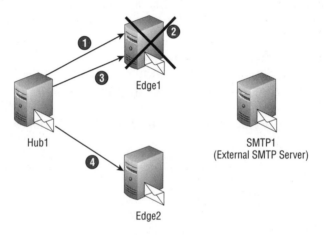

Understanding Delayed Acknowledgement

Another function of shadow redundancy is delayed acknowledgement, which is used when messages are received from SMTP servers that to do not support shadow redundancy. In this scenario, the receiving Exchange server will delay acknowledging that it has received the message from the server until the message is delivered to all of the internal transport hops. If a Hub Transport server fails during the delivery of the message, the message will not be acknowledged and the sending server will reattempt delivery. On the other hand, if the message is not delivered during the maximum acknowledgement delay, the server will send an acknowledgement to the sending server. By default, the maximum time the receiving server can take to acknowledge receipt is 30 seconds. In some environments, this default may need to be changed. In Exercise 14.1 you will use the EMC to change the `MaxAcknowledgementDelay` attribute of the default connector.

EXERCISE 14.1

Changing the Maximum Acknowledgement Delay on a Receive Connector

Follow these steps to use the EMC to change the MaxAcknowledgementDelay attribute on EX02:

1. Log onto EX02 as Administrator.

2. Click Start ➢ Programs ➢ Microsoft Exchange Server 2010 and then select Exchange Management Shell.

3. Run the following command:

Set-ReceiveConnector "Default Receive Connector"

-MaxAcknowledgementDelay 60

There are times when Exchange will acknowledge the message before the time-out even if the message hasn't been delivered to the destination. This will happen if the destination queue is in a suspended or retry state or if there are messages queued in the target queue. In the RTM version of Exchange 2010, this could lead to the loss of the message if a transport server failure occurs before the message is delivered to its destination. If Exchange 2010 with Service Pack 1 is installed, the Hub Transport server can perform shadow redundancy promotion by submitting the message to another Hub Transport server in the site, which will protect the message with shadow redundancy within the Exchange organization.

You can find more information about shadow redundancy in Chapter 12.

Understanding How the Hub Transport Role Coexists on a DAG Member

As you are aware, the purpose the DAG feature is to provide redundancy. You are also aware that you can install both the CAS and the Hub roles on DAG members. The question may come up then, Is shadow redundancy lost if a DAG member goes offline?

The answer is hopefully no. To avoid this problem, when a message is submitted from a DAG member, the active Mailbox server will attempt to submit the message to another Hub Transport server in the site rather than using the Hub Transport server located on the member. If no other Hub Transport servers are available in the site, however, the Mailbox server will submit the message to the local Hub Transport server.

As you can see, deploying redundant transport servers requires that multiple servers be deployed in each AD site. This allows shadow redundancy to protect messages during transit, and all load-balancing and rerouting of messages is handled automatically without the need of load balancing software or hardware. In fact, load-balancing the default Hub Transport receive connectors is not supported.

Deploying Highly Available Edge Transport Servers

Mail eXchange DNS records are created so that external senders can identify which servers receive email for your organization. Multiple records can be created and weights assigned to point to multiple Edge Transport servers or to Hub Transport servers receiving email from the Internet. Records that have the same weight will be load-balanced and records with higher weights will only be attempted if the lower-weighted servers are unavailable. If Exchange is deployed in multiple sites, you may assign the MX records for the primary site a low weight and then create MX records for the secondary site with a higher weight so that if the primary site is unavailable, email can be received at the secondary site.

MX records are able to provide load balancing and redundancy, which is often sufficient. In some instances, however, inbound SMTP traffic is load-balanced with NLB.

 You can find more information about MX records and how they are used in RFC 2821 and in Chapter 12.

Designing and Deploying High Availability Across Sites

You can deploy a DAG to provide failover of services between sites without needing third-party hardware or software. A cross-site DAG has the following requirements:

- As with a single site DAG, less than 250 milliseconds of latency between all DAG members.

- At least one supported domain controller in each site; however, you must consider the load and redundancy requirements and deploy an adequate number of domain controllers.

- In order to provide client connectivity to both sites, at least one Client Access server must be deployed; however, you must consider the load and redundancy requirements and deploy accordingly.

- At least one Hub Transport server in each site. In order to provide email transport to the both sites, at least one Hub Transport must be deployed; however, you must consider the load and redundancy requirements and deploy accordingly.

In the case of a complete datacenter failure, and all members in the primary site are unavailable, and a majority of the nodes are no longer online, quorum must be reestablished before the mailbox databases can be mounted. To reestablish quorum in the DAG, Datacenter Activation Coordination (DAC) must be enabled. When DAC mode is enabled, the DAG can be forced to artificially obtain quorum with the members available in the standby datacenter without having to remove the unavailable members. Even when DAC mode is enabled, the failover process requires administrative intervention. Because this is a manual failover process, it is often referred to as a switchover. In general, the switchover process is as follows:

1. If necessary, adjust DNS records for Simple Mail Transfer Protocol (SMTP), Outlook Web App (OWA), Autodiscover, Outlook Anywhere, POP3, and IMAP4. This can be completed manually or automatically using global-server load balancing.

2. Reconfigure the DAG to remove the DAG members in the primary site from the Windows Failover Cluster, and retain them in the DAG by running `Stop-DatabaseAvailabilityGroup <DAG Name> –ActiveDirectorySite <Primary Site Name>-ConfigurationOnly` in the primary site, if possible.

3. Reconfigure the DAG to use an alternate witness server to restore the functionality in the secondary site. This is completed by stopping the Cluster service on each of the DAG members in the recovery site running `Restore-DatabaseAvailabilityGroup <DAG Name>-ActiveDirectorySite <Secondary Site Name>-AlternateWitnessServer <Secondary Site Witness Server>`.

4. Start the Cluster service on each of the DAG members in the secondary site. The remaining Active Managers will then coordinate mounting databases in the secondary site.

To perform a switchover once the primary site has been recovered, the following general steps should be used:

1. Reconfigure the DAG to re-add the DAG members in the primary datacenter into the failover cluster by running `Start-DatabaseAvailabilityGroup <DAG Name> –ActiveDirectorySite <Primary Site Name>`.

2. Configure the DAG to use the primary site's File Share Witness by running `Set-DatabaseAvailabilityGroup <DAG Name>-WitnessServer <Primary Site Witness Server>`.

3. Manually reseed or allow replication to update the primary data center's database copies.

4. Schedule downtime for all mailbox databases in the DAG, and then dismount them.

5. If necessary adjust DNS records for (SMTP), OWA, Autodiscover, Outlook Anywhere, POP3, and IMAP4. This can be completed manually or automatically using global-server load balancing.

6. Move databases back to primary datacenter by running `Move-ActiveMailboxDatabase <Database>–ActivateOnServer <Server in Primary Site>`. Then mount the databases in primary datacenter.

 The initial release of Exchange 2010 only supported using DAC mode for DAGs with at least three members, two of which are located in the same site. Exchange Server 2010 Service Pack 1 introduces support for a two member DAG with a single member in each site to use DAC mode.

Designing Exchange Backup and Recovery

Before you design a backup solution for Exchange, you must first identify the use cases for the restores. You may need to perform backup for disaster recovery, long-term retention of data, deleted item recovery, or recovery from failure to a point in time. Each of these requirements can have very different solutions.

When disaster recovery is the goal, usually a second site is used to perform recovery. Although tape backups can be used to perform this sort of recovery, it rarely is the most efficient and reliable way to recover data to the secondary site. This is one of the improvements made in Exchange Server 2010, where replicating mailbox data to a secondary site is a native function of the DAG feature. For more information see the section, "Designing and Deploying High Availability for Mailbox Servers," earlier in this chapter.

Despite added features like Online Archive, Dumpster 2.0 or Single Item Recovery, and Litigations Hold, many businesses and their auditors will still require that a backup of the mailboxes be made periodically for long-term retention of data.

Deleted item recovery can often be handled with the built-in features of Single Item Recovery, assuming the deleted item retention window is configured appropriately. If specific groups of users need to recover deleted items for a longer period of time, consider configuring custom deleted item retention for those users rather than performing additional backups for archival.

Recovery of data to a point in time can be accomplished with traditional backups, and many companies will choose to do recoveries this way. Another way to accomplish this is by using lagged database copies. The lagged copy of the database receives all the transaction logs. However, they can be configured to delay applying the transaction logs for up to 14 days, essentially providing an on-disk copy of the database that can be rolled back up to 14 days if a point-in-time restore is needed. This type of recovery could be much faster than a tape-based recovery. Companies that do not require more than 14 days of backup retention may consider deploying a "backup-less" environment, assuming enough redundancy is provided within the DAG.

After determining the use cases for backup in your organization, you need to determine the recovery time objective (RTO) and recovery point objective (RPO), meaning how long it can take to recover the data and service and how much data can be lost. If the recovery point objective is seven days and the recovery time objective is three days, you may very well be able to use traditional tape backup. More realistically, most businesses would like both of these objectives to take fewer than 24 hours. If this is the case, other methods should be used to provide added redundancy.

Two features that can improve the recovery time are database portability and dial tone portability (or recovery). Database portability allows you to take a copy of a database and mount it to any other Mailbox server in the Exchange organization. This can be used if a server has a hardware failure and has only one copy of the database available. The disks can be taken out or copied from the original server to another already running Exchange Mailbox server. With dial tone portability, a blank database can be mounted on any server in the Exchange organization and the mailbox users can connect to an empty mailbox while the original database is being repaired or restored.

In the next few sections, we will cover backup and recovery specifics for the Mailbox, Hub Transport, Edge Transport, and Client Access server roles.

 For more information about Exchange backup and recovery, see Chapter 8, "Disaster Recovery Operations for Exchange Server."

Backup and Recovery for Mailbox Servers

One of the biggest changes in Exchange 2010 is the elimination of the streaming backup application programming interface (API), the interface usually used by traditional backup software for previous versions of Exchange Server. All backups must now be performed using an Exchange-aware backup provider based on Volume Shadow Copy Service (VSS). An Exchange-aware VSS plug-in has been provided for the Windows Server Backup feature; however, most companies will leverage an enterprise-class backup solution. There are some limitations that you should be aware of if you use Windows Server Backup, even when in a lab environment:

- Backups taken with Windows Server Backup occur at volume level. To back up a database and its transaction logs, you must back up the entire volume containing the database and transaction logs.
- You cannot use the Windows Server Backup with the VSS plug-in to take remote VSS backups.
- Only full backups can be taken.
- When Exchange data is restored, all databases in the backup set (minimally the databases that share the same disks) must be restored together.

Each backup solution has rules and guidelines around performing Exchange backups. Many of the top-tier backup software packages and storage providers support backing up Exchange 2010 without the limitations imposed with the free Windows Server Backup utility. You should evaluate multiple vendors and verify that the software can meet your recovery needs.

There are essentially six areas that need to be protected from deletion, corruption, or failure: messages, mailboxes, mailbox databases, public folders, public folder databases, or an entire server.

There are a number of ways to address each of these failures, as shown in Table 14.2.

TABLE 14.2 Addressing potential failure areas

Failure Type	Feature to Address
Message loss or deletion	Deleted item retention Single item recovery Traditional backup
Mailbox loss or deletion	Deleted mailbox retention Traditional backup
Mailbox database loss	Database availability group copy Database portability Dial tone portability

TABLE 14.2   Addressing potential failure areas *(continued)*

Failure Type	Feature to Address
Server failure	Database availability group copy Database portability Dial tone portability
Database corruption or point-in-time recovery	Database availability group copy Lagged database copy
Public folder deletion	Deleted item recovery (Dumpster 1.0) Traditional backup
Public folder database or server failure	Public folder replication Traditional backup

Traditional backups are covered in detail in Chapter 8. The other features listed in Table 14.2 are covered in the following sections.

Understanding Deleted Item Recovery

Deleted Item Retention has been present in Exchange since version Exchange 5.5. When deleted Item Retention is enabled, as items are deleted, they are put into the Deleted Items folder until the folder is emptied. This gives the end user the opportunity to review and recover the items before they are permanently deleted. When the Deleted Items folder is emptied, the messages are not expunged from the database; rather, they are flagged to be included in the dumpster and essentially hidden from the mailbox.

The items in the dumpster remain there for the duration set by the Deleted Item Retention policy or until the items are manually deleted from the dumpster. If the user needs to recover the data after emptying the Deleted Items folder, the user can use the Recover Deleted Items option in Outlook to retrieve the deleted data for the duration set by the Deleted Item Retention policy for the mailbox. Although this feature was often overlooked by many, the dumpster could reduce the need for database restores, especially if Deleted Item Retention was set long enough to fulfill user requests for restoration.

The dumpster in previous versions of Exchange is an excellent feature, but it has a few drawbacks:

- No quotas on the deleted items. An unlimited amount of data can exist in the dumpster, causing storage capacity planning difficulties.

- Users can manually purge the dumpster data and hide information they deleted from their mailboxes.

- Data in the dumpster is not searchable. Discovery cannot be performed against the data in the dumpster. This is essential when providing information to lawyers.

In Office Outlook 2003 and earlier, the Recover Deleted Items menu option is available only for the Deleted Items folder. This leads some to the misconception that using Shift+Delete to delete messages will permanently purge the data. On the contrary, the deleted information is moved to the dumpster for the folder from which the message is deleted. You can enable the Recover Deleted Items option in Outlook by setting a Registry key. More information on setting this Registry key can be found at http://support.microsoft.com/kb/886205.

Exchange Server 2010 introduces new behavior for the dumpster to address the previous drawbacks. These new features are sometimes referred to as Dumpster 2.0. Deleted items were flagged and hidden in the original folder, but Dumpster 2.0 is implemented as a non-IPM folder (a folder that is not visible in Outlook or OWA) in each mailbox called Recoverable Items. This folder has up to four subfolders: Deletions, Versions, Purges, and Audits.

The items that are moved to the Deletions folder are items that are soft-deleted and that would have ended up in the per-folder dumpster in previous versions of Exchange Server. To ensure backward compatibility with Outlook 2003 and Outlook 2007, the Client Access server translates any requests to the dumpster into calls for the Recoverable Items\Deletions folder. All of the data in the Deletions folder is bound by the Deleted Item Retention policy set for the mailbox. This new method allows deleted items to be indexed and searched for discovery purposes. It also allows deleted items to be moved when a mailbox is moved between databases, and a quota can be set for the maximum size for the deleted items.

The default deleted item retention period set on a mailbox database is 14 days.

To reduce the need for restores, set the Deleted Item Retention for as long as you need to support recovery of deleted items. Some companies have a four-week tape rotation and cannot restore data older than four weeks. It is possible to size the hardware and set the Deleted Item Retention to 28 days (four weeks) so the Deleted Item Retention configuration spans the same period of time that tape backups provide. However, with Deleted Item Retention data can be immediately recovered by the user rather than through performing a restore.

An online archive has a separate Recoverable Items\Deletions folder to store data deleted from the online archive.

When Single Item Recovery is enabled on the mailbox items that are purged or hard-deleted from the Deletions folder before the Deleted Item Retention has elapsed, the purged messages are moved into the Purges folder for the remaining Deleted Item Retention period. Because users cannot access this folder, this keeps them from permanently purging potentially incriminating information. However, a legal hold can enable longer-term data preservation to disable the expiration of the items. Exercise 14.2 will show you how to enable Single Item Recovery on a single mailbox.

EXERCISE 14.2

Enabling Single Item Recovery on a Mailbox Using EMS

Follow these steps to enable Single Item Recovery on a mailbox using EMS:

1. Click Start ➤ Programs ➤ Microsoft Exchange Server 2010 and then select Exchange Management Shell.

2. Run the following command:

   ```
   Set-Mailbox -Identity Brian
   -SingleItemRecoveryEnabled $True
   -RetainDeletedItemsFor 28
   ```

When either Single Item Recovery or Litigation Hold (also known as Legal Hold) is enabled, as items in the mailbox are modified, the original message is copied to the Versions subfolder. This process is called *copy on write* because as messages are modified, the original is copied to the Versions folder. Each version is kept and can be searched by a user assigned the Discovery Management role. This can be used to find messages that have been modified to hide or alter the original content of the message. However, to reduce the amount of data stored in the Versions folder, messages in the Drafts folder are not protected in this way.

Deleted items are still stored in the database and do take up storage space. It is important to understand the impact of modifying the deleted item settings. To review database sizing considerations, see Chapter 11, "Designing and Deploying Mailbox Services."

> **NOTE**   Regardless of whether Single Item Recovery is enabled or not, calendar items are by default maintained in the Recoverable Items folder structure for 120 days, with one exception. After Exchange Server 2010 Service Pack 1 is installed on the Mailbox server, the organizer of a meeting will not have versions of a meeting copied to the organizer's Versions folder when attendee tracking information is updated.

The Audit subfolder is used to store auditing information and is not specifically used to protect deleted items. Table 14.3 summarizes how the dumpster behaves depending on the mailbox configuration.

TABLE 14.3   Dumpster 2.0 behavior

Configuration	Deleted Items Protected	Versions and Hard-Deleted Items Protected	Dumpster Protected from Purge?	Automatically Purge Dumpster Items?
Single Item Recovery disabled (default)	Yes	No	No	Yes, using deleted item retention for email and 120 days for calendar items

TABLE 14.3   Dumpster 2.0 behavior *(continued)*

Configuration	Deleted Items Protected	Versions and Hard-Deleted Items Protected	Dumpster Protected from Purge?	Automatically Purge Dumpster Items?
Single Item Recovery enabled	Yes	Yes	Yes	Yes, using deleted item retention for email and 120 days for calendar items
Litigation Hold enabled	Yes	Yes	Yes	No

Understanding Deleted Mailbox Retention

Deleted Mailbox Retention is less complex than Deleted Item Retention. When a mailbox is deleted, it is kept in the database for the retention period or an administrator purges it manually. If a mailbox is deleted, the entire mailbox can be reattached to a user account using the Connect-Mailbox command. The default retention setting on a mailbox database is 30 days and may need to be changed depending on your environment to ensure that deleted mailboxes are kept long enough to be recovered using Deleted Item Retention.

Using Lagged Database Copies

A lagged database copy is a copy of a database in a DAG that does not have the transaction logs replayed as they are received from the active copy. This is configured by setting the replay lag time on the database copy, which allows an administrator to configure how many minutes to delay the replay of transaction logs into the lagged copy. The replay lag time starts after the log has been copied to the server with the lagged copy and has been successfully inspected by the log inspector.

Using a lagged database copy, you can recover a database to a point in time. For example, suppose a message is received that introduces corruption into the database, causing both the active and non-lagged copies to become corrupt. In this instance, the lagged copy can be used to recover the database to just before the corruption occurred. In some companies, combining a 14-day lagged copy with several passive copies and Single Item Recovery enabled gives them enough comfort to not perform traditional backups. This is called a "backup-less" environment.

Recovering a database to a point in time involves a number of manual tasks, such as copying the database and logs to another location and replaying the logs to the point in time from which you want to recover. If you choose to use a backup-less environment, this is usually accomplished by using a database lag copy to provide up to 14 days of lag. When a lagged copy is used as the backup in a backup-less environment, it should never be activated, even though it is possible to do so. If you activate the lagged copy, you no longer have a backup copy. Depending on the failure, this may be an acceptable risk; however, be sure you fully understand the risk before making the decision to activate the only lagged copy in a backup-less environment.

Backup and Recovery for Client Access Servers

Backup of the CAS servers is pretty straightforward. You should regularly perform a system state backup as well as have a backup of any installed certificates and the associated private keys. To be sure that any customizations you have made are also saved, you should back up at least the following folders under the Exchange installation folder:

- ClientAccess\ECP
- ClientAccess\exchweb\ews
- ClientAccess\OWA
- ClientAccess\PopImap
- ClientAccess\RPCProxy
- ClientAccess\Sync

To recover a CAS server, you can restore from backup or run Setup /m:RecoverServer from the Exchange installation media. However, usually the quickest way to recover a CAS server is to delete the nonworking CAS server and install a new one. The configuration process can be automated by creating a PowerShell script that makes any configuration changes that need to be made to the server.

Backup and Recovery for Transport Servers

As mentioned in the preceding section, backup of the CAS servers is straightforward. Backup of the Hub Transport and Edge Transport servers is similarly straightforward. You should regularly perform a system state backup as well as have a backup of any installed certificates and the associated private keys. To be sure any customizations are protected, you should back up the server data. You should be sure to back up the following files and folders under the Exchange installation folder:

- TransportRoles\Logs
- Bin\EdgeTransport.exe.config

In addition, for Edge Transport servers. you should run the Export-TransportRuleCollection cmdet to export all of the transport rules. The configuration should be exported using ExportEdgeConfig.ps1, and the resulting XML files should be copied off the server.

The Hub Transport servers can be recovered by deploying a new server with the same name and then running Setup /m:RecoverServer from the Exchange installation media. After the installation is complete, EdgeTransport.exe.config and the message tracking logs can be restored from backup, if needed.

To recover an Edge Transport server, start by deploying a new server with the same name as the failed server and then follow these steps:

1. Install Exchange.

2. Import the configuration using the `ImportEdgeConfig.ps1` script.

3. Import the transport rules using `Import-TransportRule Collection`.

4. Run EdgeSync.

5. Restore `EdgeTransport.exe.config` and any message tracking logs.

Summary

High availability is more than just a feature or a function of some software or hardware. It is an achievement that can be planned for if all the components of a messaging solution are scrutinized and adjusted to promote it.

Exchange 2010 has introduced new features such as the database availability group to provide simple-to-deploy high availability solutions. The DAG provides flexibility in the configuration process and meets the various needs of companies.

Client Access servers are more critical pieces of the infrastructure in Exchange 2010, and thus high availability is also more important. Client Access servers are load balanced using software or hardware load-balancing solutions, and Client Access arrays are created to represent the load-balanced CAS servers in Active Directory.

Transport servers now have shadow redundancy to protect messages that are in transit. This protects messages sent inside the Exchange organization as well as messages received from outside the organization.

Improvements to the backup and recovery options in Exchange 2010 show that it is possible to run a backup-less environment if it meets the needs of the business. More likely, in the near term, features like Dumpster 2.0, Single Item Recovery, deleted mailbox retention, and lagged database copies will reduce the requirement to perform restores in most environments.

Chapter Essentials

Understand the new database availability model.   Exchange 2010 now has a single database availability option, the database availability group. This one feature provides flexibility to meet the needs for most environments and is simple to set up because the Exchange installation automates the configuration of the failover cluster.

Understand Deleted Item Retention.   Deleted Item Retention provides protection for deleted and modified objects if used in conjunction with Single Item Recovery. Deleted Item Retention can greatly reduce the need for restoration.

Appendix

A

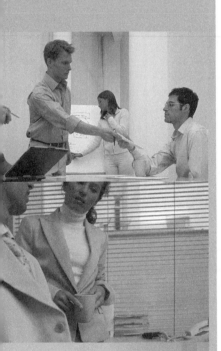

Microsoft's Certification Program

Since the inception of its certification program, Microsoft has certified more than two million people. As the computer network industry continues to increase in both size and complexity, this number is sure to grow—and the need for *proven* ability will also increase. Certifications can help companies verify the skills of prospective employees and contractors.

Microsoft has developed its Microsoft Certified Professional (MCP) program to give you credentials that verify your ability to work with Microsoft products effectively and professionally. Several levels of certification are available based on specific suites of exams. With the release of Windows Vista, Microsoft created a new generation of certification programs:

Microsoft Certified Technology Specialist (MCTS)   The MCTS can be considered the entry-level certification for the new generation of Microsoft certifications. The MCTS certification program targets specific technologies instead of specific job roles. You must take and pass one to three exams.

Microsoft Certified IT Professional (MCITP)   The MCITP certification is a Professional Series certification that tests network and system administrators on job roles rather than only on a specific technology. The MCITP certification program generally consists of one to three exams in addition to obtaining an MCTS-level certification.

Microsoft Certified Professional Developer (MCPD)   The MCPD certification is a Professional Series certification for application developers. Similar to the MCITP, the MCPD is focused on a job role rather than on a single technology. The MCPD certification program generally consists of one to three exams in addition to obtaining an MCTS-level certification.

Microsoft Certified Architect (MCA)   The MCA is Microsoft's premier certification series. Obtaining the MCA requires a minimum of 10 years of experience and passing a review board consisting of peer architects.

How Do You Become Certified on Exchange Server 2010?

Attaining Microsoft certification has always been a challenge. In the past, students have been able to acquire detailed exam information—even most of the exam questions—from online "brain dumps" and third-party "cram" books or software products. For the new generation of exams, this is simply not the case.

Microsoft has taken strong steps to protect the security and integrity of its new certification tracks. Now prospective candidates should complete a course of study that develops detailed knowledge about a wide range of topics. It supplies them with the true skills needed, derived from working with the technology being tested.

The new generations of Microsoft certification programs are heavily weighted toward hands-on skills and experience. It is recommended that candidates have troubleshooting skills acquired through hands-on experience and working knowledge.

To get your MCITP: Enterprise Messaging Administrator on Exchange Server 2010 certification, you must pass a total of two exams:

- TS: Microsoft Exchange Server 2010, Configuring (70-662)

- IT Pro: Designing and Deploying Messaging Solutions with Microsoft Exchange Server 2010 (70-663)

The detailed exam objectives, and the chapters in which those objectives are discussed, can be found in the section "Certification Objectives Map" later in this appendix.

For a more detailed description of the Microsoft certification programs, including a list of all the exams, visit the Microsoft Learning website at www.microsoft.com/learning.

Tips for Taking a Microsoft Exam

Here are some general tips for achieving success on your certification exam:

- Arrive early at the exam center so that you can relax and review your study materials. During this final review, you can look over tables and lists of exam-related information.

- Read the questions carefully. Don't be tempted to jump to an early conclusion. Make sure you know *exactly* what the question is asking.

- Answer all questions. If you are unsure about a question, mark it for review and come back to it later.

- On simulations, do not change settings that are not directly related to the question. Also, assume default settings if the question does not specify or imply which settings are used.

- For questions you're not sure about, use a process of elimination to get rid of the obviously incorrect answers first. This improves your odds of selecting the correct answer when you need to make an educated guess.

Exam Registration

You may take the Microsoft exams at any of more than 1,000 Authorized Prometric Testing Centers (APTCs) around the world. For the location of a testing center near you, call Prometric at 800-755-EXAM (755-3926). Outside the United States and Canada, contact your local Prometric registration center.

Find out the number of the exam you want to take, and then register with the Prometric registration center nearest to you. At this point, you will be asked for advance payment for the exam. The exams are $125 each and you must take them within one year of payment. You can schedule exams up to six weeks in advance or as late as one working day prior to the date of the exam. You can cancel or reschedule your exam if you contact the center at least two working days prior to the exam. Same-day registration is available in some locations, subject to space availability. Where same-day registration is available, you must register a minimum of two hours before test time.

> You may also register for your exams online at www.prometric.com. As of this writing, VUE no longer offers Microsoft exams. If you have taken Microsoft exams with VUE, continue to watch VUE's website (www.vue.com) to see if it starts offering Microsoft exams again.

When you schedule the exam, you will be provided with instructions regarding appointment and cancellation procedures, ID requirements, and information about the testing center location. In addition, you will receive a registration and payment confirmation letter from Prometric.

Microsoft requires certification candidates to accept the terms of a nondisclosure agreement before taking certification exams.

Certification Objectives Map

Table A.1 provides objective mappings for the 70-662 exam. Table A.2 provides objective mappings for the 70-663 exam. In addition to the book chapters, you will find coverage of exam objectives in the flashcards, practice exams, and videos on the book's accompanying CD.

TABLE A.1 Exam 70-662 Objectives Map

Objectives	Chapter
Installing and Configuring Exchange Servers	**1, 2**
Prepare the infrastructure for Exchange. This objective may include but is not limited to: prepare schema; prepare domain; prepare Active Directory; ensure the domain functionality level is correct; domain controller service packs; Exchange readiness check; coexistence; migration from 2003 or 2007; disable LinkState; Exchange Server Service Pack level; remove unsupported legacy components; configuring DNS to support the Exchange deployment.	

TABLE A.1   Exam 70-662 Objectives Map *(continued)*

Objectives	Chapter

Install Exchange prerequisites. This objective may include but is not limited to: install MMC 3.0, Windows PowerShell 2.0; Microsoft .NET 3.5, WinRM 2.0, IIS, Windows roles and features, use ServerManagerCMD, use Exchange prerequisite scripts.

Install Exchange roles. This objective may include but is not limited to: from the command line and the GUI; adding and modifying roles; add server roles to existing Exchange 2003 or 2007 organizations; verify Exchange installation; Security Configuration wizard (SCW); Windows Firewall, including port requirements; installing Exchange Server using standard and custom installation; installing Exchange Server using the command line; provisioning an Exchange Server and delegating server installation; troubleshooting a failed installation; adding Exchange Server roles after an initial installation

Create and configure databases. This objective may include but is not limited to: set database limits; set retention limits; set Role Based Access Control (RBAC) permissions for database creation; naming conventions; create and use GUI and Windows PowerShell; create and manage public folder databases; set default public folder database; maintenance; mount and dismount databases; create new mailbox databases; configure mailbox database settings; move the mailbox database and transaction log locations; configure public folder database settings; mount and dismount databases

Create and configure address lists. This objective may include but is not limited to: update legacy address lists; configure offline address lists; publish address lists; filterable properties; creating and configuring e-mail address policies; creating and configuring address lists; creating and configuring offline address books

Configuring Exchange Recipients and Public Folders   **4, 5**

Create and configure mailboxes. This objective may include but is not limited to: deleted items; deleted mailbox; mailbox quota; message size; warning thresholds; move from and to previous Exchange versions; online and offline moves; intra-orgs and cross-orgs; create proxy addresses; create mailboxes; configure client access protocols; configure spam confidence level (SCL) and phishing confidence level (PCL); send as permissions; delegation; forwarding; mailbox permissions; create and configure linked mailboxes

Configure RBAC. This objective may include but is not limited to: create and assign RBAC roles; define RBAC scopes; configure RBAC for specific roles, such as help desk and address list administrator

Create and configure resource mailboxes and shared mailboxes. This objective may include but is not limited to: equipment; room; permissions; set mailbox calendaring options; autoaccept; custom resource types

TABLE A.1   Exam 70-662 Objectives Map *(continued)*

Objectives	Chapter

Create and configure recipients and distribution groups. This objective may include but is not limited to: create and modify; security enabled; configure moderation, including Exchange Control Panel (ECP) options; dynamic distribution groups; create proxy addresses; configure mail-enabled users; contacts; send as permissions; forwarding

Create and configure public folders. This objective may include but is not limited to: mail-enabled public folders; configure public folder permissions; deleted items; message size; item age; public folder size; create public folders in Enterprise Content Management (EMC) and Microsoft Outlook, and OWA; configure public folder permissions; configure public folder limits

Configuring Client Access   3

Configure POP, IMAP, and Microsoft ActiveSync. This objective may include but is not limited to: enable, configure, and secure POP and IMAP; manage certificates; configure mobile device policies; autodiscover; authentication; configure the Exchange ActiveSync virtual directory; configure the external name for Exchange ActiveSync; configure client access settings for Exchange ActiveSync, including Windows SharePoint Services and Windows File Share integration; Direct Push; configure Exchange ActiveSync mailbox policies; configure autodiscover for Exchange ActiveSync

Configure Outlook Anywhere and RPC Client Access. This objective may include but is not limited to: autodiscover; MAPI; create client access arrays; certificates; Subject Alternative Name (SAN); configure virtual directories; enable and configure Outlook Anywhere on the CAS; troubleshoot Outlook Anywhere connectivity

Configure federated sharing. This objective may include but is not limited to: certificates; enrollment; DNS; calendar and free/busy; Subject Alternative Name (SAN); assign policies; create and configure a federated trust; create and configure a federated organization identifier; create and configure a sharing relationship; create and configure a sharing policy; assign sharing policies to user accounts

Configure Outlook Web App (OWA). This objective may include but is not limited to: customize the OWA interface; certificates; file share and Share-Point access; public folders; verify multi-browser support; ECP; SAN; configure virtual directories; coexistence scenarios; authentication; configure the external name for OWA; configure client access settings for OWA, including Windows SharePoint Services and Windows File Share integration; segmentation settings; configure OWA mailbox policies

TABLE A.1   Exam 70-662 Objectives Map *(continued)*

Objectives	Chapter
Configuring Message Transport	3

Create and configure transport rules. This objective may include but is not limited to: enable and configure; disclaimers; moderated transport; install the Windows Rights Management Services (RMS) pre-licensing agent; configure rights protection by using transport rules

Configure hub transport. This objective may include but is not limited to: configure transport dumpster; accepted domains; remote domains; authoritative domains; email address policies

Configure Edge transport. This objective may include but is not limited to: create, configure, and test EdgeSync; configure Edge Transport server cloning; install the Edge Transport server role; configure Edge Transport server settings; configure Edge synchronization

Configure message routing. This objective may include but is not limited to: internal and external DNS; configure routing based on sites and costs; enable, configure, and secure send and receive connectors; certificates; relay connectors; authentication; message size limits; MTLS; routing group connector for coexistence; configure accepted and remote domains; configure SMTP send and receive connectors; configure message delivery limits; configure TLS security for message delivery

| **Monitoring and Reporting** | 9 |

Monitor databases. This objective may include but is not limited to: public folder statistics; mailbox databases statistics; database status; DAG replication

Monitor mail flow. This objective may include but is not limited to: perform message tracking; DNS; manage message queues; view, retry, and delete; backpressure thresholds; resolve NDRs

Monitor connectivity. This objective may include but is not limited to: SMTP client to server; SMTP server to server; Outlook RPC/MAPI; Outlook Anywhere; Outlook Exchange Web Services (EWS); POP; IMAP; ActiveSync

Generate reports. This objective may include but is not limited to: mailbox folder statistics; mailbox statistics; mailflow statistics; formatted list and formatted table; ExBPA

Configure logging. This objective may include but is not limited to: protocol logging; store logging; configure logging levels; agent logs; message tracking logs; event logs; analysis of logging results

TABLE A.1 Exam 70-662 Objectives Map *(continued)*

Objectives	Chapter
Implementing High Availability and Recovery	7, 8

Create and configure the Database Availability Group (DAG). This objective may include but is not limited to: create and configure DAG; file share witness (FSW); replication latency; configure lag; add or remove database copies; configure failover priority; add or remove server members; configure mailbox database copies; manage continuous replication

Perform backup and restore of data. This objective may include but is not limited to: recovery database; dialtone restores; deleted mailbox retention; deleted item retention; mailbox merge; disconnected mailbox; backing up Exchange servers; creating a backup schedule

Configure public folders for high availability. This objective may include but is not limited to: add or remove replicas; schedules; message tracking; backup and restore public folder database and data

Configure high availability for non-mailbox servers. This objective may include but is not limited to: affinity; DNS round robin; MX records; NLB; configuring high availability for Client Access servers; configuring high availability for Hub Transport servers; configuring high availability for Edge Transport servers

Back up and recover server roles. This objective may include but is not limited to: hub; CAS IIS; Edge; Edge server clone configuration; setup /recoverserver; setup/recover CMS; mailbox server; restoring Exchange Servers after server failure; configuring messaging services during a server failure; backup server roles

Configuring Message Compliance and Security	6

Configure records management. This objective may include but is not limited to: custom and default managed folders; retention policy; configure and apply retention policies and retention policy tags; configure managed folders, including default and custom managed folders; configure content settings; configure managed folder mailbox policies

Configure compliance. This objective may include but is not limited to: configure RMS; configure alternate mailboxes; configure journaling; enable message classification; configure mail tips; auditing; transport rules

Configure message integrity. This objective may include but is not limited to: S/MIME; MTLS; certificates; RMS federation; transport rules

TABLE A.2   Exam 70-662 Objectives Map *(continued)*

Objectives	Chapter
Configure antivirus and antispam. This objective may include but is not limited to: file and process exclusions; transport rules; SCL; PCL; sender ID; safe sender/block sender; Realtime Block List (RBL); Sender Policy Framework (SPF) records; sender reputation list (SRL); configuring antispam agents; managing the quarantine mailbox; managing updates for content filters	

TABLE A.2   Exam 70-663 Objectives Map

Objectives	Chapter
Planning the Exchange Server 2010 Infrastructure	**10, 12**
Design the Exchange Server 2010 installation. This objective may include but is not limited to: define Exchange server physical locations; Exchange DNS requirements; plan for common namespaces; SLA requirements; Active Directory site topologies; network topology; Exchange federation; multi-domain; multi-forest; resource forest; analysis and design of ongoing infrastructure improvements due to increased capacity, performance, and requested features	
Design message routing. This objective may include but is not limited to: inter-site and intra-site hub routing; connectors; coordinate messaging topics between Exchange departments, CIO, security, and LOB providers within the enterprise; develop connectors between Exchange and other messaging applications; design and deploy hub mail flow; design and deploy Edge connectors/scoping; design message transport; reverse zone (PTR records); scale Hub Transport server performance; storage requirements (Shadow Redundancy); multi-domain; multi-forest; resource forest; accepted domains; remote domains; send connector configuration; analysis and design of ongoing infrastructure improvements due to increased capacity, performance, and requested features	
Design the Mailbox server role. This objective may include but is not limited to: plan database sizing; storage performance requirements – I/O and disk latency requirements; multi-domain; multi-forest; resource forest; public folders; design recipient, distribution group, and mailbox provisioning and deprovisioning policies; analysis and design of ongoing infrastructure improvements due to increased capacity, performance, and requested features	

TABLE A.2 Exam 70-662 Objectives Map *(continued)*

Objectives	Chapter
Design client access. This objective may include but is not limited to: local vs. remote access; mobile access policies; identify and plan for supported messaging clients such as IMAP, POP, Exchange ActiveSync; Outlook Anywhere; Web services; OWA; MAPI (RPC Client Access); MAPI on the Middle Tier (MOMT); scale CAS server performance; storage requirements; multi-domain; multi-forest; resource forest; analysis and design of ongoing infrastructure improvements due to increased capacity, performance, and requested features; plan the location and configuration of Client Access servers; plan the Autodiscover implementation; plan for Federated Sharing	
Plan for transition and coexistence. This objective may include but is not limited to: plan and investigate consolidation of Exchange servers; plan intra-org and inter-org migration; decommission legacy environment; free/busy; inter-org message routing; how to preserve the ability to reply to a message (x500, SMTP, and legacyExchangeDN); public folders (free/busy lookup, replication); identify when to use a transition rather than a migration	
Deploying the Exchange Server 2010 Infrastructure	**11, 12**
Prepare the infrastructure for Exchange Server 2010 deployment. This objective may include but is not limited to: requirements to prepare schema, prepare domain, and prepare Active Directory; legacy permissions; prepare forest; forest functional level; domain controller versions, roles (excluding RODC/ROGC) and placement; prepare DNS (MX, sender ID, federation, PTR records)	
Deploy Edge Transport server role. This objective may include but is not limited to: validate Exchange deployment; EdgeSync; configure transport agents; replace perimeter email gateway; configure address rewriting	
Deploy Client Access server role. This objective may include but is not limited to: deploy CAS hardware and protocols; deploy mobile messaging services and connectivity; validate client connectivity; validate client functionality; autodiscover; multi site/domain/forest	
Deploy Hub Transport server role. This objective may include but is not limited to: validate Exchange deployment; multi-site/domain/forest; configure transport rules; accepted domains; remote domains; send connector configuration; message and recipient limits; deploy message flow to and from the Internet; deploy email relay; configure the accepted domain; validate message transport	
Deploy Mailbox server role. This objective may include but is not limited to: database configuration and placement quota enforcement policies; deploy the Mailbox server and storage; deploy the hardware configuration for Mailbox servers; deploy the mailbox database; deploy address lists and offline address books; validate Mailbox server performance; validate Mailbox server access; deploy public folders; configure public folder replication; configure client access to public folders; configure public folder permissions	

TABLE A.2   Exam 70-662 Objectives Map *(continued)*

Objectives	Chapter
Deploy server roles for coexistence and migration. This objective may include but is not limited to: coexistence with and migration from Exchange 2003, 2007, and 2010 and third-party mail systems; coexistence with namespaces; validate Exchange deployment; server transition process; transport rule coexistence; conversion from LDAP to OPATH filtering; routing group connector (RGC) configuration	
Designing and Deploying Security for the Exchange Organization	**13**
Design and deploy messaging security. This objective may include but is not limited to: secure relaying; S/MIME; certificates; MTLS; RMS (security related to using transport rules); define message security requirements; planning SMTP connector security; planning secure routing between partner organizations; planning client-based message security; planning the integration of Active Directory Rights Management Services (AD RMS) and Exchange Server 2010; planning ControlPoint Encryption; planning Outlook Protection Rules	
Design and deploy Exchange permissions model. This objective may include but is not limited to: Role Based Access Control (RBAC) assignments, scopes, and roles; Exchange Control Panel (ECP); modification of default RBAC roles; creation of custom RBAC roles; planning administrative permissions using the built-in management roles; planning administrative permissions using custom management roles; planning remote administration of Exchange servers	
Design and deploy message hygiene. This objective may include but is not limited to: design and deploy Edge security; design antispam and antivirus solution for the messaging deployment; SPA/Sender ID; define connection, attachment, recipient, sender, and content filtering rules; safe list aggregation; block lists; phishing confidence level (PCL); spam confidence level (SCL); sender reputation level (SRL); identify the requirements for an antivirus and antispam solution; plan an antispam solution deployment; plan for ongoing management of the antispam deployment; plan an antivirus solution deployment; plan for ongoing management of the antivirus deployment; plan user communication plans	
Design and deploy client access security. This objective may include but is not limited to: design and deploy ActiveSync policies; plan certificates for Exchange CAS; alternate authentication (smart cards, client certificates, time-based two-factor authentication tokens); authentication protocols (plain text, NTLM, forms based, Kerberos); OWA segmentation	
Design and deploy Exchange object permissions. This objective may include but is not limited to: design and deploy public folder security; mailbox (send as, full access, delegation, mail flow); resource security; distribution groups; design and deploy mailbox client access security (POP, IMAP, ActiveSync, OWA, MAPI)	

TABLE A.2 Exam 70-662 Objectives Map *(continued)*

Objectives	Chapter
Designing and Deploying Exchange Server 2010 Availability and Recovery	14

Design and deploy high availability and disaster recovery for Exchange dependencies. This objective may include but is not limited to: directory resiliency; network resiliency; DNS resiliency; storage hardware resiliency; site resiliency; datacenter resiliency; plan for updates and change management

Design and deploy high availability and disaster recovery for CAS role. This objective may include but is not limited to: backup and recovery; designing and deploying CAS array; multi-site CAS deployment; DNS updates for client access during site failover

Design and deploy high availability and disaster recovery for mailbox server role. This objective may include but is not limited to: design and deploy database scoping; design DAG; design and deploy public folder replication; backup and recovery; DNS record TTL; file share witness resiliency; activation preference and auto-activation; lag copies; designing and deploying continuous replication; designing and deploying DAGs distributed across multiple locations

Design and deploy high availability and disaster recovery for Hub Transport role. This objective may include but is not limited to: backup and recovery; receive connector resiliency; send connector scoping; design and deploy high availability for Hub Transport servers; design and deploy Exchange Server configurations to mitigate the effect of a disaster; choose an Exchange Server backup solution; design and deploy Exchange Server backups; design and deploy Exchange Server data restores; restore Exchange Server role

Design and deploy high availability and disaster recovery for Edge Transport server role. This objective may include but is not limited to: backup and recovery; server placement; DNS load balancing; MX records; namespace changes; designing and deploying high availability for Edge Transport servers; designing and deploying Exchange Server configurations to mitigate the effect of a disaster; choosing an Exchange Server backup solution; designing and deploying Exchange Server backups; designing and deploying Exchange Server data restores; designing and deploying Exchange Server server restores

| **Designing and Deploying Messaging Compliance, System Monitoring, and Reporting** | 13 |

Design and deploy auditing and discovery. This objective may include but is not limited to: audit logging; admin audit logging; permissions auditing; message tracking; protocol logging; RBAC (compliance role and scope); identify requirements for discovery or auditing; plan journaling or message record management (MRM) for discovery; plan access permissions for discovery searches

TABLE A.2   Exam 70-662 Objectives Map *(continued)*

Objectives	Chapter

Design and deploy message archival. This objective may include but is not limited to: dumpster 2.0; legal hold; retention policies (MRM); retention tags; long-term backup; design and deploy managed folders; design and deploy alternate mailboxes; plan for managing messages in default Outlook folders; plan for managing messages in custom managed folders; plan a retention policy implementation; plan an AutoTagging implementation

Design and deploy transport rules for message compliance. This objective may include but is not limited to: RMS; ethical firewall; message journaling; disclaimers; mail tips, such as notification for external recipients and recipient limits

Design and deploy for monitoring and reporting. This objective may include but is not limited to: design and deploy message flow monitoring; client accessibility; SLA requirements, such as percent of email delivered in a certain amount of time within the organization; analyze message usage, number of messages, and message size; analysis and design of ongoing infrastructure improvements due to increased capacity, performance, and requested features; monitoring client access services; troubleshooting client access services

Exam objectives are subject to change at any time without prior notice and at Microsoft's sole discretion. Please visit Microsoft's website (www.microsoft.com/learning) for the most current listing of exam objectives.

Appendix B

About the Companion CD

IN THIS APPENDIX:

- ✓ What you'll find on the CD
- ✓ System requirements
- ✓ Using the CD
- ✓ Troubleshooting

What You'll Find on the CD

The following sections are arranged by category and summarize the software and other goodies you'll find on the CD. If you need help with installing the items provided on the CD, refer to the installation instructions in the section "Using the CD" later in this appendix.

Video Walk-Throughs

The CD contains over an hour of video walk-through from the authors, who show readers how to perform some of the more difficult tasks they can expect to encounter on the job.

Sybex Test Engine

The CD contains the Sybex test engine, which includes the two bonus exams, one for exam 70-662 and one for exam 70-663.

Electronic Flashcards

These handy electronic flashcards are just what you would expect. One side contains a question or fill-in-the-blank, and the other side shows the answer.

PDF of the Book

We have included an electronic version of the text in PDF format. You can view the electronic version of the book with Adobe Reader.

Adobe Reader

We've also included a copy of Adobe Reader so you can view PDF files that accompany the book's content. For more information on Adobe Reader or to check for a newer version, visit Adobe's website at www.adobe.com/products/reader/.

System Requirements

Make sure your computer meets the minimum system requirements shown in the following list. If your computer doesn't match up to most of these requirements, you may have problems using the software and files on the companion CD. For the latest and greatest information, please refer to the ReadMe file located at the root of the CD-ROM.

- A PC running Microsoft Windows 98, Windows 2000, Windows NT4 (with SP4 or later), Windows Me, Windows XP, Windows Vista, or Windows 7
- An Internet connection
- A CD-ROM drive

Using the CD

To install the items from the CD to your hard drive, follow these steps:

1. Insert the CD into your computer's CD-ROM drive. The license agreement appears.

Windows users: The interface won't launch if you have autorun disabled. In that case, click Start ➤ Run (for Windows Vista or Windows 7, Start ➤ All Programs ➤ Accessories ➤ Run). In the dialog box that appears, type D:\Start.exe. (Replace *D* with the proper letter if your CD drive uses a different letter. If you don't know the letter, see how your CD drive is listed under My Computer.) Click OK.

2. Read the license agreement, and then click the Accept button if you want to use the CD.

The CD interface appears. The interface allows you to access the content with just one or two clicks.

Troubleshooting

Wiley has attempted to provide programs that work on most computers with the minimum system requirements. Alas, your computer may differ, and some programs may not work properly for some reason.

The two likeliest problems are that you don't have enough memory (RAM) for the programs you want to use or you have other programs running that are affecting installation or running of a program. If you get an error message such as "Not enough memory" or "Setup cannot continue," try one or more of the following suggestions and then try using the software again:

Turn off any antivirus software running on your computer. Installation programs sometimes mimic virus activity and may make your computer incorrectly believe that it's being infected by a virus.

Close all running programs. The more programs you have running, the less memory is available to other programs. Installation programs typically update files and programs, so if you keep other programs running, the installation program may not work properly.

Have your local computer store add more RAM to your computer. This is, admittedly, a drastic and somewhat expensive step. However, adding more memory can really help the speed of your computer and allow more programs to run at the same time.

Customer Care

If you have trouble with the book's companion CD-ROM, please call the Wiley Product Technical Support phone number at (800) 762-2974.

Glossary

A

accepted domain   An email domain for which your Exchange servers accept inbound mail.

access control entries (ACEs)   Entries on an access control list (ACL) that define a user's permissions for an object.

access control list (ACL)   A list of users and groups allowed to access a resource and the particular permissions each user has been granted or denied.

Active Directory   A Microsoft technology that stores information on an object, this information can include: information about users, computers, and services as well as other network or domain information.

address space   The set of remote addresses that can be reached through a particular connector. Each connector must have at least one entry in its address space.

administrative group   Group that is used to define administrative boundaries within an Exchange 2003 environment.

administrative rights   NTFS permissions that determine what administrative tasks a user or group is permitted to perform on a public folder.

age limit   A property that specifies the length of time a unit of data may remain in its container (for example, a public folder).

alias   An alternative name for an object. In Exchange, an alias is usually generated for a user, based on the user's name.

All Public Folders   The name for the default public folder tree in an Exchange organization. This tree is accessible by all clients that can access public folders.

anonymous access   A method of accessing a server by logging in using a Windows account set up for general access.

anonymous authentication   See *anonymous access*.

application programming interface (API)   A collection of programming classes and interfaces that provide services used by a program. Other programs can use a program's API to request services or communicate with that program.

architecture   The description of the components of a product or system: what they are, what they do, and how they relate to each other.

archive   A location and collection of data (messages) that needs to be preserved for a given time. An archive is generally not online and immediately accessible, but it is searchable and accessible if needed.

attribute   A characteristic of an object. For example, attributes of a mailbox-enabled user include the display name and storage limits. The terms *attribute* and *property* are synonymous.

auditing   The evaluation of recorded events that are written to the Windows Security Event Log. This information can be used in troubleshooting security events.

authentication   A process whereby the credentials of an object, such as a user, must be validated before the object is allowed to access or use another object, such as a server or a protocol. For instance, the Microsoft Exchange Server POP3 protocol can be configured to allow access only to POP3 clients that use the Integrated Windows authentication method.

B

backfill   The process used in public folder replication to fill in messaging data that is missing from a replica.

backup   The process of safe guarding data by creating a copy of the data on separate media.

Bad Mail folder   The folder in which SMTP stores undeliverable messages that cannot be returned to the sender.

Basic (clear-text) authentication   A type of authentication that requires the user to submit a valid Windows username and password. The username and password are sent across the network as unencrypted clear text.

Basic over Secure Sockets Layer (SSL) authentication   A type of authentication that extends the Basic (clear-text) authentication method by allowing an SSL server to encrypt the username and password before they are sent across the network.

C

cache mode   A feature in Outlook that allows clients to work while disconnected from the Exchange server. Outlook will periodically reconnect to the Exchange server and synchronize any changes to the user's mailbox.

categorizer   A component of the Exchange Server 2010 routing engine used to resolve the sender and recipient for a message, expanding any distribution groups as needed. In previous versions of Exchange Server, this task was performed by the message transfer agent.

centralized model   An administrative model in which one administrator or group of administrators maintains complete control over an entire Exchange organization.

certificate   An electronic document that allows verification of the claim that a given public key actually belongs to a given individual. This helps prevent someone from using a phony key to impersonate someone else. A certificate is similar to a token.

certificate authority (CA)   The central authority that distributes, publishes, and validates security keys. The Windows Server 2008 Certificate Services component performs this role. See also *public key* and *private key*.

certificate store   A database that is created during the installation of a certificate authority (CA) and is a repository of certificates issued by the CA.

certificate template   A template stored in Active Directory; defines the attributes for certificates.

challenge/response   A general term for a class of security mechanisms, including Microsoft authentication methods that use Windows Server 2008 network security and an encrypted password.

change number   One of the constructs used to keep track of public folder replication throughout an organization and to determine whether a public folder is synchronized. The change number consists of a globally unique identifier for the information store and a change counter that is specific to the server on which a public folder resides.

checkpoint file   The file (EDB.chk) that contains the point in a transaction log that is the boundary between data that has been committed and data that has not yet been committed to an Exchange database.

child domain   Any domain configured underneath another domain in a domain tree.

circular logging   The process of writing new information in transaction log files over information that has already been committed. Instead of repeatedly creating new transaction logs, the Exchange database engine "circles back" and reuses log files that have been fully committed to the database. Circular logging keeps down the number of transaction logs on the disk. These logs cannot be used to re-create a database because the logs do not have a complete set of data. The logs contain only the most recent data not yet committed to a database. Circular logging is disabled by default.

client access license (CAL)   A license that gives a user the legal right to access an Exchange server. Any client software that has the ability to be a client to Microsoft Exchange Server is legally required to have a CAL purchased for it.

Client Access server   Non-MAPI clients, such as POP3, IMAP4, mobile, and web-based clients, must connect to the Mailbox servers via a Client Access server. In this way, the Client Access server is most like the front-end servers utilized in previous versions of Exchange Server. All requests from these non-MAPI clients are received by the Client Access server and then forwarded to the applicable Mailbox server for action.

cluster   A group of servers (also called *nodes*) that function together as a single unit.

cluster resource   A service or property, such as a storage device, an IP address, or the Exchange System Attendant service, that is defined, monitored, and managed by the cluster service.

cluster service   The software service used to manage all the cluster activity. The cluster service controls access to resources by the individual nodes of the cluster.

clustering   A Windows service that enables multiple physical servers to be grouped logically for high availability.

committed   When a transaction is transferred from a transaction log to an Exchange database, it has been committed.

compliance   For the purpose of Exchange, compliance is the act of complying with government, agency, or corporate policies that dictate how communications and information should be handled.

Computer Management snap-in   An administrative tool holding a variety of utilities, including Event Viewer and disk management tools.

contact   A recipient object that represents a foreign message recipient. Contacts appear in the global address list (GAL) and allow Exchange clients to address messages to foreign mail users. Also referred to as a *mail contact*.

container object   An object in the Exchange or Active Directory hierarchy that contains and groups other objects. For example, the organization object in System Manager is a container object that contains all other objects in the organization.

contiguous namespace   A common namespace shared by multiple entities. For example, Windows Server 2003 domain trees share a contiguous namespace; domain forests do not.

continuous availability (CA)   The unattainable desire to never have applications unavailable.

copy backup   During a copy backup, all selected files are backed up regardless of how their archive bit is set. After the backup, the archive bit is not changed in any file.

D

daily backup   During this backup, all files that changed on the day of the backup are backed up, and the archive bit is not changed in any file.

Data Encryption Standard (DES)   A secret-key encryption method that uses a 56-bit key.

database   A database is an organized collection of digital data. There are two types of databases in Exchange Server 2010: public databases that hold public folders meant to be accessed by groups of users; and mailbox databases that hold user mailboxes.

dcdiag   A command-line utility that can be used to analyze the state of all domain controllers in a forest and report problems that were found.

decryption   The process of translating encrypted data back to plain text.

dedicated public folder server   An Exchange server whose primary purpose is to hold public folder databases and from which the mailbox databases have been removed.

deleted item retention time   The period that items that are in a public or private database and are deleted by users are actually retained on the Exchange server.

demilitarized zone (DMZ)   See *perimeter network*.

dial tone recovery   A basic recovery that provides the ability to send and receive email but does not provide any historical email data. A dial tone recovery is used as a go-between to provide basic services and allow users to continue to work while a database restore takes place.

differential backup   A method in which all files that have been changed since the last full backup are backed up. See also *incremental backup*.

digital signature   A process of digitally signing data using public and private keys so that the recipient of the data can verify the authenticity of both the sender and the data.

directory   A hierarchy that stores information about objects in a system. A directory service (DS) manages the directory and makes it available to users on the network.

directory replication   The process of transferring directory information from one server to another. In Active Directory, directory information is replicated between domain controllers. In previous versions of Exchange, directory information is replicated between Exchange servers.

directory rights   NTFS permissions that determine who can perform modifications on the public folder object that is stored in Active Directory.

disaster recovery   The act of recovering from the loss of Exchange Server data or Exchange Server. This would require having enough data in a recoverable format, and it can be limited to the loss of a single email message or can encompass the loss of an entire datacenter.

Disaster Recovery mode   An Exchange Server 2010 setup mode that lets you recover an Exchange installation after a failure.

discovery   The actions that are taken when records are requested to comply with a given policy or form of governance.

dismounting   The process of taking a public or mailbox database offline.

distribution group   An Active Directory group formed so that a single email message can be sent to the group and then sent automatically to all members of the group. Unlike security groups, distribution groups don't provide any security function.

DMZ   See *perimeter network*.

DNS   See *Domain Name Service (DNS)*.

domain   A group of computers and other resources that are part of a Windows Server network and share a common directory database.

domain controller   A computer running Windows Server that validates user network access and manages Active Directory.

domain forest   A group of one or more domain trees that do not necessarily form a contiguous namespace but may share a common schema and global catalog.

Domain Name Service (DNS)   The primary provider of name resolution within an organization.

domain tree   A hierarchical arrangement of one or more Windows Active Directory domains that share a common namespace.

dynamic distribution group   An email-enabled distribution group whose group membership is determined by the results of an LDAP query created when the group is configured.

E

Edge Transport server   Designed to be deployed in the DMZ of your network, the Edge Transport server is used to provide a secure SMTP gateway for all messages entering or leaving your Exchange organization. As such, the Edge Transport server is responsible for antivirus and antispam controls as well as protecting the recipient data held within Active Directory.

EHLO   The SMTP command used by one host to initiate communications with another host.

encryption   The process of scrambling data to make it unreadable. The intended recipient will decrypt the data into plain text in order to read it.

enterprise CA   The certificate authority for an enterprise. Requires access to the Active Directory. See also *certificate authority (CA)*.

Enterprise Edition   The premier version of Exchange Server 2010, with support for up to 100 databases.

ethical walls   A rule or system that prevents communication between specific groups in an organization.

event log   A set of three logs (application, security, and system) maintained by Windows Server. The operating system and many applications, such as Exchange Server 2010, write software events to the event log.

Exchange Management Console   A snap-in for the Microsoft Management Console used to manage an Exchange Server 2010 organization.

expanding a distribution group   The process of determining the individual addresses contained within a distribution group. This process is performed by the home server of the user sending the message to the group unless an expansion server is specified for the group.

extended permissions Permissions added to the standard Windows Server permissions when Exchange Server 2010 is installed.

Extensible Storage Engine (ESE) The database engine used by Exchange Server 2010.

F

failback The process of cluster resources moving back to their preferred node after the preferred node has resumed active membership in the cluster.

failover The process of moving resources off a cluster node that has failed to another cluster node. If any of the cluster resources on an active node become unresponsive or unavailable for a period of time exceeding the configured threshold, failover will occur.

federated sharing The underlying trust infrastructure to enable easy and secure sharing of information across Exchange organizations and in cross-premises organizations.

file share witness (FSW) The FSW is a file share on another computer that is not part of the cluster but can be used to maintain a majority for MNS. The file share witness feature allows for the creation of another quorum resource that will work with MNS quorum resources to provide more redundancy of the quorum. This new change allows the use of two nodes for the cluster and a third server of some kind someplace on the network to provide another quorum resource to work with MNS. The file share witness is perfect for clusters that have no need for shared storage for their data. Now you can have two nodes and still have a majority available in the case of a single node failure.

firewall A set of mechanisms that separate and protect your internal network from unauthorized external users and networks. Firewalls can restrict inbound and outbound traffic as well as analyze all traffic between your network and the outside.

foreign system A non-Exchange messaging system.

forest root domain The first domain installed in a domain forest and the basis for the naming of all domains in the forest.

free/busy Terminology used in the Microsoft Schedule+ application to denote an unscheduled period of time (free) or a scheduled period of time (busy).

full-text indexing A feature that can be enabled for a database. With full-text indexing, every word in the database (including those in attachments) is indexed for much faster search results.

fully qualified domain name (FQDN) The full DNS path of an Internet host. An example is sales.dept4.widget.com.

function call An instruction in a program that calls (invokes) a function. For example, MAPIReadMail is a MAPI function call.

G

GAL See *global address list (GAL)*.

global address list (GAL) A database of all the recipients in an Exchange organization, such as mailboxes, distribution lists, custom recipients, and public folders.

global catalog A distributed data repository used to hold information about all objects in a forest. The global catalog enables users and applications to find objects in an Active Directory domain tree if the user or application knows one or more attributes of the target object.

group A collection of users and other groups that may be assigned permissions or made part of an email distribution list.

H

heartbeat A special communication among members of a cluster that keeps all members aware of one another's existence (and thus their operational states).

HELO The SMTP command used by one host to initiate communications with another host.

hierarchy Any structure or organization that uses class, grade, or rank to arrange objects.

high availability (HA) The combination of well-defined, -planned, -tested, and -implemented processes, software, and fault-tolerant hardware focused on supplying and maintaining application availability.

host bus adapter (HBA) This adapter connects the server node to the storage area network using fiber or, potentially, an iSCSI SAN.

HTML See *Hypertext Markup Language (HTML)*.

HTTP See *Hypertext Transfer Protocol (HTTP)*.

Hub Transport server The server that routes messages for delivery within the Exchange organization. When message routing is moved to another server (other than the Mailbox server), many new and needed features and functions become available in Exchange Server 2010. As an example, while messages are being routed through the Hub Transport server, they can have transport rules and filtering policies applied to them that determine where they'll wind up, such as being delivered to a compliance mailbox in addition to the recipient's mailbox, or what they'll look like, such as every outbound message being stamped with a disclaimer.

Hypertext Markup Language (HTML) The script language used to create content for the World Wide Web (WWW). HTML can create hyperlinks between objects on the Web.

Hypertext Transfer Protocol (HTTP) The Internet protocol used to transfer information on the World Wide Web (WWW).

I

IIS metabase   The database of configuration information maintained by Internet Information Services.

Inbox   The storage folder that receives new incoming messages.

Inbox repair tool   A utility (`Scanpst.exe`) used to repair corrupt personal folder (`.pst`) files.

incremental backup   The method in which all files that have changed since the last normal or incremental backup are backed up. The archive bit is cleared after an incremental backup is performed.

information store   See *Store.exe*.

infrastructure master   The operations master role that is responsible for updating references from objects in its domain to objects in other domains.

Integrated Windows authentication   Authentication that requires the user to provide a valid Windows username and password. However, the user's credentials are never sent across the network. At the Windows 2000 native domain functional level or the Windows Server 2008 domain functional level, this method uses Kerberos v5.

Internet Information Services (IIS)   A built-in component of Windows Server 2008 that allows access to resources on the server through various Internet protocols, such as POP3, IMAP4, and HTTP.

Internet Message Access Protocol version 4 (IMAP4)   An Internet retrieval protocol that enables clients to access and manipulate messages in their mailbox on a remote server. IMAP4 provides additional functions over POP3, such as access to subfolders (not merely the Inbox folder) and selective downloading of messages.

ipconfig   A command-line utility that can be used to display and modify TCP/IP information about all installed network adapters. Common uses include flushing the local DNS resolver cache and releasing and renewing DHCP leases.

K

Kerberos version 5 (v5)   The primary form of user authentication used by Windows Server 2008.

key   A randomly generated number used to implement advanced security, such as encryption or digital signatures. See also *key pair*, *public key*, and *private key*.

key pair   A key that is divided into two mathematically related halves. One half (the public key) is made public; the other half (the private key) is known by only one user.

L

Lightweight Directory Access Protocol (LDAP)   An Internet protocol used for client access to an X.500-based directory, such as Active Directory.

local continuous replication (LCR)   This is a single-server environment where the active storage group is copied to another physical disk on the same server using log shipping. This feature is discontinued in Exchange 2010.

local procedure call (LPC)   An instruction that is issued by a program and executed on the same computer as the program executing the instruction. See also *remote procedure call (RPC)*.

log file replay   A process in which Exchange examines the transaction log files for a storage group to identify transactions that have been logged and that have not been incorporated into a database. This process, also known as *playing back log files*, brings the databases up-to-date with the available transaction log files.

logical unit number (LUN)   The logical unit number is the disk structure as defined on the SAN or NAS device used to provide disk resources to a cluster. On the SAN, for example, there may be 10 physical disks combined in a RAID format. These disks are exposed from the SAN to the computer as one unit. The Windows computer then sees one large physical disk connected to it.

M

mail-enabled user   A user who has been given an email address but no mailbox.

mail exchanger (MX) record   A record in a DNS database that indicates the SMTP mail host for an organization.

mailbox   The generic term referring to a container that holds messages, such as incoming and outgoing messages.

mailbox-enabled user   A user who has been assigned an Exchange Server mailbox.

mailbox database   A database on an Exchange server that holds mailboxes. See also *database*.

Mailbox server   The primary function of the Mailbox server role is to provide users with mailboxes that can be accessed directly from the Outlook client. The Mailbox server also contains the databases that hold public folders, if you are still using them in your organization. Thus, as a point of comparison, the Mailbox server is most like the backend server from previous versions of Exchange.

majority node set (MNS) cluster   In Windows Server 2003 Enterprise Edition, Microsoft presented another option to the shared disk environment for the quorum. Instead of selecting a shared physical disk to host the quorum, it is possible to select the majority node set (MNS) option to create a server cluster. From the perspective of Windows, MNS looks just like a single quorum disk, but the quorum data is actually stored on multiple disks across the cluster. MNS is designed and built so it ensures that the stored cluster data is kept consistent across the different disks on different computers.

MAPI   See *Messaging Application Programming Interface (MAPI)*.

MAPI client   A messaging client that uses the Messaging Application Programming Interface (MAPI) to connect to a messaging server. See also *Messaging Application Programming Interface (MAPI)*.

MAPI subsystem   The second layer of the MAPI architecture; this component is shared by all applications that require its services and is therefore considered a *subsystem* of the operating system.

message state information   Information that identifies the state of a message in a public folder. Message state information consists of a change number, a time stamp, and a predecessor change list.

Messaging Application Programming Interface (MAPI)   An object-oriented programming interface for messaging services, developed by Microsoft.

Microsoft Clustering Service (MSCS)   A Windows service that provides for highly available server solutions through a process known as *failover*. An MSCS cluster consists of two or more nodes (members) that are configured such that, upon the failure of one node, any of the remaining cluster nodes can transfer the failed node's resources to itself, thus keeping the resources available for client access.

Microsoft Management Console (MMC)   A framework application in which snap-ins are loaded to provide the management of various network resources. System Manager is an example of a snap-in.

Microsoft Office Outlook 2010   The premier client application for use with Exchange Server 2010.

Microsoft Search Service   The service that performs full-text indexing of mailbox and public databases.

migration   The process of moving resources, such as mailboxes, messages, and so on, from one messaging system to another.

mounting   The process of bringing a mailbox or public database online. See also *dismounting*.

multipathing   A fault-tolerance technique used in computer storage. Multipathing is commonly used in Fiber SAN designs. Nodes will have two HBAs (remember, high availability requires redundancy) that are then joined using software. Some common products include PowerPath (EMC) and SecurePath (HP). The two HBAs can be bound together and load balanced to improve throughput from 2 GB to 4 GB for a particular node. It is also fairly common, though, that the fiber array will also use two HBAs bound together to provide 4 GB of throughput, which is then shared among all the servers that attach to the array for storage; 4 GB may not be enough. In some cases, organizations will invest and provide four fiber connections from the SAN to the fabric, thus providing 8 GB of throughput.

Multipurpose Internet Mail Extensions (MIME)   An Internet protocol that enables the encoding of binary content within mail messages. For example, MIME could be used to encode a graphics file or word processing document as an attachment to a text-based mail message. The recipient of the message would have to be using MIME also to decode the attachment. MIME is newer than UUENCODE and in many systems has replaced it. See also *Secure/Multipurpose Internet Mail Extensions (S/MIME)*.

MX   See *mail exchanger (MX) record*.

N

name resolution   The DNS process of mapping a domain name to its IP address.

namespace   Any bounded area in which a given name can be resolved.

nbtstat   A command-line utility that is used to give statistics, view cache information, resolve NetBIOS names to IP addresses, and register with NetBIOS.

netdiag   A command-line utility that is used to troubleshoot and isolate network connectivity problems by performing a number of tests to determine the exact state of a server.

netstat   A command-line utility that is used to display TCP/IP connection information and protocol statistics for a computer.

Network Load Balancing (NLB)   A feature of Windows Server that provides horizontal scalability as well as high availability. Horizontal scaling is achieved by the servers sharing the load between them. If the application becomes oversubscribed, new servers can be built and added into the NLB web farm to spread the load out even more. High availability is achieved through the NLB web farm in that if a single server fails (or even multiple servers), NLB will redistribute the load among the remaining servers.

Network News Transfer Protocol (NNTP)   An Internet protocol used to transfer newsgroup information between newsgroup servers and clients (newsreaders) and between newsgroup servers.

NNTP   See *Network News Transfer Protocol (NNTP)*.

node   In a Microsoft Management Console window, a node is any object that can be configured. In clustering, a node is one of the computers that is part of a cluster.

normal backup   A backup in which all selected files are backed up regardless of how their archive bit is set. After the backup, the archive bit is set to off for all files, indicating that those files have been backed up.

notification   Defines the event that is triggered when a service or resource being watched by a server or link monitor fails. Notifications can send email and alerts and even run custom scripts.

nslookup   A command-line utility that can be used to gather information about the DNS infrastructure inside and outside an organization and to troubleshoot DNS-related problems.

O

object   The representation, or abstraction, of an entity. As an object, it contains properties, also called *attributes*, that can be configured.

Offline Address Book (OAB)   A copy stored on a client's computer of part or all of the server-based global address list (GAL). An OAB allows a client to address messages while not connected to their server.

offline backup   A backup made while the Exchange services are stopped. When you perform an offline backup, users do not have access to their mailboxes while the backup takes place.

offline folder   See *Offline Storage (OST) folder*.

Offline Storage (OST) folder   Folder located on a client's computer that contains replicas of server-based folders. An OST allows a client to access and manipulate copies of server data while not connected to their server. When the client reconnects to their server, they can have their OST resynchronized with the master folders on the server.

organization   The highest-level object in the Microsoft Exchange hierarchy.

organizational unit (OU)   An Active Directory container into which objects can be grouped for permissions management.

Outlook Anywhere   A new mode of connecting remote Outlook clients to an Exchange Server organization without requiring the use of a virtual private network (VPN) or Outlook Web App (OWA). RPCs are passed over the HTTP connection and secured with SSL encryption. Basic authentication is used to authenticate the user and is also protected by the SSL. Outlook Anywhere was first introduced in Exchange Server 2003 as RPC over HTTP.

Outlook Web App (OWA)   A service that allows users to connect to Exchange Server and access mailboxes and public folders using a web browser.

OWA Light   A scaled-down version of Outlook Web App that was referred to as Basic in the Exchange Server 2003 version of OWA.

P

patch files   Temporary logs that store transactions while a backup is taking place. Transactions in these logs are committed when the backup is finished.

pathping   A new command that is a mix of both `ping` and `tracert`. The `pathping` command provides the ability to determine the packet loss along each link in the path and at each router in the path to the destination. This can be particularly helpful when troubleshooting problems where multiple routers and links are involved.

Performance Monitor   See *Performance snap-in.*

Performance snap-in   A utility used to log and chart the performance of various hardware and software components of a system. The Performance snap-in is also referred to as Performance Monitor, Performance tool, and System Monitor in various manuals.

perimeter network   A network formed by using two firewalls to separate an internal network from the Internet and then placing certain servers, such as an Exchange front-end server, between the two firewalls. This is also referred to as a *demilitarized zone (DMZ).*

permission   A feature that provides specific authorization or denial to a user to perform an action on an object.

Personal Address Book (PAB)   An address book created by a user and stored on that user's computer or a server.

Personal Store (PST) folder   Folder created by a user and used for message storage instead of their mailbox in the mailbox database. PSTs can be located on a user's computer or on a server, although they are not supported when accessed from a server over the network.

ping   Stands for Packet Internet Groper. The basic network connectivity troubleshooting tool that works by sending a series of ICMP Echo Request datagrams to a destination and waiting for the corresponding ICMP Echo Reply datagrams to come back. The return packets are then used to determine how many datagrams are getting through, the response time, and the time to live (TTL).

plain text   Unencrypted data. Synonymous with *clear text.*

Point-to-Point Protocol (PPP)   An Internet protocol used for the direct communication between two nodes. Commonly utilized by Internet users and their Internet service providers on the serial line point-to-point connection over a modem.

POP3   See *Post Office Protocol version 3 (POP3).*

port number   A numeric identifier assigned to an application. Transport protocols such as TCP and UDP use the port number to identify the application to which a packet is delivered.

Post Office Protocol version 3 (POP3)   An Internet protocol used for client retrieval of mail from a server-based mailbox.

postmaster mailbox   The postmaster mailbox is required in every messaging infrastructure per RFC 2822 and receives nondelivery reports and delivery status notifications.

primary domain controller (PDC) emulator   An operations master role server that is responsible for authenticating non-Active Directory clients, such as Windows 95 or Windows 98 clients. The PDC emulator is responsible for processing password changes from these clients and is also the server responsible for time synchronization within the domain.

private folder   See *mailbox*.

private key   The half of a key pair that is known by only the pair's user and is used to decrypt data and digitally sign messages.

property   A characteristic of an object. Properties of a mailbox include display name and storage limits. The terms *property* and *attribute* are synonymous.

public database   A database that holds public folders on an Exchange server. See also *database*.

public folder   A folder stored in a public store on an Exchange server and accessible to multiple users.

public folder hierarchy   The relative position of all the folders in a public folder tree.

public folder referral   The process by which a client can locate a requested public folder outside their home Exchange server.

public folder replication   The process of transferring data from a public folder data to replicas of that folder on other servers.

public folder tree   A hierarchy of public folders associated with a particular public database.

public key   The half of a key pair that is published for anyone to read and is used when encrypting data and verifying digital signatures.

public key infrastructure (PKI)   A system of components working together to verify the identity of users who transfer data on a system and to encrypt that data if needed.

public key encryption   An encryption method that employs a key pair consisting of a public and a private key.

Q

queue folder   A folder in which messages that have yet to be delivered are stored.

Queue Viewer   A part of the Exchange System Manager that lets you view and manipulate the messages in a queue.

R

recipient   An object that can receive a message. Recipient objects include users, contacts, groups, and public folders.

recovery   When it refers to Exchange databases, *recovery* means to replay transaction log files into a restored database. This action brings the database up-to-date. There are two distinct forms of recovery: soft recovery and hard recovery. *Soft recovery* occurs with a database that failed and has been repaired or is just being remounted. A soft recovery is an automatic transaction log file replay process that occurs when a database is remounted after an unexpected failure. Soft recovery uses the log files that are currently in the log file location, using the checkpoint file to determine which log files to start with during the sequential replay process. A *hard recovery* occurs after a restore of a database. The hard recovery process plays the transaction log files into a restored database to bring the database back to a consistent state. The hard recovery process uses a `Restore.env` file that is generated during recovery to determine which transaction log files must be replayed from the temporary directory to which the backup was restored. The hard recovery process then continues to replay any additional transaction log files that it finds in the current transaction log file directory of the restored database.

recovery server   A server that is separate from the organization and used as a dummy server for recovering individual mailboxes or messages from a backup.

regular expression   A string or set of symbols used to describe patterns of text. Regular expressions can be used in transport rules as a condition or exception. For example, you could use a regular expression to search message bodies for Social Security numbers and then perform an action on those messages if they had a Social Security number.

relative identifier (RID) master   An operations master role server that is responsible for maintaining the uniqueness of every object within its domain. When a new Active Directory object is created, it is assigned a unique security identifier (SID). The SID consists of a domain-specific SID that is the same for all objects created in that domain and a relative identifier (RID) that is unique among all objects within that domain.

remote delivery   The delivery of a message to a recipient that does not reside on the same server as the sender.

remote domain   An email domain outside your Exchange organization.

remote procedure call (RPC)   A set of protocols for issuing instructions that can be sent over a network for execution. A client computer makes a request to a server computer, and the results are sent to the client computer. The computer issuing the request and the computer performing the request are separated remotely over a network. RPC is a key ingredient in distributed processing and client/server computing. See also *local procedure call (LPC)*.

replica   A copy of a public folder located on an Exchange server.

replication   The process of transferring a copy of data to another location, such as another server or site. See also *directory replication* and *public folder replication*.

reserve log files   Two transaction log files created by Exchange Server that are reserved for use when the server runs out of disk space.

resolving an address   The process of determining where (on which physical server) an object with a particular address resides.

resource group cluster   A group that functions in a cluster that is not bound to a specific computer and that can fail over to another node.

restore   To return the original files that were previously stored in a backup to their location on a server. For Exchange, this generally means restoring a database backup to a recovery storage group.

Rich Text Format (RTF)   A Microsoft format protocol that gives you the ability to highlight and underline text as well as apply many other properties, such as bold and italic.

role   A group of permissions that define which activities a user or group can perform with regard to an object.

root CA   A certificate authority that resides at the top of a certificate authority hierarchy and is trusted unconditionally by a client. All certificate chains terminate at a root CA. See also *certificate authority (CA)*.

root domain   The top domain in a domain tree.

routing group   A collection of Exchange servers in which there is full-time, full-mesh, reliable connections between each and every server. Messages sent between any two servers within a routing group are delivered directly from the source server to the destination server.

routing group connector (RGC)   The primary connector used to connect routing groups in an organization. The RGC uses SMTP as its default transport mechanism.

routing group master   A server that maintains data about all the servers running Exchange Server 2000/2003 in a routing group.

rule   A set of instructions that defines how a message is handled when it reaches a folder.

S

S/MIME   See *Secure/Multipurpose Internet Mail Extensions (S/MIME)*.

scalable   The capability of a system to grow to handle greater traffic, volume, usage, and so on.

Schedule+ Free Busy public folder   A system folder that contains calendaring and synchronization information for Exchange users.

schema   The set of rules defining a directory's hierarchy, objects, attributes, and so on.

schema master   An operations master role that controls all updates and changes that are made to the schema.

secret key   A security key that can be used to encrypt data and that is known only by the sender and the recipients whom the sender informs.

Secure Sockets Layer (SSL)   An Internet protocol that provides secure and authenticated TCP/IP connections. A client and server establish a "handshake" whereby they agree on a level of security they will use, such as authentication requirements and encryption. SSL can be used to encrypt sensitive data for transmission.

Secure/Multipurpose Internet Mail Extensions (S/MIME)   An Internet protocol that enables mail messages to be digitally signed, encrypted, and decrypted.

security group   A group defined in Active Directory that can be assigned permissions and has an SID. All members of the group gain the permissions given to the group.

server license   A license that provides the legal right to install and operate Microsoft Exchange Server 2010 (or another server product) on a single-server machine.

service provider   A MAPI program that provides messaging-oriented services to a client. There are three main types of service providers: address book, message store, and message transport.

signing   The process of placing a digital signature on a message.

simple display name   An alternate name for the mailbox that appears when, for some reason, the full display name cannot.

Simple Mail Transfer Protocol (SMTP)   The Internet protocol used to transfer mail messages. It has been the default transport protocol since Exchange 2000 Server.

Simple Network Management Protocol (SNMP)   The Internet protocol used to manage heterogeneous computers, operating systems, and applications. Because of its wide acceptance and applicability, SNMP is well suited for enterprise-wide management.

single copy cluster (SCC)   This is a standard cluster much like previous server cluster implementations for Exchange. It requires use of a shared disk implementation such as a SAN to host the quorum, the storage disks, and the transaction log disks. This is a *discontinued* feature in Exchange 2010.

single-instance storage   The storage of only one copy. A message that is sent to multiple recipients homed in the same storage group has only one copy (that is, instance) stored on the server. Each recipient is given a pointer to that copy of the message.

site A logical grouping of servers in previous versions of Exchange (prior to Exchange 2000 Server) that are connected by a full mesh (every server is directly connected to every other server) and communicate using high-bandwidth RPC. All servers in a site can authenticate one another either because they are homed in the same Windows domain or because of trust relationships configured between separate Windows domains. A site is also a group of Windows servers that are connected with full-time, reliable connections.

smart host An SMTP host designated to receive all outgoing SMTP mail. The smart host then forwards the mail to the relevant destination.

SMTP See *Simple Mail Transfer Protocol (SMTP)*.

SMTP connector Using SMTP as its transport mechanism, the SMTP connector can be used to connect routing groups to one another and to connect Exchange to a foreign SMTP system.

SMTP virtual server A logical representation of the SMTP on a physical server.

SNMP See *Simple Network Management Protocol (SNMP)*.

spooling The process used by SMTP to temporarily store messages that cannot be delivered immediately.

stand-alone CA A certificate issued to users who are outside the enterprise and who do not require access to the Active Directory. See also *certificate authority (CA)* and *enterprise CA*.

Standard Edition The basic version of Exchange Server 2010 with support for up to five databases.

standard permissions Permissions that are defined in a standard installation of Windows Server 2008. Extended permissions are created when Exchange Server 2010 is installed.

standby continuous replication (SCR) A multiserver environment in which the active storage group is copied to another server using log shipping. SCR was first introduced in Exchange Server 2007 SP1. This feature is discontinued in Exchange 2010.

storage area network (SAN) A set of devices (such as disks and tapes) and servers that are connected to a common infrastructure, such as Fibre Channel. The communication and data transfer channel for a given SAN environment is commonly called a *storage fabric*. The fabric of the SAN enables multiple servers to connect to a pool of storage devices that can include multiple arrays. In a SAN, any server can be configured to access any storage device or part of a storage device. In a SAN environment, management of the environment provides security for the storage units.

storage group A collection of databases (up to five) that all share a common set of transaction logs. Exchange 2007 allows for 5 storage groups, and the Enterprise Edition allows for 50 storage groups per server. Storage groups have been removed from Exchange 2010.

Store.exe The actual process that governs the use of stores on an Exchange server. Often referred to as the information store service.

store-and-forward   A delivery method that does not require the sender and recipient to have simultaneous interaction. Instead, when a message is sent, it is transferred to the next appropriate location in the network, which temporarily stores it, makes a routing decision, and forwards the message to the next appropriate network location. This process occurs until the message is ultimately delivered to the intended recipient or an error condition causes the message to be returned to the sender.

subsystem   A software component that, when loaded, extends the operating system by providing additional services. The MAPI program, `mapi32.dll`, is an example of a subsystem. `Mapi32.dll` loads on top of the Windows 98 or Windows XP operating system and provides messaging services.

System Monitor   See *Performance snap-in.*

system state backup   A form of backup that includes the Windows Registry, the IIS metabase, and the Active Directory (if run on a domain controller). Additionally, this may include the Client Access server configuration or cluster quorum for Client Access servers and clustered servers, respectively.

T

Task Manager   An application that displays the programs and processes running on a computer. It also displays various performance information, such as CPU and memory usage.

Telnet client   A text-based command-line tool that allows you to communicate with a host remotely.

template   An object, such as a user or group, that contains configuration information that is applicable to multiple users. Objects for each user can be easily created by copying the template and filling in information.

TLS encryption   Transport Layer Security (TLS) encryption is a generic security protocol similar to Secure Sockets Layer encryption.

token   The packet of security information a certificate authority sends to a client during advanced security setup. Information in the packet includes the client's public key and its expiration information. A token is similar to a certificate.

top-level folders   The folders found in the root level of a public folder tree.

tracert   A command-line utility that uses ICMP packets to determine the path that an IP datagram takes to reach its final destination.

transaction log   A file used to write data quickly. That data is later written to the relevant Exchange database file. It is quicker to write to a transaction log file because the writes are done sequentially (that is, one right after the other). Transaction log files can also be used to replay transactions from the log when rebuilding an Exchange database. All stores in a single storage group share the same set of transaction logs.

Typical installation   This option installs the Exchange Server software, the basic Messaging and Collaboration components, and the System Manager snap-in program. It does not include the additional connectors.

U

Unified Messaging server   The Unified Messaging server role provides the following functionality to an Exchange Server 2010 organization:

- Fax reception and delivery to Exchange mailboxes
- Voice call answering and delivery of recorded voicemail files to Exchange mailboxes
- Voicemail access via a phone connection
- Message read-back via a phone connection, including replying to the message or forwarding it to another recipient
- Calendar access via a phone connection, including meeting request acceptance
- Out-of-office messages in voicemail via a phone connection

uniform resource locator (URL)   An addressing method used to identify Internet servers and documents.

URL   See *uniform resource locator (URL)*.

user object   An object in Active Directory that is associated with a person on the network. Users can be mailbox-enabled or mail-enabled in Exchange Server 2010.

V

virtual local area network (VLAN)   A VLAN is an implementation in which remote sites can be configured so that they appear to be on the same network segment.

virtual server   A group of resources that contains an IP address resource and a network name resource. The network name is published to the network so that others can attach to its name to access resources included within the group. Clients access the resources of a virtual server exactly as they would access the resources of a physical server. Whether the server is a virtual server or a physical server doesn't matter to client computers on the network.

Volume Shadow Copy Service (VSS)   A feature in the Windows Server 2008 Backup utility. It's used to back up open files as if they were closed at the moment of the backup event.

W

Web   See *World Wide Web (WWW)*.

WebReady file types   Certain file types, such as Microsoft Word documents and Adobe Acrobat PDF documents, that can be converted to HTML easily. You can configure OWA to display these file types as HTML documents, thus allowing access to them even on computers that may not have the original applications they were created in installed.

well-known port numbers   Numbers that are commonly used as the TCP port numbers for popular applications, usually under 1,024.

Windows 2000 mixed domain functional level   The domain functional level that allows Windows NT 4.0 backup domain controllers to exist and function within a Windows 2003 domain.

Windows 2000 native domain functional level   The domain functional level that requires all domain controllers to be Windows 2000 Server or Windows Server 2003 and does not provide support for Windows NT 4.0 backup domain controllers.

Windows event log   See *event log*.

Windows Internet Naming System (WINS)   A name resolution service for resolving NetBIOS names on a Windows network.

Windows Server 2003 domain functional level   The highest domain functional level in Windows 2003, which implements all the features of Windows 2003 Active Directory.

World Wide Web (WWW)   The collection of computers on the Internet using protocols such as HTML and HTTP.

WWW   See *World Wide Web (WWW)*.

X

X.400   An International Telecommunications Union (ITU) standard for message exchange.

X.500   An International Telecommunications Union (ITU) standard for directory services.

Index

Note to the Reader: Throughout this index **boldfaced** page numbers indicate primary discussions of a topic. *Italicized* page numbers indicate illustrations.

D

P

X

Wiley Publishing, Inc.
End-User License Agreement

The Perfect Companion for all Exchange Server 2010 Administrators

Contains over an hour of video walkthroughs with authors Joel Stidley and Erik Gustafson:

- The authors walk you through some of the more difficult tasks you can expect to face as an Exchange Server 2010 Email Messaging Administrator.

- See firsthand how to install Exchange Server 2010, create a distribution group, and perform a multi-mailbox search.

Search through the complete book in PDF!

- Access the entire *Exchange Server 2010 Administration*, complete with figures and tables, in electronic format.

- Search the *Exchange Server 2010 Administration* chapters to find information on any topic in seconds.

For Certification candidates, we've included practice tests for both the TS and IT Pro: Exchange Server 2010 exams

- Microsoft Exchange Server 2010, Configuring (70-662)

- Designing and Deploying Messaging Solutions with Microsoft Exchange Server 2010 (70-663)

CD also includes Electronic Flashcards to jog your memory of topics covered in the book!

- Reinforce your understanding of key concepts with these hardcore flashcard-style questions.

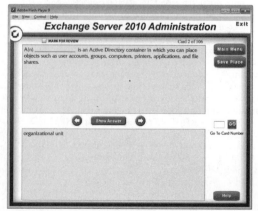